D1312404

Introduction to Social Psychology

David J. Stang

Introduction to Social Psychology

Brooks/Cole Publishing Company
Monterey, California

Brooks/Cole Publishing Company,
A Division of Wadsworth, Inc.

© 1981 by Wadsworth, Inc., Belmont, California 94002.
All rights reserved.
No part of this book may be reproduced, stored in a retrieval system,
or transcribed, in any form or by any means—
electronic, mechanical, photocopying, recording, or otherwise—
without the prior written permission of the publisher,
Brooks/Cole Publishing Company, Monterey, California 93940,
a division of Wadsworth, Inc.

Printed in the United States of America

10   9   8   7   6   5   4   3   2   1

Library of Congress Cataloging in Publication Data

Stang, David J
  Introduction to social psychology.

  Includes bibliographical references and index.
  1. Social psychology.   I.   Title.
HM251.S74   302   80-19469
ISBN 0-8185-0427-7

Consulting Editor: *Lawrence S. Wrightsman, University of Kansas*
Acquisition Editor: *Claire Verduin*
Production Editor: *Stacey Sawyer*
Manuscript Editor: *William Waller*
Interior Design: *Don Fujimoto*
Cover Design: *Katherine Minerva*
Cover Silk Screen Print: *Lynn Larson*
Typesetting: *Graphic Typesetting Service, Los Angeles, California*

Credits

This page constitutes an extension
of the copyright page.

The cover art is from an original serigraph
entitled "The Sum of Some = One," by Lynn Larson.
Used by permission of the artist.

All chapter-opening art and cartoons in this book
were drawn by Ron Grauer.

All figures and graphs in this book
were drawn by John Foster.

The following people and photo-research companies
provided the following photographs for this text:

p. 324 © John David Arms, Jeroboam, Inc.
pp. 193, 248 © Suzanne Arms, Jeroboam, Inc.
p. 108 © Philip Jon Bailey, Jeroboam, Inc.
p. 276 © Jeffrey Blankfort, Jeroboam, Inc.
pp. 188, 315 © Robert Burroughs, Jeroboam, Inc.
p. 132 © Ed Buryn, Jeroboam, Inc.
p. 366 © Eileen Christelow, Jeroboam, Inc.
pp. 311, 342 © Bob Clay, Jeroboam, Inc.
p. 379 © Vince Compagnone, Jeroboam, Inc.
p. 395 Fujihara, © Monkmeyer Press Photo Service
p. 141 Arthur Grace, © Stock, Boston, Inc.
p. 70 © Don Ivers, Jeroboam, Inc.
p. 101 © Irene Kane, Jeroboam, Inc.
p. 35 © Hank Lebo, Jeroboam, Inc.
p. 279 © Roger Lubin, Jeroboam, Inc.
pp. 18, 172 © Emilio Mercado, Jeroboam, Inc.
p. 221 © James Motlow, Jeroboam, Inc.
p. 60 © Bill Owens, Jeroboam, Inc.
pp. 151, 295 © Mitchell Payne, Jeroboam, Inc.
pp. 115, 172 © Kent Reno, Jeroboam, Inc.
pp. 21, 52, 76, 128, 259 © Stan Rice
p. 214 (top) Leonard Lee Rue III, © Monkmeyer Press Photo Service
pp. 225, 270 © Rose Skytta, Jeroboam, Inc.
p. 365 © Hap Stewart, Jeroboam, Inc.
pp. 214 (bottom), 385 David Strickler, © Monkmeyer Press Photo Service
pp. 36, 164, 351, 383 © Peeter Vilms, Jeroboam, Inc.
p. 91 © Suzanne Wu, Jeroboam, Inc.
p. 263 © Susan Ylvisaker, Jeroboam, Inc.

Preface

As an academic profession, social psychology has come of age. Literally thousands of studies of social behavior have been done, and most social-psychology texts pay homage to this research. They present study after study, attempting to represent and summarize this body of knowledge. Untrained readers of such texts, however, often feel confused and overwhelmed by the rambling vastness of the field. These readers are sometimes disappointed to find that the traditional texts offer little that seems applicable to their own lives and experiences.

Although there are now some texts that recognize the emerging parallel discipline of *applied* social psychology in that they relate academic social-psychology principles to real-world social problems, they are unfortunately few in number, because few text authors have worked in applied settings in the field and have broad, applied interests. Consequently, many students still search in vain for a text that will help them apply social-psychology principles to their own lives, to their personal problems.

This text provides what has been missing: it presents *personal* social psychology. It will help amateur social psychologists better understand their own social behavior. The book does cover traditional academic and applied social psychology, but the focus is on concepts and principles that will be useful in the daily lives of students. Professional social psychologists know that social behavior is interesting, that studying it is enjoyable, and that understanding it is useful. Students of social psychology should know this as well.

In making it personal, this book uses some new ways to present social psychology:

□ It draws from both sociologically based and psychologically based social psychology, from both academic and applied disciplines, and from both classic and contemporary research to present a balanced integration of the field.
□ It reorganizes some material (for example, traditional presentations of material on helping and hurting, and affiliation) to show conceptual, rather than historic, relations among ideas.
□ It introduces some new material in the areas of research and theory (for example, on diffusion of affect) to provide balance and currency.

☐ It deemphasizes names, dates, methods, and findings and emphasizes what is really important: ideas and understanding.

This book is designed for use in introductory social-psychology courses. It uses chapter summaries, interest boxes, and many illustrations to make the material come alive for many types of students, and it provides a glossary for students who do not have Stang and Wrightsman's *Dictionary of Social Behavior and Social Research Methods* (published at about the same time as this book).

In closing, I would like to acknowledge the following people for their help in completing this book: Wally Lambert and Roger Brown for getting me interested in social psychology as a profession; Larry Wrightsman, Claire Verduin, and Bill Hicks for getting me interested in writing this book; the reviewers—Marilynn B. Brewer from the University of California at Santa Barbara, Alfred Cohn from Hofstra University, Barry Fish from Eastern Michigan University, Harmon M. Hosch from the University of Texas at El Paso, Earl L. Jandron from San Jose State University, William W. Lambert from Cornell University, Marvin E. Shaw from the University of Florida, and Rhoda K. Unger from Montclair State College—for their constructive comments; Wade Martin of Catholic University for his assistance in preparing Chapter 7, Communication; John C. Touhey for his help in preparing the glossary; and the staff at Brooks/Cole—especially Bill Waller, manuscript editor, Stacey C. Sawyer, production editor, and Jennifer Young, production associate—for their suggestions and support.

I would also like to acknowledge my debt to two parents, a dozen typists, two dozen friends, and five dozen students, who all helped to bring this book about, and to thank my teacher, advisor, and partner, Jeanne McManus.

I like social psych. I hope that readers will, too.

David J. Stang

Contents

14

Intergroup Relations   375

Epilogue:
Employment as a Social Psychologist   405

Introduction to
Social Psychology

Social Psychology: Science and Common Sense

chapter

1

INTRODUCTION

What Is Social Psychology?   When you get up in the morning, you may decide what to wear by considering whom you will be seeing that day. Even if you eat breakfast alone, you probably use a napkin rather than your sleeve.

Driving to school, you keep to the right side of the road and stop at stop signs even when the streets are empty. Listening to the car radio, you smile and frown, hum, learn, and agree or disagree as you hear news, music, and talk shows. In class you go to the same seat you usually take and may chat with friends until your instructor begins.

Throughout the day you are influenced by others. **Social psychology**[1] is the study of how your thoughts, feelings, and behaviors are affected by the actual, imagined, or implied presence of others (Allport, G.W., 1968, p. 3). Social psychologists are interested in why you look in your mirror (trying to see yourself as others see you) or why you stop at a stop sign even with no traffic in sight.

In fact, social psychologists may be interested in any behavior that is influenced by others.

Social psychologists have discovered that people can be swayed surprisingly easily by others. In one experiment, for instance, people delivered what they believed to be 450-volt shocks to complete strangers. Moreover, people often think they have freely chosen to do something when, in fact, their behavior is fully governed by their situation. We have learned that, when people do give situations credit for their actions, they are often wrong. For instance, students who do well on a test congratulate themselves. But when they do poorly, they blame the situation—test, instructor, other students, their health, other courses, or whatever else is convenient. Not that social influence is limited to people. Chickens eat more grain when they are in groups than when alone, and ants dig faster. Cockroaches learn a maze slower when with their colleagues than when alone.

---

[1]Terms that appear in **boldface** are explained in the glossary at the back of the book.

"Lone chickens eat less than chickens in a group."

Most everything we do, then, is somehow influenced by others. Social influence and social behavior are the subject of social psychology and the subject of this book.

Common Sense. No doubt about it, **common sense** is valuable. All your life, you have been observing others. In many ways, you are an expert in social behavior. Your common sense summarizes this expert knowledge. It guides you in your interactions with others, helping you understand what they do and predict how they will behave.

In fact, it might seem that making a profession of the study of social behavior is unnecessary. You do not need a scientist to tell you not to spit into the wind. What can a social psychologist tell you that you do not already know? To find out, study Interest Boxes 1-1 and 1-2 (see pp. 6–7).

As you can see from Interest Boxes 1-1 and 1-2, common sense is not perfect. Sometimes, in fact, common sense is just plain wrong. When it is right, it often seems to be contradictory. For example, "Absence makes the heart grow fonder," "Out of sight, out of mind." If we examine our common sense carefully, we may find that it is not very good at making precise predictions, but it is fairly good at "explaining" almost everything—*after it happens.* Interest Box 1-3 points out a few contradictions in the personal theories you may hold. And you probably hold other contradictory ideas that are not even on this list (see p. 7).

The realization that personal theories and common sense are sometimes wrong was historically an important breakthrough for science. Social psychologists now generally believe in the **social construction of reality.** This is the idea that most of the things that we assume are "true facts" are merely assumptions or beliefs we have agreed on. For example, for several centuries, people in Europe believed that tomatoes were poisonous. Because this belief was widely held, people assumed it was true, and no one tested it. The toxicity of tomatoes was based on social construction, not on reality.

Our notion of **variables** is a socially constructed reality. There are no "real" variables, only ideas. One division of the world into a set of variables may not correspond exactly to another. For example, in the late 1800s, the idea of intelligence was tied to our current ideas of speed and strength. Intelligence was measured by speed in reaction time and strength of grip, among other factors. Early in this century the idea of intelligence changed, and "social intelligence" emerged, flourished, and died. As amateur social psychologists, you and I may still believe in social intelligence (people have social intelligence if they are suave, cool, and courteous). But most professional social psychologists no longer believe that social intelligence is a "real" variable.

Our personal theories or assumptions about people and the nature of the world seem to depend on our language. The Eskimos, we are told, have many

---

Interest Box 1-1.   Common Sense and the American Soldier*

Sociologist Paul Lazarsfeld (1949) has made a good case for how social-psychological research can improve on our common sense. He wrote:

> It is hard to find a form of human behavior that has not already been observed somewhere. Consequently, if a study reports a prevailing regularity, many readers respond to it by thinking, "Of course that is the way things are." Thus, . . . the argument is advanced that surveys only put into complicated form observations which are already obvious to everyone. . . . The reader may be helped in recognizing this attitude if he looks over a few statements which are typical of many survey findings and carefully observes his own reaction. A short list of these with brief interpretive comments will be given here. . . .
>
> 1. Better-educated men show more psychoneurotic symptoms than those with less education. (The mental instability of the intellectual as compared to the more impassive psychology of the man-in-the-street has often been commented on.) . . .
> 2. Men from rural backgrounds usually are in better spirits during their army life than soldiers from city backgrounds. (After all, they are more accustomed to hardships.) . . .
> 3. Southern soldiers were better able to stand the climate in the hot South Sea Islands than Northern soldiers. (Of course, Southerners are more accustomed to hot weather.) . . .
> 4. As long as the fighting [in World War II] continued, men were more eager to be

> returned to the States than they were after the German surrender. (You cannot blame people for not wanting to be killed.) . . .
>
> We have in these examples a sample list of the simplest types of interrelationships which provide the "bricks" from which our empirical social science is being built. But why, since they are so obvious, is so much money and energy given to establish such findings? Would it not be wiser to take them for granted and proceed directly to a more sophisticated type of analysis? This might be so except for one interesting point about the list. *Every one of these statements is the direct opposite of what was actually found.* Poorly educated soldiers were more neurotic than those with high educations; Southerners showed no greater ability than Northerners to adjust to a tropical climate; and so on. . . .
>
>> If we had mentioned the actual results of the investigations first, the reader would have labeled these "obvious" also. Obviously something is wrong with the entire argument of "obviousness." It should really be turned on its head. Because every kind of human reaction is conceivable, it is of great importance to know which reactions actually occur most frequently and under what conditions; only then will the more advanced social science develop [pp. 379–380].

*From "The American Soldier: An Expository Review," by P. Lazarsfeld. In *Public Opinion Quarterly*, 1949, *13*, 377–404. Copyright 1949 by the Trustees of Columbia University. Reprinted by permission of the publisher.

words for what we call *snow*. Arabs have many words for *camel*. Snow and camels are more important to them than to us, and having a variety of words makes it easier to talk and think about these things. So, too, your vocabulary of social

---

Interest Box 1-2.   How Good Is Your Common Sense?*

How much do you "know" about social behavior? Take this true/false test and see. The answers follow.

1. To change people's behavior toward members of ethnic minority groups, we must first change their attitudes.
2. Personality tests reveal your basic motives, including those you may not be aware of.
3. The basis of the baby's love for its mother is the fact that she fills its physiological needs for food and other things.
4. The more highly motivated you are, the better you will do at solving a complex problem.
5. The best way to ensure that a desired behavior will persist after training is completed is to reward the behavior every single time it occurs throughout training (rather than intermittently).
6. Children memorize much more easily than adults.
7. Boys and girls exhibit no behavioral differences until environmental influences begin to produce them.

8. Genius is closely akin to insanity.
9. The unstructured interview is the most valid method for assessing someone's personality.
10. Children's IQ scores have very little relationship with how well they do in school.

These items were taken from Eva Vaughan's Test of Common Beliefs (1977). Every single item is false, although they are regarded as true by most students. As Vaughan said: "Many students enter an introductory psychology course with considerable 'knowledge' of psychology gleaned from books, the popular media, and the proverbial grandmother's knee. Some of the knowledge is accurate. However, much of it is a collection of half-truths and untruths, supported by popular belief but refuted by psychological research" (p. 138).

*From "Misconceptions about Psychology among Introductory Psychology Students," by E. D. Vaughan. In *Teaching of Psychology*, 1977, *4*(3), 138–141. Reprinted by permission.

Interest Box 1-3.   Contradictory Proverbs

1. Honesty is the best policy.
2. Absence makes the heart grow fonder.
3. It's never too late to learn.
4. There's no place like home.
5. Work today, for the night is coming.
6. Two heads are better than one.
7. A penny saved is a penny earned.
8. Look before you leap.
9. Haste makes waste.
10. It matters not whether you win or lose, but how you play the game.
11. Birds of a feather flock together.
12. Too many cooks spoil the broth.
13. Turn the other cheek.

1. Never give a sucker an even break.
2. Out of sight, out of mind.
3. You can't teach an old dog new tricks.
4. The grass is always greener on the other side.
5. Eat, drink, and be merry.
6. If you want a thing done well, do it yourself.
7. Easy come, easy go.
8. He who hesitates is lost.
9. Strike while the iron is hot.
10. Winning is everything.
11. Opposites attract.
12. The more the merrier.
13. An eye for an eye.

behavior should expand in this course. As a result, you will be able to talk and think more easily about social behavior.

Social Psychology Can Improve Common Sense.   Common sense is not always right. But as we study social behavior, our common sense becomes better. The serious study of social behavior is worthwhile for many reasons: learning is fun, solving problems and puzzles is challenging, and understanding social behavior can be a great source of personal satisfaction.

Another reason for studying social behavior is that as amateur social psychologists we make mistakes. Our predictions about social behavior, although often right, are sometimes wrong. Social behavior can be complicated. A person may behave in a certain way for several reasons, and the reasons may change over time or across situations. Different people may have different reasons for doing the same thing. This complexity in social behavior makes it more challenging to study.

We can be more effective as persons if we better understand social behavior. Politicians, for instance, will be more effective if they understand their constituents and can anticipate their reactions. Prostitutes who understand social behavior will probably earn more and spend less time in jail. Used-car salesmen, kindergarten teachers, administrators, preachers, military leaders, historians, palm readers, football players, bank tellers, social workers, and students all benefit from understanding others. In fact, all of us can improve our situation by a better understanding of social behavior.

Social psychology improves this understanding through research. Research involves taking a personal theory and making careful, controlled observations to see if it is true. Research might find, for instance, that the theory "A watched pot never boils" is false and that the theory "There's safety in numbers" is often—but not always—true. Research helps us refine our personal theories by showing us *when* they are true and when they are not.

Research in social psychology can improve common sense by showing where it is right and where it is wrong. And, in some areas of research, common sense plays no part. Amateur social psychologists have no intuitions about the effects of physiology on behavior or about the effects of, for example, air ions. Social-psychological knowledge can also go beyond common sense. Although you may find some intuitive information in this book, other information will be new.

As social psychologists we learn to critically evaluate evidence and to reason carefully. Thus, we are better able to evaluate our own personal theories and those of others. Learning that common sense is not always right may make us more willing to critically examine it and to revise it.

Students may sometimes find social psychology disappointing. Because common sense is fairly reliable and because we use it more often to explain than predict, research findings will often agree with common sense. Much of social psychology deals with everyday events for which we already have personal theories. Because common sense is often correct, many findings agree with our intuitions. Common sense makes a strange demand of social-behavior research. If the results are what we expected or if they match a personal theory, we may complain "I already know that." If the results are completely unexpected, we are likely to think they are wrong.[2] Nevertheless, if we are to increase our understanding—improve our common sense—we need to know which personal theories are right and which are wrong.

Common Sense Can Improve Social Psychology.   Certainly, common sense has its contradictions. But as Heider said, if as scientists we accepted "such contradictions as proof of the worthlessness of common sense psychology, . . . then we would have to reject the scientific approach, for its history is fraught with contradictions among theories and even among experimental findings" (1958, p. 5).[3]

The task of social psychology is not to reject common sense but to improve it. Social psychologists pay attention to common sense, and this has some payoffs. First, common sense is the sole source of testable hypotheses; awareness of this origin should enable us to tap it systematically and creatively. Second, common sense provides a richer, more comprehensive, and more usable psychology than does science (Joysen, 1974). Without scientific psychology, people would still know not to spit into the wind. But without common sense, most of us would be run over by automobiles, beaten up, or at least covered with spit. Common sense is not only more useful than scientific psychology, it is also more used. We all have immediate access to our own common sense and can use it as needed. Formal theories, in contrast, are generally not written for reading by the public. Most are hidden in the psychologist's library. So, whether common sense is "right" or "wrong," it is influential. Common sense must be studied and understood if we are to understand the causes of behavior. As Heider said, "If a person believes that the lines in his palm foretell his future, this belief must be taken into account in explaining certain of his expectations and actions" (1958, p. 5). Social psychologists have not rejected common sense. But they have improved on it.

SOCIAL PSYCHOLOGISTS: AMATEUR AND PROFESSIONAL

The Amateur Social Psychologist.   Some of you may think of a social psychologist as a man or woman with a white laboratory coat peering through a one-way mirror. Some of you may think of someone like television's Allen Funt, making unobtrusive observations with a candid camera or clipboard. In a sense, everyone is a social psychologist. We all try to understand, predict, and control social behavior. When we hold theories of social behavior, test our hypotheses, and evaluate the evidence, we are social psychologists (see Interest Box 1-4). Those people who

---

[2]For a time, professional social psychologists seemed to have a ravenous appetite for counterintuitive (contrary to intuition) findings. Now it seems that many of these findings, such as those from dissonance theory, were either counterintuitive only for psychologists or were simply wrong. Most professional psychologists, and most amateurs, have a tendency to think that counterintuitive findings (such as support for ESP) are wrong. If your intuitions are good, trust your intuitions. If your research is better, trust it.

[3]From *The Psychology of Interpersonal Relations*, by F. Heider. Copyright © 1958 by John Wiley & Sons, Inc. This and all other quotations from this source are reprinted by permission of John Wiley & Sons, Inc.

are social psychologists *by profession* may have more complex theories that they test with greater care and rigor, but the process is the same.

The Professional Social Psychologist.   Some differences can be noted between amateur and professional social psychologists. First, social psychology is a **science.** Its researchers make careful observations in such a way that others could make similar observations under similar conditions. They carefully record these observations, objectively analyze them, and try to report them without bias. The similarities and differences between personal and formal research will become evident as you learn more about formal research.

Research reports are prepared to meet certain requirements (American Psychological Association, 1974) and then submitted to a social-psychology journal, where they are carefully considered for publication. As you might guess, these reports are usually on specialized topics. Texts such as this one attempt to summarize this huge volume of technical literature. It has been growing at a great rate, with about 1000 articles now published each year. Few social psychologists can find the time to read more than a small fraction of them.

This research establishes social psychology as a science and separates it from other fields, such as philosophy, that also deal with social behavior. Sages such as Plato and Shakespeare have made brilliant observations of social behavior over the centuries. But social psychology as a science did not begin until the 1890s (see Interest Box 1-5) and did not begin to flourish until the last few decades.

Interest Box 1-4.   Are You a Social Psychologist?

Raven and Rubin (1976) have raised the question "Who is *not* a social psychologist?" They suggest that a social psychologist is simply one who studies social psychology and that "everyone is a social psychologist. Without some ability to understand and predict the behavior of others, none of us would be able to function effectively in our social world" (pp. 11–12).

Fritz Heider was an influential social psychologist. He wrote that "In everyday life we [all] form ideas about other people and about social situations. We interpret other people's actions and we predict what they will do under certain circumstances. And though these ideas are usually not well formulated, they often function adequately. They achieve in some measure what a science is supposed to achieve—an adequate description of the subject matter which makes prediction possible" (1958, p. 5).

George Kelly agreed: "When we speak of *man-the-scientist* we are speaking of all mankind and

not merely a particular class of men who have publicly attained the stature of 'scientists' " (1963, p. 4).

Alfred North Whitehead, the mathematician and philosopher, voiced a similar view: "Science is rooted in what I have just called the whole apparatus of common sense thought. That is the *datum* from which it starts, and to which it must recur. . . . You may polish up common sense, you may contradict it in detail, you may surprise it. But ultimately your whole task is to satisfy it" (1929, p. 110).

In a similar vein, the physicist Robert Oppenheimer argued that "all science arises as refinement, corrections, and adaptations of common sense" (1956, p. 128).

When you have finished reading this book, you may think of yourself as an amateur social psychologist and be more knowledgeable and more curious about social behavior.

Social psychologists' research produces "observations" that are interpreted. Such interpretations help relate one observation to others and give it meaning. The observations and interpretations we make are guided by our previous ones, and all of them fit together—more or less—in a **system of explanation.** A particular system of explanation (such as behaviorism or phenomenology) suggests what should be studied, how it should be studied, and how to interpret the results. Such a system is useful because it gives meaning and direction to a researcher's activities. A disadvantage, however, is that some interesting observations will be overlooked, because no system can account for all observations. A system of explanation provides a useful but imperfect perspective for the social psychologist.

Although they operate from different perspectives, social psychologists make their observations according to the scientific method. Therefore, their findings are usually repeatable; that is, regardless of a researcher's system of explanation,

---

Interest Box 1-5.   The Origins of Modern Social Psychology*

Social scientists seek the determinants of social behavior
   Habit
   1890: William James, *Principles of Psychology*
   Imitation
   1890: Gabriel Tarde, *The Laws of Imitation*
   Suggestion
   1895: Gustave Le Bon, *The Crowd*
   Instinct
   1908: William McDougall, *Introduction to Social Psychology*
   Attitude
   1918–1920: W. I. Thomas and F. Znaniecki, *The Polish Peasant in Europe and America*

The first textbooks appear
   1908: William McDougall, *Introduction to Social Psychology*
   1908: Edward A. Ross, *Social Psychology*

The first journal is founded
   1921: Morton Prince's journal, *The Journal of Abnormal Psychology*, becomes *The Journal of Abnormal Psychology and Social Psychology* (later shortened to *Journal of Abnormal and Social Psychology*)

Social psychology enters the laboratory
   1897: N. Triplett, *The Dynamogenic Factors in Pacemaking and Competition*

Social psychology goes into the field
   1899: E. D. Starbuck, *The Psychology of Religion*

Social psychology is applied
   1900: H. Gale, *On the Psychology of Advertising, in Psychological Studies*

Group influences are experimentally studied
   1924: V. M. Bechterew and M. de Lange, *Die Ergebnisse des Experiments auf dem Gebiete der kollektiven Reflexologie*

Attitudes are measured
   1927–1928: L. L. Thurstone, *Attitudes Can Be Measured*
   1936: George Gallup makes the measurement of public opinion "Big Business"
   1940: Rensis Likert develops the open-end survey technique

Social psychologists espouse action research
   1936: The Society for the Psychological Study of Social Issues is founded by Goodwin Watson

Experimental group dynamics begins
   1938: Kurt Lewin and Ronald Lippitt, *An Experimental Approach to the Study of Autocracy and Democracy: A Preliminary Note*

*From *Individual in Society,* by D. Krech, R. Crutchfield, and E. Ballachey. Copyright © 1962 by McGraw-Hill, Inc. Used with permission of McGraw-Hill Book Company.

by repeating the method someone else can usually repeat the results. This makes observations far better than opinion.

Nevertheless, social-psychological theories are not "true facts." They are explanations that tie observations together. As explanations, they are tentative. They are probably better than yesterday's theories, because they typically account for more findings. But today's theories are not as good as tomorrow's will be. Why? Because we may make observations that will show how the theory needs improvement. As scientists, social psychologists are willing to revise theories that seem unable to account for new observations.

Social psychology is a science and a body of knowledge. It is also a profession.[4] Professional social psychologists get paid for doing research, for teaching, for applying their knowledge in solving social problems, and even for writing books. They have a number of professional organizations. These include the Society for Personality and Social Psychology (Division 8 of the American Psychological Association), the Society for the Psychological Study of Social Issues (Division 9 of the APA), and the Society for the Advancement of Social Psychology. Students interested in affiliating with these groups should see their instructor or write to the APA, 1200 17th Street NW, Washington, D.C. 20036.

EXPLAINING SOCIAL BEHAVIOR

The Need for Explanation.   We have a need to understand social behavior, to predict it and control it. There is ample evidence, for instance, that most of us believe some skill is involved in a game of chance. Whether it is crossing our fingers or knocking on wood, a special way of throwing the dice, rooting for a horse at the racetrack, or wearing peculiar clothes to important exams for "good luck," we all like to believe that we can control our fate. But not only do we like to *believe* we can control our fate—an illusion of control—we also like to actually control it.

Being able to choose, to control, and to have responsibility has many benefits (Lefcourt, 1973; Seligman, M., 1975). For instance, one study found that, when nursing home residents were encouraged to make choices, take responsibility, and feel in control, they became more sociable, more interested in their environment, and healthier. They actually lived longer (Langer & Rodin, 1976; Rodin & Langer, 1977). Those people who live to be 100 or more years old in the Caucasus of Russia (and several other places in the world) have continuing control over their lives. They remain active and respected, preserving an interest in life and participating in it (Kyucharyants, 1974). Other studies find that neither people (Hiroto, 1974; Krantz, Glass, & Snyder, 1974) nor rats (Joffe, Rawson, & Mulick, 1973; Overmier & Seligman, M., 1967; Seligman, M., & Maier, 1967) perform well on tasks when they learn that they cannot control the rewards or punishments they receive (see also Chapter 3).

---

[4]To some extent, social psychology is a divided profession. Some social psychologists are sociologists by training, but most are psychologists. While the *psychological* social psychologist tends to study the effects of personal and interpersonal environments on behavior, the *sociological* social psychologist commonly studies the effects of social structure—organizations and institutions—on individuals. Most social-psychology texts are written by psychologically trained social psychologists (Liska, 1977). The views and interests of both orientations to social psychology are included in this book.

There is ample evidence that most of us believe some skill is involved in games of chance.

People who believe that they have personal control over their fate and can shape the course of their life ("internals") actually do show more control than those who believe they are controlled by luck, fate or powerful others ("externals") (Rotter, Liverant, & Seeman, 1962). For instance, internals seem better able to give up smoking when they want to (James, Woodruff, & Werner, 1965). In a reformatory, internals learn more about how to get parole (Seeman, 1963). So actual control is important for us. Belief in control is, too, in part because it increases our actual control. Whether or not we find any pleasure in controlling others, we rarely find it pleasant when others control us. Rather, we feel uncomfortable and work to change our situation when others successfully predict our behavior or try to control us (Brehm, 1972; Wicklund, 1974). Personal theories give us a feeling of understanding, prediction, and control. Understanding, prediction, and control also happen to be the goals of science.

The Process of Explanation. Explanation follows a cycle involving **observation(s), induction, generalization,** and **deduction** (see Figure 1-1). Induction means that we take several specific observations, beliefs, or personal theories, find a relationship between them, and make a generalization or draw a conclusion.

Suppose you look up to see a hairy entering your room. This is the first hairy you have seen, and no one has ever mentioned them to you before. The hairy has red hair. You look back at your book, and your door swings open again. Another hairy. More red hair. Again, another red-haired hairy. And another. Before your room is filled with hairies, let me ask you a question: What color hair do hairies have? On the basis of these observations you have just made, you may conclude (induction) that they have red hair (generalization). Now, what would you guess the hair color of the next hairy to enter the room might be? You might decide that if hairies have red hair, the next hairy to come in your room would

Figure 1-1.
The construction of
social reality
through the process
of explanation

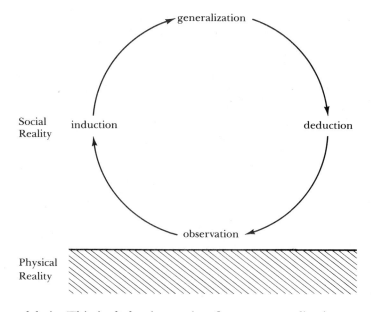

Social
Reality

Physical
Reality

also have red hair. This is deduction, going from a generalization to a specific prediction. The door now swings open. Yup, it's a hairy. And what color hair? You make an observation. If it is red, as you were expecting, your observation matches your deduction, and you support your generalization. Your confidence in your generalization is increased. But what if the next hairy has black hair? Most likely, you will want to save your generalization if you can. Is this really a hairy? Is its hair dyed? If your generalization cannot be saved, you may want to revise it a bit: maybe *most* hairies have red hair. This process is the essence of theory building and testing.

The cycle of induction-generalization-deduction-observation has no beginning or end. Any stage in the process has been affected by previous stages. For

instance, our observations are never objective views of an entire mass of information. They are selective, and we pay attention to those things we were expecting to see that might be important. That is, all observations are regulated by previous generalizations and hypotheses. And all generalizations and hypotheses are necessarily regulated and influenced by previous observations. So the process has no clear beginning. The end of the process is determined only by the limits to our curiosity and our life span.

Research reports provide us with a slice out of this process. They usually begin with a review of the literature, in which previous stages in the process are summarized, and then often state some hypotheses to be tested (deductions from this summary). They also include a method and results section, in which the observations are carefully described. Finally, there is a discussion section, in which the researcher suggests inductions that might be drawn from these observations. A research report provides us with a slice from the continuous stream of expanding explanation and understanding.

On "Proof."   Our inductive jump from observation to generalization may seem like a logical step, but it's really a leap of faith. In whatever ways a conclusion goes beyond observations, it stands the chance of being wrong. There are a number of reasons why conclusions are sometimes not completely true. For one thing, observations are time- or situation-bound[5] (maybe red-haired hairies come through *your* door, but the ones in *my* room are blond). Further, observers may view the world differently (some hairy-observers may be color-blind). Observers also affect what they are observing (maybe hairies' hair gets redder when they are stared at). And so on. Mainly, however, the problem is that a generalization always goes beyond the observations from which it was derived. Therefore, there is always the chance that some subsequent observation might not fit with it.

In short, because there is always the chance that we'll discover that a particular generalization is not true (by encountering some unexpected, unpredicted observation), we can't *prove* any generalization. All we can do is strengthen our confidence that it is adequate.

The Social Construction of Reality.   A wise old counselor once listened to a wife talk about her troubles with her husband. When she had finished, the counselor said "You're right." Then her husband gave *his* side of the story. Again, the counselor said "You're right." A young student intern who had been listening jumped up and said "But counselor, they both can't be right!" The counselor replied "You're right."

This did not really happen, but something like it happens all the time. We all have our own view of the world and are so convinced of its accuracy that it hardly seems possible that there is another legitimate view. *Within* our view, we are right. But for those standing outside our view, we may seem a little silly. For

---

[5]The idea that observations might be time- or situation-bound is a curious one. People often tell aging boxers that they aren't what they used to be. Muhammad Ali had a good retort for Howard Cosell, who had brazenly noted this. Removing Cosell's toupee, Ali asked: "Are you the man you were two years ago?" How about you? What generalizations about you have changed with time?

centuries people in the Orient practiced acupuncture, an idea that still seems odd to most of us. Yet, early in this century in the United States, barbers tried to heal the sick by applying leeches to their bodies to draw off the "bad blood." That idea may seem odd to us now, but it made perfectly good sense then. Much of "reality" is in the eyes of the beholder.

PERSONAL EXPLANATIONS

Earlier (p. 11), we saw that social psychology is an assortment of observations that are tied together by systems of explanation. Just as each professional social psychologist uses a system to understand, predict, and control social behavior, so each amateur social psychologist uses a system of **personal explanation.** "Intuition" or "common sense" is what you probably call your system of explanation. You use your intuitions about the causes of social behavior to predict and explain behavior (Ajzen, 1977). Your own system of explanation is probably similar to those used by your family and friends, but it is not identical. Your experiences and your conclusions are unique.

Your system of explanation consists of a large number of personal theories and rules that govern when to apply these theories. Personal theories are simply beliefs. (George Kelly has called them "personal constructs.") As such, personal theories are generally simpler and less elaborate than the formal scientific theories of the professional social psychologist, who would probably call your theories hunches, beliefs, attitudes, or understandings.

Types of Personal Theories.   Personal theories often describe some sort of relationship between two variables.[6] One type of personal theory is **prescriptive** (how something *should* be) or **proscriptive** (how something *should not* be). For example, "Children should be seen and not heard" argues that young people should be quiet people. In this example, age and noise are two variables. Prescriptive and proscriptive personal theories often include *should* and *ought*.

Another kind of personal theory is **descriptive** (how something *is*). For example, "The way to a man's heart is through his stomach" suggests that men like those who feed them.

Another kind of personal theory is **predictive** (how something *will be*). For example, "If you tease a puppy, it will bite" predicts biting as a consequence of teasing. Statements of these personal theories often are of the form of "if . . . then . . ."

A fourth type of personal theory is **explanatory** (*why* something is the way it is). For example, "I was late for work because the alarm didn't go off" offers an explanation for lateness based on prior events. Explanatory personal theories often include a word like "because." They most closely correspond to formal scientific theories.

---

[6]A variable is anything that can vary. *Person* is not a variable, because we can't imagine two or more states or conditions or levels of this idea. But *person size* is a variable, because we can easily imagine large people and small people. So is *age* or *sex*. Generally, any adjective you can think of has to do with the level or state of a variable implied in the sentence. For instance, a *big* person has more of the variable *size* than a *small* one. Both big and small are adjectives that describe how much size a person has (how large he or she is).

Although it is useful to distinguish types of personal theories, in everyday life we don't always make distinctions. For example, we often confuse description and explanation. "Absence makes the heart grow fonder" describes what happens when absence occurs but does not explain why it happens. Many descriptive statements ("The way to a man's heart . . .") imply a *should* or prescription ("If you want to be loved, then you should . . .").

Personal theories are important in social behavior. Not only do they help simplify and summarize observations (descriptive personal theories) and give them meaning (explanatory personal theories), they tell you how social behavior should be (prescriptive and proscriptive personal theories) and will be (predictive personal theories). Personal theories are as real as the experiences from which they were drawn. They probably have stronger influences on our social behavior than any other factor.

Characteristics of Personal Theories.   Personal theories differ in many ways. For example, some concern a process and focus on the relation between events. Some concern dispositions or motives and focus on the relation between the stable qualities of people (Laucken, 1974). For example, "People work harder if they are rewarded" is a personal theory that focuses on process. "Talkative people are assertive" focuses on disposition. Some evidence suggests that we consider both processes and dispositions when we explain the behavior of others (Bierhoff-Alfermann & Bierhoff, 1976).

Personal theories also differ in the *intensity* with which we hold them (Cantril, 1946; Hartley & Hartley, 1952). They differ in *salience*, or how obvious they are to us (Smith, M. B., Bruner, & White, 1956; Stern, 1938). For example, theories that have proverbs, clichés, or expressions associated with them are more salient than those that we could state only after considerable thought. Personal theories also differ in the degree to which they are *connected* to other personal theories (Kelly, 1955) and how much *information support* they have (Scott, W. A., 1969; Smith, T. I., & Suinn, 1965). They also differ in *certainty*, or how confident we are that they are correct (Chein, 1951). You can probably think of other ways that personal theories differ. These dimensions, as well as dozens of others, have been previously suggested as ways that attitudes differ. They were briefly reviewed by Robert Brannon (1975).

Most personal theories suggest that there are two possible relationships between variables: positive and negative. For a positive relationship, we believe that increases in one variable accompany increases in another.

Suppose we observe a large group having fun and want to explain this in terms of group size. We search for a descriptive or explanatory personal theory that matches the pattern we have found. We might say "The more the merrier" to describe this positive relationship between the variables of group size and member satisfaction. Instead, suppose we want to explain why a large group is not having fun. Again, we search for the personal theory to match this negative relationship between group size and member satisfaction. We might say "Too many cooks spoil the broth." Most proverbs and aphorisms are invoked after an observation is made, to explain it, rather than to predict an event before it occurs. We are therefore able to hold contradictory explanations in our head (see Interest Box 1-3 on p. 7).

Application Rules.   As we have seen (p. 16), systems of explanation consist of both personal theories and those *rules* that govern when to apply these theories. We know little about **application rules,** and social psychologists don't pay attention to them in their formal theories. Application rules are involved when we ask "Does this explanation *seem* to apply to this situation?" For example, when we see two similar people having fun, we know to say "Birds of a feather flock together" and know we shouldn't say "Opposites attract." Application rules include **limiting conditions**—those circumstances in which the theory doesn't apply.

   Pattern matching is one of the key application rules. Does the pattern of the event—or the behavior or relationship—we have observed seem to match with a theory that we might apply? If the match seems reasonably good, we may be content and end our search for a better theoretical pattern. If we are dissatisfied with the match, the search continues. Such dissatisfaction often leads to the construction of new theories that provide a better pattern match. For example, when we see a short and a tall person together, we search for a matching pattern. "Opposites attract" matches, but "Birds of a feather flock together" does not.

"*Typical birds of a feather flocked together.*"

SCIENTIFIC EXPLANATIONS

The personal theories of the amateur social psychologist have much in common with the more formal theories of the professional social psychologist.

What is **scientific explanation**? It is the process of establishing general concepts and the relationships between them for the purpose of description, prediction, and understanding.

Assumptions Underlying Scientific Explanations. If the process of observation, induction, generalization, deduction is continuous, then it stands to reason that what scientists write down as a formal or scientific theory represents only one (recent) stage in their thinking. Throughout their theorizing, social psychologists make many assumptions. These assumptions form the groundwork of their theories and, when unnoticed, become entangled in them. As theorists, we do best when we are aware of our assumptions. What are some of the assumptions or personal theories that social psychologists make (or should make)?

Invariance. Social psychologists often assume that relationships between variables are **invariant,** or unchanging over time and place. If college students conform more in large than small groups today in Flushing, New York, we believe they will do so in Topeka, Kansas, tomorrow. This assumption is rarely tested, and the occasional tests have yielded some surprising results. It seems likely that many findings about social behavior are true only under limited conditions and not always invariant.

Multiple causation. Why do you smile when you meet friends on the street? To show them you are happy to see them? Out of anxiety, the smile being really a defensive baring of teeth? Out of habit, with no particular intent? Because you have been taught that it is polite? Because they smiled at you and you feel it is important to reciprocate? Sometimes we behave a certain way for several reasons. Naming the reasons and the possible causes is a difficult business. It is even harder to decide which reasons are the most important.

When we explain behavior, one explanation is often enough for us. (If we are feeling guilty and are trying to explain our behavior to someone we have offended, we may go overboard with rationalizations.) Typically, our search for an explanation stops when we have discovered one explanation that appears sufficient (Jones & Davis, 1965). Our selection of an explanation probably depends on what information is salient (Kanouse, 1972) and readily available. Most social behavior has **multiple causes.** Having found one—or even two or three—we cannot be sure that there are not some additional causes waiting to be discovered. Good explanations of social behavior must recognize the fact that a single explanation is rarely enough and is usually incomplete. One explanation might be correct as far as it goes but not be a full explanation. Whenever you feel you have the explanation for something, ask yourself "Am I sure?" We need to encourage curiosity to learn about and deal with complex environments.

Determinism. Social psychologists believe that every single event they study is caused, that those causes, in turn, are caused, and so on. This belief that everything is determined—that there are no events that "just happen"—is known as the assumption of **determinism.** It is an assumption because we cannot prove that all events are caused.

It does turn out, however, that much of our behavior is complexly determined, so complexly that we often cannot discover all the causes without much effort. Further, we have little insight into our own unconscious motivations. So, although social psychologists are determinists on the job, in everyday life they sometimes lapse into explanations such as "I felt like it" or "I chose to," without worrying about identifying the causes of the feeling or choice.

Thresholds and overdetermination.   Action is often described in all-or-none terms. We go on a date or we don't. We do a favor for someone or we beg off. Yet the motivating forces that produce behavior are rarely merely present or absent. Most of the time these forces are present but vary in degree. We may then view behavior as an event that occurs if the forces are strong enough to move us to action; that is, the motivating forces exceed some **threshold** (a lower limit).

Behavior that occurs has causes that vary in strength. For example, you may get out of your comfortable chair because you are getting tired of watching television or because you have dropped a match on your lap. Either way, you get up, but with the match you had more cause pushing you up. Whether your clothing is burning or just smoldering, the lit match *overdetermined* your behavior. The causes far exceeded the threshold needed to get you out of the chair.

Now consider the case of getting out of the chair to go to bed. At 11:30 you finally decide (notice the free-will explanation!) to get up and go to bed. You are tired, and the television program is boring. But why didn't you get up at 11:20? You were nearly as tired then and the program seemed just as boring then. In fact, the behavior that didn't occur at 11:20 (getting up) still had causes for occurring but was *underdetermined.* That is, some behaviors that occur have more causes than are necessary to make them occur: they are overdetermined. In other cases, some of these influences are present but not enough to cause the behavior to occur: the behavior is underdetermined.

Let me give you another example. Suppose you are considering going to the movies. You'd like to go, but you're not sure what is playing, you don't have much money, and it's getting late. You decide not to go. Suppose you find $10 you had forgotten about. You may still not go. Here there are causes but no effect. Then suppose your doorbell rings, and there stand three of your friends insisting that you go to the movies. You decide to go, and then you discover that the movie is one you've really wanted to see. Here, the cause is more than necessary to give the effect. Even one friend at the door or even a less desirable movie might have got you to go. In short, causes may be present when effects are absent; and when an effect occurs, it is often overdetermined—there is more causal force than is needed. This simple principle of overdetermination makes accurate prediction difficult. The lack of a neat relationship between causes and effect should emphasize how tough it is to study social behavior.

As a further complication, we need to remember that our threshold for a particular action may vary across time and situations. We may be willing to help a stranded motorist if we have nothing else to do and are wearing dirty clothes.

A stranded motorist. Would you stop? What factors influence your decision?

But if we are late to a meeting and are dressed up, we probably won't stop. Further, different people may have different variables that determine their thresholds. Some may worry about their safety and others may consider whether they are likely to be able to help or have the time to help.

One last problem. Even if we ever get to the point where we can perfectly predict the occurrence of a particular behavior, there may still be additional causes we didn't know about. For instance, suppose that, after you study my helping behavior, you conclude that I will definitely stop to help a particular motorist. Sure enough, I begin to pull off the road. Suddenly, I notice this stranded motorist is my mother. Even if I hadn't planned on stopping, when I saw it was my mother I would have stopped. Your perfect prediction with a limited set of causes falls apart as we add others that add to or subtract from their effects.

Causation. Why do people behave as they do? One approach to this question is mechanistic, viewing events as the inevitable effects of certain observable previous causes. In this approach, **causation** is a "push" that one variable has on another. Behaviorism is a system of explanation that draws heavily on this viewpoint. For instance, we might explain that one person hurt another (effect) because the other had insulted him or her (cause).

The mechanistic view is too simple. People are active decision makers, not lumps or rocks. When we act, it is a result of some cognitive (mental) process in which we consider various possible actions and their possible effects. Such decisions are influenced by **reasons**—the subjective arguments related to the merits of the apparent alternatives.

Such decision making need not be conscious. In fact, we are unaware of most of our cognitive activity. "Consciousness" seems to be only a limited interpretation and simple summary of what we have just been thinking. These facts— that people are decision makers whose decision making is largely nonconscious— make the study of human social behavior very difficult. And these facts may mean that a full understanding of that behavior is not possible. But it is better to acknowledge these facts than to pretend that people are like rocks or pigeons.

Causation can be bidirectional and can be circular. For example, the thermostat in your house is a thermometer and a switch. When the thermometer drops, the switch is thrown on. The switch starts the furnace, which warms the house. The thermometer rises, and the furnace switch is shut off. The house again cools.

Many social behaviors are involved in such circular causal chains. For example, increased anxiety may result in increases in conformity, which in turn may reduce anxiety (Stang, 1972). Systems like the thermostat and furnace or like anxiety and conformity are **homeostatic** (self-regulating). They are sometimes called **feedback loops** or **control systems,** and they maintain stability for the elements of the system.

Most of our social behaviors are elements of systems. Most systems are dynamic and changing, even if the change is gradual or not detectable to those involved in it. If this is true, our theories of social behavior must recognize this.

To return to the opening statement in this section, Scientific Explanations, let's look at what formal and personal theories do have in common. For instance:

- Common origins: both develop from our previous experience and from the experience of others.
- Common interests: both are interested in the same basic puzzles of behavior.
- Common motives: both develop out of our curiosity and our need to understand.
- Common focus: both guide our observations toward some things and away from others.

On the other hand, it is important to be aware of three major differences between personal theories and formal theories:

- Formal theories are written to be tested. A good formal theory provides hypotheses that can be studied. As a result, our research can show how they can be improved.
- Formal theories are tested using the scientific method. As a result we can be more confident of our conclusions.
- Formal theories are more easily refuted and refined because their flaws are more evident. They can't "wiggle away" when they mismatch the evidence.

My intention is not to put scientific explanation down, but rather to point out how you have been scientists all along. As you discover similarities between your own explanations and scientific explanations, your self-respect should increase and the remoteness of the scientist should decrease.

SOME APPLICATIONS OF SOCIAL PSYCHOLOGY

Social Psychology Is Useful. Professional social psychologists have learned much of interest to amateur social psychologists. One of the goals of this book is to show you how useful social psychology can be in your daily life by relating its findings to common sense and by giving everyday examples of its principles. Research findings can thus be used to better understand our own social behavior and that of others.

Professional social psychologists have also learned much of interest to policymakers, social activists, planners, and other leaders. We haven't learned to leap tall buildings at a single bound, but we can evaluate people's reactions to tall buildings and offer advice to architects on what sorts of buildings will be used and enjoyed by people. Social-psychological research can also be applied to specific social problems. This application enables us to develop a broader understanding of the relation between one problem and another, guides us in considering causes of these problems, and provides research methods for assessing these suspected causes. When we intervene and try to reduce a social problem, research methods developed by social psychologists help us to evaluate the effects of our solutions.

All of social psychology can potentially be used to improve the quality of life. But that aspect of research that is *intended* to be applied and that typically deals with some problem, is called *applied social psychology*. There are several differences between *basic research* (research that can be applied) and *applied research* (research done specifically for some application).

On the one hand, basic research is typically conducted by a social psychologist from a university faculty. The research topic is selected because the researcher has a special interest in it. As a result, topics range widely. The research is often done in a laboratory, using college students and experimental designs. It is often financed by the researcher, by the university, or by a grant. Its findings are published in professional journals. Those who want to apply the findings must read these journals.

On the other hand, *applied research* is typically done by a psychologist (sometimes trained as a social psychologist) working for the government, a large industry, or a research firm. The research topic is chosen by the researcher's employer or by an agency such as the National Highway Traffic Safety Administration. The research is often done "in the field"—in the streets, in cafeterias, or wherever the problem is. College students are rarely subjects in such studies, and experimental designs are often not possible. The research is paid for by the researcher's employer or by a contract from an agency. The results are disseminated in technical reports, in-house documents, and by word of mouth. And, in general, they are put to some immediate use.

There are also major similarities between applied and basic research. Both test hypotheses and can be used to develop and refine theories. Both sometimes prove very useful and sometimes prove useless. Both are challenging and enjoyable for the researchers involved. And both are needed. In the remainder of this chapter and throughout this book, we will examine applications—actual or potential—of both basic and applied research.

Society needs applied social psychology. Every day, social problems grow larger. Every indication suggests that crime, hunger, discontentment, poverty, and injustice are quite capable of keeping up with population growth, and population is growing geometrically. If the problems are growing, then so must our efforts to solve them. Solving a problem may take money. But it also takes an understanding of the problem—its causes, its effects, and what solutions are possible. Without this understanding, money will be wasted. With this understanding, money may still be wasted. Social programs need to be objectively evaluated to determine their effects. Without such evaluation, we cannot know whether the money was well spent or not. In the next part of this chapter, I will present some brief descriptions of areas in which applied social psychologists have worked.

Not all authors cited in these pages would call themselves social psychologists. But perhaps they—and all other psychologists and sociologists—are now social psychologists at heart. As Burgess has said:

> In the final analysis, it is social interaction that has been the principal focus of social psychologists, and they have been enormously successful. Their success has reached such a magnitude that the importance of the social context, in general, and social interaction, in particular, has become increasingly evident throughout the entire field of psychology, from clinical psychology to educational psychology to developmental and physiological psychology. Certainly, these fields have much to learn about the subtlety and complexity of basic social processes, and social psychologists will, undoubtedly, have much to contribute to these areas [1977, p. 14].

The four applications of social psychology that are described on the following pages suggest its potential breadth and relevance. Other applications are discussed in later chapters.

Psychosocial Death.   From time to time in everyday life, we experience great crises. A mother or father or spouse or child dies. We lose our job. We move to another city. We get married or divorced. Many life events produce high levels of *stress*. Stress occurs whenever a great change in our life occurs, whether the change is for better or worse.

People deal with stress in many ways. At one extreme, they adapt to their new situation and cope with it very well. At the other extreme, stress leads to depression, to illness, and sometimes to **psychosocial death.** Why does stress sometimes lead to death and sometimes seem to cause little upset? We might consider three major factors that seem important.

1. *The amount of stress.* Some events are more stressful than others. The death of a significant other person is more stressful than the death of an acquaintance. But some people will find the death of a spouse more stressful than others will.
2. *Physical and emotional strength.* A person who is physically and emotionally strong is less likely to succumb to illness or depression following stress. Generally, the elderly are weaker and experience more negative consequences of stressful events.
3. *Social support.* You will read in Chapters 2 and 10 that, when people face a stressful, fear-provoking situation, they try to affiliate with others. Such affil-

iation may raise our self-esteem, reassure and comfort us, and help us appraise our situation. A person who has a network of friends who help in times of stress is better able to cope with it.

Given these three principles, let us take a look at some effects of stress.

☐ Many studies (Rowland, 1977) have found that mortality rates are high for those whose spouse has recently died. People who have lost a spouse are much more likely to die in the following year than those of the same age who have not. This effect may be due to a combination of the stress from the spouse's death and the loss of social support to deal with the stress. People who have depended on their spouse for consolation lose this support. This effect seems strongest among the elderly, who tend to be less physically resistant to the effects of stress.

☐ Moving to a strange city often results in high levels of stress. One's family and one's household goods are often the only familiar aspects of this immersion in a novel environment. Being a newcomer to groups and losing the social support of old friends also contributes to the debilitating effects of relocation.

☐ Many researchers have found high death rates for old people after their admission to an institution (Rowland, 1977). These rates range from 16% to 25% during the first month after admission.

☐ It is possible that the stress of retirement also leads to higher rates of psychosocial death, particularly if the person is in poor health. This effect may be due, in part, to the reduction in social support that comes from "loss" of colleagues at work and loss of meaning in life.

Social psychology can contribute much to an understanding of stress and psychosocial death. More research is needed on the nature of stress and the nature of our responses to it. More needs to be known about why some people are better than others at coping with it. And research is needed to better plan life events to minimize such stress and its harmful consequences. Such research could lead to social policies and reforms that might significantly increase life expectancy.

Understanding Juries. Juries have tremendous power over the fates of defendants. Few small groups have so much power. Can social psychologists provide help in understanding juries and their biases? Yes. The social psychology of juries is a rapidly growing research area. Some social psychologists have been influential in the courtroom, involved as expert witnesses or in jury selection to help stack the deck or eliminate bias (Etzioni, 1974; Rokeach & Vidmar, 1973). Others have studied simulated juries.

The findings about simulated juries have been very interesting. Researchers have learned that differences in jurors may mean differences in verdicts. For instance, jurors' "authoritarianism" (a personality trait we'll examine later) affects their judgment (Mitchell & Byrne, 1973). Researchers have also learned how aspects of the crime affect judgment. For example, murderers who mutilate their victims are more often judged insane and receive much longer prison terms (Hendrick & Shaffer, 1975b). As you might expect, factors that affect attraction affect judgments too. For instance, the similarity of attitudes held by defendant and juror may affect the juror's judgment (Griffitt & Jackson, 1973). Factors surrounding the trial also seem important. For instance, pretrial publicity affects judgment, increasing the juror's belief in guilt (Hoiberg & Stires, 1973). And, contrary to the spirit of the law, defendants who plead the Fifth Amendment may be judged more harshly than those who deny guilt (Hendrick & Shaffer, 1975a).

It is important to remember that these findings come from *simulated* juries—college students who play the role of juror in an experiment. Actual juries may behave somewhat differently.

These findings lead us to reflect on common sense. Researchers have concluded that "perceived causation in matters of law seems to have a very complex logic which rests squarely on the common sense psychology of everyday life" (Hart & Honore, 1959; Hendrick & Shaffer, 1975b). We should learn more about the common-sense psychology of everyday life and more about the thoughts, understandings, and behaviors of juries. Such knowledge could lead to changes in the legal process that would ensure justice for the accused.

Power to the Powerless: Responsibility and the Aged.   Aging brings some unpleasant changes. We find our bodies deteriorating, our friends dying, our real income shinking, and our control over our lives may decrease.

Control revisited.   The need to control our personal environment seems to be basic. We often strive for such control and for feelings of control (see also Chapter 3). There are many positive effects of control, as Langer and Rodin (1976) have reviewed. For instance:

☐   When we expect an unpleasant event that we cannot control, our physiological distress and anxiety increase (Geer, Davison, & Gatchel, 1970; Pervin, 1963). When people can choose the order of taking several tests of ability, they feel less anxious than when they cannot choose the order (Stotland & Blumenthal, 1964).

☐   When we are involved in games of chance, we tend to believe that we can control the outcome (Langer, 1975). Such an illusion of control increases our expectation of success and our confidence.

☐   People who develop feelings of hopelessness and helplessness are more prone to depression, ulcerative colitis, leukemia, cervical cancer, heart disease, and even death (Adamson & Schmale, 1965; McMahon & Rhudick, 1964; Richter, 1957; Schmale, 1958; Schmale & Iker, 1966; Seligman, M., 1975).

The aged and control.   Whereas young people typically feel that they can control their personal environments, the aged typically do not, especially those in nursing homes. As people retire and age, their familiar roles change and dissolve. Many friends in their reference groups become disabled or die. Their health typically declines. Retired, they find their fixed income shrinking relative to the cost of living and their usefulness to others fading. They find themselves no longer masters of their environments. They have become unwanted pawns.

If control is so important to health, morale, and effective functioning, then the aged who feel a loss of control find themselves without a critical resource for living. Would restoring feelings of control reduce some of the unpleasantness of growing old?

To answer this question, Langer and Rodin (1976) conducted a field study in a nursing home. Residents of the fourth floor were encouraged to make choices and take responsibility for day-to-day events. Residents of the second floor were not given this encouragement. Those on the fourth floor were asked to decide whether they would like a plant and which of several plants they would like. They were expected to take care of their plant. Down on the second floor, residents were simply given a plant, which was taken care of by the staff. Those on the fourth floor were asked to decide whether they wanted to see a movie and when they wanted to see it. Others were told when they could see it. In short, the fourth floor residents were given some control and expected to make decisions and be responsible. The second floor residents did not have such responsibility and control. Patients on both floors were given equal attention and care.

These differences in treatment may seem minor, but they were important to the patients. Three weeks after the experiment began, patients who had been urged to be responsible (the fourth floor):

- Rated themselves as happier than the others rated themselves.
- Reported themselves to be more active.
- Were rated as more alert.
- Spent more time talking to and visiting with other patients, visitors, and staff members.

Rodin and Langer (1977) did a follow-up study to see what was happening a year and a half later. Their findings were very similar to those at three weeks: inducing feelings of responsibility had many positive effects. For instance, compared to the second-floor patients, those who had been urged to be responsible were rated by nurses as more interested in their environment, more sociable, and more vigorous. Although such scores declined for both groups in the year and a half, they declined more for those not urged to be responsible. Further, the health of the fourth-floor group *increased* during this year and a half, and the health of others declined. Finally, about 15% of the responsible group and 30% of the other patients died during the 18 months.

From these studies by Rodin and Langer, it is evident that decline with aging is not inevitable. When the elderly do decline, it may be in part a result of their loss of control over their environment. All of us—both weak and strong, young and old—need to feel that we are masters of our fate.

Improving Toothbrushing. Improper dental care causes problems. Cavities develop and gums recede. An alternative to having more dentists—which would only cause congestion on our golf courses—is more toothbrushing.

The experiment. Throughout this book will be found ideas on how people might be influenced to brush better. Some of these ideas have been tested in a real-life dental hygiene program (Evans, Rozelle, Lasater, Dembroski, & Allen, 1970). In this study, almost 400 junior high students were given dental-care kits that included specific recommendations on how to care for teeth, a toothbrush, toothpaste, dental floss, and "disclosing wafers." Disclosing wafers are small tab-

"Pleasant information, repeated often, is remembered best."

lets that, when chewed, temporarily color plaque red in places missed by the toothbrush.

After these researchers gathered information on the dental practices and attitudes of the students, they attempted to improve students' toothbrushing. One group was given a persuasive appeal designed to produce high fear of the consequences of not brushing. A second group received a positive message, stressing the advantages of proper brushing—including greater popularity. A third group simply received quite detailed recommendations on proper toothbrushing.

Results.   What happened? First of all, students remembered the most information on how to brush when it was presented with the positive appeal, and they remembered the least with the high fear appeal. This finding is consistent with the Pollyanna Principle. More learning takes place under pleasant circumstances than unpleasant. As you might expect, students remembered less as time passed. This suggests that information campaigns must not only be pleasant but must also be repeated from time to time.

By using the disclosing wafer, these researchers were able to learn how well students brushed their teeth. All of the methods of persuasion used by the researchers resulted in cleaner teeth. But after six weeks there were signs that students were returning to their old brushing habits. (In Chapter 6 you will read how hard it is to change people's attitudes or behavior.) Of the various types of persuasive appeals, it turned out that the cleanest teeth resulted from the detailed recommendations and positive appeals. Thus, while fear appeals (see pp. 283–

284; 309–310) may be effective, positive appeals may be even more so (Higbee, 1969). Because fear-arousing appeals raise ethical questions, perhaps they are not necessary in dental-health education.

One of the surprise findings from this study was that how often students reported brushing their teeth was not related to how clean their teeth actually were. (The attitude/behavior consistency problem is discussed in Chapter 5.) This finding suggests that, if you want to do research on behavior change, study the actual behavior, not self-reports of behavior.

SUMMARY

Social psychology is the study of how thoughts, feelings, and behaviors are influenced by the actual, imagined, or implied presence of others. Social psychologists have found that the influence of others can be profound and is often underestimated. Studying social behavior can be useful in improving our understanding of ourselves and others.

Everyone has already studied social behavior informally and might be called an amateur social psychologist. Professional social psychologists use scientific methods in this study. This has given social psychology an identity separate from fields such as philosophy, which are also interested in social behavior.

The personal explanations of amateur social psychologists are reviewed in terms of types, characteristics, application rules, value, and shortcomings. Our systems of explanation consist of personal theories and application rules; personal theories are made up of variables and relationships between them. Most of these relationships described in personal theories are positive or negative. The major shortcomings of personal theories seem to be that they are sometimes wrong, but we do not usually have good ways to test them and discover this. Because common sense is often right, much, but not all, of what professional social psychologists have learned is intuitive and comes as no surprise to us.

Unfortunately, common sense is sometimes wrong. The conflicts between personal theories are one reason why it is important to study social behavior carefully—to refine and improve on our common sense. To improve our common sense we need to know where it is right and where it is wrong. The idea that personal theories and common sense are sometimes wrong was historically an important breakthrough for science. Sociologists are now interested in "the social construction of reality"—the idea that most of the things we assume are "true facts" are merely assumptions or beliefs we've agreed on.

Scientific explanation follows a repeating pattern of observation, induction, generalization, deduction in which we ask questions, find answers, and ask more questions. Such a process is involved in the construction of our social reality, which is a shared set of understandings of the world and behavior. Scientific explanations involve many assumptions, including invariance, multiple causation, determinism, thresholds, and overdeterminism. Some mechanistic ideas of cause and effect are questioned, and the role of expectations and decision making is emphasized. Similarities and differences can be found between personal and scientific theories and between basic and applied research. Applications of social psychology show how useful the field can be.

GLOSSARY TERMS

Define these terms in your own words, then look them up in the glossary at the end of the book.

Application rules
Causation
Common sense
Control system
Deduction
Descriptive personal theory
Determinism
Explanatory personal theory
Feedback loop
Generalization
Homeostatic
Induction
Invariance
Limiting conditions
Multiple causation
Observation

Overdetermination
Pattern matching
Personal explanation
Predictive personal theory
Prescriptive personal theory
Proscriptive personal theory
Psychosocial death
Reasons
Science
Scientific explanation
Social construction of reality
Social psychology
System of explanation
Threshold
Underdetermination
Variable

FURTHER READING

Manis, M. *An introduction to cognitive psychology.* Monterey, Calif.: Brooks/Cole, 1971.

Wegner, D. M., & Vallacher, R. R. *Implicit psychology.* New York: Oxford University Press, 1977.

chapter
2

Research

---

chapter

2

INTRODUCTION

How do people influence one another? Why are some people more influential than others? Why are bystanders sometimes helpful, sometimes not? Questions such as these are easy to ask but not always easy to answer.

In order to illustrate the difficulty of research on social behavior, I will compare the problems that confront the chemist and the social psychologist.

All chemicals have names and definite compositions. A particular chemical is exactly the same in every laboratory in the world. The chemist finds that the effects of mixing two chemicals under the same conditions can be precisely measured and will always be the same. Because the chemist can control what goes into the test tube, the effects she observes can be traced to specific causes.

The life of the social psychologist is not so simple. Four major problems in understanding "social chemistry" will always be with us:

1. *Measuring and Naming Causes and Effects.* Causes and effects in social processes are difficult to measure. Factors such as attitudes, habits, thoughts, feelings, values, and experiences are hidden inside people and cannot be seen. They cannot be named with the exactness that a chemist names a chemical, nor can they be measured with exactness.
2. *Repeatable Observations.* Because social processes are affected by history, most never occur twice in exactly the same form. Each time your family eats dinner, the members behave somewhat differently. Unlike the chemist, who can learn about the invariant effects of chemical A on chemical B, the social psychologist cannot discover such uniform relations. The effects of person A on person B may be different today than they were yesterday.
3. *Multiple Causes.* Most processes, thoughts, feelings, and behaviors have many potential causes; it is hard to separate them. It is even difficult to name all the probable causes. Unlike the chemist, who can study the effects of one pure chemical on another, the social psychologist must study processes as complex as adding a tossed salad to vegetable soup.
4. *Individual Differences.* When social psychologists study social behavior, they must be content with forming imprecise generalizations. Everyone is a bit different

Unlike the chemist, who can learn about the invariant effects of chemical A on chemical B, social psychologists can't discover such lawful relations.

and reacts to the same event a bit differently. This is different from chemistry, in which all pure bottles of chemical A are exactly the same.

Social psychologists are challenged by these difficulties in conducting their research. Most of them are **methodologists,** experts at studying a large variety of questions under difficult conditions. Because their interests are broad and the problems that interest them are complex, social psychologists have learned a great deal about how to conduct research. In fact, many of the research principles understood and accepted by social and behavioral scientists have been developed by social psychologists. This is why you will find a section on research methods in nearly every social-psychology text.

A good researcher will have to learn much more than the information presented here. This chapter is an overview of how and why research is done. Even as an overview, though, it may seem complicated. But understanding how social psychologists do research is important and worth your effort.

In the first chapter we discussed those personal theories we hold as amateur social psychologists and those formal theories proposed by professional social psychologists. How do we answer the questions we have about social behavior? Our answers come from research.

TYPES OF RESEARCH

Personal Research. The term *research*, in its broadest sense, ranges from reflecting on your own experiences or asking someone a question to conducting complex laboratory experiments or surveying thousands of people. The importance of an accurate answer to your question, your available time and resources, and your interest in the question will dictate the complexity of your research design. Generally, the earlier stages of inquiry are less rigorous than the later stages.

Personal research normally precedes **formal** (scientific) **research.** For example, we might begin our research by noticing that men tend to begin eating ice cream cones with a bite, whereas women seem to begin by licking them. Intrigued by a few casual observations made of friends, we might decide to make more observations and record what we see. Eventually, we might do more formal research, or we might decide the question was not worth much effort.

Formal Research.   Most researchers have a curiosity that takes them in two directions. First, they are interested in accurately describing social behavior, so they conduct **descriptive research.** After they have described the behavior, they then press on to explain what they have observed, conducting **explanatory research.** Researchers try to avoid confusing description and explanation.

Descriptive research.   Descriptive research takes many forms. We'll now look at four varieties—survey research, participant observation, archival research, and correlational research.

Survey research.   Survey research uses questionnaires or interviews to find answers to questions such as "Will the people in this neighborhood welcome or

Survey research uses questionnaires or interviews to find answers to specific questions. A census is an example of a survey done on an entire population.

oppose a new shopping center on Main Street?" This type of descriptive research makes an effort to **sample** (select from) a **population** (large group) of individuals in such a way that, by knowing about the sample, we can make inferences about the population. One sampling procedure is called **random sampling,** because individuals are drawn from the population at random (completely by chance). By random-sampling procedures we are able to make quite accurate guesses about a large population by surveying only a fraction of it.

Although there are many other sampling approaches, most seek to produce samples that are representative of the population. Back in 1936, the *Literary Digest* polled over 2 million voters and predicted that Alfred M. Landon would beat Franklin D. Roosevelt for president by a landslide. Remember President Landon? Remember the *Literary Digest*? This failure to predict the outcome of an election did not result from sampling too few voters. Rather, it resulted from a **biased sample.** The *Literary Digest* had used sources such as phone directories in drawing the sample. But it turned out that many people who did not own phones voted, and many of them did not vote for Landon. Today, social psychologists know that how a sample is drawn is just as important as how large it is. Using only 2000 carefully selected voters, it is now sometimes possible to predict the outcomes of presidential elections to within 1% of the votes.

Participant observation.   Surveys are not the only way to conduct descriptive research. Many researchers enter situations they want to learn about and take part in them, a technique called **participant observation.** For instance, Laud Humphreys (1970) frequented public bathrooms and acted as a lookout so he could learn about homosexuality in public places. Joy Browne (1976) attended a training seminar offered by an automobile manufacturer in order to interview used-car salesmen and learn how they work. William F. Whyte (1955) studied residents of Boston's North End and Herbert Gans (1962) did the same in the city's West End by living in these areas, attending neighborhood meetings, visiting with newfound neighbors and friends, interviewing residents, and by carefully observing neighborhood activity. Participant observation can be a very effective way to learn about a group of people. In a casual manner, we do it every day to learn about our own culture and society.

Archival research.   **Archival research** is another good way to learn about people. It lets us study what people do after they have done it, without their knowing they are being studied. We can look at graffiti on bathroom walls to learn some surprising things about men and women. We can listen to pop music from different periods or cultures and record how frequently themes such as love and sorrow appear. The great sociologist Emile Durkheim looked at records of suicide rates in different countries and seasons. In general, any written record or trace that people leave behind—even beer bottles on the streets—can be a source of information useful to the clever researcher.

Correlational research.   One goal of descriptive research is to discover averages and describe groups of people and their attitudes and behaviors. Another important goal is to discover *how* things are related, to describe naturally occurring relationships between two or more variables. The method used to do this is called the **correlational method,** because a co-relationship is examined.

For example, our casual observations might lead us to suspect that the crime rate is higher in taller apartment buildings. We might gather information on apartment projects of different heights, as Oscar Newman (1973) did. Figure 2-1 graphically shows the correlation between these variables. As building height increases, robberies per 1000 families increase, too. This is a **positive correlation** between these two variables. Sometimes a correlation between two variables results when one influences the other. For instance, building height may directly influence the crime rate. More often, though, a complex system of influences is at work, with several sets of variables actually responsible for a correlation. For example, it may be that there is greater anonymity in taller buildings and that anonymity, not building height per se, is an influence on the crime rate. It may be that tall buildings tend to have wealthier people living in them and that wealth, not height, attracts burglars. You may be able to think of other plausible explanations. Finding a correlation between two variables may pique a researcher's curiosity and lead to further research. A correlation suggests, but does not prove, that one variable is influencing another.

Figure 2-1.
Going up? Relation of robbery rate to building height. (From *Defensible Space*, by O. Newman. Copyright © 1972, 1973 by Oscar Newman. Reprinted by permission of Macmillan Publishing Co., Inc. Published in the British Commonwealth by The Architectural Press Ltd.)

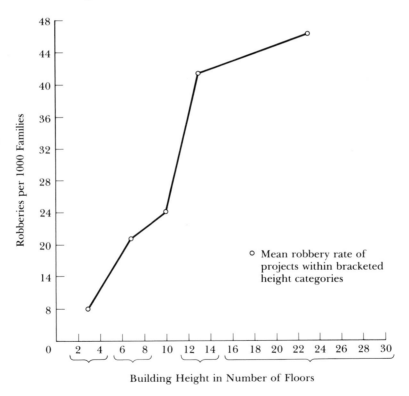

Not all correlations are positive. You will read later about a study in which students observed whether passersby would help beggars on the streets of New York City (see pp. 250–251). These students discovered that, when one person approached a beggar, helping occurred 15% of the time. Only 6% of the two-person groups helped the beggar, and none of the three-person groups did. Results (shown in Figure 2-2) indicate a **negative correlation** between group size and helpfulness. It is negative because increases in one variable (group size) accompany decreases in another (helping). As in other correlational studies, we have learned *what* the relationship between these two variables is, but we haven't learned *why* they are related. It seems unlikely that group size itself has a direct effect on helpfulness. But perhaps the size of our group affects our attitude toward helping. To see whether this is true, we need to conduct explanatory research.

Figure 2-2.
Buddy, can you spare a dime? *Buddies*, can you spare a dime?

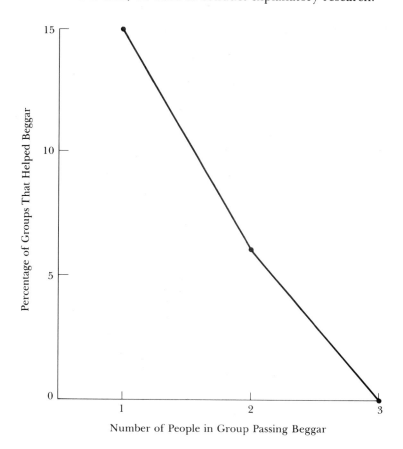

Number of People in Group Passing Beggar

Explanatory research. Social psychologists explain social behavior by describing the variables that affect it and the nature of these effects. Unlike descriptive research, which shows *if* two variables are related, explanatory research attempts to show *why* they are so related. Explanatory research uses experiments to predict and control, thus testing explanations.

Prediction is a strong test of understanding. Social psychologists make a prediction about what will happen under a certain set of circumstances and then create those circumstances and observe the results. If their predictions are confirmed, they are more confident that they understand what is happening, that their explanations are correct.

Control is also a good test of understanding. If we are able to induce subjects in an experiment to behave in a certain way, we become more confident that we understand that behavior.

The role of prediction and control in testing our understanding is demonstrated in the research of Darley and Latané (1968a, 1968b). They wondered why several dozen people could witness a murder from the safety of their apartments yet not even call the police, as has happened several times in New York City.

These researchers proposed that no one helped *because* so many bystanders were available to help. They suggested that, the greater the number of bystanders, the greater the **diffusion of responsibility** for helping and the smaller a person's obligation to help. They predicted that people would be less likely to help in large laboratory groups than in small ones or if they were alone. This prediction was tested in several experiments, including one in which smoke was pumped into the room by the experimenter. Groups of various sizes watched the smoke pour in and had an opportunity to call for help. Darley and Latané predicted that a person randomly assigned to a small group would be more likely to help a stranger than a person assigned to a larger group. This prediction was confirmed. They found that they could control a person's helpfulness by varying the size of the group. This success in prediction and control gave Darley and Latané more confidence that they understood the problem.

Prediction and control are important, but neither is necessary or sufficient proof of our understanding. To see how they are not necessary, consider the astronomer. On the one hand, astronomers have very little control over the things that interest them most, yet they understand a great deal. On the other hand, although Darley and Latané were able to predict and control helping behavior in the smoky room, this doesn't mean that they understood it. Diffusion of responsibility is a theory that "fits" their results. But so do other theories. For instance, people may feel more inhibited in taking *any* action—either helping or hurting—in a larger group. A theory may be wrong even if it seems to match our observations.

It is easier to decide if a theory is useful than to decide if it is right or wrong. Useful explanations are ones that make sense to us, that make us comfortable, that quench our curiosity about why something is the way it is, and that help us to anticipate events.

THE EXPERIMENT

A hypothesis is a reasonable guess about how two variables are related. Hypotheses (like predictive personal theories) lead us to expect to make certain observations under certain conditions. In order to see whether these predictions are correct, we must first decide how to measure the variables of the hypothesis. Any rule that translates the idea of a variable into a measuring operation is called an **operational definition**. For example, if we hypothesize that men are more aggressive than women, we need to decide how to measure aggressiveness. Will it be how they eat an ice cream cone? Will it be how fast they drive on the turnpike? Any such measuring operation provides a precise definition for the more vaguely defined abstract variable in our hypothesis.

Experiments are one means of making these observations. Experiments are very helpful in testing theories for two reasons: they create situations and they help us to understand cause and effect. For instance, when Darley and Latané wanted to study reactions of a group to smoke pouring into the room, they did not have to sit with their clipboards waiting until the building actually caught fire. By pumping artificial smoke through a vent, they created exactly the situation they wanted to study (without damaging any property).

Or consider how you might test the hypothesis that "misery loves company." Of course, you could go up to people in naturally occurring crowds of various sizes and ask them how miserable they felt. But this might be difficult. It is sometimes hard to find miserable people, and, when we do, they may be reluctant to say they are miserable. With an experiment, we don't have to wait around for a miserable person. Within the limits of ethical scruples, we can *make* people miserable and watch what they do. One great advantage of an experiment is that it allows situations to be created for study.

Two paragraphs back, I mentioned that another advantage of an experiment is that it allows an understanding of cause and effect. An experiment is a situation created by a researcher to determine if and how one or more specific variables of interest (called **independent variables**) affect one or more other variables of interest (called **dependent variables**). The dependent variables, on the one hand, *depend,* to some extent, on the values taken by the independent variables. Independent variables, on the other hand, are manipulated (controlled or caused to take certain levels) by the researcher. So their level is *independent* of that taken by any dependent variables.

In a simple experiment, the researcher divides subjects up and assigns some to an experimental condition, or treatment, and the others to a control condition. Then, the researcher makes the two conditions exactly the same in every single respect but one: the independent variable. If we tested the hypothesis that "misery loves company," for instance, we could see whether changes in misery (the independent variable) caused changes in the desire for company (the dependent variable). We might make subjects in our experimental condition miserable but not make subjects in our control condition miserable. If misery loves company, subjects in our experimental condition should desire company more than subjects in our control condition.

Correlational studies are not as clearcut in revealing cause and effect as experiments. For example, suppose we compared people who were working alone with people working in groups and found that the people in the groups were happier. Would it be because people become happier after they join a group, because happy people decide to join groups, or because sad people are excluded from groups? We wouldn't know. An experiment could test each of these hypotheses one at a time to determine what causes lead to what effects. Any well-designed experiment is better than a correlational study for understanding cause and effect.

Getting Ready for the Experiment.   Before you plan an experiment, it's worth learning what is already known about the variables you are interested in studying and the relationship between them. An experiment is usually time-consuming, so if you can learn from another researcher's experience, you can save yourself work. "Reviewing the literature" means spending time in the library.[1] For example, if you check *Psychological Abstracts* under the key word "affiliation," you'll see that Stanley Schachter has already provided an experiment on affiliation with his "misery-loves-company" hypothesis (see p. 213 for a brief review of this literature). We can use his experiment to illustrate how experiments are typically done.

Schachter began his research on affiliation with a review of the literature. But in the late 1950s, social-psychological literature was sparse, and there was little to review. Schachter concluded that "a review of the literature indicates that . . . at most, there have been two or three immediately relevant experiments" (1959, p. 1).[2] After reading about the experiences of hermits and prisoners in solitary confinement, Schachter tried a **pilot study** (a simple informal experiment) to see what would happen when students were placed in isolation. He was surprised and disappointed by the results. One subject "broke down after two hours, almost hammering down the door to get out" (1959, p. 9). But another relaxed in isolation for eight days. After calculating that 11 years might be needed to complete this experiment, Schachter decided to try another experimental design. Pilot studies are *very* useful in avoiding problems in subsequent research. Researchers can save considerable time, money, and grief by running small-scale pilot studies before plunging into full-scale experimentation.

Schachter had noticed that isolation often seemed to produce anxiety. He wondered whether "conditions of anxiety would lead to the increase of affiliative tendencies" (p. 12). Schachter decided to test this hypothesis with an experiment. To do so, he first had to think about the variables in his hypothesis and decide how to measure them. This process is called *operationalization,* because it offers a measuring operation for each variable in the hypothesis. Schachter operationalized anxiety as the effect of telling people that they would be receiving painful shocks. Affiliative tendencies were operationalized as a preference for waiting for the shocks alone or together, as measured by a questionnaire. Unfortunately, Schachter's experiment did not test his hypothesis, because he created **fear** rather than **anxiety.** As it turns out, both fear and anxiety seem to have the same effects on affiliation, and we can forgive Schachter for not thinking very clearly. Mistakes are common in research.

Assignment of Subjects.   First, Schachter randomly assigned 62 undergraduates to one of the two conditions—"high anxiety" or "low anxiety." **Random assignment** means chance placement in one of the experimental conditions. Subjects must be randomly assigned to a condition, rather than being allowed to choose it, to ensure that at the start of the experiment they are not systematically different in the two conditions. (If subjects were allowed to choose the condition they experienced, we would not know whether the difference between conditions or

[1] For advice on how to do library research, see Stang, in press.
[2] From *The Psychology of Affiliation,* by S. Schachter. Copyright © 1959 by Stanford University Press. This and all other quotations from this source are reprinted by permission of Stanford University Press.

the initial difference between subjects was responsible for the results of the study.) Random assignment means that any subject is as likely to end up in one condition as another, and it is done using a table of random numbers.

When subjects arrived at the experimental room, Schachter wrote:

> An attempt was made to prevent the subjects from talking to one another while waiting for the experiment to begin, for again it was felt that an interesting conversation or particularly friendly girl might confound the choice of "To-gether" or "Alone." As each subject entered the experimental room, she was handed a multipaged questionnaire labeled "Biological Inventory" and asked to begin filling it out. This device worked well and effectively prevented any chatter until all of the subjects had arrived and the experimenter could begin his monologue [p. 17].

Experimenters usually try to minimize **intersubject communication** (what Schachter called "chatter"), and often try to use subjects who do not know one another.

The Cover Story.   Schachter's subjects then met the experimenter, who introduced himself and delivered the **cover story** (a false explanation of the purpose of the experiment). Because an experiment is an artificial situation, the experimenter must give it realism. One kind of realism the experiment needs is **experimental realism**: Does the experiment keep the subjects awake? Do they notice what is going on? Do the procedures make sense in light of the cover story? Another kind of realism the experiment should have is **mundane realism.** Does the experimental situation have counterparts in everyday experience? Does it seem natural or artificial and contrived?

Experimenters often use some **deception** to increase both experimental and mundane realism. Deception occurs when subjects are intentionally misled about the purpose or methods of the experiment. Deception may seem like a terrible thing, but there are good reasons for concluding that honesty is not always the best policy. For one thing, deception permits the study of situations that are rare and that we simply cannot afford to wait for. For instance, if I want to learn about the conditions under which people are most helpful, through deception I can create a situation in which help appears needed without waiting for months to happen upon a similar real-life situation.

Another important function of deception is to prevent inquisitive subjects from guessing what the experimenter is up to. If Schachter had told his subjects that he was interested in learning about the relation between fear and affiliation, he might have obtained much different results. Helpful subjects would have behaved in a way to confirm what they thought were his hypotheses, while grouchy subjects might have done just the opposite. By misleading participants, Schachter assured us all that his findings were really what happens to affiliation when people are fearful and not simply reports of what people think they should do.

Although deception of some sort is often necessary, this does not mean that social psychologists are chronic liars. Researchers typically take many precautions before they use deception. These include:

- Assuring that the research problem is important and cannot be suitably studied without deception.
- Permitting subjects to withdraw from participation at any time without penalty.
- Taking responsibility for detecting and removing any harmful aftereffects of the deception.
- Fully explaining the deception to subjects after completion of the study, whenever possible.
- Making sure that, when the deception is explained, the subjects will find it reasonable and experience no loss of confidence in the researcher's integrity.

Sometimes deception takes place through **misinformation**: the experimenter lies to the subject. Sometimes the experimenter merely withholds information from subjects, thereby providing **incomplete information.** In Schachter's experiment described here, subjects were given misinformation; that is, they were told they would be receiving shocks, when in fact they were not shocked.

The Manipulation.   Schachter **manipulated** the situation to create high anxiety or low anxiety in subjects. Thus, the difference in situations in the two conditions was the independent variable. Schachter hoped that this would lead to higher anxiety in one condition than the other and that this intervening variable would in turn lead to differing affiliation preferences (the dependent variable). Schachter's hypothesis is shown in Figure 2-3. The independent variable is manipulated by the experimenter. It affects an intervening variable, which in turn affects the dependent variable.

Figure 2-3.
Independent, intervening, and dependent variables in the two conditions of Schachter's experiment

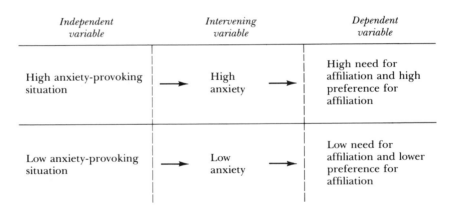

Schachter affected each subject's degree of anxiety (or fear) with his cover story. In the high-anxiety condition, subjects were frightened and convinced that they would be receiving painful shocks. The low-anxiety condition was much less frightening, as you will see below. Thus, Schachter created two "levels" of the independent variable of anxiety—high and low. He tried to make both conditions the same except for this difference in anxiety, so that differences in the dependent variables could be attributed to differences in the anxiety-provoking situation alone.

The following is a breakdown of Schachter's manipulation. It outlines the techniques he employed for both conditions or for each condition separately.

Both Conditions

Subjects entered a room to find "facing them a gentleman of serious mien, horn-rimmed glasses, dressed in a white laboratory coat, stethoscope dribbling out of his pocket" (Schachter, 1959, p. 12).

High-Anxiety Condition	*Low-Anxiety Condition*
Behind the experimenter stood "an array of formidable electrical junk" (p. 12).	No electrical apparatus in room.

Both Conditions

Dr. Zilstein (the experimenter): "Allow me to introduce myself. I am Dr. Gregor Zilstein of the Medical School's Departments of Neurology and Psychiatry. I have asked you all to come today in order to serve as subjects in an experiment concerned with the effects of electrical shock" (p. 13).

High Anxiety	*Low Anxiety*
Zilstein paused ominously, then continued.	"I hasten to add, do not let the word 'shock' trouble you; I am sure that you will enjoy the experiment" (p. 13).

Both Conditions

Dr. Zilstein continued with a seven- or eight-minute recital of the importance of research in this area, citing electroshock therapy, the increasing number of accidents due to electricity, and so on. He concluded in this vein (p. 13):

High Anxiety	*Low Anxiety*
Dr. Zilstein stated: "What we will ask each of you to do is very simple. We would like to give you a series of electric shocks. Now I feel I must be completely honest with you and tell you exactly what you are in for. These shocks will hurt, they will be painful. As you can guess, if, in research of this sort, we're to learn anything at all that will really help humanity, it is necessary that our shocks be intense. What we	"What we will ask each of you to do is very simple. We would like to give each of you a series of very mild electric shocks. I assure you that what you feel will not in any way be painful. It will resemble more a tickle or a tingle than anything unpleasant. We will put an electrode on your hand, give you a series of very mild shocks and measure such things as your pulse rate and blood pressure, measures with which

will do is put an electrode on your hand, hook you into an apparatus such as this (Zilstein points to the electrical-looking gadgetry behind him), give you a series of electric shocks, and take various measures such as your pulse rate, blood pressure, and so on. Again, I do want to be honest with you and tell you that these shocks will be *quite painful*, but, of course, they will *do no permanent damage*."

I'm sure you are all familiar from visits to your family physician."

Both Conditions

At this point, the experimenter had completed his attempt to create low anxiety in some subjects, high anxiety in others (the manipulation of the independent variable). He was now ready to measure the effects of the independent variable—anxiety—on the dependent variable that interested him—desire for affiliation. Schachter did this by telling subjects that they would have to leave the room for ten minutes while some equipment was moved in. Did the subjects wish to wait alone or together? They were asked this question:

> Please indicate whether you prefer waiting your turn to be shocked alone or in the company of others.
> _____ I prefer being alone.
> _____ I prefer being with others.
> _____ I really don't care.

This question was one **dependent measure** Schachter used (called dependent because it measured the amount of one variable—desire for affiliation—that presumably depended on the effects of another variable, manipulated earlier—anxiety). Schachter asked another question that also measured affiliation need and two questions that measured anxiety. These measures of anxiety (**checks on the manipulation**) provided a check to see if his manipulation of anxiety had been successful: Were the women who were supposed to be very anxious actually anxious? Were they more anxious than the other subjects? Schachter's use of two measures of each variable enabled him to see how much his results were an effect of his measurement methods.

Analysis of Results. What did Schachter find? First of all, his check on the manipulation indicated more anxiety in the high-anxiety condition. So far, so good. Then he looked at affiliative preferences in his two conditions. His results are reported in Figure 2-4. Twenty of 32 subjects (63%) in the high-anxiety condition wished to wait together. Only 10 of 30 subjects (33%) in the low-anxiety condition wished to wait together. Schachter's hypothesis was supported: high anxiety produced a greater desire for affiliation than low anxiety.

Was this difference between the two conditions real, or could it be due to chance? (Even if both groups received exactly the same treatment in the experiment, they would differ a bit due to unexplained factors we can call chance.)

Figure 2-4.
Relationship of
anxiety to the
affiliative tendency.
(From Table 2,
p. 18 of *Psychology
of Affiliation,* by
S. Schachter.
Copyright © 1959
by Stanford
University Press.
Reprinted by
permission of the
publisher.)

	No. Choosing		
	Together	*Don't care*	*Alone*
High anxiety	20	9	3
Low anxiety	10	18	2

$$X^2_{\text{Tog vs } DC + A} = 5.27$$
$$p < .05$$

Like other researchers, Schachter wanted to know whether or not his results were due to chance. He performed a test of **statistical significance** to find the **probability** (p) that his results were due to chance (Figure 2-4). One test Schachter performed examined the affiliative preferences of subjects in his two conditions, to see whether preferences were affected by condition. He did a "chi-square test" to compare those preferring to wait with those who either preferred to wait alone or who didn't care (χ^2_{Tog} vs $DC + A$). The computed value of chi square was 5.27, which he found (by consulting a table) to be a value unlikely due to chance. In fact, a value of chi square that is this large would occur by chance less than 5 times in 100 such tests, assuming that his two conditions were really identical in their effects ($p < .05$).

If you look at Figure 2-4, you can see how the affiliative preferences of Schachter's subjects were affected by condition: 20 of 32 (63%) high-anxiety subjects chose to wait together, whereas only 10 of 30 (33%) low-anxiety subjects had this preference. By computing chi square, Schachter found his results were "real," and not due to chance. By looking at the pattern of results of Figure 2-4, Schachter was able to determine *how* his conditions had their effect on affiliative preferences. Analysis of research results typically involves arranging data in tables, performing statistical tests, and—most important of all—carefully examining and interpreting the patterns of effects. The expression "$p < .05$" means that such a difference between conditions is very probably real, not due to chance. It means that, if the result were due to chance, you would have to repeat the experiment about 20 times before you got an effect as strong as this. Thus, Schachter concluded that his results were real effects of his manipulation and not due to chance.

Schachter did several more experiments, each of which helped lead him to new discoveries and new hypotheses to test (1959). His findings are presented in a 133-page book that is well worth reading. I will discuss affiliation again in Chapters 8 and 14.

Designing a Good Experiment.   We have now examined an experiment in some detail and followed it from start to finish. The features common to nearly all experiments were described. An **experimental design** is a plan for how an experiment will be conducted—how observations will be made, compared, and analyzed. Some designs are better than others, depending on an experimenter's needs. In this section I will discuss some experimental designs—their strengths and weaknesses.

When we conduct our own personal research, we use several different designs. In the simplest design, a **posttest-only design,** we provide a treatment and then observe the results. For example, the woman and man who put on the Flab-Away in Figure 2-5 were presumably magically transformed to look slimmer and then drawn by an imaginative artist. The biggest problem with this design is obvious: we don't know how they looked before the treatment, so we don't know what effect, *if any*, the treatment had.

Figure 2-5.
Posttest-only design

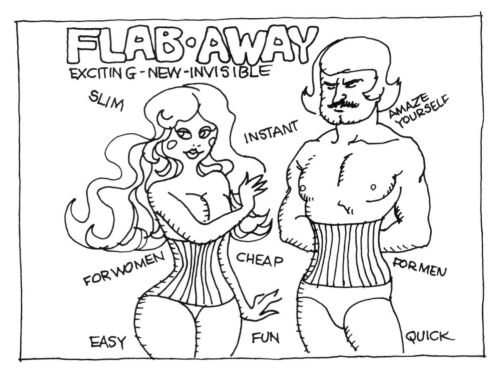

A second common personal research design is the **pretest/posttest design**, in which we make our observations before and after treatment, as in the case of the spray cleaner in Figure 2-6. The main problem with this design is separating the effects of the treatment (in this case, the spray cleaner) from the effects of other events that occurred at the same time. In other words, would a clean rag do the same job as rag plus spray cleaner? The effects of other variables may thus be **confounded** (confused) with the effects of the treatment.

A third common personal research design is a **posttest-only, control-group design.** In this design, one group receives one treatment, the other receives another. In Figure 2-7 a dirty rug is cleaned. The cleaning is done by the regular method or by a special method. Observations are then made to compare the methods.

Figure 2-6.
Pretest/posttest
design

We cannot be sure that one treatment is better than the other in this design unless we are confident that both groups were nearly identical beforehand. If one rug was *initially* dirtier, then this will affect how clean the rug looks later. One way to ensure equality is to assign individual units (rugs, people, or whatever) to treatments at random, as Schachter did. Figure 2-7 offers no assurance that this was done. When groups are randomly assigned and a number of "subjects" (rugs, in this case) are used, this design becomes important in scientific research. In fact it is the most common research design used.

A fourth common design is called the **pretest/posttest, control-group design.** This design is illustrated in Figure 2-8. First, observations of two groups (clean mops) are made. Then, each group receives a different treatment (Mop Glop versus nothing). After mopping, a second set of observations is made. Comparisons can then be made between (a) the two initial observations, (b) the initial and final observation for a given mop, and (c) the two final observations. The first comparison provides a clue to whether the third comparison is legitimate. Both the second and third comparisons provide clues about the effects of the treatment. As you can see from Figure 2-8, the experimental condition (Mop Glop) seems to pick up more dirt (the dependent measure) than the control condition (no Mop Glop). Confounding may still occur, however. The Mop Glop effect may be due to the product or to dampness. Is Mop Glop better than water sprayed on a mop?

Figure 2-7.
Posttest-only,
control-group
design

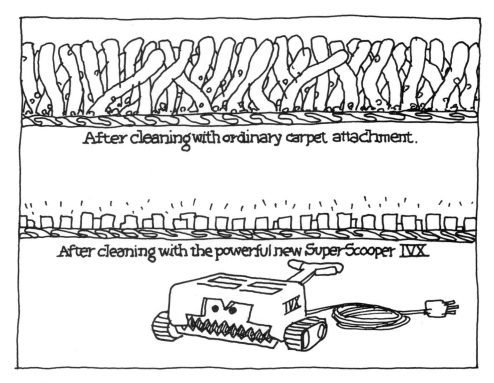

After cleaning with ordinary carpet attachment.

After cleaning with the powerful new Super Scooper IVX

We don't know from this particular experiment. To better understand the treatment effect, researchers often add additional control groups.

Field versus Laboratory.   Not all experiments are conducted in a laboratory. Many are conducted in natural settings and are called field experiments. A field experiment may have just as much control over the independent variable as does a laboratory experiment, although some have less. For example, in the laboratory, subjects can be directed to study a series of pictures or words. These pictures or words could also be displayed in a natural setting, such as in ads in magazines or posters on telephone poles, but we would not be as confident that passersby had seen them all. But whatever a field experiment may lose in control, it may gain in realism. Because field experiments take place in natural settings, generalizations from them often seem more plausible.

Another great advantage of field experiments is that they eliminate **demand characteristics.** Demand characteristics are cues that subjects notice and use to "help" the experimenter. In the laboratory, subjects may guess that the experimenter expects them to be helpful, for instance, and so try to be as helpful as possible. In a field experiment, however, subjects are unaware that an experiment is taking place and so behave more spontaneously. Field experiments are becoming increasingly popular as a research method in social psychology. Many are described in this book.

Figure 2-8.
Pretest/posttest,
control-group
design

Mop A is dry ...
Mop B has Mop-glop...

Mop B is noticeably
dirtier...

Mop B and Mop-glop
guarantee dirtier mops!

ETHICAL ISSUES

All researchers should be concerned with the ethics of research and follow the ethical principles endorsed by the American Psychological Association (1973). These principles involve many issues, of which only a few will be noted here.

Informed Consent. Every subject in a laboratory experiment should have the right to decide whether or not to participate in research that may cause stress or harm. This principle is called **informed consent.** Such a decision should be guided by accurate information from the researcher on what stress or harm may result from participation. Subjects who decline to participate should not be penalized in any way. A study such as Schachter's study of affiliation might violate this principle if subjects do not feel free to break off their participation in the experiment at any point.

Because subjects in a field experiment will not know they are in an experiment, they will not be able to decide whether or not to participate. Researchers conducting field experiments thus have a special obligation to ensure that no stress or harm occurs.

Confidentiality.   Researchers are obligated to respect the privacy of their subjects. Information that researchers acquire about individuals should not ever be presented in a way that would identify, and possibly embarrass, an individual participant. This principle is known as **confidentiality.**

Humane Treatment of Participants.   Researchers are obligated to treat participants fairly. Subjects should be protected from physical or mental stress and from exploitation.

Every subject should have the right to decide whether or not to participate in research that may cause stress or harm.

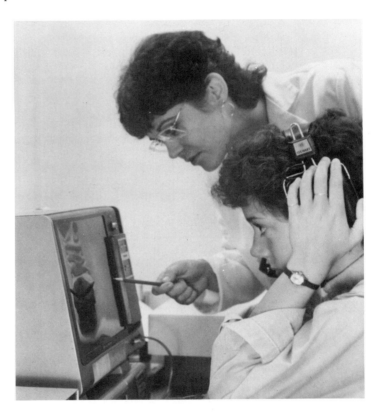

Experimentation is not easy. The researcher must know a great deal about how to do research and how to avoid problems. To avoid bias in their conclusions, researchers should:

- Choose the right method—an experiment, interviews, questionnaires, role playing, or some other technique.
- Be certain that neither their own expectations nor their subjects' subtly bias the results.
- Be certain that they will be able to generalize from their research to everyday settings of interest.
- Be certain that their research does not create ethical problems.

Researchers receive extensive training for their difficult jobs. Their training includes several courses in research methods and statistics and many courses in the subject matter they plan to investigate.

SUMMARY

This chapter on research began by describing the personal research we do every day and discussing some of its strengths and weaknesses. It then discussed reasons for doing formal research: (1) better understanding of relationships and cause and effect and (2) development of more useful explanations.

The goal of research is to discover how things are related and then why they are related. The social psychologist does research to better describe social behavior (descriptive research) and better understand cause and effect (explanatory research). When cause and effect are understood, we feel we can predict or control events. Social psychologists do research to test such predictions; if their predictions are confirmed, they feel they understand what is occurring in their research. Although prediction and control are both tests of our understanding, we can predict and control without understanding.

Common steps in an experiment include preparation, assignment of subjects to a condition, presentation of a cover story, manipulation of the independent variable(s), measurement of the dependent variable(s), analysis of results, then further research and thinking. Schachter's experiment on anxiety and affiliation illustrates this process.

This chapter also presented some common experimental designs, involving various combinations of pretests, posttests, and control groups.

The simplest design is the posttest only, which is a treatment followed by observations. The pretest/posttest design involves observations before and after treatment. In the posttest-only, control-group design, one group receives one treatment, another group another, and then both are observed. A fourth design is the pretest/posttest, control-group design. Observations are made of two groups, both are given a different treatment, both are observed for a second time, and then comparisons are made.

Experiments may be conducted in both laboratory and field settings. Wherever research is done, researchers must be concerned with ethical issues. These include informed consent, confidentiality, and humane treatment of participants.

GLOSSARY TERMS

Define these terms in your own words, then look them up in the glossary at the end of the book.

Anxiety	Correlational method
Archival research	Cover story
Biased sample	Deception
Check on the manipulation	Demand characteristics
Confidentiality	Dependent measure
Confound	Dependent variable
Control	Descriptive research

Diffusion of responsibility
Experimental design
Experimental realism
Explanatory research
Fear
Formal research
Incomplete information
Independent variable
Informed consent
Intersubject communication
Manipulation
Methodologist
Misinformation
Mundane realism
Negative correlation
Operational definition

Participant observation
Personal research
Pilot study
Population
Positive correlation
Posttest-only, control-group design
Posttest-only design
Prediction
Pretest/posttest, control-group design
Pretest/posttest design
Probability
Random assignment
Random sample
Sample
Statistical significance

FURTHER READING

Crano, W. D., & Brewer, M. B. *Principles of research in social psychology.* New York: McGraw-Hill, 1973.

Diener, E., & Crandall, R. *Ethics in social and behavioral research.* Chicago: University of Chicago Press, 1978.

Gross, A. E., Collins, B. E., & Bryan, J. H. *An introduction to research in social psychology.* New York: Wiley, 1972.

Stang, D. J. *Social research methods.* Monterey, Calif.: Brooks/Cole, in press.

chapter
3

Some Dimensions
of Differences

TWO WAYS TO EXPLAIN BEHAVIOR

In Chapter 1, we examined how explanations of social behavior are constructed. Chapter 2 discussed how such explanations can be tested. This chapter, and the remaining chapters in this book, will describe some of the regularities of human social behavior and the explanations that have been proposed for them.

As it turns out, amateur and professional social psychologists alike use two basic approaches for accounting for social behavior: a **dispositional approach** and a **situational approach.**

The dispositional approach accounts for a person's behavior in terms of traits or states of that person. (A **trait** is a stable, enduring disposition, relatively unchanging over time; a **state** is unstable and changes.) For instance, if we said that Andy drinks because he is lonely or depressed or an alcoholic, we would be using a dispositional explanation of Andy's drinking.

The situational approach accounts for a person's behavior in terms of properties of the situation. Using this approach, we might say that Andy drinks because his wife beats him, because he lost his job, or because his father drinks. In short, the dispositional approach looks inside the person for the causes of behavior, and the situational approach looks outside the person.

Most professional social psychologists prefer the situational approach. They have several reasons. First, most studies have shown only weak relations between dispositions and behavior, and many researchers believe that situations have stronger effects on behavior than personality has. (This is not always true, but it is a prevalent belief.) Another important reason is that situations can be manipulated and measured and their effects studied experimentally. In contrast, dispositions are difficult to measure, usually cannot be manipulated ethically, and can be investigated only with correlational studies. You will remember from Chapter 2 that experimental designs are much better than correlational designs for establishing causal relations. So social psychologists interested in establishing solid causal explanations of social behavior have relied largely on the experimental method and situational explanations. In keeping with that tradition, Chapters 4 through 14 of this book review the experimental study of situational influences.

Why Study the Dispositional Approach?   Approximately 5% of all social psychologists take a dispositional approach to explaining social behavior. These researchers (who often call themselves **personality psychologists** or **personologists**) are obviously outnumbered, and their views are often unrepresented in social-psychology texts and courses.

This chapter, which surveys the dispositional approach, is included in this book for several reasons. First, the dispositional approach is a valid method of explaining social behavior. Its validity is not diminished by its lack of popularity among experimental social psychologists or by the difficulty of studying dispositions experimentally.

Further, even if one is most interested in the effects of situational and social influences on a person's thoughts, feelings, and behaviors, such influences are not restricted to immediate effects. Our dispositions reflect our life experience and summarize the accumulated effects of situational influences. For example, if a parent punishes a child for failure, the short-term effects—which could be studied with the situational, experimental approach—might be quite different from the long-term effects—which could be studied with the dispositional approach. In the short run, the child might feel angry or depressed because of the punishment. In the long run, the child might develop a high need to achieve and feel guilty about failure and pleased about success.

A final reason for interest in the dispositional approach is that it makes sense to us as amateur social psychologists. We place great importance on dispositions as the cause of behavior, perhaps more than we should (Jones & Davis, 1965; Jones & Harris, 1967; Jones & Nisbitt, 1971; Kelley, 1967). This emphasis is reflected in our language, where we have about 18,000 words for dispositions and traits (Allport, G. W., & Odbert, 1936) but few words for situations. In fact, situations are difficult to describe, and their effects are not always obvious. It is often easier to use a dispositional approach.

In sum, there are three good reasons for taking a dispositional approach to the study of social psychology:

1. Dispositions are a valid method of explaining social behavior.
2. They are important in summarizing prior situational effects.
3. The dispositional approach is used by everyone in daily life in explaining the behavior of others.

HOW PEOPLE DIFFER

Because we so often depend on dispositional explanations of human behavior, we will discuss these explanations first in this book. This chapter will describe eight of the thousands of ways that people differ. Chapter 4 will discuss some of the social and cultural sources of such differences, and Chapter 5 will discuss some of the environmental factors that produce individual differences.

Before we begin, some qualifications are in order. The first is to remind you of the difference between description and explanation. To "explain" Fred's behavior by saying that he is a nice guy is not an explanation. It is a description. As amateur and professional social psychologists, we need to begin with careful description. But our curiosity should then lead us to wonder why things are the way they are. We should be careful not to use description for explanation. Generally, the dispositional approach to the study of individual differences focuses on description, the situational approach on explanation. This chapter focuses on description; other chapters focus on explanation.

Even within a given category of people, such as this family, individual differences are usually large and significant.

Individual and Group Differences.   A second consideration is this: even within a given category of people individual differences are usually large and significant. When we describe dispositions or properties of a category of people, we usually describe the "average" in the group. When we compare groups, we usually compare group averages. It is important to remember that two members of a group are likely to differ far more in any respect than are the average members of two groups. Consider the baldies who live on Nofuzz Atoll and the hairies who live nearby on Fuzz. Recently, a team of scientists, headed by Dr. Beakchecker, visited the two islands and measured the nose length of the citizens living there. Beakchecker measured 15 hairies and tallied her findings on the left side of her "data-recording sheet" (Figure 3-1). This process was repeated for 15 baldies, whose measurements appear on the right side of the sheet.

Because it is not clear whether the baldies or hairies have bigger noses, Beakchecker summarized her tallies by averaging them. To do this, she added all the measurements and divided by the number of measurements added. She found that the average hairy had a nose of 2.47 cm, whereas the average baldy had a nose of 3.53 cm. (You'll notice that, in fact, no hairy had a nose of 2.47 cm. The *average* doesn't always describe anyone exactly.)

Do baldies or hairies have the longer noses? Just looking at averages, the baldies do. The average baldy has a nose that is over 1 cm bigger than the average hairy. Does this mean that all baldies have larger noses? No. Look at the graph

Figure 3-1.
Recording data
and determining
frequency
distribution

DATA-RECORDING SHEET
Nose-Size Determinations (in cm)

Hairies	Baldies
1	5
3	4
2	2
5	5
1	1
4	3
2	4
3	2
1	4
2	5
2	2
1	5
5	4
3	3
2	4

Frequency Distribution (tallied from data-recording sheet)

Nose Size (cm)	No. Hairies	No. Baldies
1	4	1
2	5	3
3	3	2
4	1	5
5	2	4
Sum (Σ)	37	53
No. observed (N)	15	15
Average nose size (Σ/N)	2.47	3.53

in Figure 3-2. Two hairies, for instance, have a 5-cm nose. That is longer than the nose of 11 baldies. Similarly, though hairies tend to have smaller noses, four baldies had noses of 1 or 2 cm, shorter than the noses of six hairies. Some baldies and some hairies have the smallest nose (1 cm), and some of each have the largest nose (5 cm). In short, a simple question such as "Which group has the bigger noses?" deserves a complex answer.

Beakchecker's basic research might be a cause of concern for people critical of basic research. But, in fact, she established another instance of what must be seen as a very general theory: differences between groups are almost always much smaller than differences within groups. This is true on almost any variable you can think of, comparing men and women, Blacks and Whites, old people and young people, rich people and poor people, capitalists and communists, heterosexuals and homosexuals, and even baldies and hairies.

Stereotypes of Individual Differences. If you are asked how two groups of people differ, you do not look up the answer in your psychology books. You reflect a moment—or less—and present your beliefs on the matter. A **stereotype** is a set of beliefs we hold and share with others about how members of a particular

Figure 3-2.
Nose size of baldies
and hairies

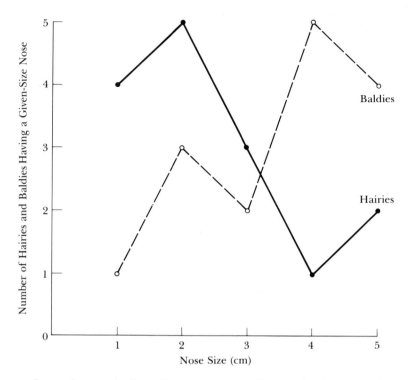

category of people are similar. Our stereotype of men, for instance, is a set of assumptions we hold about the typical personality traits, attitudes, and behaviors of men in general. We assume that most, if not all, individual men are very similar to our stereotype. Most stereotypes are shared. You and I may agree in many ways on what men are like and what women are like. In fact, we have stereotypes about racial groups, ethnic groups, religious groups, political groups, age groups, nationalities, and so on.

These stereotypes are rooted in our own experience and many may have *some* basis in truth. Some stereotypes may be entirely accurate, most have a grain of truth, and some are totally false. The trouble with stereotypes is finding where fact ends and fiction begins. Making that distinction is what education is all about.

Suppose you were asked how men and women differ. Most people would draw on their stereotypes to answer the question. Such stereotypes suggest that men and women differ in many ways. In a large number of studies, males are typically described (by both males and females) as being assertive, ambitious, competitive, competent, daring, dominant, independent, intelligent, and rugged. Females are often described as being the opposite of these male traits, as well as being emotional, expressive, gentle, helpful, kind, sensitive, tactful, understanding, and warm. These stereotypes are shared by people of various ages, marital statuses, educational levels, and religions (Abramowitz, Abramowitz, Jackson, & Gomes, 1973; Broverman, Broverman, Clarkson, Rosenkrantz, & Vogel, 1972; Elman, Press, & Rosenkrantz, 1970; McKee & Sherriffs, 1957; O'Leary, V. E., & Depner, 1975; O'Leary, V. E., & Harrison, 1975). (See Interest Box 3-1.)

Such stereotypes of men and women share many of the characteristics of the dispositional approach to explaining individual differences. They focus on internal qualities of the person (traits, attributes, and the like) while ignoring situational influences and explanations. They emphasize description rather than explanation. And they stress the differences between men and women while overlooking the great differences among men or among women on these dimensions.

Perhaps the most serious consequence of sex stereotypes is that males are seen as more highly valued than females. In one study, for instance, subjects were asked to select traits typical of men and those typical of women (McKee & Sherriffs,

---

Interest Box 3-1. Sex-Role Stereotypes in Children

Children begin learning sex-role stereotypes by the age of three or four. When I was teaching public school in Montreal, I asked 39 seventh-grade boys which of the words from the list below most often applied to girls and which ones applied to boys. Even though the list seems to have very little to do with sex, most boys agreed on which words applied to which sex. Instructions, the words, and the percentages of boys judging them to belong to each sex (or neither) are provided below.

Instructions: "Make two columns on your paper. I'm going to read a list of words. You decide whether each word I read applies to boys in general or girls in general. If it applies to both, write it in both columns. If it applies to just one, write the word in that column. If you don't think it applies to either, don't write it at all."

| Word | Percentage of boys who said word belongs to | | |
	boys	girls	both or neither
iron/steel	65	0	35
paper	11	54	35
flowers	14	70	16
blue	57	19	24
red	27	41	32
pink	0	73	27
yellow	5	57	38
black	68	0	32
corduroy	73	8	19
silk	3	76	21
lace	8	73	19
wool	22	57	21
nylon	8	62	30
study hard	22	70	8

Word	boys	girls	both or neither
strong	70	0	30
weak	0	76	24
nice	27	57	16
good	41	46	13
bad	65	14	21
athletic	70	5	25
adventurous	76	3	21
stylish	5	70	25
dirty	62	5	33
clean	16	59	25
busy	41	35	24
talkative	27	54	19
Saturday	62	16	22
Sunday	5	62	33
brave	73	0	27
sweet	0	70	30
like to sing	19	68	13
like to play ball	73	19	8
like to ride bikes	67	33	0
would like to have a family	38	59	3
would like to get a good job	70	16	14
will go to college	59	35	6
fast runners	73	5	22
gabby	5	68	27
playful	43	30	27
smart	51	49	0

It is remarkable how extensive these stereotypes of boys and girls are, covering a wide range of concepts. It is also remarkable how much each boy's stereotype was shared by the other boys in the class. But perhaps most remarkable is that these same results can be obtained today, with college students. Try repeating this study with friends. See how well their stereotypes match those of seventh-grade boys in Montreal in 1969.

1957). The results suggest that these subjects valued men more than women. Seventy-eight percent of the traits attributed to men were positive, but only 54% of the traits attributed to women were positive. Other studies have found that both men and women value men and masculine traits above women and feminine traits (Bee, Broverman, Broverman, Rosenkrantz, & Vogel, 1968; Constantinople, 1973; McKee & Sherriffs, 1957; Rosenkrantz, Vogel, Bee, Broverman, & Broverman, 1968; Sherriffs & Jarrett, 1953; Sherriffs & McKee, 1957). Such biases extend to mental-health workers, social workers, and psychiatrists. One study found that descriptions of "men" were similar to descriptions of "adults," but "women" were described much differently (and negatively) (Rosenkrantz, Vogel, Bee, Broverman, & Broverman, 1968). What's good for the gander, these therapists believed, isn't good for the goose.

Such biased values rub off on children. Parents often prefer boys to girls (Broverman, Broverman, Clarkson, Rosenkrantz, & Vogel, 1972). And they must reveal such preferences in many ways. Children learn the stereotypes and prejudices of their parents at an early age (see Interest Box 3-1). No wonder that one study found that most girls (89%) wanted to be boys but that hardly any boys (5%) wanted to be girls (Jacobson, C. J., 1974).

That men are valued more than women is reflected throughout society. The reflection shines brightest on statistics such as income. In 1972, female-headed families (father absent) had a median income of $5,380. Male-headed families (mother absent) averaged $10,350 (Howard, cited in Clifton & Lee, 1976). For equal education and equal work, women may earn between half and two-thirds of what men earn (see Figure 3-3).

Our stereotypes are closely tied to our beliefs, attitudes, and expectations. For instance, one study (Panek, Rush, & Greenwalt, 1977) found that 92% of male and female students surveyed thought psychologists were typically male. Only 40% of the people in another survey thought a woman had as good a chance of becoming an executive as a comparably qualified man (Greene, S., 1976). Should a girl be in Little League? A lot of people—boys, girls, mothers, and fathers—think not. Others see nothing wrong if she is as good as the boys on the team.

There *may* be a kernel of truth in some of these stereotypes. In some cases, a stereotype may be accurate because it is based on observation. For example, it is true that there are more male psychologists than female psychologists. But although it may be correct to say that most psychologists are men, it is incorrect to say that psychologists are men. Unfortunately, a stereotype may come to have a grain of truth through what Thomas Merton has called the **self-fulfilling prophecy** (a prediction that comes true because people act as though it were true). We tend to behave the way others expect us to behave. If we tell little boys that they are made of snails and puppy dog tails, and if we tell little girls that they are made of sugar and spice and everything nice, what opportunity will little boys have to be made of everything nice or girls to be full of mischief? Indirectly, stereotypes may have a grain of truth because they exist.

DIMENSIONS OF DIFFERENCE

The previous paragraphs have focused on sex-role stereotypes as a way of illustrating the nature and problem of stereotypes. Many other kinds of stereotypes could have been discussed, had space permitted. The same focus on sex dif-

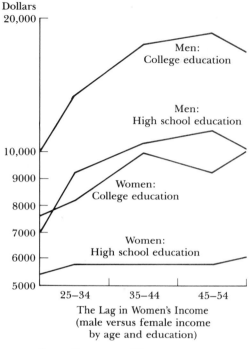

Dollars
20,000

Men:
College education

Men:
High school education

10,000

9000

Women:
College education

8000

7000

Women:
High school education

6000

5000

25–34   35–44   45–54

The Lag in Women's Income
(male versus female income
by age and education)

Source: Department of Commerce

100 percent = male income

100

Teachers, primary &
secondary schools

75

Clerical workers

Professional &
technical workers

50

Sales workers

25

1956   1960   1965   1969   1971

Women's Earnings
As a Percent of Men's
(selected occupations, 1956–1971)

Source: Council of Economic Advisors

Figure 3-3.
Sex differences in
income. (From
"Women Workers:
Profile of a
Growing Force," by
C. J. Jacobson. This
material appeared
in the *AFL-CIO
American
Federationist,* the
official monthly
magazine of the
AFL-CIO.
Reprinted by
permission of the
American
Federation of Labor
and Congress of
Industrial
Organizations.)

ferences will continue in the pages that follow, to bring some coherence to the discussion.

Eight dimensions of individual and sex differences will be presented. Some, such as authoritarianism and the achievement motive, were selected because of their historic and continuing role in the development of social psychology. Others, such as locus of control and psychological androgyny, are presented for their current interest. One, responsiveness, is presented in a more speculative way, because it has not yet gained acceptance by researchers as a dimension of difference. The section opens with a discussion of one of the most well-known and thoroughly examined dimensions of difference, the **authoritarian personality.**

The Authoritarian Personality. *He* admired those who were conservative, nationalistic, firm believers in free enterprise, friends of business, enemies of labor. He admired those with firm convictions and those who showed stability in their daily lives. He despised those who were otherwise.

She admired those who were liberal believers in social justice and equality. She admired those who were flexible, tolerant of ambiguity, and believers in individualism.

They both completed a questionnaire that contained the items shown in Interest Box 3-2, as well as others. Before you see how they scored, answer these questions yourself.

Interest Box 3-2. Attitude Questionnaire*

A. Obedience and respect for authority are the most important virtues that children should learn.
1. Strongly agree
2. Moderately agree
3. Slightly agree
4. Slightly disagree
5. Moderately disagree
6. Strongly disagree

B. Young people sometimes get rebellious ideas, but as they grow up, they ought to get over them and settle down.
1. Strongly agree
2. Moderately agree
3. Slightly agree
4. Slightly disagree
5. Moderately disagree
6. Strongly disagree

C. If people would talk less and work more, everybody would be better off.
1. Strongly agree
2. Moderately agree
3. Slightly agree
4. Slightly disagree
5. Moderately disagree
6. Strongly disagree

D. When a person has a problem or worry, it is best for him or her not to think about it but to keep busy with more cheerful things.
1. Strongly agree
2. Moderately agree
3. Slightly agree
4. Slightly disagree
5. Moderately disagree
6. Strongly disagree

E. Someday it will probably be shown that astrology can explain a lot of things.
1. Strongly agree
2. Moderately agree
3. Slightly agree
4. Slightly disagree
5. Moderately disagree
6. Strongly disagree

F. People can be divided into two classes—the weak and the strong.
1. Strongly agree
2. Moderately agree
3. Slightly agree
4. Slightly disagree
5. Moderately disagree
6. Strongly disagree

G. Human nature being what it is, there will always be war and conflict.
1. Strongly agree
2. Moderately agree
3. Slightly agree
4. Slightly disagree
5. Moderately disagree
6. Strongly disagree

H. Wars and social troubles may someday be ended by an earthquake or flood that will destroy the whole world.
1. Strongly agree
2. Moderately agree
3. Slightly agree
4. Slightly disagree
5. Moderately disagree
6. Strongly disagree

I. The wild sex life of the Greeks and Romans was tame compared to the goings-on in this country, even in places where people might least expect it.
1. Strongly agree
2. Moderately agree
3. Slightly agree
4. Slightly disagree
5. Moderately disagree
6. Strongly disagree

*Adaptation of "F-Scale Cluster" (pp. 255–257) in *The Authoritarian Personality,* by T. W. Adorno et al. Copyright © 1950 by the American Jewish Committee. Reprinted by permission of Harper & Row Publishers, Inc.

Find your score by adding the numbers of your choices. Your score can range from 9 to 54. How did you do? How do you think the two people described in the opening paragraphs of this section scored?

The nine items in the box were taken from the F scale, a personality measure developed to measure **authoritarianism.** The original scale was developed in California just after World War II by T. W. Adorno, Else Frenkel-Brunswick, D. J. Levinson, and R. N. Sanford (1950). These researchers had been stunned by the fierce anti-Semitism of the Nazis and amazed at the contrast between their own personalities and those of many Germans. Both Adorno and Frenkel-Bruns-wick had been working on the relation between personality and political extremism in Frankfurt, Germany, when the Nazi persecution of the Jews began. They eventually made their way to California, where they developed the F scale to measure tendencies toward authoritarianism.

Agreement with the nine items in the Interest Box suggests authoritarianism, and disagreement suggests nonauthoritarianism. These items represent subscales of the F scale: conventionalism, authoritarian submission, authoritarian aggression, anti-intraception, superstition and stereotypy, power and toughness, destructiveness and cynicism, projectivity, and sex. These subscales represent the nine ideas that compose the broader idea of authoritarianism.

There is a complicating factor in the quiz. If a person has a general tendency to agree with suggestions—called an **acquiescent response set**—he or she will get a higher authoritarianism score than if he or she had a tendency to disagree. Several critics of the scale have noted this problem (Bass, 1955; Berkowitz, N. H., & Wolkon, 1964; Rorer, 1965). And it seems likely that the acquiescent response set probably does affect scores on the F scale (Campbell, Siegman, & Rees, 1967).

Although other problems have been noted with the F scale and the research that produced it, this early research generated hundreds of further studies. As you might expect, scores on the F scale have been found to be related to many other things. For example, people who are authoritarian tend to be prejudiced (Campbell & McCandless, 1951). They tend to participate less in community activities (Sanford, 1950). And they volunteer less for participation in psychology experiments (Rosenthal & Rosnow, 1969). Authoritarians seem to dislike ambiguous situations (Zacker, 1973) and assume that others are very similar to them (Simons, 1966). But not all research has found advantages to being nonauthoritarian. One study, for instance, found that successful basketball and football coaches tend to be high in authoritarianism (Penman, Hastad, & Cords, 1974).

These findings are interesting, and they raise some additional questions. You will learn in Chapter 8 that similarity is an important determinant of attraction. Is authoritarianism an important dimension of similarity that affects attraction? Are your friends similar to you in authoritarianism? (To find out, you might compare your scores on the nine items of Interest Box 3-2 with those of your best friend. If your entire social-psychology class were to do this, your instructor could plot the pairs of scores on the blackboard to see if there is a relation between a person's authoritarianism and that of his or her best friend.) In Chapter 5, you will read about socialization and how parental values are transmitted to children. Do people acquire authoritarian values from their parents? How would your parents answer the nine items of Interest Box 3-2?

Dogmatism.   Most variables in social psychology, such as authoritarianism, begin with a personal theory of how or why something is the way it is. When a measuring instrument (such as the items of Interest Box 3-2) is developed, the variable moves from idea to fact. But better ideas and better measurement approaches are always possible. We have seen that there has been some criticism of the ways authoritarianism is measured. Are there problems with the idea itself?

We might wonder whether there is a connection between authoritarianism and ideology. Can an authoritarian be either left-wing or right-wing? Milton Rokeach (1960) explored the question and found that the F scale does measure conservative ideology: those with high F-scale scores are more often on the right than on the left. Believing that people can be closed-minded, rigid, intolerant, and authoritarian regardless of their political ideology, Rokeach developed the concept of **dogmatism.** He defined it as "a relatively closed cognitive organization of beliefs and disbeliefs about reality, organized around a central set of beliefs about absolute authority which, in turn, provides a framework for patterns of intolerance toward others" (1960, p. 195). His measure of dogmatism has been found to be fairly free of ideology: both conservatives of the right and communists of the left have been found to have higher dogmatism scores than moderates.

Because of the respect for authority that dogmatic people show, we might expect that people with high dogmatism scores might be more influenced by authority figures than those with low scores. This does seem to be the case (Vidulich & Kaiman, 1961). Because of the rigidity of dogmatic people, we might expect that they would not do well in situations requiring flexibility, such as bargaining. Some research supports this assumption, too (Druckman, 1967). In fact, many of the dozens of variables that have been found to be related to authoritarianism have also been found to be related to dogmatism. This is not surprising, because the two concepts are so similar.

Dogmatism and authoritarianism scales both measure some common attitudes, and each measures some unique attitudes. In the case of dogmatism and authoritarianism, they are probably unique enough to justify their continued independent existence as variables. But all personality researchers must ask themselves when proposing a new dimension of personality whether this new variable is really different from others that have already been studied. If it is not, it may be better for the investigator to devote time to the study of the existing variable.

The Achievement Motive.   Before you read further, imagine this picture: An 18-year-old boy is seated at his desk in a classroom. There is an open book in front of him, but he is not looking at it. His forehead is resting in one hand and he is looking at you thoughtfully. Now spend about five minutes writing a brief story that answers these four questions: (1) What is happening in the picture? (2) What led up to this situation? What happened in the past? (3) What is the boy in the picture thinking and feeling? (4) What will be the outcome, or resolution?

The stories of two other students are given in Figure 3-4. These stories differ considerably in what has been called the **achievement motive.** How do these stories compare with yours?

In the late 1930s Henry Murray (1938/1962) developed a theory of personality based on needs. He developed a list of 12 **viscerogenic needs** ("needs of

Figure 3-4.
Two sample stories from the TAT, one high in achievement imagery, one low in achievement imagery. (From *Motives in Fantasy, Action, and Society: A Method of Assessment and Study.* © 1958 by Litton Educational Publishing, Inc. Edited by John W. Atkinson. Reprinted by permission of D. Van Nostrand Company.)

High Story

1. This chap is doing some heavy meditating. He is a sophomore and has reached an intellectual crisis. He cannot make up his mind. He is troubled, worried.

2. He is trying to reconcile the philosophies of Descartes and Thomas Aquinas—and at his tender age of eighteen. He has read several books on philosophy and feels the weight of the world on his shoulders.

3. He wants to present a clear-cut synthesis of these two conflicting philosophies, to satisfy his ego and to gain academic recognition from his professor.

4. He will screw himself up royally. Too inexperienced and uninformed, he has tackled too great a problem. He will give up in despair, go down to the G——— and drown his sorrows in a bucket of beer.

Low Story

1. The boy in the checkered shirt whose name is Ed is in a classroom. He is supposed to be listening to the teacher.

2. Ed has been troubled by his father's drunkenness and his maltreatment of Ed's mother. He thinks of this often and worries about it.

3. Ed is thinking of leaving home for a while in the hope that this might shock his parents into getting along.

4. He will leave home but will only meet further disillusionment away from home.

the body" such as food, water, and sleep) and 28 **psychogenic needs** ("needs of the psyche" such as nurturance, sex, affiliation, and achievement). Perhaps it is a tribute to the quality of life in North America that its social psychologists have not shown much concern with viscerogenic needs.

The term **need** usually refers to a state of deficiency or deprivation that somehow arouses activity to reduce that deficit. For instance, we have a need for food; when we are deprived of food, we become aroused and take some action that leads to eating. Once we have eaten, our food need is temporarily satisfied.

Henry Murray developed the **Thematic Apperception Test** (TAT) to measure how powerful the various needs were. The TAT involves showing a person pictures (like the one described above) and asking the person to create a story (sometimes called a **protocol**) that answers the four questions you answered.

One of the needs proposed in Murray's theory was n Ach (pronounced en-atch), the **need for achievement.** This is the need to overcome obstacles, exercise power, and strive to do something as well and as quickly as possible. In the 1950s, David McClelland and his colleagues (1953) began studying the need for achievement. One way they measured it was with TAT stories like the one you wrote. They replaced *need for achievement* with the term *achievement motive*, because this new label did not suggest deprivation. People who are high in achievement motivation continue to achieve regardless of how much they have already achieved. Achievement desires are not easily satisfied.

What matters in achievement—motivation or ability? Einstein and Edison felt that genius was 1% inspiration (ability) and 99% perspiration (motivation).

For more mundane levels of academic achievement, intelligence (ability), motivation, and personality appear about equally important (Levonian, 1970). To perform any job well requires at least some minimal level of each quality.

Achievement seems to be the product of ability times motivation. When ability is 0, even high motivation means failure. When motivation is 0, even high ability means failure. When both are high, achievement is most likely.

High ability can compensate for low motivation to some extent, and vice versa. I once took a physical exam to join a volunteer fire department. In one of the tests, we had to breathe into an apparatus to measure our lung capacity. Just before this test, the medical technician asked me if I smoked. "Yes, pipes and cigars," I replied, and I felt particularly determined to demonstrate that my smoking had had no adverse effects on my lung capacity. After the test, I asked the technician if smokers generally had a smaller capacity than nonsmokers as measured by his machine. He said that the reverse was true. Apparently, he said, smokers try harder than nonsmokers to demonstrate their lung capacity—and succeed—because they do not want to believe that smoking has damaged their lungs.

People who work hard to achieve may be motivated by a desire for success, a fear of failure, or both.

A person who works hard to achieve may be motivated by a desire for success, a **fear of failure,** or both. You may know some students, for instance, who are in college because their parents expect them to be there. These students who achieve out of fear of failure may do as well as those students who have strong desires for success. People who work very hard to achieve are sometimes called **overachievers,** because they achieve more than would be expected from their ability alone.

Some people who do not achieve much may be reacting to a **fear of success** or a desire for failure. They may worry that others would disapprove of their success. Or they may have low self-esteem and secretly desire failure because they think it is more their style. Such people may have a **motive to avoid success.** People who do not strive for achievement are sometimes called **underachievers,** because they do not achieve as much as would be expected from their ability alone.

There may be sex differences in desire for achievement. Research in this area was initiated by Matina Horner (1968) using a variation of the TAT idea. Horner provided subjects with the opening of a story that they were expected to complete. The women in the study received this first sentence: "After first-term finals, Anne finds herself at the top of her medical school class." For the men, "John" was substituted for "Anne." The stories were scored as showing fear-of-success imagery if negative consequences befell either Anne or John as a result of receiving high grades in medical school. Fifty-nine of the 90 women in the study exhibited fear of success, whereas only 8 of the 89 men did.

One problem for personality researchers is developing valid measures. (A measure is valid if it actually measures what it is supposed to measure.) In the case of Horner's measure of fear of success, it may well be that women fear success more than men. But it may also be that success is less socially acceptable in women than men and that, regardless of whether men or women were writing the stories, they would indicate more negative consequences befalling successful women than men. In our society, such differences might have more than a grain of truth. Does Horner's **projective test** measure fear of success or realistic expectations of success in our culture? One way to find out would be to have women and men write stories about both Anne and John. But even with this approach, we would still be faced with several possible interpretations of the findings. The trouble with all projective tests is that we cannot be sure that they really measure what we think they do.

Research findings since Horner's study have not always been consistent. Different studies find different levels of fear of success in women (Caballero, Giles, & Shaver, 1975; Spence, 1974). This suggests that some women fear success more than others, and perhaps different methods of measuring fear of success produce different results (Alper, 1974). Other studies have not always found that women or girls fear success more than men or boys (Brown, Jennings, & Vanik, 1974; Romer, 1975; Zuckerman & Wheeler, 1975). But most studies do seem to report this finding (Caballero et al., 1975).

It is possible to interpret these studies in terms of fear of failure rather than (or in addition to) fear of success. There is some evidence that, when men succeed, they are valued more highly than women with the same level of success. But when men fail, they are seen as less competent than women who fail (Deaux & Taynor, 1973). Because of this, men have more reason to fear failure than women. If men try harder than women to succeed, it may be because men fear failure more, not because they fear success less.

What kind of success do we fear? Women may fear success in those occupations dominated by men, such as doctor, lawyer, or Indian chief. Men may fear success in occupations that are more typically dominated by women—kindergarten teacher, nurse, secretary, dental assistant. Such fears may lead the sexes away from careers in fields dominated by the other sex. And our stereotypes may draw us to those careers "appropriate" for our sex.

Why would women fear successful careers more than men? Stereotypes, prejudices, and discrimination may all be involved. To some extent, traditional

" *If men try harder than women to succeed, it may be because men fear failure more, not because they fear success less.* "

stereotypes may push women away from careers altogether. Career-oriented women may not always be well liked by male work partners (Shaffer & Wegley, 1974) and may be quite concerned about such rejection (Stewart, A. J., & Winter, 1974). Successful women have sometimes been viewed by both men and women as unattractive, immoral, and dissatisfied and are believed to experience many difficulties and conflicts (Monahan, Kuhn, & Shaver, 1974).

In any case, no one supposes that fear of success is the only thing preventing success in women. After all, it is a myth of our culture that everyone can do everything if they only try. As Depner and O'Leary have observed, "Horner's work was a major creative contribution to the field, yet it cannot and should not be expected to yield a complete understanding of the reasons why women choose the roles they do. Clearly the question is much broader than 'Why do women fail to strive for success?' " (1976, p. 267). Factors such as sex-role stereotypes, attitudes toward a woman's competence, low self-esteem, fear of failure (if you don't try, you can't fail) and role conflict may also be barriers to a woman's achievement (O'Leary, V. E., 1974).

Another barrier to achievement in women is the nature of televised models. One study (Manes & Melnyk, 1974) reported that only low-achieving women on television were depicted as having successful relations with men. Female jobholders on television were depicted as married less often than men and, if married, less likely to be successfully married. In fact, married working women were depicted as having unsuccessful marriages ten times as often as were housewives. Similar portrayals occur in children's textbooks (Child, Potter, & Levine, 1946; Jacklin, cited in Manes & Melnyk, 1974). Such a portrayal of women on television and in books must have profoundly negative consequences for a little girl's career aspirations. In short, a wide variety of factors may be responsible for sex differences in achievement.

Machiavellianism.   To some extent, perhaps, we all want to be successful and achieve. How do we achieve success? It seems that everyone has different strategies. Some people bet on the horses, buy lottery tickets, or keep their fingers crossed.

Some people have become skilled at persuading and manipulating others to get their own way. Those who are willing to use deceit and cunning to exploit others get very high scores on measures of **machiavellianism—mach** (pronounced "mock") **scales**—developed by Christie and Geis (1970a). These scales contain items such as "I do not blame a person for taking advantage of someone who lays himself open for it" and "I think most people would lie to get ahead."

A number of studies have found some remarkable differences between "high machs" and "low machs." For instance, low machs seem to be more easily influenced (Geis, Krupat, & Berger, cited in Christie & Geis, 1970a; Harris, cited in Christie & Geis, 1970a; Rim, 1966). High machs seem more influential (Christie & Geis, 1970b; Geis, 1970). For instance, one study found high-mach children more successful than low machs at getting middle machs to eat crackers with quinine (quinine has a terrible, bitter taste) (Braginsky, 1970). High machs get better grades than low machs who have the same actual ability. As Albert Harrison (1976) has observed, being a high mach is not necessarily bad. High machs are good at getting jobs done and can be just as friendly and well adjusted as anyone. Social psychologists, incidentally, are usually high machs (Christie & Geis, 1968). You might give some thought to why some people are more machiavellian than others. How machiavellian are you? Your friends? Your parents? How do you feel about people who are very high or low in machiavellianism?

Field Dependence and Independence. Have you ever been sitting in a car or train, looking out the window at another car or train, when one of them started to move? Did you find it difficult to tell which one was moving? In deciding which was moving, you may have used cues provided by your body, by your eyes, or by both. Herman Witkin has called people who tend to use such internal body cues **field independent,** because their perception is independent of the visual field (what they can see) (Witkin, Dyk, Faterson, Goodenough, & Karp, 1962/1974; Witkin, Lewis, Hertzman, Machover, Meissner, & Wapner, 1954/1972). Others are called **field dependent.** The field-independent person guesses which car or train is moving by attending to the feeling of movement. The field-dependent person would use visual cues and so might tend to be confused for a minute.

Witkin has used a variety of ways to assess field dependence. In the **rod-and-frame test** (RFT), a person in a darkened room views a luminous rod centered within a tilted luminous frame. The task is to make the rod vertical with respect to gravity, not the tilted frame. Field independents do well in this task, but field dependents are biased by the tilted frame.

In Witkin's **body-adjustment test** (BAT), people seated in a special tilted room are required to align themselves to the upright by adjusting their chairs. As in the RFT, a field-dependent person in the BAT is one who relies on the visual field rather than internal cues.

There is now a vast literature on field dependence (Goodenough, D. R., & Witkin, 1977; Witkin & Goodenough, 1977). This literature suggests that people's tendency to rely on their visual field in the RFT and BAT is related to similar tendencies in social situations. For instance, field-dependent people are more likely to be influenced by others in ambiguous situations (Birmingham, 1974). Perhaps because of this dependence on others, field-dependent people have stronger preferences to be with others (Bard, 1972; Coates, Lord, & Jakobovics, 1975). And they prefer to be physically close to others (Holley, 1972; Justice, 1970).

Just as field-dependent people are more attentive to visual cues, they are more attentive to social cues (Eagle, Goldberger, & Breitman, 1969; Fitzgibbons & Goldberger, 1971; Ruble & Nakamura, 1972). In fact, field-dependent people may be more popular with peers (Oltman, Goodenough, Witkin, Freedman, & Friedman, 1975; Wong, 1977). They may get along better (Oltman et al., 1975). And they may be more successful in occupations where interpersonal relations are important.

However, while field dependents seem to do better on social tasks, field independents do better on many cognitive (mental) tasks, especially those that require people to restructure or reorganize what they see (Witkin & Goodenough, 1977).

Witkin and his colleagues have conducted many studies in which participants included children, college students, and psychiatric patients. Once again, as in achievement motivation, sex differences in field dependence have been found. On the RFT, women tend to be field dependent and men field independent (Dreyer, Dreyer, & Nebelkopf, 1971; Hoffman, C., & Kagan, 1977; Pearlstein, 1971; Witkin et al., 1962/1974; Witkin, Goodenough, & Karp, 1967).

The study of individual differences begins by describing a way that people can differ and by proposing how such a difference can be measured. Research generally finds that such a difference is related to other differences. For instance, field dependence/independence, as measured by the RFT or BAT, is related to how people behave in social situations, as we said above. But description is not explanation. Why are people field dependent or field independent? How do such differences develop? We will examine this question in Chapter 4.

Locus of Control. The other day I met two fellows in the hall who were talking about their lives. "All sorts of things have been happening to me lately," said Ezra. "In some ways I've been really lucky, like on dates. But I got a rotten grade on that last test. The prof is a real creep."

"I didn't do well on the test either," replied Ira, "but I didn't study enough. I can do better when I try."

Ezra is not likely to do as well in college, because he doesn't appreciate the connection between hard work and success. But whether or not his instructor is a creep, the internal Ira does not blame his instructor for his failure. Ira believes that his hard work will lead to success. He may be better at adapting to new situations, may achieve more, and may be more independent.

Do you think you control your own destiny? Or are you just a pawn controlled by the fickle finger of fate? Locus of control refers to the degree to which you believe that what happens to you is under your control. People have an **internal locus of control** if they believe that things that happen to them are under their control. Those with an **external locus of control** believe that what happens to them results from luck, chance, fate, and powerful other people and is simply unpredictable. From what I overheard of their conversation, Ezra seemed to be an "external," Ira an "internal." Ezra believes that others control his fate, whereas Ira feels that he himself is in control. This idea of locus of control was proposed by Julian Rotter (Rotter, Seeman, & Liverant, 1962). In recent years the idea has become one of the major interests in personality research. The idea is important, and the variable, as measured by Rotter's (1966) **I-E scale,** appears to be related to many things.

Much of the research on internal/external locus of control suggests that being internal is related to behavior that is adaptive, achieving, independent, autonomous, and competitive. Being external is related to passive, dependent, anxious, maladjusted, and hesitant behavior (Phares, 1976a, 1976b; Thornhill, Thornhill, & Youngman, 1975).

Some studies with animals suggest how important the feeling of control might be. Dogs that learn that they cannot do anything to avoid a shock stop trying to avoid it. They also don't try to avoid unpleasant events they actually could avoid (Seligman, M., 1972, 1975). They have a **learned helplessness.** Rats who control the shock they and other rats receive may develop ulcers—an "executive rat"; but rats lacking this control become passive and withdraw (Weiss, J. M., 1971). Learned helplessness in people may also lead to passiveness and withdrawal (Dweck, 1975; Dweck & Repucci, 1973).

Research on locus of control has been growing at a tremendous rate, with a hundred or so studies published every year. To provide some flavor of the findings, a few are noted below:

- ☐ Most people are more attracted to an "internal" stranger than an "external" (Nowicki & Blumberg, 1975).
- ☐ Like field dependents and authoritarian and dogmatic people, externals are more susceptible to suggestions made by prestigious authorities than are internals (Lefcourt, 1972).
- ☐ Internals prefer positions of high power in a group, whereas externals prefer low-power positions (Hrycenko & Minton, 1974).
- ☐ Insofar as internals prefer to be in control and externals prefer to be controlled, we would expect externals to conform more and be more easily influenced by others. A number of studies find this to be true (McColley & Thelen, 1975).
- ☐ As compared to externals, internals may regard their successes and failures as more important and meaningful; thus they are more pleased by rewards and more defensive about negative reactions. Internals are usually more likely than externals to take credit for their success and sometimes more likely to accept blame for their failure (Gilmor & Minton, 1974; Krovetz, 1974; Lefcourt, Hogg, Struthers, & Holmes, 1975). For example, on receiving a poor grade, externals are more likely to blame the teacher for it (Page & Roy, 1975).

In fact, internals may be more likely than externals to feel that people, rather than situations, are the important causes of behavior. For example, internals may be more likely to blame another driver for an accident (Sosis, 1974).

Does the description of an internal sound like your stereotype of a male and the description of an external sound like your stereotype of a female? Some research suggests that women are more external than men (McGinnies, Nordholm, & Ward, 1974). But other research finds the sex difference not significant (Lefcourt, 1966, 1972; Nisbett & Temoshok, 1976). Other studies have found that Blacks, Hispanics, children, and the poor tend to be more external than other people. It may be that scores on the I-E scale are related to real differences in the amount of control people have.

Although the research is not definitive on sex differences in locus of control, studies of stereotypes find that we *believe* there is a sex difference. Good performances by women are more often viewed as due to "luck" than are good performances by men (Deaux & Emswiller, 1974), and women are more likely than men to use "luck" as an explanation of their success and failure (Bar-Tal & Frieze, 1974; Deaux & Farris, 1974; Feather, 1969). At state and county fairs—and in the laboratory—women tend to choose games of luck such as bingo, and men tend to choose games of skill such as tossing coins in dishes and tossing rings over bottles (Deaux, White, & Farris, 1975). Our understanding of locus of control as an individual difference may help us better understand differences between men and women.

Responsiveness.   Earlier in this chapter you learned that situations and dispositions are two basic classes of influence on social behavior. Typically, the situation and our own experience combine to suggest what we should do. A **responsive** person is one who pays careful attention to what the situation defines as appropriate behavior and behaves accordingly. An **unresponsive** person tends to ignore such situational cues and behaves independently of them.

The responsive person may be more willing to behave appropriately in each social situation, such as assisting others when they need help.

As we might imagine, responsive people are more sensitive to variations in the social behavior of others and variations in situations. They notice how you are feeling, what you are wearing, and so on. And they may also be more skillful at interpreting the meaning of such variations for defining "appropriate" behavior. Responsive people know when you want them to be silly, sad, or serious. The responsive person may also be more willing to behave appropriately in each social situation. Your responsive friend is willing to be silly if being silly is appropriate and willing to be serious if that is what is called for. Finally, responsive people may be more skillful at a variety of social behaviors. They may have larger "behavioral repertoires" to choose from, making the selection of an appropriate behavior easier.

Responsiveness is almost interchangeable with Mark Snyder's (1974, 1977) idea of **self-monitoring**—a person's tendencies to use impression-management tactics. (I will discuss impression management in Chapter 6.) Research on self-monitoring is just getting under way, and I am introducing the idea of responsiveness here for the first time. Responsiveness is introduced in this book in order to show how a variety of research on topics as seemingly unrelated as conformity, prejudice, and the role of status in the effects of frustration on aggression may all contribute to an understanding of a new idea. When new dimensions of individual difference are named by a theorist, there is very often already a body of literature that can be reinterpreted and reevaluated. There is a second reason for discussing responsiveness here: responsiveness may help bridge the gap between dispositional and situational approaches. If situations have stronger effects on responsive people, situational explanations of social behavior will be most apt for them.

Ralph Minard (1952) conducted a well-known study that illustrates differences in responsiveness. He estimated that about 20% of White men working in a coal mine had positive attitudes toward Blacks both in the mine and in the community. By Minard's estimate, another 20% had negative attitudes in both situations. For this 40% of the White miners, the situation did not have much effect on the expression of their attitudes. But the remaining 60% responded differently in the two situations, showing, it happens, more positive behaviors in the work situation and more negative behaviors in the after-work situation. In the mine, cooperation and positive behaviors between Blacks and Whites were useful and appropriate. It might be argued that, given the racist attitudes in the community, negative attitudes were "appropriate" for the above-ground, nonwork situation. So Minard found that about 60% of the miners studied were responsive, showing different behaviors in the two situations, and 40% were unresponsive, showing the same behaviors in the two situations.

State or trait? Is responsiveness a state (changing over time) or a trait (a stable, unchanging disposition)? It may be both. The idea of responsiveness as a state comes from our observation that, when we are tired or stressed, we may be less responsive than otherwise.

Situations themselves probably provide many cues for how responsive a person needs to be. For instance, we may earn and maintain respect by being responsive. But a person who doesn't care what others think need not be responsive.

As familiarity with the situation increases, our responsiveness to variations in it may decrease. With each exposure to a given situation, we develop and strengthen habitual ways of responding. For instance, when a situation is new to us, we may pay careful attention to it in order to determine how to respond. People in wealthy communities may rarely encounter a stalled car and may therefore respond differently to one depending on such things as its appearance (Doob, A. N., & Gross, A. E., 1968). Drivers in New York City, however, encounter hundreds of stalled cars every day. Their response—to honk or not honk—may be more bound by habit than by the status of the car (Stang, 1979). Similarly, light smokers are more responsive to the sight of cigarettes than heavy smokers, whose smoking rate seems internally determined (Herman, 1974).

In general, the behavior of the extremist is more a response to internal than to external cues. That is, whether they are heavy smokers or heavy drinkers, extremely talkative or extremely conservative, it is probable that extremists are unresponsive (to external cues). People who are very conservative, for instance, may tend to be conservative when conservatism is appropriate and just as conservative when it is inappropriate. The person who likes to sing may do so in the shower or in the church choir and be appreciated. But to sing on the subway or in an elevator is a different matter. Extremists will seem inappropriate in some situations. For example, extremely talkative people may be talkative in situations where they should be listening, and extremely quiet people may be quiet in situations where they should be talking.

People who decline to say whether they are usually talkative or quiet say "It depends on the situation." Similarly, people who are not crazy about singing but do not hate it either use the situation to determine what to do. If the situation calls for singing, average people will sing. If it calls for talking, they'll talk. If it calls for listening, they'll listen. A person who is moderate can be responsive and use the situation to decide what to do.

Extremists may have acquired their extremism through social reinforcement and may be unresponsive to those cues that would otherwise discourage them. An extremely talkative person, for instance, may find personal satisfaction and other rewards in talking but may not "read" the reactions of others who say "Shut up." Such an ability to read the reactions of others may be an aspect of "social intelligence," which, in turn, is closely related to general intelligence (Thorndike, 1936).

Some people are able to elicit greater responsiveness than others. Charismatic people, leaders, high-status males, and verbally skilled, humorous, complex, informed people elicit greater responsiveness than their counterparts. People who make eye contact with their audience, who use posture and gesture to help convey their message, who use appropriate inflections in their voice, who speak to the needs of the audience, and so on also "get attention" and get more responsiveness. Such people are in a position to be more influential. So responsiveness is, in part, a state that may be influenced by the situation itself.

Responsiveness may also be a trait. People differ in how consistent they are across situations (Bem & Allen, 1974; Campus, 1973, 1974; Long, Calhoun, & Selby, 1977). Those who insist on being perfectly consistent across situations cannot, by definition, be responsive. However, inconsistent people are not necessarily responsive, so consistency and responsivity are not opposite sides of the same coin.

As a trait, responsiveness can be measured with Snyder's (1974) self-monitoring scale (see Interest Box 3-3).[1] Responsive people are defined here as those who obtain high scores on the scale. Scores on this scale have recently been found to be related to many social behaviors. For instance:

☐ Professional actors are more responsive than college students, who, in turn, are more responsive than patients in a psychiatric ward (Snyder, 1974).

☐ Responsive people are rated by peers as better at learning what is socially appropriate in new situations (Snyder, 1974).

☐ Responsive people show more variation in their behavior in response to situational changes and can tolerate more inconsistency in their behavior across situations (Lippa, 1976; Rarick, Soldow, & Geizer, 1976; Snyder & Monson, 1975; Snyder & Swann, 1976; Snyder & Tanke, 1976).

☐ Responsive people show a variety of other differences from nonresponsive people in their social perception and social interaction (Ickes & Barnes, 1977).

☐ Obese people are apparently more responsive to a variety of cues than non-obese people (Krantz, 1977; Rodin, 1977). For instance, their eating, drinking, time estimation, pain perception, and distractibility all seem to be more affected by situational variations (Kozlowski & Schachter, 1975; Pliner, 1973a, 1973b, 1974; Rodin, 1973). The obese also score higher in the self-monitoring scale (Younger & Pliner, 1976).

Sex differences in conformity.   Throughout this chapter we have looked at sex differences in each of the dimensions of individual difference examined. Are there sex differences in responsiveness? It is not clear. For almost every study that seems to suggest a sex difference, there may be critics who note flaws or who can cite a similar study finding no sex difference. The literature on conformity is an example.

Many people believe that women are more persuasible and conform more than men, and the research literature seems in agreement (Bass, 1961; Eagly, 1978; Nord, 1969; Rosenfeld & Christie, 1974; Willis, R. H., 1961). Alice Eagly (1978) cites 10 studies in which females were more persuasible and only 1 where males were; she lists 20 studies in which women conformed more under group pressure and only 2 in which men conformed more (and a large number that found no difference between men and women). Thus, *when* a study finds sex differences, it is likely that women have been more persuasible or conforming than men. But does this mean that there is a sex difference in conformity? Many critics of this research feel that claims of sex differences in conformity and persuasibility are exaggerated. They suggest that, when sex differences are found, it is more a result of the experimental design than anything else (see Interest Box 3-4).

But it may be that women are somewhat more responsive to the demands of various social situations than are men. If women are more attentive than men

---

[1]Snyder's scale has some similarity to Nadler's (1956) Ideology of Conformity scale, which positively correlates with conformity (DiVesta and Cox, 1960). It also has some similarity to some of Crutchfield's (1955) items, which also correlate with conformity. Before more research is done using Snyder's scale, it would be a good idea to explore its relation to Nadler's and Crutchfield's scales, to see if it is really measuring something different.

Interest Box 3-3.   Snyder's Self-Monitoring Scale*

Instructions, Items, and Scoring Key for the Self-Monitoring Scale[a]

Item and scoring key[b]

1. I find it hard to imitate the behavior of other people. (F)
2. My behavior is usually an expression of my true inner feelings, attitudes, and beliefs. (F)
3. At parties and social gatherings, I do not attempt to do or say things that others will like. (F)
4. I can only argue for ideas which I already believe. (F)
5. I can make impromptu speeches even on topics about which I have almost no information. (T)
6. I guess I put on a show to impress or entertain people. (T)
7. When I am uncertain how to act in a social situation, I look to the behavior of others for cues. (T)
8. I would probably make a good actor. (T)
9. I rarely need the advice of my friends to choose movies, books, or music. (F)
10. I sometimes appear to others to be experiencing deeper emotions than I actually am. (T)
11. I laugh more when I watch a comedy with others than when alone. (T)
12. In a group of people I am rarely the center of attention. (F)
13. In different situations and with different people, I often act like very different persons. (T)
14. I am not particularly good at making other people like me. (F)
15. Even if I am not enjoying myself, I often pretend to be having a good time. (T)
16. I'm not always the person I appear to be. (T)
17. I would not change my opinions (or the way I do things) in order to please someone else or win their favor. (F)
18. I have considered being an entertainer. (T)
19. In order to get along and be liked, I tend to be what people expect me to be rather than anything else. (T)
20. I have never been good at games like charades or improvisational acting. (F)
21. I have trouble changing my behavior to suit different people and different situations. (F)
22. At a party I let others keep the jokes and stories going. (F)
23. I feel a bit awkward in company and do not show up quite so well as I should. (F)
24. I can look anyone in the eye and tell a lie with a straight face (if for a right end). (T)
25. I may deceive people by being friendly when I really dislike them. (T)

Note. T = true; F = false; SM = Self-Monitoring Scale.
[a]Directions for Personal Reaction Inventory were: The statements on the following pages concern your personal reactions to a number of different situations. No two statements are exactly alike, so consider each statement carefully before answering. If a statement is *TRUE* or *MOSTLY TRUE* as applied to you, blacken the space marked *T* on the answer sheet. If a statement is *FALSE* or *NOT USUALLY TRUE* as applied to you, blacken the space marked *F*. Do not put your answers on this test booklet itself. It is important that you answer as frankly and as honestly as you can. Your answers will be kept in the strictest confidence.
[b]Items keyed in the direction of high SM.
*From "The Self-Monitoring of Expressive Behavior," by M. Snyder. In *Journal of Personality and Social Psychology*, 1974, *30*(4), 526–537. Copyright © 1974 by the American Psychological Association. Reprinted by permission of the author and publisher.

---

to what is called for in the situation and more able and willing to deliver the proper response, then it would be reasonable that in situations demanding conformity women would conform more. Just how much women conform when a situation calls for independence has not yet been studied in the laboratory. But it is possible that, when situations call for independence, women show more independence than men. This conjecture would be an interesting idea to test in the laboratory.

Other sources of evidence provide some support for the notion that women are more sensitive, or more responsive, to social situations than men:

- A variety of studies found that women tend to be more sociable and affiliate more than men (Argyle & Dean, 1965; Ellsworth & Ross, 1975; Exline, 1972; Exline, Gray, & Schuette, 1965; Friar, 1969; Pedersen & Heaston, 1972; Rosenfeld, 1966).
- Women may be more concerned than men about their appearance. One study (Garland & Brown, 1972) found high school women more willing than men to spend money to hide a deficiency from the public.
- Males seem to eat because of hunger (internal state); females seem more affected by taste.
- When baby boys are given a bottle whose nipple has a small hole, making sucking hard, they still drink as much as with an easy nipple. But girls drink less with the small-holed nipple (Nisbett & Gurwitz, 1970). Girls seem more responsive to the difficulty of the task.
- Women seem to have more taste aversions than men. That is, they list more foods they dislike than men do (Byrne, Golightly, & Capaldi, 1963; Smith,

---

Interest Box 3-4. Sex Differences in Conformity?

There are some good reasons to be cautious with the finding that women sometimes conform more than men.

1. The percentage of studies reporting that women are more influenceable than men rose from 14% in 1940–1955 to 53% in 1961–1965, then dropped to about 20% in 1966–1970, where it now remains (Eagly, 1978). This suggests that the difference between the sexes has been changing and may continue to change. And one study (Montgomery & Burgoon, 1977) reports that **psychologically androgynous** men (see pp. 83–84) are more influenced than traditionally oriented men, whereas psychologically androgynous women are less influenced than traditional women. The changing sex differences in influenceability in recent years may be due to changes in sex roles; psychological androgyny seems to be on the rise.

2. Most of these studies contained a number of identical methodological problems that raise questions about their findings. Almost all the studies used situations that were more familiar to men than women. When people regard themselves as experts on a subject, they may feel little need to trust the judgment of others. But when they feel a lack of confidence, they are more likely to conform to the group (Stang, 1972). Moreover, when items are constructed for use in conformity experiments on which females are more confident

than men, men conform more than women (Feldman, 1974; Stang & Neer, 1975).

3. Another artifact may be that almost all the conformity experiments have been conducted by male experimenters. One researcher (Schulman, 1967) has suggested that conformity in these experiments may be conformity to the experimenter's demands (and perhaps sex-role expectations) rather than to social pressures from other subjects. Most experimenters are males, and as Eagly (1978) notes, most communicators in persuasion studies are male. (In fact, this bias is shared in television portrayal of influence situations. One study [McArthur & Resko, in press] found that most "authorities" in television commercials are men; most consumers—those influenced by the authorities—are women.) So perhaps we must qualify the conclusion of the previous research by the statement that "women conform more to male experimenters than do male subjects, and we simply don't know who would conform more to female experimenters."

As you can see, it's not easy to design an experiment that will produce results that no one can question. How would you design a fair experiment to see whether men or women conform more? What factors do you think determine whether a sex difference in conformity occurs?

W. I., Powell, & Ross, 1955a, 1955b; Wallen, 1943). Females—both people and rats—will drink more sweetened water or baby formula than unsweetened, whereas males seem unresponsive to the addition of sweetener (Nisbett & Gurwitz, 1970; Valenstein, Cox, & Kakolewski, 1967; Valenstein, Kakolewski, & Cox, 1967). Thus, there seem to be sex differences in responsiveness to taste.

☐ Women are more responsive to the costs and benefits of helping than men (Wilson, D. W., & Kahn, 1975). Changing the appearance (neatly dressed versus untidy) of the person needing help affects women's helping more than men's (Judd, Bull, & Gahagan, 1975). Similarly, women seem more responsive to situational variations in their "aggressive" behavior. Dion (1974) found that women consider a child's sex and attractiveness in choosing penalties for errors, whereas men do not.

☐ Women seem to be more responsive to being touched than men. In one study (Fisher, Rytting, & Heslin, 1975) men and women were touched briefly by a librarian as they checked out a book. When they completed an apparently unrelated questionnaire a few moments later, women who had been touched felt more positive than those who had not, but no effect of being touched was evident for men.

☐ Women seem to be more sensitive to physical pain than men and have lower "pain thresholds" (Plutchik & Bender, 1966; Sternbach & Tursky, 1964).

☐ Women show a greater diversity in judgments of others than males do, having a more **extreme response style** (Adams & Berg, 1961; Berg & Collier, 1953; Borgatta & Glass, 1961; Crandall, J. E., 1965, 1973; Deaux & Farris, 1975; Heinemann & Zax, 1968; Quereshi, Leggio, & Widlak, 1974; Soueif, 1958; Zax & Takahashi, 1967).

☐ Not only do women seem to differentiate more in their judgments of others, but they may be more accurate in some respects. One study found women consistently better than men in interpreting patterns of nonverbal behavior that included body language, facial expressions, and voice patterns (Rosenthal, R., Archer, DiMatteo, Koivumaki, & Rogers, 1974).

Other research (Bleda, undated) supports the notion that women are more *accurate* than men in assessing situational effects on their mood.

☐ Women may be more responsive to sex differences than men. A woman's behavior may be more affected by the sex of the person she's with than a man's (Kahn, Hottes, & Davis, 1971; Skotko, Langmeyer, & Lundgren, 1974).

☐ Women may be more responsive to the simple presence of others. For instance, one study of social facilitation (see Chapter 10) found that men worked about as hard on a task whether alone or with another person present, but women worked more than twice as hard when with another (Carment, 1970).

The section above has presented a rationale and some evidence for responsiveness and sex differences in responsiveness. There are undoubtedly some studies that don't find sex differences in responsiveness, and it must at present be considered an idea rather than an established principle.

If responsiveness does prove to be an acceptable principle of individual differences, then amateur and professional social psychologists alike should begin to wonder about its origins. Many different factors may all contribute to individual differences in responsiveness. Socialization practices (discussed in the next chapter) may play a major role, as may norms and expectations.

Psychological Androgyny. **Sex** refers to biological differences: we are man or woman, male or female. **Gender** refers to socialization differences: masculine or feminine. Sex differences are obviously easy to measure. Measuring gender differences is harder. Some of the "sex" differences discussed in this chapter may actually prove to be *sex* differences, but probably most have their roots in socialization practices and might better be called "gender differences."

Biology provides a more reliable and consistent effect on our sex than socialization does on our gender. Men differ considerably in how masculine they are, and women differ considerably in how feminine they are. In fact, most men show "feminine" qualities in various degrees and at various times, and most women show "masculine" qualities from time to time. Sandra Bem (1974) has proposed that, to some extent, we all possess both masculine and feminine qualities. A particular person may be both competitive and cooperative, dominant and submissive, aggressive and helpful, depending on circumstances. Bem found that a person who is high on her scale of femininity is not necessarily low on her scale of masculinity, or vice versa.

Bem calls people **androgynous** when they are about as masculine as they are feminine. Other researchers (Spence, Helmreich, & Stapp, 1975) reserve

the term *androgynous* for people who score high in both masculinity and femininity measures.

In her brilliant review of the literature on sex and gender differences, Kay Deaux (1976) notes some of the advantages of being androgynous. For instance, androgynous people have been found to be more intelligent and creative (Maccoby, E. E., 1966) and have higher self-esteem (Spence et. al., 1975). The androgynous seem to date more, receive more honors and awards, and be sick less often (Spence et al., 1975).

How much do you suppose androgynous women conform? Bem (1975) found that they conform less than feminine men and women and about the same as masculine men and women. Her experiment suggests that whatever "sex" differences have been found in conformity may be gender differences instead. If gender differences in conformity have been decreasing in the last decade (see p. 81, it may be a result of decreasing gender differences: in some ways, men have become less masculine and women less feminine. We can only speculate on this now, and we can only speculate on the future. Research on androgyny is just beginning. But considering what remarkable findings have already emerged, the future looks promising.

Other Individual Differences.   We have looked briefly at eight ways in which people differ. Social psychologists have explored dozens of such stable dimensions or traits, including "cognitive complexity," "ego strength," "manifest anxiety," "self-esteem," "self-concept," "role constructs," "repression/sensitization," and "dominance." Social psychologists have also explored a variety of needs or motives on which individuals differ, including the need for approval (approval motive), need for affiliation, and need for power. If you are interested in learning more about these variables, you should try reading the books suggested at the end of this chapter.

SUMMARY

Personality psychologists take a dispositional approach to the study of individual differences and differences between groups of people. But in spite of their efforts only a handful of the 18,000 traits we have words for have been studied carefully. Eight of these traits are discussed in this chapter. Personality research consistently finds that differences between two groups of people are smaller than differences within groups; therefore, remember that the generalizations in this chapter are just trends or tendencies.

Our stereotypes summarize our personal theories of individual differences. Sex stereotypes are far ranging, not always true, and seem to value men more than women.

Authoritarianism, measured with the F scale, refers to antidemocratic ideology. Those with an authoritarian personality are typically prejudiced, rigid, intolerant of ambiguity, conventional, superstitious, and sometimes overconcerned with sex.

Dogmatism is similar in some ways to authoritarianism but may be found in extremists of both the left and the right. A person high in dogmatism is closed minded, rigid, and intolerant.

Achievement motivation, measured with a projective test called the *Thematic Apperception Test* (TAT), refers to a person's desire to achieve and willingness to work hard for success. Some studies find that women may have a fear of success, particularly some kinds of success. Some men have a similar fear, and both sexes (but perhaps especially men) may also have a fear of failure. Success is important in our achieving society.

Machiavellianism, measured with a mach scale, refers to one's willingness to manipulate others to get one's way. High machs (those high in machiavellianism) seem more influential—and less influenced—than low machs.

Field dependence/independence, measured with the rod and frame test (RFT) and body adjustment test (BAT), refers to the degree to which we attend to internal cues (field independent) or cues from our environment (field dependent). Field-dependent people seem to do best in social tasks, field independents in cognitive tasks. Women are typically more field dependent than men.

Locus of control, measured with the I-E scale, describes a person's tendency to believe that events are under his or her control (internal) or in the hands of fate (external). Many important differences between internals and externals have been found through research. Some evidence suggests that women may typically be more external than men.

Responsiveness is a trait (and state) and can be measured with Snyder's self-monitoring scale. It refers to the extent to which we attend to (and act on) cues from the situations that define "appropriate" behavior. A growing literature has uncovered a number of ways that responsive and unresponsive people differ. Women may be more responsive than men.

Psychological androgyny, measured with masculinity and femininity scales that are scored separately and compared, refers to the extent to which a person shows both masculine and feminine qualities. Some evidence suggests that androgynous people may have special advantages (and perhaps some special problems) and that some sex differences may actually be gender differences.

GLOSSARY TERMS

Define these terms in your own words, then look them up in the glossary at the back of the book.

Achievement motive	Gender
Acquiescent response set	I-E scale
Androgynous	Internal locus of control
Authoritarianism	Learned helplessness
Authoritarian personality	Machiavellianism
Body-adjustment test (BAT)	Mach scale
Dispositional approach	Motive to avoid success
Dogmatism	Need
External locus of control	Need for achievement
Extreme response style	Overachiever
Fear of failure	Personality psychologist
Fear of success	Personologist
Field dependence	Projective test
Field independence	Protocol

Psychogenic need
Psychological androgyny
Responsive
Rod-and-frame test (RFT)
Self-fulfilling prophecy
Self-monitoring
Sex
Situational approach

State
Stereotype
Thematic Apperception Test (TAT)
Trait
Underachiever
Unresponsive
Viscerogenic need

FURTHER READING

Deaux, K. *The behavior of women and men*. Monterey, Calif.: Brooks/Cole, 1973.

Marlowe, D., & Gergen, K. J. Personality and social interaction. In G. Lindzey & E. Aronson (Eds.), *The handbook of social psychology* (Vol. 3). Reading, Mass.: Addison-Wesley, 1969.

Mischel, W. *Personality and assessment*. New York: Wiley, 1968.

chapter

4

Social and Cultural Influences

chapter

4

I n the last chapter we examined a variety of ways in which people differ. Although eight dimensions of difference were surveyed, dozens more might have been examined, if space permitted. Yet the hundred dimensions of difference that psychologists have studied represent only a fraction of the number of ways that people differ.

How do such differences arise? What influences are responsible for such variety? Two general sources of influence will be examined. In this chapter, we will look at social and cultural influences; Chapter 5 will survey some influences of the physical environment. Although this chapter will focus on social and cultural factors, we will also look briefly at some biological influences, in part to illustrate the difficulty of distinguishing between the effects of **nature** and **nurture.**

BIOLOGICAL INFLUENCES: NATURE VERSUS NURTURE

It may be best to begin with a fundamental question: are we the way we are because of our biology or because of our environment? Even the behavior of the simplest one-celled amoeba is influenced by both factors. In explaining human social behavior, biological influences are sometimes neglected by professional social psychologists, and social influences are sometimes neglected by amateurs. I will try for some balance in the explanations proposed in this chapter. Many different levels of explanation are appropriate from time to time, including biological, social, and cultural, and none is regarded by everyone as best. So the purpose of this chapter is to present a variety of forms of explanation, showing how they can be applied and how complex it is to apply them. Which explanation you use as an amateur social psychologist will depend on both the situation and your own preferences.

Hormones and Aggressiveness.   Some individual differences may be traceable to our hormones. Males have more **androgens** (male hormones), whereas females have more **estrogens** (female hormones). Androgens such as **testosterone** are produced in the testes. When they are absent in the fetus, a female develops.

When newborn female rats are injected with testosterone, they later show some male sexual behaviors. And newborn male rats who are castrated (thus removing the source of the testosterone) later show some female sexual behavior. Rather than Eve having been created from Adam's rib, it seems that testosterone creates a male from a female.

Before puberty the testosterone level is low in both boys and girls, and boys and girls are essentially the same in physical size and ability.

Testosterone has many profound effects on physical development. Before puberty the testosterone level is low in both boys and girls. The two sexes are essentially the same in physical size and ability, although girls are typically ahead of boys in intellectual and motor skills (Harris, D. V., 1976). At puberty the testes begin producing androgens, the ovaries begin producing estrogens, and further sexual differentiation takes place. One striking effect of testosterone is its impact on muscle development. It is better than any breakfast cereal for developing strength, size, and speed.

Researchers are agreed on the effects of testosterone on muscles. Many professional weight lifters, body builders, and wrestlers take it to increase their muscular development. But the other effects of testosterone are unclear. For instance, we know that men have higher levels of testosterone than women. And we also know that in most societies and at most ages males are more aggressive than females (D'Andrade, 1966; Maccoby & Jacklin, 1974a, 1974b; Whiting, B., & Edwards, 1973). In every society that one researcher (Goldberg, S., 1973) examined, men typically occupied and controlled the dominant, prestigious positions. Is this a coincidence, or are hormone differences a cause of differences in aggressiveness? We can think of several possible answers:

1. It is possible that testosterone directly gives rise to an aggressive nature. One study (Money & Erhardt, 1972) found that girls whose mothers received testosterone during pregnancy played more aggressively than other girls. However, no direct relation has yet been demonstrated between testosterone level and aggressiveness in humans (Huber, 1974). Further, there does not seem to be any good theory of *how* testosterone might directly affect aggressiveness.
2. It is possible that the effects of testosterone on aggressiveness are not so simple. For instance, it may be that testosterone affects musculature, which affects success or failure in sports, which in turn rewards or punishes competition and aggressiveness, which finally generalizes to other life activities. Strong adolescents (especially boys) learn that by playing aggressively they can win in sports, and they adopt a competitive style in other things they do. Other explanations, involving causal chains between testosterone and aggressiveness, are also conceivable.
3. It is possible that parents believe that boys should be competitive and girls cooperative and so reward their children for "sex-role appropriate" behavior and punish "inappropriate" behavior. This **sex-role socialization**, rather than testosterone, may be responsible for early differences in competitiveness that are evident in boys and girls.

   To see the complexity in explaining sex differences in aggressiveness by pointing to sex differences in hormone levels, consider what happens with age. Sex differences in aggressiveness change with age. One researcher observed that such differences blur, disappear, and may even be reversed in our 50s: "Grandpa becomes sweet, affable, but rather vague, Grandma becomes tough-minded and intrusive.... [Older women] are usually tougher than their middle-aged husbands; and they are much bolder than their younger selves" (Gutmann, 1973, pp. 62–63). Such changes might result from changing hormone levels or might result from the end of parenting, as children leave home and leave parents free to find new roles.

   The best conclusion here is this: most individual differences will be the result of several factors; thus, it is often fruitless to try to show that one explanation is best. In this chapter, we will cover a variety of "standard" explanations, which will be used in various combinations in later chapters to account for observed effects. Such explanations should be useful to you, in combination, in explaining your observations of everyday social behavior.

Hormones and Field Dependence.   Although differences in hormone levels are a popular explanation for sex differences in aggressiveness, hormones are not often viewed as influences on other individual differences. There does not seem to be any good reason why this should be so, however. In the example below, we will see how hormone level might affect cognitive functioning and just how complex such causal influences might be.

One review (Goodenough, D. R., & Witkin, 1977) suggests that sex hormones may affect the development of specialized brain capacities, which in turn may determine cognitive functioning. Some researchers studied the effects of injecting rats with hormones; others examined people with naturally occurring hormone abnormalities. The pattern of results suggests that androgens at an early age may lead to field independence, estrogens to field dependence.

Other findings from cross-cultural studies are just as intriguing. Cross-cultural research (reviewed by Berry, 1976) finds that members of migratory hunting societies are typically field independent, whereas members of sedentary agricultural societies are typically field dependent. Sex differences in field dependence seem to be absent in hunting societies but present in farming and industrialized societies. One researcher (Dawson, 1976b) has proposed that changes in diet may influence hormone levels, which in turn may affect field dependence. The reduction in protein intake that took place when societies shifted from hunting to farming and industry could have resulted in lower levels of androgens and more field dependence.

Social psychologists do not typically consider hormones in their theories of social behavior, and it may be some time before much research is done on these hypotheses. But it would not be surprising if we learned someday that many individual and sex differences are traceable in part to early differences in hormone levels. Any such finding would not require us to abandon other, more popular explanations. Rather, we would need to reaffirm what we already know about social behavior: it has multiple, complex causes.

Nature/Nurture in Perspective.   If we believe that individual differences are the result of both biological and social factors, then we might ask how important each type of factor is. This is an old question, and it sometimes arouses much emotion when it comes up. For example, some people feel that IQ is largely biologically or genetically determined. Others argue otherwise. The arguments, it seems, boil down to this:

☐ Depending on the individual difference of interest, both biological and social factors are probably important. This is certainly true in the case of IQ. Thus, any explanation of social behavior or individual differences that omits either nature or nurture is likely to be incomplete.

☐ Biological influences are complex. They include nutrition of the embryo, early hormone levels, and genetic structure. It is very difficult to separate these biological effects. The same can be said of social influences.

☐ Biological and social factors are normally intertangled. Many, such as early hormone levels and nutrition of the embryo, are difficult to even classify as biological versus social.

☐ Biological and social factors are normally correlated. Infants with the poorest biological makeup commonly grow up in the poorest social environments. This puts these children at a double disadvantage and makes it impossible to separate the biological effects from the social effects.

☐ Nearly all biological effects, no matter how large, can usually be reversed by the proper social conditions. As one researcher noted, "Under suitable conditions, the offspring of parents whose cognitive skills are so poorly developed as to exclude them from all but the most menial occupations can achieve what are regarded as distinctly high levels of cognitive performance" (Layzer, 1974, p. 1266).

☐ How important nature or nurture is depends on how much it varies. For mothers who have the same health and diet, heredity may be a big factor in an infant's birth weight, for instance. But heredity can be overshadowed by environmental effects if mothers are very different in health and diet.

Some social scientists feel that the proper task of science is not to debate the relative importance of biological and social factors, but to evaluate and improve social conditions so that all children have truly equal opportunity. Not all scientists would agree with this opinion, of course. What do you think?

SOCIAL INFLUENCES

Although biology probably has important influences on social behavior, by far the most common approach to explaining social behavior uses *social* influences. Many texts, in fact, describe social psychology as the study of social influence. Much of the remainder of this chapter will examine such influences in a general way.

A Model of Social Influence. A **model of social influence** is an abstract representation of the important components of influence, with arrows indicating which components influence which others. A model is helpful in simplifying discussion and directing thought on a topic. In the simplest model, we might have only two people, A and B, and draw arrows showing that A can influence B and that B can influence A. But a person's opinions can be influenced when his or her behavior is not, and vice versa. A model that makes opinions and behaviors separate components may be more useful. In Figure 4-1, such a model is presented. It proposes that each of the four components can influence each of the three others, so all 12 causal arrows are drawn. For clarity in discussing this model, each arrow is numbered, and the text will refer to these arrows by number.

Arrows 1 and 2 suggest that our own behavior and opinions are interrelated, with our opinions affecting behavior and vice versa. Our self-esteem, for instance, can probably be influenced by our own perceptions of our ability (arrow 1) (Coopersmith, 1967). And our self-esteem can probably have some effect on our ability (arrow 2) (Stang, 1972). Thus, if we believe that we are good at some task, we will feel better about ourselves than if we believe that we are inept at that task. Through a self-fulfilling prophecy, this opinion, in turn, can bring about good or poor performance at that task. Several studies have found a positive relationship between self-esteem and achievement in school (Brookover, Thomas, & Peterson, 1964; Wylie, 1963). And other studies report relations between ability in specific tasks and self-esteem (League & Jackson, 1964).

Of course, our opinions of ourselves are also influenced by the opinions of others (arrow 3). For example, if we encounter another person who has a low opinion of us, our opinion of ourselves may be lowered temporarily (arrow 3) (Gergen, 1966; Tippett & Silber, 1966). The opinions of others, in turn, are influenced by our opinions of ourselves (arrow 4). This mutual influence produces what Theodore Newcomb has called a **strain toward symmetry,** a pressure toward balance in the two sets of feelings. One study, at least (Miyamoto & Dorn-

Figure 4-1.
A model of social
influence

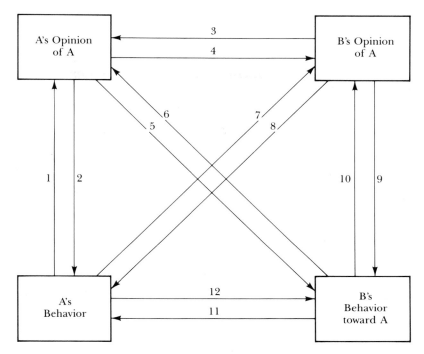

busch, 1956), reports a relationship between A's opinion of A and B's opinion of A, supporting the validity of arrows 3 and 4.

Our opinion of ourselves also influences the behavior of others toward us (arrow 5). For example, some studies have shown that students with high self-esteem are more popular and date more than students with low self-esteem.

At the same time, the behavior of others toward us has powerful effects on our feelings about ourselves (arrow 6). When we interact with others and use their behavior toward us to evaluate ourselves, we are engaged in what has been called "reflected appraisal" (Jones & Gerard, 1967) or "the looking glass self" (Cooley, 1909). Or we may use the behavior of others in a more general, indirect process of social comparison. We may simply compare their behavior, opinions, and abilities with our own. This **comparative appraisal** does not require face-to-face interaction, as does reflected appraisal. Using a simulated prison situation, Philip Zimbardo (Zimbardo, Haney, Banks, & Jaffe, 1972) found that college students who were role-playing prison guards mistreated and abused other students role-playing prisoners. The "prisoners," in turn, came to have low opinions of themselves and to feel that they as a group deserved such treatment. This study provides a powerful illustration of the effects of reflected appraisals on both guards and prisoners. (Zimbardo describes the experiment in Interest Box 4-1.)

Our behavior, of course, is a strong determinant of the opinions of others (arrow 7). Erving Goffman's writing on the presentation of self in everyday life emphasizes how much our behavior in public places influences the opinions others hold of us. At the same time their opinions seem to influence our behavior (arrow 8). This influence is sometimes mediated by the effects that their opinions

"... others can influence our self-opinion."

Interest Box 4-1.   Students as Prisoners and Guards*

In an attempt to understand just what it means psychologically to be a prisoner or a prison guard, Craig Haney, Curt Banks, Dave Jaffe and I [Philip Zimbardo] created our own prison. We carefully screened over 70 volunteers who answered an ad in a Palo Alto [California] city newspaper and ended up with about two dozen young men who were selected to be part of this study. They were mature, emotionally stable, normal, intelligent college students from middle-class homes throughout the United States and Canada. They appeared to represent the cream of the crop of this generation. None had any criminal record and all were relatively homogeneous on many dimensions initially.

Half were arbitrarily designated as prisoners by a flip of a coin, the others as guards. These were the roles they were to play in our simulated prison. The guards were made aware of the potential seriousness and danger of the situation and their own vulnerability. They made up their own formal rules for maintaining law, order and respect, and were generally free to improvise new ones during their eight-hour, three-man shifts. The prisoners were unexpectedly picked up at their homes by a city policeman in a squad car, searched, handcuffed, fingerprinted, booked at the Palo Alto station house and taken blindfolded to our jail. There they were stripped, deloused, put into a uniform, given a number and put into a cell with two other prisoners where they expected to live for the next two weeks. The pay was good ($15 a day) and their motivation was to make money. . . .

At the end of only six days we had to close down our mock prison because what we saw was frightening. It was no longer apparent to most of the subjects (or to us) where reality ended and their roles began. The majority had indeed become prisoners or guards, no longer able to clearly differentiate between role playing and self. There were dramatic changes in virtually every aspect of their of us have on their behavior towards us (arrow 9); these effects, in turn, influence our behavior (arrow 11). For example, Rosenthal and Jacobson (1968) have found that a teacher's expectations of a pupil's behavior can affect that behavior. Teachers were led to believe that some of their students were late bloomers and would show great intellectual development during the school year. The teachers behaved in such a way (arrow 9) that the children actually did show gains in intellectual performance relative to the other children (arrow 11). Other researchers (Entwisle & Webster, 1974) have suggested that teachers' expectations may influence students' actual performance (arrow 8). Teachers translate their expectations into

---

Interest Box 4-1.   (continued)

behavior, thinking and feeling. In less than a week the experience of imprisonment undid (temporarily) a lifetime of learning; human values were suspended, self-concepts were challenged and the ugliest, most base, pathological side of human nature surfaced. We were horrified because we saw some boys (guards) treat others as if they were despicable animals, taking pleasure in cruelty, while other boys (prisoners) became servile, dehumanized robots who thought only of escape, of their own individual survival and of their mounting hatred for the guards.

We had to release three prisoners in the first four days because they had such acute situational traumatic reactions as hysterical crying, confusion in thinking and severe depression. Others begged to be paroled, and all but three were willing to forfeit all the money they had earned if they could be paroled. By then (the fifth day) they had been so programmed to think of themselves as prisoners that when their request for parole was denied, they returned docilely to their cells. Now, had they been thinking as college students acting in an oppressive experiment, they would have quit once they no longer wanted the $15 a day we used as our only incentive. However, the reality was not quitting an experiment but "being paroled by the parole board from the Stanford County Jail." By the last days, the earlier solidarity among the prisoners (systematically broken by the guards) dissolved into "each man for himself." . . .

About a third of the guards became tyrannical in their arbitrary use of power, in enjoying their control over other people. They were corrupted by the power of their roles and became quite inventive in their techniques of breaking the spirit of the prisoners and making them feel they were worthless. Some of the guards merely did

their jobs as tough but fair correctional officers, and several were good guards from the prisoners' point of view since they did them small favors and were friendly. However, no good guard ever interfered with a command by any of the bad guards; they never intervened on the side of the prisoners, they never told the others to ease off because it was only an experiment, and they never even came to me as prison superintendent or experimenter in charge to complain. In part, they were good because the others were bad; they needed the others to help establish their own egos in a positive light. . . .

Individual behavior is largely under the control of social forces and environmental contingencies rather than personality traits, character, will power or other empirically unvalidated constructs. Thus we create an illusion of freedom by attributing more internal control to ourselves, to the individual, than actually exists. . . .

Each of us carries around in our heads a favorable self-image in which we are essentially just, fair, humane and understanding. For example, we could not imagine inflicting pain on others without much provocation or hurting people who had done nothing to us, who in fact were even liked by us. However, there is a growing body of social psychological research which underscores the conclusion derived from this prison study. Many people, perhaps the majority, can be made to do almost anything when put into psychologically compelling situations—regardless of their morals, ethics, values, attitudes, beliefs or personal convictions.

*From "Pathology of Imprisonment," by P. G. Zimbardo. Published by permission of Transaction, Inc., from *Society*, Vol. 9, No. 6. Copyright © 1972 by Transaction, Inc.

behavior (arrow 9) that affects the children's own expectations for themselves (arrow 6).

If the system shown in Figure 4-1 were "closed" (that is, if there were no other influences on it) and if the system had enough time for these mutual influences to adjust (as in the case of two good friends of long standing), then the system would come into balance. A's opinion of A would correspond to A's behavior, to B's opinion of A, and to B's behavior toward A. In fact, however, other influences intrude, upsetting the balance. Because of this, there is rarely a perfect match between the components of the system, and it is always in flux.

Further, even if the system of Figure 4-1 were closed, we are not totally open to the pushes and pulls of others on our opinions of ourselves. For example, we have generally more positive feelings about ourselves than we have of others or than others have of us (Matlin & Stang, 1979; Reeder, Donohue, & Biblarz, 1960). So we are likely to screen out information that contradicts this positive view and seek out information that supports it.

Joseph Luft and Harry Ingham (1955) developed what they collaboratively called the **Johari Window.** This is a matrix with columns labeled "known to self" and "not known to self" and rows labeled "known to others" and "not known to others." Because the matrix looks a bit like a window with four panes of glass—metaphorically, these "panes" differ in the clarity of the view they offer—they called it a window. There cannot be correspondence between A's opinion of A and B's opinion of A for those things to which A is blind in himself or herself. And there cannot be correspondence for those things that A knows about A but that are hidden to others. The Johari Window provides a useful reminder that the way we are is not always the way we see ourselves, or the way others see us.

We have taken enough time in describing a general model of social influence. We will now turn to a more detailed discussion of some aspects of this model.

Expectations and Roles.   As you have seen in the model of social influence (Figure 4-1), the expectations that others have of us heavily influence our own notions of how we should behave. The term **role** refers to a set of required or expected behaviors of one or more people occupying a certain position in a group (Biddle & Thomas, 1966). For example, the words *father, mother, child, housewife, waitress, cook, doctor, patient, barber, saleswoman,* and *plumber* each refers to a different role within society. People may pass into or out of a role more or less freely, as when a person occupies the role of doctor during her working hours and mother or wife after coming home (see Interest Box 4-2).

Regardless of who occupies the role, there are certain expectations for behavior in that role. For example, a doctor is expected to be honest, to be well informed about medical facts, to show some interest in the patients, and so on. Some of these expectations are more essential to a person's successful playing of a role than others. For instance, most crucial in taking the role of doctor is sound medical knowledge. Perhaps expected but less important are owning a Cadillac or Mercedes, playing golf on weekends, being busy, or keeping out-of-date magazines in the outer office.

When we take on a role, we may first "play" it and easily distinguish between our self and the role we are enacting. But after a time this **role distance** often breaks down, and the self/role distinction may be lost. Many "workaholics" have lost the distinction between their occupational role and their private selves. In the prison simulation conducted by Zimbardo (see Interest Box 4-1), college students quickly lost the role distance they had begun the simulation with.

Sex roles.   Although we enact certain roles for brief periods during the day (such as our occupational role), we carry other roles throughout life. One of the latter is our **sex role.** Our sex role exerts powerful influences on our social behavior (O'Leary, V. E., 1975), on the behavior of others toward us (Tresemer & Pleck, 1974), and on our identity. Like age and race, a sex role is **ascribed** (given to us) rather than **achieved** (earned), as an occupational role is.

Sex roles present problems for men and women. On the one hand, rigid adherence to a role limits our potential (Bem, S. L., 1976; Heilbrun, 1976; Spence,

---

Interest Box 4-2.   The Roles People Play*

Ralph Linton, a cultural anthropologist, pioneered in studying the effects of culture on personality. In the excerpt below, Linton discusses the many roles a person might occupy. In each of these positions, differences in the expectations that others hold lead to differences in the person's behavior. These differences in behavior, in turn, reinforce different expectations.

Let us suppose that a man spends the day working as a clerk in a store. While he is behind the counter, his active status is that of a clerk, established by his position in our society's system of specialized occupations. The role associated with this status provides him with patterns for his relations with customers. These patterns will be well known both to him and to the customers and will enable them to transact business with a minimum of delay or misunderstanding. When he retires to the rest room for a smoke and meets other employees there, his clerk status becomes latent and he assumes another active status based upon his position in the association group composed of the store's employees as a whole. In this status his relations with other employees will be governed by a different set of culture patterns from those employed in his relations with customers. Moreover, since he probably knows most of the other employees, his exercise of these culture patterns will be modified by his personal likes and dislikes of certain individuals and by considerations of their and his own relative positions in the prestige series of the store association's members. When closing time comes, he lays aside both his clerk and store association statuses and, while on the way home, operates simply in terms of his status with respect to the society's age-sex system. Thus if he is a young man he will at least feel that he ought to get up and give his seat to a lady, while if he is an old one he will be quite comfortable about keeping it. As soon as he arrives at his house, a new set of statuses will be activated. These statuses derive from the kinship ties which relate him to various members of the family group. In pursuance of the roles associated with these family statuses he will try to be cordial to his mother-in-law, affectionate to his wife and a stern disciplinarian to Junior, whose report card marks a new low. If it happens to be lodge night, all his familial statuses will become latent at about eight o'clock. As soon as he enters the lodge room and puts on his uniform as Grand Imperial Lizard, in the Ancient Order of Dinosaurs, he assumes a new status, one which has been latent since the last lodge meeting, and performs in terms of its role until it is time for him to take off his uniform and go home.

*From *The Cultural Background of Personality*, by R. Linton. © 1945, renewed 1973. Reprinted by permission of Prentice-Hall, Inc., Englewood Cliffs, New Jersey.

Helmreich, & Stapp, 1975). On the other hand, too much deviation from the role may also cause problems, including rejection (Hagen & Kahn, 1975; Horner, 1972a, 1972b; Shaffer & Wegley, 1974). The unpleasant fact of sex roles—or any other roles—is that people are rewarded for playing them well but often punished for deviating from role expectations.

Group roles.   Many roles are not designated by a title such as doctor but emerge to meet the changing needs of the group. Such **group roles** may include that of **task specialist** and **social/emotional specialist.** The task specialist takes responsibility for moving the group along on its task and helping it reach its goals. The social/emotional specialist maintains cohesiveness, cooperation, and pleasantness within the group. Of course, any group member may move into or out of these roles from time to time, and a single person may play both roles from time to time.

Some have suggested that men are typically task specialists in families and other groups, whereas women are typically social/emotional specialists (Parsons & Bales, 1955; Zelditch, 1955). There may be some truth in this generalization, but the correlation is far from perfect. Many women are good task specialists, and many men are good social/emotional specialists. Further, some people are able to play both roles well, and others are not.

Role conflict.   We sometimes find ourselves in situations of conflicting expectations. Such **role conflict** takes several forms (Brown, 1965).

Interrole conflict (*inter* means between) may occur when people occupy two roles that make conflicting demands on them. For instance, if your parents expect you to come home for weekends and spend time with them (your role as son or daughter) and your professors expect you to spend the weekend studying (your role as student), you will experience interrole conflict.

Intrarole conflict (*intra* means within) may occur when there are different expectations about how a person should enact the same role. For example, teachers offer one definition of your role as student, and other students offer another. These definitions differ in many ways, including how much time you should allocate to studying and to partying. These different expectations give you intrarole conflict as a student.

Sex-role expectations have been changing in recent years, and with these changes comes intrarole conflict. Sometimes a man or woman is expected to do one thing, sometimes another, and meeting one set of expectations may mean failing to meet another set. Such role conflict may have serious consequences. Before World War II, men had higher rates of mental illness than women (Gove & Tudor, 1973). Since then, women have had higher rates (reviewed in Clancy & Gove, 1974). This shift *may* be traceable to increasing female role ambiguity. When sex roles are unambiguously defined, they offer less freedom but also result in less conflict. Well-defined roles offer a legible script for how to behave. Sometimes it is easier to follow rules than to cope with ambiguity.

A third type of role conflict is the *personality/role conflict.* Here your personality and the performance required by a role may not match well. For example, your personality may not leave you well suited for studying long hours, but your role as student requires it.

Sex-role expectations have been changing in recent years, and with these changes comes intrarole conflict.

The constraining effects of sex roles are demonstrated in a study (Kidder, Bellettirie, & Cohn, 1977) that found that, when their behavior was public, women tended to be like their stereotype. They were accommodating and cooperative, generously sharing rewards with a partner who had not worked hard. In private, however, women shared the rewards on the basis of deservedness, so the lazy partner got less. Men in the study behaved in the opposite way, becoming more generous in private than in public. Sex roles do not always allow us to do what we would really like to do in public.

Sandra Bem (in press) has examined a variety of evidence suggesting that the extremes of masculinity and femininity may have negative consequences for personal, cognitive, and social functioning. She suggests that the best sex role may be psychologically androgynous, sharing the best of both masculine and feminine characteristics: strong and gentle, competent and considerate, and so on. Psychologically androgynous people, emerging evidence suggests, may be more effective and better able to adapt to a variety of situations (Bem, S. L., 1975; Heilbrun, 1968; Spence, Helmreich, & Stapp, 1975).

In the early 1960s—and it may still be true today—White college students seemed to expect that Black students would be less ascendant and more acquiescent than themselves (Katz & Cohen, 1962), and men also expected these characteristics in women (Horner, 1972a, 1972b). Blacks and women who accepted these expectations and behaved accordingly seemed to be better liked by people holding these traditional expectations than were Blacks or women who were more assertive and less acquiescent. If your personality is prone to acquiescence and your role requires acquiescence, you will not have personality/role conflict. If your personality and role don't match, such conflict may occur.

Socialization. **Socialization** is the process by which young children acquire the patterns of thought, feeling, and behavior characteristic of their parents and society. Socialization influences a child's understanding of "sex-appropriate" behavior (sex-role socialization). It also affects a child's need for achievement, degree of field dependence, and many, many other individual differences. The socialization process extends over years and involves many people who influence the child in many ways. Everything that researchers have learned about social influence could probably be useful in understanding socialization. After presenting an example of sex-role-socialization practices, I will highlight just a few key principles.

Sex-role socialization. Sex differences in personality and behavior are widely believed to be influenced by sex-role socialization, the process by which boys and girls are taught what is appropriate behavior for their sex. Such teaching may emphasize many different variables, such as:

- Nurturance—training children to be helpful toward others, especially younger children.
- Obedience—training them to obey orders and cooperate when asked.
- Responsibility—training them to perform household chores and other duties.
- Achievement—training them to desire to excel and strive toward competence.
- Self-reliance—training them to work and play independently.

Different cultures require different skills and values of adults. Thus, they differ in the ways they socialize boys and girls. In hunting societies, for instance, self-reliance and achievement may be more important than obedience and responsibility. But it seems that nearly all societies are the same in many aspects of sex-role socialization. Researchers in one classic study (Barry, Bacon, & Child, 1957) analyzed reports from 110 different cultures for sex-role-socialization practices. These researchers found that in most societies sex-role socialization emphasized nurturance, obedience, and responsibility for girls and achievement and self-reliance for boys.

Some principles of socialization. What general principles might help account for how socialization takes place? We will itemize a few here.

First, a model must be available. Children learn a great deal by imitation, and they imitate the models—such as parents—that are available. For instance, in sex-role socialization, children's books present men and women differently (Weitzman, Eifler, Hokada, & Ross, 1972). So do television commercials (McArthur & Resko, in press). These media typically present men as brighter and more competent than women. Women are depicted as more nurturant, obedient, and dependent than men. Thus, the media provide models (meaning examples, not necessarily good examples) that are important in socialization.

Imitation may also be important in developing field dependence/independence, according to numerous studies reviewed by Goodenough and Witkin (1977). Fathers tend to be more field independent, and, when a father is present in the home, boys and girls tend to be more field independent than when the father is absent. When fathers are actively involved with their children, boys are more field independent than girls, presumably because children imitate same-sex parents. In a study of polygamous African families, the more wives a father had, the more field dependent were his children (Dawson, 1967a, 1967b). This suggests that mothers (who tend to be field dependent) socialize their children for field dependence.

Another general principle of socialization is that models must set standards and make their expectations clear. Research suggests that children with high needs for achievement have parents who set high standards for excellence (Rosen, 1961; Rosen & D'Andrade, 1959). Some studies have shown that girls are encouraged by parents to be "good," whereas boys are encouraged to be aggressive (Sears, R. R., Maccoby, & Levin, 1957).

Further, models must reward children for "correct" behavior and not reward "incorrect" behavior. Several studies, for instance, have found that people who are high in need for achievement had parents who consistently rewarded success and punished failure (Child, Storm, & Veroff, 1958; Rosen, 1961; Winterbottom, 1958).

And finally, models must show affection and warmth toward children. Children are more attentive to warm models and more willing to imitate and try to please them. For instance, people who registered high in need for achievement had parents who had showed them affection (Rosen & D'Andrade, 1959; Winterbottom, 1958). Other studies have found that girls who identify with their mothers and who have good relations with them are more field dependent.

Although these general principles can probably be applied to socialization practices everywhere, they fall short of accounting for some rather interesting, specific findings. The strange case of the relation between birth order and intelligence required a special explanation and led to many new insights into socialization practices.

Birth order and intelligence. Since 1959, when Stanley Schachter published *The Psychology of Affiliation*, much has been learned about **birth order.** Birth order refers to the sequence of birth of siblings. From this research we can say that first-borns affiliate more when they are anxious (Schachter, 1959) and have a higher need to achieve than later-borns (Sampson, 1962). In fact, first-borns seem to achieve more: they do better in school (Altus, 1965) and they are over-represented in colleges and graduate schools (Schachter, 1963). Being born first is not advantageous in every respect, however. First-borns may be more dependent (Hilton, 1967) and seem to be more easily influenced, especially when they are anxious or when they are pressured (Fischer & Winer, 1969; Rhine, 1968; Warren, 1966; Wolf & Weiss, 1965).

For many years psychologists have searched for, and sometimes found, relationships between birth order and variables such as creativity, marital adjustment, tolerance of pain, and even extrasensory perception. These studies produced mixed results: sometimes one variable is found to be related to birth order, and sometimes it is not. But one variable that does seem to be fairly consistently related to birth order is **intelligence.** First-borns are more likely than later-borns to become eminent scientists (Schachter, 1963). And within lower levels of ability first-borns also outperform their siblings (Chittenden, Foan, Zweil, & Smith, 1968). Performance on intelligence tests also seems to be related to family size. Children from small families tend to be brighter, on the average, than children from large families, especially among the poor (reviewed in Belmont & Marolla, 1973).

One of the most remarkable studies in this area was conducted by Lillian Belmont and Francis Marolla (1973). They studied the birth order and intelligence scores of 386,114 Dutch men aged 19. These data were taken from the Dutch Military Examinations, and almost all of the men of that age in the Netherlands took the exams. Belmont and Marolla found that the first-born in a family of two children was brighter than the second-born, on the average. In a family of three children, the first-born tended to be brighter than the second-born, who tended to be brighter than the third. Their findings are shown in Figure 4-2. As you can see, intelligence decreases from first- to last-born and, in general, decreases as family size grows.

Figure 4-2. Birth order, family size, and intelligence. Scores on an intelligence test are lower for later borns and for large families. The lowest scores are achieved by last-borns in a family size (FS) of nine. (From "Birth Order, Family Size, and Intelligence," by L. Belmont and F. A. Marolla, *Science*, 1973, *182*, 1096–1101. Copyright © 1973 by the American Association for the Advancement of Science. Reprinted by permission.)

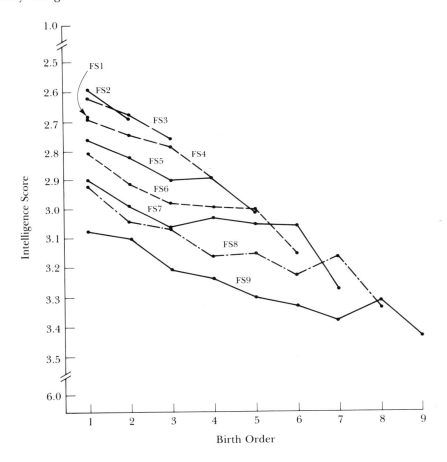

Robert Zajonc has developed a clever explanation for these findings (Zajonc, 1975; Zajonc & Markus, 1975). He points out that each person in the family is influenced by all other members and that intelligence is one thing influenced. Children learn a great deal as they mature, and their intelligence, not corrected for age, greatly increases with age. Some of this increase is because they are in an environment where there are more-intelligent people than they—their parents and perhaps older siblings and other adults. In a family of two children and two parents, the average intelligence of these four people is obviously higher than it would be in a family of two parents and six children. As Zajonc (1975) put it, "Children from large families, who spend more time in a world of child-size minds, should develop more slowly and therefore attain lower IQs than children from small families, who have more contact with grownups' minds." Zajonc also suggests that, the longer the gap between children is, the more time each older child has to develop and, therefore, the greater the rise in the average intellectual level in the family and the less disadvantaged later-born children will be. In fact, if the age gap between the first- and later-born is great enough, the later-born might be expected to be even smarter than a first-born in a small family.

Zajonc also argues that the opportunity to teach others contributes to the development of intelligence. All children but the only child and the last-born have an opportunity to teach what they know to younger siblings. This teaching allows them to solve problems and assess the adequacy of their own understanding of things. As you can see from Figure 4-2, there is a pronounced drop in the intellectual ability of the last-born from that of the next-to-last-born, and only children do not score as well as first-borns from two- or three-children families.

There are many implications to be drawn from Zajonc's theory. Zajonc himself has suggested that, if you want your children to be as bright as possible, you might stop with two. This is a poor argument, though, because the difference between the second-born of two children and the third-born of three is only about one IQ point. Also, there have been failures to replicate Belmont and Marolla's data with smaller, different samples (McCutcheon, 1977). Another implication is the effect of family size or class size on parents and teachers. If parents are raising the intellectual ability of their children, do children lower the ability of parents? If teachers of young children raise the intellectual ability of their students, do those children lower the ability of their teachers?

Explaining the direction taken by socialization.

There is a certain inevitability to socialization: it takes place in every family and has been going on for thousands of years. In fact, most mammals engage in some crude socialization practices. It is curious, however, that socialization takes place in certain directions and not others. For example, we noted earlier that most cultures socialize girls for nurturance, obedience, and responsibility, but boys for achievement and self-reliance. Why is this?

One explanation emphasizes function. If sex-role differentiation among adults is beneficial—because of the nature of the economy or family structure—then it is useful for children to be trained for this specialization. Otherwise, adolescents would have to learn new roles, skills, and attitudes (Barry et al., 1957). Such differentiation might be more effective when it magnifies basic biological differences between the sexes rather than trying to reverse them. Some theorists (Murdock, 1949) have suggested that sex-role differentiation is based on differences in physical strength. Men are typically stronger than women, it is argued, and so more suited for strenuous tasks such as hunting, fishing, mining, and herding. Women are assigned the less strenuous tasks, such as caring for babies, washing dishes, and cleaning house.

Other theorists suggest that aggressiveness, perhaps induced in part by testosterone, seems important in competition, achievement, and self-reliance. So it may make sense to encourage aggressive children to become task specialists and channel this aggressiveness into achievement and self-reliance. But every society needs a social/emotional specialist as much as it needs a task specialist, and this kind of specialization requires a gentle, nonaggressive, noncompetitive approach to life. If there is sense in encouraging and channeling aggressiveness, then there is also sense in encouraging the development of social and emotional skills.

Kay Deaux (cited in Wrightsman, 1977, p. 454) has suggested a **reinforcement-system** explanation of sex-role socialization: "Perhaps parents act differently toward boys and girls because the boys and girls treat their parents differently." Because boys are naturally very active, parents will find success (reward) in encouraging this activity and failure (punishment) in trying to squash it. Boys may thus teach their parents to encourage their activity. Every child may teach its parents what to teach! Several studies suggest a child's behavior and qualities such as attractiveness influence parental behavior (Bell, R. Q., 1968, 1971; Dion, 1974; Oshofsky & O'Connell, 1972; Yarrow, Waxler, & Scott, 1971). Perhaps more than we realize, the child controls the behavior of the parent, which in turn affects the child.

This became obvious to me one day when I was playing Old Maid with a 4-year-old. He had been matching pairs of cards, and I had been saying "good" whenever he made a match. On one match I did not say "good," and he said "Aren't you gonna say 'good'?" I realized that he had been matching cards to please me and get me to say "good," and I had been saying it to please him and get him to match more cards. Grownups sometimes think that they are acting freely and independently in dispensing rewards and punishments. But it is probably more common that they are part of a reinforcement system and are as much under the control of the child as vice versa.

Each of us has an idea of what boys and girls should be like. Such expectations color our reactions to children. That is, we may treat a little boy the way we think little boys should be treated, rather than the way *this* little boy wants or needs to be treated. There is evidence that different treatment of boys and girls begins at an early age. Researchers in one study (Rubin, J. A., Provenzano, & Luria, 1974) interviewed the parents of 15 baby boys and 15 baby girls, each less than 24 hours old. Even though these infants were not different in average length, weight, or health, parents saw the girls as smaller, softer, finer featured, and less attentive than the boys. Also, the parents believed that the boys resembled their fathers and the girls resembled their mothers. Such differences in our perception of infant boys and girls may lead to differences in our treatment of them. For example, baby girls are looked at more and talked to much more than are baby boys (Lewis, M., 1972).

What differences are desirable?   In Huxley's *Brave New World* (1933) a future is described in which individuality is sacrificed for the good of society. You should consider whether you want this kind of world or whether in socializing children you would prefer that they develop capacities to be both task specialists and social/emotional specialists. Sandra Bem and others feel that the best-adjusted person is one who is androgynous (see pp. 82–84) and who can behave with greater flexibility in a large variety of situations.

Although society may benefit from sex-role differentiation, individuals within that society sometimes suffer from it. On the one hand, boys who are trained for achievement and self-reliance will have difficulty when called on to be nurturant or obedient. Girls who are trained to be nurturant and obedient may have difficulty when called on for achievement and self-reliance. On the other hand, when children are socialized for one adult role and then find themselves as adults coping with another role, conflicts develop. Training girls for achievement and self-reliance may frustrate them as adults if roles requiring these qualities are not open to them.

SITUATIONAL INFLUENCES

We often underestimate how powerful our situation is in shaping our behavior. Carolyn Sherif tells a story about two friends walking along a sidewalk in New York some years ago. A woman approached whom one recognized as a friend of her mother's. Much to her embarrassment, though, she was unable to remember the name of the approaching woman. Finally, as they were about to pass, she leapt forward and threw her arms around the woman in greeting. The women embraced, had a brief, lively conversation, then parted. A few minutes later, she had a disturbing realization: "That wasn't a friend of my mother's. That was Eleanor Roosevelt!"

Many of our behaviors, such as Mrs. Roosevelt's greeting behavior, are largely under the control of the situation. When the behavior is "appropriate," when another does it, we reciprocate. When two joggers pass each other, both may wave, both may say "Hi!" or they may ignore each other. But it is rare that one will say "Hi" or wave without a similar response from the other.

Most of us want to have more control over our own behaviors than some situations allow. So we simply avoid some situations and seek out others. If we want to play cards, it is often easier to find a friend who likes playing cards than it is to enlist a nonplayer. If we don't like cards, we may tend to avoid people who always want to play. We may find people who are similar to us attractive because we feel in greater control: we are more likely to be influenced by them to do what we privately want to do, and it seems easier to influence them to do what we privately want to do.

The situation we are in has a complex effect on the emotions we feel. Our situation affects both our physiological arousal and our mood; situation + arousal + mood seem to determine emotion. It has taken social psychologists a long time to discover this simple equation. In one study (Schachter & Singer, 1962) some subjects were injected with adrenalin and others with a **placebo** (salty water that would have no physiological effects). Some subjects were correctly told that the adrenalin would cause their faces to become flushed, their hands to tremble, and their heart rate to accelerate. Other subjects were misled and told that the adrenalin would give them side effects such as itching, numbness, and perhaps a mild headache. Other subjects were told that there would be no side effects. Subjects then waited in a room with a confederate of the experimenters who had been trained to appear either giddy or angry and who tried to interact with them.

For those subjects who were given correct information about the effects of the adrenalin, the behavior of the confederate had little effect on their own behavior. Although they were physiologically aroused, they could attribute that

The situation we are in has a complex effect on the emotions we feel.

arousal to the drug. Subjects who were given the placebo injection did not become physiologically aroused and also did not show emotions like the confederate's.

But subjects who had been misled and given adrenalin felt aroused and did not know why. Subjects with the euphoric confederate acted somewhat giddy. The confederate may have put them in a good mood that was intensified by their arousal. Similarly, subjects with the angry confederate may have experienced a somewhat negative mood that was intensified and reflected in their behavior.

In everyday situations, the pleasantness determines our mood; the situation's excitement or the amount and nature of our own activity determine our arousal, which intensifies the mood. How do we interpret the mood? We look to the situation to see how we "should" be feeling. That interpretation names the emotional state we feel. This explanation is an expansion of Schachter's **cognitive theory of emotion**. It is a cognitive theory because thinking is viewed as a determinant of feeling; it is an expansion because Schachter did not include mood in his formulation.

Some people might find this explanation cumbersome. Don't we have different physiological reactions to different situations? Doesn't that determine our emotion and behavior? No. Many studies (see Ax, 1953) have shown that different emotions involve identical physiological responses. That is, we can't tell whether we are happy or sad or angry or delighted simply by our heart rate, our pupil dilation, our rate of breathing, or other internal changes. So, the thinking goes, if it is not distinguished in your body, it must be distinguished in your head. Only an explanation that includes physiological arousal, mood, and interpretation of the situation can be really adequate.

Schachter's finding that our physiological arousal and our interpretation of the situation affect our emotion did not go unnoticed. Elaine Walster Hatfield has suggested that sexual attraction and passionate love may be experienced when the social conditions suggest that this feeling is appropriate and when physiological arousal, no matter how induced, occurs (Walster, 1971b; Walster & Berscheid, 1971). Thus, two people who are attracted to each other may feel sexually attracted when they are physiologically aroused by gladiators killing each other (Ovid, cited in Rubin, Z., 1973). The same thing may happen when zeppelins are falling from the sky in flames (Russell, quoted in Walster & Berscheid, 1971). Or filling out questionnaires on narrow, wobbling suspension bridges over canyons may have the same effect (Dutton & Aron, 1974). Of course, social conditions for labeling this arousal as sexual attraction have to be right, too. Colliding football players are physiologically aroused yet do not fall in love at halftime.

Other studies have manipulated only people's interpretation of a situation. When subjects are led to believe that they feel a certain way, these studies find, subjects apparently *do* feel that way. A few **false-feedback studies** will be described to show how this works.

People's interpretation of their emotion can be affected by false feedback about their heart rate. In an early study (Valins, 1966) subjects were told that they would be able to listen to their heart rate with amplification equipment while viewing photographs of women. In fact, the male college students in these experiments heard a tape-recorded heart that beat at a moderate pace, beat faster, or beat slower when they viewed certain pictures. The men felt the photographs of the women more attractive when they were led to believe that the photograph had affected their heart rate (either faster or slower) than when they thought the photograph had not affected it.

Other studies using false feedback have obtained similar results. For instance, researchers in one study took advantage of the principle that we tend to spend more time looking at those we like best (Mehrabian, 1969). When subjects were misinformed about how much they had been looking at each other, they changed their ratings of attraction to the other to fit the principle (Kleinke, Bustos, Meeker, & Staneski, 1973). The more subjects believed they had been looking at another, the more they liked the other. Another study (Hendrick & Giesen, 1976) found

that, when people listening to a speech were attached to a "belief meter" (which supposedly told them whether they believed or disbelieved the speech), feedback influenced attitudes. People given false feedback showed more attitude change than others not receiving it.

The studies reviewed above suggest that both arousal and our interpretation of the situation are important influences on emotion. How does mood contribute to emotion? The evidence suggests that a positive mood may lead to any of a variety of positive emotions and positive behaviors, the exact form being determined by our interpretation of the situation. The same is true of a negative mood. This idea of diffusion of affect will be discussed in later chapters. For now, we will simply look at a few of the ways that moods affect emotion and behavior:

- We tend to like those we meet in a hot, uncomfortable room less than those met in a cooler, more comfortable room (Bell, P. A., & Baron, 1974; Griffitt, 1970; Griffitt & Veitch, 1971).
- When we view pleasant films, we may come to like those we are with more than when we view unpleasant films (Gouaux, 1971; Schwartz, R. D., 1966).
- Students who are heavily rewarded for being in an experiment may evaluate a stranger more positively than when they are not so rewarded (Griffitt, 1968).
- People who are successful at a task, or receive rewards, later behave more helpfully toward strangers (Isen, 1970).
- Many studies find that people tend to condemn the innocent victim of injustice (Berscheid & Walster, 1967; Berscheid, Walster, & Barclay, 1969; Glass, 1964; Lerner, 1970, 1971; Lerner & Simons, 1966; Walster & Prestholdt, 1966; Walster, Walster, Abrahams, & Brown, 1966).

Everyone likes a winner, but losers, even when it is not their fault, seem to be disliked. The exception to this rule seems to be when the victim's suffering means benefits for us. In an experiment where you or I must be shocked, I may like you more if you choose to be shocked (Lerner, M. J., 1968; Lerner, M. J., & Matthews, G., 1967). When we feel grateful to a victim, we like him or her more.[1]

In short, it appears that emotion and behavior are influenced by our interpretation of the situation, by our physiological arousal, and by our mood. We will have many opportunities to use this general explanation in later chapters.

CULTURAL INFLUENCES

Culture is one of those words we have heard often but may have trouble defining. Most definitions (see Interest Box 4-3) suggest that it refers to those behaviors, their causes, and consequences that are shared by a society and transmitted to

---

[1] Such studies have led Lott and Lott (1974) to propose that "liking for a person will result under those conditions in which an individual experiences reward in the presence of that person regardless of the relationship between the other person and the rewarding event or state of affairs" (p. 172). The studies of blaming the victim noted in the chapter suggest that we might also say that, when the rewards or punishments another receives do not directly determine what we receive, we like those who receive rewards in our presence and dislike those who receive punishments.

newcomers and to the next generation. In this definition, "causes" include perspectives, attitudes, habits, traditions, and customs; "consequences" include the products of behavior, such as art, music, literature, and architecture. Culture, economy, and politics are the three major activities that hold a society together. Any social behavior ultimately involves all three systems (Bunge, 1976). For instance, in writing a term paper—a cultural activity—you may use a pen and paper—products of our economic system, which in turn is regulated by our political system.

Why study other cultures? There are many good reasons. We can learn whether the personal and formal theories that have developed from within our own culture are general enough to apply to other cultures. Most likely we will discover the tremendous impact our own culture has on us, an impact now recognized by some social psychologists (Hollander, 1971) if not fully understood by any of us.

The study of differences and similarities across cultures is very important, because any inferences we might make about people in general are of doubtful validity when based on one case. A cross-cultural perspective provides a better understanding of what is happening in any one culture and a better understanding of what is basically human (Rosenblatt, 1974). In the process of studying other cultures we can also acquire new perspectives and fresh ideas from which to generate new theories. And, best of all, we can acquire perspective on ourselves, new insights and understanding. In our studies of other cultures our appreciation for others may deepen.

Such appreciation may carry over to include an appreciation of culture itself. There is a theoretical perspective in anthropology and sociology called **functionalism** that is simply enamored with every aspect of culture. The essence of this view is that everything connected with culture exists because it is useful and serves some function.

To quote the anthropologist Bronislaw Malinowski, functionalism is "the explanation of anthropological facts at all levels of development by their function, by the part which they play in the integral system of culture, by the manner in which they are related to each other within the system and by the way in which

---

Interest Box 4-3. Some Definitions of Culture

"The sum total of the knowledge, attitudes and habitual behavior patterns shared and transmitted by members of a particular society" (Ralph Linton, 1938).

"A form of nonbiological, social heritage that flows from the past, generation by generation" (Edwin Hollander, 1971, p. 303).

"That complex whole which includes knowledge, belief, art, law, morals, custom and any other ca-

pabilities and habits acquired by man as a member of society" (E. B. Tylor, 1877, p. 1).

"Everything that is produced by and is capable of sustaining shared symbolic experience" (Jaeger & Selznick, 1964, p. 663).

"A set of shared beliefs" (Loflin & Winogrond, 1976).

this system is related to the physical surroundings" (1944, p. 864).[2] Functionalists have demonstrated how imaginative they are in explaining the function of a necktie, buttons on a sleeve, or tassles on a shoe. I believe that a use can be found for almost anything, but that does not explain why that thing exists or why something else, which might be much more useful, does not exist. Nevertheless, it is a good exercise for you to think about what uses a thing has. As Edwin Hollander noted,

> In the functionalist view, therefore, even apparently non-functional elements in a culture can be imputed to have latent functions. In the instance of mechanically useless items, such as buttons on sleeves of men's jackets, there exists the latent function of preserving tradition in a symbolic sense. In short, it looks and feels "right" [1971, p. 310].[3]

Historical reconstructionists take a different approach. They suggest that many of our customs may not make much sense unless we know their origins. In earlier times, they note, travelers were often armed and prepared to fight strangers. Strangers who did not intend to fight could raise their open sword hand (the right hand) or make contact with their open knife hand (the right hand) in greeting. The wave and handshake persist today, still signifying friendship but no longer intended to reveal that the greeters are unarmed. You might be interested in speculating on the functions of other customs as well as their possible origins.

How do cultures differ? How do people in different cultures differ? In the next few pages, we will look at a sample of such differences, including visual discriminations and intelligence.

Culture and Visual Discriminations.   Abilities grow out of experience. To mechanics, the differences between two carburetors may be extremely obvious. To the rest of us, all carburetors may seem alike. People who live in different societies have different experiences and thus develop different abilities. For instance, Eskimos who hunt for a living are experienced at detecting small objects at a distance in an irregular environment. The Eskimo's ability to spot a distant seal running on an ice floe may be unfortunate for the seal, but it is essential for the Eskimo's family. Such an ability comes with practice. Farm workers, on the other hand, spend much of their lives in a regular environment of parallel rows in flat, rectangular fields. Such experience may develop many visual skills but not necessarily the same ones the hunting Eskimo develops. John Berry (1971) has found, in fact, that hunting Eskimos score better on discrimination and spatial tasks than do farm workers, even though their general visual acuity is comparable.

Our experience also structures our expectations and directs our attention. Researchers have found that people living in a **carpentered world** of straight lines and right angles are more susceptible to some illusions than are other people who live in round huts (Campbell, D. T., 1964; Jahoda, 1966; Rivers, 1901, 1905; Segall, Campbell, & Herskovitz, 1963, 1966). This may be because they are accustomed to making "corrections" in angles seen in perspective (see Figure 4-3).

---

[2]From "Social Anthropology," by B. Malinowski. In *Encyclopedia Britannica*, 1944, *20*, 862–870.

[3]This passage does not appear in the third edition of this book and therefore does not represent the author's final thinking on the matter.

Figure 4-3.
Illusion proneness of different groups on the Müller-Lyer illusion. The arrowhead horizontal line (left in the illustration) and the tailed line (right) were varied in length until the subjects taking the test judged them to be equal. The Percent Illusion is the percentage by which the left-hand line exceeded the right-hand one when they were judged to be equal. The number of cases on which the mean is based is indicated in parentheses (adult data only). (From *Comparative Perspectives on Social Psychology*, by W. Lambert and R. Weisbrod. Copyright © 1971 by Little, Brown and Company. Reprinted by permission.)

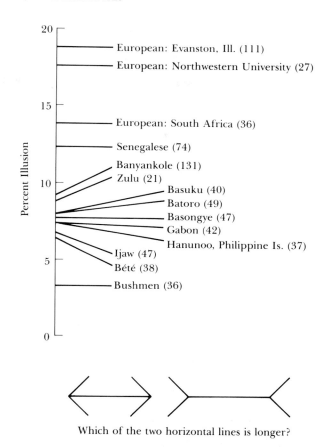

Which of the two horizontal lines is longer?

Just how this experience structures our expectations and directs our attention requires much more research. One mode of influence may be language.

Culture and Intelligence.   Intelligence refers to a specific set of cognitive abilities that are useful and important in a given culture. In our culture an ability to read and understand this book is a sign of intelligence. If a person could not read this book, would we say that person was not intelligent? Aristotle and Plato were intelligent but could not read English. Such an ability was not useful, important, or even possible in their culture. Any intelligence test must be constructed to measure cognitive abilities that are useful and important in a given culture. When a test designed for one culture is administered to people from another culture, the scores of the second culture will be lower than those of the first. Such scores may predict success in adapting to the culture for which the test was designed, but they will not measure intelligence in any general, cross-cultural sense.

Cross-cultural comparisons may reveal which cultures are higher in specific abilities. For instance, technologically advanced cultures encourage logical reasoning, generalization, abstraction, and inference (Goodnow, 1970). Methods of formal education provide practice in these tasks (Bruner, Oliver, Greenfield, et

ARISTOTLE

...in reference to cross cultural intelligence tests.

al., 1966). Hunting or farming cultures favor the development of other cognitive abilities and define intelligence differently.

Not only do we have to be careful not to impose our own definition of intelligence on others, we have to be careful when measuring their cognitive abilities. Some testing situations can produce anxiety that interferes with performance (Katz, I., 1970), particularly if the tester is from another culture. Some general abilities may also affect performance. For example, some cultures value speed, others accuracy. People who have learned to value speed may do better on speed tests. Further, how people think they should score may affect their performance. For instance, if we think we should show creativity, we will appear more creative on a test than if we think we should show traditionalism (Levine, R. A., 1970).

Other Cultural Differences.   It may be useful to briefly review some other studies to get an idea of just how much cultures can differ. As compared with people in some other cultures studied:

☐ Mothers in the United States spend more time with their babies (Minturn & Lambert, 1964) and talk to their babies more (Levine, R. A., 1970).
☐ U. S. mothers are more tolerant of a son's aggressiveness and sometimes encourage retaliation when they are attacked (Levine, R. A., 1970).
☐ Many Americans seem less accepting of male homosexuality, which apparently occurs in every society and is socially acceptable in two-thirds of all societies studied (Ford & Beach, 1951).
☐ Although Americans attach great importance to free-market capitalism, 42% of the world's population lives in socialist countries and values cooperation over competition. For many of these people, socialism implies egalitarianism, whereas capitalism implies materialism, greed, and selfishness ("Socialism: Trials and Errors," 1978).

Culture Change.   When two groups come into contact, each may make efforts to transmit its culture to the other. Some individuals will readily accept aspects of the new culture, but others will hold fast to their own culture. This process of mutual transmission of culture and the consequences of this transmission have been called **cultural diffusion, acculturation,** or **enculturation**. Such processes involve widespread attitude change, learning, and behavior change. Cultural diffusion is not always a smooth, pleasant, easy shift. It involves the acquisition of new attitudes, values, behaviors, ways of thinking, and life-styles. Confronting this newness often produces **culture shock**. Family members commonly differ in their degree of contact with the new culture and in their ability to change. Among immigrants to a new culture, the children often show greater adaptability than their parents, adopting new ways and causing tension within the family. This adaptation sometimes involves a total acceptance of the new ways but more often means partial acceptance, translating the new ways into old forms.

Much of the uniformity within a culture, like uniformity in groups (see Chapter 13), is maintained through norms and social rewards and punishments. **Folkways** or **usages** are types of uniformity that do not usually lead to punishment when violated. An example is shaking hands in greeting. Violations of **conventions**, such as wearing clothes or using a knife and fork when eating, are often punished by both laws and social sanctions. **Mores** and **taboos** refer to behavior in which there is greatest uniformity and greatest punishment for violation, as in

When two groups come into contact, each group may make efforts to transmit its culture to the other.

the universal **incest taboo**. Acculturation often means that a person breaks one norm in complying with another. People probably weigh the costs and benefits of such actions, but the situation is rarely a pleasant one.

Cultures change slowly, and any shift involves creating new norms and violating old ones, whether or not it results from contact with other cultures. Jacobs and Campbell (1961) have studied how an arbitrary, experimentally created tradition is perpetuated across generations of a laboratory microculture. In one condition of this experiment, three confederates and a subject made judgments of the distance a light apparently moved in Sherif's autokinetic situation (see p. 303). Confederates had been instructed to give the arbitrary judgments of 15 to 16 inches. As expected, the subject typically agreed and made similar judgments. The confederates were removed one at a time, and each was replaced by another naive subject who joined this microculture and made judgments. After all confederates were replaced, this replacement process continued, removing subjects in order of their seniority and replacing them with naive subjects. Not surprisingly, it took several "generations" of these laboratory groups for the tradition to shift back to where it would have been with private, uninfluenced judgments.

Traditions are maintained by **normative social influence**, as well as by prescriptive and proscriptive personal theories, and they change slowly. Because of this, they bring stability and the pleasant comfort of familiarity to daily life.

SUMMARY

This chapter has examined an assortment of biological, social, and cultural influences that give rise to differences between people. The chapter opened with a discussion of the possible role of hormones. Although it seems likely that hormones do affect aggressiveness and field dependence in some way, it is not clear how such effects take place. The relative importance of biological and social influences was also discussed.

The chapter presented a model of social influence, in which four components—the opinions and behaviors of each of two people—were shown to influence each other. This model emphasizes the complexity of the social-influence process and the importance of avoiding oversimplification in explaining social influence.

One powerful way that people influence us is through expectations they have of us. When such expectations come to be shared, they define *role*, a set of required or expected behaviors of a certain position in a group. Sex roles are carried with us for life, whereas group roles may be carried only when we are acting members of a particular group. But all roles have the potential for conflict, when expectations, desires, and personality do not all match up.

Socialization is the process by which young children acquire the patterns of thought, feeling, and behavior of adults. The processes involved are extremely complex and extremely important. In addition to imitation, reinforcement, and other forms of influence, children learn by teaching others. Why socialization takes the direction it does is still a mystery, although functional, reinforcement-system, and expectation explanations provide some tentative answers. The section on socialization closed with a discussion of what form of sex-role socialization may be most desirable.

Situations have powerful effects on social behavior and emotion. Research suggests that situations affect both our physiological arousal and our mood. These two factors, in combination with our interpretation of the situation, may determine the emotion we feel and the things we do.

In addition to biological, social, and situational influences, culture has strong effects on our thoughts, feelings, and behaviors. To illustrate these effects, the relationships between culture and visual discriminations and between culture and intelligence were discussed.

GLOSSARY TERMS

Define these terms in your own words, then look them up in the glossary at the back of the book.

Acculturation
Achieved role
Androgen
Ascribed role
Birth order
Carpentered world
Cognitive theory of emotion
Comparative appraisal
Conventions
Cultural diffusion
Culture
Culture shock
Enculturation
Estrogen
False-feedback study
Folkways
Functionalism
Group roles
Historical reconstructionism
Incest taboo
Intelligence
Interrole conflict

Intrarole conflict
Johari Window
Model of social influence
Mores
Nature
Normative social influence
Nurture
Placebo
Reinforcement system
Role
Role conflict
Role distance
Sex role
Sex-role socialization
Social/emotional specialist
Socialization
Strain toward symmetry
Taboos
Task specialist
Testosterone
Usages

FURTHER READING

Shaffer, D. R. *Social and personality development.* Monterey, Calif.: Brooks/Cole, 1979. An intriguing, scholarly review of social and personality development.

chapter
5

The Physical Environment and Social Behavior

chapter
5

Prepared with the assistance of Jonathan Charry

INTRODUCTION

People who have lived all their lives in a small town find a visit to New York City distressing. They find too many people, too much noise, and too much traffic. People drive too fast, walk too fast, and talk too fast.

New Yorkers who venture into a small farming town experience distress, too. Nothing seems to be happening. Nobody much is around, and those who are talk slowly, amble slowly, and do nothing slowly. People are actually able to find parking spaces in front of their houses, and they don't have to get up at 6 A.M. to move their cars.

It is obvious that people differ in how much stimulation they are comfortable with. City dwellers find the country distressingly boring, and country dwellers find the city overstimulating. It is also true that people can adjust to various levels of stimulation. Most people who move to the country or the city eventually adapt to the available stimulation and come to accept it.

In this chapter we will look at the effects of stimulation on people, especially on their social behavior. We will be concerned with both the nature of stimulation and the nature of those stimulated. You will learn about what happens to people when they are isolated for days or weeks in a laboratory or months at a polar station. You will learn about some of the effects of noise, crowding, heat, and air pollution on behavior. These sources of influence are not social in nature, like peer pressure or authority, but they have important effects on social behavior. If we are to develop a comprehensive understanding of social behavior, we must understand something of all of the major sources of influence, not simply the social ones.

It would be a formidable task to review all of the possible effects of all of the possible sources of stimulation. Rather than attempt that, I will review some effects of some sources of stimulation and do what I can to integrate the many findings into a coherent framework.

A FRAMEWORK FOR UNDERSTANDING

Our general thesis in this chapter is that too much or too little stimulation from the environment may be unpleasant and even harmful. Too much stimulation will affect behavior, which may, in turn, be directed toward reducing that stimulation. Too little stimulation will also have behavioral effects, which may be oriented toward increasing stimulation to some optimal (best) level. We will use the term **sensory overload** to refer to the condition of too much stimulation and **sensory restriction** to refer to the condition of not enough stimulation. **Stress** will refer to "a condition of physical or mental strain which produces changes in the autonomic nervous system" (Wolman, 1973, p. 359). A **stressor** is an event that produces stress. Stressors are unpleasant, and we usually try to avoid them. Sensory overload and sensory restriction are stressors.

The general framework we will use was proposed by Kurt Lewin (1936). He suggested that behavior is a function of (that is, depends on) both the person and the environment. This proposition is so obviously true that it may seem unnecessary to state it. But we should remember that as amateur social psychologists we often forget the environment when we make an internal attribution and forget the person when we make an external attribution (see pp. 167–169). Both person and environment affect behavior. Further, behavior may affect the environment, and both environment and behavior affect the person.

For example, people living near airports may be bothered by the noise (arrow A of Figure 5-1). When planes fly overhead, the people may stop talking (arrows C and F). Those who feel distress at the noise (arrow A) may close their windows (arrows C and F), which in turn may both cut down the noise and change the temperature (arrow E).

In general, the environment affects people in two major ways—first, by the amount of stimulation that it provides and, second, by the nature of the stimulation. We will look at both of these effects in this chapter.

Figure 5-1. Reciprocal influence model of environment, person, and behavior

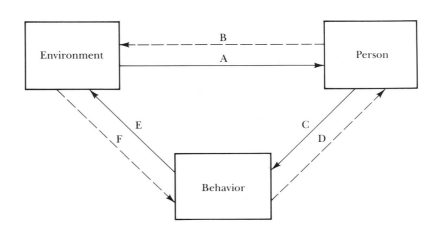

The Amount of Stimulation.   How much stimulation does an environment provide? How do we react to that amount? Two theories offer an answer: the optimal-level-of-arousal theory and the adaptation-level theory.

Optimal level of arousal.   People differ in their preferred level of stimulation. For example, if you like a particular song on the radio, you may raise the volume. Your parents may not feel as positively about it and ask you to lower it. Some of your desire to have the music louder may stem from your interest in that music. And some of your desire may be motivated by what Marvin Zuckerman (1969) called **sensation seeking**. People who like their music loud may also like driving cars fast and watching action programs on television. Individuals differ in their characteristically preferred level of stimulation. This preferred level has sometimes been called the **optimal level of arousal.**

The idea of **arousal** has been explored by a number of investigators (Bindra, 1959; Duffy, 1941, 1951, 1962, 1972; Freeman, G. L., 1948; Hebb, 1955; Malmo, 1959; Schlosberg, 1954a, 1954b). These investigators have used terms such as *degree of arousal, level of arousal, level of activation,* and *degree of energy mobilization* to refer to a continuum of brain excitation that ranges from deep sleep (at the lower end) to intense emotions, panic, and seizures (at the upper end). According to Donald Hebb (1955), stimulation from the environment has two general effects. It influences our arousal level, and it influences our reactions to the environment. According to his theory, at intermediate levels of arousal a person's ability to perceive and discriminate is at its maximum.

Different levels of arousal are associated with different behaviors, ranging in Figure 5-2 from sleep (low arousal) to behavioral disorganization (high arousal). Activities such as driving that require alertness and rapid thinking are likely to be carried out well under moderate levels of arousal. That is, for tasks requiring complex coordinations and careful thinking, the optimal level is in the middle of the arousal range. For sleep, on the other hand, the optimal level is much lower. Optimal level of arousal reflects the amount of activation required for a given task in a given situation. For example, if the radio is on, the lights are bright, and you have been drinking lots of coffee, your arousal will be fairly high. Not a good situation if you are trying to fall asleep. However, if your professor turns out all the lights in the classroom, shows you some fuzzy black-and-white slides of the brain, and talks in a monotone, your arousal level may drop considerably. Not a good situation for learning.

If we are at the optimum level of arousal, we will find doing an activity more pleasant than if our arousal is too low or too high. For example, it is more unpleasant to take notes in class when we are almost falling asleep than when we are wide awake. The relation between arousal and satisfaction may look like that of Figure 5-3. Thus, we are motivated by both a desire to do a task well and a desire to enjoy doing it, to be at our optimal level of arousal on each thing we do.

If there is a best level of arousal for performing a particular task, we might wonder how people regulate their arousal to bring it to this optimal level. Sometimes we can raise or lower our arousal through fantasy. If we need to raise our level, we may find ourselves with stimulating fantasies. You may have had such fantasies while reading this book, during sex, and at other times when you wanted to raise your arousal level. Similarly, we can lower our level through fantasy.

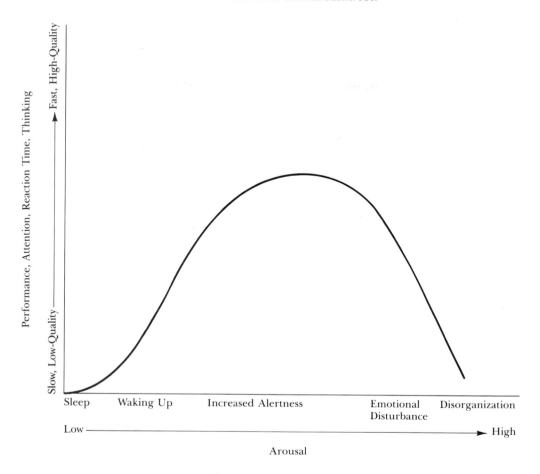

Figure 5-2.
Arousal curve.
(Adapted from
"Drives and the
CNS (Conceptual
Nervous System),"
by D. O. Hebb,
Psychological Review,
1955, *62*, 243–254.
Copyright 1955 by
the American
Psychological
Association.
Reprinted by
permission.)

Counting sheep is a classic recommended fantasy for falling asleep. Fantasies are an internal means of regulating our arousal level, to help keep it near the optimum.

Another means of regulating our arousal is through seeking or avoiding physical stimulation. You may have your hand against your face as you read this, which is an effective means of providing both your hand and face with stimulation and raising your arousal. You may be drinking coffee or tea, which contain caffeine, a chemical that raises arousal level. On other occasions, when your arousal is too high, you may avoid stimulation. Perhaps you turned the radio off or shut the door before you began reading. Zuckerman (1969) has suggested that people differ in how much arousal control they get from fantasy and how much they regulate arousal by regulating physical stimulation. Outward focusers may have a higher need for environmental stimulation than inward focusers.

Whether we are focusing on an internal or external source of stimulation, we actively select stimulation that meets our arousal needs. Bored at a party, we seek out an interesting person or interesting topic of conversation. While talking

Figure 5-3.
Relation between
arousal and
satisfaction

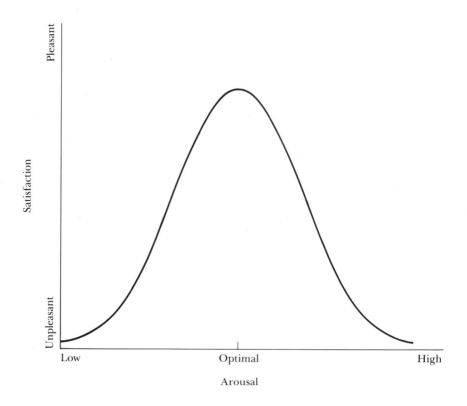

in a small group, we may find ourselves overhearing another conversation and miss what someone was saying to us. This cocktail-party phenomenon emphasizes our ability to direct our conscious attention to one source of stimulation and avoid others that may also be available. You may not be aware of many noises as you read this, but if you stop and listen, you may hear plenty.

To summarize, we are able to control the stimulation we experience in several ways: by behavior that creates, stops, or changes an external source of stimulation; by fantasy; by shifting our focus from outside ourselves to inside or back; and by selecting from the many available sources of stimulation. All of these efforts enable us to maintain a level of arousal that is near the optimum for the task we are engaged in. Regulating arousal is a process of **reciprocal influence** among environment, person, and behavior (Figure 5-1).

Adaptation level. The man who lives next to me has driven a doughnut truck for 20 years. Does he eat a lot of doughnuts? No, he got sick of them. Almost everything seems to follow this principle: when familiarity breeds contempt, absence makes the heart grow fonder. We enjoy some variation in our lives, although it, like everything else, is usually best in moderation.

How we react to the environment is influenced by our experience with it. For instance, consider an environment with a temperature of 78 degrees. This

...you can read this despite the external stimulations.

may be pleasant to a camel driver who has just ridden across the desert, a mild stressor to an office worker, and a severe stressor to an Alaskan wearing earmuffs. Because of these individual differences in affective response (mood), we can expect differences in behaviors. The camel driver might feel generous because he is in such a good mood. The office worker might feel slightly irritable and be neither helpful nor aggressive. The Alaskan might feel extremely irritable and express anger and hostility. Environments have powerful effects on our moods, and our moods have powerful effects on our behaviors.

The comfort or discomfort we experience from environmental stimulation affects our mood, which determines how we will evaluate that stimulation. But we seem to be able to **habituate** (adjust) to many sources and levels of repeated or continuous stimulation. When our camel driver enters the room he may feel cool at first, but after a while he "gets used to it." So does the Alaskan. Then, when they eventually go back outside, they may have to readjust to the outside temperature. This same effect occurs with all of our senses: taste, touch, smell, hearing, and vision.

Harry Helson's (1964) **adaptation-level theory** proposes that what we've "gotten used to" is our **adaptation level**. Because people naturally seem to enjoy small variations in the environment, slight changes from that adaptation level seem pleasant at first, and we seek them out (see Figure 5-4). After continued exposure to that new level or type of stimulation, though, it diminishes in pleasantness, becoming a new adaptation level, and we may again look forward to a slight change.

Figure 5-4.
The butterfly curve. Slight discrepancies from our adaptation level are pleasant, and extreme discrepancies are unpleasant. When we are exposed to a new and pleasant level of stimulation, it may decrease in pleasantness until we become indifferent to it. At that point, a slight change in stimulation becomes pleasant. (From "Discrepancy from Adaptation-Level as a Source of Affect," by R. N. Haber. In *Journal of Experimental Psychology,* 1958, *56,* 370–375. Copyright 1958 by the American Psychological Association. Reprinted by permission.)

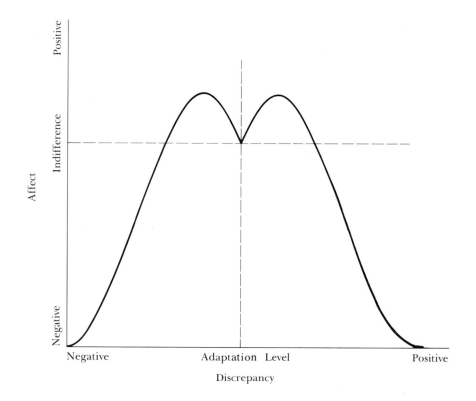

Helson suggests that large changes from that adaptation level may not seem so pleasant. For example, if you are adjusting the temperature of the shower before you step in, you may find 100 degrees a pleasant change from your current room-temperature adaptation level. At the same time, you might find 110 degrees unpleasantly hot.

After you have been in the shower a few minutes, you adapt to 100 degrees and may find yourself raising the temperature to 110 degrees. Again, Helson's prediction is confirmed: your adaptation level has shifted, and you find change from that new level pleasant.

If you were to stand in the shower for half an hour, how hot could you set the water temperature? Probably not above 180 degrees! The theory does not explain why, but common sense does: you would burn yourself if it got too hot. Your body sets limits on the usefulness of the theory. Further, the theory predicts that a change in either direction from your adaptation level may be equally pleasant. But few people find themselves lowering the water temperature after they've gotten used to it. Again, our sense organs have their preferences, the **butterfly curve** of Figure 5-4 is not always symmetrical, and the adaptation-level theory has its limitations. But within these limits it is useful.

The adaptation-level theory seems to apply to all kinds of stimulation. For example, a music lover may usually set the volume on the radio to a particular intensity. Slight changes within the music, from slightly louder to slightly softer, are very pleasant. But substantial changes in the volume can be unpleasant. This preferred level may be affected by many things. For instance, when we are trying to talk, we may prefer a lower volume; when we are trying to wake up in the morning, we may raise the volume. Our situation affects our interpretation of the environment.

The Nature of Stimulation. Optimal-level-of-arousal theory and adaptation-level theory offer accounts of how we are affected by the *amount* of stimulation we experience. How does the *nature* of this stimulation affect us? Diffusion-of-affect theory suggests an answer.

Diffusion of affect. Later in this book (Chapter 13), we will discuss in some detail a process called **diffusion of affect**. We will introduce the idea here, how-ever, because it bolsters the explanatory framework used in this chapter.

Diffusion of affect refers to the fact that moods have many different effects on behavior, as well as on thought. The diffusion-of-affect theory suggests that:

1. Although we have many names for our moods, there may be only two basic types: pleasant (happy, delighted, contented, appreciative, relaxed, comfort-able) and unpleasant (unhappy, depressed, angry, resentful, frustrated, ir-ritated, frightened).
2. Many seemingly different events can have very similar effects on our moods. For instance, it seems likely that such events as eating a tasty meal, receiving praise, or getting an unexpected check in the mail all produce a similar effect on our mood: we feel good. Similarly, many different events can make us feel bad. For example, hot, polluted air, a worm in an apple, or an "F" on an exam may all put us into a similar bad mood. It is also plausible that, when we experience more or less stimulation than we desire, we feel unpleasant.
3. A particular mood may have a variety of behavioral effects. For example, when we are in a good mood, we are more likely to be generous, cooperative, helpful, and loving than when we are in a bad mood. When we are in a bad mood, we are more likely to be aggressive, angry, resentful, and competitive.
4. In general, good moods make us more active than bad moods. In a good mood, we are likely to be more talkative, more interested in going places, more likely to do things. People who are in bad moods may feel inactive.
5. Mood is not the only determinant of behavior, of course. We usually try to respond appropriately to the situation. For instance, if a friend asks to borrow money, we are likely to be more generous if we are in a good mood than if we are in a bad mood, but we may loan money regardless of our mood. If the friend doesn't ask for money, of course, we are not likely to offer it, regardless of our mood.
6. A particular mood may also have some general cognitive effects. Good moods seem to make thinking, learning, and remembering easier, and bad moods seem to make these tasks more difficult.

We can relate these general principles to the idea of optimal level of arousal. If understimulation and overstimulation are both unpleasant and if both can put us in a bad mood, then some of their effects will be similar to other effects of being in a bad mood. For instance, we might expect that people who are under- or overstimulated would be irritable, easily angered, competitive, and so on. We might expect that their performance on tasks requiring thinking, learning, and remembering would suffer. Does the theory work? You will find out in the pages that follow.

SENSORY RESTRICTION

We have all had our escapist fantasies: a cottage in the country, a deserted beach in Tahiti, a quiet ski lodge in the Alps. Many of these fantasies occur when we are feeling overloaded and under stress. They are healthy. They also raise a good question: would we be happy under such conditions? Individually, we will not know until we try it. But some research has been done that suggests an answer.

Many of us have escapist fantasies when we are under stress. But would we really want to live in those fantasy worlds?

Research in sensory restriction began in the late 1950s, when scientists were worried about whether astronauts would suffer from their confinement in a tiny space capsule.

Types of Sensory Restriction.   Three general methods have been developed for studying what happens when we don't get enough stimulation. In **sensory-deprivation** experiments, stimulation may be greatly reduced by total immersion in warm water. Another method is to place the subject in a soundproof room, lying on a soft bed, with arms and legs immobilized in a comfortable, loose-fitting straightjacket, wearing a mask to eliminate sight.

In studies of **social isolation**, the subject is removed from other people. Such studies help determine what effects a particular type of stimulation—the companionship of others—has on our thoughts, feelings, and behaviors. Social isolation doesn't require a laboratory for study. We can study people who are in solitary confinement, those who have sailed a small boat around the world, or those who have been lost in storms.

In studies of **small-group confinement**, a group can be isolated from society for periods of time. Many groups naturally undergo such isolation, including polar and mountain-climbing expeditions, tracking-station crews in outlying areas, and crews on submarines and spacecraft.

Obviously, studies of small-group confinement and social isolation are important, so that we can understand what happens when this isolation or confinement occurs and develop methods of combating the negative effects. Because sensory restriction (partial deprivation) often accompanies social isolation or confinement, the effects of these two sources of stimulation are usually confounded (see p. 48). For instance, the prisoner in solitary confinement experiences social isolation as well as a very barren physical environment. Thus, studies of sensory deprivation are important to help determine the relative importance of sensory and social stimulation.

Sensory deprivation. If you were placed in a tank of warm water and floated on your back in a dark room, how long do you suppose you could stay there before begging the experimenter to stop the test? Your **endurance** in this situation could be used as a measure of how distressing the experience is. Studies using different methods of producing sensory deprivation have found that people can endure deprivation with some methods better than with others.

Immersion in water tanks has been found to be particularly difficult for subjects. In one experiment fewer than 40% of the subjects were able to continue for three hours (Francis, 1964). Floating face down and breathing with a mask appears even more stressful. In one study 71% of the subjects lying on their back were able to stay submerged for six hours, but only 20% of those floating face down were able to stay this long (Shurley, 1966). Even the slightest amount of visual stimulation (in the face-up condition) seems to make a considerable difference. Our face has many nerve endings in it, and it appears to be an important mechanism for maintaining an optimal level of arousal.

Most people who try floating in warm water in a darkened room quickly discover it to be very stressful and show little endurance. They often report anxiety, fantasies, visual sensations, and even hallucinations in some cases (Zuckerman, 1969). Subjects placed in soundproof cubicles with their eyes, ears, and limbs covered have reported fear, anxiety, and distress (Leiderman, 1962; Zuckerman, Albright, Marks, & Miller, 1962). They also experienced visual and auditory disturbances (Biase & Zuckerman, 1967). Sensory deprivation also induces intellectual impairment, including difficulties in concentration, clear thinking, and learning and memory (Suedfeld, 1969).

Social isolation. Social isolation is a second form of sensory restriction. Just as with sensory deprivation, the effects of social isolation increase with the degree of isolation. For instance, patients in iron lungs often feel lonely, but many endure this situation for months. In one study of healthy subjects in an iron lung, an observer was present and could respond to subjects. Seventy-one percent of subjects were willing to continue the experiment 8 hours, and 35% endured 24 hours (Wexler, Mendelsohn, Leiderman, & Solomon, 1958). In contrast were the endurance records of subjects in an experiment with no observer present. Here, only 40% persisted for 8 hours, and only 10% persisted for 24 hours (Mendelsohn, J., Kubzansky, P. E., Leiderman, P. H., Wexler, D., Dutoit, D., & Solomon, P., 1960). We might compare these effects with the endurance of unacquainted male subjects who were isolated in pairs and permitted to talk to each other. Here, 90% remained in the experiment for ten hours (David, J. M., McCourt, Courtney, & Solomon, 1961). Together, these three studies suggest that the effects of social isolation are quite strong. The less socially isolated we are, the longer we can endure an otherwise unpleasant situation.

Such a conclusion may be too hasty, however. Social contact does not always increase endurance. One study (Davis et al., 1961) placed married couples side by side in iron lungs and found that only 10% of these couples endured ten hours, the shortest rate of endurance of the studies described here. It appears that the married couples discussed their discomforts and supported each other in the decision to end the experiment, whereas the unacquainted males felt competitive, tried to outlast each other, and did not discuss their problems. We may conclude that the nature of our contact with others affects our *willingness* to endure sensory restriction.

The nature of our contact also affects our *ability* to endure sensory restriction. The married couples mentioned above who persisted in the experiment had fewer hallucinations, mental lapses, and other symptoms than the male strangers. In fact, the pairs of unacquainted males had reactions comparable to males in complete isolation. Another study (Altman & Haythorn, 1967) provided a direct test of this compatibility hypothesis. It found that males paired for compatibility experienced lower stress from sensory restriction than males paired for incompatibility. The U. S. space program has considered such findings in planning trips. Astronauts usually do not go alone; teams are selected for maximum compatibility, in part to prevent the negative effects of sensory restriction.

Small-group confinement.   In the studies of isolation discussed above, subjects were confined to iron lungs, or their movement was otherwise restricted. What happens if more movement is permitted? What would life be like in a fallout shelter, submarine, or tree house? Studies of confinement in a small room find that subjects can endure much longer than they can under conditions of sensory deprivation (such as floating in a tank of water) or sensory restriction (such as lying in an iron lung). Some studies have found that pairs of subjects were able to endure ten days in a small room with fixed activity schedules (Altman & Haythorn, 1965, 1967a, 1967b; Haythorn & Altman, 1967a, 1967b; Haythorn, Altman, & Meyers, 1966).

But as anyone knows who has been hospitalized or sick at home for this length of time, confinement can be very distressing. Pairs of subjects confined to a small room typically show considerable hostility and interpersonal friction (Cowan & Strickland, 1965; Smith, S., 1969). Naturally enough, they are bored (Cramer & Flinn, 1963; David, 1963). And they suffer from depression and sleeplessness

(Alluisi, Chiles, Hall, & Hawkes, 1963; Farrel & Smith, 1964; Hammes, 1964). Such symptoms have also been noted in natural confinement situations such as hospitals, submarine voyages, and polar expeditions; again, compatibility counts. Pairs of subjects matched for compatibility typically endure longer than pairs matched for incompatibility. It seems that compatibility reduces the negative effects of confinement.

Summary. Studies of sensory deprivation, social isolation, and small-group confinement all reduce environmental stimulation to some degree. Small-group confinement restricts our sensory input somewhat by reducing the variation offered in the physical environment and the variety of things we can do. Its effects, if it is prolonged, include boredom, depression, loneliness, irritability, hostility, sleep disturbances, fatigue, and, sometimes, headaches and nausea. Social isolation is more difficult to endure because social stimulation is reduced or eliminated. If continued as long as small-group confinement, social isolation would probably produce the same effects, but they would probably be more intense. Most people find sensory deprivation extremely difficult to endure, because here even physical sensations are reduced or eliminated. In a brief period of time, sensory deprivation impairs learning, memory, and performance. It leads to fantasies and hallucinations, anxiety, and fear.

Explaining the Effects of Sensory Restriction. The idea of optimal level of arousal may explain some of the effects of sensory restriction. It seems likely that any particular task—such as watching television, reading a book, programming a computer, or driving a car—requires a particular level of arousal in our brains. Too much or too little arousal may interfere with performance. For instance, you can be very relaxed while watching television but need to be thinking carefully while driving a car. Driving may require more arousal than viewing.

Where does that arousal come from? Some may come from the activity itself. When we are chased by an angry dog or ride a roller coaster, a considerable amount of arousal may come from the task. But many tasks do not produce all the arousal they require. For instance, classroom learning demands a lot of attention and critical thinking. That requires arousal. But some classes are boring. What do you do in those classes to help keep alert? Some of the arousal our brain requires must come from the stimulation provided by our body movements, eye movements, and fantasies. Moving around in your desk, looking around the room, and thinking about what you are going to have for lunch may all help raise your arousal level so that you will be more effective in learning.

In sensory-restriction studies, there may not be enough stimulation to maintain our arousal at an optimum level. Because complex tasks require more arousal than simple ones, performance on them may deteriorate sooner. And that is exactly what studies find (for example, Goldberger & Holt, 1958).

Further, we might expect that subjects in sensory-deprivation studies would have tremendous fantasies, simply to maintain their arousal. And fantasies and hallucinations do occur. If their brains are fighting to stay awake, we would not expect subjects to be in very pleasant moods. Just as one part of the brain sends another part the signal "I'm cold," which leads us to do something to warm it, one part of the brain may send another part the signal "I'm bored," which leads us to stimulate it. If we can't, because we are stuck in a sensory-deprivation experiment, we may feel frustrated in reducing this boredom, becoming irritable and sometimes hostile.

The diffusion-of-affect theory can also account for some of the findings from sensory-restriction studies. Being understimulated is unpleasant, and the bad mood that results can lead to depression, irritability, and hostility. This bad mood may also interfere with tasks requiring thinking, learning, and remembering. Many studies do find that such intellectual functions deteriorate.

Boredom, which results from understimulation, can lead to depression, irritability, and hostility.

We might expect that, the longer subjects experience sensory restriction, the more negative their mood would become. According to the diffusion-of-affect theory, this should result in decreased activity levels over time. Zuckerman (1964) reported that the amount a subject says decreases over time in isolation studies, a finding consistent with diffusion of affect.

We do not know which is the best explanation of sensory-restriction effects. The optimal-arousal theory and the diffusion-of-affect theory both explain some of the findings, but neither explains all of them. Perhaps several mechanisms are involved in sensory-restriction effects. If so, the best explanation will be one that draws from several theoretical frameworks.

SENSORY OVERLOAD

So far we have discussed only sensory restriction—what happens when we do not have enough stimulation. The optimal-arousal curve of Figure 5-2 suggests that we can also get too much. Too much stimulation can be just as unpleasant and stressful as too little and can affect our performance as well. We will discuss two common sources of overstimulation: noise and crowding.

Noise.   The dictionary tells us that **noise** means loud, unpleasant sounds. Our reactions to sounds seem to depend on their meaning, their intensity, and their expectedness.

In part, we react to loud sounds through their meaning to us. A teenage fan of the Bubblegum Five may love to hear their records played very loudly, but that teenager's parents may not.

Regardless of the meaning of a sound, when it is loud enough, it becomes unpleasant. A 50-watt amplifier turned to maximum volume would be distressing to everyone in a small car, regardless of what music was being played. In fact, prolonged exposure to loud sounds can lead to hearing loss. Rock musicians, jackhammer operators, and factory workers are often victims.

Unexpected noises can be upsetting, no matter what they are and how loud they are. If you are studying hard or dozing at the pool and a friend comes up quietly and says "Hello," you may be startled and upset. Research has shown that college women exposed to unpredictable loud or soft noise had much more difficulty concentrating on tasks or performing them accurately than women exposed to predictable noise of the same volume (Glass, Cohen, & Singer, 1973).

Noise probably raises our arousal level, particularly when it has an unpleasant meaning (for example, a baby crying), is loud, or is unexpected. Such heightened arousal may interfere with performance. Noises may also put us into a bad mood, and the mood may interfere with performance in other ways. It may also lead to more aggressiveness and less helpfulness. Such predictions have been tested in the research described below.

In a series of important studies on the effects of unpredictable noises on task performance (Glass & Singer, 1972, 1973) we may find some evidence for the optimal-arousal theory. These experiments found that subjects' physiological responses increased sharply when noises occurred, especially when they were unpredictable. Such changes suggest that the noise initially raised the subjects' arousal level. After continued exposure to these bursts of noise, the subjects no longer showed sudden physiological changes with each noise burst. This reduced responsiveness to stimulation is called habituation. In terms of the adaptation-level theory, the subjects seemed to become indifferent, but the bursts of noise may have maintained their arousal at fairly high levels. The researchers found that performance on complex tasks such as verbal reasoning suffered. But performance on simple tasks that did not require as much thought did not deteriorate.

To further test the hypothesis that unpredictable noise leads to difficulty in concentrating on tasks or performing them accurately, these researchers conducted a field study comparing reading-achievement scores of children who lived on various floors of tall apartment buildings (Glass et al., 1973). These buildings stood near a busy expressway, and from the lower floors the sounds of the traffic were moderately loud. The researchers found that reading achievement improved from lower to higher floors. Children on the 5th to 11th floors, for instance, scored in the 51st percentile, whereas those on the 26th to 32nd floors were in the 85th percentile. This difference was apparently not due to differences in the children when they moved there, because the relation between reading achievement and apartment height held only for children who had lived there four years or more. It apparently takes some time before noise has noticeable effects on reading ability.

But was noise really responsible for the effects observed in this field study? Perhaps. Or perhaps there was more pollution from passing cars on lower floors, and pollution affects reading performance. Perhaps it was easier for the children on lower floors to go outside and play, and they did not do as much homework. Such plausible rival hypotheses are not ruled out by this field study. Perhaps further studies controlling for such factors might provide more assurance that traffic noise interferes with a child's learning.

Just *how* noise interferes with learning also needs to be studied. In the case of the apartment children, the distracting effects of noise may have made homework more difficult. The effects of noise on auditory discrimination may have thwarted learning in the classroom. The noise may have raised arousal to the point that learning at home was impaired. Or it may have produced negative moods in the children, interfering with their desire and ability to do their homework. Again, more research on the effects of urban noise would be useful.

You will recall that the diffusion-of-affect theory suggests that, when we are in an unpleasant mood, we are less likely to do positive things such as being helpful and more likely to do negative things such as being aggressive. If noise makes us feel unpleasant, then we could expect it to have the same effects as negative moods. Researchers in one study (Sherrod & Downs, 1974) asked subjects to perform tasks in either a noisy or quiet laboratory, then asked these subjects if they would be willing to provide additional help to the experimenters. As you might expect from the diffusion-of-affect theory, those in the noisy condition were less helpful than those in the quiet condition. Another study reports similar findings in both a laboratory experiment and a field experiment on city streets (Matthews & Canon, 1975). A study that looked at the effects of noise on aggression found what would be predicted from the diffusion-of-affect theory: a noisy experimental condition produced more aggressiveness than a quiet condition (Geen & O'Neal, 1969). Other research (Glass & Singer, 1972) found that, when people were exposed to unexpected noise, they seemed to become frustrated more easily. As you will see in Chapter 9, frustration sometimes leads to aggression. You might want to make some predictions about other effects of noise, particularly unpleasant, loud, or unexpected noises.

Crowding.   How physically close others are to us is a physical aspect of our social environment. The term **density** refers to the number of people occupying a given space. **Crowding** refers to the unpleasant feeling that develops when we feel density is too high. At a cocktail party or football game density may be high, but we may not feel crowded. In fact, high density may make a party or game more enjoyable. When we are stuck in traffic after the game, however, we experience crowding. We are "too close for comfort." Can you think of a circumstance when you feel crowded even though density is low?

Before we review some of the findings from studies of crowding, it may be helpful to see how the theoretical framework of this chapter can be applied. Our approach combines optimal-arousal theory, the adaptation-level theory, Schachter's cognitive theory of emotion (see Chapter 4), the diffusion-of-affect theory, and one new assumption. The new assumption is that arousal level increases with increases in density. With higher densities, our breathing may become more rapid, our heart may beat faster, and our digestion may slow.

Crowding vs. Density

From the adaptation-level theory we might expect that people will be able to adapt to a particular density, become indifferent to it, and find changes in that density somewhat pleasant. When a few people arrive at or leave a party, the result may be interesting and pleasant. But if everyone gets up and leaves at once or if 40 more people come in at once, the change may be upsetting.

From the optimal-arousal theory we might expect that performance on some complex cognitive tasks would deteriorate under high density.

Schachter's cognitive theory of emotion suggests that, the higher our arousal, the more intense our emotion. So if we are feeling pleasant when density increases, arousal will increase, and we will feel even more pleasant. If we are feeling unpleasant when density increases, the increased arousal will lead to more intensely unpleasant feelings.

The diffusion-of-affect theory suggests that our mood will have many effects on our behaviors. For instance, if an unpleasant mood is intensified, aggressiveness and competitiveness should increase; if a pleasant mood is intensified, cooperativeness and generosity should increase.

This framework makes many predictions. How good is it? Are these predictions confirmed in research? The available evidence is reviewed below.

Density and arousal.   Our first assumption is that arousal increases with increases in density. One researcher has found that high density may lead to an enlargement of the adrenal glands in animals (Christian, 1950, 1955, 1959, 1963; Christian, Flyger, & Davis, 1960; Christian, Lloyd, & Davis, 1965). These glands produce adrenalin, a hormone that increases our arousal level.[1] This evidence is too indirect to get very excited about, however. It would be nice to have some research that directly examines the effects of density on arousal.

The prediction that density increases our arousal squares with common sense. Part of the feeling of being crowded is a flight, or escape, response: when we feel crowded, we want to put more distance between ourselves and others. Increased arousal prepares the body for an escape reaction.

Adapting to density.   Although long-term high-density conditions may increase the size of adrenal glands (in other animals, at least), it may also produce a different and somewhat opposite effect on our interpretation of the situation. We may learn to adapt to crowded conditions. Visitors to New York City may find their first subway ride terrifying. Native New Yorkers may not be crazy about the subway, but those who ride it endure it quite calmly. Like people, rats and mice are able to adapt to density. When they have been reared under high-density conditions, these animals often appear to be less emotional in stressful circumstances than those who have been reared alone (Ader, Kreutner, & Jacobs, 1963; Morrison & Thatcher, 1969; Thiessen, 1964; Thiessen, Zolman, & Rodgers, 1962). We may tentatively conclude that experience in crowding is important. Like the

---

[1]This might lead us to suppose that long-term crowding produces chronically high arousal levels, which might lead to stomach ulcers or other damaging physiological effects. In fact, Christian has suggested that populations may be self-regulating by this means: crowding produces enlarged adrenals, which produce higher arousal, which in turn interferes with sexual activity and lowers the fertility rate, as well as weakening the body and raising the mortality rate. These effects would reduce crowding and, in turn, reduce the size of the adrenal glands.

city and country mouse, we may come to prefer the stresses we are accustomed to. We may find, as adaptation-level theory would predict, that large changes from our accustomed level of stimulation are unpleasant.

Density and task performance.   The optimal-arousal theory suggests that, for anything we do, there may be a best level of arousal. On very simple, repetitive tasks, the task itself may not contribute much to our arousal level, and we may seek other stimulation. For such tasks, the presence of many others may actually improve performance, because it raises arousal to the level needed to perform well. However, a complex task may be arousing in itself, and any additional arousal provided by high density might produce overload, interfering with performance. That is, if density raises our arousal, then it may improve our performance, leave it unchanged, or impair it, depending on how well learned the task is. Such mixed effects have been observed (Freedman, Klevansky, & Ehrlich, 1971; Paulus, Aunis, Seta, Schkade, & Matthews, 1976; Rawls, Trego, McGaffey, & Rawls, 1972). More research is needed to determine whether these effects depend on the interaction of arousal and task complexity.

Density and mood.   Our theoretical framework proposes that an increase in density leads to an increase in arousal, which in turn intensifies our moods. In a direct test of this hypothesis, Jonathan Freedman (1975) gave some groups of subjects a difficult task and told them they had not done as well as others: the "failure condition." Other subjects were given easier tasks and told they had done better than others: the "success condition." Freedman found that crowding intensified the success or failure experience, making the success more positive and the failure more negative. Crowding affected the subjects' willingness to participate in the experiment again and their judgments of the boringness, liveliness, and overall quality of the experience. Freedman's findings neatly fit our theoretical framework.

We might also wonder whether density has other, more direct effects on mood. The fact that the terms *crowding* and *density* are often used interchangeably suggests that we often find high density unpleasant. A number of laboratory experiments have looked at this possibility. Some have found that subjects feel discomfort or stress under high density (Griffit & Veitch, 1971; Stokols, Rall, Pinner, & Schopler, 1973). But others have found few emotional effects of high density (Freedman, Levy, Buchanan, & Price, 1972; Sundstrom, 1973). As Irving Altman (1975) has suggested, because these experiments provided only brief encounters between strangers, their effects might be smaller and different from those of the long-term crowding of some urban living. Most of the correlational studies done in natural settings have found that people living in densely populated areas report somewhat more anxiety, stress, and strain than those in areas of lower density (for example, Marsella, Escudero, & Gordon, 1970; Schorr, 1963; Zlutnick & Altman, 1972).

One influence on our reactions to high density seems to be control. If we have chosen to be in a high-density situation, then we may find it pleasant. If we are forced to be in a high-density situation, we may find it unpleasant. People who love where they live have often chosen to live there. Those who hate where they live may have been brought there by some circumstance such as a job transfer.

In general, high density takes away our control over the situation. This may lead to that unpleasant feeling of reactance (see p. 295). With traffic moving freely, you are able to change lanes and drive at a variety of speeds. In a traffic jam, you are trapped in the conveyor belt of cars. In an empty subway car, you can freely choose a seat and look around the car. When it is crowded with commuters, you may have to stand and even have your vision restricted in order not to meet the glances of others. When density means loss of control, it may be unpleasant.

Density sometimes results in other unpleasant side effects. For instance, a crowded room may become too warm, smoky, or noisy. In a crowded place you may have difficulty moving about or finding a seat. So density may be somewhat unpleasant because of other factors associated with it.

Men and women *may* differ somewhat in their reactions to density. Women seem to have more social skills and may find density pleasant, whereas men may feel more competitive or aggressive (Schettino & Borden, 1976; Stokols et al., 1973). Men have been found to be more threatened by being jostled by a crowd and to find density unpleasant (Freedman et al., 1972; Ross, Layton, Erickson, & Schopler, 1973). If women tend to enjoy crowding more than men, the diffusion-of-affect theory would predict that women's judgments of others should be more positive than men's under crowded conditions. One study found this effect in a jury simulation: women became more lenient with crowding, whereas men became somewhat less lenient (Freedman et al., 1972).

Density and helpfulness.

Density and helpfulness.   If high density typically produces unpleasant feelings, then the diffusion-of-affect theory would predict that people who feel crowded should be less helpful. In a dormitory situation it has been found that high density is often unpleasant (Baron, Mandel, Adams, & Griffen [cited in Baron, R. A., & Byrne, 1977]; Baum & Valins, 1973; Valins & Baum, 1973). One study found that students in crowded dorms were less likely to return a lost letter that they had found than were students in uncrowded dorms (Brickman et al. [cited in Baron, R. A., & Byrne, 1977, p. 634]). Rural/urban differences in rate of helping behavior will be discussed in Chapter 9. Such differences, when they occur, are not necessarily due to crowding, although they may be.

Density and aggressiveness.   The diffusion-of-affect theory predicts that, when high density is pleasant, aggressiveness should be lower than when high density is unpleasant. Many people seem to believe that high density usually leads to crime. It is true that cities have higher crime rates than do small towns, and it is also true that cities usually have higher densities than small towns. So it may come as no surprise to learn that many studies have found positive correlations (see Chapter 2) between density and crime rate (Lander, 1954; Lettier, 1938; Marsella et al., 1970; Schmid, 1969, 1970; Schmitt, 1957; Watts, 1931; White, 1931). This correlation does not necessarily mean that high density causes crime. It is likely that much of the relation is a result of the operation of other factors associated with density and with crime. For instance, wealthy people do not live in high-density areas and may have more police per capita, better burglar alarms, and so on. So it may be that income rather than (or in addition to) density has a causal effect on crime rate.

Not every study has found a relation between density and crime rate (Freedman, Heshka, & Levy, 1973, 1975; Pressman & Carol, 1971). One important study

There seems to exist a correlation between density and crime rate!

found that crime was more closely related to density measured as people per room than as measured by residences per acre (Galle, Gove, & McPherson, 1972). *How* density is measured influences what it is related to. Further, whether factors such as ethnic background, education, occupational level, and income are statistically controlled (held constant, so they do not bias the results) seems important. Studies that control for such factors do not always find a correlation between density and crime (Freedman et al., 1973, 1975; Pressman & Carol, 1971).

Crime is one form of aggressiveness. Are other forms of aggressiveness influenced by crowding? Some laboratory and field studies have been done, again with mixed results. Sometimes crowding leads to more aggressiveness (Freedman et al., 1972; Hutt & Vaizey, 1966; McGrew, 1970; Rohe & Patterson, 1974). Sometimes it leads to less aggressiveness (Freedman et al., 1972; Loo, 1972). And sometimes there is no effect (Price, 1971). It may be that crowding leads to increased aggressiveness only when the situation is already somewhat unpleasant. A pleasant, crowded situation might actually lower aggressiveness. But research is needed to test this hypothesis. All we can safely say now is that there is no simple, straightforward relation between crowding and aggression.

Density and judgments of others. When we are feeling good, our judgments of others tend to be more positive than when we are not, through diffusion of affect. If crowding raises our arousal and intensifies our mood, then it should also intensify our judgments of others. People we like moderately under uncrowded conditions should be liked more under crowding, whereas people we initially dislike should be liked even less. This is exactly what happened in several studies.

In a first study, Jonathan Freedman (1975) asked subjects to deliver a prepared speech before an audience of five to nine persons. In one condition, audiences were instructed to make only negative comments on the speech; in the other condition, only positive comments were to be made. Some of these groups met in a large, uncrowded room, and others met in a small, crowded room. In the pleasant-feedback condition, crowding led to greater liking for the others, greater willingness to participate again, and greater liking for the other speeches. In the unpleasant-feedback condition, crowding had just the opposite effect. These results are shown in Figure 5-5. Freedman (1975) reported a similar second study with even stronger effects.

Figure 5-5.
Density and
intensity. Crowding
makes reactions
more positive when
subjects receive
positive feedback
and more negative
with negative
feedback. (Adapted
from *Crowding
and Behavior*, by
J. L. Freedman.
Copyright 1975
by W. H. Freeman
and Company,
Publishers.)

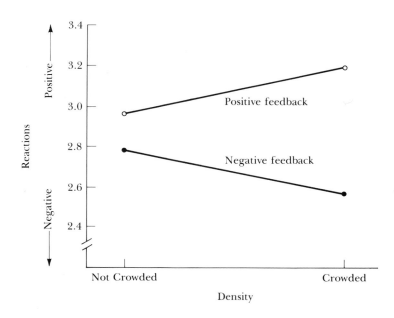

NOXIOUS ENVIRONMENTS

So far, this chapter has focused on the quantity of stimulation we experience and its effects on us. We find that too little or too much stimulation is unpleasant and affects our mood, our performance on tasks, and our behavior. Some stimulation from the environment doesn't differ only in amount, however. It also differs in *quality*. The air, for instance, may be fresh or polluted, cool or hot. In the next few pages we will look at some of the effects of two aspects of the environment: heat and air.

Heat. How does heat affect you? Many people find themselves listless and irritable on a very hot day. We don't need formal theories or research to tell us that heat makes us irritable. This is common sense, a personal theory held by nearly everyone. When the riots occurred in the summers of the late 1960s and early 1970s, some people blamed the heat. Others proposed that conditions in the social environment (such as poverty or unfulfilled rising expectations) were aggravated by the heat, leading to the riots. As students of social behavior, you'll probably be able to find shortcomings in such explanations. For instance, why are there no riots in some years? Why does a riot occur exactly when it does and not on some other, hotter day? Why didn't the hottest cities have the most riots? But such explanations do emphasize the prevalence of the heat variable in personal theories.

    The diffusion-of-affect theory would make two general predictions about the effects of heat on social behavior. First, very high temperatures are unpleasant, and unpleasant moods produce unpleasant results—aggression, anger, resentment, and competitiveness. But the theory also predicts that bad moods lead to less motor and cognitive activity than good moods. Such predictions might at first seem contradictory. Would the theory predict that people will be more aggressive in the summer or less aggressive (because they are less active)? It is not clear.

Fortunately, we do not use theories to answer questions, but to raise them. Researchers have shown considerable curiosity about the effects of heat on social behavior. We will review some of that research below.

Some research has been done on the effects of heat on mood. One study (Griffitt, 1970) found that high temperature (90.6° Fahrenheit) reduced positive feelings, decreased interpersonal attraction, and decreased elation, concentration, and vigor, as compared with normal (67.5° F) temperature. Other research (Griffitt & Veitch, 1971) found that heat had adverse effects on mood and interpersonal attraction. These studies support the hypothesis that heat produces negative moods.

Do heat and the bad mood it produces make us more aggressive? When it is hot, are we more likely to get "hot under the collar" and be "hot headed"? Common sense says yes, but laboratory research says maybe. The first study in

Do high temperatures cause us to be more aggressive?

this area (Baron, R. A., 1972) found that high temperatures (91–95° F) actually reduced aggression. The researcher had predicted that provoking subjects to anger, exposing them to heat, and then giving them an opportunity to behave aggressively would result in aggression. The fact that subjects behaved less aggressively in the hot condition than in the cool condition was explained by the researcher as due to the extreme discomfort produced in subjects by the heat and the desire of subjects to leave the experimental atmosphere as rapidly as possible.

A follow-up study (Baron, R. A., & Bell, 1975) yielded somewhat different results. These investigators not only provoked subjects before they entered the hot or cool room but also provided an aggressive model to facilitate an aggression response. These researchers found that, when subjects were provoked, exposed to the hot condition, and observed an aggressive model, their aggression was significantly *reduced*. When subjects were only exposed to heat without prior provocation or a model, their aggression *increased*.

Using the same basic procedure, these researchers later reported that high temperature increased aggression only when other sources of irritation (such as prior provocation) were absent (Baron, R. A., & Bell, 1976). When other sources of irritation were present, aggression was reduced in the hot condition.

An additional finding came out of this study and was followed up in a later investigation. When subjects were put in a bad mood before exposure to heat, they were *less* aggressive than when they were not put in a bad mood first. Such findings don't seem to fit our intuitions.

The studies mentioned above were all conducted in a laboratory. What about riots? Is there a relation between rioting and heat? Yes, reports one study (Baron, R. A., & Ransberger, 1978). Riots are more likely when the temperature is between 81 and 90° F than when it is hotter. Another study (Schwartz, 1968) found that more violent political activity seems to take place during periods of moderate temperature than in hotter periods.

Taken together, these studies show that heat affects mood as well as aggression, but the effects on aggression are complex. The findings suggest that the diffusion-of-affect theory is incomplete.

It seems plausible that what the theory lacks is an attribution component. When people are in a bad mood because it is 95° out, they know why they feel as they do and attribute their mood to the temperature. When it is uncomfortable—80° or so—they may misattribute their bad mood to the actions of another, because the effects of heat on their mood are not so noticeable. Similarly, in the study in which subjects were provoked and irritated before being subjected to heat and given an opportunity to be aggressive, they may have attributed their bad mood to the provocation. The diffusion-of-affect theory suggests the general direction of behavior resulting from mood, but our own attributions will guide the specific form of our behavior. Our behavior is affected by our environment and our interpretations. Further research is needed to examine this explanation of previous findings.

Air Quality.   Heat, it appears, can significantly affect mood and social behaviors such as aggression. Heat is often assumed to be the most important aspect of the weather that affects us. But it is often present during other unpleasant weather conditions, such as high humidity and pollution, and is accompanied by changes in the electrical charge of the air. Thus, heat is often confounded with other factors that may be responsible for some of its apparent effects. In order to fully understand how our physical environment affects us, we need to study each of these effects carefully. Unfortunately, many of these effects have not yet received much research attention.

Atmospheric ions and social behavior. Some years ago, two studies reported some remarkable effects of weather on social behavior. One found that the onset of hot, dry winds was accompanied by increased suicide, crime, and automobile accidents in Israel (Sulman, Pfeifer, & Hirschman, 1964). The other, conducted in Europe, found that hot, dry winds were accompanied by a loss of concentration and attention on the job and increased industrial accidents(Muecher & Ungehever, 1961). It has been suggested that the friction generated by the hot, dry, rapidly moving air creates positive air ions and that they are responsible for these behavioral effects.

What are these villains? An **atmospheric ion** is a tiny particle of air with a positive or negative charge. The smallest of such ions are biologically and psychologically active (Krueger, A. P., & Reed, 1976), which means that they can affect social behavior. Although the research findings are sometimes contradictory, they generally show that negative air ions improve attention and concentration and enhance the formation of positive moods, whereas positive air ions have negative effects (Charry & Hawkinshire, 1976; Halcomb & Kirk, 1965; Slote, 1962). This may be one reason why a shower (which produces negative ions) is such a refreshing experience and one reason why hot days (with their positive ions) drag us down.

This is not to say that positive ions always have negative effects, or vice versa. It now appears that there is an optimal ratio of small air ions, perhaps five positive to four negative. Change in this ratio may be unhealthy.

There is also some reason to believe that atmospheres containing numerous small positive and negative ions may be more beneficial than atmospheres where small ions are lacking. Some evidence suggests that perhaps between 500 and 1000 small ions per cubic centimeter of air may be an ideal level.

How do small ions produce their effects? No one really knows yet. But there is evidence for the following: (1) Air ions produce disturbances in the central nervous system. (2) Both negative and positive air ions change brain waves (Silverman, D., & Kornblueh, 1957). (3) Negative air ions induce hemispheric synchronization, a sign of increased relaxation (Assael, Pfeifer, & Sulman, 1974; Sulman, Assael, Alpern, & Pfeifer, 1974). Further, levels of serotonin (a powerful chemical involved in the firing of nerve cells in the brain) are lowered by positive or negative air ions. This finding may be important, because lowered levels of serotonin have been found to be associated with depression and suicides (Coppen, 1973; van Pragg & Korf, 1973). They have also been linked to sleep and dream disturbances (Dement, 1969; Jouvet, 1969; Zarcone, Hoddes, & Smythe, 1973). And they have been found to be related to chronic schizophrenia (Wyatt, Vaughan, Kaplan, Galanter, & Green, 1973).

Where do air ions come from? In addition to the rain (which produces negative ions) and dryness (which produces positive ions), there are many manmade sources. These include electrical activity (such as electric motors or high-tension wires), heat (from car engines, furnaces, and so on), and radiation (from microwave ovens, television sets, smoke detectors, and the like). Further, dust and pollution may reduce the number of small ions, because these particles in the air attract the small ions into these larger clusters.

Much technology affects air ions. Where people are crowded together, technology has its greatest impact on air ions. If air ions are important influences on behavior, then they deserve much more attention by researchers. Some part of the difference between behavior in the city and in the country may be due to differences in the atmospheric ions there.

Air pollution.   Air pollution that we can see, smell, or taste is unpleasant. The diffusion-of-affect theory would predict that such unpleasant moods might give rise to various "unpleasant behaviors." In fact, studies have found that judgments become more negative with pollution (Rotton, Barry, Frey, & Soler [cited in Baron, R. A., & Byrne, 1977]). And task performance is impaired with pollution (Lewis, J., Baddeley, Bonham, & Lovett, 1970). Increased levels of air pollution are accompanied by declines in recreation (Chapko & Solomon, 1976) and increases in psychiatric admission (Strabilevitz, Strabilevitz, & Miller, 1979). Of the various types of air pollution, carbon monoxide may be one of the worst, because it increases irritability, impairs thinking and memory, and can cause brain damage and even death.

When we add up the number of stressors in an urban environment, it becomes understandable that cities have multiple social problems. This is not to say that the experience of living in cities is negative. Most city dwellers seem to love their city. They appreciate the cultural opportunities and the adventures that are always available. For many city dwellers, the city provides an optimal level of stimulation.

SUMMARY

This chapter has examined the effects of the physical environment on social behavior. Three theories were used to account for a variety of findings: the adaptation-level theory, the optimal-level-of-arousal theory, and the diffusion-of-affect theory. Each of these perspectives helps account for a portion of the findings. Taken together, they provide some coherence and meaning.

Sensory restriction is one important effect of some physical environments. Studies of sensory deprivation, social isolation, and small-group confinement provide some evidence of what happens under different types and degrees of sensory restriction. The effects of such restriction range from boredom and depression to deterioration in task performance, hallucinations, anxiety, and fear.

Sensory overload is the other side of the coin. Physical environments often provide too much stimulation, and the effects can be as unpleasant as sensory restriction. Two common sources of overload are noise and crowding. Loud, unexpected, and meaningless noises disrupt our performance, may lead to learning problems, and put us in bad moods. High density may be pleasant or unpleasant, depending in part on whether we are able to control our exposure to it. When density is unpleasantly high, it is called crowding. Like noise, crowding raises our arousal level. Like noise, it can be adapted to up to a point. And like noise, it may put us in a bad mood, making us less helpful and more aggressive.

The quality of the stimulation we experience also affects us. Excess heat may make us irritable and, in some cases, more aggressive. Positive air ions and air pollution may have similar effects.

GLOSSARY TERMS

Define these terms in your own words, then look them up in the glossary in the back of the book.

Adaptation level
Adaptation-level theory
Arousal
Atmospheric ions
Butterfly curve
Crowding
Density
Diffusion of affect
Endurance
Habituate
Noise

Optimal level of arousal
Reciprocal influence
Sensation seeking
Sensory deprivation
Sensory overload
Sensory restriction
Small-group confinement
Social isolation
Stress
Stressor

FURTHER READING

Freedman, J. L. *Crowding and behavior.* New York: Freeman, 1975. A very well-written, easy-to-read, informative, somewhat opinionated book.

Schultz, D. P. *Sensory restriction: Effects on behavior.* New York: Academic Press, 1965. A well-written review of over 250 studies of sensory restriction.

chapter
6

Impressions

chapter

6

Prepared with the assistance of Pat Castell

INTRODUCTION

Forming impressions of others and explaining their behavior is an important part of everyday life. The impressions we form are never simple summaries of the information that reaches our senses. Throughout the entire process of impression formation, we actively modify, interpret, and transform our sensory intake. As a result, the impression that is formed is only a partial reflection of the actual characteristics of the person being described. It also reflects the characteristics of the person doing the describing.

We transform our sensory intake into meaningful units by the process of **perception**. When we meet another person, his or her presence bombards our senses with huge quantities of sensory information—a continually changing pattern of colors, shapes, and sounds. Perception is a construction process through which this information is organized. Through the process of perception we are able to recognize that the object in our view is a person rather than a tree, that it is female rather than male, that she is young rather than old, and so forth. Through the process of perception we are able to recognize that sounds are words and sentences rather than noise, that they are poetry rather than prose, that they are understandable rather than incomprehensible, and so forth. So it is through perception that we impose meaning on the numerous events we experience.

Because we experience particular objects, people, and sounds in a certain way, we develop our own personal theories that reflect that experience. If your interactions with New Yorkers have been pleasurable, your personal theory about them will reflect that experience. Often, your personal theories about the social world may be too broad or too restrictive. For instance, it is just as erroneous to say that *all* New Yorkers are nice as it is to say that *no* New Yorkers are nice.

Our concern in this chapter is perception of people. Although we believe that the cognitive processes involved in the perception of physical objects and social objects are similar, we also believe that social perception is more complicated. This complication is due in part to the dynamic nature of social objects. We will first look at a general model of perception and then discuss social perception.

Sometimes our perceptions lead us to form a generalized expectancy about a group of individuals. This expectancy is referred to as a stereotype. After we discuss the development and accuracy of stereotypes, we will look at impression formation. Three factors affect impression formation—the person perceived, or stimulus person; the perceiver; and the social context. Finally, we will look at how we attempt to create the impression that others have of us. We manage others' impressions of us by what we say and do. The various aspects of generating an impression—self-disclosure, self-presentation, self-monitoring—are covered in the last part of this chapter.

PERCEPTION

Perception is the process by which we transform sensory information into organized impressions. The process of perception involves a number of stages. Perception, therefore, is a process rather than an event.

A General Model.   First, some object, or stimulus, in the world may give off sound energy or reflect light energy. When this energy strikes our sense organs, it is transformed into a complex pattern. This pattern is stored very briefly as a meaningless likeness of the stimulus in what might be called **image storage**. Here, the flood of information that bombards the senses begins to be simplified and organized. Within fractions of a second, some analysis of the visual, auditory, and other images begins. The analysis and organization of the image depend on the concepts, categories, and expectancies of the perceiver. The image is evaluated as valuable or worthless, pleasant or unpleasant, worthy of attention or not. Analysis of the stimulus' pleasantness and intensity may occur before analysis of other parts of its meaning.

Images worth further attention are transferred in some new form into **short-term storage**. Because we experience so much and can store so little, relatively little is passed on to short-term storage. The images in short-term memory are available for immediate use. But they reside in short-term memory for only a few seconds. Images are then either forgotten or transferred to **long-term storage**.

Because much of the information we experience is needed only briefly, it is beneficial to "forget" most of what we have experienced. Although we sometimes get angry at not being able to remember the phone number we have just looked up, we would be in a mess if we remembered every one we had ever looked up. If something is important to us and we need to remember it, it is **encoded** (translated) into a form our brain can **store**. **Rehearsal** (thinking about an experience) helps us transfer what we have experienced into long-term storage, where we can find it later when we need it. In order to withdraw information from long-term memory, a search procedure is required. Once the information is located, it is **decoded** into words. A center for cognitive control and decision making, closely linked to long-term storage, determines what will be selected for further processing. This description of the process of perception is theoretical. The stages, procedures, and processes involved in perception cannot be examined directly. But this theoretical description seems to be compatible with what we know about how people learn and process information.

Social Perception.   Our model of perception has obvious implications for how we perceive people. For instance, we hypothesized that image storage can hold only a small proportion of what we experience and that short-term storage can hold only a small proportion of that. In **social perception**, then, we are likely to become aware only of the central, important features of another person. Our perception of others is likely to omit the small details that only Sherlock Holmes could catch. For example, although someone's accent is noticed immediately, whether he or she is right- or left-handed may be overlooked for weeks. Not only do we focus on central traits, or features, of the person, but even this limited focus is easily disturbed. It is difficult to attend to something if there is a great deal of extraneous stimulation. For instance, it is hard to hear a teacher when a radio is playing (or hard to hear the radio when the teacher is talking). When too many sensations occur at the same time, we experience sensory overload. In contrast, too few sensations produce sensory restriction. Neither overload nor restriction is very pleasant, and we usually try to obtain some intermediate amount of stimulation (see Chapter 5).

Once sensations are encoded and move from short-term memory to long-term memory, they are stored with similar elements, events, or experiences. During this transfer, the uniqueness of the sensation is lost, and it becomes more similar to other images already in long-term storage. This process is referred to as **categorization.**

The categorization process can influence our social experiences in a variety of ways. For example, we sometimes attach a particular meaning to a behavior no matter who performs it. In reality, of course, the reason for performing the behavior varies. Categorization can also influence us to "see" a behavior as characteristic of a group. In other instances, we may "set up" a situation so that some behavior is forthcoming.

Perception is an active process. The physical object that we sense, attend to, and perceive is not an exact replica of the physical object in space. We add to or subtract from the stimulus' traits, qualities, or characteristics. Thus, the impression of a physical object only resembles the objective features of that object.

STEREOTYPES

Introduction.   One of the ways that we categorize information is on the basis of similarity. When we encounter something new, we analyze the traits and characteristics. We assess the qualities of our impression of a physical object and try to find a **cognitive** category that seems to match it. So an animal we see may appear to be similar to a cat but more similar to a dog. We decide that the animal fits in our "dog" category and label it a dog.

What if no such category exists? Is a moped a bicycle or a motorcycle? It may deserve its own category, and if we encounter mopeds often enough we may create a new cognitive category to store them.

Associated with each category are personal theories about variables related to that category. We see a creature and decide it is a hairy (categorization). We believe that hairies have bad breath (personal theory). So we assume that this particular individual also has bad breath. We step back and don't find out. This

Perception is an active process. The physical object that is perceived is not an exact replica of the physical object in space.

dual process of categorization and inference is called **stereotyping**. Stereotypes are overgeneralized beliefs or expectations about how certain sorts of people think, feel, and behave. Stereotypes lead us to expect something we have just experienced to be similar to other things we have previously experienced or have learned about indirectly. If someone tells you that she is a preacher, prostitute, or pool player, you may jump to the conclusion that she has all the traits you attribute to those groups. This can lead to a difficulty for both of you.

We usually do not test to see if the traits we use to describe a group are really correct for each member we meet. The guesses that we make about specific people are often wrong for the particular case, even though they may have a kernel of truth for the stereotyped group as a whole. Most hairies may have bad breath, but does the hairy you have just met? This assumption can damage your relationship. Because of your stereotype, however, you probably will not even establish a relationship.

Meeting someone for the first time is made easier by categorization. Stereotypes relieve us of processing each individual thoroughly. These means of classifying others are very important in the way we perceive and behave toward others.

Do you hold stereotypes? Take the simple test in Interest Box 6-1 and see for yourself.

Interest Box 6-1. Stereotypes of Talkative People

Below is a list of traits. Place a sheet of paper over the whole right side of the page, leaving only the list uncovered. Next to those traits that you feel are typical of a talkative person, place a letter *T*. Next to those traits that you think are typical of a quiet person, place a *Q*. To see whether your ideas about talkative and quiet people match those of others, uncover the right side. If you were able to place some *T*s and *Q*s on the list, you have a stereotype of talkative and quiet people. If your *T*s and *Q*s match those of the right side of the page to some extent, then you share that stereotype with others who have described typical talkative and quiet persons.

| | Study 1 | | Study 2 | | | | Study 3 | | |
| | Stereotype | | Self-Description | | Stereotype | | Role Playing | | |
	T	Q	T	Q	T	Q	T	Q	X^2
active	55	0	77	67	90	0	100	0	53.1
adventurous	—	—	41	60	76	0	78	8	33.6
aggressive	70	2	35	20	94	2	100	3	63.2
ambitious	—	—	82	73	62	2	69	33	7.5
anxious	—	—	47	87	28	32	75	59	
appreciative	—	—	71	87	20	22	38	67	4.9
argumentative	—	—	47	20	98	0	91	3	52.3
articulate	42	10	—	—	—	—	—	—	
assertive	—	—	29	0	82	2	91	5	48.8
best ideas	3	20	—	—	—	—	—	—	
boastful	—	—	6	0	86	0	81	0	46.6
bored	5	23	—	—	—	—	—	—	
bossy	—	—	12	27	86	0	54	4	23.5
calm	—	—	47	73	0	84	9	69	23.5
cautious	—	—	47	80	0	70	19	87	30.7
cheerful	—	—	82	73	50	2	97	36	25.6
clever	—	—	53	80	36	8	88	36	17.3
confident	48	8	41	47	70	12	84	26	22.0
conservative	—	—	18	33	0	60	9	69	23.4
considerate	—	—	82	93	2	38	28	82	18.8
cooperative	—	—	77	80	14	34	41	77	8.2
determined	—	—	82	87	54	6	81	34	11.5
discreet	—	—	18	40	6	62	16	72	20.1
dominant	—	—	24	7	86	0	81	3	42.9
egotistical	—	—	12	13	64	4	69	3	32.2
emotional	40	12	94	53	40	18	—	—	
energetic	—	—	59	60	68	0	91	21	31.9
enthusiastic	—	—	65	60	74	0	84	15	30.9
excitable	—	—	76	40	76	0	78	21	21.2
extroverted	82	0	—	—	—	—	—	—	
fast talker	55	0	—	—	—	—	—	—	
fearful	13	32	24	27	8	44	8	44	11.1
forceful	—	—	24	13	74	0	54	7	20.8
friendly	45	2	82	80	70	6	91	54	9.7
gentle	—	—	65	73	2	60	31	82	16.7

Interest Box 6-1. (continued)

| | Study 1 | | Study 2 | | | | Study 3 | | |
| | Stereotype | | Self-Description | | Stereotype | | Role Playing | | |
	T	Q	T	Q	T	Q	T	Q	X^2
good leadership ability	43	0	—	—	—	—	—	—	
good speaking ability	55	3	—	—	—	—	—	—	
humorous	—	—	88	60	66	0	60	13	17.7
impulsive	—	—	53	40	74	0	78	5	36.7
inactive	0	27	—	—	—	—	—	—	
individualistic	—	—	53	67	36	12	75	44	5.9
inhibited	—	—	41	60	2	80	9	87	39.6
intelligent	8	23	88	80	18	14	57	52	
interested	35	18	—	—	—	—	—	—	
interesting	15	7	—	—	—	—	—	—	
interests wide	—	—	88	60	29	12	75	26	15.2
introverted	0	90	—	—	—	—	—	—	
kind	—	—	82	80	12	26	41	69	4.7
loud	—	—	41	7	92	0	62	2	33.0
loud voice	57	0	—	—	—	—	—	—	
meek	—	—	12	33	2	72	5	50	17.3
mild	—	—	12	47	2	70	9	85	36.9
moderate	—	—	47	33	8	40	16	67	16.6
modest	—	—	29	73	4	60	13	67	19.0
most ideas	48	2	—	—	—	—	—	—	
noisy	—	—	29	7	80	0	60	0	34.2
obedient	0	25	—	—	—	—	—	—	
opinionated	72	0	35	47	80	2	75	23	17.0
optimistic	23	2	—	—	—	—	—	—	
outgoing	—	—	88	40	92	0	91	3	52.3
outspoken	—	—	65	0	90	2	84	0	49.6
patient	—	—	53	53	2	66	22	77	19.2
peaceable	—	—	59	73	2	66	22	67	12.4
persistent	—	—	59	60	49	10	75	33	10.6
popular	50	2	—	—	—	—	—	—	
quarrelsome	—	—	12	0	66	0	41	2	17.0
quiet	—	—	0	100	0	80	0	100	67.0
reasonable	—	—	53	87	10	30	43	50	
reserved	—	—	18	60	0	90	6	90	45.8
respectful	0	45	—	—	—	—	—	—	
responsible	5	28	77	80	14	22	41	69	4.7
self-confident	—	—	41	40	70	4	81	18	25.8
self-controlled	—	—	41	73	14	60	30	57	4.9
sensitive	—	—	94	80	8	64	34	82	14.8
serious	—	—	77	73	4	60	41	69	4.7
show-off	—	—	41	7	76	0	40	0	25.8
shy	0	80	24	73	0	86	3	87	46.4
silent	—	—	6	60	0	94	0	82	44.5
sincere	—	—	82	60	10	40	38	77	9.7
slow talker	0	33	—	—	—	—	—	—	

Interest Box 6-1. (continued)

	Study 1		Study 2				Study 3		
	Sterotype		Self-Description		Stereotype		Role Playing		
	T	Q	T	Q	T	Q	T	Q	X²
sociable	—	—	88	80	88	2	97	21	38.4
soft voice	2	52	—	—	—	—	—	—	
spunky	—	—	29	7	68	0	35	2	13.6
submissive	—	—	35	33	2	76	11	46	10.2
sympathetic	—	—	94	60	8	34	24	48	3.9
talkative	—	—	100	0	96	0	100	0	67.0
thoughtful	—	—	53	73	8	38	25	69	12.1
timid	—	—	6	47	0	84	3	61	28.0
trusting	7	35	71	67	12	26	24	54	6.5
understanding	—	—	100	87	6	36	38	74	8.3
uninhibited	—	—	35	13	66	2	51	0	27.8
versatile	—	—	65	47	58	0	72	23	˙15.0
withdrawn	—	—	12	33	0	82	0	72	35.0
zany	—	—	59	20	67	0	49	0	25.8

These three studies (published here for the first time) explored the relationship between talkativeness, self-perception, and social perception. In Studies 1 and 2, a total of 112 students used adjective checklists to indicate their stereotypes of talkative and quiet people. The list in Study 1 had 39 adjectives; the one in Study 2 had 300. In Study 3, 83 students role-played talkative and quiet people using an adjective checklist. These stereotypes fairly closely agreed with each other and matched self-descriptions provided by talkative and quiet students in Study 2. Both stereotypes and self-descriptions agreed with previous published findings on talkative/quiet differences. These results suggest a large measure of truth in these stereotypes (see Chapter 7). They also suggest a few interesting variables on which self-perception and social perception considerably differ. And they provide a systematic source of hypotheses for further research.

Interest Box 6-1 demonstrates that stereotypes are often very complex sets of assumptions about how a category of people behaves and feels. Sorting people into categories (Black/White, male/female, talkative/quiet, old/young, believer/infidel) is one first step in simplifying our view of a very complex world, making it easier to deal with and understand. Our beliefs that relate specific traits to specific categories come from indirect sources such as parents, the news media, and friends. Our own direct experience with a representative of a certain type of person is another important source for our beliefs about others. We make conclusions about the personality characteristics for an entire category of individuals after contact with a few of them. These conclusions frequently develop after only limited contact. But they may be formulated after considerable contact with many members of the group, as in the case of our stereotypes of talkative and quiet people.

Stereotypes are not easily changed. The little information we have when we form a stereotype has a greater impact than subsequent information has in changing a stereotype. This has been called the **prior-entry effect** (Jones & Gerard, 1967). One reason stereotypes resist change is that they are confirmed every so often and receive partial reinforcement. For instance, every so often I meet a hairy with bad breath, confirming my stereotype of hairies as foul-mouthed little beasts. Another reason that stereotypes resist change is that we tend to selectively seek out information that confirms our stereotypes and ignore information that disconfirms them. Some **prejudiced** people would rather feel right than be right.

Another reason that stereotypes resist change is that they guide our behavior, which in turn shapes the behavior of others. Thus, a stereotype acts as a self-fulfilling prophecy. This fact was demonstrated several years ago in a laboratory experiment (Snyder, Tanke, & Berscheid, 1977). Investigators asked a male and a female to chat briefly over a telephone so that the experimenters could observe the "getting-acquainted process." The males were provided with a photo that they were led to believe was of their female partner. A standard picture was presented, so that the men thought they were interacting with either an attractive or unattractive partner. These pictures were not pictures of the actual women in the study, and, in fact, the women did not know that they were in "attractive" or "unattractive" categories.

The men who believed they were talking with an attractive woman acted differently from the other men. They were more sociable, warm, interesting, independent, bold, outgoing, humorous, and socially adept. Females paired with these males acted differently from the females paired with males who believed they were chatting with an unattractive partner. The "attractive" females displayed greater confidence, animation, enjoyment of the conversation, and liking for their partner than the "unattractive" females. Another important finding of this research was that the two groups of women were rated differently only on the personality characteristics that distinguished attractiveness from unattractiveness according to each male's personal theory of attractiveness. It seems that people will extract from another's behavior the characteristics that are related to their personal stereotype (Snyder et al., 1977).

In the study just described, the males acted in such a way that their own personal stereotype of a particular type of female—either attractive or unattractive—was confirmed. Such self-fulfilling prophecies are frequent occurrences in everyday life. Our personal theories of other people guide our behavior toward them. Our behavior affects their behavior. And we unwittingly confirm our personal theories. This effect can be dramatic and sometimes tragic. Rosenthal and Jacobson (1968) concluded that teacher's expectations of how well students would perform were translated into all sorts of behaviors that helped the pupils perform as expected.

Both of these studies demonstrate how stereotypes influence interactions with others. Even more profound is the fact that we are usually unaware that our stereotypes intrude on our interpersonal exchanges. Once a stereotype of a certain person or group is formed, misconceptions may be difficult to correct. Let us look at research concerned with the accuracy of stereotypes.

Accuracy of Stereotypes. Are our stereotypes correct? Sometimes yes (Schuman, 1966), sometimes no (LaPiere, 1936). Because stereotypes are overgeneralized expectancies, there is often evidence to support them. The notion that there is some degree of accuracy in stereotypes has been called the **kernel-of-truth hypothesis** (Zawadzki, 1948).

.. *grow David* ... *grow Betty* ... *grow Lee* ... *grow David* ...*g*

Do teachers' expectations affect students' performances?

Stereotype accuracy is no doubt affected somewhat by our familiarity with the group. If you are Polish and you know many Poles, your stereotypes of Poles are likely to be quite correct. If you are not Polish, have never met a Pole, and have only heard about Poles through Polish jokes, your impression is probably quite inaccurate. There may be a kernel of truth in every stereotype you hold. For some of the stereotypes you hold, this kernel is larger—the stereotype is more accurate—than for others.

We often convince ourselves that our stereotype is an accurate description of a group. This occurs in part because of a phenomenon called observer bias. That is, observers perceive selectively. And the qualities and traits that we become aware of are the ones that support our current beliefs. We remember the particular person or event or time that supports our stereotype. In our previous example of a stereotype, we stated our belief that hairies have bad breath. We may have observed this in some hairies. Or we may have observed one hairy who at times had bad breath. As we remember it, however, bad breath was always noticeable.

Stereotypes may appear to be accurate for another reason. Our self-descriptions often match the way we are described by others (Triandis, 1971). This implies that stereotypes sometimes, but not always, match facts.

There are situations that encourage the development of an accurate stereotype. When contact with another involves observing behavior in a variety of situations, our information about that other increases. We have more things to say about him or her and more data with which to make judgments. Stereotypes become more refined when the amount of contact with the stereotyped group increases and when we learn about members by direct experience (Triandis & Vassilou, 1967). Increasing our contact with a group is not enough to assure that our stereotypes will be accurate. Other forces may interfere, so that increased contact does not produce an accurate stereotype (see Chapter 14).

When we have strong feelings about a specific group, our perceptions about them tend to be biased. Both strong positive and strong negative feelings can "blind" or distort perception. The less extreme our opinions of the group, the more likely our perceptions are to be accurate.

We can expect that our view of a similar other person will be more accurate than for a dissimilar one. We often project our own characteristics onto others. When you play tennis with someone whose ability is comparable to yours, you may predict how a point will develop or predict the scores of the sets. The accuracy of judging someone on a given dimension depends on similarity of them to you on that dimension. For a person who is similar in tennis ability, you may be accurate in your judgments of how well they would do against other tennis players you know. To a lesser extent, you can often predict how well that person would do in another sport. To estimate your tennis-playing colleague's intellectual ability, however, you would have to use other information.

Another factor that affects the accuracy of a stereotype has to do with the circumstances under which it is formed. When our contacts are exclusively with low-status members of a group, we are more likely to form a negative stereotype than when the contacts are with high-status members (Allport, G. W., 1954; Bem, D. J., 1970). Perhaps the prevalence of males in high-status positions and females in low-status positions has something to do with our sex-role stereotypes. Interest Box 6-2 gives you another chance to test your stereotypes. Then you might want to discuss their "truth" with a friend of the other sex.

When our stereotypes are correct, we may take credit for being careful observers and astute social theorists. But stereotypes are often quite wrong. We are aware of this and have disclaimers at hand when they fail; for example, we may say "There is an exception to every rule."

Inaccuracy in our impressions of others is sometimes disastrous. Our stereotypes lead us to prejudge others, which influences our interactions in subtle ways. We may limit our contact with some individuals because of their group membership. Thus, we prevent ourselves from getting to know anyone in that group better. When we believe that all members of a group possess negative attributes, we prevent ourselves from finding those who do not have such qualities.

The influence of prejudgment is not always so subtle. Archie Bunker lets almost everyone know how he feels about particular groups. All of us are a bit like Archie when we evaluate friends and foes. Those who are members of our group are kind, considerate good guys. Non-members are unkind, inconsiderate bad guys.

Humor frequently reveals our stereotypes. Two social psychologists collected jokes from students in Belgium, Hong Kong, and the United States. They found that all had other groups to which they attributed negative qualities. In the aggressive jokes, a stereotype of someone from another country was the butt of the joke. It was interesting to realize that Western Europeans stereotyped Americans as insensitive and overbearing (Castell & Goldstein, 1977).

Stereotypes of People in General.   Also involved in our stereotyping of particular groups of people is our stereotype of people in general. What is your theory about human nature? Do you tend to think that most people are basically good, as Carl Rogers (1957, p. 200) has described them: "positive, forward moving, constructive, realistic, trustworthy" (see p. 183)? Or do you tend to agree with Sigmund Freud (1960) that "with a few exceptions, human nature is basically worthless"? All of us have what Wrightsman (1964a) has referred to as "philosophies of human nature." Do you find most people to be trustworthy or untrustworthy? Helpful or selfish? Independent or conforming? Strong-willed and rational or passive and irrational? Very similar to one another or very different? Very simple or very complex? These six ways of viewing people, Wrightsman suggested, are among the most important ways that we think of others.

Other researchers report that people use three dimensions to describe objects, ideas, and others (Osgood, Suci, & Tannenbaum, 1957). These three basic dimensions are evaluation (good/bad), potency (strong/weak), and activity (active/passive). When we are involved in social perception, evaluation is most important. Although impressions of people can be described using any of the three dimensions, evaluation is most often used. In addition, more than either of the other

---

Interest Box 6-2.   Exploring Your Sex-Role Stereotypes

How do you think that men and women differ? In the space below are 13 adjective pairs with five-point rating scales. For each scale, place an *M* where you think the typical male falls and an *F* where you think the typical female falls. To see how your stereotypes match those of other undergraduates, see below.

weak	1	2	3	4	5	strong
brave	1	2	3	4	5	cowardly
leader	1	2	3	4	5	follower
dominant	1	2	3	4	5	submissive
attractive	1	2	3	4	5	ugly
bad	1	2	3	4	5	good
masculine	1	2	3	4	5	feminine
competitive	1	2	3	4	5	noncompetitive
happy	1	2	3	4	5	sad
honest	1	2	3	4	5	deceitful
aggressive	1	2	3	4	5	nonaggressive
independent	1	2	3	4	5	dependent
small	1	2	3	4	5	large

Forty male undergraduates enrolled in an introductory psychology course at Pennsylvania State University (McGovern, Ditzian, & Taylor, 1975) believed that males were stronger, braver, more often leaders, more dominant, less attractive, less good, more masculine, more competitive, happier, less honest, more aggressive, more independent, and larger than females.

two dimensions, our feelings reflect evaluative judgments. To some extent, most of the 18,000 English adjectives we use to describe people are either complimentary or insulting (Allport, G. W., & Odbert, 1936; Cattell, R. B., 1951). Philosophies about human nature and our way of describing others influence our stereotypes about specific groups of people. If we think that most *people* are basically good, we are more likely to also think that Jews or Buddhists or Blacks or Whites are basically good. Our own particular philosophy of human nature not only influences our beliefs about a group of individuals but also influences our perception of a particular individual. The next section will describe the process of impression formation.

IMPRESSION FORMATION

When we form impressions of other people, we begin with a very limited amount of information. Some of this information enables us to place them in one or more categories. For instance, a person who enters the room may fit the categories *short*, *White*, *old*, and *woman*. Our stereotypes about individuals who possess these traits provide us with additional tentative information. The process is very rapid and very complex.

The two major characteristics of the other person, or stimulus, that influence the process of **impression formation** are physical appearance and the other's behavior, including his or her reactions to us. We attempt to organize the observations from these characteristics into a consistent picture. When something a person says or does is inconsistent with our expectations, we often invent an explanation that resolves the inconsistency. Or we ignore or distort the inconsistent information. These strategies are possible in social perception because we can focus on any of an enormous number of traits, characteristics, or qualities in others. The complexity of people as stimulus objects makes the study of impression formation a complicated task. Even more restrictive, however, is the fact that direct examination of the thoughts and feelings of the perceiver is not possible. And there are an infinite number of situations in which impressions are formed. We will now examine three factors that influence impression formation: the stimulus person, the perceiver, and the situation.

Influence of the Stimulus Person.   There are many characteristics of others that are important in impression formation. We will examine just three—similarity, competence, and central traits.

Similarity.   What kinds of similarity matter to you in your attraction to another person? Different people no doubt find different kinds of similarity more important than others. For example, members of the Ku Klux Klan undoubtedly especially value similarity of race in their friendships. College professors may especially value similarity in intelligence.

Many dimensions of similarity have been found to be important in choosing friends, lovers, and marriage partners. Some of these are:

● Ability (Senn, 1971).

- Age (Bowerman, 1965; Hollingshead, 1951).[1]
- Agreement with us (Byrne, 1971; Griffitt, 1974; Kaplan, 1972).[2]
- Attitudes (Byrne, 1971; Byrne & Nelson, 1965; Griffitt, 1974; Griffitt & Veitch, 1974; Schachter, 1951).
- Authoritarianism (Rubin, Z., 1974).
- Behavior (Reagor & Clore, 1970; Senn, 1971).
- Experience (Clore & Jeffrey, 1971).
- Intelligence (Richardson, H., 1939).
- Physical dimensions (Pearson & Lee, 1903).
- Race (Schmitt, 1971; Triandis & Davis, 1965).
- Religion (Bumpass, 1970; Glick, 1960; Rubin, Z., 1964).
- Socioeconomic status (Byrne, Clore, & Worchel, 1966; Dinitz, Banks, & Pasamanick, 1960; Sundal & McCormick, 1951).

There are many levels at which we can discover similarity between ourselves and another. At each of these levels, we may choose to learn more and get to know the person better or choose to stop learning about the person and let the relationship fade. At the first level, there is similarity of physical appearance and overt behaviors: he or she looks like us and acts like us. Assuming that there is sufficient similarity here, we may begin talking to the other and search for additional obvious similarities. These include similarities of interest, values, and likes and dislikes. If sufficient similarity is discovered at this level, then interaction may proceed to the point where both of us try to understand how the other thinks.

Similarity may be more important in the initial stages of getting to know somebody than in later stages. If people feel somewhat anxious when they meet a stranger, they find comfort in knowing that the stranger is very much like them. Discovering similarities makes it possible to rapidly draw many inferences that would not be possible if we discover that the person is very different from us. Typically, when we are getting to know someone, if we want them to like us, we first present ourselves as quite similar to them. Later on, as we get to know someone better, we are feeling comfortable enough to share the ways that we are different. In fact, as we become comfortable with another, we may even seek out areas of disagreement to maintain our interest. But in the initial stages of attraction, certainly, similarity is very important.

Competence.   When we see someone perform a task or activity well, we are usually impressed. And we form a positive impression of that individual. Competent people are liked more than less competent ones, in general. Other things being equal, the competent are more often sought out as friends. For instance, one study of 2,800 schoolchildren found that the brighter children tended to be more popular, regardless of their family's income (Sells & Roff [cited in Hartup, 1970, p. 394]). One obvious example of this is what happens after a football game. During the game the battle may have been close and the crowd evenly divided in its enthusiasm for the two teams. Finally in the last few minutes one team pulls ahead and wins. Fans of the winning team pour down onto the field and express

[1]In mixed-sex pairs, males tend to be somewhat older.
[2]We like those who agree with us more than those who disagree.

their enthusiasm for (and high level of attraction to) the winning team. The cameras follow the winners down into the locker room. Fans of the losers leave the bleachers quietly. The research literature supports the view that we like competent others (Iverson, 1964; Spence & Helmreich, 1972; Stotland & Dunn, 1962; Stotland & Hillmer, 1962). Incompetence may lead to disliking and negative impressions. For many cultures, grounds for divorce include economic, sexual, or some other form of incompetence (Murdock, 1950).

But what about the importance of similarity in attraction? Not all of us are extremely competent. How do we feel about people who are very competent but in other ways are similar to us? Some research suggests that they may make us feel uncomfortable (Nadler, Jazwinski, & Lau, 1976). If we feel threatened by similar but very competent others, we may look for ways to downplay their competence or their similarity. Several studies have found that when extremely competent people make a minor mistake such as spilling coffee, they are liked even more (Aronson, Willerman, & Floyd, 1966). Perhaps this is because their error makes them seem more similar to us and less threatening. In contrast, this research suggests that, when people low in competence make an identical mistake, our attraction to them decreases. Perhaps this is because we do not see people as similar to us when they are low in competence, and committing a blunder lowers their competence still further, decreasing their similarity still more.

We may feel greatest respect for those high in competence and feel greatest affection for those who are moderately high in competence.

Central traits. Our impression of another is often influenced by one outstanding characteristic that the other person possesses.

Traits such as warmness and coldness have a great impact on impression formation. They are referred to as **central traits**. Solomon Asch, who pioneered in impression-formation research, thought that some traits are central and others peripheral. He also thought that some traits can be either central or peripheral, depending on the other traits with which they are associated.

The warm/cold dimension plays a major role in how we perceive others (Nisbett & Wilson, 1977) and how we act toward them (Simonson, 1973). Nisbett and Wilson asked students to view a college instructor who spoke English with a European accent. When he acted and spoke in a warm fashion, students rated the accent and other qualities about him as appealing. When he said exactly the same things but acted coldly, students rated the same attributes as irritating. It appears that we let our global impressions of others influence our evaluations of specific attributes. The warm/cold dimension was influential in the way the students viewed the instructor.

The warm/cold dimension also influences how we act toward others. Subjects were told either that they would be talking with a "warm" therapist or a "cold" therapist. The therapist acted the same for both groups of subjects. Those subjects who believed that they were talking with a warm therapist revealed more personal information (self-disclosure) than did the others (Simonson, 1973).

Influence of the Perceiver. We will examine two types of influence the perceiver has on social perception—perceptual biases and cognitive factors.

Perceptual biases.   The more we initially like someone, the higher we will judge his or her intelligence, health, status, competence, attractiveness, and so on. Through a diffusion of affect, our overall impression can color many specific aspects of our impression. The result is that our evaluation is less finely differentiated and more global than it should be. The phenomenon of rating someone either too high or too low because of one outstanding trait is referred to as the **halo effect**. Halo effects reduce ambivalence, which may be pleasant, but also lower objectivity. Those who believe "my country, right or wrong" have let a halo cloud their vision.

We tend to believe that traits are related: a person who has X tends to have Y and Z. This, in fact, may be true for people in general but not true for specific individuals. We will be committing a **logical error** if we assume that, because a person has property X, he or she must have properties Y and Z. A personal theory some people hold is that bright people are generally witty. If Sally is bright, they assume Sally is witty. If she is not actually witty, they have committed a logical error.

"I never met a man I didn't like". A positivity bias by Will Rogers.

The **positivity bias**, or **leniency effect**, is another bias that occurs during social perception. This refers to the fact that we make more positive judgments than negative ones (an instance of the Pollyanna Principle, described in Chapter 7). To believe that most people are basically good or to say, as Will Rogers did, that you have never met a man you didn't like, is to express this positivity bias.

Assumed similarity is another tendency that leads to error in social perception. When others are similar to us in basic ways, such as age, race, and socioeconomic status, we may assume that they are similar in other ways, too. Assumed *dis*similarity occurs for those who differ in some obvious ways.

The phenomenon of attributing our own feelings and thoughts to another person is called **projection**. Projection results in distorting our perceptions of the other. Rather than seeing ourselves as others see us, we tend to see others as we see ourselves.

Another interesting bias occurs when we describe others. Each of us has a set of **favored descriptors**—terms we like to use. For instance, Bob might describe Ted and other friends as warm and bright. Jack might tend to describe these same people as witty and healthy. As a consequence, my descriptions of a variety of people may suggest that they are all quite similar. Your descriptions might suggest the same. But comparing our descriptions, it might look as if we are talking about different people. Beauty and most other qualities are in the eye and mouth of the beholder.

These **perceptual biases** demonstrate the influence that the perceiver has during social perception. It seems that the perceiver has as much effect on the description of a person as the characteristics of the person. Even more important, however, is the way that the perceiver and stimulus person interrelate.

So far we have taken a **static view** of the social-perception process. It is as though we were examining one frame of a movie film. This approach does not give us a very rich picture of what may occur during an interaction. Impressions change over time, even within a brief encounter. For example, suppose you are in a fantastic mood on the way home from school. Seeing a friend, you stop to chat. Your friend, it seems, is caught in a dilemma and tells you about the problem. You want to be helpful. So, you give your solution. When your friend finds fault with your suggestion, you try again with a different idea. But again your friend finds fault. As the moments slip by, you find your good wishes and sympathy for your friend also slipping away. Your impression of your friend may also shift. Real-life social perception is a **dynamic**, ever-changing process and not a single, static event. In fact, each of us continues to form and reform our impression of others and to behave in ways designed to influence the impression others form of us.

Cognitive processing.   As we have seen, our perceptual biases affect our impressions. Our cognitive processes also influence our impressions, and this section will describe some of the ways this happens.

Prior-entry effect.   First impressions of another person or some other social stimulus (for example, a speech made by a politician on an issue we have not thought about much) are very important to us. There is often no simple category in long-term storage in which our perception can be stored. Consequently, we must create a new category. This category construction will be affected by particular aspects of the social stimulus that are assumed to be true. If you are well-dressed when I meet you, I will assume that you usually are. One of the elements of the cluster of "truths" I will hold about you is that you dress well. I reach that conclusion from that first meeting. But on the occasion when we met, you might have been more well-dressed than usual. I may have been mistaken in the category I created for you (or sorted you into). If you are poorly dressed on the next occasion when we meet, I may tend to see this as merely an exception to my rule about the way you dress. If I repeatedly see that you are poorly dressed, I may finally revise my rule. The fact that first information contributes more to category formation than later information will contribute to change of the category is referred to as the prior-entry effect. This effect describes an error in social categorization.

Primacy and recency effects.   Even though we know that first impressions are important, we also know that they fade. When we give ourselves or others the advice to "put the best foot forward," we are relying on the **primacy effect** to benefit us. *Primacy effect* refers to the tendency for the material that is presented at the beginning of a sequence to have greater influence than material presented later.

We also know that recent events can change our perceptions of others. This **recency effect** may occur because recent impressions are more vivid and vivid recollections are easier to retrieve from long-term storage.

Which effect—primacy or recency—is more important? The answer, apparently, is that it depends on many things. One factor seems to be memory. The longer the interval between first impression and most recent impression, the more influential the recent impression is. In addition, if a number of distractions were present during the first meeting, learning about the other person would be difficult and incomplete. In such instances, we would expect recent information to be more influential (Luchins, 1957b; Mayo & Crockett, 1964; Rosenkrantz & Crockett, 1965). Also, recent events will have a major influence if the cues have not previously been presented by the other or attended to by us.

If you were a lawyer in a courtroom defending a client, would you want to speak before or after the prosecuting attorney had spoken?

In summary, many factors influence whether first impressions will count most heavily (a primacy effect) or whether the most recent impression will count most heavily (a recency effect) in forming an overall impression.

Selectivity. In our description of the perception process, we noted that in each phase of perception a selection occurs. We do not attend to all of our sensations. We do not perceive all of the characteristics of those objects to which we attend. Perceptions are selective, and some information is favored over other information. If selectivity in perception did not occur, we would be in big trouble. Very often, our processing seems to favor the pleasant over the unpleasant and, sometimes, the intense over the mild. As we look at a crowd of people, we are likely to notice those who seem happy more than those who seem sad, as well as noticing those who seem to be showing the most intense emotions. The other blank expressions may fade into the sea of faces. These meaningful features of the social stimulus—pleasantness and intensity—are qualities related to our needs. They are probably processed before we become consciously aware of the stimulus' full denotative meaning, and they influence whether a stimulus is processed further or ignored.

One interesting aspect of selectivity that has been studied in the laboratory is called **perceptual defense** and **perceptual vigilance**. In these studies, students are shown a series of words with a machine (tachistoscope) that displays them for only a fraction of a second. The words are not presented long enough for anyone to be confident about what was seen. Typically, students are better at guessing what the pleasant words are than the unpleasant, somehow "defending" against unpleasantness, being "vigilant" for pleasantness, or both.

There are other aspects of perceptual selectivity that influence social perception. For instance, there is evidence that it is harder to learn something unpleasant than something pleasant. Also, we are more inclined to think about pleasantness than unpleasantness. Most of our evaluations of other people tend to be pleasant or positive. On those occasions when we do form a negative impression, many of us avoid revealing that impression or try to find something pleasant to say (Matlin & Stang, 1978).

Early impression-formation research demonstrated the importance of selectivity in social perception. If you are told several things about a person you don't know, including the fact that he or she is "warm," you'll form a much more positive impression of that person than if you are given exactly the same description with *cold* substituted for *warm* (Asch, 1946). *Warm* and *cold* seem to be words that give us general positive or negative impressions of a person.

Implicit personality theories. Insofar as we do have other objective information about the person, we are likely to draw on our personal theories about what variables are related to warm or cold people. Are warm people considerate of others or self-centered, popular or unpopular, good-natured or irritable, social or unsociable? We seem to believe that people are consistent in their "goodness" or "badness." If we are told that a person has one good quality, we assume that person has others; if we are told that the person has a bad quality (and told nothing else), we assume that person has other bad qualities. We try to form a consistent impression.

All of us develop a notion of what traits regularly appear together. For instance, when I observe someone who is intelligent, I assume that he or she will be talented in at least one other area—athletics, music, art, and so forth. I assume that intelligence and achievement are related. I have developed an **implicit theory of personality** (Bruner & Tagiuri, 1954). An example of such a theory concerns people who wear glasses. They are viewed as more intelligent, industrious, and reliable than those without glasses (Manz & Lueck, 1968). Implicit personality theories develop because they let us form integrated views of others.

How do we develop such theories? Why do some traits seem to correlate with certain other traits? We will look at how we combine the pieces of information that we learn about another.

Combining information. We would expect a track coach to pay more attention to a person's strength than to musical ability or esthetic propensity. We would also expect a beggar to care about someone's generosity rather than someone's humor. However, the coach and the beggar use all the information available when they "size up" another. How do people combine that information to form an overall impression? One way seems to be through simple addition. Each trait has a value associated with it. We sum the values of the descriptive traits to form an overall impression. With this approach, a person who is decribed as "fairly pleasant" ($+1$ in positiveness) and "very smart" ($+3$ in positiveness) does well: $1 + 3 = 4$.

The sum of the value of descriptive traits equals an overall impression.

Another way that information about others is combined to form an overall impression is by averaging (Anderson, N. H., 1965, 1974; Anderson, N. H., & Anderson, 1971). This model asserts that people form an impression by averaging every piece of information into a total impression. We recognize that a person has both good features and bad, and our overall impression lies somewhere in between. A person who is "fairly pleasant" ($+1$) and "very smart" ($+3$) comes out at $+2$. Evidence suggests that the adding model is sometimes the best description of what really happens and that other times the averaging model is the best.

But is there such a thing as a single overall impression of a person? Very often we have mixed feelings about people. This implies that we have not fully averaged or added. We have not fully integrated all the information we know about them into one coherent picture. Mixed feelings are not always pleasant to have. We often resolve them by ignoring traits that make the picture inconsistent. As we get to know somebody, we learn both good things and bad things. Although we do know the bad things, if we like the person a lot, we may not pay much attention to them. If something should happen and we come to dislike the person, these bad things will suddenly come to the surface. We will amaze ourselves with how much negative information we know about the person. We will wonder how we could have liked him or her so much for so long.

We are still gathering information about how people combine information when they form an impression of another. It appears that we sometimes average information, add information, ignore information, or distort information.

As active seekers of information we usually try to find information consistent with our views. When we like somebody, we want to know more about his or her good points. When we dislike someone, we want to know more about the bad points. Such selectivity in information seeking helps us to develop consistent pictures of people. It helps us reduce our mixed feelings.

Attributing causes of behavior. At first, investigators of social perception focused on the traits of the perceiver that contribute to accuracy in social judgments. But then a researcher (Cronbach, 1955) pointed out that social perception, rather than being a global ability, involves at least four separate abilities. This criticism shifted research away from the perceiver's traits and toward the *process* the perceiver uses. A number of models have been developed to explain these processes. One family of models can be thought of as the **attributional approach to social perception.**

One theory focuses on the way that people make inferences about another's personality traits (Jones & Davis, 1965). To figure out what "caused" an act (what trait or characteristic of the individual was underlying the act), we use pieces of information about that specific person and other similar people, and we form our own hunches. One of these bits of information is the degree to which the act produced desirable effects. Another is the number of "noncommon effects" produced by the act. (Noncommon effects are those resulting from one alternative but not the others.) For example, if Al knows that Bob bought a motorcycle rather than a moped, Al might conclude that Bob is adventurous. Al arrives at that dispositional inference by knowing first that Bob wanted to please himself (desirability of effects). Secondly, Al knows that either choice provides Bob with transportation (common effects) but that the motorcycle also provides an opportunity to obtain thrills that the moped does not (noncommon effects). It is possible to make an attributional error, though. Perhaps the reason that Bob bought the motorcycle was for safety. Perhaps Bob read an article contending that mopeds are dangerous.

Someone who engages in an activity and another person who observes that activity often come to different conclusions about its meaning. This discrepancy is called the **actor/observer divergent-perspectives hypothesis** (Jones & Nisbett, 1971). Actors (those who perform the behavior) are more likely to attribute their behavior to environmental conditions. Observers are more likely to attribute the actor's behavior to some disposition—trait, characteristic, attitude—of the actor. This is especially true when the act either pleases or displeases the observer. When an act has an effect on the observer, it is said to have **hedonic relevance**. When an actor's behavior pleases or displeases us and also directly benefits or harms us, that act has a high degree of **personalism**.

Our feelings about others are the result of both their behavior toward us and our evaluation of their motives. When another's behavior is helpful and we feel that the other's motives were positive, our liking for that person increases. When another's behavior is helpful but we suspect the motives, we tend to feel repelled and resentful (Tesser, Gatewood, & Driver, 1968). When another's behavior hurts us but we believe that his or her intentions were good, we are forgiving. In fact, even though a competency rating of the person may be very low, our attraction for him or her may not change much. Finally, when a person hurts us and we feel it was intended, we tend to dislike that other. When we evaluate others, our interpretation of their motives is sometimes more important to us than the consequences of their actions.

An observer will often try to explain an act either in terms of external influences or internal (actor's qualities) influences. For example, if a friend tells you she is going to a folk festival in North Carolina next weekend, she could have a lot of reasons. It may be that she likes to go away for weekends—anyplace, anytime. It may be that she hasn't been to North Carolina but has always wanted to go. Or perhaps she has been to North Carolina many times and looks for any opportunity to go there again. Or she may like to drive and so drives to distant places often. And so on.

According to Kelley's covariation model (Kelley, 1967), an observer uses three criteria to figure out what the particular cause of a behavior is. They are:

1. Consensus

2. Distinctiveness

3. Consistency

Some people, but certainly not everyone, like folk music. When **consensus** is low, we ordinarily make an internal causal attribution rather than an external one. So you might conclude that folk music is important to your friend. But if all people respond in the same way to an object (high consensus), the behavior seems to be due to the object and not to any unique quality of the individual. When observers use knowledge about other people's reactions to an entity to judge whether the cause of an act should be attributed to the actor or environment, they are using the consensus criterion.

If you know that your friend has not traveled great distances to attend other mass gatherings—revival meetings, state fairs, and so forth—you conclude that folk music must have quite an appeal for her. After all, its performance is causing her to drive to North Carolina. Knowledge that one object causes a certain response from someone, whereas similar objects don't, helps the observer make a causal attribution. When an individual responds differently to similar entities, we can conclude that there is something **distinctive** about those entities for that person. The distinctiveness criterion helps an observer decide whether a behavior is due to internal sources. When one object stimulates a response that other similar objects don't, we should make an external, or entity, attribution; that is, the object is in some way distinctive.

The other criterion used to make causal attributions is that of **consistency**. If you know that your friend attends lots of musical events—band concerts, rock concerts, classical concerts, and some jazz concerts—you notice a great deal of consistent behavior in her "music-attending behavior." And you become more certain that she is attending the festival for love of music, rather than for some other motive.

Underlying the attributional approach is the notion that we have a need to understand our world and be able to make predictions about what will happen in the future. So if you know you will have contact with someone in the future, you are interested in developing some theory about what makes that person tick. You will be interested to learn what traits you can use to describe the person. This knowledge gives you better control over your world. The main tenet of the attributional approaches is that our thoughts and behaviors are based on a mastery of the causal network of the environment.

Influence of the Social Context.   In addition to the influence of the stimulus person and the influence of the perceiver, the social context of an act also affects our formation of impressions.

Timing of the interactions.   Do your feelings about a stranger depend on whether you expect to be with him or her in the future? If you are like the women in one study, the answer is probably yes (Darley & Berscheid, 1967). In that study, women who were led to believe that they would actually meet another woman later rated her higher than women who did not expect such a meeting.

Even when we dislike another person, the knowledge that we will have further dealings with him or her makes our impressions more favorable than if we do not expect future interactions. One study (Tyler & Sears, 1977) found that liking for a dislikable or ambiguous person increased when subjects anticipated further interaction. These authors noted that many of our relationships involve a situation in which we have no choice but to continue the relationship. One aspect of the Pollyanna Principle (see Chapter 7) is to make the best of a bad situation. Because interacting with someone we dislike is unpleasant, if we must interact with them it is helpful to like them. We might increase our liking for those we can't avoid by emphasizing their positive qualities and by reinterpreting their negative qualities.

Reactions of others.   Another way that the context can influence our perception of another person has to do with the way that others react to him or her. For instance, we like those who have favorable reputations but are less eager to like those with unfavorable ones (Jones & Shrauger, 1970). When others express the same opinions about another that we do, we are more confident in the accuracy of our judgment (Goethals, 1972). The phenomenon of social support for opinions or judgments is referred to as **consensual validation**.

Similarity of perceptions.   Earlier in this chapter we described how the behavior of one person influences the behavior of another. The way a male talked with an "attractive" female elicited behaviors from her that corresponded to his stereotype (Snyder, Tanke, & Berscheid, 1977). In that experiment, males were asked to indicate how physically attractive they believed the female was. The women, however, were not asked for their impression of the male's impression. That is, the females did not indicate their perception of what score the male would use to rate their physical attractiveness. Nor were the females asked how attractive they believed they were.

When two people have similar perceptions of each other and similar views of what each is trying to express, we would expect the interaction to flow smoothly. When they have differing views of what the other is trying to accomplish, however, we can expect conflict, misunderstandings, or uncomfortable feelings to develop. Problems in an interaction can occur because a number of impressions of each interactant are formed. These impressions are formed on various levels of abstraction. On the first level, you form an impression of the other. The other also forms an impression of you. On the next level, you form an impression of what you think the other thinks of you. The other person involved in the interaction will probably do the same. On still another level, you form an impression of what the other thinks you think about them. The other person also engages in that kind of impression formation. The point to all this **reflexive thinking** is that we are concerned with what others think of us. By what we say and do, we try to present the proper cues so that others develop the impression of us that we want them to have. This presentation is referred to as **impression management**.

IMPRESSION MANAGEMENT

When we know we will be seeing a particular person, we sometimes rehearse what we will say, do, and wear. We are also aware that we seem to show different sides of ourselves to parents, friends, teachers, rivals, and so on. We often try to make the person who is perceiving us receive the message we want. This conscious attempt to create the image of us we want the other to have has been called impression management.

Defining the Self.   When we are involved in impression management, with what are we dealing? How can we define the self? How is the self formed? How do we know ourselves? As we move through our lives, we are aware that we change. We can reflect on the kind of person we were in high school and see how we are the same or different now. Although we can enumerate these differences, we still believe that we remain the same "self."

William James (cited in Gordon & Gergen, 1968) divided the self into three parts—the material self, the social self, and the spiritual self. Included in James' notion of the "material me" was almost anything and anyone that could be counted as part of my property or possession. The social aspect of a "self" is the recognition one gets from others. James believed that we are really many "social selves" rather than just one. He suggested that, to each group of people that we care about, we show one of our "selves." We may show our friends the very playful side of ourselves while showing our parents and other adults our serious, hard-working self. By the "spiritual me" James meant the entire collection of states of consciousness.

Self-Disclosure.   One of the ways we have to control someone's impression of us is by what we say about ourselves. *Self-disclosure* is the process of verbally revealing information about the self to another person. Altman and Taylor (1973) hypothesized in their **social-penetration theory** that gradual disclosure from superficial to intimate self-information produces more positive effects than rapid disclosure. That is, revealing ourselves by degrees seems to lead to more stable relationships than does an opposite strategy. So the way that we reveal ourselves affects the impression of us that others form. In addition, how much or how little we reveal also influences impression formation.

Both overdisclosure and underdisclosure produce negative effects (Castell & Taylor, 1977). Overdisclosure reveals too much or too soon or too many or in an inappropriate setting. The impression that overdisclosure produces is that of a blabbermouth who is insensitive and lacks social skills. Underdisclosure also generates a negative impression. This person discloses too little personal information in any social setting. He or she is viewed by others as cold, untrusting, and distant.

When a disclosure is properly timed, a positive impression of the discloser occurs. That is, when we as recipients of a disclosure believe that some quality of ours encouraged the disclosure, we attribute the cause of that disclosure to ourselves (Braunstein, Gould, & Taylor, 1978). When it appears that we have been singled out for a disclosure, both liking for and reciprocal disclosure to the discloser are likely to occur.

When individuals exchange self-information, they seem to be governed by a **norm of reciprocity**. The amount that is revealed and the intimacy level of what is revealed is about equal. Davis (1976) demonstrated that one of the participants of a conversation usually assumed control in guiding the intimacy level of the statements. And the level established by that person was matched by the other partner. This effect of disclosure on one partner producing disclosure in the other has been termed the **dyadic effect** (Jourard, 1964), or **reciprocity.**

A variety of factors affect the appropriateness of disclosing. For example, what we disclose depends on who the recipient is—friend or stranger. What we disclose also depends on the context—whether we are alone or in a crowded elevator. Another factor that determines the appropriateness of the disclosure is the role relationships that the discloser and the recipient are enacting. Goffman (1959) advanced the thesis that *all* our interactions with others are examples of role playing: our performance is designed to create a particular impression in our "audience." The appropriateness of different types of self-disclosure varies as a function of the particular role we are playing at the time. As Goffman has noted,

The appropriateness of different types of self-disclosure varies as a function of the particular role we are playing at the time.

it is singularly inappropriate for a salesperson to disclose personal information to a customer, unless it is directly related to the transaction. Some role relationships institutionalize or even demand self-disclosure. For example, patients reveal to doctors, and clients disclose to therapists. Other role relationships inhibit intimate disclosure. For example, some disclosures from students to professors are considered beyond propriety.

What we disclose to another influences what the other thinks of us. But other factors influence the development of another's impression of us. As we said earlier, we all engage in impression management. We all hope that others see us as we want them to see us. The way we are in private or with friends is usually at least a little different from the way we present ourselves in public. Goffman (1959) has described this phenomenon and refers to it as **self-presentation**.

Self-Presentation.   When we appear in public, we create and maintain a public self. We engage in self-presentation. Interactions between two or more people go well when each person performs a behavior appropriate for that setting. Each has to accept and support the role that the other enacts. The complete pattern of verbal and nonverbal actions that each person brings to an encounter is called a **line.** A line differs from situation to situation. We are able to express our views of the situation, other participants, and ourselves with our line.

One rule of interpersonal interaction is that those involved are mutually committed to carry out the interaction. All the participants have a responsibility to conduct themselves in such a way that each participant's *face* is maintained. Face is a major part of each person's line and is a public expression of self. Each of us has an interest in saving our face. There is an implicit rule of reciprocity that those involved in an encounter will protect each other's face.

Presentation of the self is always a mixture of role and real self. At one extreme we might be almost totally consumed by our role, but we still focus enough attention on our true characteristics so that we don't expose undesirable material. At the other extreme we might be involved in honestly disclosing ourselves, but we still have some awareness of role requirements that restrict our disclosures. Therefore, we maintain a balance between self-awareness and role awareness.

As I said before, others learn about us from the things we say, but they also learn about us from the things we do. Social psychologists have recently been looking at the degree to which individuals adapt their pattern of behavior to a situation. People differ in their ability and desire to engage in impression management. They differ in the degree they engage in self-monitoring (Snyder, 1974) (see Chapter 3).

SUMMARY

In this chapter, we described a general model of perception. We examined the variety of factors that influence social perception. Although we form impressions of others instantaneously, the process is very complex. Social and physical dyads provide stimuli for the perceiver. We believe that some of the same processes that are involved in the perception of physical objects are also involved in social perception. But social perception differs, because the stimulus is changeable. In addition, the perceiver is often involved in understanding or inferring another's internal state. Based on direct and indirect experience, we develop a set of generalized expectancies, or stereotypes, about various groups of individuals.

Our stereotypes sometimes develop after experience with only a few individuals from an entire group. Our experience may have been with individuals who are not representative of the group. When our behavior toward another is influenced by our stereotype, we often elicit behavior from the other that confirms the stereotype.

Developing an impression of someone begins as soon as we meet him or her. We often develop impressions of others based on what we have heard about them. A variety of factors are involved in impression formation. First, characteristics of the others—their behavior, language and physical appearance—influence the impression-formation process. Second, the perceiver contributes to impression formation with such factors as perceptual biases and cognitive processing. The time-and-place context is another major element that influences the process.

Perception of another is complicated by the fact that both the perceiver and the perceived are involved in impression management. That is, both try to "send" messages so that the other will develop the impression that the sender intended. We try to manage the other's impression of us by what we say—self-disclosure—and how we act—self-presentation.

GLOSSARY TERMS

Define these terms in your own words, then look them up in the glossary at the back of the book.

Actor/observer divergent-perspectives
   hypothesis
Attributional approach to social
   perception
Categorization
Central traits
Cognitive

Consensual validation
Consensus
Consistency
Decode
Distinctiveness
Dyadic effect
Dynamic

Encoded
Favored descriptors
Halo effect
Hedonic relevance
Image storage
Implicit theory of personality
Impression formation
Impression management
Kernel-of-truth hypothesis
Leniency effect
Line
Logical error
Long-term storage
Norm of reciprocity
Perception
Perceptual bias
Perceptual defense
Perceptual vigilance

Personalism
Positivity bias
Prejudice
Primacy effect
Prior-entry effect
Projection
Recency effect
Reciprocity
Reflexive thinking
Rehearse
Self-presentation
Short-term storage
Social-penetration theory
Social perception
Static view
Stereotype accuracy
Stereotyping
Store

FURTHER READING

Anderson, N. H. A simple model for information integration. In R. P. Abelson, E. Aronson, W. J. McGuire, T. M. Newcomb, M. J. Rosenberg, & P. H. Tannenbaum (Eds.), *Theories of cognitive consistency: A sourcebook.* Chicago: Rand McNally, 1968, pp. 731–743.

Hastorf, A. H., Polefka, J., & Schneider, D. J. *Person perception.* Reading, Mass.: Addison-Wesley, 1970.

Shaver, K. G. *An introduction to attribution processes.* Cambridge, Mass.: Winthrop, 1975.

Vallacher, R. R., & Wegner, D. M. *Implicit psychology: An introduction to social cognition.* New York: Oxford University Press, 1977.

WHAT I'M SAYING IS . . .
WHAT HE THINKS I MEAN IS . . .
DID HE UNDERSTAND THAT ?
WHAT SHE MEANS IS...
WHAT SHE THINKS I THINK, IS...
NO!

chapter
7
Communication

chapter
7

INTRODUCTION

More college-age Americans will die this year from car accidents than from any other cause. More Americans will be killed on the highways than died in all of the years of the war in Vietnam. Most of these accidents involve two drivers. The accidents often occur when one does not correctly predict what the other will do. Such predictions require experience, good judgment, and *communication*—the exchange of information between people. In order to avoid an accident, you have to be a *sender*, telling other drivers what you're planning to do. You also have to be a *receiver* and understand what they're telling you. And you can't afford a mistake.

It seems evident from the number of automobile accidents that we often do make mistakes in communicating with others. Such mistakes are frequent in other situations that the word "communication" brings to mind. Both what we say and how we say it are often misinterpreted. Such errors—and their consequences—make the study of communication valuable.

Some communication, such as television commercials or newspaper editorials, puts one person into the role of sender and one or more others into the role of receiver. But in most communication, as in driving, we are both senders and receivers. In a typical household situation Sally (sender) asks Bill (receiver) to wash the dishes. Bill has trouble hearing because the phone is ringing. This "noise" (distracting, irrelevant information) makes communication difficult. Bill (sender) objects, then answers the phone. Sally suggests that he do the dishes later. He agrees. Each learns something about the other from this feedback. Sally learns that Bill heard her but doesn't want to wash the dishes. She learns that he is willing if he can put the job off. Bill learns that Sally wants the dishes washed. He finds that he can get out of it (at least temporarily) by putting it off.

In this chapter, you will be mainly a receiver and, ideally, will learn something from our communication. First, you will be told about several ways that social psychologists describe communication. Then, various aspects of verbal and nonverbal communication will be explored.

DESCRIBING COMMUNICATION

There are many ways to describe communication: we can look at its intended and perceived meanings, its accuracy in transmitting information, its amount, and its content. It can also be described with content-analysis techniques. We will begin by looking at the differences between intended and perceived meaning.

Meaning: Intended versus Perceived. What I say has an **intended meaning**—what I want you to understand. It also has a **perceived meaning**—what you understand me to mean. There is generally a fairly good match between intended and perceived meaning, and we have effective communication. The receiver will sometimes pick up less meaning than was intended by the speaker, because of the listener's inattention or the speaker's poor organization, low volume, or unfamiliar accent. Conversely, more meaning will sometimes be perceived than intended, because of a listener's insightfulness, attention to nonverbal cues, and so on. And sometimes perceived and intended meanings will simply differ. "You may think you understand what I meant when I said what I did, but in fact what I meant was not what you understood"—I may think.

The difference between intention and perception is not easy to detect. How can we be certain that we accurately understand what another wants us to? We have several methods. First, as senders, we are **redundant** (we repeat the same information). The end of a sentence can be guessed by knowledge of the beginning, and a missing word can be guessed from knowledge of words before and after. To see how redundant communication is, cross out every 20th word in a magazine article, then read it to a friend. Can your friend supply the missing words? What if every tenth word is crossed out? Every third word? Such redundancy assures that, even if our receiver misses part of the message, the missing parts can be guessed fairly accurately. And such redundancy increases our ability to say what we mean.

Another method for assuring that perception and intention match is to use feedback. Both the sender and receiver want to be sure that intention and perception match. A teacher may simply ask "Are there any questions?" He or she may also use nonverbal cues from students to assess understanding. Well-timed nods are a sign of understanding; puzzled looks are not. In all types and sizes of groups, each person wants to understand the others, and feedback plays an important role in both assessing and improving understanding.

How do we know what we mean to say? By what process do we grasp our own intention? We cannot answer this question, because our insight does not "see in" far enough. It is as if our intention and planning were produced by processes of which we are unaware. Such nonconscious processes also select our words and organize our sentences. These hidden processes also mysteriously produce a "meaning" for our consciousness to consider, evaluate, and report on if it chooses. But we cannot be sure that the meaning we detect is a cause of what we say or simply a *post hoc* (after-the-fact) explanation of it, a reasonable accounting or rationalization.

It often *seems* as if our actions are consciously determined, because action and awareness are correlated, and awareness sometimes precedes some actions. But the error in this conclusion is evident when you examine your own speech.

Are you aware of an entire typical sentence before you utter it? No, probably not. Your awareness does not go much beyond listening to yourself, deciding to change topics, deciding to increase your eye contact, and other such matters. Our awareness of what we are saying may actually come from listening to ourselves! Studies that delay the sound of the speaker's voice reveal how difficult it is to speak without hearing. Perhaps we do not fully know what we have said until we have heard it.

If we are listening to someone else speak, we can decide what he or she means ("slow processing") while we simultaneously do other things, such as look around the room, bite a fingernail, or decide how we should respond. But the act of speaking requires incredibly fast processing. We must consider the receiver's background knowledge, select the ideas we will present, remember what we have already said, determine the general form for expressing the ideas, select appropriate words from our vocabularies of thousands of words, remember how each word is pronounced, then deliver these words in a smooth flow, adding inflection, emphasis, pauses, and hand motions. We can be grateful that nonconscious processes take care of this effort for us. Consciousness of each step in this process would be like listening to a hundred conversations at once and remembering them all.

Because our consciousness cannot probe what makes it tick, we are not in a position to explore directly the rules that guide the thought that leads to speech or writing. Formal grammatical rules for writing are far better defined, prescribed, and practiced than those for speech. In speech, we permit more freedom of expression than in writing.

There seem to be two good reasons for this difference between the rules for speech and writing. First, writing may be reflected on by both the sender and the receiver. The written word can also be edited mentally by both, permitting greater conformity with grammatical rules. Second, writing does not offer the feedback that speech does, so the writer only has one chance to reach the audience. The only feedback the writer gets is imagined by the writer while writing.

You will remember from Chapter 1 that social psychology is the study of how thoughts, feelings, or behaviors are influenced by the actual, imagined, or implied presence of others. The actual feedback that we receive when we speak affects our speaking behavior (as well as our thoughts and feelings). The imagined feedback authors get when they write "to the audience" influences their behaviors. Speaking and writing are indeed different forms of social behavior, fit for study by social psychologists.

Accuracy: Leveling, Sharpening, and Assimilation. A **rumor** is a shared explanatory personal theory. Rumors arise in puzzling situations, where the need for explanation is high. People ask themselves and one another for an explanation of the situation, and any explanation that seems plausible may become rapidly shared. Even though a rumor itself may be an unpleasant explanation of a situation, it may still be preferable to no explanation at all.

Because a rumor is a shared personal theory, it may give rise to uniform behavior within the group. For instance, if everyone believes a dam has broken (see Interest Box 7-1), everyone may be inclined to run in the same direction. When a personal theory is not shared (for example, "The sky is falling!"— C. Little), such uniformity in behavior does not develop.

When rumors are transmitted, at least three processes often occur. First, there may be **leveling**, or a reduction in detail with each retelling. **Sharpening** is also common, in which a central focus to a story emerges, and details are added to support that focus. Finally, **assimilation** may occur, in which the story is modified to fit better with the teller's personal theories, to make "more sense." G. W. Allport and L. J. Postman (1958), who proposed these terms, studied rumor transmission in the laboratory, using illustrations such as the one in Figure 7-1. They found leveling (descriptions of the scene became greatly simplified), sharpening (descriptions came to focus on the two standing men), and assimilation (some White students "moved" the razor from the White man's left hand into the Black man's hand, consistent with their prejudice). Leveling, sharpening, and assimilation make stories easier to remember and more interesting, but also make them less accurate and trustworthy!

Amount: Talkativeness.   Before you read any more, take a look at Interest Box 7-2 (see next page).

It is obvious that *what* we say influences the reactions of others. Not so obvious are the influences of *how much* we say. Talkative people are believed to be quite different from quiet people.

For example, in one study (Stang, 1973) college women listened to tape-recorded conversations of other college women and rated the speakers. *What* the speakers said was superficial small talk (they were reading carefully prepared scripts), and how much they said was deliberately varied. One speaker had

---

Interest Box 7-1.   The Day the Dam Broke*

Here is an excerpt from James Thurber's story "The Day the Dam Broke":

Suddenly somebody began to run. It may be that he had simply remembered, all of a moment, an engagement to meet his wife, for which he was now frightfully late. Whatever it was, he ran east on Broad Street (probably toward the Maramor Restaurant, a favorite place for a man to meet his wife). Somebody else began to run, perhaps a newsboy in high spirits. Another man, a portly gentleman of affairs, broke into a trot. Inside of ten minutes, everybody on High Street, from the Union Depot to the Courthouse, was running. A loud mumble gradually crystallized into the dread word "dam." "The dam has broke!" The fear was put into words by a little old lady in an electric, or by a traffic cop, or by a small boy: nobody knows who, nor does it now really matter. Two thousand people were abruptly in full flight. "Go east!" was the cry that arose—east away from the river, east to safety. "Go east! Go east!". . . .

. . . A tall spare woman with grim eyes and a determined chin ran past me down the middle of the street. I was still uncertain as to what was the matter, in spite of all the shouting. I drew up alongside the woman with some effort, for although she was in her late fifties, she had a beautiful easy running form and seemed to be in excellent condition. "What is it?" I puffed. She gave me a quick glance and then looked ahead again, stepping up her pace a trifle. "Don't ask me, ask God!" she said.

*Copyright © 1933, 1961, by James Thurber. From *My Life and Hard Times*, published by Harper & Row. Originally printed in *The New Yorker*.

Figure 7-1. Who dunnit? Study the picture for one minute, then describe the scene to a friend. The friend should then describe the scene to another friend, who should write down the story. Can you find instances of leveling, sharpening, or assimilation in the final story? (From *The Psychology of Rumor*, by Gordon Allport and Leo Postman. Copyright © 1947 by Henry Holt & Co., Inc. Renewal © 1975 by Holt, Rinehart and Winston. Reprinted by permission of Holt, Rinehart and Winston.)

a long part, one had a short part, and one had an intermediate-length part. The raters attributed the most leadership in the group and the most leadership ability to the talkative speaker. The least talkative speaker was given the lowest leadership ratings.

How much did raters think they would like each speaker? The speaker with the intermediate-length part received the highest ratings. Talkativeness seems to affect how we are perceived by others.

A series of experiments using this same approach has expanded our understanding of the stereotypes of talkative and quiet people. Tape recordings were made of two people talking; the speakers talked either 80%, 50%, or 20% of the time on the tape. People who spoke 80% of the time were evaluated by college students as being domineering, outgoing, selfish, inconsiderate, inattentive, impolite, and cold. The people who talked 50% of the time were liked best, being rated as likable, attentive, polite, and warm (Kleinke, Kahn, & Tully, undated).

Interest Box 7-2. A Conversation*

Short: "What courses are you going to take next term?"

Long: "Well, I want to take 304, 362, and 348, but I'm not sure I'll be able to. 304 is given Monday and Wednesday at 11, and 362 is given Monday, Wednesday, and Friday at 12. That's a pretty long walk for ten minutes. Do you know when 348 will be given?"

Medium: "I'm taking that too, but I don't know either. The notice said it would be announced."

After you have read this script, ask yourself these questions: Who seems to be the leader of this group—Short, Long, or Medium? Whom do you think you would like most? After you have made your decision, return to the text.

*From "The Effect of Interaction Rate on Ratings of Leadership and Liking," by D. J. Stang. In *Journal of Personality and Social Psychology*, 1973, *27*(3), 405–408. Copyright © 1973 by The American Psychological Association. Reprinted by permission.

How well do our stereotypes of talkative and quiet people match with the facts? Is there a kernel of truth in our stereotypes? Some of our stereotypes were suggested by Interest Box 6-1 in the previous chapter. Researchers have found that some of those stereotypes do have a basis in truth. As compared with quiet people, talkative people appear to have higher self-esteem (Morrison & Thomas, 1975). They have higher self-confidence (Borgatta & Bales, 1956). They are more persuasive (Bass, 1949; Riecken, 1958). And they are better liked (Stang, 1973). Talkative people may also be more opinionated (Borgatta & Bales, 1956) and may have less difficulty being assertive (Rosenwein, 1970). Such findings are all consistent with our stereotypes.

Not all research findings agree with our stereotypes, however. For example, our stereotype suggests that quiet people may be shyer than talkative ones, but at least one study finds no relationship (Rickfelder, 1970). Our stereotypes give quiet people the credit for having the best ideas and talkative ones credit for having the most ideas. But research has found that group members often judge talkative members as having both the best and the most ideas (Bales, 1953; Bass, 1949; Norfleet, 1948; Riecken, 1958; Slater, 1955). Such studies are important in revealing the shortcomings of common sense. Common sense, in turn, can both suggest hypotheses for investigation by researchers and be improved on by the findings of such studies.

It is evident that we hold different stereotypes of talkative and quiet people. Less evident is the extent to which our view of people in general is influenced by the thoughts, feelings, and behavior of talkative people. Survey researchers attempt to describe some population on the basis of returned questionnaires, and they may be biased in their conclusions if respondents and nonrespondents are different in significant ways. (For instance, when a researcher wants to learn how many honors and awards the average psychologist has received, perhaps those who have received the most will be most likely to respond. Thus, the researcher may overestimate the frequency with which the average psychologist has been honored.) Similarly, a teacher may form an impression of the entire class based on the impression formed from talking to a few talkative students. How do you think talkative and quiet people differ? How do your stereotypes affect your thoughts, feelings, and behavior toward talkative and quiet people?

Content: The Pollyanna Principle.　Pollyanna was the cheerful young heroine of a series of novels and later a Walt Disney movie. She always managed to look on the bright side of things and count her blessings. People may differ in how cheerful or optimistic they are, but to some extent we all show evidence of a **Pollyanna Principle** (Matlin & Stang, 1978a, 1978b). *Pollyanna* has come to refer to those who see roses where others see thorns. And research has revealed evidence that most of us are, to some extent, Pollyannas.

Newspapers and gossip abound with scandals, sorrow, and desperate situations. But everyday conversations do not. Instead, we seem to take the advice of the third monkey in the famous trio, who says, hand over mouth, "Speak no evil." Some research suggests that we are reluctant to transmit bad news to people when it concerns them but willing to transmit it when it does not (Rosen & Tesser, 1970; Tesser, Rosen, & Conlee, 1972). In everyday life, we can find evidence of this principle. The newspapers, for instance, do not find it difficult to report on fires or floods or car accidents. But a reporter may find it very difficult to tell a family that their house was destroyed by a fire or that a relative was killed in a car accident.

Not only are we reluctant to transmit bad news, but we seem reluctant even to use words that are negative in meaning. For instance, how often do you use the word *good*? How often do you use the word *bad*? Chances are you say or write *good* considerably more often than *bad*. In fact, studies have shown that positive words are used about five times more often than their negative opposites. *Able* occurs more often than *unable*, *polite* more often than *impolite*, *add* more often than *subtract*, and so on. This effect occurs for both written and spoken English, for children and adults, for scientific writing and popular writing, and for every language examined—English, German, French, Spanish, Chinese, Hindi, and Russian (Matlin & Stang, 1978a).

It is not easy to explain why pleasantness predominates in our speaking and writing, but there are several partial explanations we should consider. One is that for some reason it seems easier for us to think of pleasant than unpleasant words. In an early study of free associations, researchers asked subjects to listen to a neutral word and say whether the first idea that came to mind was positive or negative (Washburn, M. F., Harding, Simmons, & Tomlinson, 1925). Subjects said they had more positive than negative ideas come to mind. Interestingly, cheerful subjects had more positive ideas than those who were depressed, a finding consistent with diffusion-of-affect theory (see Chapter 5). Other studies have found that pleasant stimuli produce more responses—and produce them faster—than negative stimuli do (reviewed in Matlin & Stang, 1978a).

Another explanation for why we prefer to "speak no evil" is that, when we do say positive and negative things, the first words we say tend to be more positive than later words. A team's record of victories is reported before its losses, and parliamentarians ask for the ayes before asking for the nays. When last is not least, we may feel obliged to say so, for even in the dictionary, first means best (Matlin & Stang, 1978a). If you look at this paragraph and the one before it, you will see this effect: the positive word usually comes before the negative, and sometimes the negative is only implied by the sentence. In only two sentences does a negative word occur without a positive, and in each case one negative makes another negative positive ("no evil," "not least"). You might try an experiment with a few friends to see how this works. Pick a category, such as television programs, colors, or games, and ask friends to write down five or ten items from that category. Then ask them to rate each item for how much they like it. The first they list will usually be their favorite and the last their least favorite.

The fact that pleasant things seem to be easier to think of and that they seem to come out first when we talk or write provides a partial explanation of the greater frequency of pleasant words in speech and writing. But we still might wonder why pleasant things are easier to think of. One reason is that they seem to be easier to learn and to be better learned (Matlin & Stang, 1978a). But our curiosity should lead us to question why that is so. Right now, we simply don't know. What we do know is that the Pollyanna Principle shows up in many other situations. Some of the outcroppings (scattered visible evidence of something larger underneath) of the Pollyanna Principle are mentioned in Interest Box 7-3.

Process: Analyzing Interactions.   Every day in our lives we interact with others, we observe others and ourselves interacting, and we reflect on our observations. Our analysis of the interaction process is often sensitive and profound. But we generally use the same observational method and, because we have become so familiar with the task, give little thought to what we are doing, how we are doing it, or even why we are doing it. Using a different method can get us out of this rut and help us to make new discoveries.

One of the first social psychologists to formalize a useful method of analyzing interaction processes was R. F. Bales (1950a, 1950b). Like any other observational method, Bales' method requires that observations be **reduced to data**—numbers that can be analyzed. Such analysis inevitably discards some information, because not everything can be counted at once. But by discarding unimportant information the observer can concentrate on accurate observations of a few things. Such accuracy and persistence in focusing on selected types of information has yielded some very interesting findings.

Interest Box 7-3.   Outcroppings of the Pollyanna Principle*

There is a great variety of evidence that supports the idea that the pleasant predominates in human communication. Some of the evidence not mentioned in the text is detailed here (Matlin & Stang, 1978b, pp. 56, 59):

1. People seek out the pleasant and avoid the unpleasant. For example, they avoid looking at unpleasant pictures whenever they have a choice.
2. People take longer to recognize unpleasant or threatening stimuli.
3. The pleasant member of antonym pairs became a part of the English language before its unpleasant opposite. The first entry for "good" in the *Oxford English Dictionary* dates from the year 805; for "bad," 1297.
4. The pleasant member of antonym pairs is likely to be linguistically "unmarked": it is used more generally and in more basic ways than the unpleasant member. For example, we ask "how good" something is (a restaurant, a movie, a book) rather than "how bad."
5. Even when people have seen pleasant and neutral stimuli equally often, they report that the pleasant stimuli were more frequent.
6. People judge pleasant events to be more likely to occur than unpleasant events, even when the actual probabilities are equivalent.
7. People judge pleasant objects to be larger in size than unpleasant or neutral stimuli.

8. People memorize and recall pleasant items more accurately than less pleasant items.
9. People supply the judgment "good" faster to pleasant items than they supply the judgment "bad" to unpleasant items.
10. People tend to think about pleasant items more often than unpleasant items.
11. People remember events as more pleasant with the passage of time.
12. People overestimate the importance of pleasant events and underestimate the importance of unpleasant events.
13. People consider the majority of the events in their lives to be pleasant.
14. Most people describe themselves as optimists, claiming that their present mood is positive, and that their lives are happy at work and at home.
15. The average person rates himself or herself as "better than average," even though this is mathematically impossible.
16. People tend to evaluate other people—students, instructors, strangers—positively.
17. People give high ratings to inanimate objects; even distilled water is judged to have a rather pleasant taste.

*From "The Pollyanna Principle," by M. W. Matlin and D. J. Stang, *Psychology Today*, 1978, *11*(1), 56, 59, 100. Copyright © 1978 Ziff-Davis Publishing Company. Reprinted by permission.

How does **interaction-process analysis** work? Three kinds of information are recorded about everything that everyone says in the group. The first is simple: who is talking? The second is a little more difficult: who is being spoken to? This is more difficult because the observer, to be certain of who is being addressed, must take note of eye contact, who spoke last, who speaks next, and what is said. Sometimes the group as a whole is being addressed, in which case the observer must record that. The third kind of information that the observer must record is the nature of what has been said. In Bales' system, there are 12 different categories, clustered into four broader categories. The categories are shown in Interest Box 7-4.

As you will see by examining this system, categories A and D are opposites (for example, 3 versus 10, 2 versus 11), as are B and C. Researchers who use this system have found that everything that people say can be sorted into one of these 12 categories. As Bales (1970) noted, the system is a type of **content analysis** that classifies behavior act by act, focusing on the role played by each act in the group process.

Interest Box 7-4 shows the relative frequency with which communication in face-to-face small groups falls into each category. You can see that people in these

---

Interest Box 7-4. Categories of Interaction-Process Analysis*

In the table below, the 12 interaction-process-analysis categories are shown. In 1970, Bales changed the names (and definitions) of some of the categories. Where a name has been changed, the old name (listed first) and the new name are separated by a comma. The percentage column indicates the percentage of 22,970 communication acts that Bales (1950) scored in each of the 12

categories. For instance, Bales scored 1% of all communication as "shows solidarity."

*From *Personality, and Interpersonal Behavior,* by Robert Freed Bales. Copyright © 1970 by Holt, Rinehart and Winston, Inc. Reprinted by permission of Holt, Rinehart and Winston.

		Percentage
A.	Positive (and Mixed) Actions	
	1. Shows solidarity, seems friendly	1.0%
	2. Shows tension release, dramatizes	7.3
	3. Agrees	12.2
B.	Attempted Answers	
	4. Gives suggestion	5.2
	5. Gives opinion	30.0
	6. Gives orientation, information	21.2
C.	Questions	
	7. Asks for orientation, information	5.4
	8. Asks for opinion	3.5
	9. Asks for suggestion	0.8
D.	Negative (and Mixed) Actions	
	10. Disagrees	6.6
	11. Shows tension	4.4
	12. Shows antagonism, seems unfriendly	2.4
	Total	100.0%

studies agree twice as often as they disagree (12.2% versus 6.6%); they show tension release such as laughter almost twice as often as they show tension (7.3% versus 4.4%). These two effects are consistent with the Pollyanna Principle. Yet group members seem to show antagonism more often than they show solidarity, not consistent with the Pollyanna Principle.

Some other interesting findings are evident. For instance, it seems that people are quite willing to give advice, even when it has not been asked for (compare the Attempted Answers and Questions categories). In fact, making statements seems to be much more common in the groups studied than is asking questions.

Another finding concerns the amount that each person in the group talks (the method isn't very good at measuring how much each person listens!). It turns out that group members make unequal contributions. Regardless of the size of the group, some talk more than others. For instance, in the typical eight-person group, the most talkative person contributes about 40% of the time, the second most talkative contributes 17%, and the third most talkative contributes only 13% (Bales, 1970). Thus, 38% of the group contributes 70% of the conversation. Typically the least talkative in an eight-member group initiates less than 3% of the conversation. You can probably see this effect in your classroom: a few students do most of the talking, most talk infrequently, and some never talk. Teachers usually find it impossible to get everyone to talk an equal amount.

You can try a simplified version of interaction-process analysis with your class, your family, or your friends. Simply make a table that has one horizontal row as well as one vertical column for every group member. Write a member's name to the left of the first row, and at the top of the first column. Do the same for each other group member. The row names are the names of the speakers; the column names are the names of those spoken to. Because members will sometimes address the group as a whole, you might want to add an extra column for the group. Each time a person speaks, record with a check mark who spoke and to whom he or she spoke in the appropriate cell. After five minutes of practice, you will be able to keep up with a lively conversation. By adding across columns, you will be able to see how much each person talked. By adding down rows, you will be able to see how often each person was talked to. There will be other interesting findings from your study. For instance, you might want to see if there are any empty cells (indicating that one person was not talking to another). You might want to see if some cells are much fuller than others (indicating that one person was talking a lot to another). You might want to see how much talking was reciprocated (for example, did John talk to Mary as much as Mary talked to John?). Compare your results with your intuitions. Are there any surprises?

Researchers who use the 12 categories of interaction-process analysis usually use a simple machine called an interaction recorder (Bales & Gerbrands, 1943). This is a little box that contains a roll of adding-machine paper that slowly moves past a window. Twelve labels are positioned on the machine next to the window; these labels represent the 12 categories. As the paper moves through the recorder, the observer writes the code letter of the person speaking and the person spoken to in the appropriate space. In this way, the recorder is able to keep track of the order of events.

Using this method, studies find that positive categories are more common at the beginning and the end of a group session than in the middle (Matlin &

Stang, 1978b). It would be interesting to speculate on why this is true. I suspect that groups capitalize on primacy and recency effects this way, assuring that what is remembered best—the first and last parts of the meeting—will be positive and still being able to get the important problem solving and discussion completed. Whatever the explanation, studies have found that other aspects of the interaction process also change over time.

VERBAL AND NONVERBAL COMMUNICATION

As we speak, we do more than list words in a meaningful sequence. We vary our rate, volume, and pitch and use pauses to help give meaning to what we say. This aspect of communication is called **paralanguage** (*para* means alongside of). We also vary our distance from the person we are talking to (called **kinesics**). We vary our eye contact, and move our hands, arms, legs, and torso (called **body language**). Paralanguage, kinesics, and body language are all components of **nonverbal communication**.

Body language is one form of paralanguage.

Nonverbal communication and **verbal communication** occur at the same time and often present the same information. For example, we may tell people that we like them by what we say and by how we say it. In this capacity, nonverbal communication can enrich and give added meaning and emphasis to verbal communication. Sometimes, though, these two forms of communication will mismatch. For instance, we may say we are not angry but may sound and look angry. When verbal and nonverbal messages appear to disagree, we may be confused and sometimes disbelieve the verbal message. Thus, both types of communication are of interest to social psychologists.

The meaning of verbal communication is also affected by the social situation. Suppose someone praises your work. Here, your interpretation of the motives behind the compliment will influence the meaning you attach to it. The compliment could mean that the sender believes you did well on the job; or it could mean that the sender thinks you pulled off the appearance of doing well even though the sender doesn't really think the work was good. It could also mean that the compliment was paid only to get on your good side, in which case you may resent the remark. Each of these different meanings is a product of a different context for the communication. The dictionary, nonverbal communication, and the context work together to determine the meaning of verbal communication.

In the remainder of this chapter, we will first discuss verbal (including written) communication, then turn to a discussion of nonverbal communication.

Verbal Communication and Language. Verbal communication is important in social interaction. What verbal communication is and how it plays a role in the various forms of social interaction are the topics of this section.

Forms of verbal communication. "Speech is the most common form and medium of interpersonal behavior" (Krech, Crutchfield, & Ballachey, 1962, p. 274). It is primarily through speech that people communicate and through communication that most forms of social behavior take place.

But not everyone can speak. Washoe was born without a pharynx, the space just above the voice box that changes shape to help produce speech sounds. Allan and Beatrice Gardner taught her the American Sign Language, and by the age of 4 she had learned the signs for 160 words and could use them well enough in sentences that visiting deaf people could communicate with her (Rensberger, 1974). This would not be very remarkable, except that Washoe was a chimpanzee.

Other psychologists have since taught chimps to communicate in other ways. Ann and David Premack have used pieces of plastic of various colors and shapes to represent words. Their chimp, Sarah, learned over 130 words and could construct sentences using them, such as "Ann give apple Sarah." Sarah could also understand and comply with requests written with these symbols, such as "Sarah insert apple pail banana dish," using her knowledge of sentence structure to put the apple in the pail and the banana in the dish, rather than putting the apple, pail, and banana in the dish. Sarah even learned conditional relations, such as "If Sarah take banana, then Mary no give chocolate Sarah" (Premack & Premack, 1972).

Another approach used in communicating with chimps has been tried by Duane Rumbaugh with Lana. She learned to speak to a computer by pressing keys that represented various concepts. Only if her sentence construction was correct would the computer respond to her request. For instance, if Lana pushed the buttons "Please, machine, give milk," the automatic milk dispenser—complete with straw—filled with milk. But if she said "Please, machine, make milk," nothing happened. In the language rules she had been taught and the computer was programmed to accept, machines do not make milk, they give it. Lana and her computer communicated quite well. At night, when the researchers went home and she was alone with her computer, she sometimes asked "Please, machine, move into room" and "Please, machine, tickle Lana" (Rensberger, 1974).

Washoe, Sarah, and Lana have convinced everyone that chimps are much brighter than we once thought. They have convinced many researchers that chimps can acquire language. And they have reminded us that speech is not the only way to communicate.

All languages are systems of symbols that are *shared* with some consistency by the members of a community (Kinch, 1973). By this definition, all human societies have a language. Most of these languages are written and read as well as spoken.

There are some great differences between writing and speaking (see the earlier section in this chapter on Meaning: Intended versus Perceived). When we write, we typically have an opportunity to polish what we say. We can give careful thought to the best choice of words and phrase things so that they conform to grammar rules. Speech does not offer such a luxury. If you have ever listened to a tape recording of yourself, you may have been surprised at how many grammatical rules you violated. An unedited transcript of our conversations can be very embarrassing.

This gap between the rules of grammar and the facts of natural conversation raises some questions. What does the gap mean? Some behaviorists (psychologists who focus exclusively on measurable behavior) seem uninterested in linguistic rules. But most psychologists have the idea that we understand many communication rules (language) but do not always adhere to them when we speak. Such psychologists accept a distinction between language and speech. There is also a third possibility. It may be that what we traditionally call **language** refers to the rules that govern *written* communication. In this view, speech does not follow these rules because it has its own rules. For instance, in writing we use commas to separate ideas. In speech, we pause to take a breath. In writing we require periods every so often, and many rules tell us where. In speech, we get by just fine with "run-on sentences," and no one ever objects. Therefore, we are still competent speakers even though we may not adhere strictly to the rules of "language."

The study of language behavior.

Psycholinguistics is the area of study that overlaps **linguistics** (the study of language) and psychology. Psycholinguists study a language's **phonology** (the sounds that are used), **lexicon** (the words, pronunciations, and definitions), and **grammar** (the rules regulating how the lexicon will be put together to be meaningful). Psycholinguists are interested in how languages are learned by children (and as second languages by adults). They are interested in how language usage affects our impressions of others and our attitudes and behaviors toward them. In short, they are interested in the relations between language and behavior.

The sound of some words suggests their meaning. *Moo* is not just the word for the sound a cow makes, it is almost the sound itself. *Quack, woof, meow,* and *purr* are other obvious examples. But other words have sounds that suggest their meaning. Some researchers have suggested that there may be sound/meaning linkages that are constant across languages and people (Brown, Black, & Horowitz, 1955). In a study conducted by these researchers, U.S. college students did better than chance in matching Chinese, Czech, or Hindi word pairs with English word pairs such as *warm* or *cool, heavy* or *light*. For example, given the English pair *bright/dark* and the Hindi pair *chamakdar/dhundhala*, 90% of the students guessed which Hindi word meant bright. Can you?[1] One reason for this match between the meaning of a word and its sound may be memorability: if a word sounds like its meaning, it may be easier to remember.

---

[1]Bright = chamakdar.

There exists a relationship between language and behavior.

A word has two kinds of meaning. Its **denotative meaning** is what is pointed to by a word, the objective thing referred to. The **connotative meaning** is the subjective emotional reaction elicited by a word. The denotative meaning of *atheist*, on the one hand, is "one who does not believe in God." The connotative meaning of *atheist*, on the other hand, is often negative for theists (those who believe in God) and positive for atheists themselves. Many other words such as *lesbian* or *communist* have denotative meanings that most people agree on and connotative meanings that differ from one group to another.

Phrases usually carry much different and more complex denotative and connotative meanings than any of the words that they include. It is from a phrase that we are often able to determine the meaning of a word and from a word's meaning that we can determine the meaning of a phrase. For example, consider the phrase *cabinet filing* in the sentences below.

- "He photographed the President's cabinet filing out the doorway."
- "In this cabinet I keep my lunch and books, in that cabinet filing."

The study of how words are combined in meaningful units is the study of *syntax*.

Thinking, speaking, and social behavior. How does our language affect our thinking? After many years of debate on the question, it now seems that language is not necessary for thinking. We know that monkeys and some other animals show good evidence of abstract reasoning. We know that preverbal children (those too young to talk well) can memorize, reason, and plan without language (Conrad, 1971). We know that totally deaf children are able to solve problems very well (Furth, 1971). Further, we know that we are able to think quite well without speaking. When we are alone, we think well but usually do not speak. It seems that neither knowing words nor using them is necessary for thinking.

This is not to say that words do not improve thinking. Just as having the right word for something makes communication easier, having the concept represented by that word may make thinking easier.

Our language is influenced by our culture, and our culture is influenced by our language. On the former point, there can be no doubt that language reflects our interests and preoccupations. There are about 6,000 Arabic words associated in some way with "camel" (Thomas, W. I., 1937). The availability of a word makes it much easier for us to conceive of, and refer to, its denotative meaning. For instance, an Arab's concept of a mean old camel can be expressed in a single word by an Arab and in three words by an English speaker, but it requires many words for someone who has never seen a camel.

Sapir (1929) suggested that our language shapes our understandings and that different languages give rise to different perceptions of the world. Along these lines, Whorf (1956) has suggested that the Eskimos, having many words for different kinds of snow, are better able to perceive and discriminate between types of snow. Whether such a correlation between linguistic and cognitive categories exists and, if so, whether the relation is causal, has been questioned by social psychologists (Brown, R. W., & Lenneberg, 1954).

Both the number of words we have for snow and our ability to discriminate between one type of snow and another come from a third variable: the amount of snow in our life. Because Eskimos walk in snow, hunt in snow, eat in snow, sleep in snow, and build igloos from snow, they naturally develop many words for it. And they naturally learn to recognize many different kinds of snow. You and I can recognize "snow that makes good snowballs," "snow that a dog has been in," and "snow that will melt when stepped on," even though we do not have special words for these snows. With practice, we could probably learn to distinguish snows as well as Eskimos. And with practice we might invent names for these types. Having the names would make it easier to talk about the types of snow.

Emotion and speech.   One of the most basic questions we might ask about speech is why people choose to speak when they do. Optimal-arousal theory (Chapter 5) suggests a preliminary and partial answer. If talking raises our arousal level and listening lowers it, then people may alternately talk and listen to maintain their arousal at a comfortable level. People who tend to be quiet may find talking too arousing; people who like to talk may find being quiet not arousing enough.

As with many good hunches about social behavior, most of the support for this hypothesis is anecdotal. You know that talking can be very arousing, particularly if you have to address a large group. Listening is much more relaxing, especially in a large group. These observations are supported by a study that found that personal inhibitions against speaking increased with group size (Gibb, J. R., 1951). This may be partly due to the increased risk of embarrassment and partly due to the fact that the opportunity for group members to talk decreases with group size (Zimet & Schneider, 1969). In larger groups we have less opportunity to talk and may feel greater frustration as a consequence (Miller, N. E., Jr., 1952). When our opportunity to participate decreases, so may our satisfaction with the group (Marquis, Guetzkow, & Heyns, 1951). One reason may be the reduced opportunity for expressing feelings and reducing tensions in larger groups. Another reason may be the reduced opportunity we have to raise our arousal by talking.

What about the hypothesis that a listener's arousal decreases as group size increases? As a student and listener, you know that you have to pay attention in a small class. In a large class, you can relax more. In a large group speakers are less likely to direct their remarks directly at any given listener, as suggested by the greater frequency with which members of larger groups disagree and show antagonism (Bales & Borgatta, 1955; O'Dell, 1968; Slater, 1958). Your teacher talks to you less in a large than in a small class, and such classes may be less cohesive and enjoyable than your smaller ones. The greater anonymity of the larger group not only reduces the listener's arousal but may reduce involvement, making it easier to avoid social responsibilities such as helping others or contributing to group performance and productivity (Ingham, Levinger, Graves, & Peckham, 1974).

Does a listener's arousal decrease as group size increases?

Most research on small groups has ignored individual differences. But it is certainly plausible, as mentioned above, that different people prefer different-sized groups. For instance, an introverted person with low self-confidence may find participation in large groups too arousing and feel most comfortable in a two-person discussion group. An extroverted, self-confident person may seek larger discussion groups to avoid the boredom of a smaller group. This is consistent with the finding that quiet people feel more anxious and timid and are viewed as feeling less calm and confident than talkative people.

The optimal-arousal hypothesis, then, may account for how much people say and what size group they prefer. Because arousal is a component of emotion, we may conclude that emotion affects the *amount* we say. Do emotions affect *what* we say, too? Diffusion-of-affect theory suggests an answer. This theory (see Chapter 5) suggests that our mood may have two effects on our conversations. First, it may determine how much we say. When we are in a bad mood, we are less inclined to speak than when we are in a good mood. This may be partly because of some cognitive effects of mood. For instance, thinking is harder when we are in a bad mood. It may also be a result of some norms related to the Pollyanna Principle: "If you can't say anything nice, don't say anything." So we may feel inhibited from expressing ourselves when we are in a bad mood.

The second type of effect predicted by diffusion-of-affect theory is that what we say will evaluatively match our mood. If we are in a good mood, we are more likely to say pleasant things than if we are in a bad mood. So powerful is this effect that we are usually able to guess people's mood by what they are saying.

In summary, both optimal-arousal theory and diffusion-of-affect theory make predictions about what and how much we will say. But neither offers very precise predictions about exactly what a person will say. Such predictions are probably best made in the specific situation by the others present, in their role of amateur clinical psychologist.

Special languages.   "Special languages" are developed by groups within a society. To some degree, they differ from the language of the larger society and are oriented toward the special tasks of the groups. Doctors, sky divers, psychologists, auto racers, soldiers, and members of various minority groups, for instance, all develop special languages. (Doctors, for instance, have many names for nerves, bones, operating procedures, and so on that most of us aren't interested in.) A

WE   THEY

group's special language not only makes communication within the group easier but also helps bind the group with a feeling of solidarity. Because only group members tend to know the special language, it becomes a basis for differentiating "we" and "they."

Language is a powerful social force, drawing together people who speak the same language, building walls between people who do not. Americans feel a special bond with people from other English-speaking countries such as Canada, England, or Australia. Within a language community, dialects create subcommunities, uniting some people and partially separating them from others. Such dialects or special languages may differ in pronunciation, grammar, word usage and so on. From dialects we can often infer a speaker's race, education, social class, and geographic area of origin.

What do these words have in common: *bad, bent, clean, crib, hammer, hit on, ride, tackhead, tight*? All these words are familiar to White students in what is called (by Whites) "standard English." But these words also have totally different meanings in what is termed "Black nonstandard English," "nonstandard Black dialect," "Black English," "ghettoese," and so on. (Some of them have become common in White slang, too.)

The differences between Black English and White English shouldn't obscure their similarities. Both have similar (but not identical) **phonologies**, **lexicons**, and **grammars** (see p. 190). However, Black English, particularly of Blacks from lower socioeconomic backgrounds, differs from White English in many ways. Whether the differences are small enough to justify viewing one as a dialect of the other or large enough to justify regarding them as distinct languages is not our concern. But the differences should be acknowledged and examined.

Some researchers have wondered whether the difference between White and Black English means that the language of Whites is "better." It would be just as sensible to ask "Is the language of Blacks better?" But no researcher seems to have posed that question. A number of Whites have argued that the language of Whites ("standard English") is better. These White scholars, echoing some nonscientific popular feelings, have argued that Black ghetto children essentially lack any regular language. Some argue that language development is determined by biological factors with some influence of the environment (Lenneberg, 1967; McNeill, 1966). Others argue that Blacks are genetically inferior in the intellectual abilities that determine language (Jensen, 1969). And it is argued that "impoverished" childhood environments will make this inherited problem worse. In this view, difference equals deficit.

The difference-as-deficit view is both ridiculous and dangerous. To understand the absurdity of the situation, imagine the shoe on the other foot. You are on another planet and find it very difficult to understand the language. One day a scientist comes up to you and, through an interpreter, explains that you lack any regular language (after all, the scientist can hardly understand you), that this is because you are biologically inferior (after all, your nose has two nostrils rather than one), and that your impoverished childhood environment (you didn't have any robot parents to take care of you and you ate sugar-frosted cereal every morning) has made your inherited problems worse. Who wants to argue with a 450-pound Martian scientist who has studied the languages of the entire universe? You can see, though, that this Martian can't understand you any better than vice versa, that Martian heredity and environment are inferior to yours by your standards (and vice versa), and that there is nothing scientific about this narrowmindedness. If the Martian weren't so big, you might dismiss the situation as ridiculous. Difference as deficit is a dangerous point of view because it gives "scientific" support to racist views some Whites have of Blacks (or vice versa).

There have been a large number of studies on whether speakers of "nonstandard English" are deficient in verbal "standard-English" skills. Unfortunately, the results of most of these studies can't be interpreted because of problems in their design. When Black and White children are properly matched for social class and nonverbal intelligence, they may do equally well in recalling standard-English words and sentences. On nonstandard English sentences, Blacks may perform significantly better than Whites (Genshaft & Hirt, 1974). Studies that don't match for social class and nonverbal intelligence may find either White or Black children superior in some ways in standard or nonstandard English, depending on which group is of higher social class and nonverbal intelligence.

One consequence of special languages is that they tend to distance people who do not share them. If Blacks and Whites have trouble understanding each other, they may be less likely to interact. Infrequent interaction makes it even more difficult to understand each other, permits differences to emerge, and especially permits the *perception* of difference to grow. Birds who don't flock together may conclude that their feathers are more different than they really are.

Black nonstandard English is rarely used by teachers in the classroom and almost never rewarded. The consequence is that Black children must either become bilingual or remain silent. Becoming bilingual is difficult, and when the two languages are very similar, one may interfere with the other. A number of writers (see Saville, 1971) have suggested that cognitive and emotional interference puts the Black child at a disadvantage in the standard-English classroom, where competition is with White children who have spoken standard English all their lives. Some have suggested that, if texts and tests were written in nonstandard English, speakers of nonstandard English might understand them much better (Baratz & Shuy, 1969). Tests of this plausible assumption have not been as supportive as we might expect (Marwit & Neumann, 1974).

How shall we educate our Black and White children? Integrated classrooms, in which users of standard and nonstandard English are encouraged to become bilingual, would seem ideal. Integrated classrooms in which everyone must learn standard English but in which nonstandard English is regarded as inferior or improper could have damaging effects on the self-concepts of Black children and could foster feelings of racial superiority among White children. Such classrooms might produce more racial problems than segregated classrooms, "equal" or otherwise. This concern is underscored by a recent court decision requiring the use of Black English in the school system of Ann Arbor, Michigan.

Spatial influences.   The distance between us and others has important effects on what we say to them, how much we say to them, how we say it, and what attributions others make from this conversation. Edward T. Hall (1966) has noted four general distance limits used by North Americans when interacting with one another: intimate (0 to 18 inches between persons), personal (18 inches to 4 feet), social (4 to 12 feet), and public (greater than 12 feet). Some research has questioned how exact the distances of Hall's zones really are. But it is has supported the idea that the ordering of these distances is correct, that these distances vary in terms of the types of social interactions that take place in them, and that smaller distances mean greater intimacy (Dosey & Meisels, 1969; Leginski & Izzett, 1976; Little, 1968; Sommer, 1962; Willis, F. N., 1966). Thus, for a given distance we have a basic expectation that certain kinds of interactions will occur.

Many factors appear to affect how close we stand to another for a particular kind of interaction. For example, the more two persons like each other, the closer they tend to stand (Evans, G., & Howard, 1973; Mehrabian, 1968; Rosenfeld, H. M., 1965). And it seems that physical distance corresponds to social distance (Adler & Iverson, 1974). Sex is another influence on interpersonal distance: women tend to stand closer than men (Adler & Iverson, 1974; Aiello & Aiello, 1974; Heshka & Nelson, 1972; Tennis & Dabbs, 1975; Willis, F. N., 1966). They apparently feel less stress under high-density conditions (see Chapter 5), engage in more physical contact with each other (Elzinga, 1975; Jourard, 1971), and feel less stress than men when touched (Nicosia & Aiello, 1976). Some of the studies of these sex differences are rather interesting. In one, researchers found people less willing to step into the personal space of a man than a woman in order to press an elevator button (Buchanan, Jahnke, & Goldman, 1976). In another, 4-year-old children approached female experimenters more closely than male experimenters to ask the experimenter to turn on a game for them (Eberts & Lepper, 1975). This study, as well as others (Tennis & Dabbs, 1975) suggests that patterns in our use of distance may begin at an early age.

What else affects our interpersonal distance? Hall (1966) observed considerable differences between cultures in what distances were preferred. Other factors, such as the amount of control we feel in the situation, our age, the topic of conversation, the social setting, the task, and even the lighting also seem important in determining interpersonal distances (Edney, Walker, & Jordan, 1976; Sommer, 1961; Tennis & Dabbs, 1975; Willis, F. N., 1966). At present, there is no good theory of why people choose the distances they do. Given the number of known influences on this variable, a good theory may be difficult to develop.

Interpersonal distance is actually part of the interaction. We know that we are more comfortable talking with friends at close distances. We are also more likely to discuss personal topics with friends and provide them with pleasant behaviors when we are close to them. So distance correlates with the type of interaction.

An important effect of distance noted by Hall in his early work (which has not received much attention by social psychologists) is also evident in many of the examples here. When we change interaction distance, our senses give us different information about the other person. This results in a change in what other nonverbal behaviors are important. As distance changes, all nonverbal (and verbal) behaviors change in how easily we can sense them and how important they are compared with other behaviors. For instance, it is harder to see small changes in people's expression when they are 12 feet away than at 12 inches. Also, because at 12 inches we see mainly their face, we can conclude that their body would be more salient at greater distance.

What happens during an *invasion* of personal space? One researcher (Garfinkel, H., 1964) asked students to select a friend, begin talking to him, and in the course of the conversation, without indicating that anything unusual was happening, bring his face up to the other person's face. Regardless of sex, this approach

apparently motivated, in both the experimenter and the subject, attributions of sexual intent on the part of the other. Attempted avoidance, bewilderment, and acute embarrassment were characteristic, being especially pronounced among males. Frequently the experimenters were unable to restore the situation by explaining that it was an experiment. Each subject then wanted to know why he in particular had been chosen.

Thus, we see that distance has many basic effects on the kinds of communication that occur in social interaction.

Distance and disclosure.   In general, the closer we are standing or sitting to another person, the more intimate our conversation is. This effect is probably circular: a desire for intimacy draws us closer, and when we are closer, we are more inclined to be intimate.

In the discussion of self-disclosure, we noted that women typically disclose more than men. If this is true, then we might expect that they would naturally stand somewhat closer to people when they talk than men do. In fact, we might predict that two women would stand closer to each other than a man and a woman, and two men would stand farthest apart of all. Several studies confirm these predictions (Hartnett, Bailey, & Gibson, 1970; Horowitz, M. J., Duff, & Stratton, 1970; Liebman, 1970; Sommer, 1959). It is not clear, though, whether women stand closer because they wish to disclose more, whether they disclose more because they stand closer, or whether some other factors affect both disclosure and distance.

If friends disclose more to each other than strangers and if disclosure is best done at small interpersonal distances, then we might predict that friends stand or sit closer to each other than do strangers. Research has revealed some interesting supporting evidence. For instance, friends and people who are sexually attracted to each other stand closer than others do (Aiello & Cooper, 1972; Allgeier & Byrne, 1973). This effect is so common, though, that it is part of common sense. People may be "close friends," "distant relatives," "insiders," and the like. We understand that interpersonal distance is a sign of intimacy. So when we want to show people that we like them, we may choose smaller distances (Lott, D. F., & Sommer, 1967; Patterson, M. L., & Sechrest, 1970). And we may use interpersonal distance to determine how much someone likes us or how much two people like each other.

Because physical interpersonal distance is a sign of social distance or intimacy, we are careful in selecting it and want others to show the same care. For instance, if we are standing on a street corner and a stranger comes up to us and stands very close, we may feel uncomfortable. On an empty sidewalk, this distance is inappropriate among strangers. One study found that, when an experimenter did this to people standing on the corner, they crossed the street much faster than usual (Konečni, Libuser, Morton, & Ebbesen, 1975). Not only may we feel some discomfort when a stranger is too close, but we may also feel some discomfort if a friend is too far away.

We also show respect for the interpersonal distances of others. You might try a little experiment with a friend to see how this works. Stand in a hallway or on a sidewalk on campus, facing each other and talking. As others come along, see what they do. If your experience is like mine, you may find that passersby will often go around, even if this is an inconvenience to them. If they go through, and "violate" your interpersonal space, they may duck their heads or apologize. I have found that men are more likely to go through than women, that high-status people are more likely to go through than low-status people, and that more people go around two high-status people than around two low-status people. The distance you stand from your partner, whether or not you are talking, and the difficulty of going around also seem to have the expected effects.

How do people feel when they have been forced to get too close to someone? In one study, we guessed that, if people are forced to go around, they might feel slightly angry because their path was blocked. If they were forced to go through, we thought, they might feel a little guilty because they had violated a norm. To test this, we "forced" them through in one condition and around in another (using a chair to block one route). Then we asked them to do us a favor after they had passed by. We predicted more helping with guilt than anger, and we found just that. You might try such an experiment, too.

Just how close is close? Too close? Too far? The answer is defined by you, by the situation, and by your social class and culture. Each person probably has his or her own ideas of appropriate distances for various situations: some of us feel comfortable at smaller distances than others. Nevertheless, we generally conform to class and cultural norms. Members of the middle class in the United States seem to prefer greater distances than members of the lower class, regardless of their race (Aiello & Jones, 1971; Scherer, 1974). And White Americans seem to prefer greater distances than Hispanics (Baxter, 1970). It seems likely that each culture has somewhat different norms defining what is the "right" interpersonal distance (Hall, 1959, 1966).

Seating position and leadership.   Figure 7-2 is a view of a room, looking down from the ceiling. Who do you suppose is the leader at Table 1? At Table 2? At Table 1, the best guess is Person A. At Table 2, either D or H is most likely to be the leader. There are several reasons for this.

First, even if people are randomly assigned to seating positions, those people in positions A, D, or H are likely to be most talkative, perhaps because they have the best eye contact with others and because eye contact is essential in getting someone's attention before speaking (Silverstein & Stang, 1976; Ward, 1968). Talkativeness, in turn, is related to and often results in leadership (see Figure 7-2). This may simply be because in the act of speaking you momentarily exert leadership, and the more you speak, the more you lead (Stang, 1973).

A second reason: because it is easier to speak to the group from some seating positions than from others, those wishing to speak (the leaders) tend to *choose* those positions that face the most other group members (Hare & Bales, 1963;

Figure 7-2. Leadership positions. (From "Seating Position and Interaction in Triads: A Field Study," by C. H. Silverstein and D. J. Stang, *Sociometry*, Vol. 39, 1976, Figure 1 on p. 166. Copyright 1976 by the American Sociological Association. Reprinted by permission.)

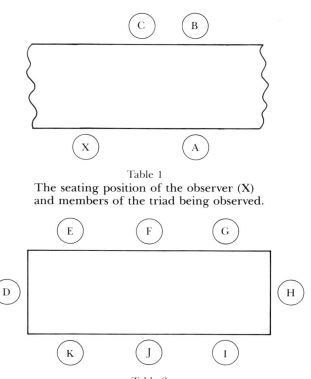

Table 1

The seating position of the observer (X) and members of the triad being observed.

Table 2

Where are the leaders seated?

Sommer, 1961; Strodtbeck & Hook, 1961). When you were young, your father and mother probably sat in positions D and H at the dinner table, your brothers and sisters and you along the sides. At committee meetings, the chairperson typically sits at D or H, others at the sides of the table. When D is occupied by the leader, position H may be avoided, if no one is interested in challenging the leader.

A third reason for guessing that A, D, and H are the leaders is simply common sense. The preceding two paragraphs put into words things that amateur social psychologists have known all along. The hostess, the teacher, and even the author of the Apostles' Creed[2] recognize the effects of seating position on leadership.

Communication networks.   We have just seen that seating position has effects on talkativeness and leadership emergence. Such effects may occur because certain positions around the table make it easier or more difficult for the people sitting there to talk. In everyday life, we may find it easy to talk to some people and difficult or impossible to have access to others. Researchers studying this topic have described it in terms of **communication networks**, or patterns that define

---

[2]In the Apostles' Creed, Jesus is described as sitting at the right hand of God.

whether a **channel** between two positions is *open* or *closed*. For example, in Figure 7-3, a variety of networks are shown. In each, a circle defines a position (person), and a line indicates that the two positions connected by it are able to communicate with each other; that is, the channel is open. If no line connects two positions, that channel is closed, and no communication is permitted. In real life, factors such as status, proximity, and similarity determine how much two people talk to each other, if at all. In the laboratory, channels are opened or closed by using intercoms or by passing written notes.

Although a variety of communication patterns are possible, it may be convenient to think of them all in terms of their degree of **centralization** or **decentralization**. A central position is one that has many open channels. The boss's secretary, for instance, is usually very central in an organization, because he or she can talk to nearly everyone else with little difficulty. A noncentral position has few open channels. The janitor who comes in to clean the offices at night is in such a position. In a centralized organization, there is a great difference between the most central and least central position (for example, the *wheel* in Figure 7-3 is the most centralized). In a decentralized network, there may be no difference between most central and least central (for example, the *circle* of Figure 7-3). How centralized is the *Y*? The *chain*?[3]

Figure 7-3. Some communication patterns in four- and five-member groups. Each circle indicates the *position* of one group member; each link between circles represents a two-way *channel* of communication between two members. (Adapted from Leavitt, 1951, and M. E. Shaw, 1954a.)

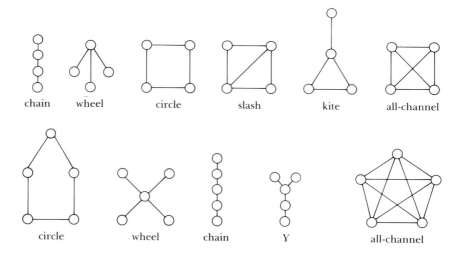

Effects of centrality. Laboratory studies of communication networks find that a person's **centrality** has many effects on him or her. People who are central in the network send the most messages (Leavitt, 1951) and are the most influential and least influenced (Goldberg, S. C., 1955). They have the highest morale and highest status (Bavelas, 1953; Christie, Luce, & Macy, 1952; Leavitt, 1952; Shaw, 1954a; Trow, 1957).

---

[3]The *Y* is less centralized than the *wheel*. The *chain* is less centralized than the *Y*. The *circle* and *all-channel* are completely decentralized.

Other studies find that the degree of centralization has effects on group functioning. As compared with decentralized groups, centralized groups develop internal organizations more rapidly and show more agreement on who the leaders are (Leavitt, 1952). Centralized groups seem to be more satisfying to group members (Leavitt, 1952). And they are often more efficient at solving problems (Cohen, A. M., & Mennic, 1961). But no single communication network seems to be most efficient for all tasks (Heise & Miller, 1951; Macy, Christie, & Luce, 1953; Shaw, 1958; Shaw, Rothschild, & Strickland, 1957).

In many small groups and most organizations, communication is somewhat restricted. Not everyone can talk to everyone else with equal ease. In an effective organization only those who need to communicate with one another are able to. Ideally, those who need not communicate should find communication difficult, if unnecessary communication interferes with their work and creates "noise."

Just as the channels of communication bind a group or organization together, they also bind a nation. Suppose you receive a letter from a stranger describing someone you do not know. The description includes the name, city, and occupation. You are instructed to mail the letter to an acquaintance who might be more likely to know the person than you. How many people would be needed before the letter you received eventually reached the person described? You may be surprised to learn that in the United States it takes only five or six intermediaries to link together any two strangers (Milgram, 1967). Through chains of acquaintances, information, news, and rumor may pass fairly quickly, even in a "group" the size of the United States.

Power and the amount and direction of communication.   If the *amount* that we speak gives us power in a small group, then by speaking we acquire power, and by allowing others to speak we give power. Most communication is probably between people of equal status. But when it is across status lines, it is more likely to be initiated in an upward rather than downward direction. That is, low-status people are more likely to initiate a conversation with high-status people (gain power) than vice versa (share power) (Cohen, A. R., 1958; Hurwitz, Zander, & Hymovitch, 1953; Kelley, 1951; Riley, Cohn, Toby, & Riley, 1954; Thibaut, 1950). One result of this tendency toward upward communication is that, the higher a person's status, the more information he or she has access to. Having more information may mean a greater ability to solve problems (Collins & Raven, 1969). Because knowledge is power, upward communication patterns help the powerful acquire more power. Presumably, upward communication is most likely when people want to improve their status and when they see such communication as providing such an opportunity. Downward communication should be most likely among people not concerned with their status, those with high self-esteem, and those not fearful that such communication will reduce their status.

But this may be an oversimplification. Upward and downward communication may differ in content and style. Upward communication is usually more positive and more polite, and we are reluctant to transmit bad news, especially upward. After all, higher-status people may reward or punish, depending on what they learn. Legend has it that Greek runners bearing bad news sometimes lost their heads (literally)! Low-status group members may feel discomfort, and much of what they say may be intended to make them feel more comfortable (Hurwitz et al., 1953).

Nonverbal Communication. Spoken language is the most common form of social interaction. When we interact with other people, we attend primarily to what they say and mainly think about what we say. Many nonverbal behaviors are noticed only when they are unusual or unexpected. And perhaps nonverbal behaviors are more likely to be misinterpreted than verbal behaviors. One fact is certain: when we interact, we often need to spend most of our attention concentrating on what the other person says and what we say in return. There may simply not be enough mental capacity left to use the full variety of nonverbal behaviors which occur. However, researchers now realize that even with this emphasis on talking the other behaviors in social interaction are also important.

One of the early pioneers in the study of nonverbal behavior was the anthropologist Edward T. Hall, author of *The Hidden Dimension* and *The Silent Language*. His interest in nonverbal behavior came about in part because of the variety of nonverbal behaviors he saw when watching interaction between people from other cultures. He noticed it because it was different. Once the variation in nonverbal behavior became apparent, social psychologists and others became aware that it was indeed an important part of communication. Psychologists now generally agree that inner feelings, emotions, and conflicts can be detected with some accuracy by a sensitive observer of nonverbal behavior (Baxter & Rozelle, 1975).

Because there is no one system, or "language," of nonverbal behavior, it has been more convenient to study the various parts of the body or types of behaviors that seem to play an important role in communication. Four basic areas have been commonly used: interpersonal distance, facial expression, gazing behavior, and paralanguage. It is possible that the main message of a given behavior is related to what causes the sender to perform the behavior in the first place. We call this similarity between cause and message the *primary meaning*. Thus, if one person's emotional state is primarily responsible for his or her facial expression, we would expect a second person to notice the facial expression and wonder about the emotional state behind it. Every nonverbal behavior can be examined both in terms of what causes it in the first place (a study of the sender), and in terms of the impact it has on a person exposed to it (a study of the receiver).

Distance. Perhaps the most basic and important nonverbal channel is the distance we use in interacting with other people. Two general areas are included in the study of interpersonal distance—**personal space** and **interpersonal space**. Personal space is defined as that area around your body that you feel control over and into which another person may not come unless you allow it. The implication of this for communication is that we react very differently to people depending on how they treat our personal space. Personal space is always carried with the person, as opposed to territory, which has a particular physical location that remains constant.

Facial Expression. We all know the importance of reading another's feelings by watching his or her face. Much of the time during interaction is spent looking at some part of our coactor's face. The most important type of information gained from the face is the expression and communication of emotions. Knowing what emotion a person feels can obviously help us in a social situation. When a friend opens a letter, his or her expression may reveal the content of the letter. A second consequence of determining the emotion is that it allows us to predict the future

"*Violation of personal space.*"

behavior of the person observed. A happy face over an income-tax refund tells us that it is a good time to ask the recipient for a loan.

Given that knowledge of emotional states is so important to social interaction, psychologists have asked how accurately we identify emotional states from facial expressions. The general answer is that we are probably not as good as we think we are. Several problems exist with providing a simple answer to this question of accuracy. One major issue is defining what the basic emotions are. In fact, early psychologists wanted to go the opposite way. They wanted to determine what emotions existed by studying facial expression. When we ask people to judge a particular expression, we might give them a series of photographs posed by actors (it is very hard to create true emotions in the laboratory). Then we could provide them with a series of labels (happy, sad, angry, fearful) with the hope that matching the labels with the photos will give an accurate index. The best research in this area has used films or videotapes of people in actual emotional situations and provided judges with basic labels. The early work of Woodworth and Schlossberg has not been improved on significantly, however. There is general agreement among theorists that the basic emotions expressed in the face are happiness, sadness, fear, anger, disgust, and surprise (Ekman & Friesen, 1971).

The *meaning* of a facial expression may be different for the person making the expression than for the person perceiving it (see Figure 7-4). If there is agreement, it is because both have learned to attach particular meaning to the facial expression. For example, we usually interpret a smile as a sign of pleasure. Some therapists, however, agree that certain "inappropriate smiles"—for which Richard Nixon was famous—signal tension, anger, and hostility. Interestingly, the resemblance between the smile and the snarl is striking. When a filmmaker wants

Figure 7-4.
Is this man laughing? The meaning of a facial expression may be different for the person making the expression and for the person perceiving it. (*Feel All Right*, 1980, © Melinda Gebbie.)

a chimpanzee to "smile," she may threaten the chimp, who responds by the bared teeth (smile?) of counterthreat.

Although the meanings of many nonverbal expressions have been socially constructed, there is often widespread agreement on these meanings. Some of our facial expressions, in fact, have the same meanings in all cultures studied. For instance, lowered eyebrows accompany aggression in children (Blurton Jones, 1971; Brannigan & Humphries, 1972), dominance or threat in monkeys and apes (Andrew, 1963; Van Hooff, 1967), and anger or dominance among adults of various cultures (Ekman & Friesen, 1971; Keating, Mazur, & Segall, 1977). Raised eyebrows signify surprise, submission, recognition, or fear. Some authors, including Charles Darwin (1872), have proposed that many of our facial expressions are not learned but have biological origins that may date back hundreds of thousands of years.

But whether or not the meaning of a particular facial expression is culturally defined, our accuracy in interpreting that meaning is influenced by our understanding of the social context and what is "appropriate." For instance, if we can see a man smiling and if we know that he is talking to someone he does not like, we are more likely to see those aspects of the smile that make it "plastic." In one study (Cline, 1956) the actual interpretation of any given facial expression (he used simple drawings) was dependent on what type of second facial expression it was paired with. A smile paired with an angry face was seen as belonging to a "gloating bully," whereas one with a sad face was seen as comforting.

In conclusion, it seems that, rather than being a primary indicator of another's feelings, facial expressions probably allow us to double-check our guess about the person's emotional reaction to the situation that we already have knowledge of.

Gazing Behavior.   The most frequent target of our gaze within another person's face is the eyes. Mutual gazing, sometimes called eye contact, occurs when two persons look at each other's eyes at the same time. What does it mean to look at someone's eyes? Why do we spend so much time during interaction—sometimes as much as 60% of the time—looking at the other person's eyes? The most reasonable answer comes from the concept of primary meaning introduced earlier. The main determinant of our gaze direction, whether we are looking at someone's face or at the sky, is our attention. When we want to know about something, we look at it. This can occur even when there is no information to be gained by looking (Kahneman, 1973). Because what we are thinking about determines where we look, it only makes sense to assume that, if someone watches our eyes, they can tell with some accuracy what we are attending to. In fact, most of the variables that indicate the meanings we attach to gaze direction (liking, power, listening, thinking) are really reflections of the way attention varies.

One of the traditional areas where gazing is important is attraction. If we examine gazing as a response to some internal feelings, we find a fair amount of evidence that our level of attraction toward another person determines how much we will look at them, and at their eyes. Our first reaction when we see someone we like—a physically attractive person, a friend, someone who is nice to us, someone who is familiar, or generally any person whom we would consider to be likable—is to look at them. The more we like someone, the more eye contact we make (Coutts & Schneider, 1976). Further, the more attractive a stranger of the opposite sex is, the more we seem to look at him or her (Coutts & Schneider, 1975; Kleck & Rubenstein, 1975). Although it is natural to assume that attraction therefore determines gaze direction, that conclusion is a bit hasty. One study (Martin, 1974) has found that, if you need to know what someone thinks, you will watch his or her eyes whether you like the person or not.

Even when we examine the meanings for where people look, we find that most of them have something to do with how much the other person is attending to us. In one study (Ellsworth & Carlsmith, 1973), an experimental assistant gave the subject one of two types of evaluation—a very good one or a very bad one. When the assistant gave a good evaluation, she was liked more if she looked at the subject a lot than if she looked at her very little. When the evaluation was bad, however, the opposite effect was found: less looking produced greater liking than more looking. We can easily interpret this to mean that we want people to attend to us when we do well and not to attend to us when we are told we did badly. This dimension of attending through visual behavior is so basic to our everyday lives that we frequently ignore the attending dimension and concentrate on more specific states. Yet as Goffman has said, interaction itself is often defined by an "eye-to-eye . . . huddle," meaning that we know a person is interested in interaction by the fact that he or she looks at us (Goffman, 1966).

In fact, where we are looking is often so much below our awareness that many of us probably do not know about the basic relationship between gazing and distance. Both British and Americans look at one another more the farther apart they stand (Argyle & Dean, 1965; Patterson, M. L., 1973). You probably have noticed that it is more difficult to stare at someone who is very close, but you probably have not realized that the amount of gazing you do changes with distance.

Michael Argyle (Argyle & Dean, 1965) has suggested that for any interaction there may be a "psychological distance" that is most desirable for each participant. A person can increase that distance by avoiding eye contact, moving farther away, turning sideways, or moving so that a barrier (such as a desk or table) is in the way. The psychological distance may be decreased by increasing eye contact, moving closer, facing the other, smiling, and so on. As two people approach each other from a distance, the theory predicts, their eye contact will begin to decrease when they are too psychologically close. This effect has been found in the lab on many occasions (Coutts & Ledden, in press; Coutts & Schneider, 1975; Lesko, 1977; Patterson, M. L., 1973). But it does not always occur (Chapman, 1975).

Paralanguage. Whenever we speak, we do so to communicate our ideas to another person through sounds that have an accepted meaning. But we also produce a wealth of information through the patterning of the sounds that is not necessarily symbolic in value. The sounds that accompany speech are called paralanguage, or paralinguistic cues. Examples of these cues include the rate of speech, loudness, inflection, and clearness of pronunciation. Even pauses between words are considered to be paralanguage. Often many of these cues are combined, and both speaker and listener may use or respond to them without being aware that they are nonverbal. For example, when the same sentence is given with emphasis on different words, we can completely change its meaning. So we see that the basic impact of paralanguage is to allow for clearer interpretation of the messages we normally exchange in social interaction.

We may not always be consciously aware of paralinguistic cues, but we are nevertheless influenced by them, For example, in one study researchers found that, when interviewers asked long questions or made long comments, so did job applicants (Matarazzo, Wiens, Saslow, Dunham, & Voss, 1964). When they made short comments or asked short questions, so did applicants. This paralinguistic cue of "utterance length" was reciprocated by applicants. In another study (Matarazzo & Wiens, 1967), the longer the interviewer's pause before speaking, the longer the inverviewee's pause. Even though we may be unaware of such paralinguistic cues, we are affected by them.

Another very important social aspect of paralanguage is personal identification. Most of us can recognize our friends, relatives, and well-known people by their voices. The ability to recognize voices with which we are familiar is probably due mainly to paralanguage. Even so, we cannot overlook the impact of our knowledge of the situation and expectations of who may be speaking to us. When the phone rings, if you are not expecting a call from an old friend, you may find it hard to recognize the voice. There are some who believe that the visual representation of a voice, using a machine called a spectrograph, allows foolproof identification. As is often the case, the research is not conclusive. Some research has shown that just listening to a voice compares very favorably on identification accuracy with the spectrograph or computer analysis of the sound waves.

Most of the interest in paralanguage has been directed at other consequences of communication. The two other types of socially relevant information that have received the most attention as being derived from paralinguistic cues are the communication of emotions and personality. The real problem with paralinguistic cues to emotion is that they take second place to facial expressions. One study (Leavitt, 1952) found that, when emotions communicated in the face and in paralanguage were compared, subjects gave most weight to the face. Perhaps this is because we tend to consider the voice as being more under conscious control, a condition which over our social experiences would lead us to believe that something that is controlled is not necessarily a true expression of feelings.

A variety of specific cues are associated with specific judgments about personality types. We are familiar with the fact that we can generally judge the sex, age, and cultural background of a speaker through paralinguistic cues. Some research suggests that such cues can also be used with some accuracy to judge intelligence and overall appearance (reviewed in Kramer, E., 1963). In fact, such identifications may then lead to judgments of specific personality traits based on our general stereotypes of a person in that group. In Canada, speaking English with a French accent can lead to being rated as lower in intelligence, likability, dependability, and character than someone who speaks without a French accent. This effect is found even among French-Canadians and with the speaker in both cases delivering the same formal message.

Because we have mentioned the importance of paralanguage for face-to-face interaction, we cannot complete this section until we note that one of the basic events in interaction—taking turns in speaking—is heavily influenced by vocal cues accompanying words. Dropping one's voice usually indicates a willingness to listen, especially when it is accompanied by a pause. Although the gaze direction is also important in this regulation of interaction, the fact that we converse quite well on telephones indicates that the regulatory powers of paralanguage are quite sufficient to allow the normal give and take characteristic of interaction.

There is more to normal communication than meets the eye. And more than meets the ear. Many researchers have spent their lifetime studying communication, but many more are needed. After all, we all spend our lifetimes communicating. More communication research, writing, and teaching can improve this important social process.

SUMMARY

Communication—the exchange of information between people—is a basic, important social process. It can be described in many ways. For instance, it has both an intended meaning and a perceived meaning. Effective communication occurs when these meanings match; factors such as redundancy and processes such as feedback help assure effective communication. In rumors and other forms of communication, leveling (reduction in detail), sharpening (the addition of detail) and assimilation (modification of a message) occur to help make a message more meaningful, but these processes also reduce the accuracy of our stories.

Talkativeness is another dimension of communication. Research suggests that our stereotypes of talkative and quiet people are only partly true. One characteristic of much of our spoken and written communication is the Pollyanna Principle: pleasant words such as *good* are more common than unpleasant words such as *bad*. Many of these characteristics of communication, as well as others, may be studied by interaction-process analysis.

Verbal communication—speaking and writing—and nonverbal communication are the two major forms of communication. They usually, but not always, present similar or complementary information. Speech is probably unnecessary for thought, although it may make thinking easier; both thought and emotion have powerful effects on speech. Where we sit, whether or not we face others, and how far we are from them affects our verbal behavior and the reactions of others to us. The communications network itself affects satisfaction and productivity in small groups and large organizations.

Nonverbal communication involves distance, facial expression, gazing behavior, and paralanguage. Each of these factors has been found to be related to the impressions others form of us and their reactions to us.

GLOSSARY TERMS

Define these terms in your own words, then look them up in the glossary at the back of the book.

Assimilation	Kinesics
Body language	Language
Centrality	Leveling
Centralization	Lexicon
Channels, open and closed	Linguistics
Communication network	Nonverbal communication
Connotative meaning	Paralanguage
Content analysis	Perceived meaning
Data reduction	Personal space
Decentralization	Phonology
Denotative meaning	Pollyanna Principle
Grammar	Redundancy
Intended meaning	Rumor
Interaction-process analysis	Sharpening
Interpersonal space	Verbal communication

FURTHER READING

Chertkoff, J. M., & Esser, J. K. A review of experiments in explicit bargaining. *Journal of Experimental Social Psychology*, 1976, *12*, 464–486. Bargaining is one situation in which communication is very important. A considerable amount of research and theory in this area is reviewed in this scholarly article.

Matlin, M. W., & Stang, D. J. *The Pollyanna Principle*. Cambridge, Mass.: Schenkman, 1978. A thorough discussion of this principle for readers interested in more details.

"EXCUSE ME, YOU APPEAR TO BE VERY COMPETENT AND ATTRACTIVE. IF YOU'RE AVAILABLE WE COULD EXAMINE OUR SIMILARITIES AND THRU INTERACTION OFFER EACH OTHER A FEW SOCIAL REWARDS."

chapter
8

Affiliation, Liking, and Loving

We are born in the family of humankind and are members of that family all our lives. We need one another and depend on one another. Without the love, caring, and helpfulness of others, our lives would be nasty, brutish, and short. We are social animals.

This does not mean that we are lonely when we are alone. Sometimes we seek the company of others, and sometimes we seek solitude. In the first part of this chapter we will seek an answer to the question of why we **affiliate** (seek out the company of others).

In a laboratory experiment, we are assigned to one of the conditions. In real life, we are sometimes "assigned" to particular situations or people, such as roommates or lab partners. But very often we choose our situations and choose our friends. In the second part of this chapter we will briefly examine **availability** and **social desirability** as factors important in these choices. Proximity is important for availability, and similarity, competence, and attractiveness are important for desirability.

Why are these factors important? Similarity, competence, and attractiveness are rewarding; we interact more with those who are desirable and reward us. We also interact more with those who are available and in our proximity. Proximity facilitates interaction, interaction leads to familiarity, and familiarity leads to attraction. In the third part of this chapter we examine details of these and related processes.

Love is the source of some of life's greatest joys and most wretched sorrows. In the fourth part of this chapter we ask what is this thing called love? Then we examine love and sex, passionate love, and love and emotion.

In the final part of the chapter, we will take another look at just how important similarity—and difference—is to attraction.

WHY DO YOU AFFILIATE?

Sometimes we feel a need to be with others. This need for affiliation may be experienced and expressed in various ways: we may feel lonely, have fantasies about being with others, call friends on the phone, or seek them out. When we are with them we may be talkative, self-disclosing, or appear very interested in them. Our need for solitude may be experienced and expressed in just the opposite ways: we may feel "crowded" or "cramped," and we may have fantasies in which we are alone.

Affiliation and Arousal.   One reason we affiliate with certain people at some times but not at others is related to the notion of optimal arousal (see Chapter 5). At any given time there is some level of excitement or calm (arousal) we most prefer. When we choose to affiliate with certain others, it may be because we expect that they will help us to reach some optimal (best) level of arousal. For instance, if you want stimulation, you may seek out an acquaintance who is somewhat unpredictable and exciting. If you are feeling stress and want to lower your arousal, you may seek out a familiar, comforting friend. Or you may prefer to be alone.

Being with others, especially certain novel others, may raise our level of arousal, and being alone or with certain familiar others may lower it. For these reasons we will sometimes feel a need for affiliation with specific others or a need for solitude from specific others.

How is it that others can raise our arousal level when we are bored and lower it when we are too excited? How can affiliation either excite or calm us? When we are extremely excited, those we affiliate with tend to be calmer than we. Through a diffusion of affect (see Chapters 5 and 13) we become somewhat calmer and they become somewhat more excited; that is, the group members shift toward a group average and become more uniform. When we are extremely bored, others we affiliate with tend to be more excited than we are. Again, the group members may shift toward an average. Such shifts probably occur with other emotions, as when a depressed person joins a group and "throws a wet blanket" on its fun.

In Chapter 2 you learned about Schachter's study (1959) of anxiety and affiliation. Many social psychologists have been intrigued with Schachter's work and have continued this line of investigation (Becker, 1967; Buck & Parke, 1972; Firestone, Kaplan, & Russell, 1973; Gerard & Rabbie, 1961; Helmreich & Collins, 1967; Miller, N., & Zimbardo, 1966; Rabbie, 1963; Ring, Lipinski, & Braginsky, 1965; Sarnoff & Zimbardo, 1961; Wrightsman, 1960b; Zimbardo & Formica, 1963). Most of this research has found that, when people are feeling fearful or anxious, they may wish to be with others (see Interest Box 8-1). This is especially true if the situation is one that doesn't embarrass them and if affiliation seems appropriate at the time. When we are worried, our preference may be for others who are facing the same situation. In fact, no matter how we are feeling, we may prefer others who feel that way.

Affiliation with others in stressful situations may give us an opportunity to talk about our feelings; self-expression often calms strong feelings. Thus, affiliation when we are overly aroused may help to lower our arousal level.

Why should we choose to affiliate with others who are experiencing the same stressful situation we are? There are four good reasons. First, affiliation with similar others may be a good strategy to ensure that they will understand our situation and be empathetic. The second reason is more complex. People try to make good impressions and typically appear less anxious than they feel. Thus,

Young baboons
seem to affiliate
when they are
anxious.

This human child is
also seeking relief
from its distress.

being with others who have experienced the same stressful situation may lead you to conclude that they are not feeling very anxious. You may therefore reinterpret your own state as one of lower anxiety than you would if they appeared very anxious or if you were alone. After all, you might say, would the others behave calmly if they felt anxious? If they feel calm, shouldn't I?

A third explanation for why similar people affiliate is that, when we affiliate with people who *appear* calm, we may reduce our anxiety or fear through **imitation** and **self-perception**. When you are with others, you tend to behave the way they do. They serve as models for your behavior. If others are behaving calmly, you may imitate their calm behavior and behave calmly yourself. When you see that you are behaving calmly, you may come to feel calm through self-perception. A fourth explanation—and perhaps the most obvious one—is that the response of similar others in ambiguous but stressful circumstances tells us how we should respond to those circumstances.

Affiliation and Social Comparision.　Being with others is useful. For example, Festinger's (1954) **social-comparison theory** suggested that we have a need to evaluate our opinions and abilities; when objective evaluation is not possible, we compare ourselves with appropriate others. When physical reality is not available for self-evaluations, social reality—the opinions of others—turns out to be very important.

Five-year-olds might directly check with others to evaluate their abilities in games such as Old Maid or basketball: "Am I good, Daddy?" College students evaluate their opinions through a similar process, by finding out if friends agree. Those we respect and who are similar to us provide social reality and form the comparison group we use to evaluate our opinions and ability. We often seek out similar others for social comparison. Comparing ourselves with dissimilar others seems silly. No marathon runner would evaluate her ability by comparison with a 5-year-old. Not only do such comparisons give you direct verbal information on your own abilities and opinions, but the company you keep in making these comparisons helps strengthen your evaluations. Interest Box 8-2 summarizes the research findings on social comparison.

Interest Box 8-1.　Anxiety and Affiliation in Rats and Students

Davits and Mason (1955) have found that the presence of an unafraid rat reduces the fear of another rat under stress. Zajonc (1965) suggested that the fearful animal may be calmed by imitation of the unafraid animal's calm behavior. Perhaps both rats and people in stressful situations in which an unstressed other is placed observe the calm behavior of the other, imitate that calm behavior, and then observe their own calm behavior and conclude that they are calm.

Are you more likely to seek out others when you are anxious than when you are not? Berscheid and Walster (1969) have suggested a simple experiment that you might try after you have studied this. Try coming to class a few minutes early on the day of an exam and a few minutes early on a day when no exam is being given. On an exam day, when people are anxious, you might hypothesize that students will arrive earlier than on a nonexam day, will be seated closer together, will engage in more conversation, and will seem friendlier. Any truth in these hypotheses?

WHOM DO YOU CHOOSE TO BE WITH?

In the first part of this chapter, we looked at why people choose to be together much of the time. But *whom* do you choose to be with? Everyone is different, of course, and has unique preferences. But regardless of the situation or task, the

---

Interest Box 8-2.   Social Comparison and Affiliation*

Social psychologist Ladd Wheeler (1974) has summarized the research on social comparison and affiliation in this way:

1. *Opinions.* There is evidence that uncertainty about an opinion leads to affiliation; that individuals doubting the accuracy of their opinion choose to affiliate with others in agreement with them and with others whom they expect to be correct; that prior disagreement increases attraction toward someone who agrees; and that agreement is most closely related to attraction if the issues are nonverifiable and nonobjective. Agreement by a dissimilar other increases confidence more than agreement by a similar other on belief issues: the opposite is true for value.

2. *Emotions.* In general, the evidence indicates that emotional arousal (usually fear) leads to affiliation with others in the same situation and with others who are responding with the same emotional intensity. This tendency is heightened if the subject's reactions appear to be erratic. Being with others results in a homogenization of emotional intensity within the group.

There is some evidence that older and wiser people are preferable to peers for purposes of emotional comparison.

Under some circumstances, emotional arousal leads to a reduction in affiliation. These circumstances have not been adequately specified, but they may include motives such as embarrassment about one's emotional response, depressive reactions, lack of emotional support, and fear of further emotional stimulation.

3. *Abilities.* There is evidence that uncertainty about an ability leads to affiliation, particularly with someone of similar ability; and that people of nonaverage ability have difficulty making an accurate judgment of their performance and may, therefore, have unusually strong affiliative preferences.

4. *Personality traits.* If subjects are uncertain about the possible or actual range of a personality trait, they choose to learn about other subjects at the extremes. If they know the upper and lower limits of obtained scores, there is a shift toward learning about the most similar scores, but there is still a tendency to choose extreme scores even when they provide very little information. This is probably a defensive choice. There is additional evidence that when subjects receive unexpectedly negative information about themselves, they want to learn about someone who is worse off.

Some personality similarity with another person makes him more salient as a comparison person and more able to elicit positive or negative affective responses.

5. *Individual differences.* There is some evidence that first-born children have stronger affiliative needs under emotional arousal than do later-borns. First-borns also like those with whom they share stress, and they avoid affiliation when it might stimulate negative emotions. First-borns affiliate more than later borns with both a supportive and a neutral other under both conditions of embarrassment and fear. First-borns who affiliate were found in one study to have a higher level of self-esteem than those who did not affiliate.

Extroverts have been found to be more affiliative under stress than introverts (though not under normal conditions). Finally, individuals low in chronic anxiety affiliated more in a study when they were emotionally aroused due to the anticipation of self-disclosure or the sucking manipulation; the reverse was found for individuals high in chronic anxiety [pp. 326–327].

*From "Social Comparison and Selective Affiliation," by L. Wheeler. In T. L. Huston (Ed.), *Foundations of Interpersonal Attraction.* Copyright 1974 by Academic Press, Inc. Reprinted by permission.

research suggests that you choose someone who is:

1. Available
2. Desirable, including
   a. similar
   b. competent
   c. attractive

Availability.   Although there are billions of people in the world that you might choose to be with, to like, or love, there are practical difficulties in meeting them all. In fact, you will actually meet only a small fraction of the world's people and can only expect to like or love a portion of those you meet. Those people you encounter often enough to get acquainted with have been called the **field of availables** (Kerckhoff, 1964). Your friendship choice within the field of availables will focus on those you find most desirable, the *field of desirables*. Before we discuss the field of desirables, though, we should look at a major influence on the field of availables—**proximity**, or closeness in space.

Proximity and attraction.   You and I may be "drawn together" and become "close friends." Or we may "drift apart." Most of us have "distant relatives." The idea of social distance uses a spatial metaphor to indicate degrees of intimacy. The metaphor may be apt, because there is evidence that contact between people may have strong effects on their liking for each other. When we were children, most of our friends probably lived down the block—our block—rather than on some block across town. As adults, the same principle still holds (see Figure 8-1).

Figure 8-1. Partying patterns. Whyte's study of the social columns in the newspaper in one suburban community found that people who lived near one another tended to party together. The map above shows partying patterns for a six-month period. (From *The Organization Man*, by W. H. Whyte, Jr. Copyright © 1956 by William H. Whyte, Jr. Reprinted by permission of Simon & Schuster, a Division of Gulf & Western Corporation.)

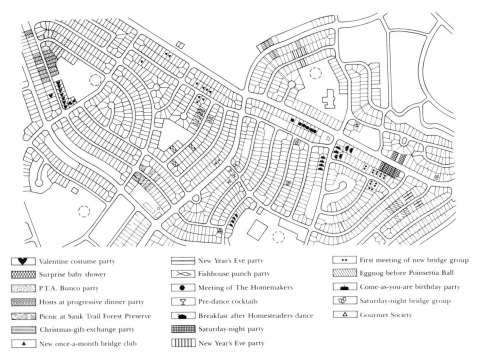

Valentine costume party	New Year's Eve party	First meeting of new bridge group
Surprise baby shower	Fishhouse punch party	Eggnog before Poinsettia Ball
P.T.A. Bunco party	Meeting of The Homemakers	Come-as-you-are birthday party
Hosts at progressive dinner party	Pre-dance cocktails	Saturday-night bridge group
Picnic at Sauk Trail Forest Preserve	Breakfast after Homesteaders dance	Gourmet Society
Christmas-gift-exchange party	Saturday-night party	
New once-a-month bridge club	New Year's Eve party	

Research has shown that people who work or live near one another often wind up liking one another (Athanasiou & Yoshioka, 1973; Caplow & Forman, 1950; Kipnis, 1957; Merton, 1947; Nahemow & Lawton, 1975; Rosow, 1961; Whyte, 1956). Similar effects of proximity on attraction occur in small groups (Blake, Rhead, Wedge, & Mouton, 1956). They have also been documented in classrooms (Byrne & Buehler, 1955) and dormitory rooms (Segal, 1974). Within a city people who live near one another are more likely to intermarry than are those who live farther apart, even though the number of people available to marry increases as the square of the distance from one's home (Bossard, 1932; Katz, A. M., & Hill, R., 1958). Thus, one study (Bossard, 1932) found that one-third of 5000 couples applying for marriage licenses lived within five blocks of each other at the time of application. Half lived within 20 blocks. (Today, of course, our norms have changed, and many people who decide to marry are living in the same bedroom when they apply for a marriage license. Proximity leads to attraction and attraction leads to proximity.)

Proximity isn't the only determinant of availability. Other factors such as marital status are also important. And some factors may be confounded with proximity. For instance, people are more likely to marry others of similar socioeconomic status. Our segregated residential patterns often mean that people of similar socioeconomic status live closest to each other. And, of course, proximity doesn't always lead to friendship or romance. For instance, Festinger (1950) cited a study of a government housing project where residents felt they had been forced to live: "Many residents . . . had not expected to like the type of person who lived [there]. . . . There was a surprisingly great amount of hostility expressed toward neighbors in the project" (p. 161).

You will not like everyone you find yourself living or working near. Proximity seems to work to increase the amount of **interaction** we have with people. Interaction, in turn, tends to intensify initial feelings. Most first impressions are fairly positive, so interaction turns most acquaintances to friends. But some initial impressions are negative, and interaction sometimes makes these impressions worse. Thus our most intense feelings seem to be for those we are closest to (Schiffenbauer & Schiavo, 1976). These feelings are often—but not always—positive.

Proximity thus increases the amount of interaction we have with another. This increase may be partly a result of the reduced costs—in time and effort—of interaction. It's easier to talk to someone who is across the room than someone who is across the country. We'll look at the relation between interaction and attraction later in this chapter.

Desirability.   From the field of availables some people will be more desirable than others. It is from a field of availables who are also desirable that we choose our friends and lovers. What defines the field of desirables? Three factors are probably most important: **similarity, competence,** and **attractiveness.** The reasons for their importance will be discussed in the third part of the chapter. Other factors in social desirability include health, wealth, power, and intelligence; these will not be discussed.

Measuring Liking.   What do we mean when we say we like someone? Zick Rubin (1970, 1973) offers an operational definition of liking that includes perceived similarity, affection, and respect. He has used a "liking scale" (Interest Box 8-4) to measure liking.

Another method of measuring liking is with a technique called **sociometry** developed by Moreno. In a small group, such as your class, who is most attracted to whom? The study of attraction in small groups often begins by studying the friendship choices of each group member (sometimes also called sociometric choices). In these studies each group member is typically asked to write down the names of one or two persons with whom he or she is closest in the group. Individuals are then given code letters (such as their initials), which are arranged on a sheet of paper. Arrows are drawn between the code letters to indicate who has chosen whom as best friend in the group. The resulting diagram is called a **sociogram**. Most groups have **stars** (people who are chosen as friends by a relatively high proportion of other group members) as well as **isolates** (those who are underchosen). In Figure 8-2 individuals A and B are stars, and C and D are isolates. Individuals E, F, and G have what Heider has referred to as an imbalanced relationship, and individuals G, H, and I are in the state of balance with respect to one another.

Figure 8-2.
Sociogram. Arrows indicate the two choices of best friend each of these nine students has made.

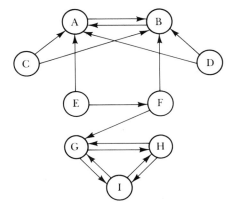

EXPLAINING YOUR ATTRACTION

Liking another may seem like "doin' what comes naturally," but in fact it is a complex process. Figure 8-3 diagrams the attraction process. Each major variable is enclosed in a box, and arrows indicate which variables affect which. Other variables and arrows could be added, but this model is already very complex. Each variable and arrow will be discussed below, starting with similarity.

Similarity and Proximity.   Because we prefer similar others, we choose situations where we will find them (arrow 1 of Figure 8-3). We choose to live in neighborhoods that are populated with those who are similar to us in social status, ethnic or racial identity, and probably other dimensions (Duncan & Duncan, 1960; Lieberson, 1963; Taeuber & Taeuber, 1965). Because of this preference, neighborhoods become homogeneous, and residential segregation occurs. Such homogeneity of our social environment extends to the clubs and groups we join, our choice of work environments, and so on. Similarity, in short, leads to proximity.

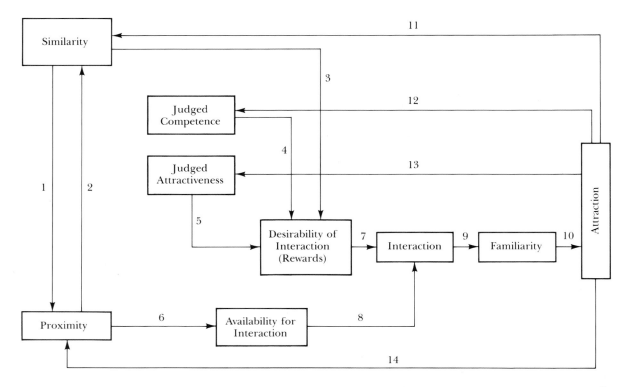

Figure 8-3.
Factors in
attraction. Each
arrow indicates that
one variable affects
another. Numbered
arrows are taken up
sequentially in the
text.

Conversely, proximity to others probably does increase their similarity to us (arrow 2 of Figure 8-3), but the processes are complex. Much of Chapter 13 will explain how groups come to be uniform. By being a member of a group ("proximity"), we are influenced by it, and we become more similar to other members in the group.

Similarity, Competence, and Attractiveness Bring Rewards. As mentioned previously, similarity, competence, and attractiveness are the three most important factors in social desirability. Why are these factors important? We find similarity, competence, and attractiveness to be rewarding (Chapter 4). **Social rewards** refer to pleasures, satisfactions, and gratifications (Homans, 1950, 1956, 1961; Thibaut & Kelley, 1959). Social rewards also include compatibility, respect, trust, and liking (Newcomb, 1956, 1959, 1961). **Social costs,** or punishments, occur when rewards are withdrawn or not given. Social rewards lead to increases in the behaviors that seem to produce them, whereas social costs lead to a reduction in such behaviors.

We like those who give us social rewards and dislike those who give us costs or punishments (Lott, A. J., & Lott, 1965). We most often choose as group leaders those who have rewarded us (Hollander, 1958; Hollander & Julian, 1970). And, in fact, we reward those who reward us. Rewards and punishments are exchanged, or reciprocated.

Reciprocating rewards. The following is a quote from Aristotle:

> Most men wish what is noble, but choose what is profitable; and while it is noble to render a service not with an eye to receiving one in return, it is profitable to receive one. One ought, therefore, if one can, to return the equivalent of services received, and to do so willingly [cited in Tedeschi, 1974, p. 211].

Being liked is one kind of reward we can receive from others. People seem to have a natural tendency to reciprocate in relationships. We do unto others as they do unto us, an eye for an eye, a tooth for a tooth, a kiss for a kiss. When others like us, we tend to like them in return. Other things being equal, the more others like us, the more we like them; the more others dislike us, the more we tend to dislike them (Backman & Secord, 1959; Festinger, Schachter, & Back, 1950; Lott, A. J., & Lott, 1965; Newcomb, 1963). We find it much more pleasant to be with those who like us than with those who do not. So we spend more time with people who are pleasant, who like us, who respect us, who say positive things to us. As Rosenberg has put it, "Friendship is the purest illustration of picking one's propaganda" (1968, p. 343).

Rewards and punishments tend to be reciprocated. One researcher has suggested that interaction often involves "resource exchange" and that the major classes of resources are love, services, money, goods, information, and status (Foa,

People often don't enter into a relationship unless they believe that there is a good potential for reciprocity.

1971; Turner, Foa, & Foa, 1971). When we offer one of these six kinds of resources, apparently we are most likely to receive the same kind in return (Turner et al., 1971). From this analysis it appears that we are more likely to love someone who offers us love than we are someone who performs a service or gives some other resource.

Within a class of resources, one may be exchanged for another. For instance, when people make a positive evaluation of us, we may be inclined to reciprocate with a positive evaluation of them. But we are also likely, through a diffusion of affect, to value them as a work partner, to be more attracted to them, and to adopt a more positive mood (Bell, P. A., & Baron, 1974).

If we find that others like us more than we like them, we tend to increase our level of liking. If we find they like us less, we tend to decrease our liking. We also may engage in behaviors to help them like us more or less, so that their liking for us matches ours for them. Very often we do not enter into a relationship unless we believe that there is some good potential for reciprocity: nobody likes to be shot down.

When other people's attraction to us seems to be increasing, we may like them more than when their attraction remains the same. If their first impressions of us are somewhat negative but if they come to like us over time, we may appreciate their affection far more than if they had liked us very much from the very beginning (Aronson & Linder, 1959; Berkowitz, L., 1960; Clore, Wiggins, & Itkin, 1975). One explanation for these "gain/loss" findings is that change attracts our attention. A change in another's affection for us will be noticed, and our behavior may respond to the change (Berkowitz, L., 1975). When you were young, you may not have thought of your allowance until one week when you did not get it. Then you noticed—and responded.

Our interpretation of the situation can be as important an influence on us as the situation itself. When people reward us, our interpretation of their motives is important. If you believe people have praised you because they were trying to manipulate you or because they felt such praise was expected or required, how do you feel? You probably are not as flattered as when you think praise is freely given. Any reward that we think is given voluntarily means much more to us than one we think is expected or required. People who praise us voluntarily and with no apparent selfish gain are seen as more sincere, and they are more likely to receive our praise in return (Goranson & Berkowitz, 1966; Iverson, 1968; Jones & Davis, 1965; Nemeth, 1970). The meaning of a reward, how we feel about it, and how we behave in return hinges on our interpretation of the rewarder's motives.

Let us look at how similarity, competence, and attractiveness each brings us rewards.

Similarity is rewarding.   Because similarity is so important in attraction, we should suspect that there are several reasons. (We should suspect multiple causes for any strong relationship.) One set of reasons for the similarity/attraction relationship we might label *psychological*. Similarity makes interaction desirable and is rewarding (arrow 3 of Figure 8-3) for several reasons. First, we are more confident that similar others will like us (Insko, Thompson, Stroebe, Shaud, Pinner, & Layton, 1973; Walster & Walster, 1963). And we are confident that they

"We are more likely to praise those who have voluntarily praised us".

will approve of us (Nelson, 1965). Second, similar others tend to agree with us, and this agreement assures us that our own opinions are correct. This **consensual validation** may be important in attraction (Byrne, 1969; Festinger, 1957; Johnson, Gormly, & Gormly, 1973; Newcomb, 1961). Third, when others are similar to ourselves, we attribute to them additional positive qualities we see in ourselves (Fishbein & Ajzen, 1972; Stalling, 1970). Through projection, we see in those we like what we like in ourselves, and, perhaps, in those we dislike what we dislike in ourselves. Whatever the processes, our liking for others seems to be in proportion to the degree to which they agree with us (Byrne, 1969).

Most of us enjoy being "close" to another and sharing our feelings, experiences, and ideas. With a similar other, such sharing is more likely to be reciprocated and thus rewarded. Through reciprocation and mutual reward, self-disclosure moves to more intimate levels and greater liking for the other. Thus, there are many reasons for preferring people similar to us. Can you think of others?

These reasons for preferring similar others lead to norms that develop to summarize the collective wisdom that similarity has a psychological value. These norms become prescriptive personal theories: "You should choose similar others as friends and marriage partners." When this norm is held strongly, sanctions for violating it may also exist. Religious families, for instance, may express strong negative feelings toward a member considering a spouse of another religion and in some cases may disown and effectively segregate a deviant family member.

Freeman has found that those who married or dated outside their own group were often quite alienated from that group, and "a self-perpetuating cycle was built up in which deviation intensified rejection and rejection enhanced deviation" (1955, p. 372). Another researcher (Heiss, 1960) reported that deviation in the form of interreligious marriages was most common among people from families having a weak religious influence. Interreligious marriage can seriously strain relations with religious parents. To summarize, the psychological advantages of similarity give rise to norms, which, in combination with rewards and punishments, strengthen the similarity/attraction relationship. By choosing similar others, we receive social rewards and avoid social punishments from our friends and family. These rewards and punishments affect the probability of our interaction with the other (arrow 7 of Figure 8-3).

Competence is rewarding.   We are rewarded for interacting with competent others (arrow 4 of Figure 8-3). We may find, for instance, that competent others are more likely to be correct, so by being with them we obtain more accurate information. Competent people are more likely to have social power, wealth, and influence and thus be in a better position to share these resources with us. As we are judged by the company we keep, others may think we are competent when we are with others of known high competence.

Attractiveness is rewarding.   We are also rewarded for interacting with attractive others (arrow 5 of Figure 8-3). Being with an attractive person is good for self-esteem. Through social comparison we are able to conclude that we must be attractive if this attractive person would be willing to be with us. Further, we are likely to be judged desirable by others for the attractive company we keep. How often have you seen a good-looking man or beautiful woman with an unattractive older person and concluded that "the unattractive person must be rich or something"? Several studies have found that men rise in status—in the eyes of their peers—when they are involved with beautiful women (Bar-Tal & Saxe, 1976; Hartnett & Elder, 1973; Sigall & Landy, 1973). People who are attractive but have low self-esteem may avoid trying to go out with extremely attractive people out of anxiety that they might be rejected because they are not "good" enough.

Attractive others seem to have a greater capacity than unattractive others to reward or punish us (Sigall & Aronson, 1969). As a consequence, if those we are with normally reward us, attractive others may be liked more than unattractive others, because they are typically more rewarding.

To summarize, people who are similar to us, whom we judge as competent and attractive, can give us social rewards. We desire to interact with them and do so (arrow 7 of Figure 8-3). Remember, although similarity, competence, and attractiveness make interaction *desirable*, our interaction is limited to those who are *available*. Proximity to others is a major factor in their availability for interaction (arrow 6 of Figure 8-3). Both desirability (arrow 7) and availability (arrow 8) determine the likelihood of interaction. We are most likely to interact with someone who is *both* desirable and available.

Interaction Leads to Attraction.   A classic study of proximity and attraction was conducted by social psychologists Leon Festinger, Stanley Schachter, and Kurt Back (1950). They studied what happened when couples who had been assigned to apartments in a housing complex made friends with others in the complex. These researchers found that those who lived in very accessible locations such as near the stairways and mailboxes got to know more people than did those in less

The more opportunities for interaction, it seems, the more likely it is that people will become friends.

accessible locations. They also found that next-door neighbors were much more likely to become friends than neighbors two doors away and that they, in turn, were much more likely to become friends than neighbors three doors away. The more opportunities for interaction, it seems, the more likely it is that people will become friends. Several studies have found, for instance, that eye contact between two persons tends to increase their **interaction rates** (the amount they say to each other) (Hearn, 1957; Silverstein & Stang, 1976; Steinzor, 1950).

Interaction with others, in turn, often increases our liking for them (Lott, A. J., & Lott, 1965). As Homans said, "Other things equal, the more a man interacts with another, the more he likes him" (1961). Presumably this applies to women, too.

Some of you might object to this proposition, for as we learn about the other through interaction, there is always the possibility that we will discover more dissimilarity than similarity of values and interests. In this case interaction may not lead to attraction. But, in general, interaction leads to liking. For example, one study found that undergraduates in discussion groups liked most those other students who had talked most (Stang, Castellanetta, Constantinidis, & Fortuno, 1976). The correlation between judged talkativeness and judged likableness was .72, a strong relationship. Other studies have found that people who talk more tend to be liked more (Bass, 1949; Borgatta & Bales, 1956; Lott, A. J., & Lott, 1961; Norfleet, 1948; Slater, 1955).

Other evidence suggests that we do not necessarily prefer the *most* talkative person in the group—he or she may seem like a "big mouth" (Bales, 1953, 1970;

Stang, 1973). And, if we are talkative ourselves, we may prefer friends who are good listeners. Further, we might wonder why talkative people are liked. Is it admiration for their competence? Do we feel relief that we are not pressured to keep up the conversation? Or is it that people we like we reward for talking, and therefore they talk more? It may also be that norms develop in some groups that regulate how much a person should say and that people who violate that norm may be liked less than those who do not. In a newly created group, which lacks such norms, the most talkative person may be best liked. But in an established group, we may grow weary of the most talkative person. *What* people say is probably more important than *how much* they say.

Interaction, familiarity, and attraction.   One possible explanation of the effects of interaction on liking is that interaction with others increases our familiarity with them (arrow 9 of Figure 8-3), and familiarity generally increases our attraction (arrow 10 of Figure 8-3). Are you more attracted to those people you are familiar with? Yet we have heard that sometimes "familiarity breeds contempt" and "absence makes the heart grow fonder." Under certain conditions each of these pieces of folk wisdom is undoubtedly true.

Mae West's formula is that, "When caught between two evils, I like to take the one I never tried." **Novel** stimuli (people, places, things) are interesting, attract our attention, and sometimes raise our arousal level more than familiar stimuli. They may or may not be pleasant. Nevertheless, given a choice between exploring a novel stimulus and a very familiar one, we generally prefer to explore the novel one if we are fairly relaxed or bored or if both stimuli are fairly simple. We may prefer to explore the familiar stimulus if we are fairly anxious or frightened or if both stimuli are quite complex.

In the process of looking at, listening to, or otherwise being exposed to a novel stimulus, we learn about it. We feel comfortable with things we know about and find them pleasant, although they aren't generally as exciting as things we don't know about. Holding other factors constant, the more we see it, the more we learn about it—and the more we like it (Stang, 1975a). Whether or not learning is involved, these positive effects of familiarity on liking seem to occur with all sorts of stimuli. Studies have been done involving real people (Brockner & Swap, 1976; Saegert, Swap, & Zajonc, 1973). They have also been done with photos of strangers (Wilson, W., & Nakajo, 1965), with public figures (Harrison, 1969), and with candidates for student government (see Interest Box 8-3). And other studies have involved nonsense words (Stang, 1974b; Zajonc, 1968; Zajonc & Rajecki, 1969), ideographs (Moreland & Zajonc, 1976), and past U.S. presidents (Stang, 1977). After you have become very familiar with the stimulus and learned most of what you will learn about it, you may begin to avoid exposure to it. If you must continue being exposed to it, you may find the stimulus becoming less pleasant. After an absence of exposure, however, this unpleasantness may diminish, and you may like it again (Stang, 1975b).

We might summarize these propositions as follows: Although we may find novel stimuli somewhat discomforting, we may attend to them. During this attention we learn about them, and this learning is reinforced through an increase in stimulus pleasantness. After we have learned about them, we normally turn our attention elsewhere. But if we must continue looking at them, increased familiarity

Interest Box 8-3. Foot Powder Elected Mayor: Familiarity and Voting

Robert Zajonc has reported an extensive political "saturation campaign on behalf of one unknown fellow [conducted] by flooding the city with signs saying *three cheers for Pat Milligan*. . . . The advertisement of the slogan went on for months, and on election day Pat Milligan was the undeniable winner. What else but the effects of mere exposure?" (1970, p. 62). In an even more extreme example, the news agency Reuters (cited in Ornstein, undated) reported that a foot powder named *Pulvapies* was elected mayor of an Ecuadorean town of 4100. During the election campaign, the foot-deodorant firm used the slogan "Vote for any candidate, but if you want well-being and hygiene, vote for *Pulvapies*." The town of Picoaza elected the powder by a clear majority.

To study the effects of repeated exposure in political campaigns, three researchers conducted a phony election (Schaffner, Wandersman, & Stang, 1978). College students were asked to rank-order six "candidates" for editor of a proposed university literary magazine. The students were asked how likely they were to vote for each candidate in the upcoming "elections." These candidates were actually six nonsense words that pretesting had found to be equally pleasant: Mecburi, Nijaron, Borulce, Tavhane, Bozulma and Kadirga. After the initial poll, the college-town area was plastered with campaign posters for these candidates. On the next day, additional students were polled and asked how likely they were to vote for each candidate in the upcoming elections. Each candidate had either 0, 20, or 200 posters displayed; half of the candidates were represented by dittoed posters and the other half by higher quality mimeographed posters. We found that a pretest group of college students—who had not seen any posters—ranked all the "candidates" about the same. A posttest group of students who said they did not see any poster did not differ from this pretest group. But those students who did see any posters ranked most favorably the "candidates" with the most posters. Further, candidates with the high-quality posters received more votes than those with low-quality posters.

In a parallel unpublished study, Perlman, Shann, and Stang looked at a real campus election to see whether the number of posters that candidates had displayed was a better predictor of how many votes the candidates received than was their status as incumbent or nonincumbent. In an analysis of the six races within this election, we found that the actual number of posters displayed was a better predictor. Further, the relationship between number of posters and number of votes was strongest for freshman and lower sophomores and weakest for upper juniors and seniors. This suggested that, the longer the candidates had been on campus, the less dependent they were on posters for their election victories and the more they benefited from previous publicity, social networks, incumbency, and so on.

In some respects, political campaigns are similar to advertising campaigns (Hiebert, Jones, Lotito, & Lorenz, 1971; McGinnis, 1968). And voting behavior is similar to consumer behavior (Roshwald, 1957). Exposure to the names of unknown candidates may result in the learning of their names; the more exposure of a name, the more people were likely to learn it. The better a name is learned, the more it will be liked. This greater liking may emerge as votes cast by the previously uncommitted voters. Of course no amount of simple-minded exposure is going to affect those voters who have direct knowledge and abundant information regarding particular candidates. Unfortunately, most of us are uninformed about most candidates in most elections, leaving the outcome of such elections open to the influence of repeated exposure. Votes require exposure and exposure costs money. How many votes can money buy?

Familiarity through repeated exposure might take place in a variety of ways. For instance, candidate expenditures on advertising are believed to be important by candidates (Bullit, 1971), journalists (MacNeil, 1968) and campaign consultants (Agranoff, 1972), perhaps because advertising increases familiarity. Media exposure, incumbency, campaigning in prior elections, and notoriety through previous occupations (such as sports or entertainment) all mean increased familiarity. There is now substantial evidence that each of these forms of familiarity is important in influencing voters (Grush, 1978; Grush, McKeough, & Ahlering, 1978; Jacobson, G. C., 1975; Schaffner et al., 1978; Wanat, 1974). These effects of familiarity on voting seem to be especially important in primaries, where candidates are in the same party. In national

---

Interest Box 8-3.   (continued)

elections, many people vote along party or ideological lines, and the effects of advertising may be largely to strengthen voting intentions rather than change them (Klapper, 1961; Sears, 1969; Weiss, W., 1969).

Because candidates are not restricted in using their personal funds to finance their campaigns, wealthy candidates are likely to have a great advantage. The new evidence that money buys familiarity and familiarity brings votes has many important implications for our political process. A number of writers have recognized that the present system of private financing of election campaigns makes equal access impossible. Applied social psychology can take credit for increasing our understanding of this process.

---

breeds contempt. Then with the absence of exposure our "hearts" may once again grow fonder. Let me illustrate these principles by using them to explain the rise and fall in popularity of pop music.

Feelings about popular music seem to be strongly influenced by familiarity. Recall how you react to pop-music selections as you drive along in the car. The first time you hear a song, you may listen to it but not like it very much. If passengers in the car are talking or if you've had a bad day, you may even switch to another station to hear something more familiar, particularly if the song is very complicated, the words difficult to understand, and so on.

Eventually, you'll hear that song again as it rises on the charts. As you hear it, you'll learn the words and learn little variations in the melody. You'll be able to hum along and you may come to enjoy the song.

Assuming you have come to like it through repeatedly hearing it, you may eventually get sick of it, depending on how often you've heard it, how familiar you are with similar songs, how complex the song is, and so on. But as you get sick of it, you'll start changing the station when it comes on to avoid hearing it. Often this strategy won't completely prevent further exposure (the song on another station could be worse), and soon you'll hate the song. Fortunately, this experience happens to most everyone, and the song drops on the charts and is no longer played on the station. What you can't hear doesn't bother you, and a month or two later the song is an oldie but goodie—it's enjoyable to hear again. This time, however, you'll get sick of it a lot faster than you did the first time.

This phenomenon has been observed with stimuli other than pop music, such as food tastes (Stang, 1975b), platform shoes, midi-dresses, and all sorts of fads. Does it apply to people, too?

Our exposure to novel or familiar people and things is sometimes beyond our control, but we usually do have control over this exposure. We can often choose whether or not to be exposed to a stimulus, avoiding things we are tired of and seeking things we are interested in. This often results in "spontaneous alternation" between stimuli: we don't eat the same food, even our favorite, all the time, or see the same person, even our best friend, all of the time. Novelty and newness are the spice of life. Long-term relations or marriages must cope with these facts by regulating (sometimes limiting) contact between partners and by introducing other sources of novelty such as meeting new friends, visiting new places, and being involved in new activities.

The difference between something we feel bored with and something we feel comfortable with may be small. Not only does familiarity breed contempt, it also breeds comfort. There is no place like home for boredom, but also for relaxing at the end of a stressful day. Much of our home life is designed as a quiet refuge from our daily stresses; our arousal level is raised at work, reduced at home. Whereas people who have stressful jobs may find the familiarity of the home comforting, those who are unemployed may find home life dull, tiring, and depressing. Much of the joy or pain in life comes from being able to tread that line between too much novelty, excitement, and stress and too much familiarity, dullness, and calm.

Other Factors in the Attraction Process.   So far, we have reviewed the processes describing arrows 1–10 of Figure 8-3. How about arrows 11–14?

Attraction affects similarity and judged similarity.   Not only are we attracted to similar others, but we become more similar to those we are attracted to (arrow 11 of Figure 8-3). Much of the evidence for this is presented in Chapter 13.

In addition to increases in actual similarity, there are increases in judged similarity. When we like people, we tend to assume that they are more similar to us than they really are. For example, we may assume that they agree with us more and have attitudes more similar to our own than is actually the case (Levinger & Breedlove, 1966). We also assume that people we like are more similar to us than people we dislike (Fiedler, Blaisdell, & Warrington, 1952).

Why do we assume that our friends are more similar to us than they really are? One reason may be that they know we like similar others, they want to be liked, and so they selectively present us with those aspects of themselves that are most similar to us. The experiences, feelings, attitudes, and personal theories they present may be chosen because they are similar and presented in such a way as to make them similar.

One way that we get to know someone is by discovering whether that person describes a third person in the same way we do (Duck, 1977c). You may learn how others think by asking for their views on other **attitude objects**, such as cars, dogs or houses. But because people are more complex than these attitude objects, personal descriptions of them are more self-revealing. When we discuss other people with our friends, we learn whether their personal theories are similar to our own. As stated in Chapter 1, discovering another's personal theories is the essence of learning about their "personality," the self-disclosure that matters most in forming and maintaining friendships.

Attraction affects judged competence.   Attraction also affects judged competence (arrow 12 of Figure 8-3). When we come to like others, our judgments of their competence become more positive. For instance, when we like people, we are more likely to hire them (Griffitt & Jackson, 1970) and to rate them as doing well on some task (Smith, R. E., Meadow, & Sisk, 1970). We are less likely to punish them for mistakes (Banks, 1976), more likely to recommend them for a raise (Griffitt & Jackson, 1970) and even more likely to approve them to receive a loan (Sung, 1975). In short, as our affection for others increases, our respect for them and our perception of their competence also seems to increase.

Such judgments may be self-justified by a self-fulfilling prophecy. A loves B, thinks B very competent, and communicates this belief. B tries to deserve the impression and becomes more competent. A then finds evidence to support the belief in competence, the belief is strengthened, and the cycle continues.

Attraction affects judged attractiveness. If beauty is in the eyes of the beholder, arrow 13 of Figure 8-3 represents this adage. For example, we may judge those who agree with us to be more physically attractive than those who disagree (Walster, 1971a) and those who like us to be more physically attractive than those who do not.

Other studies find that, when people are asked to consider the height of a male political choice, they overestimate in relation to their estimates of the heights of his opponents (Kassarjian, 1963; Ward, 1967). In fact, in every election between 1900 and 1968 the taller of the two U.S. presidential candidates won. Even ethnic groups we like are judged as taller than groups we dislike (Koulak & Tuthill, 1972). One researcher introduced a male "guest lecturer" to five different groups of Australian college students (Wilson, P. R., 1968). For one group, the guest was introduced as a professor of psychology at Cambridge. For a second group, he was introduced as a senior lecturer. For other groups, he was introduced as a lecturer, a demonstrator, or a student. Following this introduction, the college students in each group estimated the height of the visitor and their regular teacher. Although all five groups generally agreed on the height of their regular instructor, when the guest was introduced as a professor from Cambridge, he was judged to be 2½ inches taller than when he was introduced as a student. Similar results have been obtained by other researchers (Dannenmaier & Thumain, 1964).

Folklore may be right; we may assume that "the bigger the better." Tall males, at least, are judged to be more attractive than short ones (Berkowitz, W. R., Nebel, & Reitman, 1971). Tall men are probably more likely to get jobs than short men and often receive higher starting salaries (Knapp, 1972). It may be that we assume that this condition operates in reverse: "the better the bigger." Even though we might have greater respect for tall than short people, respecting people does not make them taller. It should be evident that our inferences from one attribute to another are not always valid. There are always exceptions to our generalizations: some good things come in small packages. Presumably, though, being tall is desirable for politicians who want to be elected and for men who want to be liked. The effects of height on the judged attractiveness of women need to be studied. But one study, at least, finds that, whereas boys worry about being too short, girls are more likely to worry about being too tall.

Attraction affects proximity. How about arrow 14 of Figure 8-3? When we like people, we stand closer to them (Allgeier & Byrne, 1973; Byrne, Ervin, & Lamberth, 1970). We lean toward them rather than away (Mehrabian, 1968b). And we look at them more (Efran, 1969). Physical contact is much more likely among friends. Because attraction leads to proximity, various measures of proximity can be used as measures of attraction. Baron and Byrne have reasoned that, "Because the physical distance we place between ourselves and others is often not a conscious decision, such behavior may sometimes serve as a more sensitive measure of attraction than what we say" (1977, p. 240).

As amateur social psychologists, we can often guess how much people like each other by how close they are. We would guess that those standing several feet apart, making occasional eye contact, and not touching each other are acquaintances. Those who are standing close together gazing into each other's eyes are probably lovers.

A Cross-Cultural Perspective. Throughout this chapter the importance of choice in our attraction to others has been emphasized. In the United States, Canada, and Western Europe, there is considerable freedom of choice in many social behaviors. Where there is freedom of choice, our attraction to others is a prime factor in being with them, having them as friends, and marrying them. But many cultures have limited free choice. In these cultures, attraction is suppressed as a factor in mate selection, and marriages are often arranged (Rosenblatt, 1974). This suppression of attraction is often produced by segregating the sexes, severely punishing premarital sexual activity, and socializing children to accept arrangement rather than attraction as a basis for marriage (Goode, 1959).

It may be hard for us to imagine how people could marry when they do not feel attracted to each other, but this happens all the time in many societies. The fact that marriages in these other societies are so stable compared to our own, where a large percentage of marriages end in divorce, suggests that attraction may make marriage more fun but not necessarily more stable.

LOVE AND LOVING

Amateur social psychologists have acquired first-hand familiarity with romantic love. Such familiarity does not make for expertise, however. Many people find themselves "falling" in and out of love, overwhelmed by positive feelings and, sometimes later, by mixed or negative feelings. Ignorance is not bliss, though. Almost everyone who has ever been upset by a romantic attraction would benefit from understanding it better. This section may add to that understanding.

Definition and Measurement. What is **love**? Philosophers, theologians, and other thinkers have puzzled over that question. The answer is hard to put into words. Love is strong positive attitudes, thoughts, feelings, and behaviors toward another. Love is a felt and expressed warmth. It often includes feelings of sexual attraction toward the other. Rubin (1974, p. 385) and others have suggested some attributes of romantic love. These often include:

- Desire to focus attention on the other, forgetting the world.
- Desire to be exclusively attached to the other, sometimes to possess the other.
- Desire for intimacy with and knowledge of the other and physical and psychological contact.
- Desire to selflessly give and care for the other.
- Desire that these desires and behaviors be reciprocated.

Rubin (1970, 1973) was one of the first social psychologists to measure and study love. (Interest Box 8-4 presents a few items from his *love scale* and his *liking scale*.) Rubin's scale, which is his operational definition of love, includes needs for affiliation and dependency, a desire to be helpful, and feelings of exclusiveness and absorption in the other.

Rubin administered his liking and loving scales to 182 dating couples at the University of Michigan. Some of his findings seem consistent with our common-sense notions of love. For instance, he found a great deal of reciprocation in love, with men loving their partners about as much as women loved theirs. But, perhaps surprisingly, women *liked* their partners more than men did. There was a fairly close relationship between how much the man and woman loved each other but a weaker relationship between how much they liked each other. Further, how much they loved each other was fairly closely related to estimates of how likely it was that they would get married. Liking scores were more weakly related with the likelihood of marriage. Rubin also found that men and women had equal liking for same-sex friends, although women were more willing than men to report love for same-sex friends.

Love and Sex.   Premarital or extramarital sex has effects on attraction and love and is more restricted in some societies than others. According to the literature (Rosenblatt, 1974), premarital sex is less restricted among the poor and among societies where family authorities have a minimal influence in mate selection. Sexual intercourse may have both positive and negative effects on attraction. Often it increases commitment; sometimes it induces guilt; and sometimes it produces unacceptably high levels of responsibility and involvement. Sexual attraction may sometimes be confused with other kinds of attraction. It may be less stable than other forms of liking and loving and may lead to more rapid escalation and then decline of relationships.

If you are like college students in a recent study you probably underestimate your parents' sexual activity. In Figure 8-4 are the findings of a study of the impressions of 646 Illinois State University students and actual findings reported by Alfred Kinsey (1948, 1953). Sons and daughters appear to have underestimated the amount of their parents' sexual activity. One reason for this underestimation, suggest the researchers, is that many parents avoid showing physical affection to

---

Interest Box 8-4.   Measuring Loving and Liking*

A few Love-Scale and Liking-Scale items:

Love Scale

1. I feel that I can confide in _____ about virtually everything.
2. I feel responsible for _____'s well-being.
3. It would be hard for me to get along without _____ .

Liking Scale

1. I would highly recommend _____ for a responsible job.
2. Most people would react favorably to _____ after a brief acquaintance.
3. _____ is the sort of person whom I myself would like to be.

*From "Measurement of Romantic Love," by Z. Rubin. In *Journal of Personality and Social Psychology*, 1970, *16*, 265–273. Copyright 1970 by the American Psychological Association. Reprinted by permission.

Psychometric data on the two scales can be found in Rubin (1970). In his current research, Rubin is making use of nine-item versions of the two scales.

Figure 8-4.
Some things you
never wanted to
know about sex.
(From "Is There
Sex After 40?" by
O. Pocs, A. Godow,
W. L. Tolone, and
R. H. Walsh,
Psychology Today,
1977, *4*(1), 54–56,
87. Copyright ©
1977, Ziff-Davis
Publishing
Company.
Reprinted by
permission.)

DAUGHTERS' BELIEFS VERSUS KINSEY'S FINDINGS

Type of Activity	Thought mother did	According to Kinsey	Thought father did	According to Kinsey
Premarital petting	63%	99%	80%	89%
Premarital coitus	10%	50%	33%	92%
Extramarital coitus	2%	26%	7%	50%
Oral/genital sex	25%	49%	29%	59%
Masturbation	31%	62%	62%	93%

SONS' BELIEFS VERSUS KINSEY'S FINDINGS

Type of Activity	Thought mother did	According to Kinsey	Thought father did	According to Kinsey
Premarital petting	69%	99%	81%	89%
Premarital coitus	22%	50%	45%	92%
Extramarital coitus	2%	26%	12%	50%
Oral/genital sex	30%	49%	34%	59%
Masturbation	49%	62%	73%	93%

each other when their offspring are around and even fail to mention that sex is
enjoyable when they are having discussions of sex with their children. If we believe
that sex is "wrong," then we can understand how parents might avoid discussions
of it and not want to know what their children are doing. And we can understand
why children seem to behave the same, not discussing it with their parents and
avoiding knowledge of their parents' activity.

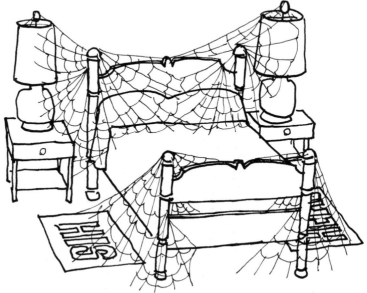

"Student's estimate of parents' sexual activity."

Passionate Love.   **Passionate**, or romantic, **love** can be defined as a positive, intense emotional involvement between two people, involving affection, respect, and sexual attraction.[1] Passionate love seems to be experienced sooner or later by everyone in our culture. Because of its intensity and because it is so poorly understood, it seems to cause emotional upset in most of us.

We fall in love. We fall out of love. These statements suggest that passionate love is less stable and shorter lasting than other forms of attraction. To fall in or out of love suggests that we are not prepared to take credit for our emotional state and would prefer to think of it as something that happens to us. Why do we fall in love? For one thing, passionate love involves liking. So everything I have said about liking in the previous pages probably applies to love, too.

Other special factors may be involved. For one, a **state of readiness** to fall in love may be useful: we are more likely to fall in love at certain times than others ("on the rebound," between the ages of 15 and 25, when we are dissatisfied with an existing relationship, and so forth). Fantasy and imagination play a role too: rewards and pleasures we expect to give and receive may prove even more important than those actually received. Mystery may be important: believing that we do not know all there is to know about the other may be more critical in continued interaction than is our actual level of knowledge.

Other factors that promote feeling and growing in love relate to **selectivity**. We may selectively attend to the similar features of the other, enhancing the other's attractiveness. We may selectively seek out additional dimensions of similarity. We may selectively rehearse in our minds the positive features of the other, enhancing our attraction still further. And we may selectively present to the other aspects of ourselves that will increase his or her liking for us. When we fall out of love, selectivity still operates, but it shifts toward negative attributes. For instance, we may selectively attend to the dissimilar features of the other, which we had previously ignored or repressed, causing a drop in our attraction.

As will be suggested later in this chapter, being "in love" involves labeling an emotional state. Some people are more cautious than others in their use of such labels, even though they may feel the same way. Researchers (Dion & Dion, 1973, 1975) have found that women are more likely than men to *report* being in love. Also, people who believe that their behavior is largely controlled by their environment—externals—more often report being in love than those who believe that they are in control (internals). And for some reason those with low self-esteem more often report being in love.

What causes the shift from falling in love to falling out of love? Through personal growth some of the couple's needs may change, becoming less complementary. Some values may change, becoming less similar. **Satiation** may occur: when we are no longer learning about the other or believe that there is no more mystery about the other, we may grow bored. (Some part of passionate love is novelty and arousal-seeking behavior.)

A change in circumstances may sometimes cause a falling out. Diffusion of affect suggests that, when the context becomes less pleasant (as when you return

---

[1]Berscheid and Walster (1974) have suggested that the main difference between romantic love and **infatuation** is that the latter refers to a relationship that has ended. When we are in love, we may call it "romantic love" or "love"; if and when we fall out of love, we decide to call it "infatuation." Hindsight is 20/20.

from the honeymoon, see your spouse unshaven or in curlers, and begin washing floors) your feelings about the other may become less pleasant, too.

Some factors work to hasten the decline. For instance, **reactance** (an unpleasant feeling that accompanies a perceived loss of freedom) may result. In my slight withdrawal from you, you may cling more desperately; I may feel trapped and withdraw further, causing you to cling more frantically. Another factor may be the Pollyanna Principle (see Chapter 7): we don't like to face unpleasant situations and so try to avoid them. If we have problems or negative feelings, we have trouble discussing them. Our difficulty in coping with the unpleasant means that we fall out of love much faster than we fall in love, for interaction may simply cease as we avoid the unpleasant.

When people have been in love for some time, they may fall out of love. But they may also grow to love more. Although the early stages of successful relationships may be filled with blind passion, later stages reflect a deepening attachment, a growing respect for the other's nature and abilities, and a tireless concern for the other's welfare (Rubin, Z., 1974). These qualities sustain relationships, make them so worthwhile, and distinguish between "in love" and "loving."

POSTSCRIPT: HOW MUCH SIMILARITY IS IMPORTANT?

Although many studies have shown that similarity is important in attraction, social psychologists have not begun to explore the question of *how much* similarity is important. Even though the literature convinces us that most of us do *not* prefer as our friends people who are totally different from us, our intuition tells us most people would not prefer carbon copies of themselves either. We need to feel somewhat different (Fromkin, 1972; Fromkin, Dipboye, & Pyle, 1972). We don't want to be made to feel self-conscious or inadequate by very similar others (Lerner,

"*Loving qualities sustain relationships.*"

M. J., & Agar, 1972). And we don't want others to be so similar that we are bored with them. How similar do you like your friends to be? I once asked 84 students to think of an *ideal* same-sex friend. I then asked them how similar this ideal friend would be to them. The percentage of students choosing each answer appears in Figure 8-5. How would you answer?

From Figure 8-5 it looks as if few people would have someone either completely different from or identical to them as an ideal friend. Most prefer someone moderately similar. And it looks as if similarity of values is more desirable than similarity of appearance.

Some studies have found that similarity of attitudes may be more important for friendship among people who are unsure of themselves (Worchel, P., & McCormick, 1963) and who are worried about being liked (Walster & Walster, 1963). Other factors, such as race, will sometimes override the importance of attitude similarity.

Similarity of Race and Attitudes and Attraction. Interaction between Blacks and Whites is less frequent than our intuition tells us it is. At the same time, it does not seem that we interact very often with those whose attitudes are extremely different from ours on important issues.

Several studies have found that under certain circumstances similarity in attitudes may be more important than racial similarity in the forming of casual friendships (Hendrick, Bixenstine, & Hawkins, 1971; Rokeach, 1960; Rokeach & Mezei, 1966). In more-intimate social choices, such as those involving marriage, racial similarity may be more important than attitude similarities (Triandis & Davis, 1965; Willis, R., & Bulatao, 1967). These studies are valuable not so much for their suggestion of which factor is more important (for this is likely to be a consequence of the particular experimental design) but rather because they show that both variables are very important and that their relative importance seems to depend on many situational factors. For example, prejudiced people are likely

Figure 8-5.
How much
similarity is best?

Questions Asked Regarding Ideal Same-Sex Friend	Completely different	Moderately different	Slightly different	Extremely similar	Identical
Question 1: How similar would this person's values be to yours?	1%	37%	10%	52%	0%
Question 2: How similar would this person's physical appearance (height, weight, hair color, hair length, facial features, and so on) be to yours?	7%	46%	41%	7%	0%
Question 3: How similar would this person's clothing be to yours?	3%	59%	19%	18%	1%

to consider racial similarity a far more important aspect in friendship formation than do unprejudiced or relatively unprejudiced people. An added difficulty with these studies is that the studies artificially bring together Black and White students and force them to interact. In real life, such interracial interaction is so infrequent that there is limited opportunity for Blacks and Whites to discover how much their attitudes have in common. Without this opportunity for mutual discovery, friendship has very little opportunity to develop, and misconceptions of the views and characteristics of the group avoided will persist.

We might view the whole affair as a **filtering process** in which race sorts people into *potential friends* and *others*; then, physical attractiveness again sorts the *potential friends* into two categories—*potential friends* and *others*. These filters will lead to interaction with selected others. Following initial interaction, *apparent* attitude differences and other factors work to still further reduce the size of the *potential-friends* category. There may be some people, of course, for whom one or more of these filtering stages is absent. For instance, a blind person is not likely to be interested in physical attractiveness; some people may prefer to seek racial dissimilarity among their acquaintants; and attitude similarity is more important for some than for others. In general, the filter model may work in this fashion.

Complementarity and Attraction.   If "birds of a feather flock together," can "opposites attract"? The answer is "sometimes." Similarity may be very important in affiliation for arousal reduction, whereas complementarity may be important when one affiliates for increased arousal. People who are quite different from us are certainly interesting. (Berlyne has shown that novel stimuli receive higher "interestingness" ratings than do familiar stimuli. This might apply to people as well.) Robert Winch posed a theory of mate selection in which he argued that **complementary needs** are important in the choice of a satisfactory mate (Winch, 1952; Winch, Ktsanes, & Ktsanes, 1954). If you like to be motherly, then you might be happiest with someone who would like to be mothered. If you like to dominate, then you might be happiest with someone who likes to be submissive.

These qualities do not need to be permanent traits of the individual, however. Relationships work most satisfactorily for both people if each is able to adjust his or her behavior to meet the needs of the other. Sometimes your friend may need to be taken care of, and your relationship will prosper if you are able to take care of your friend. Sometimes you may need to be taken care of, and your relationship will prosper if your friend is able to do that caring. It is important to be able to express your own needs and find someone who will help you meet them, and it is important to be sensitive to the needs of that person and be able to meet them yourself. There are not many satisfactory relationships where one person is always dominant and the other always submissive. Good partners in a relationship will be sensitive to the needs of others and responsive to them.

Several years ago 60 Canadian students were asked: "In general, are your best friends more talkative, about the same, or less talkative than you usually are?" The answers suggested that the students who rated themselves as *above* or *below* average in talkativeness tended to see their best friends as complementary—not similar—to themselves in talkativeness (Stang & Russell, 1976). This finding is consonant with Winch's (1958) views of need complementarity in friendship and mate selection. However, although the notion of need complementarity seems reasonable, most of the research on this hypothesis has not supported it. Rather, it seems that similarity of needs is sometimes more important than complementarity. We may need to take a closer look at the attraction process to see just when complementarity seems to be beneficial, then revise our theory a bit.

SUMMARY

Much of our daily life is spent with others; some is spent in solitude. Two major explanations are offered for this selective affiliation. Affiliation may help us maintain an optimum level of arousal, raising our arousal when we are bored and lowering it when we feel stress. Through social-comparison processes, affiliation helps us to evaluate our opinions and abilities.

Not only do we choose when to be with others, but we also choose those we will be with. Both availability and desirability are important in the latter choice. Our field of availables is influenced by our proximity to others. Those with whom we frequently make contact are likely to become attracted to us and vice versa. Some of those who are available are more desirable as friends and lovers than others. Those in our field of desirables are typically similar to us, competent, and attractive. Our liking for others can be measured in many ways, such as with sociometry or with liking scales.

Attraction is a complex process, and the explanation for it is necessarily complex. Much of our attraction may be a result of familiarity, which in turn results from interaction. Interaction is most likely to occur when it is rewarding and when we are available for it. Availability is determined by proximity, and rewardingness is determined by similarity, judged competence, and judged attractiveness. It is likely that each of these variables also has some effect on the others.

Love is difficult to define, much less explain. Passionate love seems to benefit from a state of readiness for love, selective attention to the positive qualities of the other, and labeling our emotional state as love. Falling out of love seems almost as common as falling in love and may be a result of factors such as satiation and reactance.

Some limitations of these generalizations were discussed in the final section of the chapter. Although similarity has been found to lead to attraction in dozens of studies, there are probably limits to this effect. Opposites may attract when people have complementary needs or wish to raise each other's arousal; birds of a feather may flock together when they have similar interests and values or wish to lower each other's arousal.

GLOSSARY TERMS

Define these terms in your own words, then look them up in the glossary at the back of the book.

Affiliation	Complementary needs
Attitude object	Field of availables
Attractiveness	Filtering process
Availability	Imitation
Competence	Infatuation

Interaction
Interaction rates
Isolate (sociometric)
Love
Novelty
Passionate (romantic) love
Proximity
Reactance
Satiation
Selectivity

Self-perception
Similarity
Social-comparison theory
Social costs
Social desirability
Social rewards
Sociogram
Sociometry
Star (sociometric)
State of readiness

FURTHER READING

Berscheid, E., & Walster, E. H. *Interpersonal attraction* (2nd ed.). Reading, Mass.: Addison-Wesley, 1978. One of the best-written little books in social psychology.

Huston, T. L., & Levinger, G. Interpersonal attraction and relationships. *Annual Review of Psychology*, 1978, *29*, 115–156. An up-to-date, comprehensive, and balanced review of the research.

chapter
9

Helping and Hurting

chapter

9

INTRODUCTION

Our newspapers are filled with stories of aggression and violence and also of bystanders' failing to provide help when it is needed (see Figure 9-1). These sensational accounts disturb us, in part because we would like to believe better of ourselves and others. Statistics seem to agree with the newspapers: we live in violent times. In a recent year, for instance, the U.S. Bureau of Alcohol, Tobacco, and Firearms, made 3,495 arrests for violations of federal firearms laws. Over 10,000 firearms were seized, including 1,278 gangster-type weapons such as machine guns, sawed-off shotguns and rifles, and assassination devices (U.S. Law Enforcement Assistance Administration, 1978). In a given year in the United States over 10,000 people are murdered with firearms alone, and over 100,000 robberies are committed using firearms. During the period 1963–1968, at least 2,000 people participated in terrorism against Blacks and civil rights workers, resulting in 112 casualties (and only 97 arrests!) (*New York Times Encyclopedic Almanac*, 1969). Why are people so cruel? Why are they not more helpful? Such questions lead us to a study of helping and hurting.

Of course, the newspapers may give us the wrong impression of what people are like. Whether the crime rate is high or low depends on one's viewpoint. In a given year about 16% of Americans over 14 years of age contributed their labor to some form of health, education, or welfare services for the general good (U.S. Department of Labor, 1969). This voluntary helping is not continuous, though. In a given week the percentage may be only 5% or less, and on a given day the percentage is less. Are these percentages high or low? As with the crime rate, it depends on one's viewpoint. Most people rarely engage in violence or in great acts of altruism. Many people never do. A few people sometimes do. Most of us fairly often do little things that help or hurt.

All things considered, life in the United States is neither utopian nor "nasty, brutish, and short." We can find examples of both great helpfulness (see Figure 9-2) and brutal violence. So we are led to refine our question: What factors lead us to helping or hurting behavior? How can we get people to be more helpful and less hurtful?

An Albany, New York, man was saved from a suicide leap by the coaxing of his seven-year-old nephew while onlookers jeered, "Jump! Jump! Jump!" Among the curious crowd of about 4000 were people challenging him to jump, "C'mon, you're chicken," "You're yellow," and betting whether he would or not. Instructive is the comment by one well-dressed man, "I hope he jumps on this side. We couldn't see him if he jumped over there."

© 1964 by The New York Times Company. Reprinted by permission.

50 in Area of Murder, But No One Is Talking

NEW YORK, Oct. 25 (UPI) — Police say they have been stymied in their efforts to solve the murder of a 42-year-old Brooklyn plumber because none of the 50 persons who may have witnessed the slaying has been willing to talk.

Angelo Treglia was getting into his truck, which was parked down the street from his home Saturday, when a car pulled alongside and a gunman shot him three times in the head and once in the shoulder.

Police said about 50 of Treglia's friends and neighbors were in the area at the time, but that subsequent questioning of them failed to provide any clues to the gunman's identity. Police said that the slaying apparently was over a private matter.

From the *Washington Post* 10/26/77. Reprinted by permission of United Press International.

A Model's Dying Screams Are Ignored At the Site of Kitty Genovese's Murder

By Robert D. McFadden

While at least one neighbor heard her dying screams and did nothing, a 25-year-old model was beaten to death early Christmas morning in her New Gardens, Queens, apartment, which virtually overlooks the scene of the murder of Catherine Genovese 10 years ago.

The 10-story red brick building where the latest murder occurred was the residence of many of the 38 witnesses who heard or saw the knife-slaying of Miss Genovese on the street below in the early morning hours of March 13, 1964, and neither called the police nor took any action.

The celebrated case was the subject of books and many articles detailing and analyzing the inaction of the witnesses, many of whom cited a fear of becoming involved.

The latest victim, Sandra Zahler of 82-67 Austin Street, was apparently slain about 3:20 A.M. Wednesday, when a woman in the next-door apartment on the fifth floor said she heard screams and the sounds of a fierce struggle.

But the murder was not reported until about 2 P.M., yesterday, when Miss Zahler's boyfriend, George Boguslaw, 24, let himself into the one-and-a-half room apartment and discovered the body sprawled on a sofa.

© 1974 by The New York Times Company. Reprinted by permission.

Figure 9-1.
How people don't help

In this chapter we will look at both helping and hurting. There are several reasons for thinking about both at once. Research on both relates to the same general question of what people are like, and why they do positive or negative things. Conceptually, helping and hurting are the poles of a prosocial/antisocial continuum. Because of this, they seem to have some common causes. Also, hurting sometimes leads to helping and vice versa. For instance, when a country mobilizes for war or a neighborhood organizes to combat crime, cooperation and helping within the country or neighborhood may increase. A threat from an out-group may lead to increased helpfulness and cohesiveness in the in-group.

Figure 9-2.
How people help

In Arlington County
Volunteers Up For Red Cross

By Lorraine Thompson
Special to the Journal

Arlington Red Cross has released its 1977-78 service report which shows impressive increases both in community services rendered and in volunteer participation.

Leading the list of successes are the blood services statistics for the year that ended June 30. Arlington's collection of blood increased 9 percent to a total of 11,099 pints.

The department's gain, according to blood director Marguerite Gully, is especially significant since 22 percent of the county's population is at least 65 years of age and the population growth has stabilized. Gully said her 84 volunteer aids put in 9,054 hours.

Nursing services, another major area, showed an increase of 8 percent, with 15 new volunteer nurses on the roster. Also, 68 R.N.s gave 3,400 hours of volunteer time working at bloodmobiles, health fairs and clinics, teaching and taking blood pressures. Blood pressure screenings during the fiscal period numbered 9,000, up 3,000 over last year.

From the *Fairfax* (Virginia) *Journal*, August 16, 1978.
Copyright 1978. Reprinted by permission.

DEFINITIONS

Helping is any behavior that benefits another person, whether or not it benefits the helper. **Altruism** is a special kind of helping behavior in which one freely acts with the intention of helping another, with the expectation of personal costs but without the expectation of benefits to oneself. Because of these special requirements it is difficult to determine when helping is altruistic, and altruism is less common than other forms of helping behavior. **Aggression** can be defined as any behavior that causes harm to another. **Violence** is one type of aggression in which harm includes physical pain.

These definitions refer to behaviors rather than to motives. A purely *motivational definition* of helping would be "any action *intended* to cause benefit to another, whether or not benefit actually occurred." A purely *behavioral definition* would be "any action that causes benefit to another, regardless of intention." Similarly, a motivational or behavioral definition of aggression could be offered by replacing *benefit* with *injury*. Social psychologists have preferred behavioral to motivational definitions, simply because behaviors are far easier to measure than motives. When people label some behavior as helpful or aggressive, however, they generally consider *both* some analysis of motives and the consequences as well (see Interest Box 9-1). Helping one person may mean hurting another (or vice versa), so defining an action or intention as hurting or helping is not always easy.

Why do people help one another? Why do they hurt one another? Most thinkers who have considered one of these basic questions have ignored the other,[1] and there has been little research designed to test some general explanation of both helping and hurting.

This is not to say that there is little research on helping or aggression! There is now a sizable literature on helping, and it is growing larger rapidly (reviewed by Berkowitz, L., 1972, 1973; Bryan, J. H., & London, 1970; Huston & Korte, 1975; Krebs, 1970; Macaulay & Berkowitz, 1970; Midlarsky, 1968).

Research on aggression and hurting dates back to the thinking done by John Dollard and his colleagues (Dollard, Doob, Miller, Mowrer, & Sears, 1939). Today there is a tremendous literature, and many exciting findings are made each year. We are probably now at a point when it is possible to compare the effects of various factors on helping and hurting. We will do just that in the remainder of this chapter. We have already seen (Chapter 4) how early experience and learn-

---

Interest Box 9-1.   Helping or Aggression?

Decide whether each of the following situations is aggression or helping. Then discuss your answers with other members of your class.

Is This Aggression?

1. Suicide.
2. A police officer's gun goes off during the arrest of a drunk, wounding the drunk.
3. An unarmed hijacker takes over an airplane, but releases all unharmed.
4. Terrorists plant a bomb in a hotel. It explodes, but there are no injuries.
5. Students burn their draft cards.
6. Bystanders do nothing while a murder takes place.
7. Your grandmother cheats at canasta and wins.
8. A car rolls down a hill because the parking brakes were not set and kills a child playing in his front yard.

On which situations do you agree? Disagree? Why? Did you use motivational definitions? Or behavioral definitions? Or both?

Is This Helping?

1. A mechanic repairs an exhaust system without charging the customer; the customer is later asphyxiated by it.
2. A waiter serves a customer and is tipped.
3. A Girl Scout directs traffic at a parade.
4. Someone plans to give blood but is rejected because of low blood pressure.
5. A witness to a crime calls the police.
6. Lassie jumps in a raging river to save a drowning child.

---

[1]There are some exceptions, such as Gaertner (1976), who reviews both topics in the same chapter.

ing affect a person's helpfulness or aggressiveness. In this chapter we will look at the effects on helping and hurting of personality, internal state, the situation, the characteristics of the other person, and our previous behavior. Before you begin, you might think about how helpful various professions are by doing the exercise in Interest Box 9-2.

EFFECTS OF PERSONALITY ON HELPING AND HURTING

Contemporary social psychologists do not often refer to *personality, disposition, mentality,* and so on. Some of their distaste for such terms stems from the research designs they use, which treat individual differences as "statistical error." By creating powerful manipulations and chronically using homogeneous college students, they increase the impact of situations and reduce the impact of individual differences. But there *are* individual differences in helpfulness and in aggression. On the one hand, researchers have found that the people most likely to help are also likely to

☐ "Have a strong sense of moral and social responsibility, a spirit of adventurousness and unconventionality, sympathy for others, and a tendency to reduce [their] distress by social actions designed to reduce the distress of another" (Huston & Korte, 1974, pp. 34–35).
☐ Be a first-born (Staub, 1971a) from a small family (Staub, 1971b), have moralistic parents (London, 1970), and believe that their parents practiced what they preached (Rosenhan, 1970).
☐ Be at a higher stage in "moral judgment" (McNamee, 1974) and belong to a service group (Horowitz, I., 1971).

Interest Box 9-2.   Measuring Altruism

Rank the following professions in order from most altruistic (1) to least altruistic (10):

auto mechanic
member of clergy
college professor
judge
union official
physician
politician
television reporter
army general
used-car salesperson

Now compare your responses with the following responses of subjects (including almost 300 college students) who were studied by Rotter and Stein in 1971. (Note that the Rotter and Stein study took place almost ten years ago. If your ranking of the professions listed in this interest box agrees with the ranking of the subjects studied by Rotter and Stein, what are the implications of that agreement?)

1. member of clergy
2. physician
3. judge
4. college professor
5. union official
6. television reporter
7. army general
8. auto mechanic
9. politician
10. used-car salesperson

☐ Have higher interest in others. Social interest, defined as empathy, sympathy, and "interest in the interests of mankind," seems closely related to the idea of responsivity. People who score high in social interest (Crandall, 1975) have been found to be more cooperative and more willing to donate time to help others.

On the other hand, people are more inclined to be aggressive when

☐ They have attitudes condoning the use of punishment and focus attention on themselves (and these attitudes) (Carver, 1975).
☐ They are frequently frustrated.
☐ They lack those qualities associated with altruism in the list above.

EFFECTS OF OUR INTERNAL STATE

Physiology.   Think back about the last time that you hurt or helped some people. How did you feel? When you hurt them, you may have been feeling an emotion that you had labeled anger, rage, jealousy, frustration, or pain. When you helped them, *they* may have been feeling all or any of these emotions, but the emotion that *you* most likely experienced you labeled empathy, compassion, or sympathy. In Chapter 4 we considered how people label their physiological states. Whether you are helping or hurting, your physiological state may be just the same—namely, a condition of high arousal. After a car accident, whether you were an observer or participant, your heart is likely to be pounding, your digestion slowed, your breathing faster, and so on.

So one physiological state of high arousal may underlie many different emotions and many different behaviors. Our heart and lungs probably cannot tell whether we are being "warm hearted" and helping or "cold hearted" and hurting. But when we are aroused, we are more likely to take *some* action than when we are not (Piliavin, J. A., & Piliavin, 1975).

Frustration.   Physiology is one part of our internal state. Our cognitive processes are another. One important cognitive process is setting goals and directing behavior toward reaching them. Reaching these goals is important to us, and we feel upset when we are **frustrated** (prevented from doing so). This experience is so common than it is easy to empathize with others who are frustrated.

In some of the situations in which you hurt others, *you* had been frustrated (prevented by them, by someone else, or by some event from reaching some goal). In some of the situations where you helped others, *they* have been prevented from reaching some goal.

Of course, not all aggression is motivated by frustration. There are many situations in which we hurt other people intentionally with the ultimate purpose of trying to help someone. Such situations include removing a splinter from a friend's hand, amputating a leg that has become gangrenous, acting under orders as a soldier or member of a firing squad, giving a student a bad grade for poor performance so that he or she will study harder and learn more, or spanking a child with the goal of improving the child's behavior. Arnold Buss (1966) reported an experiment that further suggests that we may sometimes hurt others in order to help them. Subjects were led to believe that another person's learning of the task would be improved if that person received shocks. These subjects then shocked the learner more than other subjects who had been led to believe that shocking interfered with learning. If the intent of the shocking had been only to harm the learner, we would have expected the opposite results.

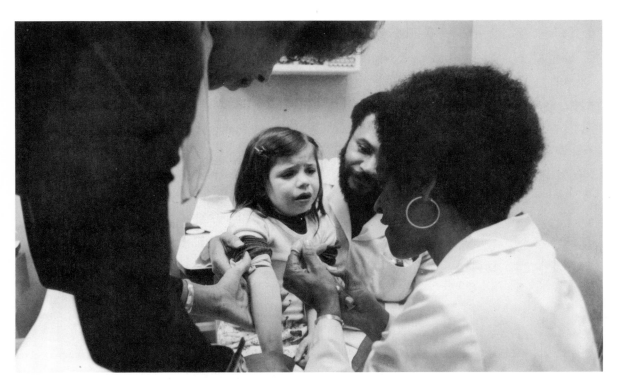

Sometimes we hurt others in order to help them.

Frustration does not always lead to aggression (Miller, N. E., 1941), nor does any other emotion. Nor does great attention to someone else's plight always lead to helping. Our particular definition of the situation determines whether hurting or helping (or something else) is "appropriate." Sometimes what is appropriate has been learned through childhood experiences and depends on the behavior of others or on the degree to which they seem to be deserving of being helped or being hurt.

The actual process that occurs when one behaves aggressively is probably complex. The immediate effect might be to reduce tension, relax muscles through activity, and create a sense of justice that would reduce one's need for further aggression. At the same time, however, the aggressor may find this reduction of tension pleasant and decide that aggression toward this and other targets is appropriate. So one effect of aggression might be **catharsis**. But another effect might be to make future aggression easier.

Further, aggressors may become accustomed (habituated) to the unpleasantness of the aggressive actions, making it easier to aggress further. If people can be induced to behave somewhat aggressively, it may be possible to then induce them to behave a little more aggressively, and so on—a "foot-in-the-door" approach to aggression induction. Stanley Milgram reported an experiment (see Chapter 13) in which subjects were ordered to shock a confederate of the experimenter, each shock increasing slightly in its intensity. Milgram reports that many of his subjects continued in the experiment until they believed that they were administering 450-volt shocks. This seems astounding, but it must be remembered that their shocking of the confederate had proceeded with gradual increments of only 15 volts each. Most subjects would probably have refused to administer 450-volt shocks at the start of the experiment. Repeated exposure to violence probably causes us to be less upset each time we observe it. Most of us have now seen so much violence in the movies and on television that it takes an extremely gory scene to really make us wince.

Mood.   Our own mood seems to have a strong effect on whether we help or hurt. Our behaviors are consistent with our mood. On the one hand, several studies have found that people are more helpful when they are in a good mood than when they are not (Aderman, 1972; Isen, 1970; Isen, Horn, & Rosenhan, 1973; Isen & Levin, 1972; Levin & Isen, 1975). On the other hand, you can recall days when you were in a bad mood and would do nothing but grumble, kick the dog, yell at your spouse, or insult your best friend. Anger is probably a major cause of aggression (Konečni, 1975).

With the passage of time, moods change. When we are angered, our physiological arousal increases. If we "count to ten"—or wait even longer—much of our arousal and our initial anger may subside, along with our aggressiveness (Konečni, 1975). However, repeated frustrations may slowly build our anger to the point at which we explode. Our aggressiveness sometimes seems out of proportion to the particular event that preceded it.

Our mood may be affected by the weather, and the weather, therefore, may have indirect effects on the rate of helping or hurting. Hot weather seems to be most conducive to violence. For instance, the U.S. Riot Commission (1968) reported that 38% of the disorders studied occurred on days of 79° F or more (see Chapter 5). Because more people are outside on hot days, there is greater chance for heat-induced violence to occur and be modeled by others. One study found that aggression is imitated more under hot (93° F) than comfortable (79° F) temperatures (Berkowitz, L., & Geen, 1966). High temperatures produce discomfort, which may be labeled as anger. Anger, in turn, may result in aggression (Ellsworth & Carlsmith, 1973). No one has yet studied the effects of temperature on helping.

EFFECTS OF THE SITUATION

Some explanations of behavior focus on consistencies and differences in individual behavior. With this approach we might conclude that some people are more helpful than others. Boy Scouts, for instance, are supposed to "help other people at all times," whereas, we are told, "God helps those who help themselves."

A study of individual differences alone, however, will not be very useful in helping us accurately predict when others will help. You, who know yourself better than anyone, may have some difficulty predicting when you will or will not help someone else. Consequently, social psychologists have turned to a study of situational influences on helping and the relationship between individual differences and situational influences. A similar approach has been taken in the study of aggression.

Four of my undergraduate students conducted two field studies that you might try yourself.[2] In both studies these students observed whether or not passersby (108 groups in study 1, 2215 groups in study 2) stopped to help various beggars at work on the sidewalks of Manhattan. Some of the results may surprise you. For example, the larger the groups of passersby, the *less* likely it was that at least one person in the group would give money. One person passing by helped 15% of the time, but only 6% of the two-person groups helped and *none* of the three-person groups helped. As some other studies have found, men were more likely to help than women (7% versus 4%) (see Bryan & Test, 1967; Piliavin, I. M., Rodin, & Piliavin, 1969; Thayer, 1973).

Similarity of the beggar to the passersby seemed to have an effect on helping. For example, beggars between the ages of 30 and 50 received more help than younger or older beggars from these passersby, whose average estimated age was 38.

"SO I READ THIS REPORT THAT SAYS ONE PERSON GIVES 2.5 TIMES AS OFTEN AS TWO PERSONS".

[2]Study 1: Tammy Goldberg and Stephanie Workman; study 2: Kathy Braile and Alvita Liktorius.

Further, although Black and White beggars were helped about equally often overall, Blacks were more likely to help Blacks, and Whites and Orientals were more likely to help White beggars (see Figure 9-3). It should be noted that a previous study (Thayer, 1973) did not find this same-race helping effect. However, another study (Huang & Harris, 1974) found considerable similarity between Chinese and White Americans in their helping behavior.

Figure 9-3.
Helping beggars

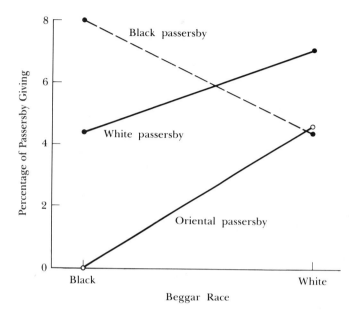

The degree of need for help also appeared to influence helping. Three amputees were helped most often (7.7% of the time), two blind beggars next most often (2.5%), and one with no apparent handicap was helped least often (1%). Five persons collecting for charity (Salvation Army, leukemia, or a religious group) did about as well as the amputees (7.6%).

Although many of these effects are very interesting, we still do not know very much about helping behavior. Information on the sex, race, and age of both beggars and passersby proved to be of little value in predicting when help would occur, even when a computer and fancy statistical techniques were used.

Costs and Benefits.   In addition to considering whether the situation is appropriate and calls for helping or hurting, we often make a quick cost/benefit analysis of what may be involved in helping or hurting.

In general, when the expected costs of any behavior are reduced or the expected benefits are increased, that behavior becomes more likely (Baron, R. A., 1970; McGovern, Ditzian, & Taylor, 1975a; Midlarsky & Midlarsky, 1973; Moss & Page, 1972; Piliavin, J. A., & Piliavin, 1972; Pomazal & Jaccard, 1976; Wagner & Wheeler, 1969; Weiss, R. F., Buchanan, Alstatt, & Lombardo, 1971). Reducing costs and increasing benefits is like lowering a "hurdle." For example, in one study students who believed that giving blood is painful or unpleasant (high expected cost) were less likely to donate blood than students who did not expect such side effects (Pomazal & Jaccard, 1976). Rewarding a person for helping by saying "thank you" (a benefit) has been found to make subsequent helping more likely (McGovern et al., 1975a; Moss & Page, 1972).

We also are likely to consider costs and benefits when we aggress against another. Anthony Doob and Alan Gross (1968) studied how we respond when a stalled car blocks our path. These researchers found that a frustrated driver honks sooner at a rundown old car than an expensive, new one. One reason may be that we have learned to inhibit our aggressive responses to powerful people because we can get in trouble. The costs of a skinny runt's fighting back when a big bully has kicked sand in his face at the beach may be greater than the benefits. Some body-building ads suggest that, by reducing this discrepancy in size and strength, one could reduce the costs and increase the benefits of retaliation. Rewarding people for aggression increases their aggression (Bandura, 1973; Geen & Pigg, 1970; Geen & Stonner, 1971). And the same effect occurs in rats (Ulrich, Johnston, Richardson, & Wolff, 1963).

Costs and benefits are like punishments and rewards. When we consider the costs and benefits of helping or hurting another, we are likely not only to look at the particular situation and its consequences but also to reflect (perhaps subconsciously) on previous situations in which we have been rewarded or punished. Social reinforcement resulting from previous experiences can shape what form our helping or hurting takes. For instance, women are not often rewarded and sometimes are punished for picking up hitchhikers. Judging only from the infrequency with which they do, one might conclude that women are not very helpful people. Yet in many, many situations women prove to be far more helpful than men, those situations being ones in which they were rewarded for helping. Some children, especially boys, may be rewarded for being *physically* aggressive, and other children may learn to be *verbally* aggressive.

Anonymity. Our model of helping and hurting requires that we pay attention to those we will help or hurt. Staring leads to attention. Among people, other primates, and other mammals, staring under the right conditions can lead to aggression, whereas looking away ("gaze aversion") can inhibit aggression (Bolwig, 1964; Exline & Yellin, 1969; Van Hooff, 1967). Staring at a caged monkey, for instance, often gets the monkey very angry. Nevertheless, there seem to be conditions in which eye contact leads to helping or a reduction in hurting (Ellsworth & Carlsmith, 1973). If you are trying to pull your car into traffic, eye contact with another driver may result in his or her letting you in. I suspect that the key factor in whether helping or hurting occurs is whether your eye contact and other body language are interpreted as a threat or as a request for help.

When we are anonymous—when the other cannot see us (and cannot retaliate)—our need to help seems to drop, as does our reluctance to hurt (see Figure 9-4). Researchers found that moans and groans from the victim reduced aggression (Buss, 1966; Milgram, 1965). Presumably, moans and groans also increase the chances of being helped.

Population Density. Another variable that is related to both helping and hurting is the number of people living in a given area. Several studies find that, the

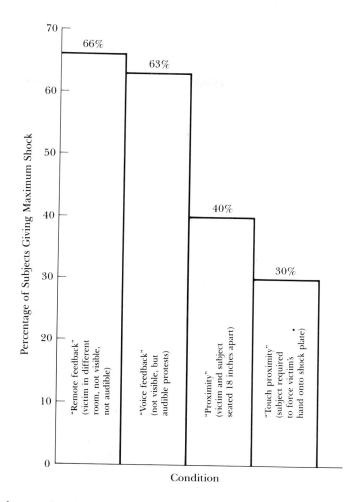

Figure 9-4. Psychological distance and aggression in Milgram's obedience experiments. (Copyright 1965 by Stanley Milgram. From the film *Obedience,* distributed by the New York University Film Library.)

less densely populated the area, the more likely one is to help in a given situation (Gelfand, Hartmann, Walder, & Page, 1973; Korte & Kerr, 1975; Krupat & Coury, 1975; Latané & Darley, 1970; Milgram, 1970; Schneider & Mockus, 1974; Thorngate & Love, 1974). That is, a passerby in a city is less likely to offer help than one in a small town. This fits our expectations. One study (Schneider & Mockus, 1974) surveyed college students and found that most of them expected that people are more likely to be helped by a stranger in a small town than in a big city. However, it seems that the density of passersby is more important (Krupat & Coury, 1975). Whether in a city or small town, passersby who are crowded help less than when they are few and far between. At the same time, the per-capita incidence of crime in the United States increases with city size (National Commission on the Causes and Prevention of Violence, 1969, p. xvii). The same is true in Canada (Bell-Rowbotham & Boydell, 1972).

A partial explanation of this may have to do with the frequency with which one encounters those needing help or encounters appropriate targets of one's aggressive feelings. In the small town, if you do not help a person needing help, that person may have to wait a long time before being passed by another person. At the same time, you may encounter very few people in need of help in a small town. Life is much different in the city, where there may be a beggar on every other block, frequent motorists in distress, and so on. In the city, if you stopped every time you encountered someone in need of help, you would never get to where you are going. Yet people may be helped more often or more rapidly if they are in distress in the city than in the country, because there are usually more passersby to help them. Similarly, if you are feeling angry and aggressive in a small town, you may not encounter an appropriate target of aggression until the feeling has subsided. In a densely populated city there are many possible targets of aggression available.

"anger and frustration have many outlets in a large city vs a small town."

Ambiguity of the Situation.   If our interpretation of the situation is important in determining how we will react to it, then situations we find very ambiguous and have difficulty defining also give us difficulty in choosing how to act. Ambiguous situations will often not give rise to any action at all, helping or hurting. One study found that every group of bystanders tested offered assistance when a maintenance man fell and cried out in pain (Clark, R. D., & Word, 1972). But not all groups responded with help when the maintenance man fell but did not cry out. In the latter case the situation was more ambiguous: if he was hurt, why didn't he cry out?

A fascinating study by Bibb Latané and John Darley capitalized on the action-inhibiting effects of an ambiguous situation (Latané & Darley, 1968). Subjects either waited alone, with two other "naive" subjects, or with two passive confederates as a pungent smoke puffed through a small vent in the wall. Latané and Darley were interested in learning whether people act more quickly in an emergency when they are alone or with others. They were also interested in knowing whether, if the others are passive and do not act, this will delay a person's own helpful actions. Figure 9-5 shows the proportion of subjects in each condition who had reported the smoke at any point after the introduction of the smoke. As you can see, 55% of the subjects who were alone had reported the smoke within two minutes. But only 12% of the three-person groups had acted within two minutes. The line showing "hypothetical three-person groups" is calculated to show how fast three-person groups would respond if each group member acted as fast as he or she did when alone. The chance of someone's acting rapidly in a group is theoretically higher than with only one person in the group. But as you can see, three naive subjects took much *longer* to act and were *less likely* to act than did one subject alone.

In this experiment, there was some uncertainty about whether the situation was an emergency and an uncertainty about how to behave. As you can see from Figure 9-5, most subjects made their decisions about how to act in the first few minutes after the introduction of the smoke. When subjects decided not to act, they were likely to remain with that decision. Latané and Darley describe the reactions of the subjects below:

> Subjects who had reported the smoke were relatively consistent in later describing their reactions to it. They thought the smoke looked somewhat "strange," they were not sure exactly what it was or whether it was dangerous, but they felt it was unusual enough to justify some examination. "I wasn't sure whether it was a fire but it looked like something was wrong." "I thought it might be steam, but it seemed like a good idea to check it out."
>
> Subjects who had not reported the smoke also were unsure about exactly what it was, but they uniformly said that they had rejected the idea that it was a fire. Instead, they hit upon an astonishing variety of alternative explanations, all sharing the common characteristic of interpreting the smoke as a nondangerous event. Many thought the smoke was either steam or air-conditioning vapors, several thought it was smog, purposely introduced to simulate an urban environment, and two (from different groups) actually suggested that the smoke was a "truth gas" filtered into the room to induce them to answer the questionnaire accurately. (Surprisingly, they were not disturbed by this conviction.) Predictably, some decided that "it must be some sort of experiment" and stoically endured the discomfort of the room rather than overreact.
>
> Despite the obvious and powerful report-inhibiting effect of other bystanders, subjects almost invariably claimed that they had paid little or no attention to the reactions of the other people in the room. Although the presence of other people actually had a strong and pervasive effect on the subjects' reactions, they were either unaware of this or unwilling to admit it [1968].

This may well be because the situation was so ambiguous: "If this is an emergency, why are these other people just sitting there so calmly? Perhaps this isn't an emergency at all!"

Figure 9-5. Cumulative proportion of subjects reporting the smoke over time. (From "Group Inhibition of Bystander Intervention in Emergencies," by B. Latané and J. M. Darley, *Journal of Personality and Social Psychology*, 1968, *10*, 215–221. Copyright 1968 by the American Psychological Association. Reprinted by permission of the authors and publisher.)

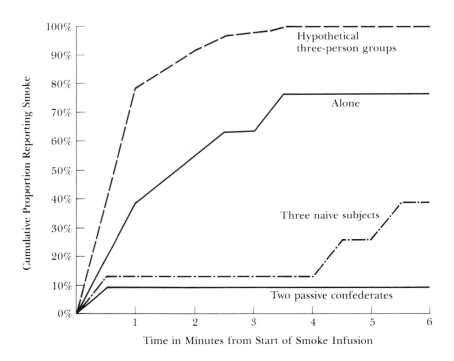

Another factor that seems to be important in our decision about what is appropriate is the behavior of the other person. If another person helps us, then it is quite appropriate, it would seem, for us to help in return. And if someone hurts us, then it would seem appropriate to hurt in return. Several studies, in fact, do show that both helping and aggression are reciprocated (Borden, Bowen, & Taylor, 1971; O'Leary, M. R., & Dengerink, 1973). We help those who help us, meet force with force, and fight fire with fire. This norm of reciprocity (Gouldner, 1960) captures some of the spirit of both the Old and New Testaments. What is normal, it seems, is to exchange an eye for an eye and a tooth for a tooth. But if you want to take control of the situation, you may do unto others as you would have them do unto you, knowing that they may feel obligated to reciprocate and behave as you did.

But reciprocation is rarely an exact trading, with kisses or threats measured carefully and exactly one eye traded for one eye. If it were, there would be little change in our social relations from day to day. Rather, we live in a world with people who are willing to trade three kisses for one and governments that are sometimes willing to go to war in response to insults or assassinations. Because we do not keep careful count of debts or credits, our relationships often intensify, leading sometimes to considerable helping and sometimes to considerable hurting.

Our familiarity with a situation may affect how much we are influenced by others. In a very strange situation we may be uncertain how to act. One way to reduce this uncertainty is through social comparison. We look at others and study their reactions. How they are behaving and seem to be feeling are clues for how we "should" behave and feel. What we may not realize when we are making these observations is that the others may be equally uncertain of how to behave and may be looking to us for clues on what is "proper." This is an example of **pluralistic ignorance**. As a consequence, you might expect that, the more novel the situation, the more people will engage in social comparison and the more similar or uniform will be the behavior of individuals in the group. In a very familiar situation, of course, we act confidently. We know how to behave, because we learned it in previous situations. In familiar social situations, then, there might be a wider range of individual differences in behavior, as different people have had somewhat different previous experiences with these situations.

Another thing that probably occurs when we are in a novel situation and unsure of what to do is that we tend to follow the guiding principle "When in doubt, do nothing." Many animals "freeze" when they are confronted with a novel situation. Laboratory studies of reaction time show that, the greater the number of alternatives to choose from in making a decision, the longer it takes to make that decision. In a strange situation there are many things we might do that we must weigh and evaluate. We may conclude that no single action is clearly better than any other and simply choose not to act. When we combine these hypotheses of inactivity in novel situations and social comparisons in social situations, the result is sometimes a uniformly passive group of people in a novel social situation.

In the case of situations in which someone requires the help of a group, pluralistic ignorance may work in another way to prevent action. Because most of us think that most people are basically good, we are likely to assume that someone else will help and that it will not be necessary to provide help ourselves. This idea has been called the diffusion-of-responsibility hypothesis. The larger the group, the more diffuse is this feeling of responsibility (Darley & Latané, 1968; Latané & Darley, 1968). As a consequence, people may first assume that, if help is needed, someone else will provide it; if no one appears to be helping, it may be because help is not needed.

Another factor that may be involved, one that has not been considered much by previous researchers, is that our initial behavior has a profound effect on later behavior in that same situation. If we begin a conversation with a stranger in a serious or giddy or angry state, the conversation is likely to remain at that level, for example. When we enter an emergency situation, whatever we do in the first few minutes is likely to affect how we behave throughout that emergency. Through self-perception, our early behavior probably suggests a temporary personal theory about how we should continue to behave (see Interest Box 9-3). Much social comparison also takes place when a group is about to become a victim. In a theater fire, for instance, everyone may exit quietly and peacefully. (Perhaps most people feel an urge to run but observe that others are behaving calmly and decide that they should feel calm, too.) But sometimes people do start to panic and run. Their behavior is very visible to others, and through social comparison others may conclude that they should also be running and feeling panicky. The result can be disastrous.

The importance of our **definition of the situation** in our decision to help another has been emphasized in two studies (Bickman, 1969, 1971a). In these studies, confederates defined a potential helping situation as a *crisis* ("She's not answering; something must've fallen on her—she's hurt"), as *ambiguous* ("I hope it's nothing serious; I hope she's OK"), or as *not needing help* ("Something must've fallen on the intercom; I guess she'll tell the guy it's not working; we'd better wait for him to tell us what to do next"). When subjects were led to believe that the situation was a crisis requiring help, they were much more likely to help than if the situation was ambiguous and their help might or might not be needed. And the ambiguous situation produced more helping than the situation in which subjects did not believe help was needed.

When the person needing help is not present but is overheard, it may not be clear whether help is needed or whether someone else will provide it. In this case, larger groups seem to inhibit helping (Darley & Latané, 1968; Latané & Darley, 1968; Latané & Rodin, 1969; Ross, A. S., 1971; Ross, A. S., & Braband, 1973; Ross, A. S., & Burke, undated). When the victim is present, however, there is no ambiguity in the need for help, and larger groups give rise to more and faster helping (Piliavin, I. M., Rodin, & Piliavin, 1969; Piliavin, J. A., & Piliavin, 1972; Ross, A. S., & Burke, undated).

It may well be that the activity or inactivity of others affects us most when our own definition of the situation is very ambiguous. When we are not sure how to respond, we are most likely to engage in social comparison and look to others for views on how we should behave. But when we know that helping or hurting is called for, we are likely to focus our attention on the problem and ignore the behavior of others. This hypothesis is consistent with various findings (Bickman, 1969, 1971a; Clark, R. D., & Word, 1972).

Interest Box 9-3.   Fighting a Fire and Fighting Inertia

I was once returning to my office when I noticed a small building on campus that seemed to be burning. It was late in the afternoon, and no one was around. I ran and asked a secretary to phone the Fire Department, then grabbed a fire extinguisher and began to squirt the flames with it. Because this was an emergency that required more than the help of one person, as others arrived, I suggested that they also grab fire extinguishers. Each of the early arrivals on the scene had the model of us volunteer fire fighters to follow. Eventually, however, there were half a dozen of us squirting the fire in this small shed, and as others arrived, they simply watched. These observers were partly inhibited from fighting the fire by the fact that the shed stood in a muddy field behind a waist-high fence that had to be climbed.

Eventually, we ran out of filled fire extinguishers and needed more. We needed help from the group of bystanders. I suspected (from reading social-psychology texts!) that addressing the group as a whole and asking "Would someone please go and get a fire extinguisher?" would not produce the desired result. So I asked a friend in the group if he would take one other student, go to another building, and bring back two fire extinguishers. Even with that specific request for help, he was extremely reluctant to move. I suspect that what he had decided was "proper" had already been clearly defined for him by his previous behavior and by the behavior of the large group of spectators in whose midst he stood.

Has this person locked his keys in the car, or is he trying to break into someone else's car? Would you stop to check? It may be that the inactivity or activity of others affects us most when our own definition of the situation is ambiguous.

If our definition of the situation is important in our decision to help or hurt someone else, then it is important to consider what might affect this definition. One factor may be our liking or respect for the person in need of help. If we like the person a lot, we may be more likely to define the situation as serious and needing our help than if we do not. Similarly, we may define the situation as more serious when the person is the same race as we are, particularly if we are prejudiced. Sex may also play a role in our definition of the situation. If we tend to view females as more helpless and dependent than males, then we may generally assume that, if a woman is in distress, she is in greater need of help than a man in the same predicament. Our own sex may enter into the definition too: the average woman may see herself as having less ability to help in many situations than the average man and may be inclined to define situations differently.

EFFECTS OF CHARACTERISTICS OF THE OTHER

Similarity. People who appear similar to you and share your opinions may be more likely to receive help from you, other things being equal (Baron, R. A., 1971a; Clark, M. S., Gotay, & Mills, 1974; Doob, A. N., & Ecker, 1970; Hodgson, Hornstein, & LaKind, 1972; Hornstein, Masor, Sole, & Heilman, 1971; Karabenick, Lerner, & Breecher, 1973; Pandey & Griffitt, 1974; Sole, Marton, & Hornstein, 1975). In one illustrative case campaign workers for President Richard Nixon and Senator George McGovern conducted an experiment during the 1972 presidential race by pretending to drop campaign literature near voting booths (Karabenick et al., 1973). These researchers found that passersby more often helped them if their political preference was the same as that of the campaign workers. In another study, similarity of physical appearance proved to be important, with "hippie" and "straight" subjects receiving more dimes when they requested them from those of similar appearance.

Aggression, however, may be more likely to occur toward dissimilar others in situations where both similar and dissimilar others are available as possible targets of aggression (Donnerstein & Donnerstein, 1975). But crime statistics suggest that more aggression is directed toward similar others than dissimilar others. For instance, more crimes are committed by Blacks against Blacks (and Whites against Whites) than by Blacks against Whites or Whites against Blacks. This is probably because, as we have seen earlier, we are most often in contact with others similar to ourselves.

Familiarity. Naturalistic studies of disasters such as tornadoes have found that people are inclined to help their families before others and that friends and neighbors are helped before strangers are (Form & Nosow, 1958). Other studies have found that people who have had a brief opportunity to become acquainted with each other are more likely to help each other than are complete strangers (Latané & Darley, 1970; Latané & Rodin, 1969; Macaulay, 1975).

Other studies have found that, the more familiar we are with a victim, the more likely we are to help the victim (Geer & Jarmecky, 1973; Korte, 1969; Moriarty, 1975). The more familiar we are with the environment, the more likely we are to offer help (Latané & Darley, 1970). No wonder "charity begins at home."

Moreover, the more unfamiliar the victim, the more likely we are to hurt him or her. Studies of mice have found that fighting becomes more likely when their cage is cleaned, making it less familiar by removing odors; when a familiar mouse is removed and then reintroduced; or when a new mouse is introduced (Cairns & Nakelski, 1970). Newcomers are very often the subject of hostility until they have become more familiar to group members.

In everyday situations, however, familiarity is related to opportunity. If we are angry enough to hurt someone, chances are that familiar people—family and neighbors—will be available and possible targets of our aggression. Thus, availability, rather than familiarity, may account for the high rates of violence reported between close friends and relatives. With availability held constant, as in the studies of mice mentioned above, aggression may be most likely to be directed toward unfamiliar others.

Attractiveness. A person's physical attractiveness seems to be another factor in whether or not help or harm will be forthcoming. Physically attractive people are more likely to receive help than unattractive people (Benson, Karabenick, & Lerner, 1975). This is particularly true when help is greatly needed (West & Brown, 1975). However, the physically unattractive are likely to receive more punishment than the physically attractive. In one study (Dion, 1972; see Chapter 14) college women gave the benefit of the doubt to beautiful children who had allegedly misbehaved, whereas unattractive children were not given this benefit, and punishments were recommended for them instead.

As you saw in Chapter 8, similarity, familiarity, and attractiveness are all factors that lead to liking. Several studies have found that, under some conditions at least, we are most helpful to those we like (Daniels, L. R., & Berkowitz, 1963; Epstein, Y. N., & Hornstein, 1969; Gross, Wallston, & Piliavin, 1975; Staub & Sherk, 1970). Most of those factors that lead to affection probably also lead to helping. Factors that reduce our affection probably make aggression more likely. The relation is not perfect, though. Sometimes we hurt those we love, and we do not always give most help to those we like best (Wright, 1942).

Sex. Men and women differ in the ways they help and hurt. Study after study has found that women are more likely to be helped than men (Latané & Dabbs, 1975; Pomazal & Clore, 1973; Samerotte & Harris, in press; Snyder, Grether, & Keller, 1974; West, Whitney, & Schnedler, 1975). But women are not necessarily more helpful (Krebs, 1970). In contrast, men are more likely to be the victims of aggression than women. Men, it seems, are also much more physically aggressive than women (Feshbach, S., 1970; Gaebelein, 1973, 1977; Harris, M. B., & Siebel, 1975). In societies in which people earn their living by hunting and gathering, men hunt and women stay home. Such a division of labor persists in most agricultural and industrial societies. But this does not mean that the males of a hunting species *must be* a specialized hunting class. Among chimpanzees, males do the hunting; among lions it is the females. Among wolves and African wild dogs, adults of both sexes cooperate in hunting.

EFFECTS OF OUR PREVIOUS BEHAVIOR

Throughout this chapter we have looked at factors affecting helping and hurting. One cause of helping and hurting may also be a consequence of them. That is, if we have just helped—or hurt—someone, our chances of helping—or hurting—someone else may change.

The catharsis hypothesis, which dates back to Aristotle, proposes that, by observing aggression or by behaving aggressively, we reduce our tendency toward further aggression. It is a nice hypothesis, for it justifies socially disapproved aggression on the ground of long-term reductions in it. The research literature, unfortunately, does not support the hypothesis. Observing aggression does not always seem to make us less aggressive (reviewed in Bandura, 1973). And acting aggressively does not always seem to reduce subsequent aggression.

There is no comparable catharsis hypothesis for helping behavior. But it seems as if helping on one occasion may make us more or less likely to help on another. Here are some general principles that might hold for both helping and hurting.

1. When we engage in a new helping or hurting behavior, we learn the behavior. Because we can only do those things we know how to do, such learning will make that behavior more probable in the future.

2. When a situation arouses us to help or hurt, with the simple passage of time our tendency to help or hurt will decrease.

3. When we are physiologically aroused by nearly anything (such as erotic stimuli or strenuous activity) and interpret the situation as one requiring

helping (hurting), we may interpret our feelings as desires to help (hurt). Such arousal may thus make helping (hurting) more likely. Thus, when we are angered and engage in strenuous activity, our aggressiveness increases (Zillman, Katcher, & Milavsky, 1972).

4.   When we are rewarded by another person or "rewarded" by a good mood for helping or hurting, that behavior becomes more probable. When we are punished (by another or by a bad mood such as guilt), that behavior becomes less probable. For instance, when we see our aggression hurt another, we are "punished" and our aggressiveness may decrease (Doob, A. N., 1970). When we see our help actually help another, we are rewarded, and our helpfulness may increase.

5.   Generally, even when we voluntarily stop behaving aggressively, we will still feel somewhat angry. After the anger subsides, we will still have some negative attitudes toward the one we have hurt (Buss, 1961). When we voluntarily stop helping someone, we will still continue to feel good. After that pleasant feeling subsides, we will still have some positive attitudes toward the one we helped. This residue of feeling can persist for a long time.

Some other principles could probably be developed. In the meantime, it would be valuable to test each of these experimentally.

SOME ISSUES TO CONSIDER

Helping and Hurting: Spontaneous or Premeditated?   The long discussion of physiological responses, definitions of the situation, cost/benefit analyses, and other factors suggests that decisions to help or to hurt may take a long time to make. This is probably not the case. We have had much experience with these decisions, and they come almost automatically. Our decision to hurt (and sometimes our decision to help) often seems very spontaneous. For example, it seems that very few murders are carefully planned, that most are spontaneous (Mulvihill & Tumin, 1969; Wolfgang, 1968).[3] If this is so, it explains why the threat of capital punishment is not much of a deterrent for murder (Walker, N., 1965).

Although *individual* helping or hurting may be most commonly spontaneous, the helping or hurting a society provides is often premeditated. Fire departments are organized to help put out fires. Similarly, our preparation for hurting is considerable. War is carefully planned; punishments such as imprisonment are given only after costly trials.

The Ethics of Research on Helping.   Researchers have created many situations to study behavior, including these:

- A subway rider collapses on the floor of the car (Piliavin, J. A., & Piliavin, 1972).

[3]Just how often is helping or hurting "premeditated"? Two researchers have estimated that "probably less than 5% of all known killings are premeditated, planned or intentional" (Wolfgang & Ferracuti, 1967, p. 189 [quoted in Middlebrook, 1974, p. 302]). The other 95% occur "in the heat of passion or as the result of one person's intention to harm but not to kill another." Although there are no data available, it may well be that much of our helpful behavior is also unpremeditated, unplanned and unintentional.

Our decision to hurt often seems spontaneous.

- Smoke pours into a room filled with college students (Latané & Darley, 1968).
- A loud crash in the next room is followed by sobbing (Staub, 1971a).
- Someone falls from a ladder (Bickman, 1972).
- A person suffers an "epileptic seizure" (Horowitz, I., 1971).
- A person experiences severe electric shock (Clark, R. D., & Word, 1974).
- A person twists an ankle and falls to the ground (Shotland & Johnson, 1974).
- A person is found lying in a doorway, groaning (Darley & Batson, 1973).

How would you feel if you passed by such a situation without helping? Or what if you did help and later learned that it had been "just an experiment"? Would you hesitate to help in another emergency, thinking that it, too, might be an experiment? What are the costs and benefits to participants in such research? If you feel that these costs outweigh the benefits, are the benefits to science or society adequate? Would you like to do such research? If not, how should we study helping behavior?

Researchers have wrestled with these questions for years, and the answers they have offered are arrived at with difficulty. Many feel that, whenever research puts participants under stress or causes them any unpleasantness, it is important to "debrief" participants. Debriefing involves discussing what was done and why. Participants are assured that their behavior—whatever it was—was normal, reasonable, and acceptable. Researchers try hard to enable participants to leave an experiment in the same state as when they entered, just a bit older and wiser. Most researchers feel that any experiment that places a participant under stress should be carefully considered. If the benefits to science and to that participant do not seem to clearly outweigh the expected costs to the participant, the experimenter often decides not to conduct that particular experiment.

Researchers have been assisted in their ethical decision making by Human Subjects Review Committees, which monitor research done in institutions—such as your college—that receive federal funding. Although such committees take some spontaneity out of designing and conducting research, they also add an additional measure of responsibility and concern for the welfare of participants. But whether or not there is a committee available to review their research plans, investigators have a heavy responsibility to be certain that the welfare of human subjects is safeguarded.

SUMMARY

Our newspapers are filled with stories of helping, failing to help, and hurting. Why are people so kind? So cruel? What factors lead to helping and hurting?

Helping and hurting can be viewed as the poles of a prosocial/antisocial dimension. Many factors that influence one also influence the other. The chapter reviewed some of these factors, with the following conclusions:

1. Rewarding helping or hurting makes it more likely; punishing it makes it less likely.
2. There are probably some personality differences between the very helpful and the very aggressive.
3. When we feel frustrated, we are more likely to behave aggressively; when we see someone else frustrated, we are more likely to behave helpfully.
4. Good moods favor helpfulness; bad moods favor aggression.
5. Situations may have the strongest effects on helping and hurting.
6. The lower the costs for helping (or hurting) relative to the benefits, the more likely we are to help (or hurt).
7. Anonymity reduces helping and increases hurting.
8. Helping rates are lower and hurting rates higher in cities than in small towns.
9. The more ambiguous the situation, the less likely we will help or engage in any activity.
10. We are more likely to help, and less likely to hurt, those who are similar, familiar, and attractive.

The chapter closed by raising some questions for discussion: Is helping and hurting spontaneous or premeditated? Is research on helping ethical?

GLOSSARY TERMS

Define these terms in your own words, then look them up in the glossary at the back of the book.

Aggression (motivational and behavioral definitions)	Frustration
	Helping (motivational and behavioral definitions)
Altruism	Pluralistic ignorance
Catharsis	Psychological distance
Cost/benefit analysis	Violence
Definition of the situation	

FURTHER READING

Helping:

Huston, T. L., & Korte, C. The responsive bystander: Why he helps. In T. Lickona (Ed.), *Morality: Theory, research, and social issues*. New York: Holt, Rinehart & Winston, 1975. A fine review with perspective.

Latané, B., & Darley, J. *The unresponsive bystander: Why doesn't he help?* New York: Appleton-Century-Crofts, 1970. The book that sparked research interest in that area.

Macaulay, J., & Berkowitz, L. (Eds.). *Altruism and helping behavior*. New York: Academic Press, 1970. A fine collection of influential readings.

Milgram, S. The experience of living in cities. *Science*, 1970, *167*, 1461–1468. A well-written classic.

Hurting:

Bandura, A. *Aggression: A social learning analysis*. Englewood Cliffs, N.J.: Prentice-Hall, 1973. A contemporary analysis.

chapter 10

Attitudes and Behavior

INTRODUCTION

Every day in our lives we are bombarded with attempts to change our attitudes. Television accounts for a significant fraction of these attempts. A. C. Nielsen (1977) has found that the average American under 5 years of age watches television 23.5 hours a week; the average adult watches 44 hours a week. A high school graduate has devoted at least 15,000 hours to television—4200 more hours than he or she has spent in school! In those 15,000 hours of viewing, he or she has witnessed 18,000 murders and been exposed to over 350,000 commercials (see Interest Box 10-1). But television, radio, newspapers and magazines, and billboards and posters account for only a portion of the attempts to change our attitudes. Perhaps more common and more effective are the actions of our friends and relatives.

Attitudes do change, but most of these attempts have little or no effect. Imagine what it would be like if you changed your attitude every time someone made an effort to change it. Perhaps we should be amazed at how stable attitudes are in the face of so many efforts to change them. Nevertheless, it is attitude change rather than attitude stability that has interested social psychologists.

Attitude change is sometimes sudden and dramatic, as in a religious conversion. But more often the change is gradual and subtle. We may be more aware of these changes when we look back at how we were when we were younger; the change we see we may call growth or maturation. In fact, we may want to attribute whatever change we acknowledge to a rational decision we have made, the result of increasing wisdom and experience. We are not as comfortable with the idea that other people influence us every day. Or with the idea that perhaps our "growth" is simply change and that our attitudes may be no "better" now than when we were younger. But our discomfort does not mean that the idea is false. Your values, tastes, ideas, opinions, attitudes, and behaviors are similar to those of your family and friends, in large part because these people influence you. To some extent, too, you are similar to your friends and family because you have influenced them. You are no more immune to their influence than they are to yours. In our interdependent world, influence is mutual. We all sell ourselves, our ideas, and even a little snake oil from time to time. And from time to time we buy from others. This chapter offers some understanding—and some practical advice, if you will read between the lines—on how to influence, how you are influenced, and how to resist influence.

Why Study Attitudes?   One main reason that researchers study attitudes—and have since 1888 (Allport, G. W., 1935)—is the belief that, if attitudes cause behavior, knowledge of them will help in understanding, predicting, and controlling behavior. For example, if we know that worker satisfaction (attitude) causes lower absenteeism, fewer on-the-job accidents, and less turnover (behaviors), then we can use our knowledge to understand and control these behaviors. We can take steps to increase satisfaction in order to control (reduce) absenteeism, accidents, and turnover.

Most researchers assume that attitudes are useful to the people who hold them. This view is most explicit in the statements of functional theorists (Katz, D., 1960, 1968; Katz, D., & Stotland, 1959; Sarnoff, 1960; Smith, M. B., Bruner, & White, 1956). Some attitudes serve a **utilitarian adaptive function.** We have positive attitudes toward people and things that help us reach our goals, negative attitudes toward people and things that block us (Katz, D., 1960). Positive attitudes toward others help us to identify with them and build or maintain positive relationships with them (Kelman, 1958; Smith et al., 1956). Attitudes may serve an **ego-defensive function,** justifying the expression of behavior we cannot otherwise justify. For example, people who cannot accept their own aggressive feelings

---

Interest Box 10-1.   New York Destroyed by Martians

On the evening of October 30, 1938, thousands of Americans became panic stricken. The Martians had landed and were beginning to destroy New York City. You may not have read about this devastation in your history books, but about 1,200,000 radio listeners were excited, frightened, or terrified. So serious was this reaction that it became the subject of a classic book on the psychology of panic (Cantril, 1940). As these listeners soon learned, it was not a news broadcast, as they had thought, but a radio play entitled *War of the Worlds*.

If the media are so powerful, you might ask, why have there not been other panics since 1938? The answer is that producers are now aware of their power and show some self-imposed restraint. This restraint may even make the media more influential by increasing their credibility and by restricting their influence to more subtle effects.

How much power do the media have? Some contend that, although they have strong overall effects, the impact of any single message is greatly reduced by the number of messages conveyed. In a single evening of television watching, we are likely to be exposed to advertising of several different kinds of aspirin, several different kinds of automobile, several different kinds of deodorant, and so on. The net effect may be that Americans buy more aspirin, cars, and deodorant than they ordinarily would, even though the sales of a particular product are not as dramatically affected in all cases by advertising.

The effects of a particular television commercial on one person are probably miniscule. Personal contact and face-to-face conversation are probably much more persuasive than the media (for example, see Eldersveld & Dodge, 1954). But no advertiser could possibly afford personal contact with everyone. When the miniscule effect of one commercial on one person is multiplied by the huge number of people who see a given commercial and the huge number of commercials a person sees, the total impact of advertising might be tremendous. For many types of products, the best-advertised ones are also the best sellers.

Because influence is so important, understanding influence is important.

may become militant pacifists or dislike people who behave aggressively. Because everyone holds a unique set of attitudes, attitudes also serve to help people establish and express identity, an **expressive function.** Finally, attitudes function as personal theories, helping one understand and deal with the world, a **knowledge function.**

WHAT IS AN ATTITUDE?

There are probably as many definitions of **attitude** as there are social psychologists who have offered definitions. Most of these definitions have suggested that an attitude is an acquired predisposition to behave in certain consistent ways. We assume that an attitude exists when we observe general patterns of consistent behaviors in a person. In fact, "Consistencies in behavior are evidence of, and are caused by, an underlying attitude" is an explanatory personal theory that most social psychologists hold.

The theory is not testable, because we cannot directly measure an attitude. An attitude, said Gordon Allport (1935, p. 810), "is a mental and neural state of readiness, organized through experience, exerting a directive or dynamic influence upon the individual's response to all objects and situations to which it is related." Mental and neural states of readiness cannot be measured. The fact is that *attitude* is what we sometimes call a **hypothetical construct** (an idea proposed as an explanatory device). If we agree that attitudes cannot be measured, then how do we account for the thousands of pages written on "attitude measurement"? The best explanation is that *attitude measurement* is probably a misnomer. Our "measures" are really indexes or indicators, because they offer clues about what attitude might exist, without ever being very convincing. Still, it is hard to swim upstream. If others want to call attitude indicators attitude measures, we might as well, too. So to make life easier in these pages, we will call any device that purports to measure an attitude an *attitude measure* and any device that purports to measure only opinions an *opinion measure*. Because **opinions** are an indicator of attitudes, most opinion measures will probably be viewed by some researchers as attitude measures as well. Some methods of attitude measurement are shown in Interest Box 10-2.

Although we can measure consistencies in behavior, most of this measurement is done with our brains rather than on clipboards. As amateur social psy-

---

Interest Box 10-2.   Some Methods of Measuring Attitudes

Since Louis Thurstone proposed in 1928 that attitudes can be measured, a great number of measures have been developed. We will review a few here briefly.

Paper-and-Pencil Measures

The most common measures use paper and pencil and really measure opinions, from which attitudes may be inferred. Common methods include:

Thurstone Scales. Thurstone (1928) proposed that attitudes can be measured as follows: First, a list is made of 100 or more opinions representing all possible attitudes toward a particular attitude object. The opinions are sorted by judges into 11 ordered piles, ranging from strongly opposed to strongly in favor. From these piles are selected about 20 statements, which form the final scale. People then indicate which statements they agree with, determining their scale position.

Likert Scales. Rensis Likert (1932) proposed an easier method for measuring attitudes. In a Likert scale, several items are offered that refer to different aspects of the same general attitude. Instead of answering each item with *agree* or *disagree*, as in the Thurstone method, subjects answer each item using a five-point or seven-point scale. In the five-point scale, typical response alternatives include *strongly approve, approve, undecided, disapprove,* and *strongly disapprove.* Scores on each item (ranging from one to five if there are five alternatives) are added to find a total score. Likert-type scales are now more popular than Thurstone scales, and the evidence suggests that they may be more reliable (Seiler & Hough, 1970) and perhaps faster to construct.

Semantic Differential. Osgood, Suci, & Tannenbaum (1957) developed the semantic differential as a method of separating out aspects of semantic meaning. In this method, a concept (such as *apartment living*) is rated on one or more seven-point scales, whose extremes are labeled with adjectives such as *good* and *bad* or *pleasant* and *unpleasant.* Scores can be added in various ways.

Behavioral Measures

Four general forms of behavioral measures have been used from time to time to measure attitudes:

Behavioral intentions can be collected by simply asking respondents what they plan to do in such and such a situation;

Behavioral observations can be used to learn what people actually do in relation to the attitude object. For instance, LaPiere traveled around the country to see how hotel proprietors treated Chinese guests;

Behavioral indicators can be collected after the behavior has occurred. For instance, garbage cans might be examined to see what people drink and how much they drink in order to learn something about their attitude toward alcohol;

Behavioroid measures ask respondents to report what they usually do in a certain situation. They are called "behavioroid" because they are only indirectly and inexactly measuring behavior.

Physiological Measures

A variety of physiological measures have been used to learn about attitudes. Some researchers have measured the galvanic skin response (GSR). This method takes advantage of the fact that, when people are under stress, their skin changes slightly in its ability to conduct a small electrical charge. Topics that make people feel some stress or discomfort can be determined by careful study of these physiological measures. Other researchers have looked at pupil dilation as a measure of arousal produced by various topics.

chologists, we observe that some behaviors seem related to others. We see a secretary who delays filing assignments and photocopying and conclude that he has a negative attitude toward work. We discover that he enjoys drafting letters and may conclude that he has a negative attitude toward certain kinds of work. If he changes supervisors and then seems to enjoy filing and photocopying, we might conclude that he has a negative attitude toward certain kinds of work under certain kinds of supervision. Some other observer, who saw more or less than we, might have inferred the existence of some other attitude. Both observers are involved in the construction of personal theories and social reality rather than the discovery of physical reality.

Whether or not attitudes—as defined by anybody—exist, some cognitive processes take place to determine behavior. We would like to know about those processes that give rise to both the consistencies and inconsistencies in behavior. The search for understanding of these cognitive processes has been the focus of much social-psychological research for many years. In fact, Gordon Allport (1954a, p. 45) has referred to the idea of attitudes as "the primary building stone in the edifice of social psychology." It may be that this search will never produce complete understanding, because cognitive processes are hidden from view, and only some of their effects can be seen. But along the way in our search for the unknowable we have learned and will learn much about ourselves.

WHAT WE SAY VERSUS WHAT WE DO

What is the relationship between what we say (expressed opinions) and what we do (behaviors)? Figure 10-1 shows how complex the question really is. From this model we can see that attitudes are but one of the causes of expressed opinions and other behaviors. In this model:

1. Expressed opinions affect attitudes ("I said that little car is cute, so I must like it"—arrow 1).
2. Attitudes affect expressed opinions ("I felt that small cars are fuel efficient, so I said so"—arrow 2).
3. Other behaviors affect our attitudes ("I just bought this little car, so I must like it"—arrow 3).
4. Attitudes reflect various behaviors other than opinion expression ("I just loved the little car, so I bought it"—arrow 4).
5. Factors other than attitudes also affect the expression of opinions ("Bob just said he likes small cars, and I usually agree with him; I'll agree now"—arrow 5).
6. Our behaviors affect other influences on us ("Perhaps Bob said he likes small cars because I bought one"—arrow 6).
7. Other factors than opinion expression affect behaviors ("Bob was happy with his car, so I decided to buy one"—arrow 7).
8. Our behavior affects our expressed opinions ("I bought this little car, so I'd better say something good about it"—arrow 8).
9. Our opinions, when expressed, give rise to compatible behaviors ("I've been saying nice things about small cars for so long, I guess I'll buy one"—arrow 9).

Figure 10-1.
Influences on what
we say and do

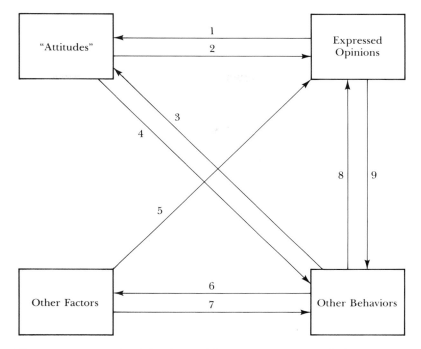

The term *expressed opinion* is used here to refer to verbal statements, and *attitude* refers to predisposing factors that give rise to these verbal statements. For instance, if I say "I like motorcycles," I have just expressed an opinion. You can use that expressed opinion to make inferences about my attitude toward motorcycles. But expressed opinions are not attitudes. There are many reasons why I might express such an opinion. For instance, if 14 big guys with leather jackets and boots were to ask me if I liked their motorcycles, you can be sure I would consider saying yes (expressed opinion), regardless of how I really felt (attitude).

Because attitudes and other cognitive processes are not directly measurable, we do not know to what extent a given expressed opinion or behavior reflects the influence of a given attitude. So the question regarding the relationship between attitudes and behavior is really a question of the relationship between expressed opinions and behavior. Are expressed opinions and behavior related? Yes or no, depending on what opinions and behaviors you have in mind. Our opinion of the Republican Party is probably unrelated to the number of peanuts we will feed an elephant, the party's symbol. Our opinion of candidates for office, however, is usually closely related to our voting behavior.

As two researchers have noted, "A given behavior is assumed to be consistent or inconsistent with a person's attitude on the basis of largely intuitive considerations" (Ajzen & Fishbein, 1977, p. 889). We do not *expect* to find more Republicans than Democrats feeding elephants at the zoo, but we do expect differences in the way they vote. Such expectations come from personal, rather than scientific, theories.

So generally, we might say, we *expect* to find a relation between certain expressed opinions and certain behaviors. This expectation has led to a certain casualness in our research. Researchers who assumed that expressed opinions and behaviors are related found it easier to measure expressed opinions than behaviors. As increasing numbers of social psychologists have moved toward laboratory experimentation, they have tended to focus more and more exclusively on paper-and-pencil measures of opinion. McNemar (1946), Wicker (1969, 1971), Fishbein and Ajzen (1975) and others have emphasized that over the last 75 years only a handful of studies have explored the relationship between questionnaire measures of opinions and other behavioral measures. (Technically, completing a questionnaire is a behavior, and it is but one of many possible ways to measure opinions. Other methods include measuring heart rate, measuring choices and preferences, and recording what people actually do in various situations. Not many studies have used both questionnaires and other measures to determine how the two types are related.) Thousands of studies have relied only on questionnaires.

But then, studies and reviews began to accumulate that suggested that our assumption was wrong. Very often, opinions and behaviors seem hardly related at all (Deutscher, 1965; Kutner, Wilkins, & Yarrow, 1952; Saenger & Gilbert, 1950; Tittle & Hill, 1967; Vroom, 1964; Wicker, 1969). At the same time, evidence was accumulating that paper-and-pencil measures of personality are often unrelated to behaviors (Bem, D. J., & Allen, 1974; Mischel, 1968; Wiggins, J. W., 1973). Many researchers changed their opinion toward the value of opinions in predicting behavior.

One result of this dismay with the weak opinion/behavior relation was to shift from dispositional approaches to situational approaches. As this shift took place, social psychologists discovered that situations can exert powerful influences on behavior. You have already read about Milgram's research on obedience and Zimbardo's research in a simulated prison environment, and these studies will be examined again later.

Another side effect of this discouragement is that social psychologists have begun to try harder to understand how opinions and behaviors are related (for example, see Ajzen & Fishbein, 1977; Albrecht & Carpenter, 1976; Calder & Ross, 1973; Campbell, D. T., 1963; DeFleur & Westie, 1958, 1963; Ehrlich, 1969; Kelman, 1974; Liska, 1974; Norman, 1975; Perry, Gillespie, & Lotz, 1976; Rokeach, 1967; Tittle & Hill, 1967).

There are many good explanations for the weak relation between opinions and behavior sometimes observed. We will review three here briefly and then look at a few others more carefully.

First, perhaps consistency is in the eye of the beholder. There are a variety of reasons why we might be wrong in our intuition that opinions and behaviors are related (reviewed by Bem, D. J., & Allen, 1974). We believe that people are and should be consistent, and we have many personal theories about what traits are related to what other traits (reviewed in Schneider, 1973). These personal theories guide our perception, helping us to see consistencies where they do not exist—through selective attention, reinterpretation, and selective recall. Further, we see others in a limited range of situations, all of which include us. Across situations, and with ourselves absent (and our consistency-adding effects on them absent), they may behave differently.

Second, perhaps our measures should be improved. If our measure of expressed opinion or behavior is low in *validity* (the relation between the thing being measured and the measure of it), then the relation between expressed opinion and behavior *measures* must be weak (see Lemon, 1973; Liska, 1974; Wicker, 1971 for reviews).

Third, perhaps *some* people will show consistency between a particular expressed opinion and behavior, and others will not. Our research designs may be wrong because they ignore individual differences in what opinions are related to what behaviors. Researchers might shift their attention from measurement of consistency across individuals to consistency within individuals and study fewer people more carefully. Possible individual differences in consistency or responsivity were discussed in Chapter 3.

Four additional explanations of the weak relation between expressed opinions and behaviors are discussed below: the effects of other variables, hurdles to action, the correspondence of measures, and reinforcement.

Variables Other Than Attitudes.   One of the strongest explanations for the weak relationship between expressed opinions and behaviors is that they do not always share the same causes. In Figure 10-1 you can see how variables other than attitudes can influence expressed opinions (arrow 5) and behaviors (arrow 7). Although there has been little systematic study of both attitudes and other factors as predictors of behaviors (Wicker, 1969), social psychologists are now coming to believe that "attitude is only one of many factors determining behavior. Although this position reaffirms the importance of attitudes, it leads to the expectation that attitudes will often be unrelated to behavior" (Ajzen & Fishbein, 1977, p. 888). With lowered expectations, we should be less often disappointed with our findings.

What other factors influence opinions and other behaviors? These **other variables** (Wicker, 1971) include such things as the expected outcome of the behavior and the desirability of that outcome (if I say or do something, how will others feel about me?). Often, norms are present that regulate our behavior, and we may choose to comply with them even if our behavior does not quite match our private attitudes (Ajzen, 1971; Fishbein, 1967). As Wicker (1969) has noted, "Social norms and role requirements, whether internalized by the individual or externally enforced, may contribute to inconsistency in a number of different ways" (Brookover & Holland, 1952; Chein, 1949; Cook & Sellitz, 1964; DeFleur & Westie, 1963; Deutsch, 1949; Fendrich, 1967; McGrath, 1964). Goffman (1955) has alerted us to the probability that, when most of us communicate (including expressing opinions), we engage in a self-presentation, which reflects how we want to be seen, how we think we ought to behave, and so on. And most of us, by now, know quite well what sorts of opinions and behaviors are socially desirable in what situations (Crowne & Marlow, 1964; Edwards, A. L., 1957). When our opinion or behavior is measured in a public situation, it is much more likely to be influenced by social desirability and group pressure than when it is measured privately and confidentially (Hyman, 1949). And so measuring a behavior in public and an opinion in private—or vice versa—may result in apparent inconsistency between the two.

Previous chapters, especially Chapter 1, argued that everyone is an amateur social psychologist. It can also be argued that much of what professional social

How many
youngsters really
believe smoking is
good? Our behavior
is much more likely
to be influenced by
social desirability in
a public situation
than in private.

psychologists have learned regarding the experimental situation can be applied to everyday situations. For instance, we now know some things about biasing factors in the experiment that influence the behavior of subjects. Some of these factors may be seen as "other factors" of the model of Figure 10-1.

Every situation we encounter probably contains some demand characteristics of the sort suggested by Martin Orne (1962) for the experimental situation: those cues that define the roles and rules, or "appropriate," "expected" behavior. Most situations may induce lesser degrees of compliance than does the experimenter in an experiment, but demand characteristics bring about roles and rules in everyday situations, nonetheless.

Experimenters often behave unwittingly in ways that lead subjects to confirm their hypotheses and expectations. Robert Rosenthal (1964, 1966) has alerted us to these **experimenter-expectancy effects.** An opinion expressed is not exactly the attitude felt, because subjects want to please the experimenter and confirm the experimenter's expectations. In everyday situations, what I expect you to say is a strong other factor that may influence what you actually say.

Opinions expressed in everyday life are not so much forthright, blunt statements of opinion as they are an interchange in which opinions are gradually expressed. Opinion expression often takes the form of simply agreeing with an opinion expressed by another group member. You and I may differ in our tendency to agree—our acquiescent response set (Couch & Keniston, 1960, 1961; Edwards & Walker, 1961; Rokeach, 1963; Rorer, 1965; Taylor, J. B., 1961). But you and I do tend to agree in public, even if we may privately disagree (see

Chapter 7 for a discussion of the Pollyanna Principle). Our agreeableness is yet another factor that reduces the match between attitudes and expressed opinions.

Habit is another important influence on opinions and behavior. *Habit* shares some properties with *attitude*. Both are hypothetical constructs used to explain consistencies in behavior. As such, they are both useful and unmeasurable. *Habit* seems to be used as an explanation for a consistent, established pattern of behavior when no other causes are obvious to either outside observers or oneself.

Habits differ from attitudes in at least two ways. First, the behavior from which we infer the existence of a habit can occur in a number of different settings but looks just the same across these settings. For example, you put your shoes on in the morning in the same way (for example, right foot first) that you put them on after a shower. The behaviors from which an attitude is inferred, however, may differ in form. For example, you may show your evaluation of shoes in general by the frequency with which you wear them, the number of pairs you own, your interest in shopping for them, and so on. Second, behaviors caused by habit may or may not imply evaluation; behaviors caused by attitudes always do (Lemon, 1973). For example, putting your right shoe on first does not mean that you like shoes more or less than if you put your left shoe on first. When an attitude and opinion are changed, habit accounts for why other behaviors do not immediately change (Fleishman, Harris, & Burtt, 1955; Greenwald, 1965, 1966; Janis & Feshbach, 1953; Maccoby, N., Romney, Adams, & Maccoby, 1962).

The "other variables" of Figure 10-1 are numerous and often very powerful. LaPiere (1934) traveled across the United States with a Chinese couple (he was Caucasian) and found that nearly all of the restaurant and motel owners accepted the couple as guests ("other behavior" of Figure 10-1). Over 90% of the 128 proprietors later said in response to a letter from LaPiere that they would *not* accept Chinese as guests ("expressed opinion"). He concluded:

> In the end I was forced to conclude that those factors which most influenced the behavior of others towards the Chinese had nothing to do with race. Quality and condition of clothing, appearance of baggage (by which, it seems, hotel clerks are prone to base their quick evaluations), cleanliness and neatness were far more significant for person-to-person reactions in the situations I was studying than skin pigmentation, straight black hair, slanting eyes and flat noses. . . . A supercilious desk clerk in a hotel of noble aspirations could not refuse his master's hospitality to people who appeared to take their request as a perfectly normal and conventional thing [1934, p. 232].[1]

In short, LaPiere believed that variables other than race were important influences on the behavior that he observed, although race seemed to have an important effect on the written replies. (We might also consider the possibility that the owners who answered LaPiere's letter were more prejudiced than the desk clerks.) Although LaPiere's interpretation of his findings took the other-variables approach, other interpretations have been offered (Ajzen, Darroch, Fishbein, & Hornick, 1970; Dillehay, 1973). Donald Campbell provided an interesting interpretation in his notion of **hurdles**.

[1] This and all other quotes from this source are from "Attitudes vs. Action," by R. T. La Piere, *Social Forces*, 1934, *13*, 230–237. Copyright 1934 by University of North Carolina Press. Reprinted by permission.

Hurdles.   To begin, let us take a closer look, in his own words, at what LaPiere did:

> In something like ten thousand miles of motor travel, twice across the United States, up and down the Pacific Coast, we met definite rejection from those asked to serve us just once.... To provide a comparison of symbolic reaction to symbolic social situations with actual reaction to real social situations, I "questioned" the establishments which we patronized during the two year period.... To the hotel or restaurant a questionnaire was mailed with an accompanying letter purporting to be a special and personal plea for response. The questionnaires all asked the same question, "Will you accept members of the Chinese race as guests in your establishment?".... 92% of the [restaurants and cafes] and 91% of the [hotels, auto-camps and tourist homes] replied "no." The remainder replied "Uncertain; depend on circumstances" [1934, pp. 232–233].

Campbell had this to say about LaPiere's study:

> In LaPiere's ... study, he and the Chinese couple were refused accommodation in .4 percent of places stopped. The mailed questionnaire reported 92.5 percent refusal of Chinese. The first thing we note is that the two diagnostic situations have very different thresholds. Apparently it is very hard to refuse a well-dressed Chinese couple traveling with a European in a face-to-face setting, and very easy to refuse the Chinese as a race in a mailed questionnaire.... But this is no evidence of inconsistency. Inconsistency would be represented if those who refused face to face accepted by questionnaire, or if those who accepted by questionnaire refused face to face. There is no report that such cases occurred [1963, p. 160].

Campbell has suggested that different opinions and behaviors may have different **thresholds** for their occurrence; just as some hurdles are easier to jump over because they are lower, some actions or opinions are easier to express than others. It may have been easy for LaPiere's hotel proprietors to say no in a letter (low threshold, so the behavior occurs) but hard to say no in person (high threshold, so the behavior does not occur).

Results similar to LaPiere's have been obtained under conditions that made it hard to reject guests in person and relatively easy over the telephone (Kutner, Wilkins, & Yarrow, 1952).

This notion of different hurdles can be applied to other situations, too. For instance, it is easier to offer to help (low hurdle) than to actually help (high hurdle). Many studies have found that more people volunteer to help than actually help (Gross, Wallston, & Piliavin, 1975; Kazdin & Bryan, 1971; Nemeth, 1970; Pliner, Hart, Kuhl, & Saari, 1974; Schellenberg & Blevins, 1973). Other studies have found that people say they would help more than they actually do help (West & Brown, 1975). One researcher asked college students if they would return a dime left in a phone booth to someone who claimed it (Bickman, 1971b). Ninety-five percent of these students said they would return it, but they thought only 72% of others would return it. In fact, only 58% of subjects in the experiment actually

Just as some
hurdles are easier
or harder to jump
over because they
vary in height, some
actions or opinions
are easier or harder
to express than
others.

did return it. Other studies have found that, although people say they would not hurt someone if ordered to do so, in the real situation they may. (See the discussion of Milgram's studies of obedience in Chapter 13.)

In summary, people often behave as if they were jumping hurdles of various heights. Given an attitude to jump, they will go over the low, easy hurdles but may not jump the high, difficult ones. When a behavior that expresses an attitude has many benefits and few costs, the hurdle is low, and the behavior occurs. When costs are high and benefits are few, attitudes do not lead to jumping, and behavior consistent with the attitude may not be expressed. Considerations of cost and benefit are often involved when we make decisions to act. We often take the course of action (or inaction) that gives us the highest expected benefit with the lowest expected cost. Such considerations often override the influence of attitude on behavior.

Correspondence of Measures.   Some of the mismatch between what people do and what they say they would do may come about because the two **measures** do not really **correspond.** For instance, LaPiere's hotel proprietors responded in person to a specific Chinese couple accompanied by him, but they responded by letter to "members of the Chinese race." It could well be that they *generally* did not accept Chinese but did *on occasion* accept Chinese, particularly well-dressed individuals accompanied by Caucasians.

This is essentially the argument advanced by Ajzen and Fishbein (1977). These theorists proposed that opinions and behaviors each have four elements: the action, the target of the action, the context of the action, and the time of the action. When any of these four elements do not correspond, the relation between the attitude measure and the behavior measure is reduced. For instance, the target of LaPiere's proprietors' behavior was a specific couple, but the target of his questionnaire was "members of the Chinese race." Because the targets only partially corresponded, the relation between opinion and behavior was weakened. Ajzen and Fishbein reviewed over 100 different opinion/behavior studies to determine the degree of correspondence between opinion and behavior measures and the degree of relation found between these measures. They concluded that, at least for target and action elements, the better the correspondence between opinion and behavior measures, the better the relation between them.

One way that correspondence is increased is by matching the specificity of the opinion and behavior measures. (Typically, opinion measures are very general, and behavior measures are very specific, as in LaPiere's study.) Researchers have agreed for some time that specificity is important for correspondence between opinion and behavior (reviewed in Haeberlein & Black, 1976).

This does not mean that we will be able to perfectly predict behavior from corresponding measures of opinion. Ajzen and Fishbein contended that opinions predict **behavior intentions** and that behavior intentions predict behavior. Behavior intentions, they argued, are also affected by the person's subjective norms and other situational factors (Ajzen & Fishbein, 1973; Fishbein & Ajzen, 1972, 1974, 1975). You might consider whether intentions are either necessary or sufficient for behavior, because we often act without thinking and sometimes find it necessary to act differently than we had planned. Whether necessary, sufficient, or neither, behavior intentions are often found to be good predictors of behavior.

Reinforcement.   If we reward a behavior, we increase the chances that it will take place again. If we withhold reward for a behavior, it is less likely to occur. This is Thorndike's **truncated law of effect.** Research suggests that the best way to change behaviors is by **reinforcing** desirable ones. Such a procedure has been used to reduce the "criminal" behavior of delinquents (Schwitzgebel & Kolb, 1964) and to reduce aggressiveness in children (Brown, P., & Elliott, 1965).

The effectiveness of social rewards on behavior change was shown in a study by Calvin (1962). Students in his psychology class gave social rewards to other students wearing clothing of specified colors. These rewards, comments such as "My, that is a nice-looking sweater" or "That coat certainly is attractive" increased the percentage of students wearing blue from 25% on a given day to 38%. After red-wearers were rewarded, the percentage rose from 12% to 19% wearing red. Your class might try Calvin's experiment.

Rewards and punishments probably affect behavior by affecting the cognitive processes that give rise to it. As a consequence, some rewards and punishments may produce changes in both attitudes and behaviors. If rewards are delivered consistently in response to a particular behavior, such as wearing red clothing, the receiver has an opportunity to learn that, "If I wear red, I will be complimented." This descriptive personal theory may lead to behavior change. It may also lead to a prescriptive personal theory: "I should wear red." This unexpressed prescriptive personal theory is an attitude. So consistent rewards (and punishments) may lead to consistencies between attitudes and behaviors. In this example, consistent rewards lead to wearing red (behavior) and having a positive attitude toward red clothing.

Sometimes, though, we are given different rewards for opinions and behaviors. Verbal behaviors most commonly are the means for rewarding or punishing verbal behavior. For example, you may say "good" or "I agree" when a person expresses an opinion consistent with your own. Other behaviors are generally used to reward similar other behaviors: you smile at me, I smile at you; you touch me, I touch you. Because entirely different classes of **reinforcers** determine much of our opinions and other behaviors and because these reinforcers may be inconsistent, the opinions and behaviors produced may be inconsistent with each other. For example, LaPiere's hotel proprietors were probably verbally rewarded by their prejudiced peer group—there was a lot of anti-Chinese sentiment in the United States in 1934—for expressing anti-Chinese opinions. But these same proprietors may have been monetarily rewarded for accepting Chinese as guests. Consistency between an opinion and a behavior should occur when rewards for the two are consistent.

The messages that parents give children are often inconsistent. Parents may expect children to "do as I say, not as I do." The father may not eat spinach because he doesn't like it. The mother may leave her room a mess. They interrupt each other during dinner. But Junior is told, "Eat your spinach, it's good for you"; "Clean up your room"; and "Don't interrupt." Junior may learn—because he was rewarded for it—that spinach is good for him, that a clean room is desirable, and that interrupting is not polite. But he may not learn to change any behaviors. After all, spinach still tastes terrible, cleaning your room is as much a pain as ever, and the only way to get a grown-up's attention seems to be by interrupting (see also Krantz & Ustler, 1974).

The rewards for attitudes and behaviors are consistent when both develop out of the same direct, personal experience with the attitude object. Rewards may be inconsistent when they develop out of different experiences or develop with vicarious (indirect) experience. For instance, two researchers found a close relation between housing attitudes and behavior in students who had personally experienced a housing crisis. But they found a weak, nonsignificant relation in students who had heard about, but not experienced, the crisis (Regan & Fazio, 1977).

ATTITUDE CHANGE

If attitudes exist and are acquired, then presumably they can be changed. How do we change attitudes?

Although social psychologists have developed a number of hypotheses of attitude change and a number of different approaches, there has not really been much conflict among these different perspectives. It turns out that each approach has dealt with a different piece of the puzzle or viewed the whole puzzle from a different angle. Rather than trying to show you what these pieces and angles have been, it will be easier to integrate them into a single view that looks at the whole puzzle. That integrated view is the goal of the pages that follow. Figure 10-2 describes the approach of this section.[2]

[2]Readers interested in more detail are urged to consult Insko, 1967; McGuire, 1968, 1969, 1972; Wrightsman, 1977.

Figure 10-2.
An overview of the attitude-change process. The cognitive process of attitude change is a sequence of events, all of which must occur for attitude change to occur. If, at any of these stages, the process "breaks down" and doesn't pass to the next stage, we will not experience attitude change. Acceptance means changing our attitude to be consistent with the message (stimulus). Rejection means no change.

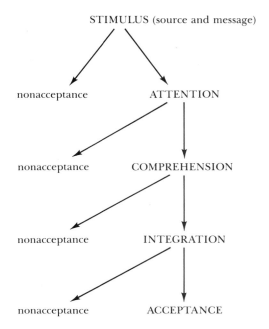

The Stimulus.   In looking at the attitude-change process, it may be helpful to distinguish between the **source** (the communicator, or originator of the persuasive communication), the **message** (the content of the persuasive communication), the *medium* (the method of presenting the message, such as television, radio, magazine ad, or speech to an assembled group) and the *audience* (those who see or hear the message). The **stimulus** to attitude change consists of the source and the message.

Most studies have found that sources who are credible (trustworthy, believable, and expert) are more influential than sources lacking credibility (Aronson & Golden, 1962; Choo, 1964; Hovland & Weiss, 1951; Karlins & Abelson, 1970; Kelman & Hovland, 1953; Watts & McGuire, 1964). This is especially true if members of the audience are dogmatic (Harvey, J., & Hays, 1972) or have an external locus of control (McGinnies & Ward, 1974; Ritchie & Phares, 1969). Prestigious sources increase the likelihood of a persuasive communication's being accepted. They also produce more positive evaluations of statements and objects (Das, 1960; Duncker, 1938; Farnsworth & Misumi, 1931; Goldberg, H., & Iverson, 1965; Hastorf & Piper, 1951; Lorge, 1936; Pastore & Horowitz, 1955; Saadi & Farnsworth, 1934). This **prestige suggestion** is often used in advertising, as where a football star patronizes a certain car-rental firm and nine out of ten dentists surveyed recommend a brand of chewing gum.

Suppose the Muttmeat Dog Food Company wants you to buy their fine product for your pooch and decides to place an ad (stimulus) in your favorite magazine. You pick up the magazine and flip through it. If the ad is located in the right spot and is well designed, you may notice it (attention). If not, you can't accept the message and decide to buy Muttmeat. Suppose you do see the ad. Do

"*Prestigious sources increase the likelihood of accepting persuasive communication.*"

you understand that Muttmeat is made *for* dogs, not *from* dogs? Do you understand other parts of the ad? If not, there is little chance you'll buy it. If you do, you must then integrate the message with your other beliefs: Is Muttmeat more nutritional/tasty/economical than your pooch's current dinner? Will your dog eat the stuff? Such important questions must be answered satisfactorily before you accept the ad's message.

Your dog may go through the same steps in deciding whether to eat Muttmeat: He must notice (attention) the stimulus (dish of Muttmeat), understand it is food (comprehension), and fit this fact in with others, such as whether or not he's hungry and whether or not he would eat something that looked and smelled like Muttmeat. If Muttmeat passes these tests, he'll accept the mess and start eating. With this graphic example in mind, let's look at some more abstract aspects of the attitude-change process.

The importance of the credibility of the source of the attitude-change process seems to diminish over time (Hovland & Weiss, 1951; Kelman & Hovland, 1953). Low-credibility sources usually do not produce much attitude change either immediately or after some delay. High-credibility sources produce some change immediately, but their effects diminish with time, in part because we dissociate (lose the connection between) message and source.

This dissociation principle may be used by television advertisers who have cartoon cats meowing over their favorite food. The immediate effect of the commercial may be to capture your attention and teach you the product name; the delayed effect may be to induce you to buy, if you can't remember whether it was a dancing cat or a neighbor who recommended the product. Even in the short run, advertisers know, if you are distracted and not paying attention, a high-credibility source (a cat-club president, for instance) may be no more effective than a low-credibility source (Brock & Becker, 1965).

We are probably also more easily persuaded by sources who are physically attractive (Mills, J., & Aronson, 1965; Snyder & Rothbart, 1971). This is also true of sources we are fond of and those we regard as most similar to us.

Attention.   **Attention** is the first stage in the attitude-change process. In order for us to be influenced by a personal communication, we must notice it and attend to it. (Without some degree of attention, the next stage in attitude change—**comprehension**—is not possible.) If our own attention is distracted and we do not hear or see the message well, attitude change is less likely (Baron, R. S., Baron, & Miller, 1973). The principles of learning that are known to affect attention presumably also operate in attitude change (Hovland, Janis, & Kelley, 1953).

Advertisers have found many ways to get your attention. Handsome men rope cattle, surf, or sky-dive, then take a break with the advertiser's beer or cigarettes. Beautiful women stand near cars, and cats talk and dance around cat food. And where do they do these feats? On prime-time television, on billboards you see when stuck in traffic, and on the back covers of magazines. Advertisers spend a fortune getting your attention.

One good way to get people's attention is to surprise or frighten them. Many experiments have found that sources, messages, or presentations that arouse fear are effective in producing attitude and behavior change (reviewed in Higbee, 1969; Leventhal, 1970). Even informing people that they are frightened by means of false physiological feedback produces attitude change (Hendrick, Giesen, & Borden, 1975). The effects of fear arousal may stem from the fact that our attention is captured. The frightened person may say: "This is frightening! I'd better pay attention and learn this. Maybe it's important!"

Loudness is another way to get someone's attention. When we are confident of what we are saying, our loudness tends to increase. Our audience may take such increases as a sign of our confidence, pay closer attention, and be persuaded. Moderately loud communications seem to be more persuasive than quieter ones (Packwood, 1974), a principle that radio and television sometimes use by raising the volume in commercials. (The effects of overheard whispers suggest a limit on this generalization, though.)

If you are listening to a long speech, you are more likely to remember the first part and the last part than the middle. The same may go for poems you learned in high school or arguments made in court. This is the well-known **serial-position effect** in learning: the first and last items in a series are easier to learn than the middle items. A great deal of research has been focused on whether the first items have a greater effect (a primacy effect) or the last items have a greater effect (a recency effect) (Anderson, N., 1959; Anderson, N., & Hovland, 1957; Crano, 1973; Cromwell, 1950; Hovland & Mandell, 1957; Insko, 1964; Knower, 1936; Lana, 1963a, 1963b, 1964a, 1964b; Lund, 1925; Miller, N., & Campbell, 1959; Rosnow, 1966; Rosnow & Robinson, 1967; Thomas, Webb, & Tweedie, 1961; Wilson, W., & Miller, 1968). For much of everyday life, we experience a steady barrage of attitude-change attempts, and the issue of whether primacy or recency is more important may not matter much. However, there are occasions—such as in the courtroom or in a debate—when it does matter. Until the research clarifies the conditions under which primacy is stronger than recency (and vice versa), the safest conclusion is that both are important. When planning a speech, for instance, you might put your best arguments first and summarize them at the end.

Comprehension.   If we have been paying attention and have heard or read the message as presented by the source, the next question is, do we comprehend it? Obviously, if you do not understand the message it cannot have much of an effect on your opinion. At least one study has found that greater comprehension can lead to greater influence (Thistlewaite & Kamenetsky, 1955). In everyday conversation, we make special efforts to be understood and to understand the other person who is talking to us. Because we cannot have such a conversation with a television commercial or billboard, advertising is usually carefully pretested to be certain it is understandable.

We do not understand how we understand things, but it must be a complex process. When we hear a persuasive communication—or most conversations, for that matter—we have to remember what we have heard, then translate the words and phrases used into words and phrases *we* use. When someone is advocating a position we are not familiar with, the entire position must be somehow translated into our own perspective. Such a mental translation may find not word equivalents but meaning equivalents. When we feel we have completed the pattern matching "successfully," we may experience a pleasant feeling—the internal counterpart to a "smile of recognition"—that rewards the cognitive process. Thus, learning may be intrinsically rewarding (Stang, 1975a).

Feelings of understanding are not the same as understanding. Much of our acceptance of a persuasive communication may occur because we have reinterpreted the persuasive communication to "fit" the patterns already in our head. Consider the statement, "I hold it that a little rebellion, now and then, is a good thing, and is as necessary in the political world as storms are in the physical." When we believe Jefferson is the source of this message, we may understand it (reinterpret it) to refer to peaceful political change. If we believe Lenin to be the source of this message, then it might be understood to mean revolution. We might agree with the first interpretation but disagree with the second. Solomon Asch (1940, 1948, 1952) has suggested that such a perspective is useful in understanding a variety of situations in which attitude change does or does not occur. Asch suggested that this process of interpretation results in "a change in the object of judgment, rather than in the judgment of the object" (Asch, 1940, p. 458). Because we interpret everything in order to understand it, misunderstanding will sometimes give rise to apparent agreement or disagreement. We might misunderstand (and think we agree with) a statement attributed to Jefferson or misunderstand (and think we disagree with) the same statement attributed to Lenin.

Integration.   Does the message "fit" with the ideas and opinions and facts that we carry around in our heads? The first step in this **integration** may be to examine our **counterarguments.** Do we have any reason for believing that the viewpoint expressed by the source is wrong or should be rejected? We may already have reasons to disagree with the source about this topic, in which case the source may present some counterarguments. If not, we are likely to try to think of reasons why the viewpoint is in error, to develop our counterarguments. If no counterarguments come to mind or if they do not seem to be particularly good, we are much more likely to accept the message and change our attitude (or form one) than if good counterarguments are on hand.

As McGuire has persuasively argued, when we are confident about widely shared beliefs—"cultural truisms"—then we may be highly vulnerable to attack (Anderson, L. R., & McGuire, 1965; McGuire, 1961, 1964, 1967, 1968; McGuire & Papageorgis, 1961; Papageorgis & McGuire, 1961). For instance, few of us have thought about why we should not brush our teeth, so an argument that advocates not brushing may be particularly effective in attitude change. Many children who attend parochial school later discover that they cannot effectively deal with counterarguments to their religious beliefs. "Inoculating" ourselves by practicing counterarguments, McGuire suggested, should help develop resistance to persuasion.

Whether you try to develop counterarguments at all depends in large measure on your initial views on the subject. If the message is similar to messages that you endorse (that is, if it falls within what some researchers have called a **latitude of acceptance**), you may be more likely to accept it and distort it so that it seems more compatible with your views. If the message is contrary to views you endorse and falls within what some researchers have called a **latitude of rejection,** you are likely to distort it so that it seems even more incompatible with your views, and then reject it (Hovland, Harvey, & Sherif, 1957; Sherif, C. W., Sherif, & Nebergall, 1965; Sherif, M., & Hovland, 1961). However, a number of experiments have found that, when a great change in opinion is advocated, more change results than when smaller change is advocated (Fisher & Lubin, 1958; Fisher, Rubinstein, & Freeman, 1956; Goldberg, S. C., 1954; Hovland & Pritzker, 1957). *Latitude of*

acceptance is another convenient hypothetical construct and, like *attitude*, probably cannot be measured. If we are not much involved with the issues, our latitude of acceptance is likely to be fairly wide, and we will be fairly agreeable. If we are quite involved with the issue already, we will have strong attitudes before we even hear the message, and our latitude of acceptance will be small (Sherif, C. W., et al., 1965).

Another process in integrating a new attitude with those already held seems to be **consistency assessment.** We seem much more willing to adopt an attitude that appears similar to those we already hold than to adopt one that appears inconsistent. Rejecting inconsistent attitudes or beliefs is one way of maintaining cognitive stability. This will be discussed later in this chapter. If consistency is important, then you will be most persuasive when you maximize the apparent similarity between you and your audience on every important dimension related to the attitude you want to change.

Just as consistency is important in attitude change, it can be important in attitude formation. For instance, if we learn that a politician is a member of our party and religion and has advocated a position consistent with our own, this consistency helps us create a positive attitude toward her. If she were inconsistent with us in these respects, our emerging attitude would be more likely to be negative.

As you can see, the process of integrating a new idea, attitude or belief with our old ones is complex. Many conditions must be met before we accept this stimulus and "change" our attitude. More likely than not, little permanent change will occur. Rather, we may accept it in some modified form, seek more information, or reject it outright. Such options help us cope with a world full of propaganda and permit attitude stability.

ATTITUDE STABILITY

This chapter opened by suggesting that, although we are bombarded by attempts to change our attitudes, they are remarkably stable. Although attitude change may appear to occur in the laboratory, field studies suggest considerable **stability of attitudes** (Hovland, 1959). Further, little attention has been directed at how long lasting laboratory-induced attitude change is. But it seems likely that most attitude change dissipates soon after it is measured, and former attitudes are reinstated (Ronis, Baumgardner, Leippe, Cacioppo, & Greenwald, 1977). And although several have raised the question, few have been concerned with the effects (if any) of lab-induced attitude change on subsequent behavior change (Cohen, A. R., 1964; Festinger, 1964a; Greenwald, 1965).

A variety of evidence suggests that attitudes are not very easily changed. For instance, since the surgeon general warned us that smoking is dangerous, a tremendous campaign has been waged to reduce smoking. But cigarette smoking in the United States continues to climb. Every week millions of Americans attend religious services in which they are exhorted to love one another. The effect seems small (see Interest Box 10-3). Even the total institution of the prison does not seem to have much effect on attitudes toward crime. Although one function of prisons is rehabilitation, half of all prisoners in the United States will go back to prison on another offense after they are released. Finally, as Etzioni has noted, "Initially all of the 150-odd compensatory education schemes that have been tried either have not worked at all or have worked only marginally or only for a small proportion of the student population" (1972, p. 214).

It is probably easier to change behavior by changing our situation than by changing our attitudes. Etzioni (1972) contended that driver education is far less

---

Interest Box 10-3.   Religion and Racism

Are people who attend church regularly less racist than those who do not attend church? If church attenders are influenced by religious teachings, one might expect this to be the case, as most religions teach love toward others, and only about 10% of clergy oppose civil rights (Hadden, 1969). However, research on this subject suggests that those who do attend church or synagogue once or twice a month are *more* prejudiced than those who do not attend at all (although those few who attend three or more times a *week* tend to be least prejudiced) (Allport, G. W., & Ross, 1967; Struening, 1963). Other studies have found that those who attend church regularly, as compared with infrequent attenders, are *less* likely to accept Christian ethics (Glock & Stark, 1966; Hadden, 1969; Stark & Glock, 1968). Large proportions of White regular churchgoers, these studies find, do not want Blacks in their churches, would move if Blacks moved into their neighborhoods, and think that Blacks should be grateful for what they have and stop protesting.

Of course, this does not mean that religion causes prejudice. As with any correlation, it may be that some other factors are responsible for the relationship. For example, a functional explanation might suggest that people who are insecure may be prejudiced as a means of reducing this insecurity and may also find religion helpful in giving them a feeling of security. Stark & Glock (1969) have suggested another explanation. A central belief in Christianity is that individuals act freely and are capable, through the choices they make, of shaping their destinies and getting to heaven. This belief requires that social, situational, and historical influences on one's fate be overlooked. If people are poor, it must be because of actions they have taken. People with strong beliefs in free will may blame victims.

How do you feel about free will? Social psychologists, who are accustomed to studying social influences on behavior, are inclined to believe that behavior is not simply and entirely determined by "free will," are consequently interested in social reforms, and, incidentally, are not generally religious (McClintock, Spaulding, & Turner, 1965).

cost-effective than seat belts in saving lives. In a similar way, the controversial Antabuse (a drug that makes you sick if you drink alcohol after taking it) appears more effective than therapy or advertising campaigns in reducing drinking, and the controversial methadone appears more effective than jail or therapy in reducing heroin addiction.

Why is it so difficult to change behavior by changing attitudes? There are at least two good reasons. First, attitudes are but one influence on behavior. Any behavior takes place in a context of influences, an interdependent system of cause and effect. Such systems tend to be relatively stable and compensate for shifts in their components. That is, when an attitude changes and puts pressure on a behavior to change, other influences on behavior may come into play, preventing the change. Even if I decide that doughnuts are fattening (attitude change) and that I should not eat them, my hunger, the suggestion of a friend, their presence, habit, and other factors may lead me to eat just as many.

If we want to change a particular behavior, we must find its causes and which of these causes are most easily changed. There will often be multiple causes, and the behavior will be embedded in a system of behaviors. Intervention at a single point will not always be adequate. When it is, an attitude-change campaign may sometimes be the most efficient means of changing behavior, sometimes not. Punishing a behavior does not always reduce its probability. But rewarding a behavior seems effective in increasing its probability.

The second reason it is difficult to change behavior by changing attitudes is that attitudes themselves are probably very resistant to change, maybe more resistant than behaviors. As you saw in previous pages, many conditions must be met before an attitude will change. And as soon as it does, mysterious forces, such as other attitudes, begin working on undoing the change. Attitudes are stable in part because we have a need that the new attitude be consistent with (a) our other existing attitudes, (b) our current behaviors, (c) our previous behaviors, (d) the attitudes of our friends and family, and (e) even the earlier attitude(s) that are being replaced. Thus, a new attitude must be integrated neatly into a larger pattern for it to be accepted. Because consistency plays such a major role in maintaining attitude stability, we should spend some time looking at theories and findings related to consistency.

Consistency Theories and Findings.   People seem to behave in a way that will provide them with some optimum level of consistency among their attitudes. Sometimes we strive toward feelings of greater consistency, and sometimes we seem to relish inconsistency.

A feeling of consistency is not the same as consistency. It is quite possible for us to hold two or more logically inconsistent attitudes or personal theories in separate, logic-tight compartments. Logic, after all, is not the only factor affecting our beliefs. **Wishful thinking**—holding beliefs consistent with our desires and wishes—is also important (McGuire, 1960a, 1960b, 1960c). To some extent, we believe what we want to believe. Also, we are often able to keep our inconsistent beliefs from encountering each other and exposing the inconsistency. McGuire suggests that, when we become aware of inconsistencies, we may try to reduce them—a "Socratic effect."

Another reason why people are not always perfectly consistent is that consistency requires considerable cognitive effort, constant adjustments in attitude and behavior, and so on. When this effort exceeds the apparent benefits, we may find it preferable to live with inconsistencies.

Balance theory. Fritz Heider (1944, 1946, 1958) was apparently the first social psychologist to call our attention to a simple fact: if I like you, I tend to like what you like. Take cats, for instance. If I like you and you like cats, then I tend to like them (Figure 10-3.1). Heider calls this pleasant state **balanced.** Suppose I don't like you and you like cats. I'm likely to come to dislike cats (Figure 10-3.2). This is also balanced. If I don't like you and you don't like cats, I may find it more pleasant to like them (Figure 10-3.3). My enemy's enemy is my friend (balanced). You will note that, for balance to occur, either 0 or 2 bonds must be negative.

Figure 10-3.
Balance theory and attitude change

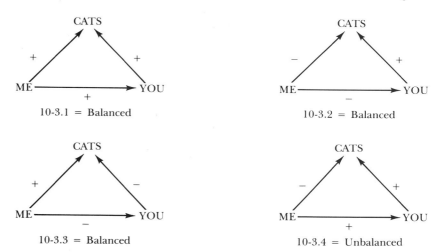

10-3.1 = Balanced

10-3.2 = Balanced

10-3.3 = Balanced

10-3.4 = Unbalanced

What if I like you, you like cats, and I don't (Figure 10-3.4)? Heider calls this **unbalanced** (or imbalanced), and theoretically it is unpleasant. Such unpleasantness, Heider proposed, leads to action: I might change my attitude toward you or toward cats. We might not discuss cats. I might reinterpret your statements about cats to mean something less positive than you meant. I might decide that cats are not important. And so on.

Such a charming idea as **balance theory** has led to half a dozen major theories, scores of propositions, thousands of published studies, and just as many sleepless nights for researchers trying to resolve the inconsistencies between their theory and data (see Abelson & Rosenberg, 1958; Aronson, 1968; Brehm & Cohen, 1962; Cartwright & Harary, 1956; Feather, 1964; Festinger, 1957, 1964; Newcomb, 1953; Osgood & Tannenbaum, 1955).

Dissonance theory. In 1957, Leon Festinger proposed his **cognitive-dissonance theory.** Its assumptions are similar to those of other consistency theories: people presumably find inconsistency (Festinger called it **dissonance**) unpleasant and will therefore act to reduce it. Festinger proposed that two **cognitions** (thoughts, knowledges, beliefs, attitudes, values, personal theories) are dissonant when they appear to be psychologically contradictory. The thought "I am an athlete" and the thought "I don't smoke" are consonant (consistent), because one follows the other: good athletes should not smoke. But the thought "I am an athlete" and the thought "I smoke heavily" are dissonant. Dissonant cognitions make us uncomfortable, according to the theory, and motivate us to action.

There are many actions we can take to reduce dissonance. For instance, we can

1. Reduce the *importance* of the dissonant cognitions. We can say "I never wanted to be a great athlete, just a good one."
2. Reduce the *number* of dissonant cognitions. "Maybe the studies are wrong, and smoking isn't so dangerous. Maybe smoking is only dangerous when one smokes more than I do."
3. Increase the *number* of consonant cognitions. "Although I smoke, I take care of myself other ways. I wear a seat belt, get plenty of sleep, take vitamins, and exercise regularly."
4. Increase the *importance* of consonant cognitions. "Good diet is much more important for good health than not smoking is."
5. Drop one or both cognitions from conscious awareness. When we are made aware of inconsistencies between our cognitions or between our attitudes and behaviors, on the one hand, we are likely to try to reduce these inconsistencies (Rokeach, 1973; Rokeach & McLellan, 1972). By becoming *unaware* of the inconsistent cognitions (say, by forgetting), on the other hand, it seems possible that we can reduce the dissonance they create.

Not long after Festinger published his theory, Brehm and Cohen improved on it. They proposed that "a person will try to justify a commitment to the extent that there is information discrepant with that commitment" (1962, p. 300). **Commitment,** here, means decision, choice, or action. We are most inclined to bring our attitudes and actions into line with each other, suggest Brehm and Cohen, when our commitment has been made freely, our behavior not forced. When someone casually asks us to do something and we do it, we may feel that we have chosen to do it. If it is the obverse of an attitude we hold, we may experience dissonance and change our attitude to make it more consistent with our behavior.

Suppose someone casually asks us to write an essay supporting a position we disagree with and offers to pay us $1. We agree and say to ourselves: "Why am I writing this essay? For the money? No, $1 isn't enough. Perhaps I really agree with the essay I've written." Result: attitude change. Now suppose the experimenter had offered $20 to write such an essay. No one would wonder why he or she was writing such an essay: it would be for the money. Result: no attitude change. In fact, such results have been repeatedly obtained using this **forced-compliance** procedure. It happens when people are asked to write essays on topics they disagree with (Brehm & Cohen, 1962), when they are asked to eat grasshoppers (E. E. Smith, 1961), when college students are asked to go without food for a long period of time (Brehm & Cohen, 1962), or when students are asked to tell others that a boring experiment is interesting (Festinger & Carlsmith, 1959) (see Figure 10-4).

Figure 10-4.
You don't always
get what you pay
for. (From
"Cognitive
Dissonance," by
L. Festinger.
Scientific Offprint
#472, p. 6.
Originally
published in
Scientific American,
1962, *207*(4),
93–102. Copyright
© 1962 by Scientific
American, Inc. All
rights reserved.
Reprinted by
permission of W. H.
Freeman and
Company,
Publishers.)

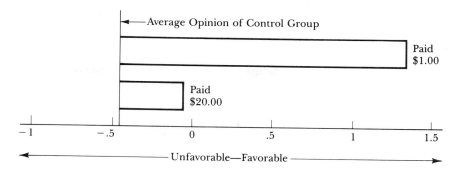

Consequences of lying are found to vary, depending on whether the justification for the lie is large or small. In this experiment students were persuaded to tell others that a boring experience was really fun. Those in one group were paid only $1 for their cooperation; in a second group, $20. The low-paid students, having least justification for lying, experienced most dissonance and reduced it by coming to regard the experience favorably.

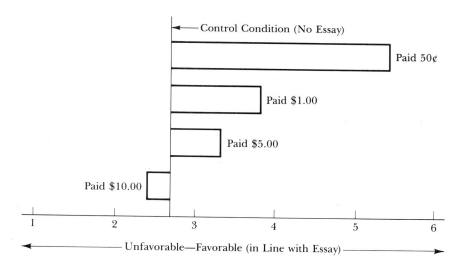

Graded change of opinion was produced by paying subjects various sums for writing essays advocating opinions contrary to their beliefs. When examined later, students paid the least had changed their opinion the most to agree with what they had written. Only the highest paid group held to their original opinion more strongly than did a control group.

Because *dissonance* is another cognitive process like *attitude* or *habit*, it cannot be measured directly, so we cannot be sure it exists. Dissonance is assumed to have existed when certain events that are believed to reduce it are observed. One such event is attitude change, which occurs to make an attitude more consistent with a behavior. Another event is behavior change, to make the behavior more consistent with the attitude. And a third event is seeking out information that should reduce dissonance or avoiding information that increases it. There is little clear experimental evidence that this selective exposure to information takes place.

Dissonance theory has been very useful in generating research and ideas. But because dissonance cannot be measured directly and because there are so many ways one can theoretically reduce it when it is aroused, dissonance theory has been hard to test unequivocally. As Aronson has said, "While the theory has generated a great deal of data, it has not been easy to define the limits of the theoretical statement to determine the specific predictions that can be made" (1973, p. 225). In fact, many findings in research generated by dissonance theory are open to nondissonance interpretations, and there has been considerable controversy on which interpretations are best (Chapanis & Chapanis, 1964). In the last 20 years, there have been several major restatements of dissonance theory (Aronson, 1968; Brehm & Cohen, 1962; Wicklund & Brehm, 1976). And the theory has gradually shifted in several ways to maintain consistency with the findings it has generated (reviewed in Greenwald & Ronis, 1978).

Two other interpretations of dissonance findings, *self-perception* and **mere thought,** illustrate the shift in dissonance theory.

Self-perception theory.   Can our behaviors affect our attitudes (arrow 3 of Figure 10-1)? Can our expressed opinions affect our attitudes (arrow 1 of Figure 10-1)? Daryl Bem (Bem, 1965, 1966, 1967, 1972) has proposed an intriguing theory of self-perception. He suggested that our actions sometimes give rise to our attitudes, rather than vice versa. We may not have an attitude on a particular subject, and the situation may call for some behavior on our part. Having behaved, we observe our behavior, just as we observe the behavior of others. Just as we infer attitudes of others from their behavior, we may infer that we have particular attitudes consistent with the behavior we have just engaged in. For example, you visit a friend, who feeds you a bowl of Sugarglop Puffs. As you munch through this bowl of cereal, you quietly think to yourself "I eat things that I like and I am eating this. Therefore, I must like it." Another example: you are sitting in the drive-in and your friend leans over, embraces you, and kisses you. You naturally kiss back and conclude: "I am kissing this person. Maybe I like this person."

It seems likely that we infer both attitudes and other internal states from observations of both our behavior and other external cues. Observing our own behavior may lead to attitude formation or change when we believe that our behavior was freely chosen, when there seems to be little external justification for the behavior (so we conclude "I must have done it because *I* wanted to"), and when the consequences of the behavior are important (reviewed in Collins, 1973).

Evidence that our behavior can affect our attitudes comes from an experiment by Bem and two of his students (Bandler, Madaras, & Bem, 1968). They administered a series of electric shocks to paid volunteer subjects and asked them to report how painful each was. For each shock, subjects were given a choice to endure it or escape after a time by pressing a button. Although this seemed like a "free choice" to subjects, in fact, Bem was able to control the choice simply by subtly suggesting to subjects whether he preferred them to endure or escape. Self-perception theory predicts that subjects would judge shocks they chose to escape as more uncomfortable than shocks they chose to endure, right? That is what happened, even though all shocks were actually identical in strength (of course, by choice of the subject, the endured shocks lasted longer).

"Sometimes there seems to be little justification for behavior."

Bem suggested that, the less apparent external motivation is provided for an action, the more likely a person will assume that the action was internally motivated. For instance, when people go through a difficult initiation to join a group (such as a fraternity hazing) they may conclude that they must really want to be in the group—why else would they have done it? People, in fact, do seem to like groups that are hard to get into more than those with easier entrance requirements (Aronson & Mills, 1959; Gerard & Mathewson, 1966). Other types of effort also seem to increase value. For instance, when we pay more for a product, we may come to believe it is worth more and like it better (Doob, A. N., Carlsmith, Freedman, Landover, & Tom, 1969).

There may be limits to the self-perception effect. When we are given feedback that suggests that we hold an attitude very different from the one we initially held, behavior seems more likely to change than attitudes (Nisbett & Schachter, 1966); Storms & Nisbett, 1970; Valins & Ray, 1967). When the feedback is somewhat consistent with the attitude initially held or when the initial attitude is very weak, the effects of behavior on attitudes may be stronger (Bandler et al., 1968; Taylor, S. E., 1975; Valins, 1966). It is difficult to reverse an attitude even through laboratory manipulations of self-perception. Similarly, attitudes that are very important are probably carefully assessed before being changed, and again, the influence of self-perception may be reduced (Taylor, S. E., 1975). If we accept self-perception theory, we do not have to reject dissonance theory. Both are useful ways of understanding attitudes and behavior. And they have much in common. Both, for instance, deal with the effects of behavior on attitudes. How strong are these effects?

The effects of our behavior on our attitudes may be very strong. Insko has suggested that "it may indeed turn out that most of the consistency between attitudes and behavior is due not to the effect of attitudes upon behavior but of behavior upon attitudes (1967, p. 348). Nigel Lemon echoed this sentiment: "Because of the tenuous nature of subjective experience, knowledge of previous behavior is likely to exert a powerful influence on an individual's judgment of his own attitude; and prediction of an attitude from behavior is likely to be more effective than the other way round" (1973, p. 245).

Mere-thought theory.   Another explanation of dissonance theory is that the conditions in dissonance research lead to conscious or nonconscious thought of some sort and that **mere** repeated **thought** affects our attitudes toward what we are thinking about. A considerable amount of literature now indicates that mere repeated exposure usually leads to attraction (reviewed in Stang, 1974b). When we are exposed to an object, we naturally think about it, so we might also say that repeated thought leads to attraction. In fact, Abraham Tesser has found this to be true, when the initial attitude is somewhat positive (Stang, 1978c; Tesser, 1975; Tesser & Conlee, 1975; Tesser & Cowan, 1975; Tesser & Johnson, 1974). In most dissonance studies, subjects are likely to give their actions considerable thought. When subjects make their choices that lead to attitude change, it is usually from among initially attractive alternatives (Ehrlich, Guttman, Schönbach, & Mills, 1957). This thought alone may make the object of the thought more attractive. But after a choice is made, thought is much more likely to focus on the alternative chosen than on the one(s) not chosen—and often no longer present. More thought about the chosen alternative than about others should lead to greater preference for it. This finding is what many researchers have noted.

For example, one study (Knox & Inkster, 1968) found that bettors at the $2 window of a race track thought they had a fairly good chance of winning *after* placing their bets (liked their horse more?) but only a fair chance of winning *before* betting. Most bettors probably think relatively more about the horse they have bet on after betting than they do before deciding how to bet. Indirect support for this notion can be found in a study done by Ehrlich and colleagues (Ehrlich et al., 1957). They found that before buying a car people usually read all sorts of ads and seek out facts on many different makes and models. But after buying a car they seek information more selectively, and ads for cars not chosen tend to be avoided. Differences in exposure to information may enhance differences in thought and liking about the choices.

Thinking about something does not always lead to increased liking, though; sometimes we seem to come to dislike it more. Thinking about an upsetting experience may make us grow more and more angry. This leads us to suspect that mere thought may polarize our attitudes, causing our likes to grow more positive and our dislikes more negative.

Mere-thought theory is being proposed on these pages for the first time, so there is no research that tests it as an explanation of the findings of dissonance research. It is presented to demonstrate how new theories can always come along to challenge or elaborate on old explanations of findings generated by those older theories.

Reactance theory. Many of the situations studied by dissonance and self-perception researchers involve subtle forced compliance. That is, a researcher gets people to do something and lets them believe they have chosen to do it. Then they find that they like what they are doing. When people try it, they like it. Sometimes, though, we feel forced to do something or feel prevented from doing something. When this happens, we feel unhappy. Jack Brehm (1966, 1972) called these unpleasant feelings **psychological reactance.** Reactance, Brehm suggested, develops when we feel a loss of freedom. We work to regain a feeling of freedom and to avoid feelings of reactance (Worchel & Brehm, 1971). Brehm has found that, if your free choice among several alternatives is restricted and you are denied one of the alternatives, that alternative will become more desirable (Sensenig & Brehm, 1968). At the same time, when you are forced to do something, that alternative becomes less desirable than when you can freely choose to do it.

For example, suppose you are undecided whether to spend your Easter vacation at home with your parents or travel to Florida. If your parents call and insist that you come home for the vacation, your freedom to choose how you will spend the vacation has been taken away. Reactance theory suggests that you will now prefer to take the vacation in Florida. Through reactance, Prohibition may increase the desirability of drinking, censorship may increase the value of the films or literature censored, and a parent's demands may increase the chances that children and adolescents will want to do just the opposite of what the parent wants. The grass seems to become greener when the fence is built.

Neither dissonance theory nor self-perception theory deals with why people dislike an alternative when it is forced on them. Reactance theory simply says that these negative feelings are a consequence of people's *need* to feel they have free choice (the need is not explained further). The mere-thought explanation suggests that yes, indeed, being forced is unpleasant and that unpleasant things become more unpleasant with repeated thought. For instance, Taylor (cited in Cook, S. W., 1957) found that Whites who felt favorably toward Blacks before any Blacks lived in the neighborhood became even more favorable after Blacks had been living there for several weeks. Good things get better with repeated thought. However, those Whites with initially negative feelings became more negative after contact. Negative feelings become more negative with thought. It may turn out that the mere-thought theory is another consistency theory. Inside our heads new, positive attitudes and beliefs may associate with and become attached to existing positive attitudes and beliefs, and negative may become attached to negative.

Perhaps we should not assume that there is some invariant relationship between attitudes and behavior, attitudes and opinions, or opinions and behavior. The relationship will sometimes be weak or nonexistent, sometimes quite strong. Our attitudes are sometimes so strong that they lead us beyond simple expressions of opinions in discussion. The protest movements throughout our history have developed out of strong attitudes that could not be soothed by discussion. Strong attitudes have led to a variety of remarkable behaviors.

Some attitudes
result in remarkable
behaviors.

POSTSCRIPT

How Much Consistency Is Best?   How much consistency do you prefer in
yourself and in others? How do you achieve such consistency? When do you prefer
inconsistency? Why? These are good questions to think about, though very little
research has been done on these issues.

How Much Influence Do Situations Have?   The situation you are in has a
stronger effect on your behavior at some times than at others. If we see our
behavior as being forced by the situation (see discussion of attribution theory,
Chapter 6), then we are not likely to infer our attitudes from our behavior. If we
believe that we are acting out of free will, then there is greater possibility for our
behavior to influence our attitudes. Most of us seem to greatly underestimate the
magnitude of the effect of situations on our behavior; that is, we think we are
acting out of free will when we are really forced. Because we attribute our behavior
to free choice rather than situational forces, our awareness of our behavior probably has a major effect on our attitudes. Even social psychologists may underestimate the magnitude of the effect of situations on behaviors, because a given
situation may affect different people differently and cause them to behave differently. Our belief that we act out of free will, not governed by situations, is very
strong. But is this belief justified by the facts: how free are we? In the next chapter
we will see that situations can have unpleasantly powerful effects on our behavior.

SUMMARY

Attempts to change our attitudes are never-ending, daily occurrences, ranging from television commercials, newspapers, billboards, and radio programs to action and conversations with friends and relatives. Some attitudes do change, but for the number of attempts made it is rather amazing that our attitudes remain fairly stable. Nevertheless, understanding when and how attitudes change is important, because it helps us understand and control behavior.

As it turns out, however, attitudes do not always seem very useful in predicting behavior. Four major reasons were offered to explain the mismatch between what we say and what we do.

In addition to attitudes, other variables may influence behaviors. For example, norms, our desire to make good impressions, demand characteristics, and habits all affect behavior, too. The more behavior is influenced by these other variables, the less it will show the effects of attitudes.

Hurdles for action are usually higher than hurdles for opinions. Actions speak louder than words, because many things are easier said than done. For instance, it is easy to offer to help (low hurdle) but harder to actually help (high hurdle). Talk is cheap, and we must tell our children to do what we say, not what we do.

Correspondence of measures should be high if we are to find a relation between attitude and behavior. For instance, if we want to predict whether a person will help a woman open a door (a behavior), we should measure that person's attitude toward helping women and toward opening doors for others. If we were to measure attitudes toward women or doors, our attitude measures would not be as closely related to our behavioral measures.

Reinforcement is important, too. If we are rewarded for saying one thing and rewarded for doing another, there will not be much match between what we say and what we do. If we are rewarded for both saying and doing the same thing, there will be more consistency between our words and deeds.

Attitude change usually takes place in a series of steps, as follows:

The stimulus consists of the source (the communicator) and the message (the content of the communication). Sources that are credible (trustworthy, believable, and expert) are most persuasive.

Attention is the first part of our response to this stimulus. Without attention, no attitude change can occur. Effective advertisements, public speakers, and teachers work at capturing the audience's attention.

Comprehension (understanding) is also necessary for attitude change. In order to accept a persuasive communication, we must not only pay attention but also understand it.

Integration is the process of fitting the message with our old ideas and attitudes. The better the fit and the better the consistency with what we already believe, the more likely we are to accept the message and change our attitudes.

With so many critical steps involved in attitude change, it is no wonder that attitudes are so stable, so resistant to influence. Often, it seems, it may be easier to change behavior by changing situations than by changing attitudes.

There is a consistency between our attitudes, but they are not completely consistent. For instance, we may value our health, know that smoking endangers our health, and still smoke. Various consistency theories approach the problem from different angles.

Balance theory suggests that people try to make their feelings about an attitude object the same as those of a person they like and different from those of a person they dislike. So if I like you and you like smoking, I will probably come to like smoking.

Dissonance theory suggests that, when people discover that they have done things inconsistent with their private beliefs, they may change those beliefs to reduce the inconsistency. For instance, if I smoke and then become aware that this behavior is inconsistent with my beliefs, I may change some beliefs or change the behavior. For instance, I might decide not to smoke, decide to cut down, or decide that perfect health is not so important.

Self-perception theory suggests that we observe our behavior to infer our attitudes. For instance, if I smoke, I may conclude that I like smoking. So opinions follow from behavior, and opinion change follows from behavior change. If the price of cigarettes gets too high and I decide to stop smoking, I may conclude that I did not really like smoking very much.

Mere-thought theory suggests that our attitudes become stronger as we think about them. If I like smoking a little, as I smoke I think about smoking. The more I think about it, the more I come to like it. If I stop smoking and think about it less, I may come to like it less. If I decide smoking is not healthy, the more I think about it, the more unpleasant the idea becomes.

The chapter concluded with a discussion of reactance, the idea that people cherish their freedom and will work to restore it when it is taken away. When we are told that we cannot do something, we may want to do it all the more.

GLOSSARY TERMS

Define these terms in your own words, then look them up in the glossary at the back of the book.

Attention	Habit
Attitude	Hurdles
Attitude stability	Hypothetical construct
Balance theory	Integration (in attitude change)
Balanced state	Knowledge function
Behavior intentions	Latitude of acceptance
Cognition	Latitude of rejection
Cognitive-dissonance theory	Mere thought
Commitment	Message
Comprehension	Opinion
Consistency assessment	Other-variables approach
Correspondence of measures	Prestige suggestion
Counterargument	Psychological reactance
Dissonance	Reinforcement
Ego-defensive function	Reinforcer
Experimenter-expectancy effects	Serial-position effect
Expressive function	Source
Forced compliance	Stimulus

Thresholds
Truncated law of effect
Unbalanced (imbalanced)

Utilitarian adaptive function
Wishful thinking

FURTHER READING

Bem, D. J., & Allen, A. On predicting some of the people some of the time: The search for cross-situational consistencies in behavior. *Psychological Review*, 1974, *81*, 506–520. A thoughtful review of the topic.

Zimbardo, P. G., Ebbesen, E. B., & Maslach, C. *Influencing attitudes and changing behavior* (2nd ed.). Reading, Mass.: Addison-Wesley, 1977. A great little paperback. Interesting, easy reading. Highly recommended.

chapter
11

Interdependence and Influence

chapter

11

INTRODUCTION

In a social-psychology laboratory in the northeastern United States, seemingly normal men and women from all walks of life deliver 450-volt shocks to a stranger with a heart condition, because an experimenter has asked them to. In a laboratory in California, normal college students have locked other students in a "prison" in the basement of the Psychology Building and are making them do push-ups for insubordination. In the middle of the country, a psychologist is amazed to find that one-third of the college students in his study are willing to give completely wrong answers to easy questions, simply because others who have answered them first were giving those incorrect answers.

These three studies have much in common. All show the amazing power people have over others, the power to influence and control. All were done by social psychologists studying social influence, one of the topics in the final part of this book.

How would you study social influence? Throughout this century, social psychologists have used a range of strategies.

For instance, Norman Triplett, a bicycle buff and psychologist, found that bicycle racers usually achieve faster times when competing against one another than when racing against the clock. Triplett discovered a similar effect in social psychology's first laboratory experiment: children wound fishing reels faster when they were with other children than when they were alone (1897). In short, it seemed that people may do things faster together than they do them alone.

Triplett's pioneering work in social facilitation was extended by Floyd Allport (1920, 1924). He found that, although the presence of others may increase the *rate* at which we perform an activity, it may also reduce our accuracy. Young pianists often find that they play faster and make more mistakes during recitals than when alone. Allport (1934) studied some effects of social influence in natural settings. He found that, when a norm is well defined and most people comply with it, the *frequency* of deviation from it decreases very rapidly with increases in the *degree* of deviation. For instance, Allport found that nearly every driver came to a full stop at a stop sign, a few almost stopped, and very few went through without slowing. (Some of Allport's findings are shown in Figure 11-1). Today, the norm has shifted, so that in some cities such as New York and Boston most people slow to a few miles an hour, but few stop completely. Allport's interesting studies of conformity could be repeated in your town. How have the norms changed?

Figure 11-1. Conformity by drivers at a stop sign. In 1934, conformity with a traffic regulation resembled a backward *J*, a **J-curve of conformity**. Today, the norms may be different. (Adapted from "The J-Curve Hypothesis of Conforming Behavior," by F. H. Allport, *Journal of Social Psychology*, 1934, 5, 141–183. Copyright 1934 by The Journal Press. Reprinted by permission.)

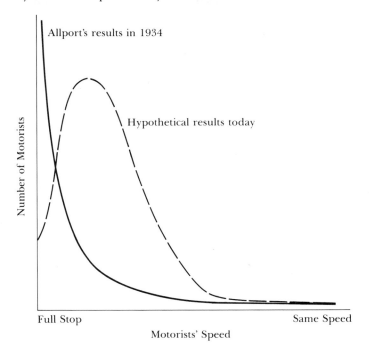

M. Sherif (1935) used a somewhat different technique to study conformity. He placed groups of subjects in a completely darkened room and exposed a small point of light at the far end. Lacking any frame of reference, it *appears* (because of the way the eyes function) that this light moves slightly when it is closely watched. In fact, the light does not move at all. This apparent movement is called the **autokinetic effect.** Sherif found that subjects disagreed with one another on their initial judgments of how much the light appeared to move. With each subsequent exposure to the light, subjects' individual judgments of the amount of movement shifted toward a group average. It is interesting that Sherif's subjects seemed unaware that they were being influenced by the others in the room. Further, this influence was long lasting. The day after the experiment, solitary judgments were similar to judgments made in the group. In a repetition of Sherif's study, Rohrer, Baron, Hoffman, and Swander (1954) found that the effects of this group influence persisted up to a year.

In Sherif's study, the effect of the group was **uniformity** (more similarity of judgments) and moderation (a shift toward a group average). It seems that, given an ambiguous, unstructured situation—whether involving the autokinetic effect or not—norms develop, judgments stabilize, and the group becomes more uniform (Pollis, Montgomery, & Smith, 1975). However, moderation does not *always* occur when a group's opinions or behaviors become more uniform. If one or two members of the group persuasively take similar and extreme positions, much of the change in group behavior may be toward this extreme. Consider this example: During a riot the most extreme members of the group may influence the mob most. When they start shouting a slogan, others join in. When they lead a charge on the police, others may follow. When they build a bonfire in the middle of the street, others may contribute debris. The rioters become more uniform in the early stages of the riot by becoming more extreme. As the riot cools, the crowd becomes more moderate in its actions, loses some of its uniformity, and begins to disperse.

So, group members can become more uniform by becoming more moderate (as in Sherif's autokinetic situation) or by becoming more extreme (as in the riot). Conformity is the process that underlies such shifts to uniformity.

One well-known study of conformity was conducted by Solomon Asch (1955, 1958). He asked subjects seated in small groups to make perceptual judgments using drawings such as Figure 11-2. Subjects were asked a question such as "Which of the lines on the left is the same length as the test line?" It seems to be a fairly

Figure 11-2.
The Asch problem. Which line on the left is the same length as the test line? How would you answer if you saw the lines only briefly, and everyone else said "line 2"? (Adapted from S. E. Asch, "Effects of Group Pressure upon Modification and Distortion of Judgments." In *Groups: Leadership and Man,* by Harold Guetzkow. Copyright 1951 by Carnegie Press. Reprinted by permission.)

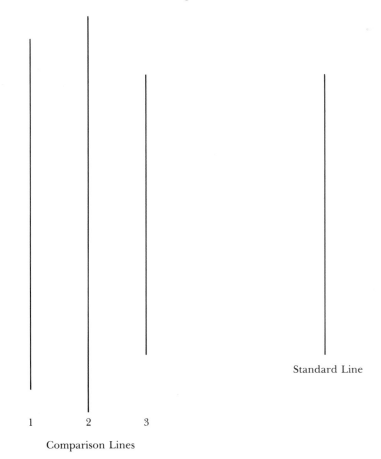

Standard Line

1   2   3

Comparison Lines

simple task, but in many of the judgments almost every subject made an error. (What the real subjects did not know was that other "subjects" seated around the table were not subjects at all, but paid **confederates**—experimental helpers—who were instructed to make these errors.) After five or six "subjects" had guessed that line 2 was the same length as the test line, the real subject was in a dilemma. Should he or she choose the answer that seemed right or the answer that the others were choosing? Perhaps not surprisingly, about one-third of all the estimates made were errors identical with or in the direction of the distorted estimates of the confederates.

Some problems can be found with Asch's conformity studies. For instance, they are very low in external validity: when do we ever encounter a situation in real life similar to this one? It is thus almost inevitable that some subjects will become suspicious. Suspiciousness of the experimenter's stated intent may not have been too common when these studies were done by Asch, but it seems to be common now (Stang, 1976c). A second problem is that the experimental design is inefficient: many confederates are needed to study one subject. A problem with Asch's conformity study, which also occurs in the research designs of Sherif, Crutchfield (see below), and others (Bovard, 1951), is that subjects were not functioning as members of a group in any simple or obvious manner and probably did not feel like group members, sharing group goals and the like (Deutsch & Gerard, 1955). Thus, we may wonder how much of what researchers learn in these artificial laboratory situations can be applied to groups in real life. Some researchers have found that people are more influenced by groups when they are participating members than when they are anonymous observers (Deutsch & Gerard, 1955).

The method used by Asch for studying conformity has been modified and made more efficient through the use of a device developed by Richard Crutchfield (1955). In the **Crutchfield apparatus**, subjects are seated in private booths side by side with a display panel of lights and switches before them. An Asch-type slide or one displaying multiple-choice questions is projected on a screen before all subjects. Each subject is led to believe that the others are answering first. But the experimenter, in fact, supplies artificial answers for these others. This efficient design makes it possible to "run" several subjects at once and does not require any confederates.

If you do not mind studying conformity with a group when the group is imaginary, then you do not even need the Crutchfield apparatus. Several computer programs are available that enable you to test a subject at a computer display screen (Hirsig, 1974; Seligman, S. R., & Stang, 1975). Subjects are led to believe that other subjects are seated at similar screens in other rooms and are giving their answers first. But in fact, the computer supplies the real subjects with both the questions and the answers from the other "subjects." The computer also records the answers of the one subject actually taking part in the experiment. This is but one of several possible uses of the computer as experimenter (Stang & O'Connell, 1974).

A wide variety of procedures are used to study social influence. Researchers have conducted literally thousands of studies (Stang, 1974c). We will look at some of these findings in this chapter. First, we will examine the source of influence on our behavior. Next, we will take up the target of influence—us—and how our characteristics affect the way we are influenced. That will be followed by a discussion of how source and target interact. The chapter will close with a look at methods used to influence others and an examination of how the situation affects conformity.

THE INFLUENCE SOURCE

Expectations.   Others hold expectations about how we should behave (prescriptive personal theories), should not behave (proscriptive personal theories), and will behave (predictive personal theories). Such expectations are the major social influences on our behavior. The essence of **conformity** is uniformity of behavior resulting from adherence to social expectancies (Beloff, 1958; Hollander, 1971).

The expectations that others have of our actions in a particular situation define the role we play. In our family, for instance, we have one role as a son or daughter, perhaps another as brother or sister, and perhaps another as grandson or granddaughter. In each of these positions we may be expected to behave in certain ways.

Within a group, some general expectations for behavior come to be shared and apply to all group members. For instance, in the family all members might be expected to remove their own dishes from the dinner table or make their own beds. These **normative behaviors** come about through **normative expectations** and **normative control.** Normative expectations are simply those expectations shared by the group. Each member of our family may expect us to remove our dishes from the table. If we don't, someone may try to get us to. This normative control may be in the form of rewards (one parent points out that dessert will be served when the table is cleared) or punishments (one parent notes that people who can't clear the table can't watch television).

Normative control often exerts its effects simply through subjective expectations that such control might be used. For instance, fines or jail terms are sanctions against nonconformity (forms of normative control) used by the legal system. These sanctions attempt to maintain conformity to expectations called laws. However, such control seems to have low effectiveness if we consider the recidivism rates of those who break laws—that is, engage in punishable deviant behavior. The *fear* of punishment seems to be more effective than punishment. Most people who stop at stop signs have never been punished by the legal system for failure to stop. But *anticipated* punishment, in the form of a fine or a collision, does seem to be important in inducing the habit of stopping at stop signs. Habits, in turn, seem important in whether or not one stops at stop signs. This reasoning suggests that groups—including our legal system—would increase normative behavior by increasing the *perceived* probability of receiving rewards and punishments.

Power.   Expecting to get a reward or punishment has a strong influence on what we do. The expectations of others are especially effective when they have power over us. Power refers to the use of effective initiative in the interactive process, activities, and decision making of group members. It can be defined as the relative effectiveness of attempted influence over time (Sherif, M., & Sherif, 1969). When we feel attracted to someone, we want them to like us and approve of us. We may want to be more similar to them, because similarity leads to attraction. As a result

"Anticipated punishment is important in inducing the habit of stopping at stop signs."

of our identification with them, we may accept their influence with some eagerness and internalize their values. In this process the other person comes to have what French and Raven (1959) have called **referent power.**

Other forms of power also lead to influence. For instance, those officially in authority in a given situation have **legitimate power** in that situation. In the classroom, a teacher has some legitimate power over students taking the course, even if some students are off-duty police officers. On the road, a police officer has legitimate power over drivers, even if some are college professors.

When people of high and low status meet or talk, those of high status (for example, doctors, generals, administrators) tend to be more influential (and less influenced) than low-status people (for example, nurses, privates, secretaries) regardless of the topic of discussion (Bass, 1954; Bass & Wurster, 1953a, 1953b; French & Snyder, 1959; Torrance, 1954). In laboratory studies in which status is created by the experimenter, the same effect occurs: high-status people seem to conform less than medium- or low-status people (Berkowitz, L., & Macaulay, 1961; Harvey, O. J., & Consalvi, 1960; Julian & Steiner, 1961; Sabath, 1964; Wiggins, J. A., Dill, & Schwartz, 1965). This status effect, however, seems most pronounced when the discussion is related to topics in which the authority has expertise. Among equals, one study has suggested that high-status equals are more influential *and* more influenced than lower-status equals (Faley & Tedeschi, 1971). That is, they allow themselves to be persuaded more easily and are more persuasive, too. Those who control resources that can be used to reward or punish are probably more influential (Bennis, Berkowitz, Affinito, & Malone, 1958). And those who depend on others for such effects are probably more influenced (Jones & Gerard, 1967).

Whether or not we have the legitimate power of an authority, we often have **reward power,** through promises or rewards we might offer, and **coercive power,** through threats or punishments. Possessing knowledge, presenting it skillfully and developing a reputation for having such knowledge are the bases of **expert**

power. Such expertise can result in considerable influence, especially when we depend on others for information (Hollander, 1960; Jones & Gerard, 1967).

Exchanged power is power that exists because it has been given to one person by another out of previous exchanges. Exchanged power is sometimes created by agreement. For instance, when a group elects a leader, it agrees to transfer some decision-making power to that leader. Exchanged power is sometimes created by indebtedness. When you perform a service for me, I "owe" you, and, until I pay you back, you have some power over me. Exchanged power is sometimes attained by gaining affection and respect. If we make a favorable impression on others, behave competently, and conform to group expectations, we accumulate **idiosyncrasy credits** (Hollander, 1958). That is, we are free to behave (within varying limits) in idiosyncratic ways, without such behavior being perceived as unacceptable. In fact, the idiosyncratic behaviors of U.S. presidents, movie stars, and rock singers are sometimes so acceptable that they set new styles. The more power we have, the more we are accepted by others and the greater our freedom to deviate from group norms without receiving sanctions. In general, high-status, respected, and liked people have considerable idiosyncrasy credit and usually have exchanged power.

Other power-classification systems (Dahl, 1960) are based on the resources of power, such as money and credit, control over jobs, control over information, and social standing. A more interesting and meaningful approach considers the motives of a person who complies. After all, if person A doesn't comply with B, then B doesn't have power over A. M. Hamilton (1977) has described 19 such types of social power.

These various types of power have several features in common. Most involve an asymmetrical relationship in which one person is dependent on another, is influenced by him or her, and changes, whereas the other person tends to be independent, uninfluenced, and unchanging. Most forms of power are pleasant to have, although individuals differ in their desire for power and their ability to get it. Most forms of power are interrelated; for instance, people often obtain legitimate power through the use of their expert or reward power. People who are powerful tend to be popular, respected, of high standing, competent, intelligent, and in control of resources such as money, information, or the judicial process (Dahl, 1961; Lasswell & Kaplan, 1950).

Such power may be used to maintain itself and gather more power. For instance, the wealthy can afford skilled accountants who minimize their income taxes and increase their wealth and power. Successful researchers use grant money to pay students to conduct their research and pay secretaries to type reports of their research. Such reported research increases their influence, their expert power, and their chances for further successful grant applications. Powerful people are less likely to receive criticism (Thibaut & Riecken, 1955) or aggression (Doob, A. N., & Gross, A. E., 1968) when they make mistakes and may even be protected from criticism or unpleasant information by subordinates. Much of the Watergate scandal involved efforts by subordinates to cover the mistakes of President Nixon to protect his power.

Peers, Parents, and Influence.   Our peers and our parents are the most important influences on our attitudes. Researchers have found, for instance, that our political attitudes are often similar to those of our parents (Jennings & Niemi, 1968) as well as those of our peers (Newcomb, 1943; Newcomb, Koenig, Flacks, & Warwick, 1967; Rose, P., 1957). Our racial prejudices also tend to match those of our parents (Epstein, R., & Komorita, 1966; Horowitz, E., & Horowitz, 1938) and those of our peers (Margolis, 1971).

Do peers or parents exert a stronger influence on attitudes and behaviors? One study (Kandel, 1973) found that marijuana use was slightly more common (37%) among teenagers who *thought* their parents used some drugs (for example, tranquilizers) than among other teenagers (24%). But actual parental drug usage was unrelated to teenage marijuana use. However, there was a strong relation between teenagers' drug use and their friends' use of drugs. The more a teenager's best friend reported using marijuana, the more likely it was that the teenager used it. In fact, this study found that friends were more similar in marijuana use than in any other activity or attitude measured. Does this mean that peers are more influential than parents? No, because teenagers can choose their friends and because preferences may be for similar others (see Chapter 8). The relations found in this study may be more due to friendship choice than peer influence.

Whether one's peers or one's parents have a stronger influence on one's values, attitudes, and opinions may be different for different people. It does seem that, as we grow up, we also grow out and away and that growing older is accompanied by increasing peer influence and decreasing parental influence. In one study, for instance, researchers found that, as children grow older, they become more willing to go along with the misconduct of their friends (Bixenstine, DeCorte, & Bixenstine, 1976). This seems particularly true for those children with negative attitudes toward adults. In another study, preference for the political party of one's father declined from 80% for elementary school children to a little over 50% for college students (Goldsen, Rosenberg, Williams, & Suchman, 1960; Hess & Torney, 1967). In his classic studies, Newcomb found that, whereas students at Bennington College generally came from conservative families, their professors were mostly liberal New Dealers (Newcomb, 1943; Newcomb, Koenig, Flacks, & Warwick, 1967). With each passing year on campus, students became more liberal. This change was strongest for those students who developed close ties with friends on campus and depended on friends more than family for emotional support. Newcomb's follow-up study found that those attitudes that changed during college remained changed through later life, by and large (Newcomb et al., 1967). That is, students who had been raised in conservative homes and then became liberal at Bennington remained liberal over the next 2½ decades of their lives and married liberal men. How have your friends and instructors influenced your attitudes since you have been in college?

THE INFLUENCE TARGET

A variety of individual differences seem to be related to how easily a person is influenced. We will consider two such differences: anxiety/fear and self-esteem/self-confidence.

Anxiety and Fear. Many of our actions in everyday life seem designed to maximize our benefits while minimizing our costs. When we learn that we are doing something that may be harmful or not doing something that could help us, we are often motivated to change our behavior. Tedeschi and Lindskold (1976) cited a number of studies showing that people often seem to change their attitudes, their behavior intentions, and sometimes their behaviors when they are frightened. The studies examined fears of the danger of tetanus (Dabbs & Leventhal, 1966), improper dental care (Haefner, 1956), poor driving (Berkowitz, L., & Cottingham, 1960), cigarette smoking (Insko, Arkoff, & Insko, 1965), tuberculosis (DeWolfe & Governale, 1964), not using the handrail on stairways (Piccolino, 1966), and even viewing the sun during an eclipse (Kraus, El-Assal, & DeFleur, 1966). We may be gamblers at heart, but few of us will gamble our health and safety when the deck seems stacked against us and the stakes are high.

Arousing a person's fear seems most effective in changing behavior when the person believes that something can be done (Rogers & Thistlethwaite, 1970) and knows how to do it (Leventhal, Singer, & Jones, 1965; Leventhal, Watts, & Pagano, 1967). The person must also *believe* the fear-arousing information that is presented. Janis and Feshbach (1953) tried to convince their subjects in a high-fear condition that improper tooth care would lead to "arthritic paralysis, kidney damage, or total blindness." High disbelief, rather than high fear, may have occurred in this condition of the experiment, explaining the low levels of attitude change that resulted (Katz, D., 1960). Attitude or behavior change is probably a function of our fear of the consequences of a behavior multiplied by our belief that those consequences will occur. A smoker who believes that the consequences of smoking can be dreadful but who thinks it unlikely that he or she will suffer these consequences will probably not be motivated to stop smoking. A smoker who comes to believe that the consequences are fearful and certain and is shown how to quit just might quit.

Anxiety and fear act much like low self-confidence in their effects on conformity. When we are anxious or fearful, we may feel insecure and want to seek out others for company and comfort. Some studies have found that, when people are anxious, they tend to conform more (Walters & Karol, 1960; Walters, Marshall, & Shooter, 1960). Other studies find that mild fear leads to conformity too (Darley, 1966).

Extremely high levels of fear cannot be studied in the laboratory, of course; it would not be ethical. But we can see the effects of high fear in everyday life. During theater fires, the audience is likely to panic and, with great uniformity, plunge toward the door. Sometimes there is fear but no visible panic, and people file out the doors quietly, also with great uniformity.

Because we often try to hide our fear or anxiety and appear calm, we may look calmer than we feel. In *The King and I*, Anna whistles a happy tune so no one ever knows she's afraid. The result of this bravado is that, like us, others may look calmer than they feel. When we are fearful or anxious, we may imitate the behavior of those who appear calm out of the belief that they know what they are doing and are in control of the situation. Such imitation may reduce our fear or anxiety. Of course, if they feel fearful and we appear calm, they may copy us. Result: uniformity. (Incidentally, by acting calm, we may reevaluate our own feelings and feel calmer. For a discussion of self-perception, see pp. 292–294.)

Self-Esteem and Self-Confidence. A few studies have found that high self-confidence or high self-esteem is positively related to conformity, **persuasibil-**

ity, or attitude change (Cox, D. F., & Bauer, 1964; Gelfand, 1962; Lindskold & Tedeschi, 1971b; Silverman, I., 1964). And a few have found no relation between self-esteem and conformity (Painter, 1968). But most have found that, the higher the self-confidence or self-esteem, the lower the persuasibility (Berkowitz, L., & Lundy, 1957; Boomer, 1959; Cohen, A. R., 1959; Croner & Willis, 1961; Crutchfield, 1955; Ettinger, Marino, Endler, Geller, & Natziuk, 1971; Geller, Endler, & Wiesenthal, 1973; Hochbaum, 1954; Hovland, Lumsdaine, & Sheffield, 1949; Janis, 1954, 1955; Janis & Field, 1959; Janis & Rife, 1959; Julian, Regula, & Hollander, 1968; Klapper, 1961; Krech, Crutchfield, & Ballachey, 1962; Lazarsfeld, Berelson, & Gaudet, 1948; Lesser & Abelson, 1959; Linton, H., & Graham, 1959; Mausner, 1954a, 1954b; Meunier & Rule, 1967; Ross, Bierbrauer, & Hoffman, 1976; Smith, T. I., & Suinn, 1965; Stang, 1972; Stukat, 1958; Tuddenham, 1959).

People whose self-esteem or self-confidence is low and who want to be correct in their judgment will probably attribute the difference between the group's opinion and their own to their own error. By conforming, they believe, they increase their chances of being correct. People whose self-esteem is moderate may be uncertain whether they or the group are right and conform moderately. Those with high self-esteem may be confident that they are right and attribute the difference between their opinion and the group's to an error on the part of the group. Given such an interpretation, it would be wisest for them to ignore the group and its opinions. In fact, people who see themselves as more competent than the group conform less than those who see themselves as less competent (Costanzo, Reitan,

People with high self-confidence try to influence others and often succeed; those lower in self-confidence are influenced. By accepting the opinions of those who are self-confident, we may increase our confidence.

& Shaw, 1968; Endler, Coward, & Wiesenthal, 1975; Endler, Wiesenthal, & Geller, 1972; Ettinger et al., 1971; Fagen, 1963).

Thus, our self-confidence and self-esteem may affect our judgment of who is in error, and independence or conformity may both be viewed as strategies for assuring correctness. When we choose to remain independent, our confidence may decrease, whereas when we choose to conform, our confidence may increase (Hochbaum, 1954). Thus, whether conformity is positively or negatively related to confidence may depend on whether confidence is measured before or after an opportunity to conform.

INTERACTION OF SOURCE AND TARGET

The most important aspects of influence probably concern neither qualities of the target alone nor qualities of the source alone but both sets of qualities considered together. For instance, power like beauty is to some extent in the eye of the beholder. Our perception of others as powerful or not powerful determines their influence on us and their effective power over us. How much power they actually have over others is only one factor in how much power we perceive in them. Your social-psychology teacher has more power than you in the classroom, but you are equals when you are trying to get your cars repaired down the street. In this brief section we will consider two **collative variables**—factors that depend on characteristics of *both* target and source. These variables are similarity and attraction.

Similarity and Attitude Change.   Many of the factors that are responsible for our attraction to another also influence our attitudes. For example, we saw that we are more attracted to those who are similar to us than to those who are dissimilar to us. Those who are similar to each other tend to influence each other more than those who are dissimilar. For instance, one study found that handicapped people conformed more to others who were handicapped than to nonhandicapped, and for nonhandicapped people this was reversed (Linde & Patterson, 1964). Other studies of groups have also found greater conformity with greater similarity along other dimensions (Festinger & Thibaut, 1951; Gerard, 1953).

One researcher (Brock, 1965) examined similarity and attitude change in a paint store. One salesman told customers that he had recently purchased about 20 times as much paint as the customer was considering purchasing. He ended up selling less paint than a salesman who said he had recently purchased about the same amount of paint as the customer. Here, similarity rather than "expertness" seems to have been important in selling paint. In another study (Nesbitt, 1972) college students went door to door trying to persuade residents to oppose the war in Vietnam. The researcher found that residents were *less* opposed to the war after being visited by the radical-appearing students than they were before the visit—a **boomerang effect.** Note that these studies suggest that, if you try to influence other people, you should begin by establishing your similarity to them.

Of course, the effects of similarity on attitude change are greater for some kinds of similarities than others. Similarities in eye color or handedness are probably of little importance, but similarity of certain important values and beliefs may be extremely important. The dimensions of similarity that are important may vary from situation to situation.

Dressing like those you admire and like is one way of identifying with them and increasing their liking for you. Whether or not "clothes make the man," clothing does seem to make us more or less influential. In one study conventionally dressed students received more signatures on a petition from conventionally dressed adults than did "hippie" students (Keasey & Tomlinson-Keasey, 1973). And a hippie obtained more signatures on a petition from antiwar protesters than did a conventionally dressed student (Suedfeld, Bochner, & Matas, 1971). In each of these studies, students were most influential in getting people to express their views on a controversial issue when they dressed like those they were trying to influence.

Attraction and Influence.   We are influenced by those we like, and we like those who influence us. This seems to be common knowledge (Rittle & Cottrell, 1967) and a common research finding in both natural settings (Janis & Hoffman, 1971; Stang, Castellanetta, Constantinidis, & Fortuno, 1977) and the laboratory (Harper & Tuddenham, 1964). A closer look, however, often reveals that in a group the *best* liked are not always the *most* influential (Bales, 1958; Hollander & Webb, 1955; Radloff & Helmreich, 1968). The relationship is positive, though, and there is a strong tendency for influence and liking of individuals to go hand in hand.

Although the studies just cited look at liking for *individuals* and their influence, other studies suggest that *groups* we are attracted to are also usually more influential over us (Back, 1951; Berkowitz, L., 1957; Festinger, 1953; Festinger, Gerard, Hymovitch, Kelley, & Raven, 1952; Festinger, Schachter, & Back, 1950; Gerard, 1954; Lambert & Lowy, 1957; Lott, A. J., & Lott, 1961; Schachter, Ellertson, McBride, & Gregory, 1951; Thibaut & Strickland, 1956; Wilson, R. S., 1960). Further, the influence of attractive groups seems to last longer than that of other groups (Berkowitz, L., 1954; Gerard, 1954).

Why should those people and groups we like be more influential? Attractive, cohesive groups sometimes put more pressure on their members for uniformity (Schachter, 1951). Not only is there greater pressure, but there may also be greater desire. Accepting the influence of others is one way we can show we like them. Friends may try harder to be pleasant together, and agreement is more pleasant than disagreement (Gerard, 1961).

Finally, of course, we spend more time with friends, understand them better, are more similar to them, and may be more attentive to them. Each of these factors may lead to greater influence.

Some studies indicate that people we dislike can also influence us. In one study, for example, a disliked communicator insulted the audience, and the members of the audience moved farther away from the speaker's position than they were before they heard the message—a boomerang effect (Abelson & Miller, 1967). Boomerang effects may not occur, however, if the speaker can get you to do something he or she wants you to do (and you do not want to). If a person you dislike can get you to do something that you are opposed to doing, you may be more likely to decide that you are not really opposed to it. Why? You might reason that you did it because you liked it rather than as a favor to this disliked person. When someone you like gets you to do something you do not like, you might believe that you did it simply as a favor. This principle is illustrated in a study in which either a belligerent experimenter or a nice one attempted to get army reservists to eat fried grasshoppers (Zimbardo, Weisenberg, Firestone, & Levy, 1965). Those reservists who ate the grasshoppers judged them more pleasant when the belligerent experimenter had been the instigator than when the nice experimenter had been. (This is an example of cognitive-dissonance research that seems to pose problems for diffusion-of-affect theory.)

METHODS OF INFLUENCE

Gentle Persuasion: The Foot in the Door.   A proverb says "The warm, gentle sun will get a man to remove his coat faster than a strong, cold wind." Freedman and Fraser (1966) have explored a step-wise persuasion technique that they call the **foot-in-the-door technique.** They found that, if you can get somebody to agree to a small request, he or she will be more likely to agree to a slightly larger request than if you had made the larger request first. In their study homeowners were first asked to sign a petition encouraging safe driving and later asked to place a large, ugly sign on their front lawn that read *Drive Carefully.* More people who had signed the petition agreed to post the sign than did people who had not been asked to sign the petition. Other research suggests that, if you want someone to do a moderate-sized favor, you ask them to do a small favor first, rather than a large one (Snyder & Cunningham, in press). Raven and Rubin illustrated how the Nazis in World War II used the foot-in-the-door technique against the Dutch Jews.

> First of all, they required the Jews to wear yellow Stars of David . . . then the Jews were forbidden to use public parks; then they were restricted in their employment; then they were forbidden to live in certain areas; then they were forced to move into a restricted ghetto area; then that area was sealed off with barbed wire and gun emplacements. Then, the Nazis spirited the first Dutch Jews to "work camps" in Germany [1976, p. 241].

Several factors may be at work in the foot-in-the-door technique. The first may be self-perception. ("I didn't object when they made the Jews wear yellow stars. Perhaps I don't like them as much as I thought.") A second factor is that in the early stages of this persuasive technique the power and legitimacy of the influence source are established. ("The Germans have the right to make Jews wear yellow Stars of David. Nazis have authority over Jews.") Another factor in this incremental form of persuasion is that of the situation. With enough experience we can grow accustomed to almost anything. Even though it is difficult for us to imagine that we could become accustomed to the idea of Jews being forbidden to use public parks, not long ago in parts of the United States Blacks were accustomed to separate parks, lunchrooms, restrooms, schools, churches, water fountains, residential areas, swimming pools, and so on. One of this author's Black students was removed from a "White" church by the police when she was a girl.

One-Sided or Two-Sided?   Should you present both sides of an argument or just your side when you are trying to persuade someone? There are two sides to

With enough experience we can grow accustomed to anything.

the answer. On the one hand, presenting an opposing viewpoint may make your presentation seem fairer and more open-minded. Your listeners may feel that you are giving them a choice of positions, and they may like you more and go along with your own position. On the other hand, some people may already agree with you and not know the opposing arguments. Giving them both sides of the story might have a boomerang effect and weaken their initial agreement with your position. Thus, whether it is better to present a **one-** or **two-sided communication** depends on what your listeners already know and believe (Hovland et al., 1949). It may also depend on such things as their intelligence and sophistication.

Repetition, Familiarity, and Group Size.   Many advertisers believe that, the more often you hear a persuasive communication, the more attention you will give it, the better you will learn the argument, and the more likely you will be to accept it. One effect of repetition of a message or of increasing group size is to attract our attention. **Social-impact theory** (Latané, 1973) suggests that, with increases in the number of other persons, their effect on us increases. This effect of group size is evident in one study (Bassett & Latané, 1976), which found that college students playing the role of newspaper editor allotted more space in the newspaper to stories involving larger numbers of people.

Advertising studies often show that repetition of a message increases one's learning of it (Cromwell & Kuchel, 1952). Does this learning always result in increased agreement with the message? The evidence is mixed but suggests that repetition is most likely to cause attitude change when the messages are similar but not identical (McCullough & Ostrom, 1974), the source is credible, the argument is strong (Weiss, W., 1969), and the argument is sufficiently complex that it cannot be fully comprehended in a single exposure. When Richard Nixon ran for reelection to the presidency, his television campaign made use of this principle, repeating the sound track and varying the visual presentation. When you watch television this week, pay attention to the commercials and you will see how advertisers repeat a message, sometimes with slight variation. How does this repetition affect your learning of the message? How does it affect your attitude toward the product?

Repetition leads to attitude change. Advertising leads to sales. Campaign posters lead to voting. Do large groups produce more conformity than small groups? Not always. When others in the group are unanimous in their opinion, it is difficult to disagree with them. But unanimity is hard to achieve.

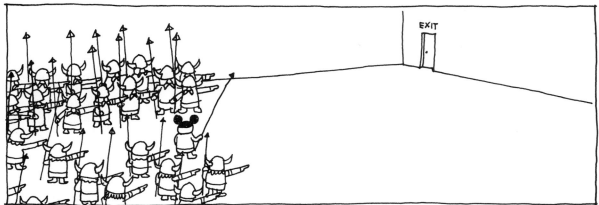

"When the opinion of the group is unanimous, then disagreement with it is difficult!"

Larger natural groups do not always produce greater uniformity among members. In fact, larger groups may be less able to achieve consensus than smaller groups (Feldman, R. A., 1974; Hare, 1952; Zimet & Schneider, 1969). They may also take longer to reach consensus (Chapko & Revers, 1976) and may be somewhat less uniform, on the average. (In a humorous vein, judging from how ponderous decision making in committees becomes with increases in committee size, it has been calculated that the most efficient size of a small group is $7/10$ of a person (Olds, 1946). Parkinson (1957) made a similar argument for a negative relation between group size and productivity.) This lack of uniformity may result because the large group size restricts communication among all members, reducing the opportunity for influence. Nevertheless, when a group does achieve consensus and is unanimous in its position, large groups are powerful. The probability of social influence increases with increases in the size of a unanimous group, perhaps because a large unanimous group is assumed to be more likely to be correct in its judgments than a unanimous but smaller group (Stang, 1976b; see also Nordholm, 1975). If this is so, by agreeing with the majority we increase our own chances of being correct. This process has been called **informational social influence**.

When a group does achieve some uniformity, norms are established, and there are sometimes mild rewards for complying with these norms and mild punishments for deviating from them. A large, unanimous group may be able to offer more rewards and punishments than smaller groups; hence, **normative social influence** may increase with group size.

Though large groups may be more influential than small groups, individuals within a large group are probably less influential than those in smaller groups. Your influence on group opinion or behavior probably decreases with increasing group size (Hare, 1952; Tannenbaum, 1962; Ziller & Behringer, 1959).

THE SITUATION

Earlier I suggested that conformity, or informational social influence, may be a good way to increase our chances of being correct. If so, we might expect more conformity in those situations in which we do not know what is right. Ambiguous situations, in which it is difficult or impossible to know the correct answer, seem to result in more conformity (Asch, 1952; Crutchfield, 1955; Luchins, 1945; Luchins & Luchins, 1955; Nordholm, 1975; Walker, E. L., & Heyns, 1962; Wiener, 1958). Similarly, when the task is difficult, we are less sure of the correct answer and more likely to conform (Blake, Helson, & Mouton, 1957; Coleman, Blake, & Mouton, 1958; Crutchfield, 1955; London & Lim, 1964; Luchins & Luchins, 1963). When we think we have high ability to deal with a situation, we are less likely to conform (Gerard, 1961; Goldberg, S. C., & Lubin, A., 1958; Mausner, 1954a, 1954b).

In the play *Annie Get Your Gun*, country girl Annie finds herself at a society party, uncertain how to greet others. This uncertainty leads to social comparison. She observes that, when people are introduced, one says "Delighted," and the other says "Enchanted." She does the same and seems to pass as a society woman. If you find yourself in a situation that is familiar to others present and unfamiliar to you, you will probably accept their behavior as useful information for how you should behave. When in Rome, do as the Romans do.

Traits versus Situations: The Conformity Controversy. It has been suggested that conformity is a personality trait. If that is the case, some people are "conformers," some are "nonconformers," and others fit in between these extremes. If conformity is a personality trait, then we might expect people to show the same levels of conformity across different situations. That is, some people would conform a great deal in most situations, some a moderate amount, and some very little. Not so. Studies show little evidence of stability across situations (Back & Davis, 1965; Vaughan, 1964).

We would also expect that, if conformity is a personality trait, there would be stability over time in the same situation. This seems to be true only if a person's role in the group does not change, because role seems to have strong effects on conformity. For instance, older children are more influential and less influenced than younger children. As long as a child remains at the same age relative to the other group members, that child's amount of conformity may remain about the same. But a 10-year-old may conform more in a group of 12-year-olds than in a group of 8-year-olds.

If conformity is a personality trait, then it should be related to some other personality traits. Study after study has found conformity to be either weakly related or not related at all to such other traits as need for affiliation, need for achievement (Samelson, 1958), scores on personality tests (Barron, 1953; Crutchfield, 1955), dominance, and so on (Barocas & Gorlow, 1967; Mann, 1959).[1]

Furthermore, studies with positive results tend to be published and studies with negative results not published. If only a few of the published studies have found a relationship between conformity and personality, even fewer of all studies done are likely to have found such a relationship. Likewise, personality may interact with situations (Endler, 1975; Endler & Hunt, 1966; Hunt, 1965). That is, in different situations personality may be related in different ways, and in some situations it may not be related at all. To view conformity as a personality trait not influenced by situations, we would need evidence that conformity and a given personality trait are related across several situations (Goldberg, L. R., & Rorer, 1966). Such evidence has not been sought. Even if we were able to establish that some people conform more than others do in general, we would not have gained in our understanding of conformity. To say that a person is a conformer is to *describe* his or her behavior, not to explain it.

POSTSCRIPT

Attitudes, opinions, and behaviors *can* be caused or changed as a result of classical conditioning and extinction (extinction is the process in which an attitude, opinion or behavior ceases to exist or occur through lack of reinforcement), by imitation, and by other processes. It would be nice to know just how important each of these influences is. What percentage of attitudes is established and modified by each of these influences? Research has not yet answered this question.

Conformity: Good or Bad?   Do you think that conformity is "good" or "bad"? Many people like to see themselves as independent, free-willed people, as "internals," or "field independents," not conformists. But everyone is influenced by others. Being responsive and accepting such influence is useful; we increase our wisdom, our chances of being correct, and our chances of being accepted and liked by others.

Nevertheless, independence and free expression are necessary to protect civil liberties. Hollander (1975) has argued that "the expression of individual views is essential to the creation of an atmosphere in which free speech and other civil liberties may thrive. . . . Where such expression is not encouraged and protected, there will be a waning of these liberties" (p. 56). Hollander noted that there are six hurdles to surmount in being independent and expressing oneself freely: (1) risks of disapproval, (2) lack of perceived alternatives, (3) fear of disrupting the

---

[1]This may be a result of the way that conformity is measured or the personality traits are measured. Self-ratings of adjustment and extroversion, for instance, seem related to conformity, but other measures are not (Mann, 1959). Different paper-and-pencil measures of the same trait may show different relations between that trait and conformity (Stang, 1972). Because our measurement of personality is not very satisfactory, we cannot definitely conclude that conformity and personality are unrelated. We can conclude that research has not yet found consistent relationships.

group, (4) an absence of shared communication, (5) an inability to feel responsible, and (6) a sense of impotence.

Perhaps the best balance is a society in which people typically show regularities in their behavior and conform, yet feel free to act independently when this seems best. Conformity may be a good idea when the group seems correct or seems to be acting for the good of society. Conformity is bad when the group seems incorrect or does not seem to be acting for the good of society. But we cannot make a general value judgment of conformity as a class of social behaviors, because everyone does it. You might want to discuss the pros and cons of conformity with a friend or with your class.

Public Compliance versus Private Acceptance.   A distinction is sometimes made between **public compliance** and **private acceptance**. Compliance refers to a change in behavior that makes it more acceptable to the group. Private acceptance, as you might guess, refers to any change in one's personal theories or attitudes that results in greater similarity to those of the group. We have already learned that attitudes and behaviors do not always match up perfectly. In many situations we may change our attitudes (private acceptance) without changing our behavior (compliance), or vice versa.

How does what you say in public differ from what you do in private? Some years ago a researcher studied a little rural village that he called "Elm Hollow" (Schanck, 1932). Schanck found that in public the residents of Elm Hollow almost

"When we share private feelings and beliefs, we often feel a sense of relief."

uniformly said they were strongly opposed to smoking, drinking, and playing
cards. He also found that many residents did these things in the privacy of their
own homes with the doors closed and the blinds drawn. It was apparently the
influence of the small church in town, and in particular that of the minister and
the widow of the former minister, that had so influenced the public statement of
attitudes. People said what they felt they should say but quietly and privately did
what they wanted to. Because their smoking, drinking, and card playing were all
done in the secrecy of their homes, however, when people were asked what other
people actually did, their opinions matched what other people said should be
done. That is, residents did not realize that others privately smoked and drank
and played cards. This ignorance, which the researcher called pluralistic ignorance, was nourished by the fact that, because people were not supposed to smoke,
drink, or play cards, they could not admit to others that they did.

Most of us now smoke, drink, and play cards without any second thoughts
and are not the least bit reluctant to admit this to others. But we still have many
private behaviors that most of us do not readily discuss in public and that, therefore, we may assume that others do not engage in. It is probably true that almost
everyone reading this book has sexual fantasies, but they are rarely appropriate
topics for public discussion. Others sometimes discover our private behaviors or
feelings, and we feel a sense of shame or concern. But when we discover that their
private behaviors or feelings are the same as ours, we feel a sense of relief.

SUMMARY

Social influence has long been a major interest of social psychologists. Studies by
Triplett, Allport, Sherif, and Asch provide classic demonstrations of a variety of
ways in which people have powerful effects on one another. The influence source
has been the subject of much investigation. Researchers have learned that others
influence us through the expectations they hold, translated into normative control.
Others also influence us through various forms of power, such as referent power,
expert power, reward power, coercive power, and exchanged power. Those who
have power are influential; those who lack it are influenced. Studies find that our
parents and our peers are both influential, with parental influence typically declining as we mature.

The influence target has also been well studied. Those who are anxious,
fearful, or low in self-esteem or self-confidence are more easily influenced than
others. Accepting influence when one is anxious or low in self-confidence may be
a rational means of increasing one's correctness.

We can probably make the most accurate predictions of who will influence
whom if we know about both the source and the target. The greater the similarity
or attraction between source and target, the greater the influence. Some exceptions
to this principle have been found in research, however.

The manner in which one tries to influence another also determines how
much influence there will be. For instance, if we want a large favor done by
another, we may be more successful if we request a small favor first—a principle
called the foot-in-the-door technique. Depending on the audience, sometimes a
one-sided presentation of your position will be most effective, and sometimes a
two-sided presentation will be. Repetition increases the likelihood of influence,

particularly if the source is credible and the argument is complex and strong. Similarly, the larger the unanimous group, the more difficult it is to resist its influence attempts.

Some aspects of the situation also affect influence. We are more likely to be influenced in situations that are ambiguous or unfamiliar and in tasks that are difficult. Although it seems likely that some people are more easily influenced than others, the source, the situation, and the interaction between source and target have received most of the attention in recent research.

GLOSSARY TERMS

Define these terms in your own words, then look them up in the glossary at the back of the book.

Autokinetic effect
Boomerang effect
Coercive power
Collative variable
Confederate
Conformity
Crutchfield apparatus
Exchanged power
Expert power
Foot-in-the-door technique
Idiosyncrasy credit
Informational social influence
J-curve of conformity
Legitimate power

Normative behavior
Normative control
Normative expectations
One-sided communication
Persuasibility
Power
Private acceptance
Public compliance
Referent power
Reward power
Social-impact theory
Two-sided communication
Uniformity

FURTHER READING

Asch, S. E. Opinions and social pressure. *Scientific American*, 1955, *193*(5), 31–35.

Emerson, R. M. Social exchange theory. *Annual Review of Sociology*, 1976, *2*, 335–362.

Hollander, E. P. Independence, conformity, and civil liberties: Some implications from social psychological research. *Journal of Social Issues*, 1975, *31*(2), 55–67.

chapter

12

Groups

INTRODUCTION

We belong to
groups from an
early age.

What is a **group**? Olmsted has offered a useful definition: "A group . . . may be defined as a plurality of individuals who are in contact with one another, who take one another into account, and who are aware of some significant commonality" (1959, p. 21). Group members typically share some goals, values, needs, and

interests. As a group, they are often interdependent in meeting their needs and working toward their goals.

Social psychologists typically study **small groups**,[1] ranging from two persons (the **dyad**) or three (the **triad**) up to ten or more. Social psychologists find that small groups are easier to study in small laboratories and happen to occur more frequently in everyday life than larger groups. For example, students scanned newspapers and magazines and noted the number of groups of various sizes (as illustrated by Figure 12-1). In a sample of 1060 photos, there were 423 photos of individuals alone, 183 photos of two-person groups, and so on. The larger the group, the less frequently a group of that size occurred. This effect is also true of naturally occurring groups, not just their pictures. One researcher (Aveni,

Figure 12-1. Newspaper and magazine photographs of small groups are more common than those of larger ones.

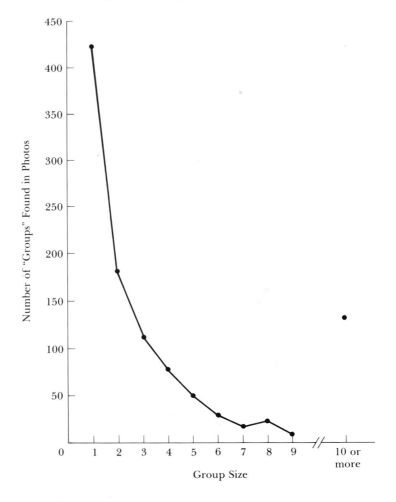

[1]These groups may be small, but the literature is not. In 1969 Raven catalogued over 5000 studies of small groups, almost four times as many as he had counted a decade earlier. Seven or eight new studies of small groups are reported each week.

1977) interviewed 204 people milling on the street after a football game. He found that 26% were alone, 54% with one friend, 18% with two, 16% with three, and 12% with four or more (see Figure 12-2).

In fact, small groups frequently form temporary smaller groups. In a group of four, for instance, two pairs may form to talk and then recombine. Subgroups sometimes form out of special needs or interests or through situational effects. For instance, at a party two people may discuss a job that one knows about and the other wants (effect of needs). Two market economists may discuss recent influences on currency exchange rates (effect of interests). And two or three others who meet at the punchbowl may begin a discussion of hyperimbibation (getting loaded) (situational effect). Such subgroups dissolve, and new subgroups form. So for every large group, at any moment, there are often a number of smaller subgroups.

You might ask whether two people at the punchbowl really make a group. By Olmsted's definition (1959, p. 21), they do. The punchbowl talkers

☐ "Are a plurality of individuals." Two or more make a plurality, and the punch-bowl group has two.

☐ "Are in contact with one another." This contact may be psychological or physical; the punchbowl group may have both forms of contact.

☐ "Take one another into account." Each is influenced by the other; that is, one person's statements and behavior will be affected by the statements and behavior of the other at the punchbowl, and vice versa.

Figure 12-2.
Small groups are common at football games. Adapted from A. F. Aveni, 1977. (From "The Not-So-Lonely Crowd: Friendship Groups in Collective Behavior," by A. F. Aveni. In *Sociometry*, 1977, *40*, 96–99. Copyright 1977 by the American Sociological Association. Reprinted by permission.)

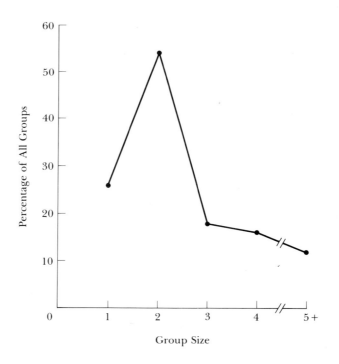

□ "Are aware of some significant commonality." The punchbowl group has at least one common interest, drinking punch, and the market economists and those exchanging job information have other common interests. Such interests may seem petty to you but may be "significant" to the group members.

Olmsted's definition of *group* is quite inclusive. The people at the punchbowl might not be considered a group by other definitions. You might give some thought to what groupings of people should or should not be considered a group.

This chapter will continue with a setting out of various types of groups. Next, the formation and breakup of groups will be examined, followed by a look at group structure and leadership. How groups function, particularly with respect to their size and productivity, will then be discussed. The chapter will close with a look at a particular kind of group, the crowd.

TYPES OF GROUPS

Groups are so common in everyday life and so important to us that several ways have been developed to classify them. The most common classifications are the primary/secondary and reference/membership distinctions.

Primary and Secondary Groups.   The idea of a **primary group** was first discussed by the sociologist Charles Cooley, who wrote:

By primary groups I mean those characterized by intimate face-to-face association and cooperation. They are primary . . . in that they are fundamental in forming the social nature and ideals of the individual. . . . Primary groups are primary in the sense that they give the individual his earliest and completist [*sic*] experience of social unity [1909, pp. 23–24, 26–28].

Primary groups are usually small, and their members show loyalty and solidarity. The group, in turn, may provide a high degree of social support and strength for members. The primary group in the armed forces supports and sustains soldiers during the stress of warfare (Shils, 1950). And those primary groups we all belong to help us cope with more conventional life stresses. Primary groups include the family, communes, the play groups of children, and the intimate work or play groups of their parents.

Secondary groups tend to be larger, impersonal, more formal, and sometimes shorter lasting. Participation in such groups is often contractual and done in exchange for some goods or services (Olmsted, 1959). Corporations, professional associations, political parties, and small groups created for a study by researchers are examples of secondary groups. Other examples, which emphasize the formal nature and short duration of such groups, include the clerk/customer, announcer/audience, and performer/spectator "groups." Primary and secondary groups differ in many respects, and some groups are not very easy to classify because they have some of the properties of both.

Reference and Membership Groups.   **Reference groups** are those important groups that are used by a person in making a self-evaluation. For example, suppose you very much value the opinion of your professors. They serve as a reference group for you. When you find yourself disagreeing with them, you may question the validity of your attitude and perhaps change it so that it matches their attitudes. In this example, the professors serve as a positive reference group. A group that you disagree with strongly may also affect your attitudes, but as a negative reference group. For instance, if you regard yourself as a feminist and find yourself in agreement with an antifeminist group on some issue, you might reevaluate that attitude and change it to increase your dissimilarity to this negative reference group. As you can see, reference groups can be influential.

As you will recall, our social comparisons are often made with those of similar opinions (positive reference groups) and similar or slightly greater ability. Status comparisons are similarly made "horizontally." We keep up with the Joneses, who are similar to us, rather than comparing ourselves with those of greatly different status. Because of this choice of reference groups, it is possible that those with great ability, wealth, status, attractiveness, or strength are no more satisfied with themselves than those less fortunate.

When we change our attitudes, we sometimes also change reference groups in order to support those attitudes. When our reference groups change their attitudes, we may try to change our own or change reference groups. Reference groups are chosen to give support to our own beliefs. To see this more concretely, consider the effects of wealth on attitudes and reference-group choice. Money can buy happiness if it enables people to make more-positive self-evaluations. Very often, though, a person who has acquired wealth changes to a wealthier reference group and in the end may be none the happier. At the same time, the newly wealthy person's old friends may experience some mixed feelings. One person's gain in status is someone else's loss.

Membership groups are simply those groups we belong to: our family, our clubs, our college, a fraternity or sorority, and so on. The difference between membership and reference groups is simple: if you belong, it's a membership group; if you compare, it's a reference group; if you both belong and compare, it's both a membership and a reference group. Primary groups are always membership groups and are usually reference groups; secondary groups may be membership groups and may be reference groups, but they need not be.

The reference group/membership group distinction implies that people do not need to belong to a reference group and that they need not use a membership group for social comparison. Very often, however, a reference group is also a membership group. For example, psychologists often compare themselves with other psychologists (reference group) and belong to one or more organizations of these psychologists (membership group).

Two Groups in Psychology.   Many psychologists have shown considerable interest in two other kinds of groups: the encounter group and the laboratory group.

Encounter groups.   Encounter groups come in many forms, such as the T-group, sensitivity group, consciousness-raising group, experiential workshop, and so on. Most make efforts to be primary groups, membership groups, and reference groups all at once. Most have goals relating to self-improvement through increased social awareness, understanding of self and others, and expression of repressed and suppressed feelings. All may be viewed as forms of group therapy, although the leaders of these groups (usually called facilitators) commonly lack formal training in psychotherapy or psychology. Encounter groups are praised by many who have taken up this social movement, but they have created some cynics and critics as well. One study found that about 17% of the members who were studied dropped out, and 10% of the members lost self-esteem, trust in others, and the ability to cope with problems and relationships. Only 33% of those studied were considered (by themselves and others) to have benefited from the experience (Lieberman, Yalom, & Miles, 1973). Encounter groups nonetheless form a potentially important part of the mental-health movement and are a social phenomenon of interest to social psychologists.

Laboratory groups. The **laboratory group** is a secondary group. It is an artificial grouping of a few unacquainted college students who meet for an hour or so and follow the directions of a researcher. Such groups are created to help solve some of the research problems that occur in real groups. Laboratory groups permit easier and better observation and recording, especially through the use of **one-way mirrors**[2] and videotapes. Some experimental manipulations are easier in the laboratory, where cause and effect can be studied more rigorously.

But studying small groups is *very* difficult. Why? First, other areas of research focus on a *behavior* and seek to explain it, so research may emphasize one dependent measure (such as helping behavior) and ignore others. But because small groups are *systems* in which many behaviors occur, the student of small groups has more to study and more to explain. Second, explanation is more difficult. The behaviors in a small group are components of interdependent *processes*; their causes are many and spread over time. So any researcher who wants to know about the effects of variable X must study both immediate and delayed effects; delayed effects may have additional—or other—causes. Further, one effect may serve as cause for another. If you tell a joke and I laugh hard, you may tell another one. If I don't laugh, you may not tell another joke. In an interdependent system it is difficult to find a truly independent variable. Cause and effect are more difficult to study.

This leads to a paradox. Because most social behavior takes place in small groups, understanding the small group may be the most important task of a social psychologist. Yet the main research method of the social psychologist—the experiment—is not well suited for studying most small-group phenomena. Much experimental work in this area has focused on obvious but possibly unimportant variables such as seating arrangements, group composition, and group size. Most variables in small groups do not "hold still" as group size or seating position do, and they are more difficult to study experimentally. Although group processes may be more interesting and important than group outcomes or products, researchers have tended to study the latter (O'Dell, 1968). For example, you will learn later in this chapter about research on how group size (independent variable)

[2]A one-way mirror is a special window between two rooms. When one room is darkened, people can see those in the illuminated room, but from the illuminated room, the window looks like a mirror.

affects satisfaction (a dependent variable, outcome, or product). Little research has been done on how this happens (process).

GROUP FORMATION, MAINTENANCE, AND DISSOLUTION

During the course of the day, you will probably enter and leave several groups. Some of these are temporary. They form, continue briefly, then dissolve, never to form again. Examples of such temporary groups include crowds and laboratory groups. You will probably also be a part of several ongoing groups. In such groups, members have a clear expectation that the group will continue and that they will continue as members.

Why do people choose to join or leave a particular group? Differences in attractiveness is one reason. If joining a group seems more attractive than staying out, you will probably join. People join groups because they expect them to be satisfying. People avoid dissatisfying groups. For instance, when morale in an organization is low, absenteeism and tardiness rise; when morale is high, absenteeism and tardiness drop.

Newcomers.   When a group first forms, everyone is a newcomer to it and faces the same problems. But newcomers to established groups may find difficulties that the oldtimers didn't experience. R. Crandall (in press) has reviewed a number of problems that newcomers face:

1. Newcomers may be seen as potentially disloyal (Schuetz, 1944) and may be initially disliked (Feshbach, N., & Sones, 1971; Ziller & Behringer, 1961). This reaction may be related to the unpleasantness of novelty (Stang & Crandall, 1977). As a result of the oldtimers' negative reactions to the novel newcomers, they may be treated with hostility. The low status of newcomers may mean they are given low-status work, as was found in one study (Walker, T. G., 1973).
2. The negative behaviors on the part of the oldtimers may produce negative feelings on the part of newcomers. Migrants and immigrants, for instance, sometimes become depressed (Rossi, R., 1971). Depression, in turn, inhibits activity; newcomers often feel inhibited in free expression and show restraint in their actions (Washburn, R. W., 1932).
3. Newcomers may be extremely low in idosyncrasy credit (see Chapter 11) and quite aware that oldtimers may not appreciate much deviance from group norms. As a consequence, newcomers often show the greatest conformity to group norms (Nash & Heiss, 1967; Nash & Wolfe, 1957). This conformity may include acquiring the prejudices of the group being joined. Individuals from minorities, when seeking to become assimilated into a majority culture, often take on the attitude that the majority holds toward the minority from which they came. For example, Blacks trying to become accepted by White culture may acquire some prejudices toward Blacks. Whites seeking to identify with Blacks may acquire some negative attitudes toward Whites. Through this process of identification and conformity, individuals may develop negative attitudes toward the group from which they came and perhaps even toward themselves (Allport, G. W., 1954b; Lewin, 1935, 1941).

Newcomers may anticipate negative reactions from oldtimers and, in response to this expectation, may band together, become more cohesive, and feel more positive about each other and more negative about the oldtimers. These effects are sometimes evident among immigrants and minorities. They apparently occur even without any negative reactions from the oldtimers. In one study (Crandall, R., & Moreland, 1978) researchers formed groups of strangers and told some that they were newcomers to an established group. The above effects (banding together and so forth) occurred for those who were told that other group members were oldtimers, but they did not occur for others in the group.

Getting Acquainted. How do temporary, informal groupings coalesce into ongoing groups? In a temporary group, individuals interact fairly spontaneously and creatively. Because the responses of others are fairly novel, each person is forced to analyze them and decide on appropriate courses of action. Such cognitive activity is challenging, sometimes tiring, and sometimes stressful. But it may produce a satisfying result. If so, when the group dissolves, it may make plans to meet again. With each successive meeting, several things happen:

1. As members learn about one another, they become more skilled at predicting one another's behavior.
2. As members become skilled at predicting one another's behavior, they learn to anticipate how to respond. Sometimes roles become differentiated. Sometimes members develop habits that decrease spontaneous, thoughtful behavior and therefore make it easier for members to predict one another's behavior.
3. As members become more predictable, others come to *expect* such behaviors. Such expectations are shared (norms) and come to influence such behaviors (normative control). When people do what they believe is expected, expectations are confirmed.
4. As people become familiar with one another, their attraction increases. This attraction further cements the group together. The processes of attraction described in Chapter 8 all are relevant to this discussion of group formation and dissolution (including the discussion of romantic attraction; the change from "a couple on a date" to "a dating couple" is a change from a temporary group to an ongoing group).

Cohesiveness. As individuals become increasingly attracted to one another, they spend increasing amounts of time together. Boy meets girl. Girl meets boy. They date a little, then often. Over time, this mutual attraction builds to the point at which the group is recognized as such. They go steady or are engaged or married. Initiation ceremonies provide formal recognition of an individual's interest in a group and serve as a commemoration of membership.

Just as individuals may become more (or less) attracted to each other over time, they may become more (or less) attracted to groups of individuals. Attraction is commonly reciprocated, so it often happens that a group becomes more (or less) attractive to its members.

This attraction to a group has been studied for many years and is called **cohesiveness.** Cohesiveness can be defined as "those forces which keep a person in the group and prevent him from leaving" (Collins & Raven, 1969, p. 120). You

DON'T THEY MAKE A LOVELY GROUP ?

can think of cohesiveness as the degree to which group members "stick together," giving the group unity. Cohesiveness is manifested in many ways. For instance, researchers have found that, the more attracted we are to a group, the longer we remain members and the more meetings we attend (Libo, 1953; Sagi, Olmstead, & Stelsek, 1955). Other researchers have found that, the more attracted we are to a group of others, the more they influence us (Back, 1951; Berkowitz, L., 1954; Festinger, Gerard, Hymovitch, Kelley, & Raven, 1952; Schachter, Ellertson, McBride, & Gregory, 1951).

Many different factors may influence cohesiveness. Your attraction to the group is one, of course. But factors such as the motivation of the group to succeed on a task, its prestige, and its efficiency in working toward its goals affect cohesiveness (Back, 1951). Another influence is the degree to which attitudes are shared by group members; the more they are shared, the greater the group's cohesiveness.

Stress can have positive or negative effects on cohesiveness. Some groups cope with stressful situations better than others. Long-standing groups, with well-developed internal structure and affection among members, seem to weather a crisis better than newly formed, disorganized groupings (French, 1941; Torrance, 1954). Moderate stress may actually bring some groups closer together, increasing friendliness and cooperation (Lanzetta, 1955). But with very high stress most groups may find it difficult to survive. For instance, during a battle a seasoned company of soldiers may draw together and work cooperatively and supportively. A company of new recruits, on the other hand, sometimes becomes disorganized, as soldiers adopt an every-man-for-himself response to the stress.

How would you measure cohesiveness? Researchers have tried many ways, but no method seems satisfactory. Some have used the consequences of cohesiveness (such as attrition or attendance rates). Others have used indicators of satisfaction or attraction to group members, as compared with attraction to nongroup members. But because the concept of cohesiveness is a little vague and very broad, valid measurement has been difficult. Measured or not, cohesiveness is very useful in thinking about the many sources and effects of group unity (Newcomb, Turner,

& Converse, 1965). A systematic program of research would probably reveal that all of the principles of attraction between two people are applicable to a person's attraction to a group. Nonetheless, groups are not individuals. Groups have special properties that make them different from the sum of their parts. They develop their own special norms, roles, traditions, and structures.

GROUP STRUCTURE

After a group forms, it develops some internal structure over time. **Group structure** consists of the roles that develop within the group and the types of relationships that result from these roles. For instance, in a family an older sister might take a motherly role toward a younger brother and a daughterly role toward her mother. In her classroom this same girl would take the role of student rather than mother or daughter.

Relationships within a group require communication. In any group some pairs of members interact more often than others, and all pairs interact a bit differently. The nature of these interactions defines the group structure.

Frederic Thrasher studied 1100 gangs—a type of small group—and came to the following conclusion:

> Every member of a gang tends to have a definite status within the group. Common enterprises require a division of labor. . . . As the gang develops complex activities, the positions of individuals within the group are defined and social roles become more sharply differentiated [1927, p. 328].

Division of Labor.   Societies and, to some extent, small groups as well produce specialists. Specialists are trained for a particular task and consequently perform it better than others. The specialist requires certain resources produced by other specialists and produces certain resources. The baker uses flour to make cakes and pies. Such **division of labor** thus leads to interdependence: the baker depends on the products of the miller and depends on many people for the sale of baked goods. The public, in turn, depends on the baker. As Durkheim has suggested, this "division of labor produces solidarity . . . because it creates . . . an entire system of rights and duties which link [people] together in a durable way" (1947). Within the small group, two interesting types of specialist have been identified—the *task specialist* and the *social/emotional specialist*. Robert Bales (1958), Philip Slater (1955), and Fred Strodtbeck (1951, 1958) were among the first to study this role differentiation. Their findings, as well as those of more recent investigators (Burke, 1968), are summarized in the following three paragraphs.

Task specialists, on the one hand, have high competence in a particular task in which the group is engaged. They tend to speak and be spoken to a great deal. While working on the task, they generate many ideas, give considerable guidance, and make many influence attempts. In laboratory studies of mixed-sex groups, task specialists tend to be men. Task specialists are reasonably well liked, are quite influential, and are often given high leadership ratings by other group members. We might expect them to be relatively high in need for achievement.

Social/emotional specialists, on the other hand, are very well liked by other group members, more so than task specialists. They tend to be more positive, asking more questions and making fewer problem-solving attempts. They are good at keeping relations warm and friendly and at soothing hurt feelings. We might expect them to be relatively high in need for affiliation. Research suggests that social/emotional specialists in small, mixed-sex groups tend to be women.

These sex differences in role within the small group have been found in studies of the family (Strodtbeck, 1951, 1958), small laboratory groups (Slater, 1955), and simulated jury deliberations (Strodtbeck & Mann, 1956). It is not clear whether these patterns are as strong today as they were in the 1950s. Depending on factors such as group size and the nature of a group's activities, a variety of members may take one or both of these roles from time to time. Several members will sometimes occupy the same role. But whether one sex or both sexes are associated with each of these roles, both are important in maintaining productivity, satisfaction, performance, and morale in the small group. People in these roles interact and agree more with one another than with other group members. Both roles are useful in group functioning.

Status.   **Status** refers to the respect one receives from others. It reflects the degree to which one possesses qualities that others value. For instance, if others in the group value daring and if you are daring, you will have the group's respect. You will be of higher status in that group than if you were not daring. In a particular group, you might be able to guess each member's status if you knew what qualities each member valued, how important each was, who had how much of each quality, how much each quality was evident, and so on. It might be simpler, though, to ask group members whom they most respect or who has what status. Among Americans the most commonly valued qualities include task competence, social skills, education, occupation, wealth, and background. In other cultures some variables affect respect and status differently. For instance, the elderly receive less respect in the United States today than in Japan.

Social animals such as chickens, monkeys, and wolves also show status differences. They are similar to people in that higher-status individuals typically are

THERE GOES ONE HELLUVA CHICKEN!

more influential and have more power, more control, and easier access to limited resources such as food, mates, and nesting areas. It is interesting to note all these "fringe benefits" of high status. On the basis of just a few brief fights, a hen's access to the food trough over a long period of time is determined: the winner may eat whenever she pleases, and the loser must wait. Similarly, people with prestigious occupations (high in the "pecking order") may be more influential in small groups than those with lower-status occupations (Bass, 1965; Strodtbeck, James, & Hawkins, 1957). A person who is respected for one attribute comes to be respected for others, and through this halo effect respect and status increase. The rich get richer.

Status, influence, and *leadership* are three concepts that have much in common. Status refers to the respect a person is given; influence depends on such respect. Thus, high-status people tend to be influential. **Leadership** in one sense simply refers to the influence process. Leaders tend to have respect and be of high status. We will turn now to a discussion of leadership, a subject on which much has been written (Kymissis & Stang, 1975).

Leadership. The word *leadership* is so common that we may not feel much curiosity when we hear it. But this frequency of usage leads to a great variety of dictionary meanings and some sloppiness in our usage. After reviewing over 3,000 studies of leadership, one researcher concluded that "there are almost as many different definitions of leadership as there are persons who have attempted to define the concept" (Stogdill, 1974, p. 7). Early research in leadership was guided by the intuition that there are leaders and followers; early researchers sought to list the general qualities of these people (Cowley, 1931; Sanford, 1950; Shartle, 1949). But their results were disappointing. Most social psychologists now believe that, if a general leadership trait exists, it is not very helpful in predicting who will be chosen as leader. We can make more-accurate and more-useful predictions from knowledge of the group's situation. In fact, leadership is least likely to be predicted from the traits of the individual leader, more likely to be predicted from the situation, and most likely to be predicted from an examination of both the individual and the situation.

Failing to find much evidence that leaders have different characteristics from nonleaders or unsuccessful leaders, social psychologists began looking at **leadership style.** At first it was assumed that considerate, person-oriented behavior by a leader would result in greater satisfaction among group members than a task-oriented leadership style. This may often be true, but satisfaction does not always increase productivity. Sometimes it lowers it (Stogdill, 1974). Current thinking favors the idea that leadership results from special combinations of individuals and situations. This shift in focus is reflected in changing definitions of leadership. Unfortunately, a major problem with this approach is that we still have no adequate way to classify situations to understand their effects. Further, good leaders have multiple styles (Hill, W. A., 1973). They adapt their behavior in response to the situation (Hill, W. A., & Hughes, 1974) and the behavior of others (Farris & Lim, 1969; Greene, C. N., 1975; Lowin & Craig, 1968). For example, in a particular situation a good leader might give some group members firm direction, offer others suggestions, and seek out others for advice. In another situation the effective leader might seek advice from the entire group—or no one at all—before making a decision.

In fact, it may be better to think of leadership as activities such as support, guidance, and influence that all group members perform from time to time in an effective group. Thus, leadership is a shared function that some group members do more of than others.

Although thousands of leadership studies have been done since the start of World War II (McCall, 1977), we seem to have established few principles. As Warren Bennis has said, "Of all the hazy and confounding areas in social psychology, leadership theory undoubtedly contends for top nomination. And, ironically, probably more has been written and less known about leadership than about any other topic in the behavioral sciences" (1959, cited in McCall, 1977). McCall has made the same point: "Researchers are still a long way from an integrated understanding of leadership processes, and are equally far from providing organizational leaders with integrated and validated models of leadership" (1977, p. 6).

What do leaders do?   Current theories of leadership may have failed partly because the theorists lacked experience with real leaders in management and administration. Some theoretical problems may also be traced to the unnatural laboratory settings typically used for leadership research. Studies of real managers (McCall, 1977) reveal some interesting facts that should be considered in leadership research. (Not all leaders are managers, though, so we should not generalize.)

Pace.   Studies have found that foremen and managers may average between 200 and 500 activities in a single day (Guest, 1955–1956). Each activity lasts only a short time, with very few lasting more than half an hour (Carlson, S., 1951; Mintzberg, 1973). Managers need to be able to change tasks rapidly and to waste little time in "getting going."

Control.   This frantic pace is largely the consequence of interruptions, of contacts with others that those others initiate. Managers may initiate only one-third of their contacts with others (Mintzberg, 1975). And more time is spent reacting to situations than planning them. Most managers probably have an internal locus of control (Chapter 3), so this lack of control can be frustrating.

Contact.   Managers need verbal ability, because perhaps 60 to 80% of a manager's day is spent talking to others (Brewer, E., & Tomlinson, 1963–1964; Burns, 1954; Dubin, 1962; Dubin & Spray, 1964; Mintzberg, 1973). Managers may spend 30 to 60% of this contact time with subordinates (Dubin, 1962; Mintzberg, 1973), 10 to 20% with superiors (Brewer, E., & Tomlinson, 1963–1964; Mintzberg, 1973), and the remaining time with peers and colleagues. Most of this contact apparently involves exchanging information; very little involves giving orders or instructions (Horne & Lupton, 1965; Mintzberg, 1973). Most contact is via spoken word (Dubin, 1962). Not only is spoken contact more frequent than written, but it is more influential.

A leadership trait?   Will people who show leadership in one situation show leadership in others? There is some evidence that this leadership is a general trait, but it may depend on how *similar* the situations are. For instance, leaders in a reasoning task may also show leadership in other intellectual tasks but not show much leadership in tasks not requiring such verbal or cognitive skills (Carter, Haythorn, & Howell, 1950). Leaders are task specialists and can show effective leadership only in those tasks in which they are more competent than other group members.

If leadership *is* a general trait, then people should agree in their judgments of the leadership of others. Some evidence shows that group members do agree on who the group leaders are (Carter et al., 1950; Stang, 1973; Stang, Castellanetta, Constantinidis, & Fortuno, 1976). However, people who do not see the group in operation do not generally agree with group members on group leadership judgments (Carter et al., 1950). This suggests that "leadership" is much more than "leadership ability." It is also motivation, attitudes of other group members, and particular task-specific knowledge and skills. In fact, Robert Merton has emphasized that leadership is "less of an attribute of individuals than of a social exchange. . . . Leaders assist their associates in achieving personal and social goals. In exchange, they receive the basic coin of effective leadership—trust and respect. You need not be loved to be an effective leader, but you must be respected" (1969, pp. 2615–2616). Leadership is *not* a general trait, though to some extent leadership ability may be.

Qualities of leaders. Many studies have searched for attributes of task leaders, or qualities they typically possess. Interest Box 12-1 lists some of the findings. Most of these studies have assumed that, the more one has of a given quality, the greater one's task-leadership ability. This may be true for task-leadership *ability*, but not true for task leadership. People may wish to be led by those they both like and respect. Because our liking is greatest for similar others, we may vote for those who are better—but not too much better—than we. The best man or woman does not always win. One researcher has noted that "the evidence suggests that every increment of intelligence means wiser government, but that the crowd prefers to be ill-governed by people it can understand" (Gibb, C. A., 1969, p. 218). Thus, the relation between variables such as size, intelligence, or attractiveness and leadership may actually be **curvilinear** (increasing to a point, then decreasing). For instance, people with moderate levels of intelligence may be preferred as leaders to those with more or less intelligence.

Men, women, and leadership. Much of the literature on leadership assumes that leaders are men: "the leader and his group" (Berkowitz, L., 1953), "the leader is the man who acts when the situation requires action" (Whyte, W. F., 1943), "the great man theory of leadership" (Borgatta et al., 1954), and so on. Everyday language does likewise: *chairman, congressman,* and the like. This assumption even guides research on leadership, which historically has focused only on male leaders (Eskilson & Wiley, 1976) and more often uses male than female subjects. Because it also happens that most researchers of leadership are men, it might be suggested that this is simple sexist bias.

Although that is one interpretation, another is that the stereotype is based on fact. Steven Goldberg (1973) suggests in *The Inevitability of Patriarchy* (discussed in Chapter 3) that men are more aggressive than women (through biological differences) and that this aggressiveness pushes them into positions of task leadership.

Another possibility is that men become task leaders because they are more influential than women. (This may sound circular. Informal leadership is influence. But influential people are often "promoted" to positions of formal leadership and authority.) If men are generally more influential than women, they may be more likely to be both informal task leaders and formal (appointed or elected) task leaders.

Some studies do find that men are more influential (Kenkel, 1957; Strodtbeck et al., 1957; Tuddenham, MacBride, & Zahn, 1958; Whittaker, 1965; Zander & Van Egmond, 1958). If men are more influential, it may be because cultural

---

Interest Box 12-1.   Some Findings from Leadership Research

Variable	*Finding*
Activity level	Leadership takes a lot of energy, and influence requires activity. Leaders may be more active than others (Gibb, C. A., 1969; Terman, 1904).
Attractiveness	Attractive people tend to be more influential and better liked and thus may be more often chosen as leaders (Partridge, 1934; Terman, 1904).
Height and weight	Leaders are often taller (reviewed in Stogdill, 1948); for instance, insurance-company executives may be taller than policy holders (Gowin, 1915). Leaders may also tend to be heavier, particularly where size or strength is important (reviewed in Gibb, C. A., 1969).
Intelligence	Many studies (reviewed in Mann, 1959) have found that leaders are more intelligent than others, though they are not always the most intelligent group members. Competence in the special tasks of the group may be more important than general intellectual ability.
Personal adjustment	There is much evidence that leaders are better adjusted (reviewed in Mann, 1959). Well-adjusted people may be chosen as leader, and leaders may find it easier than others to be (or appear) well adjusted.
Popularity	If leaders tend to possess all these desirable qualities, it should come as no surprise that leaders are well liked, popular, and congenial (for example, see Borgatta, Couch, & Bales, 1954; Gibb, C. A., 1950; Terman, 1904). Recent research indicates that, although chosen leaders are well liked by group members, they are not always the best liked (for example, see Bales, 1953; Borgatta, 1954).
Self-confidence	Self-confidence is indispensable in influencing others; leaders have been found in a number of studies to have more self-confidence than others (reviewed in Gibb, C. A., 1969). As with adjustment, leadership may be both the cause and effect of self-confidence.
Talkativeness	Leaders are talkative (Bales, 1953, 1970; Bass, 1949; Bavelas, Hastorf, Gross, & Kite, 1965; Borgatta & Bales, 1956; Borgatta et al., 1954; Carter, Haythorn, Shriver, & Lanzetta, 1951; Ginter & Lindskold, 1975; Goodenough, F. L., 1930; Jaffee & Lucas, 1969; Kirscht, Lodahl, & Haire, 1959; Morris, C. G., & Hackman, 1969; Norfleet, 1948; Shaw, M. E., & Gilchrist, 1956; Slater, 1955; Stang, 1973; Stang et al., 1967; Zdep & Oakes, 1967).

norms, traditions, and stereotypes of their sex as more competent give them an advantage in respect and status.

Still another possibility is that women do not assume the task-leadership role because they feel it to be inappropriate. Even when placed in such roles, they may engage in less "leader-like" behavior and be less likely than men to choose themselves as future leaders (Eskilson & Wiley, 1976).

Whatever the explanation, it appears that men are more often in positions of task leadership than women, that our stereotypes may exaggerate this sex difference, and that our stereotypes may put men at a further advantage in task leadership.

GROUP FUNCTIONING

Now that we have some idea of how a group is structured, we can examine how it functions. We will look at two aspects of the functioning of a group—the effects of its size and how its productivity is affected by various factors.

Group Size. First, I will take up the effect of a group's size on its members' satisfaction. Then I will discuss the effect that size has on the performance of members.

Effect on member satisfaction. Is there a relationship between group size and member satisfaction? Common sense suggests "The more the merrier," perhaps because "There's safety in numbers" or "Two heads are better than one." But it also suggests that "Three's a crowd," no doubt because "Too many cooks spoil the broth." If common sense appears contradictory, so does the research.

One researcher (Hare, 1952) reported greater satisfaction with their decisions among members of 5-person groups than 12-person groups. Another researcher (Miller, N. E., Jr., 1952) found no relationship between group size and three measures of satisfaction. A third researcher (Ziller, 1957) found members of 4-person groups to be more satisfied with their part in the discussion than members of groups of 2, 3, 5, or 6. Yet another researcher (Slater, 1958) found fewer complaints about group size in his 5-person groups than in other groups ranging in size from 2 through 7. Not surprisingly, another study (Hackman & Vidmar, 1970) reported conflicting results. By some analyses, satisfaction decreased with group size, groups of 2 being most preferred. With other analyses, groups of 4 or 5 were most preferred. On some but not all of their measures of satisfaction, other researchers (Frank & Anderson, 1971) found groups of 3 or 5 more preferred than groups of 2 or 8. And so it continues! Although these studies are far from consistent, the majority thus suggests that perhaps 4 or 5 members is an optimum group size for member satisfaction, with both smaller and larger groups being somewhat less satisfying.[3]

To test this hypothesis, two conceptual replications (a replication of a study using a different method to test the same hypothesis) of these studies were conducted (Stang, 1978a). In the first, 53 undergraduate students in a social-

---

[3]This generalization may only apply to small groups of 10 or fewer members, however. One study reports that, as group size increased from 10 to 60, satisfaction increased (Osborn & Hunt, 1975). The generalization may also be limited to certain tasks.

psychology course took part as experimenters. Each experimenter opened a newspaper or magazine and selected the first 20 photographs of individuals or groups of people he or she saw. Experimenters then snipped these photographs out and asked two friends to rate them on a seven-point scale for how happy the people in each picture seemed.

Across all 1060 pictures, the rated happiness of the individuals in the pictures increased from 4.4 for single individuals to a high of 5.0 for a group size of four. It then declined and leveled off as group size increased to 9 or 10 or more (see Figure 12-3). This pilot study, then, suggests that members of groups of four may be happier than members of smaller or larger groups (or that, for some reason, students more readily imagine them to be happy).

Another conceptual replication attempted to see whether this relation would hold up using different methods. Two hundred twenty-eight undergraduates were asked several questions, including "If you could be in a group of friends of any size now, how many people, including yourself, would be in the group?" As you can see from Figure 12-4, more people preferred a group size of four than any other size. So it seems that our intuition about group size and member satisfaction might be revised a bit. For groups under four, "The more the merrier." For groups over four, "Too many cooks spoil the broth."

If you compare preferences for even- versus odd-sized groups in both studies, you will find that two members may be more satisfying than three. So "Two's company, three's a crowd" may be correct. (And four's company, five's a crowd, six's company, seven's a crowd . . .) Some other research suggests that this proverb

Figure 12-3.
The relationship between group size in magazine and newspaper photographs and judged happiness. The number of groups of each size is indicated in parentheses.

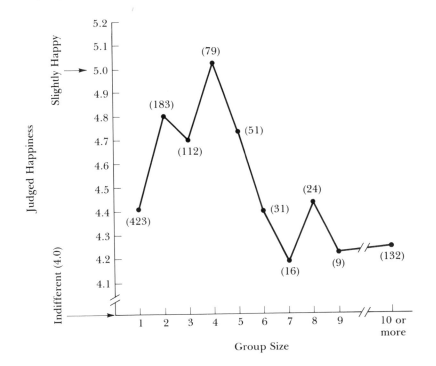

Figure 12-4.
Number of college
students most
preferring groups
of various sizes

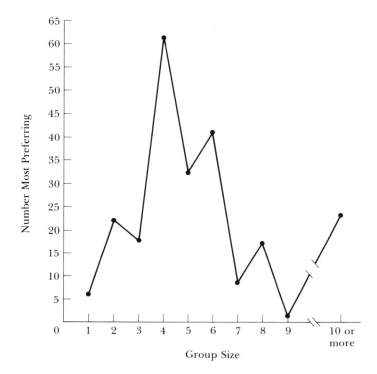

is true. One researcher (Mills, T. M., 1953) studied the interaction of 48 triads over time and found that in many of these groups two people tended to become mutually attracted and to communicate most with each other, excluding the third member (Simmel, 1902). Coalitions often form within larger groups. When they do, even-sized groups (two, four, six, eight, ten members) may be more stable than odd-sized groups. Even-sized groups can always break into dyads, whereas in odd-sized groups one member may become excluded from other relationships, become dissatisfied, and leave the group (creating an even-sized group).

However, even-sized groups may not always be preferred (Bales & Borgatta, 1955; Frank & Anderson, 1971; O'Dell, 1968). When a group has to reach consensus in its task, odd-sized groups can break into majority and minority coalitions. This imbalance may make it easier to come to a consensus through "majority rule." Small, even-sized groups may be more likely to form even-sized coalitions and become stalemated. So whether two's company or three's company may depend on whether consensus is important.

Why should groups of four be preferred to larger or smaller groups? Several explanations will be considered below. Each may account for some of the relationship, even if none is alone a sufficient explanation.

The first explanation borrows from the idea of optimal arousal. Most people prefer to spend their lives somewhere between low arousal (for example, boredom) and high arousal (for example, terror) and may even choose groups that help them to maintain some desired, intermediate level of arousal. When we speak to

In a triad, dyads
often form.

a group, our arousal (anxiety, fear, excitement) probably increases with group size. However, when we are listening in a group setting, our arousal decreases with group size. If an intermediate level of arousal is preferred, then both speakers and listeners should most prefer some intermediate-sized groups.

The optimal-arousal hypothesis may account for only some of the relationship between group size and member satisfaction, and we might also consider the possibility that the nature of the task interacts with group size in determining member satisfaction. For instance, brainstorming tasks may be most satisfying in larger groups, because, for producing ideas, two heads are better than one, three better than two, and so on (up to some point) (Gibb, J. R., 1951). Other tasks require members to reach consensus or make a decision. Several studies have shown that the likelihood of consensus decreases with increases in group size (see Chapter 7).

We might expect that, if consensus is important to member satisfaction, members might be most satisfied with smaller groups. Further, member satisfaction with a group decision is related to the extent of that member's participation in and influence on that decision, which decreases with increases in group size (Hare, 1952; Hoffman, L. R., Burke, & Maier, 1965).

These conclusions parallel some analyses of cities of different sizes. Smaller communities have higher rates of participation in community activities (Verba & Nie, 1972) and higher rates of perceived ability to influence local political decisions (Finifter & Abramson, 1975).

One area of research that might be reexamined is that of group cohesiveness, which is sometimes defined as the attraction (satisfaction?) of a group for its members. There is evidence that large groups are usually less cohesive. They are more likely to break up into cliques (small, close-knit groups) (Berkowitz, L., 1954; Hare, 1952; Miller, N. E., Jr., 1952). And they are more likely to have higher absence and termination rates (Indik, 1963). And so on. Whether cohesiveness is a linear decreasing function of group size, as is sometimes suggested (Berkowitz, L., 1954), remains to be seen.

Effect on performance. Member satisfaction is one goal of most groups. Performing some task well is often another goal. Does group size affect performance? When are two heads better than one? The answer is as follows:

☐ When a group is making a judgment or learning material in which *accuracy* is most important, such as guessing the number of beans in a jar, the larger the group, the more accurate will be the judgment (Dashiell, 1935; Gordon, 1924; Lorge, Fox, Davitz, & Brenner, 1958; Perlmutter, 1953; Perlmutter & de Montmollin, 1952). To some extent, at least, this may be a statistical artifact rather than a group effect (Gordon, 1923, 1924; Stroop, 1932; Zajonc, 1962, 1966). For instance, by averaging five individual judgments from one person, one person might be as accurate as a group of five.

☐ When a group is engaged in a task in which speed is important, small groups may often be more effective than larger groups, particularly if performance requires consensus. Consensus is more difficult to achieve in larger groups, and much problem-solving time may be devoted to resolving initial differences of opinion. The wag who suggested that a camel is a horse or cow designed by a committee must have had considerable experience with committees and the difficulties of achieving consensus. Research has found groups slower and less efficient than individuals in a variety of tasks, including tests of recall (Perlmutter, 1953), planning (Fox & Lorge, 1962), reasoning (Klugman, 1944), and some other types of problem solving (Davis & Restle, 1963; Taylor & Faust, 1952).

☐ When each group member has something unique to contribute to the solution of a problem, groups will generally be more effective at solving problems than individuals (Kelley & Thibaut, 1969). For instance, in solving a series of anagram tasks, each group member may quickly solve an anagram that has the others stumped. Through this pooling of insight, the series of tasks is solved faster than by individuals alone (Faust, 1959). In brainstorming, larger groups generate more ideas (Gibb, J. R., 1951).

☐ When performance of the group is contingent on the performance of a single member, the group may be better or worse than the average member. On the one hand, if the task requires a special skill such as open-heart surgery, and one of the group members is a surgeon who performs the operation, the patient will probably do better than if the operation were conducted by the average group member. On the other hand, if the task requires that people swim a river and the group contains a nonswimmer, the average member will swim the river before the group as a whole does. Whether a group performs as well as its best member or as poorly as its worst depends in part on the task and the rules (Frank & Anderson, 1971). In decision-making tasks the group may perform nearly as well as its most competent member if the group does not interfere with that member's performance and if that member's solution is rapidly accepted by the group (Dashiell, 1935; Kelley & Thibaut, 1969).

☐ In tasks requiring physical or mental effort and permitting relative anonymity and diffusion of responsibility, per-capita efficiency decreases with increasing group size. For instance, two people may pull a rope much harder than one, but not twice as hard (Ingham, Levinger, Graves, & Peckham, 1974; Moede, 1927). This is the **Ringleman effect.**[4] Two people may cheer much louder than one, but not twice as loud. A brainstorming group produces more ideas than an individual, but not as many ideas as the members would collectively if they were working alone (Bouchard, 1969; Bouchard & Hare, 1970; Dunnette, Campbell, & Jaastad, 1963; Renzulli, Owen, & Callahan, 1971; Taylor, D. W., Berry & Block, 1958). And workers in a car factory produce less per person as group size increases (Marriott, 1949). In fact, in tasks such as this, individual effort or contribution seems to decrease with increases in size. Some of this effect may result from a diffusion of responsibility and some from difficulties in coordinating the group's effort.

In summary, groups perform better than individuals when accuracy or creativity is important. Individuals may perform better than a group when speed is important, especially if consensus is required by the task.

Group Productivity.   *Group productivity* refers to the amount and quality of the work produced by a group. Because it affects both producers and consumers, productivity is of interest to us all.

Effect of satisfaction.   We have looked at the relationship of group size to satisfaction and performance. How are satisfaction and performance related? Satisfied groups are more cohesive and more attractive to their members. They establish stronger norms, which regulate performance. Such norms may raise or lower the overall quality of performance and make it more uniform across members (Berkowitz, L., 1954; Schachter et al., 1951; Seashore, 1954). In an office where morale is low, some secretaries may work slowly and others diligently. In another office, where morale is higher, everyone may be working at a similar pace—either fast or slow. Satisfaction also tends to increase a person's activity level, and thus, apart from any effects of norms, performance often tends to be higher in satisfied, cohesive groups (Lott, A. J., & Lott, 1965). Other evidence, however, suggests that successful management efforts to raise productivity may also introduce **evaluation apprehension** and lower satisfaction (Latham & Yukl, 1976).

Finally, because satisfied, cohesive groups tend to produce greater uniformity among members (see Chapter 11), critical, careful, independent thought among members may be reduced in an effort to achieve consensus. Such consensus may be both pleasant and destructive. When satisfaction leads to this uncritical consensus, which Irving Janis (1971, 1974) has called **groupthink,** the results may

---

[4]Named after the student who discovered the principle.

be quite negative.[5] With groupthink, group performance is no wiser than that of its leader. And it can be much slower. In summary, the relation between satisfaction and performance is complex.

Effect of productivity norms.

Suppose you were given the job of your dreams—sewing on buttons in a pajama factory. And suppose that after practice you could sew 100 buttons an hour. If others in your work group averaged 70 buttons an hour, how many do you suppose you would average? As an amateur social psychologist, you should think of group norms and group pressure and guess 70. At least that is what you might guess if you were predicting someone else's behavior.

Not only might the other workers slow you down, but you might have the effect of speeding them up. The effects of an individual on a group are probably greatest when the group is small and newly formed. An interesting example of this comes from a study of ants. Chen (1938) found that, when working alone under a variety of conditions, the individual ants that he was studying worked at an amazingly constant pace, hauling soil from one point to another. Some ants, it seemed, were constantly faster than other ants, and this work rate seemed to be physiologically determined. However, if Chen placed a fast-working ant together with a slow-working ant, the slow-working ant increased its work speed and the fast-working ant decreased its work speed. Uniformity in behavior of group members does not seem to be limited to human groups. (For a discussion of other **coaction effects,** see pp. 346–348).

Productivity norms probably operate everywhere that groups engage in tasks, even in pajama factories. In a study of work groups in a pajama factory, researchers observed that a new worker quickly learned her job and began working at a rate considerably faster than the group norm (Coch & French, 1948). Soon, however, her work had slowed to better coincide with the group norm. When these researchers removed this new worker from her group and let her work on her own, her work level rose again. When she returned to the work group, her productivity fell back down again. Individuals satisfy their personal preferences for work rates when they work alone, but when they join groups, they eventually adopt the rates shared by other group members. The same probably occurs for opinions and behaviors. In school, how much one does and how well one does may be affected by group norms (Backman & Secord, 1968; Hughes, Becker, & Geer, 1962). In industry settings, at least, productivity norms may be so strong that piecework incentives have weak effects (Roethlisberger & Dickson, 1947). After all, if incentives raise your productivity, you have shown the management that more productivity is possible. Management might then expect this high productivity without such incentives.

To summarize, in small work groups norms develop that regulate productivity. Those who are more productive than the average group member—the "rate

---

[5] Janis blames groupthink for the Bay of Pigs invasion and other administrative catastrophes. Rudyard Kipling's poem "Charge of the Light Brigade" reminds us that groupthink is not new. Soldiers in the Light Brigade died because "theirs not to reason why, theirs but to do or die."

busters"—are not appreciated. Nor are the "chiselers," those who do not do their share.

Effect of social facilitation.   What effect does the simple presence of another have on our behavior? One type of social influence is **social facilitation.** Social facilitation has been observed in ants, cockroaches, chickens, rats, dogs, and people. An understanding of it is essential for an understanding of other more complex problems of social influence and interaction.

If you ever had to speak before a large group of people, you know that the mere presence of others can have a profound influence on your own thoughts, feelings, and behavior. **Audience effects** are one form of social facilitation. The home-field advantage is one of the best-known audience effects. In baseball, football, hockey, and basketball, teams win more home games than games away from home (Schwartz, B., & Barsky, 1977). The home advantage is especially pronounced in the indoor sports of hockey and basketball, where effects of members of the audience are magnified by their proximity to one another and to the players. One study of hockey found that, out of every 100 home games, 53 were won, 30 lost, and 17 tied. Further, crowd size seemed to determine the size of the advantage: with a small audience (20% or less of the stadium filled), the home team won about 48% of the time in baseball. With a medium-sized audience, the home team won 55% of the time. With a large audience (40% or more of the stadium filled), the home team won 57% of the time (Schwartz, B., & Barsky, 1977).[6]

Coaction effects are another form of social facilitation. They occur when people or animals engaged in the same task behave differently because of the presence of others. The very first experiment in social psychology happened to be an experiment in social facilitation and coaction effects. At the end of the 19th century Triplett (1897) began an investigation of social facilitation in bicycle racing. A bicycle buff himself, he was familiar with the speed records of the League of American Wheelmen and became intrigued by the observation that the fastest speeds were recorded for riders competing against one another. There were slightly slower speeds for riders assisted by a pacer but not competing. After further study, Triplett proposed a theory that assumed that

> the bodily presence of another rider is a stimulus to the racer in arousing the competitive instinct; that another can thus be the means of releasing or freeing nervous energy that he cannot of himself release; and further, that the sight of movement in that other is perhaps suggesting a higher rate of speed, is also an inspiration to greater effort [1897].

Competition provides a plausible explanation for the behavior of two bicyclists in a race, but it may not be plausible as an explanation of coaction effects among animals. For example, if chickens are allowed to eat until they eat no more and if a hungry chicken is then introduced to the cage, the full chickens will resume eating and may eat two-thirds again as much grain as they had already

---

[6]Because crowd size was not controlled by the experimenters, it is possible that crowds are drawn to games where the home team has the best chances of winning, accounting for this relation.

eaten (Bayer, 1929). Similar effects have been recorded for a large variety of animals, including armadillos, dogs, monkeys, opossums, and rats (Rajecki, Kidd, Wilder, & Jaeger, 1975).

D. W. Rajecki (Rajecki et al., 1975) has suggested that we perform best when the performance context matches the learning context. Thus, when we have learned to do something in the presence of others, we do it best when others are present. But when we learn something alone, we may perform it best alone. Social animals—which spend much time together—learn to eat together and thus eat more when together. When animals that have been reared alone are placed together, they eat less than they do alone.

Rajecki (Rajecki et al., 1975) has also suggested that novel situations may produce anxiety, which inhibits behavior. Further, whatever anxiety is produced by a novel situation seems to be reduced as the situation becomes familiar. Speakers learn that stage fright disappears after they have been speaking two or three minutes. One of the most interesting coaction effects has been reported by Chen (1938) in a study mentioned earlier. Chen carefully measured how much sandy soil ants moved when they were working alone, in pairs, or in threes building nests. He found that the average ant moved more soil when working in a group than when working alone.

Effect of social interference.   Coaction effects do not always produce social facilitation. Sometimes they produce **social interference.** Social facilitation is any increase in performance resulting from social interaction; social interference is any decrement in this performance. Social interference seems to occur when we are doing something that we do not do very well. Inexperienced public speakers find an audience very distressing and often develop stage fright. Experienced speakers, in contrast, often prefer large audiences.

Even cockroaches do not perform particularly well when they are learning in the presence of other cockroaches. In one study (Gates & Allee, 1933) researchers measured how long it took for cockroaches to run an E-shaped maze in isolation or in groups of two or three. As you may know from what happens when you turn on the light in your kitchen, roaches prefer darkness and will scramble to find it. The roaches were rewarded for running the maze correctly and were able to escape into a dark bottle on one arm of the maze. Figure 12-5 indicates that, when cockroaches were alone, they learned the maze faster than when in groups of two; groups of two learned the maze faster than groups of three.

Some social interference may occur as a result of *distraction*. When cockroaches are trying to learn a maze in groups, we might imagine that they are also stopping to say hello to each other and gossip. When males learn or perform tasks, they do better in the presence of an unattractive female experimenter, perhaps because an attractive experimenter is more distracting (Hartnett, Gottlieb, & Hayes, 1976). In fact, even though we may eat more when with others (social facilitation), we may also eat more slowly (social interference), because we spend time talking, listening, or otherwise interacting with the other.

It may be hard to distinguish conformity and productivity norms (see Chapter 11) from social-facilitation and social-interference effects. Group members very often adjust their performance to a common level, which means that some

Figure 12-5.
Maze learning in
isolated and
grouped
cockroaches. (From
"Conditioned
Behavior of Isolated
and Grouped
Cockroaches on a
Simple Maze," by
M. J. Gates and
W. C. Allee, *Journal
of Comparative
Psychology*, 1933, *15*,
331. Copyright
© 1933 by the
American
Psychological
Association.)

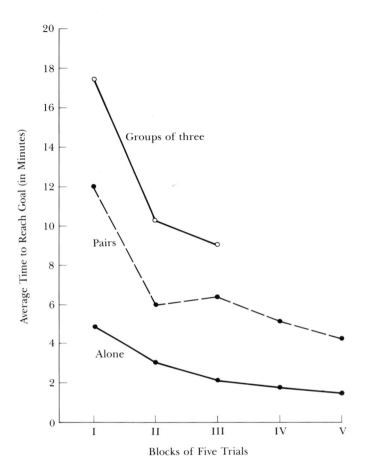

members are raising their level (facilitation) and others are lowering theirs (interference). If you eat more when you are with a group of hungry friends, is it because of conforming to the group norm or because of social facilitation? In a given situation, we simply may not know.

CROWDS

Though many definitions of **crowd** have been offered, it is easiest to think of a crowd as a large, temporary group. Crowds engage in **collective behavior,** the relatively unplanned, spontaneous, and somewhat disorganized and unpredictable behavior of a large, informal grouping of people. Crowds often contain smaller groups of friends within them (Aveni, 1977). The study of crowds and collective behavior has attracted the attention of thinkers for centuries. And in fact, the first textbooks in social psychology spent many pages describing and analyzing the behavior of crowds (McDougall, 1908; Ross, E. A., 1908).

There are many reasons for studying the collective behavior of crowds (Milgram & Toch, 1969). First, collective behavior often brings individuals beyond the actions they would take if acting alone. Our capacity for destruction and for heroism becomes more obvious when we look at the behavior of individuals in crowds. These heroic and destructive capacities are illustrated in this newspaper account (Claiborne [cited in Huston & Korte, 1975, p. 3]):

> Robert Mayfield . . . became involved in an argument with another motorist. According to police, Mayfield became enraged at the taunting by a small crowd, pulled a gun and fired blindly into the crowd, mortally wounding a four-year-old boy and injuring another man.
>
> A woman began screaming, "He killed my baby," and an off-duty policeman, Earl Robinson, ran up and ordered Mayfield to drop his gun. Mayfield shot Robinson in the chest.
>
> Suddenly, according to Robinson's account, the crowd of bystanders closed in on Mayfield, knocking him to the ground and kicking him relentlessly. Two other policemen arrived, and while attempting to pull Mayfield from the crowd and into the safety of an alley, they were injured by the mob.

Studying collective behavior may show, for instance, that fads, crowds, and social movements are often agents of social change, and by studying these agents we can see how our society evolves. In studying collective behavior we may also be in a better position to control it. Crowds and lynch mobs cause enormous damage to people and property. Even groups with the best intentions can be dangerous. Fads have enormous implications for business; for instance, anticipating a preference for Hula Hoops would give a company a great edge in the market, but overproduction when the fad was fading would result in a great loss.

Collective behavior is fascinating to study. Can a crowd behave, or is it only individuals in the crowd? Theorists have argued this for a century, and both schools of thought have some merit. On the one hand, technically, only individuals behave. The behavior of the crowd is really the behavior of its members, seen as a whole. Although it may not be accurate to speak of crowd behavior, there is some sense in describing it. To study only what separate individuals in a crowd do is to miss some of the impact of these individuals as a group. But individual behavior should also be studied, because the crowd is not a single entity, and there are always interesting and sometimes important differences in the behavior of individuals in the crowd.

Many theorists have also puzzled and fought over the idea of a group mind. Does a group have a mind that guides and directs it? The answer must be no. But we must also acknowledge that individuals sometimes behave very differently in a crowd than when alone. Crowd members often show incredible uniformity in their behavior, a uniformity rarely seen in other circumstances. It is *as if* the crowd had a single mind. But this is only a metaphor, an expression of our astonishment at the tremendous uniformity shown by individuals.

You may have wondered why crowds sometimes seem to be so emotional and irrational. Theorists of collective behavior have discussed and investigated this issue for years. The observation is correct, it seems: many crowds do show more emotion and less good judgment than individuals alone, or in small groups do. Several factors are probably at work in producing this effect.

As I have said elsewhere, the presence of others is sometimes physiologically arousing. When we stand in a large mass of people, shoulder to shoulder, our hearts beat faster, our breathing quickens, and our adrenalin flows. If the crowd is running, cheering, or engaged in other activity, the physiological effects are even stronger.

When we are physiologically aroused, we have difficulty thinking clearly. And when we are in a crowd of people who seem sure of what to do, we can look to others for guidance. So a crowd may make independent thinking more difficult and make it seem less necessary. The result is that crowds may sometimes seem irrational.

We look to the situation to decide how to label our physiological arousal. Often the crowd and situation provide an answer. We may decide that we are angry, frightened, or delighted, depending on what is happening. For instance, if we are rushing from a burning building with the crowd, we surely label our emotion fear. Demonstrators charging a police barricade label that same internal state anger.

Because we are often among strangers and anonymous in a large crowd, we don't feel the same inhibitions we would feel acting alone. If you were to throw a brick into a bank window when standing alone on the sidewalk, you would be caught and punished. In the crowd, with others doing it, you're much safer. There

"The anonymity of being in a crowd releases our everyday inhibitions."

is a diffusion of responsibility and sense of security. In fact, we may feel insecure if we don't go along with the crowd and comply with its norms.

Members of groups who are angry or hostile often try to lose their identity—a process called **deindividuation**—perhaps so they will feel less guilty about their actions (Cannavale, Scarr, & Pepitone, 1970). With such anonymity, studies find, college students are more willing to shock others (Zimbardo, 1969) and more willing to make obscene remarks (Singer, Brush, & Lublin, 1965). The hood and gowns of the Ku Klux Klan protect its members from recognition, leaving them unrestrained in their aggression. In fact, people may be attracted to groups that enable them—through anonymity—to overcome their inhibitions (Festinger, Pepitone, & Newcomb, 1952). Angry groups and mobs make it clear that we do not learn all there is to know about people by studying them one or two at a time.

Perhaps the most amazing feature of crowds and mobs is the incredible uniformity in the behavior of group members:

- People often join crowds for the same reasons, so uniformity results, to some extent, simply through self-selection.
- Once a person joins a crowd, he or she feels a subtle obligation to behave as other crowd members do—a social contract.
- Once in the crowd, people observe the actions of others and through imitation engage in those actions themselves.
- Some crowds have leaders who direct action. Obedience to these leaders increases uniformity.

Perhaps the most amazing feature of crowds and mobs is the incredible uniformity in the behavior of group members.

- Crowd members who do not conform to the actions of others may be rejected. In a crowd listening to a comedian, people may turn to someone who is not laughing and say "What's the matter with you?"

In addition to these general explanations of crowd behavior, we might note some specific features unique to crowds that promote uniformity.

One frequent circumstance surrounding the behavior of a crowd is uncertainty and ambiguity. Members of a mob have had little experience in such a situation and are unsure what to do. Sherif and Harvey (1952) suggested that, the more uncertain the situation, the greater the tendency of group members to converge in their behavior.

This ambiguity often leads to the rapid spread of rumor, which in turn shapes uniformity of behavior. As was said in the chapter on interdependence, we have a need for information. In an ambiguous situation, our need becomes overpowering. Imagine you were returning to your home and found eight police cars parked in the street, with a crowd standing about. Your curiosity would lead you to ask a bystander what had happened. The bystander had had the same need and probably asked someone else. Though the entire crowd may have had the same explanation for the presence of the police cars, each person's explanation may have been formed largely from what someone else said. The first bystander on the scene may not have known the facts, though, and simply guessed. Bystanders in many situations are often quite wrong. Nevertheless, their beliefs, developed out of rumors they have heard, may be shared by others and guide common action.

Collective behavior is difficult to study. Large crowds cannot be simulated in the laboratory, although exit panics have been simulated (Kelley, Condry, Dahlke, & Hill, 1965; Kruglanski, 1969; Mintz, 1951). Field observation (see Chapter 2) may be more realistic, but it is also more difficult than laboratory simulation.

SUMMARY

Groups are important to us in everyday life, having both positive and negative effects on us. Various types of groups serve our various needs. For instance, reference groups help us to evaluate ourselves through social comparison. People often join groups out of the expectation that membership will be rewarding and leave when they find more rewarding alternatives. As a group develops from its first meeting, members learn about one another, norms develop, and roles become differentiated. Interaction gradually becomes more intimate and includes more and more areas of interest. This process of social penetration is part of group formation. The result may be a cohesive group—one to which its members are attracted. But initially, newcomers to groups may experience some negative reactions from other group members.

As a group develops, roles become differentiated and interrelated, forming a group structure. Such a division of labor sometimes produces task specialists and social/emotional specialists. Leadership has been defined in various ways, but it seems to include the ability to influence others in a group, often because of a special competence with a task and with social interaction. Although leaders may have some distinguishing qualities, such as being more active and better adjusted, leadership is probably better viewed as activities such as support, guidance, and influence that all group members perform from time to time.

Group functioning was discussed in terms of group performance and member satisfaction. Member satisfaction is related to many characteristics of the group, but only the relation to group size was discussed in any depth. Some studies suggest that a group size of four may often be preferred to other sizes. Group size also affects performance but in complex ways, depending on the task, the members, and so on. Performance, or productivity, seems to depend, in part, on productivity norms, and it is influenced by social facilitation and social interference.

There are many reasons for studying the behavior of crowds. They sometimes have powerful effects on individuals and society. They are fascinating, and what we learn about them can be used to help control their destructiveness. Some issues were discussed, such as Does a crowd behave? Does a crowd have a mind? and Why are crowds emotional? The chapter concluded with a brief review of factors that promote uniformity in crowds.

GLOSSARY TERMS

Define these terms in your own words, then look them up in the glossary at the back of the book.

Audience effects	Leadership
Coaction effects	Leadership style
Cohesiveness	Membership group
Collective behavior	One-way mirror
Crowd	Primary group
Curvilinear relationship	Reference group
Deindividuation	Ringleman effect
Division of labor	Secondary group
Dyad	Small group
Evaluation apprehension	Social facilitation
Group	Social interference
Group structure	Status
Groupthink	Triad
Laboratory group	

FURTHER READING

Davis, J. H., Laughlin, P. R., & Komorita, S. S. The social psychology of small groups: Cooperative and mixed-motive interaction. *Annual Review of Psychology,* 1976, *27* 501–541.

Marx, G. T., & Wood, J. L. Strands of theory and research in collective behavior. *Annual Review of Sociology,* 1975, 363–428.

Turner, R. H., & Killian, L. M. *Collective behavior.* Englewood Cliffs, N. J.: Prentice-Hall, 1957.

chapter
13

Uniformity in Groups

13

INTRODUCTION

In a recent interview, a visitor from outer space recollected some impressions of earthlings. "It's not that they're all alike," she said. "But small groups of earthlings do seem to be quite uniform. The differences within a group seem small. Between groups, the differences are sometimes great." She had met Republicans and Democrats, sky divers and streetwalkers, Chinese-Americans and Blacks, chess players and beer drinkers, bureaucrats and migrant farmers. Each belonged to one or more groups of similar others. Few seemed well acquainted with many members of other groups. Discovering the causes of such phenomena is part of the delight of social psychology, and it is the purpose of this chapter.

Like other powerful social facts, uniformity in groups is a result of many different influences. These influences combine, in complex ways, to produce the net effect: groups are uniform in many ways.

This uniformity seems true of all groups everywhere, although groups differ in the special ways that they are uniform. Further, though uniformity changes slowly over time, we often seem unaware of our own great similarity to other group members.

How easily are you influenced? We like to see ourselves as open-minded, rather than closed-minded, and as having opinions and not going along with the crowd. Within our own groups we may conform, but we don't like to see ourselves as the same as everyone. Nevertheless, in spite of our need to see ourselves independent, we very often show considerable interdependence with others. We, like others, contribute to uniformity in groups.

Some of the factors that lead to uniformity have been touched on already in this book, but others will be introduced now. As each explanation is covered in a section of this chapter, you should ask whether it makes sense. When you have completed the chapter, you should ask whether other good explanations have been omitted.

How are groups uniform? The uniformity that seems to be most evident is the stuff of which social psychology is made—that of thoughts, feelings, interests, attitudes, values, and behaviors. Because uniformity occurs along many different dimensions, it is quite possible that some factors affect some dimensions and other factors affect other dimensions. For example, an authority may command obedience, resulting in uniformity of behavior but not uniformity of interests. As an amateur social psychologist, you may want to think about what types of uniformity result from the various influences discussed below.

UNIFORMITY THROUGH SELECTION

People are attracted to people who are similar to them and, naturally, join groups of people who are similar to them. Of course, we are sometimes assigned to groups or are "forced" to join them (as in the laboratory experiment that uses random assignment or the family group in which we were raised). But usually we *choose* the groups we belong to, just as we choose what we read or watch on television. For example, many psychologists join the American Psychological Association, social psychologists join the Society for the Advancement of Social Psychology, and other birds of a feather flock together. We might call this process in which people choose membership groups **self-selection.**

Self-selection is an important source of uniformity in groups. It may have the strongest effects when people know a great deal about the group before joining. Many employers try to take advantage of this effect by carefully and accurately describing their company and the nature of the work to job applicants. Job applicants who do not feel suited to the position may withdraw their applications or may not try quite as hard in the interview. Self-selection is more difficult when little is known about the group. Secret societies are usually small, in part because they do not advertise, and few apply.

"Secret societies are usually small."

Self-selection is not always possible. There are circumstances in which we are "assigned" to a group (a draftee into the army, a blind date, or a new baby in a family) and other circumstances in which our choice is not totally free. For instance, your choice of college was probably limited by factors such as geography, cost, parental preferences, the nature and amount of information you had on various schools, and others.

Not only do people select groups, but groups select people. **Member selection** often follows self-selection. You apply for membership in Psi Chi or some other organization (self-selection). Then the organization decides whether to admit you as a member (member selection). Sometimes member selection comes first. Baseball teams send scouts to observe players on other teams; employers sometimes send out "feelers" to prospective job candidates, discretely inviting application. But whether member selection occurs before or after self-selection, it is important in creating and maintaining group uniformity.

Every membership group (see Chapter 12) has its own procedures for member selection. A committee may review a written application, an employer may interview an applicant, a team may observe a prospective member during tryouts and practice. Groups probably use about the same criteria for member selection as individuals use in selecting groups. Factors such as similarity on important dimensions, expected benefits and costs to the group, and compatibility with other group members all play a role.

THE SOCIAL CONTRACT

After we have selected and been selected by a group, a principle we might call **social contract** comes into play. A social contract is simply an unspoken agreement that we will comply with the wishes of others and meet their expectations and that they will do the same for us. A social contract is an unwritten agreement to accommodate, cooperate, exchange, and trade off. For instance, when you see a stranger at a distance and make eye contact, both you and the stranger may honor the social contract of "gaze aversion." It is "not polite to stare," so you both look away. Such a social contract promotes uniformity in groups.

Normative Expectations.   There are several forms of social contract. One is the agreement that we will behave in accordance with the expectations of the group. These normative expectations can be far reaching. For example, as a group member, we may be expected to express views consistent with those of the group. It is known that the voting patterns of the public are closely related to party membership (Campbell, A., Converse, Miller, & Stokes, 1960). So are roll-call votes of legislators (Turner, 1970) and even the impeachment voting by members of the House Judiciary Committee in 1974 (Granberg, 1975).

Normative expectations lead to the dignified behavior of dignitaries, the painful persistence of pugilists, and the receptiveness of receptionists. Through an unwritten social contract, we agree to meet the group's expectations and behave as the group behaves. This inevitably increases uniformity.

The Norm of Reciprocity.   Another form of social contract is the *norm of reciprocity* (Gouldner, 1960), which refers to the understanding that, whatever you have done for, with, or to me, I am obligated to do for, with, or to you. "An eye for an eye, a tooth for a tooth" is an example of this norm. We speak when spoken to, look into others' eyes when they look into ours, toss a ball back to someone who has tossed it to us, and express appreciation to someone who has done us a favor. Each of these exchanges suggests the operation of this norm of reciprocity. The norm increases uniformity in groups.

We need not simply be passive responders who comply with this norm, of course. We may initiate an exchange that results in reciprocity. If we want someone else to do us a favor, we might first simply do one for him or her. Kissing someone is a good way to get kissed. This insight is reflected in the teaching "Do unto others as you would have them do unto you."

Unlike normative expectations, which are gradually developed by a group, the norm of reciprocity seems to be carried with us. Reciprocity occurs from the moment a group forms. When you meet a stranger on the elevator and he or she says something about the weather, you are likely to say something about the weather, too.

Rewards and Punishments.   What do groups do when members honor or violate their social contract? How are social contracts enforced? Through rewards and punishments. In general, groups reward conformity to normative expectations, and punish deviance.

It may be easier to get uniformity by rewarding compliance than by punishing noncompliance. Compliance has been found to increase with increases in rewards (Crosbie, 1972; Lindskold & Tedeschi, 1971a). The probability of receiving a reward for compliance is also important. One study (Zipf, 1960) suggests that compliance depends on the probability of reward times the magnitude of reward and that different groups respond differently to rewards of different types such as praise or candy (see Interest Box 13-1 on p. 360).

Two of the most important rewards that groups offer their members are respect and affection. Such rewards are often given for compliance with group norms. John F. Kennedy once remarked:

> We enjoy the comradeship and approval of our friends and colleagues. . . . We realize, moreover, that our influence in the club—and the extent to which we can accomplish our objectives and those of our constituents—are dependent in some measure on the esteem with which we are regarded by other Senators: "The way to get along," I was told when I entered Congress, "is to go along" [1956, p. 3].

We may make our opinions or behaviors more similar to those of others to increase our attractiveness to them and to help us identify with them. As you saw in Chapter 8, we are more attracted to others who hold similar opinions and who behave in a similar way. So conformity may be a rational strategy to increase our attractiveness to others. Edward Jones (1964) has suggested that there may be some optimal level of conformity for producing attraction. If we conform too much, we may be suspected of conforming simply to get others to like us, what Jones called **ingratiation.** If we conform too little, others may find us too different to be much attracted to us. If we conform somewhere in the middle of these two extremes, we may be best liked, Jones suggested.

Edwin Hollander (1958, 1964) has suggested that, through conformity and demonstrations of competence, people accumulate idiosyncrasy credits. These credits can be used later to permit deviation from group norms to go unpunished. We are usually more tolerant of differences and idiosyncrasies among those we like; we like those who are similar, competent, and familiar and hence permit such people more nonconformity.

Group cohesiveness (see Chapter 12) helps determine the power of groups to reward, punish, and influence members. Highly cohesive groups have lower absenteeism and turnover (Van Zelst, 1952). And in some cases they may meet more often, giving them more opportunities to build and enforce expectations through rewards and punishments. Further, members of highly cohesive groups are more inclined to attempt to influence one another and are more willing to accept this influence (Collins & Raven, 1969). They produce a more clear-cut, powerful set of norms. Because norms are stronger in cohesive groups, behavior and opinions tend to be more uniform than in less cohesive groups.

Although groups often reward uniformity, they may reward other behaviors too. For instance, in many work settings people are paid for the amount of work they produce (piecework), for the quality of their work, or for the accuracy of it. Some studies suggest that rewarding people for accuracy may increase their accuracy but also their independence from the group, thus decreasing uniformity (Kelman, 1950; Luchins & Luchins, 1961; Mausner, 1953, 1954a, 1954b).

Interest Box 13-1. If Deviance Results in Punishment, Does Threat of Punishment Reduce Deviance?

Social deviants are frequently punished. Punishment through fines, imprisonment, or the death penalty is used, some say, to deter crime. According to this view, the more severe the punishment, the less likely the crime. This view is not supported by the facts. Homicide rates in states that have capital punishment are no lower than homicide rates in other states (Katzenbach, 1968). Another study, which looked at differences between countries, found no relationship between crime rate and degree of punishment (U.N. Department of Economic and Social Affairs, 1962). In fact, the United States punishes crime more severely than many other countries but still has a higher crime rate than some of them.

Why is punishment not more effective in deterring crime? One reason is that not everyone who commits a crime is punished. Only some are caught, only some of them are found guilty, and only some of *them* are punished. When we consider an action, we consider not only the costs but the probability of the costs. Pickpockets were once hanged in England, but pickpockets were rampant at public hangings for their colleagues, perhaps because the probability of punishment was so low. When the probability of punishment for noncompliance with a rule, request, or law is high, compliance is high (for example, see Horai & Tedeschi, 1969).

Some evidence suggests that criminals rarely weigh the magnitude of punishment when contemplating a crime but do seem to focus on the probability of arrest. Also, psychologists know that, although immediate rewards and punishments may have strong effects on our behavior, delayed rewards and punishments have weak effects, if any. Punishment for a crime may not begin until many months later. Another reason that punishment does not deter crime is that punishment is much less effective in shaping behavior than are rewards.

IMITATION

Imitation (copying the behavior of another) can be an important source of uniformity in groups. In one study researchers asked college students to sign a petition after asking another person, who either signed or refused to sign (Helson, Blake, & Mouton, 1958). When the first person—who was a confederate of the experimenter—signed, 53% of the students did, too. But when the first person refused, only 10% signed. Similarly, when we step into an elevator and others are looking at the floor, we may do the same. When we sign a petition, if previous signers have used their first initial and last name, we may, too. Imitation has powerful effects on uniformity, yet we are often unaware that we are imitating others.

Imitation can occur in almost any setting where one person is able to observe the behavior of others. It does not require any formal relation, interaction, or group setting. In one study researchers observed cars turning at an intersection (Barch, Trumbo, & Nangle, 1957). They recorded whether or not a lead driver (the **model**) signaled a turn and whether the driver of the following car did the same (imitation) or did not. When the first driver signaled a turn, 66% of the second drivers signaled. When the first driver did not signal, only 54% of the following drivers signaled. Thus, we imitate the driving of others, and others imitate our own driving. This imitation leads to uniformity.

Other research shows that pedestrians are just as imitative as drivers. In one study, when a confederate jaywalked, the percentage of pedestrians who jaywalked increased. Whereas only 1% jaywalked with no jaywalking model, 4% jaywalked with a poorly dressed, low-status model, and 14% jaywalked following a well-dressed, high-status model (Lefkowitz, Blake, & Mouton, 1955). Thus, both the nature of another person's behavior and his or her characteristics determine how much imitation will occur. In general, we are more inclined to imitate those we respect; children imitate adults and older children, but adults have their heroes, too.

Imitation is not restricted to humans. The schooling of fish is a well-known example. Fish that school observe the direction and speed of other fish and adjust

their direction and speed accordingly (Hunter, J. R., 1969). The same can be said of birds in flight, grazing sheep, and other animals. Imitation occurs in rats, too. In one study rats were trained to select one of two doors in a Y-shaped maze in order to get a drink (Konopasky & Telegdy, 1977). They were also trained to follow a leader rat. When the leader chose the incorrect door, followers did likewise 60% of the time. When the leader was not present, they chose the wrong door only 34% of the time. Rats, like people, imitate others.

Why, then, does imitation occur, if it sometimes leads us through the wrong door? Probably because we are more often right than wrong, more often rewarded than punished when we imitate.

Imitation does not always lead to being objectively right or wrong. Rules of etiquette, customs, traditions, fashions, and group norms all define a subjective social reality of right and wrong. By imitating others, we are able to be "right" as defined by the group. "When in Rome, do as the Romans do" is good advice.

THE NEED FOR INFORMATION

Groups are important sources of information for us (Deutsch & Gerard, 1955; Festinger, 1950; Kelley, 1952). Social-comparison theory assumes that groups are important in providing members with useful information for evaluating, validating, or revising their personal theories, attitudes, beliefs, and values.

But the possession of information is a source of power. Because groups satisfy our **need for information,** they are capable of informational social influence (Deutsch & Gerard, 1955). Such influence may affect our behavior. Suppose that the group is engaged in some task and that others seem to have greater ability than you. It makes sense to do it their way, for you to increase your chances of doing it right. Such influence may affect our opinions, too. Perhaps your parents told you that asparagus is tasty and good for you. As a child, you could not argue with "good for you." You accepted this as true. However, you were in a position to argue about the taste, because your taste buds work as well as theirs. Parents find that not all of the information they provide is accepted as fact.

What factors determine informational social influence? Deutsch and Gerard (1955) suggested that, the more certain we are of the correctness of the judgment of the group, the greater its influence; the more certain we are of the correctness of our own judgment, the less its influence. When we lack confidence in our own judgment, we tend to listen and accept the views of others. When we are quite confident, we tend to speak and try to influence the views of others. Religious and political zealots spend considerable effort trying to influence others.

In 1974, the House Judiciary Committee held hearings, debated, and voted to recommend impeachment of President Richard Nixon. Prior to these hearings, the *New York Times* published a chart indicating how each committee member felt toward impeachment: strongly opposed, mildly opposed, undecided, mildly in favor, strongly in favor. From this chart, Carlos Fortuno and I obtained an "opinion extremity score" for each committee member, and from the *Congressional Record* we determined how often each member spoke. We discovered that those with extreme opinions (either for or against impeachment) spoke more often than those with milder opinions. It may be, on the one hand, that disagreement with others produces stress and arousal that leads to higher levels of activation, reflected in higher rates of participation in group discussion. The very act of defending a position, on the other hand, may strengthen our belief in it through self-perception. It may also increase our self-confidence and lower our level of stress if we successfully defend our position. But if the argument goes badly, we may experience a loss of self-confidence and still higher levels of stress.

DIFFUSION OF AFFECT

Social-comparison processes lead to uniformity in opinions and beliefs, as we have suggested above. Diffusion of affect may also lead to uniformity of feelings and such feelings may, in turn, lead to some uniformity of behavior. Two propositions from diffusion-of-affect theory account for affective (emotional) uniformity in groups:

1. A wide variety of pleasant events outside a person tend to put him or her in a pleasant mood; unpleasant events tend to lead to unpleasant moods.
2. Pleasant moods lead to a wide variety of positive behaviors, and negative moods may lead to a wide variety of negative behaviors.

You might wonder why these propositions bother to mention mood at all. Why not simply say that pleasant events lead to positive behavior and unpleasant events to negative behavior? The answer is that mood seems to act like a filter. If a person is in a good mood when an unpleasant event occurs, his or her behavior will be more positive than when unpleasant moods and events combine. Our mood gives our behavior some stability over time, making it less reactive to an unstable environment. Nevertheless, few studies have examined propositions 1 and 2 separately. Most have examined the effects of environmental pleasantness on behavioral pleasantness. It is these studies, therefore, that we will review.

When people view a pleasant film, they are more attracted to strangers than when they view an unpleasant film (Gouaux, 1971; Schwartz, M. S., 1966). They are more attracted to strangers in a comfortable room than a hot room (Griffitt & Veitch, 1971; Veitch & Griffitt, 1976). And they are more attracted to strangers under other pleasant circumstances (Amir, 1969).

When people experience success, they reward themselves more than when they experience failure. They are more expectant of future success than others (Feather, 1966; Mischel, Coates, & Rastoff, 1968). And they seek more positive information about themselves (Mischel, Ebbesen, & Zeiss, 1973).

When people are rewarded for being in an experiment, they feel more attracted to strangers present (Griffitt, 1968). When they are told that they are correct in a rating task, they make more positive ratings of strangers (Marx & Marx, 1978). Other events that lead to positive words also lead to positive feelings toward strangers (Clore, 1975; Clore & Byrne, 1974; Veitch & Griffitt, 1976).

When people heard about President Kennedy's assassination, their philosophies of human nature became more negative (Wrightsman & Noble, 1965). Another study found that people were less likely to return a lost wallet after Robert Kennedy's assassination than before.

A variety of studies have found that people are more likely to be helpful when they are in good moods than when they are not (Aderman, 1972; Aderman

& Berkowitz, 1970; Isen, 1970; Isen, Clark, & Schwartz, 1976; Isen & Levin, 1972; Moore, Underwood, & Rosenhan, 1973).

When people in one study received a gift (a 29-cent note pad or pair of nail clippers) and were then asked to rate their car and television set for performance and overall service, they gave more positive performance and service ratings than did people not receiving the gift (Isen, Shalker, Clark, & Karp, 1978).

People who smile often are liked more than those who smile little (McGinley, McGinley, & Nicholas, 1978). When an experimenter smiled at a stranger getting on an elevator, the stranger stood closer than when no smile was offered (Lockard, McVittie, & Isaac, 1977). When waitresses in another study gave a broad smile to customers, they received much larger tips and were more likely than nonsmiling waitresses to receive a "departure smile" from the customer (Tidd & Lockard, 1978).

When animals such as rats and monkeys are given footshocks in an experiment, they are observed to fight with other animals (Azrin, Hutchinson, & Hake, 1963, 1967; Ulrich & Azrin, 1962), bite inanimate things in the environment (Azrin et al., 1967; Azrin, Hutchinson, & Sallery, 1964; Azrin, Rubin, & Hutchinson, 1968; Hutchinson, Azrin, & Hake, 1966; Pear, Moody, & Persinger, 1972), and even bite their own feet (Hineline & Harrison, 1978).

Propositions 1 and 2 in the diffusion-of-affect theory suggest that environmental events lead to behaviors that are positive when the event is pleasant, negative when the event is unpleasant. Such effects might account for much conformity in groups. For instance, when Al tells Bob a funny story, Bob is likely to

A standard classroom: Obedience and uniformity.

do things such as smile, laugh, tell Al a funny story, reward Al, agree more often with him, like him more, and so on. Any such positive responses from Bob are likely to lead Al to a variety of positive behaviors. This positive cycle is a source of uniformity in this group. Negative cycles also occur during disagreements, quarrels, and fights. Many factors may lead to positive or negative cycles, and many specific behaviors may occur in them. But one consequence is that group members tend to be uniform in the positiveness or negativeness of their thoughts, feelings, and behaviors.

OBEDIENCE

Another reason for uniformity in a group may be that members are all **obedient** to the same authority. In a religious service members of the congregation rise in response to "Please rise" and are seated in response to "Please be seated." In the classroom students learn to speak when spoken to and to raise their hands for permission to speak at other times. In large groups such as these such obedience to authority is important. Obedience can help the group achieve its goals efficiently. Without obedience, disorder and chaos would be common. Even in the "open classroom," where students are not confined to their desks or to some common activity, obedience to rules such as "Speak quietly" is necessary.

An open classroom: How much obedience? How much uniformity?

Obedience is very important in our crowded, interdependent, complex society. As a result, we have been rewarded many times for obedience and have learned to obey. Those in authority—the police officer directing traffic, the teacher

giving a lecture—obtain obedience without any questions asked. Power refers to this ability to control others.

Obedience is not always a positive force. Hitler used the obedience of some (the Gestapo, for instance) to ensure the obedience of others (Jews, for instance). Millions died (in part) because of this obedience. The problem of obedience is not restricted to Germany, though, as Stanley Milgram has taught us.

Milgram's Shocks.   In Milgram's well-known studies of obedience (1963, 1974) the experimenter asks a subject to take the role of "teacher" and deliver shocks to a "learner" whenever the learner makes an error. The teacher watches while the learner (actually a confederate of the experimenter) is seated and electrodes are connected to his arm and leg (see Figure 13-1). The experimenter then leads the teacher to an adjoining room, is shown how to use the shock apparatus, and is given a small sample shock. The shock generator (see Figure 13-2) consists of a panel of switches which are labeled with voltages ranging from 15 volts to 450 volts in 15-volt increments. Labels indicate that 195 volts is a "very strong shock," 255 volts an "intense shock," 345 volts an "extreme intensity shock," and 375 volts is "danger: severe shock." What, then, could a 450-volt shock be called? Simply "XXX."

Suppose you were a "teacher" in this experiment. The first time you test the learner and the answer is wrong, you are told by the experimenter to give a shock of 15 volts. For each additional wrong answer, you must increase the shock level by 15 volts. Would you go all the way to 450 volts if the experimenter told you to? At what shock level do you think you would defy the experimenter and stop the experiment?

Milgram found that samples of psychiatrists, students, and middle-class adults thought they would stop at about 135 volts, on the average. Not one person of 110 surveyed predicted that he or she would deliver more than a 300-volt shock. (For an account of how one subject responded, see Interest Box 13-2.) With an experimenter present and the learner (victim) in the next room, a very high percentage of Milgram's subjects went all the way, giving 450-volt shocks. In Milgram's first experiment (1963), the average subject stopped at 405 volts, but 65% of the subjects went all the way to 450 volts. As the Pollyanna Principle suggests, we may like to think better of ourselves than is justified by the facts.

Repercussions.   Some people have wondered whether this high level of obedience occurs in other countries as well. In a study done in Munich, Germany, 85% of subjects gave 450-volt shocks (Mantell, 1971). In Sydney, Australia, 54% gave 450-volt shocks (Kilham & Mann, 1974). In Amman, Jordan, 63% continued to the end (Shanab & Yahya, 1978). Thus, destructive obedience to authority *may be* a cultural universal.

Milgram's first experiments were done with male subjects. Are males more obedient than females? Several studies have found no sex differences (Milgram, 1974); one has found that males are more obedient than women (Kilham & Mann, 1974); and one has found the reverse (Sheridan & King, 1972). It is probably safe to conclude that men and women are equally obedient in this situation.

Several variations on Milgram's basic experiment have revealed some interesting factors that affect obedience. One series of studies (Milgram, 1974) has

Figure 13-1. What would you have done? The person on the left is the subject, helping the experimenter (right) attach electrodes to the man in the middle. The victim was actually a confederate of the experimenter. (Copyright © 1965 by Stanley Milgram. From the film *Obedience*, distributed by the New York University Film Library. Reprinted by permission.)

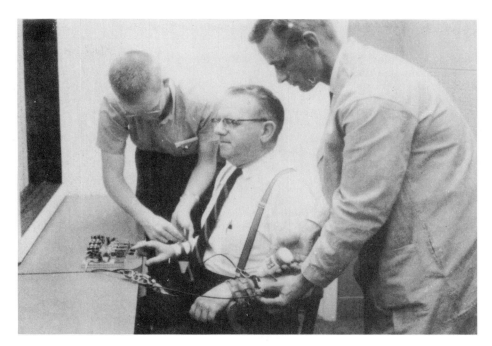

Figure 13-2. Milgram's "shock generator." (Copyright © 1965 by Stanley Milgram. From the film *Obedience*, distributed by the New York University Film Library. Reprinted by permission.)

Interest Box 13-2.   Would You Electrocute a Stranger?*

Stanley Milgram's (1963) research on obedience is graphically described in the partial transcript of one experiment, presented below. The "teacher" is a polite, casually dressed heavy man. He has just flipped the 180-volt lever (Meyer, 1970).

Learner (who, from the teacher's point of view is heard but not seen, an offstage voice): Ow, I can't stand the pain. Don't do that. . . .

Teacher (pivoting around in his chair and shaking his head): I can't stand it. I'm not going to kill that man in there. You hear him hollering?

Experimenter: As I told you before, the shocks may be painful, but—

Teacher: But he's hollering. He can't stand it. What's going to happen to him?

Experimenter (his voice is patient, matter-of-fact): The experiment requires that you continue, Teacher.

Teacher: Aah, but, unh, I'm not going to get that man sick in there . . . know what I mean?

Experimenter: Whether the learner likes it or not, we must go on, through all the word pairs.

Teacher: I refuse to take the responsibility. He's in there hollering!

Experimenter: It's absolutely essential that you continue, Teacher.

Teacher (indicating the unused questions): There's too many left here, I mean, Geez, if he gets them wrong, there's too many of them left. I mean who's going to take the responsibility if anything happens to that gentleman?

Experimenter: I'm responsible for anything that happens to him. Continue please.

Teacher: All right. (*Consults list of words.*) The next one's "Slow—walk, truck, dance, music." Answer, please. (*A buzzing sound indicates the learner has signaled his answer.*) Wrong. A hundred and ninety-five volts. "Dance." (*Zzumph!*)

Learner: Let me out of here. My heart's bothering me! (*Teacher looks at experimenter.*)

Experimenter: Continue, please.

Learner (screaming): Let me out of here, you have no right to keep me here. Let me out of here, let me out, my heart's bothering me, let me out! (*Teacher shakes head, pats the table nervously.*)

Teacher: You see, he's hollering. Hear that? Gee, I don't know.

Experimenter: The experiment requires. . . .

Teacher (interrupting): I know it does, sir, but I mean—hunh! He don't know what he's getting in for. He's up to 195 volts! (*Experiment continues, through 210 volts, 225 volts, 240 volts, 255 volts, 270 volts, delivered to the man in the electric chair, at which point the teacher, with evident relief, runs out of word-pair questions.*)

Experimenter: You'll have to go back to the beginning of that page and go through them again until he's learned them all correctly.

Teacher: Aw, no. I'm not going to kill that man. You mean I've got to keep going up with the scale. No sir. He's hollering in there. I'm not going to give him 450 volts.

Experimenter: The experiment requires that you go on.

Teacher: I know it does, but that man is hollering in there, sir.

Experimenter (same matter-of-fact tone): As I said before, although the shocks may be painful . . . .

Teacher (interrupting): Awwww, he—he—he's yelling in there.

Experimenter: Start with "Blue," please, at the top of the page. Continue, please, Teacher. Just go ahead.

Teacher (concentrating intently on list of words in front of him, as if to shut everything else out): "Blue—boy, girl, grass, hat." (*Buzz indicates answer.*) Correct. "Night—day, sky, job, chair. (*Buzz*) Wrong. The answer is "day." Two hundred and eighty-five volts. (*Zzumph!*)

Learner: Ohhhuhhoohhh!

Experimenter: Continue, please.

Teacher: "Fat—man, lady, tub, neck." Answer, please. (*Buzz*) Wrong. The answer is "neck." Three hundred volts. (*Zzumph!*)

Learner: Ohhh. I absolutely refuse to answer any more. (*Shouting urgently, now*) Let me out of here. You can't hold me here. Get me out. Get—me—out—of—here.

Experimenter: Continue. The next word is "Green," please.

Teacher: "Green—grass, hat, ink, apple." (*Nothing happens. No answering buzz. Just gloomy silence.*)

Teacher: I don't think he is going to answer.

Experimenter: If the learner doesn't answer in

Interest Box 13-2.   (continued)

a reasonable time, about four or five seconds, consider the answer wrong. And follow the same procedures you have been doing for wrong answers. Say "Wrong," tell him the number of volts, give him the punishment, read him the correct answer. Continue, please.

Teacher: "Green—grass, hat, ink, apple." Answer, please. (*More silence. Teacher just sits there.*)

Experimenter: Go on with the procedure, please, Teacher.

Teacher: Three hundred and fifteen volts. The answer is "ink." (*Zzumph!*)

Learner: Ohh. Ooohh.

Teacher (relieved to hear response): Next one . . . .

Learner: I absolutely refuse to answer.

Teacher: You got to. You get a shock if you don't answer. (*Experiment continues with learner refusing to answer, and, finally, failing even to grunt or groan. At 375 volts, the teacher stands up. Has he had enough? Will he break off the experiment? Will he disobey?*)

Teacher: I think something's happened to that fellow in there. I don't get no answer. He was hollering at less voltage. Can't you check in and see if he's all right, please?

Experimenter (same detached calm): Not once we've started. Please continue, Teacher.

Teacher (sits down, sighs deeply): "Cool—day, shade, water, paint." Answer, please. Are you all right in there? Are you all right?

Experimenter: Please continue, Teacher. Continue, please. (*Teacher pushes lever. Zzumph!*) . . . (*Teacher returns to his list, starts running through words*

as rapidly as he can read them, works through to 450 volts.)

Teacher: That's that.

Experimenter: Continue using the last switch on the board, please. The four-fifty switch for each wrong answer. Continue, please.

[*The teacher protests further but ultimately obeys.*]

Teacher (now at a furious pace): "White—cloud, horse, rock, house." Answer, please. The answer is "horse." Four hundred and fifty volts. (*Zzumph!*) Next word, "Bag—paint, music, clown, girl." The answer is "paint." Four hundred and fifty volts. (*Zzumph!*) Next word is "Short—sentence, movie . . . ."

Experimenter: Excuse me, Teacher. We'll have to discontinue the experiment.

(*Enter Milgram from camera's left. He has been watching from behind one-way glass.*)

Milgram: I'd like to ask you a few questions. (*Slowly, patiently, he dehoaxes the teacher, telling him that the shocks and screams were not real.*)

Teacher: You mean he wasn't getting nothing? Well, I'm glad to hear that. I was getting upset there. I was getting ready to walk out.

(*Finally, to make sure there are no hard feelings, friendly, harmless Mr. Wallace comes out in coat and tie. Gives jovial greeting. Friendly reconciliation takes place. Experiment ends.*)

*Copyright © 1965 by Stanley Milgram. From the film *Obedience*, distributed by the New York University Film Library. Reprinted by permission.

found that, if the subject can hear the "learner" making vocal protests ("I can't stand it." "Let me out of here"), obedience decreases. Obedience decreases still further if the subject can see the learner. And it is lowest when the subject must put the learner's hand down on a "shock plate" to deliver the punishment. But even in this "touch proximity" condition, 30% of the subjects gave 450-volt shocks. Another finding is that, if the experimenter leaves the room and gives orders over the telephone, obedience drops—only 29% gave 450-volt shocks in one experiment. It appears that destructive obedience is less likely when the "victim" gets closer or the authority moves farther away.

The subjects in these remarkable experiments did not believe that they were immoral or ruthlessly obedient. They thought of themselves as average people. During the experiments many felt extreme stress. Most argued with the experimenter and said they wanted to stop. Yet as we have seen, most obeyed the experimenter. Many people believe that these experiments are unethical in causing such high levels of stress in subjects (Baumrind, 1964; Elms, 1972; Katz, J., 1972; Kelman, 1967; Milgram, 1974; Ring, Wallston, & Corey, 1970). Social psychologists have argued the issue in print, and students who have seen Milgram's film *Obedience* have argued the same issues in class. This research, however, has taught us some important facts about some conditions under which people will not obey. This alone is adequate justification for the research, many researchers feel. Further, we have all become aware of the destructive effects of obedience. Some argue that the terrors of Nazi Germany could not happen here. Milgram's research suggests that the potential for destructive obedience is not restricted to long ago and far away.

Other evidence helps bring this conclusion home. One study of 1000 adult Americans found that 51% said they would shoot *all* of the inhabitants of a Vietnamese village suspected of aiding the enemy, including children, women, and old men, if ordered to do so (Kelman & Lawrence, 1972). What we do is often less "socially desirable" and noble than what we say we would do. Perhaps the real terror of any massacre we may read about comes from the realization that it was not the first atrocity and that in some form or other—in Jonestown, the Mafia, the army—it will happen again.

Other social psychologists have been concerned that obedience of the sort Milgram found could take place only in an experiment, where people trust the experimenter and know that experimenters will safeguard subjects (Masserman, 1968; Orne & Holland, 1968). But in many other situations authorities are assumed to know what they are doing and take responsibility for the negative side effects of their orders. For instance, one study found that 21 of 22 nurses were prepared to administer *twice* the recommended dose of a drug—which did not even appear on the hospital's approved drug list—when ordered to do so over the phone by an *unknown* physician (Hofling, Brotzman, Dalrymple, Graves, & Pierce, 1966). Destructive obedience is an everyday fact of life in the armed forces during war. It occurred in Jonestown, Guyana. Can you think of everyday situations in which it sometimes occurs?

INTERDEPENDENCE THROUGH A THIRD PARTY

Related to the idea of obedience is the idea of **interdependence through a third party.** Two people may become similar in thoughts, feelings, and behavior through the common influence of a third person or the media. Millions of people view world events through the eyes of Walter Cronkite, get to know interesting people with Barbara Walters, follow the sports reported by Howard Cosell, and believe that name-brand aspirin is better than generic because of the advertising of several big companies. Television is a powerful force in our understanding of the world. Its potential impact is suggested by these facts (Nielsen, 1977):

☐ As of September 1, 1977, the total number of U.S. households was estimated at 74.7 million. Of these, 98% (72.9 million) had at least one television set.
☐ More than three out of four TV households had a color set.
☐ Almost 50% of the TV households had two or more sets.
☐ One household in six had cable TV. (This is expected to grow rapidly in the next few years.)

- Color and multiset ownership continued to be highest in urban households, while cable TV was highest in rural areas.
- Color and multiset ownership tended to be highest in households that are large (five or more members), have high income ($15,000+), have children, and are better educated.

UNIFORMITY THROUGH REJECTION

Just as self-selection and member selection bring groups and members together to create and maintain uniformity, the reverse of these two processes also serves to maintain uniformity. Members sometimes find that the group they selected does not meet their expectations and choose to drop out of it. When members leave large organizations (as in the case of many academically oriented psychologists now leaving the increasingly clinically oriented American Psychological Association), the group usually increases in uniformity. When members choose to leave very small groups (as in a divorce), the group may dissolve.

Rejection, like selection, is a mutual process. Groups may put pressure on deviant members to become more uniform. When this pressure fails, members may be rejected and expelled from the group. Universities do not grant tenure to those who do not conform to certain standards. Bridge clubs may drop poor or unpleasant players, employers fire employees, and so on. As unpleasant as it is, rejection is a fact of social life.

Sometimes rejection is a one-sided affair. Psychologists who drop out of the American Psychological Association get "Dear Colleague" letters that attempt to woo them back. And groups sometimes reject members who want to remain. But

over time these feelings often come into balance; the employee who was fired may later say "I'm glad I quit!"

Although the rejection process is sometimes one-sided, it may be more common that both the member and the group play a contributing role in the rejection process. A person might sense (perhaps incorrectly) that he or she is not appreciated and do something deviant to test this hypothesis. Group members might take this deviance as a sign that they are being rejected and punish it. The deviant, in turn, takes this as proof of not being wanted, devalues the group (Kelley & Shapiro, 1954) and deviates further. The cycle might continue until the deviant leaves the group or is expelled.

Perhaps this has happened to you on a blind date that did not work out. Your date may have done something that you interpreted as a sign of dislike or lack of interest. Whether or not your interpretation was correct, you may have reciprocated and done something to show your lack of interest. That convinced your date that you were not interested. Before long, the miserable evening ended, with mutual rejection. No more dates with that person, you vowed. Your date felt the same.

Several studies have found that, as a person disagrees with a group, his or her attractiveness decreases (Emerson, 1954; Levine, J. M., Saxe, & Harris, 1974; Schachter, 1951). Disagreement reduces similarity, which is important for attraction. At some point, dissimilarity may be so high and attraction so low that the group simply dislikes the disagreeing member and wishes to expel him or her. Diffusion-of-affect theory would suggest that being with a disagreeable, unpleasant person is unpleasant, and the Pollyanna Principle suggests we try to avoid unpleasant situations. This process probably takes place in declining relations between lovers, in organized groups such as country clubs, and in society as a whole.

SUMMARY

Uniformity in groups is pervasive. Group members everywhere are more similar to other members of their groups than to members of other groups. Several factors are probably responsible for this effect.

When people join groups, they select groups, and groups select them. Both self-selection and member selection operate to maintain a group's uniformity, avoiding the need for much change on the part of the new group member.

Uniformity also results from a social contract, an unspoken agreement to meet the expectations of others. Normative expectations alone bring about some uniformity, and they are strengthened by normative control in the form of rewards and punishments. The norm of reciprocity is one simple type of expectation: we generally are obligated and permitted to do to/with/for others what they have done to/with/for us.

Imitation is a simple form of social influence that does not require any interaction. We simply observe and copy the behavior of another through modeling. Many social animals such as birds, rats, and some fish show imitation.

Our need for information leads us to seek out similar others, engage in social-comparison processes to evaluate our opinions, and revise those opinions when they seem to differ. Such processes offer a feeling of correctness and promote uniformity.

Many behaviors in a group are positive or negative, pleasant or unpleasant. Through a diffusion of affect one positive behavior leads to another, and one negative behavior leads to another. Mood helps stabilize such positive or negative cycles, bringing further uniformity to groups.

Some uniformity occurs when all members are obedient to the same authority. A number of studies offer strong and perhaps disheartening evidence that under certain conditions most "normal" people will be obedient to malevolent authorities, hurting people when ordered to do so. This research may also provide clues to reducing such destructive obedience.

Rejection is a final solution for how groups can eliminate members that break their uniformity and how members can deal with groups that no longer meet their needs. Rejection occurs when influence fails.

GLOSSARY TERMS

Define these terms in your own words, then look them up in the glossary at the back of the book.

Ingratiation
Interdependence through a
    third party
Member selection
Modeling

Need for information
Obedience
Rejection
Self-selection
Social contract

FURTHER READING

Milgram, S. *Obedience to authority.* New York: Harper & Row, 1974. Provides information on and insight into some of social psychology's most fascinating, disturbing, and controversial findings.

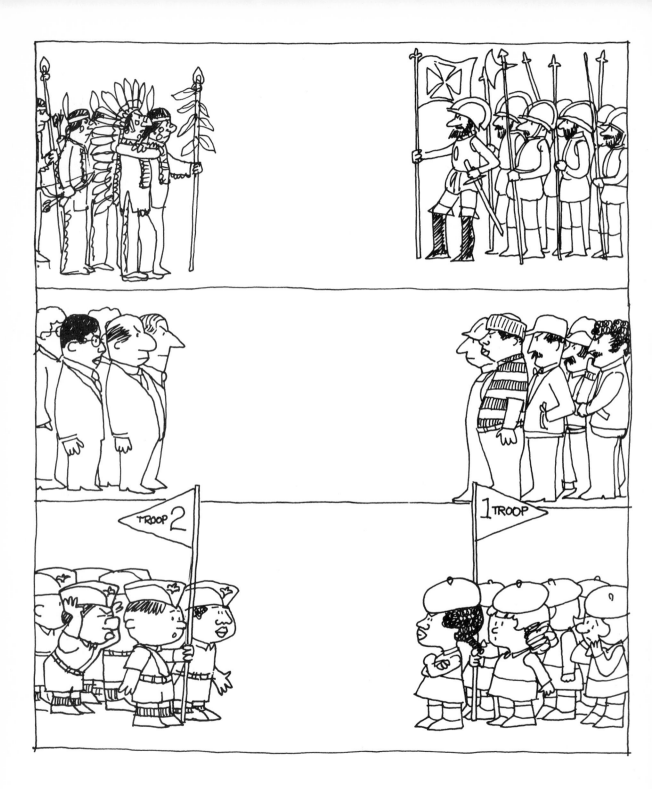

chapter
14

Intergroup Relations

chapter

14

Intergroup relations are interactions between two or more groups and their members. The study of peace and war, cooperation and competition, alliance and enmity, prejudice, discrimination, racism, and sexism involves the study of intergroup relations. Such processes are part of social psychology: our thoughts, feelings, and behaviors toward members of another group are influenced by their behavior toward us as well as by the opinions and behaviors of our own group members.

Because the topic of intergroup relations is vast and this chapter cannot be, I will focus on just two critical aspects of intergroup relations—prejudice and discrimination. This chapter will discuss such conflict between groups, first describing the problem, then presenting explanations for it, and finally outlining some proposed solutions.

THE PROBLEM

Conflict and violence exact tremendous costs in the destruction and disruption of life and property. The costs in terms of lingering animosity, resentment, and hatred cannot be measured. But the evidence is obvious: the Middle East, Northern Ireland, Bangladesh, Cyprus, and the U.S. Civil War all attest to the fact that conflict does not always end in brotherly love. Other conflicts such as economic, sexual, and racial discrimination are sometimes less obvious, although their costs may be even greater than the costs of strife between nations. Those who are young or old or female or Black or poor or unattractive or overweight are discriminated against by those who are not. To make it clear that intergroup conflict is not something long ago or far away, we will look at such discrimination briefly.

Age Discrimination. It is sweet to be 16. It is fine to be 29. But when you're 2, you are a "terrible 2." When you are 70, you may simply be unwanted. Age discrimination in our society makes it tough to be very young or very old.

We sometimes treat the very young the way we treat property or pets (see Interest Box 14-1). We don't usually question whether children should have a

Interest Box 14-1.   Do We *Really* Like Children?

If we do, indeed, like our children, we may find it difficult to account for some of the things we do to them. Parents have the "right" to tell them what to wear, what to do and not to do, and with whom they can or can't do it. Parents can force their children to eat their peas, and if they don't, may spank them or send them to bed. Parents can insult or terrify their children, then punish them for "talking back." We all condone this in others, perhaps because as children we had few human rights. We are commanded to honor our father and mother, but not so commanded to honor our children. And yet, in spite of evidence that we do *not* like children, we still profess otherwise. The gap between what we say and what we do is extraordinary, as both Kenneth Keniston and Wayne Sage point out in the following excerpts.

Do Americans really like children?[a]
I wish to pose a question that has preoccupied me for the last couple of years: Do we Americans *really* like children?

After considerable reflection, I suggest that the answer is: Yes, *if* our sentiments are to be taken as evidence. Yes, we do like children, and even love them—if the test is in the values we profess and in the myths we cherish, celebrate, and pass on from generation to generation. However, I am prepared to assert that in spite of our tender sentiments, we do *not* really like children. We do not as a nation really love them in practice, and I am sure that all of you will agree that what we do must finally provide the evidence that answers the question.

Why *is* it that we, as a nation, allow so much inexcusable wretchedness among our children in practice, while at one and the same time we, as individuals, nurture and profess such tender and loving and solicitous sentiments for our children?

Broadly, I think that the answer is this: Our sentiments for children have been rendered ineffective by the stronger influences and forces of the economic system that have grown up willy-nilly among us.

I have been preoccupied with the subject of American children since I joined the Carnegie Council on Children three years ago. The Council has been attempting to understand the unmet needs and problems of American children and families. Such is the assignment that sent me looking for an answer to the question, Do Americans *really* like children? Now let me give you a bit more detail about the practices that impel me to the negative answer I just offered.

Let me start by mentioning our scandalously high infant mortality rate. Our rate is the fifteenth among 42 nations having comparable data, which is almost twice the rate of Sweden. Infant mortality rates for American nonwhites are much higher than the national average, and mortality rates for nonwhite infants born in America's 20 largest cities approach the rates in urban areas of underdeveloped countries. We are among the very few modern nations that do not guarantee adequate health care to mothers and children.

Next let me mention malnutrition. A United States Department of Agriculture survey shows that between 1955 and 1965, a decade of rising affluence and agricultural productivity, the percentage of diets deficient in one or more essential nutrients actually increased. Millions of American children today remain hungry and malnourished.

So it goes; our sentiments of caring to the contrary.

We say that children have a right to the material necessities of life, and yet of all age groups in America, children are the most likely to live in abject poverty. In fact, one-sixth of them live below the officially defined poverty line. One-third live below that level defined by the government as "minimum but adequate." And we are the *only* industrial democracy that lacks a system of income supports for families with children. In this area, we are an underdeveloped nation.

Our school system, of course, is supposed to equalize opportunity for all children, poor and rich. Yet, on a variety of standard achievement tests the absolute gap between rich and poor, and between black and white students as well, is greatest at the twelfth grade level. Far from equalizing opportunity, our school system augments the inequalities with which children enter schools.

Violence in the Children's Room[b]
Even by conservative estimates, more children under the age of five die at the hands of their own

---

Interest Box 14-1. (continued)

parents than are killed by tuberculosis, whooping cough, polio, measles, diabetes, rheumatic fever and hepatitis combined.

There have always been abused children. In earlier centuries, they were crippled and mutilated to make them more pathetic and, therefore, more profitable beggars. Until the 1800s, dead or abandoned infants were almost commonplace on city streets. And as late as 1892, 200 foundlings and 100 dead infants were found on the streets of New York City alone.

Until very recently, children have had little legal protection of any sort. The first child-battering case ever brought to the courts in this country was tried under regulations prohibiting cruelty to animals. The New York Society for the Prevention of Cruelty to Animals argued that a child named Mary Ellen, starved and kept in chains, was "a hu-

man animal" and therefore could not be so treated. There were no laws to prohibit mistreating children. The situation had changed little until 1963 when New York passed the first law requiring physicians to report cases of child abuse to police and social agencies while providing doctors immunity from lawsuits for making such reports. Today, all 50 states have such laws, in varying forms. The result has been the criminalization of child abuse and, in some cases, the battering by the legal system of abusive parents, who actually need even more help than their children.

[a]From "Do Americans *Really* Like Children?" by K. Keniston, *Today's Education,* November/December 1975. Reprinted by permission.
[b]From "Violence in the Children's Room," by W. Sage, *Human Behavior,* July 1975. Copyright © 1975 *Human Behavior* Magazine. Reprinted by permission.

---

voice in adoption, foster placement, desegregation, probation, corporal punishment in the schools, or even compulsory schooling. We don't question whether a store or theater owner may prevent children from entering without their parents or whether children may be allowed to vote, drive a car, drink, or smoke. Children don't decide on their bedtimes or the color of their rooms. They are told that

WERE YOU THINKING OF GETTING A BOY OR A GIRL?

Age discrimination in U.S. society makes it tough to be very young or very old.

they should be seen but not heard and that they should honor their parents. This situation would seem absurd if women proposed that men be treated this way or vice versa.

Children don't seem to have many rights. They don't have much power, either. They can't afford lawyers, and they can't get on talk shows to discuss their cause. They are too little to resist parental violence. It may be that children don't have basic human rights because we don't think of them as humans but rather as something like puppies or hamsters. It is interesting to note that the New York Society for the Prevention of Cruelty to Children was organized ten years after the Society for the Prevention of Cruelty to Animals.

Our treatment of the elderly is similar to our treatment of children, in some ways at least. Our retirement requirements may prevent the elderly from working and earning a decent living. Social security allowances, never adequate in the past, haven't kept pace with the cost of living, and many people who have worked hard all their lives find themselves, in their old age, shivering in cold apartments and dying as paupers. The elderly must watch their health deteriorate, their bodies stiffen, their memories fail, and their self-respect disappear.

But, unlike our treatment of children, our treatment of the elderly is more often a matter of neglect and disdain than direct abuse. We fear aging as we fear mental illness or violence, so we ship the elderly off to places where they'll be out of sight and out of mind—like the mentally ill or the violent—that is, to nursing homes, old age homes, and retirement communities.

Such treatment of the young and the old may be unique to highly industrialized societies such as ours. Before the 15th century, children of 5 or 6 years of age were regarded as small adults and granted the same rights and responsibilities (Aries, 1962; Plumb, 1972). Elders were respected for their wisdom and understanding, just as they still are in nonindustrialized societies today.

Discrimination against Women.   Many analogies might be drawn between the way children are treated and the way women are treated, although American women now have far more legal rights than children do. This gap was not always so large. It was once possible to deny a person the right to vote, join a club, or attend a particular college on the basis of sex as well as age. Yet in spite of legislative progress discrimination against women continues.

Prestigious, high-status jobs in our society are typically held by White men. Jobs that command less respect are held by members of minority groups and White women. This crowding of women and minorities into less desirable occupations means that the supply of workers exceeds the demand, driving down salaries and leaving many jobless. The unemployment rate of women and minority groups is higher than that of men year after year. The difference between male and female unemployment rates has increased in recent years (U.S. Department of Labor, 1974). You can see from Figure 14-1 that, although men and women have completed nearly the same number of years of education, employed women earn about $100 less a week than men. Their unemployment rates are considerably higher.

Some of these effects can be seen in a look at the American Psychological Association, where at the end of a recent year 78% of the lowest-paid employees, but only 7% of the highest-paid employees, were members of minority groups. Of the lowest-paid employees 67% were women, but of the highest-paid only 43% were women. The APA is like most organizations in that minorities are concen-

Figure 14-1.
Earnings, education, and unemployment rate

	Non-White M	F	White M	F	All M	F	All Non-White	White
Median weekly earnings 1977[1]	$201	147	259	157	253	156	171	217
Median school-years completed 1977[2]	11.3	11.4	12.5	12.4	12.5	12.4	11.4	12.5
Unemployment rate, Jan.–April 1978	11.4	13.1	4.7	6.2	—	—	12.2	5.3

[1]From the U.S. Bureau of Labor Statistics *News*, November 2, 1977.
[2]From *Statistical Abstract of the United States*, 1978, by the U.S. Department of Commerce, Bureau of the Census.

trated in the lowest-paying jobs, White women work at middle-level jobs, and White men dominate the top jobs (see Figure 14-2).

This pattern comes about through hiring practices that overlook women as potential contenders for high positions. In a recent search for a new APA executive officer (the top position), the all-White board of directors selected an all-White, all-male search committee, which in turn considered a number of candidates, all of whom were White males. Not surprisingly, the candidate chosen had been hand-picked by the retiring executive officer. Even if the search committee had nominated a woman or a member of a minority, the facts of the selection process usually give a position to a personal favorite similar in many ways to the person or committee making the hiring. Thus, men bring men into power.

Chances are that most of your college professors are men. Where are the women? Although women typically get higher grades than men in college, they are less likely to go on to graduate school. Those who do receive doctorates are less likely to hold full-time jobs in prestigious schools. Although many explanations have been suggested, one possibility is that women are discriminated against.

To test the hypothesis that women are discriminated against in hiring practices in psychology, Linda Fidell (1970) conducted an experiment. Each of 228 psychology-department chairs was asked to indicate at what level (from full professor to lecturer) each of 10 psychologists should be hired. What the chairs didn't know was that two forms of the questionnaire had been prepared. In one form a given paragraph supposedly described a male (for example, James Ross), and in the other form the same description was supposedly of a woman (for example,

Figure 14-2.
APA's central-office work force. Percentage at each salary-grade level who are women and minorities.

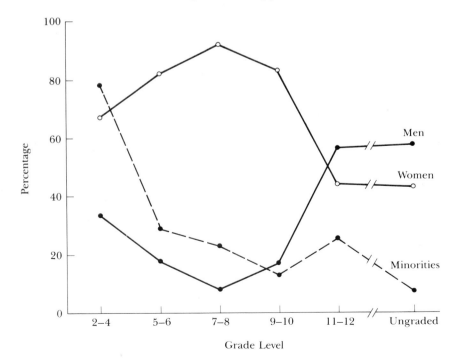

Janet Ross). So the only difference between the two forms was in the sex of the psychologist described.

Fidell found that chairs believed that women should be offered positions of lower rank than men. For instance, most thought that James Ross should be offered a position as associate professor, and most thought that Janet Ross should be an assistant professor. The hypothetical men received more academic positions leading to tenure, and only men were offered full professorships. These findings do not prove that women are discriminated against. But they make charges of discrimination very believable.

Other studies are in agreement with Fidell's findings. For instance, people evaluate men more favorably than women whose performance is identical (Dipboye, Fromkin, & Wiback, 1975; Rosen, B., & Jerdee, 1974a, 1974b; see also Chapter 3). In hiring decisions males are often preferred to females (Dipboye et al., 1975) and, when hired, are often given higher positions or higher salaries (for example, Terborg & Ilgen, 1975). The same bias favors Whites over Blacks. Differences in status within an occupation are another subtle indicator of discrimination. In general, the more-prestigious occupations have higher percentages of men than women (for example, Boss [cited in Deaux, 1976]) and higher percentages of Whites than Blacks. Some have suggested that the percentage of White men in an occupation is a factor in setting the prestige of that occupation.

Fidell's study measured opinions, using an experimental design. Another way to look at discrimination is by measuring actual salaries, using questionnaires. That is what I did in a recent survey of 4868 psychology faculty members from 274 departments (Stang, 1978c).

Several studies have found that male academic psychologists earn more than females, perhaps as much as $3500 more on the average (Bryan, A. I., & Boring, 1947; Fields, 1974; Stang, 1978c). This is partly due to sex differences in rank: women tend to work at lower ranks than men (Fields, 1974; Stang, 1978c). It is possible that women are discriminated against in promotions; certainly, some discrimination in promotions does occur. But there is another good reason why women are at lower ranks than men: women faculty members are younger than men (Stang, 1978c). Because people advance in rank and salary with age, if women are younger, they should be expected to earn less.

Why would women be younger? For one thing, higher percentages of women are now entering the profession than in previous years. These new faculty members are young and start as assistant professors. Another reason may be that women do not stay in the profession as long as men, leaving (for various reasons) before retirement.

Research such as that reported in this section can be helpful in understanding sex discrimination. Such research can tell us where women are most and least likely to be discriminated against and where they are favored over men. By knowing these details, we are in a better position to stop such discrimination. After we have done research to determine what needs to be done, other types of research can suggest how to do it.

Race Discrimination.   For many readers the evidence that Whites discriminate against Blacks is so overwhelming that it seems superfluous to even mention it. For other readers, such evidence is unconvincing. For them, presenting such

Sexism, like other forms of prejudice, often springs from the best of intentions.

evidence is a call to arms. The issue, though, is not Does race discrimination ever occur? (for it certainly must from time to time), but How often does it occur, what are its effects, and what can be done to reduce such effects?

In effect, *race discrimination* is a causal explanation of a particular action. As with other causal explanations, it is customary to attempt to rule out other plausible explanations. Unfortunately, this is usually not possible. A Black who applies for a job and is told that the job has just been filled or that he or she does not qualify may wonder whether the interviewer is telling the truth. But no one can afford to spend his or her life filing court suits to test the statements made by employers.

And even employers who decide to hire a White over a Black may have difficulty determining their real motives. Did they do so because of prejudice, a difference in qualifications, or both? Or were there other factors, such as the personality or appearance of the applicant? In the individual case it is often difficult to determine whether an action is discriminatory.

It is usually easier to determine that actions are discriminatory when they are repeated many times. If 30 percent of the adults in an area are Black and only 3% of a company's employees are Black, it seems likely that some discrimination may be occurring. But even then it may be necessary to examine the applicants for these positions. What percentage of applicants were Black? How did their qualifications compare with those of White applicants? When courts have examined such information, they have concluded very often that discrimination did occur. In the eyes of the courts race discrimination is a fact of American life.

Discrimination against the Poor.   Wealth in our society is not evenly distributed. The wealthiest 10% of our population earns about 27 times as much as the poorest 10% does (Kolko, 1962), a gap that is increasing each year. Many people feel that, because the rich pay so much in taxes and the government spends so much in welfare programs, this disparity in income somehow evens up. This is not the case. Americans earning less than $4000 a year actually pay more in taxes than they receive in welfare (Kolko, 1962).

Income disparity may be great in the United States, but the gap between rich and poor is even more evident in global comparisons. A few miles from the Texas border, a Mexican laborer may earn $3.40 a day and face a family food bill of $4 a day, making it necessary for several in the family to work. In India, a landless farm worker may earn less than $200 a year (*Poor versus Rich*, 1975). The average American earns over 50 times what the average native of India earns. Such poverty is difficult to comprehend. But it is both a source and sign of conflict. Third-World nations have charged, with some justification, that colonial exploitation first stripped their lands of natural resources and destroyed their social structures, then offered foreign aid that undermined dignity and self-sufficiency. The result was pockets of privileged elites addicted to Western luxuries and standards of living (*Poor versus Rich*, 1975). Such exploitation has planted the seeds of conflict, so evident in the "Yankee-go-home" attitude.

Even in buying a used car, the poor are more likely to be cheated than the rich. Only 3% of the U.S. public feels that the $33-billion used-car industry is doing a good job of serving the consumer (Skidmore, 1978). And the poor seem to be the most likely victims of this fraud. Not only are they more likely to buy a used car than are the wealthy, but those with annual incomes under $6000 pay almost 10% more for the same used car than those with incomes over $24,000. Although they pay more, they have to spend more on repairing their car after buying it and report lower satisfaction with their purchase (McNeil, Nevin, Trubek, & Edelman, 1978; Skidmore, 1978). Further detailed study is needed to learn why the poor pay more for less.

Discrimination against the Unattractive.   Physical attractiveness is believed, in our assumptions about people, to be related to all sorts of good things. We believe that attractive people are more popular, smarter, and wealthier than the unattractive. Handsome men are given more positive ratings than unattractive ones on such things as sexuality, "datability," and marriageability (Byrne, Ervin, & Lamberth, 1970). Attractive people are viewed as being more outgoing, more pleasant, and higher in self-esteem and as having higher occupational status, too (Adams, G. R., & Huston, 1975). We see attractive people as more sensitive, kind, interesting, strong, modest, and sociable and as having more-pleasant futures to look forward to (Dion, K. K., Berscheid, & Walster, 1972). Attractive people are viewed as more friendly, warm, attentive, and likable (Kleinke, Staneski, & Pipp, 1975). And they are expected to achieve more in educational settings (Clifford & Walster, 1973). Even the essays attributed to attractive authors are judged more positively! (Landy & Sigall, 1974). Perhaps through diffusion of affect the pleas-

The poor are the most likely victims of fraud.

antness we feel from the presence of attractive people spreads to everything we feel and say about them and everything we do regarding them. To put it another way, we seem to be prejudiced against unattractive people.

Such stereotypes give attractive people a strong advantage in social relations in everyday life. For instance, one study found that physically attractive candidates received about three times as many votes as unattractive candidates in an election (Efran & Patterson, 1974). Even among children the attractive seem more popular than their peers (Dion, K. K., & Berscheid, 1971; Mussen, Conger, & Kagan, 1969). Attractive adults are more influential and can get us to work harder for them (Kahn, Hottes, & Davis, 1971; Sigall, Page, & Brown, 1971). And we are more eager to offer them help when they request it (see Chapter 9). Unattractive people are at a strong disadvantage in everyday social relations.

In the United States, at least, many people seem to believe that what is beautiful is good. Karen Dion (1972) showed students photographs of children who, she said, had been misbehaving. In deciding what punishment should be given these children, college women felt that the beautiful children should be given the benefit of the doubt. After all, thought these women, the unattractive children (who had misbehaved in exactly the same way) were more likely to misbehave in the future. Even the naughty behavior was viewed as naughtier when committed by an unattractive child.

Several studies have found that we judge attractive people as more responsible for behavior we approve of and less responsible for behavior we disapprove of (Efran, 1974; Seligman, C., Paschall, & Takata, 1974; Sigall & Ostrove, 1975). Diffusion of affect may be at work here; our positive evaluation of attractive people spills over and colors our other evaluations of them.

When attractive defendants have been accused of burglary or cheating on an exam, simulated juries like them better than less attractive defendants. They are viewed as less guilty and are given less severe punishments (Efran, 1974). When misfortunes happen, the attractive receive more sympathy (Shaw, J., 1972). Although these studies are simulations, they suggest a bias in our behavior as parents, judges, or jurors.

Physical attractiveness seems to be extremely important in the early stages of attraction to another person. We are likely to strike up conversations with those we find attractive and avoid those we find ugly. Obviously, the initial conversation is necessary before we can get to like somebody. Even if in a long-term relationship we do not judge someone on his or her looks, in an initial stage of acquaintance looks count.

In several studies people were randomly assigned blind dates, supposedly through a computer matching system. After the dates the daters were asked how much they would like to go out with the same person again (Brislin & Lewis, 1968; Walster, Aronson, Abrahams, & Rottmann, 1966). There was an extremely strong relationship between how physically attractive the date had been and how much the person wanted to go out with him or her again. In fact, one study (Walster et al., 1966) found that attractiveness—not intelligence, personality, or attitudes—was the sole influence on attraction. The more attractive the men or women, the more they were liked and subsequently dated by their computer date. Another study found that a woman's physical attractiveness was strongly related to her dating frequency, though this relation was weaker for men (Berscheid, Dion, Walster, & Walster, 1971). It appears that for many young people physical attractiveness is more important in attraction and forming a positive impression of another than is intelligence, personality, or similarity of attitudes.

Such findings raise many questions. Do handsome men or beautiful women make better friends and better marriage partners? Are they likely to really be more healthy, wealthy, and wise? The studies on such questions are just getting under way. We do know that attractive people have more sexual experience, less anxiety about dating, more dates, more friends of both sexes, and happier marriages (Berscheid et al., 1971; Curran & Lippold, 1975; Kirkpatrick & Cotton, 1961). And attractive children seem to have higher self-esteem (Maruyama & Miller, 1975). We also know that people who regard themselves as attractive have higher self-esteem, more dates, and expect to marry at an earlier age (Minahan, 1971). Prisoners who have had cosmetic surgery to improve their appearance are apparently less likely to commit the same crimes again (Kurtzberg, Safar, & Cavior, 1968). This effect may occur because these ex-convicts are treated differently in society or because they feel better about themselves. Another study found that mental patients were less attractive than others and that unattractive patients had more severe diagnoses, were hospitalized longer, and had fewer visitors than attractive patients (Farina, Fischer, Sherman, Smith, Groh, & Mermin, 1977).

Because physical attractiveness is so valued, it may be an important ingredient in upward social mobility. An attractive high school senior who comes from a poor home may be able to trade attractiveness for a classmate's potential wealth and marry someone who will become prosperous. One study (Elder, 1969) found that women whose social status was improved by marriage tended to be prettier as teenagers than women whose status did not change. Those people who are unattractive may have difficulty in obtaining certain jobs or getting promotions.

Physical attractiveness can overcome some of poverty's stigma.

Following this line of reasoning, we might expect people in wealthy neighborhoods to be more attractive than people found elsewhere. Researchers in one study took random photos of 120 people as they left either a fast-food restaurant or an expensive restaurant (Zibaida, Sieretzki, & Stang, 1976). The pictures were shuffled, the backgrounds were masked out, and then the subjects were rated for attractiveness, wealth, and education. Some college students rated the slides for face and body, others saw face only, and a third group rated body only.

Regardless of whether students saw photos of face, body, or both, they rated the diners at the expensive restaurant as significantly more attractive, wealthy, and educated than diners at the inexpensive restaurant. Judgments about attractiveness and wealth for these two settings differed most when students were rating face and body, and education judgments differed most when face alone was available for rating. Thus, college students use different cues in judging qualities such as attractiveness and education. But a more interesting suggestion of this study is that people found in wealthy areas look wealthier, more educated, and more attractive.

Much of physical attractiveness is something that money can buy: new clothes, new hairstyles, cosmetics, frequent dental care from an early age, face-lifts, diet, and so on. Without money, it is hard to obtain these aids to attractiveness. Further, the poor often suffer in attractiveness from working in difficult or dangerous occupations or in the hot sun and from improper diets. Physical attractiveness probably has strong effects on one's actual and perceived socioeconomic level. Welfare reform might consider this and permit expenditure of public money by the poor on cosmetics, clothing, and other things which would increase physical attractiveness. Upward mobility might then be easier.

Discrimination against the Overweight.   In every culture attractiveness affects attraction (Brislin & Lewis, 1968; Byrne, London, & Reeves, 1968; Ford & Beach, 1951; Huston, 1973; Kleck & Rubenstein, 1975; Walster et al., 1966). This is not to say that every culture shares the same definition of beauty. In the United States today, for instance, magazine cover women seem to be dying of malnutrition, and "thin is in" (Cahnman, 1968; Lerner, R. M., 1969; Lerner, R. M., & Gellert, 1969; Richardson, S. A., Goodman, Hastorf, & Dornbusch, 1961; Wells, W., & Siegel, 1961). In cultures where death from malnutrition actually occurs with some frequency, plumpness means beauty, perhaps because it means health and wealth.

Thin people and those of average weight discriminate against fat people. Fat applicants are much less likely to be accepted into top colleges than are others with the same grades and abilities (Harris, T. G., 1978). Students were suspended at Oral Roberts University because they would not (or could not) lose weight. Five crew members of a submarine were kept out of sight during a presidential inspection of their ship because they were "too fat to be seen by the President" (Cook, A., 1978).

Psychologists have sometimes used Sheldon's (1940, 1942, 1949, 1954) classification of **body types** in describing people. **Mesomorphs** are strong and muscular; **ectomorphs** are thin and delicate; **endomorphs** are soft and round. Our stereotypes are most positive toward mesomorph males, most negative toward endomorphs. For example, mesomorph males are assumed to be the best leaders, the best soldiers, and the best athletes and are the most desired as friends (reviewed in Montmayor, 1978).

Studies have found that, if body type is related to anything, the relation is very small—much smaller than our stereotypes suggest. Some studies have found that mesomorph boys are more likely to become delinquents than other boys (for example, Cortes & Gatti, 1972; Sheldon, 1949). Other studies have found ectomorphs may have a bit more verbal ability than others and may be more likely to attend college (reviewed in Montmayor, 1978). But on the whole, research has found little evidence that body type affects behavior. Nevertheless, our stereotypes persist.

We justify our prejudice against the obese with the belief that they are weak willed and that they simply will not control their eating. The belief is wrong. Obesity is largely genetically determined. If both of your parents are obese, you are 11 times as likely to be fat as if both are "normal" in weight. With one obese parent, you are five times more likely to be fat than if both are "normal" (Harris,

T. G., 1978). When twins are raised apart, their weight tends to match that of their genetic parents, not their foster parents (Harris, T. G., 1978).

The prejudice shown toward fat people, like that shown toward Blacks, women, the poor, and other groups, often turns to self-hatred or self-contempt. People who are fat often have low self-esteem. Although some people think that fat people eat because they are depressed, it is more likely that they are depressed because they are fat. Like you and me, they eat because they are hungry.

EXPLAINING CONFLICT

The previous pages in this chapter present a dismal view of humanity. We are rough and cruel and selfish at times. We hold prejudices that have no basis in fact. Social psychologists do their best to be objective in their study of **conflict** and tension. To do this, it may help to begin with some definitions.

Prejudice is an undeserved negative emotional reaction or dislike directed toward some person or group. As Gordon Allport has noted, prejudice is "based upon a faulty and inflexible generalization. It may be felt or expressed. It may be directed toward a group as a whole or toward an individual because he is a member of that group" (1954b, p. 10).

Discrimination refers to those behaviors that result from prejudice and adversely and unjustly affect the target of prejudice.

Many approaches have been taken in an attempt to understand conflict, prejudice, and discrimination. As Gordon Allport argued,

> By far the best view to take toward this multiplicity of approaches is to admit them all. Each has something to teach us. None possesses a monopoly of insight, nor is any one safe as a solitary guide. We may lay it down as a general law applying to all social phenomena that multiple causation is invariably at work and nowhere is the law more clearly applicable than to prejudice [1954b, p. 212].

Characteristics of the Target.   One of the most common explanations of prejudice is offered by prejudiced people. They argue that the target of their dislike deserves to be disliked. They tell you that it is rational and reasonable to dislike Blacks or Jews or some other group because of the characteristics of that group.

For example, those who oppose giving aid and opportunity to the poor frequently assert that the poor are poor because they do not work as hard as the wealthy. Although this may be true for particular cases, it is not true for the poor as a whole. Irwin Garfinkel, Robert Haveman, and Betson (1977) have examined **earnings capacity,** which they define as the income that would be generated by a household if it employed its human and physical assets to capacity. **Capacity utilization** refers to the percentage of earnings actually used. For example, if you could earn $20,000 a year and are only making $15,000, your capacity utilization is 75%. Garfinkel, Haveman, and Betson report that capacity utilization for the average U.S. household is nearly 75% if the value of housework is included. Men, they find, usually have higher rates of capacity utilization than women (because many women who could work outside the home choose to work inside). But poor families have the same rates of capacity utilization as wealthy families: they *are* working just as hard. And for a given social class Blacks have slightly *higher* rates of capacity utilization than Whites. In other words, the poor are no "lazier" than the wealthy, Blacks no "lazier" than Whites.

Confronted with such evidence, prejudiced people may seek other justifications for their feelings. The poor may work as hard, they tell you, but they're not as smart. They spend their money on the wrong things. They don't have any moral values. You can't trust them. And so on. The prejudiced are not particularly interested in findings that seem to run counter to their beliefs. For a good explanation of prejudice, we must look elsewhere. Prejudice is not caused by characteristics of the target.

Characteristics of the Prejudiced.   Personality theorists are inclined to look at the prejudiced person, rather than the target of prejudice, for an explanation of prejudice. One popular explanation focuses on the authoritarian personality (see Chapter 3). Another focuses on ethnocentrism. Other explanations look at the similarity between target and prejudiced person or at the familiarity of target to the prejudiced person.

The authoritarian personality.   Sigmund Freud's psychoanalytic theory suggests that prejudice may be a consequence of a person's own insecurities. According to this view, when people are unwilling to accept their own weaknesses or needs, they may deny or repress them and project them onto others. Thus, according to psychoanalytic theory, people who are prejudiced may really be unhappy with themselves. By blaming others and using them as scapegoats, people may feel better about their own frustrations and inadequacies.

As we said in Chapter 3, a group of psychologists at Berkeley, California, took this approach to understanding prejudice in the late 1940s. After a very ambitious series of studies and much work, they published their findings in a book called *The Authoritarian Personality* (Adorno, Frenkel-Brunswick, Levinson, & Sanford, 1950). From many interviews these investigators concluded that authoritarian people tend to have a general prejudice against all other groups, not simply one or two specific groups.

Authoritarian people may have other things in common besides their prejudice. They tend to see people as weak or strong, good or bad. They may be submissive, respectful, and polite to superiors but dominating, contemptuous, and authoritarian toward "inferiors." Authoritarian people generally hold conventional values, are conservative, and are intolerant of ambiguity. They deny weakness or inadequacy in themselves and introspect little. People on the other end of the authoritarian dimension generally lack these attributes.

Although there has been substantial criticism of weaknesses in the methods used by these researchers (for example, Christie, R., & Jahoda, 1954), the psychoanalytic interpretation of prejudice they proposed remains a powerful, useful tool in understanding. At least some racial and ethnic prejudice does indeed seem well explained by psychoanalytic theory. Nevertheless, no single theory can explain everything.

Ethnocentrism.   **Ethnocentrism** is a "view of things in which one's own group is the center of everything, and all others are scaled and rated with reference to it." So wrote the sociologist William Graham Sumner in 1906 (p. 13). Recent research suggests that ethnocentrism exists in many cultures. Marilyn Brewer (1979) reported that in 20 different areas studied—including northern Canada, West Africa and the South Pacific—people typically feel more positive about their own groups (the **in-group**) than they do about other groups (**out-groups**). In-group ratings are usually more positive than out-group ratings on dimensions such as obedience, friendliness, beauty, potency, industry, virtue, honesty, and love of peace. In short, we believe that our own group is more morally virtuous and trustworthy than other groups. Further, Brewer found, when our group does see another group as better in some way, we minimize the difference. When we see our group as better, we maximize the difference. Love is not blind, but our positive feelings toward members of our own groups do interfere with clear vision.

Why does ethnocentrism occur? It seems likely that, by holding lower opinions of "them" than we hold of "us," we boost our satisfaction with our group and thus feel better about ourselves. The belief that we are better than they is not often tested objectively; after all, if we are better than they, why waste time with them? Without such opportunities for disconfirming beliefs, beliefs are permitted to persist.

Can ethnocentrism account for prejudice toward the young, old, women, the unattractive, and so on? Perhaps the idea can be extended this far. But perhaps ethnocentrism does not account at all, but rather simply describes. We do like our own groups best. Why? Two explanations seem likely: similarity increases attraction, and so does familiarity. These effects are discussed below.

Similarity,, attraction, and prejudice. Many interpersonal conflicts arise from people's dissimilarities. Our moral judgments, for example, are often based on how similar others' actions are to our own. As Emile Durkheim commented,

> In more advanced societies . . . the absences of some likenesses [to others in our group], however, is still a sign of moral failure. . . . If a criminal is the object of reprobation, it is because he is unlike us. Likewise, in lesser degree, acts simply immoral and prohibited as such are those which evince dissemblances less profound but nevertheless considered serious [Durkheim, 1947, cited in Hare, Borgatta, & Bales, 1965, p. 7].

We have seen in the previous chapters that we are attracted to people who are similar to ourselves. We join groups of people who are similar to ourselves. And group processes operate to maintain and even increase the similarity between members. The result of all these forces is a greater similarity within groups than between groups.

The same effect is true for some groups that we do not join but rather are "assigned" to by the facts of our birth. Our age group has many things in common. Our "sex group"—male or female—also makes us more similar to some people than others. The same may be said for race, ethnicity, social class, and even physical appearance. To some extent, such characteristics may directly influence our thoughts, feelings, and behaviors through biological forces. But more importantly, such characteristics have powerful indirect effects on our lives by determining how others will think, feel, and behave toward us.

If it is true that we tend to like most those we believe are most similar to us, it is also true that we tend to like least those we believe are most dissimilar to us. The similarity/attraction principle may be a powerful cause of prejudice in everyday life.

Familiarity, attraction, and prejudice.   The effects of familiarity on attraction have also been discussed in previous chapters. In brief, it seems that the greater our familiarity, the greater our attraction; when we are unfamiliar with members of another group, we may feel uncomfortable when we encounter them. This discomfort may be properly attributed to our lack of familiarity, but more often it is misattributed to the group itself. We may conclude that we do not like this unfamiliar group because of its characteristics rather than because of our lack of familiarity with it.

Such dislike can be counterproductive. If we dislike a group because it is unfamiliar and avoid it because we dislike it, we will be stuck with our uninformed prejudice. Such prejudice may be reduced through contact with others if conditions are right, as we will see later.

Characteristics of Social Processes.   We will consider two ways in which social processes contribute to intergroup conflict: labeling and competition/cooperation.

Labeling.   "Sticks and stones can break my bones, but names will never hurt me." **Labeling** theorists would disagree. Labeling is the process of giving a name—usually derogatory—to a class of people. Some studies suggest that labeling can affect the attitudes or behaviors of others (Buikhuisen, Buikhuisen, & Dijksterhuis, 1971; O'Connor, 1970; Rosenthal, R., & Jacobson, 1968; Schwartz, R. D., & Skolnick, 1964). (Intuitively, we would suppose that delinquency or other behavior syndromes could develop without such labeling effects, and several studies offer support for this [Clinard, 1952; Lemert, 1967; Sutherland, 1949]. Labeling may be a sufficient but not necessary condition for the creation of some behavior syndromes.)

Labeling might affect delinquency like this: A boy tries shoplifting because his friends are doing it. He is caught and arrested. His upset parents call him a delinquent. He begins to feel like a delinquent and look to the behavior of other boys who have been so labeled as a guide for his own behavior. There is some evidence that with each arrest the effects of labeling become more pronounced. After the first offense, with low labeling, there is low **recidivism** (repetition of the action that led to court action) (Klein, 1974). With each subsequent arrest (if there are more), the chances of recidivism increase. Of course, other factors also affect recidivism.

Members of an oppressed group sometimes acquire the negative attitudes held by their oppressors. Research has found anti-Semitism among Jews (Sarnoff, 1951) and prejudice against Blacks among Blacks (Asher & Allen, 1969; Clark, K., & Clark, 1947; Maliver, 1965; Morland, 1970). Many female secretaries still insist on referring to themselves as "girls." Can you think of other examples in which an oppressed group has acquired the negative attitudes of the oppressors?

Discrimination reduces opportunities, resources, and valued attributes. These less positive characteristics, in turn, are used by others to justify further discrimination. For example, women have traditionally been "the weaker sex." This weakness was a sign of femininity and was actively encouraged in women by both men and women for many years. But weakness leads to weakness. For instance, many of those who opposed college educations for women in the 1800s "felt that higher education would . . . physically debilitate the weaker sex" (Kistiakowsky, 1976). As a result of such arguments, women were excluded from college, further diminishing their social worth.

Competition, cooperation, and diffusion of affect.

When two groups compete for a limited resource (such as a prize in a game of tug of war), members become concerned that their group may lose. Losing sometimes results in bad feelings, as may the tension produced during competition. Diffusion-of-affect theory might predict that these negative feelings will spill over onto the opponents. A group that loses may feel more negative about the winners than it felt before the competition began.

Cooperation between two groups that leads to mutual success in reaching a mutual goal should have far different effects than competition. Diffusion-of-affect theory would predict that, if cooperation and reaching the goal are pleasant, these pleasant feelings may spill over onto those who are cooperating. Thus, competition is likely to increase tension and may create prejudice; cooperation is likely to reduce tension and may create good will.

Muzafer and Carolyn Sherif studied the effects of cooperation and competition on intergroup relations in a series of well-known field experiments (Sherif, M., Harvey, White, Hood, & Sherif, 1961; Sherif, M., & Sherif, 1953; Sherif, M., White, & Harvey, 1955). The best-known of these experiments took place in a summer camp in the mountains of Pennsylvania, a place called Robbers Cave. The Sherifs divided 22 11-year-old boys into two groups—the Bulldogs and the Red Devils. Separate activities were arranged for these two groups to allow members to get to know one another and to allow the groups to develop internal structures. After a short while the boys began to show preferences for their own group.

In the next phase of this experiment the groups were offered a variety of opportunities to compete (cleaning the camp, tug of war, and the like) and prizes for winning. It did not take long for name-calling and intergroup conflict to occur. This tension escalated in a subsequent phase of the experiment, in which the two groups were frustrated in various ways. Interestingly, as out-group tension increased, so did in-group cohesiveness and solidarity.

In the final phase of the Robbers-Cave experiment, peace was restored between Bulldogs and Red Devils. Both groups were given some common goals that required cooperation. For example, the water truck stalled in the mud. Because both groups needed the water, they worked together to push it out. Such successful cooperation reduced intergroup tension and prejudice.

These findings, which have held up in studies of adults (Blake & Mouton, 1961), suggest that the social processes of competition and cooperation may be important in creating or reducing intergroup conflict. But it is difficult to isolate exactly what produced or reduced the conflict. Was it the cooperation/competition, some aspect of it (for example, shared versus nonshared goals), or some byproduct of it (for example, winning versus losing or good mood versus bad mood)? Perhaps more research will help explain how cooperation and competition affect intergroup relations.

Diffusion-of-affect theory does not explain why conflict should improve *intra*group relations. The theory, in fact, predicts the opposite. But it is useful in integrating other conflict phenomena. For example, it suggests that a variety of negative responses may be made to a variety of negative inputs. These responses may include intrapersonal responses (depression, anger, despair), intragroup responses (friction, dissent, disorganization), responses directed toward appropriate targets (those groups or individuals responsible for the negative input), and responses directed toward inappropriate targets (scapegoating, blaming the victim, and the like). Thus, in regard to intergroup relations, diffusion-of-affect theory might account for findings such as:

- Deprivation, insults, frustrations, and attack often lead to anger, aggression, and dislike (reviewed in Konečni, 1979).
- Similarly, droughts and other natural disasters may lead to such varied responses as feuding (Hart, D. M., 1954; Lewis, W. H., 1961), looting, or voting against political incumbents (Abney & Hill, 1966).
- Gasoline lines during shortages in the United States have been an apparent cause of insults, dented fenders, fist fights, increased prejudice toward Arabs, and reduced popularity of the President.
- Frustration or uneven distribution of resources by one person sometimes leads to prejudice, insults, and physical aggression against others (Cowen, Landes, & Shaet, 1958; Miller, N. E., & Bugelski, 1948; Thibaut, 1950).

Because competition and cooperation have such strong effects on intergroup conflict, I will return to this subject later in the discussion on proposed solutions to conflict.

Characteristics of the Social System.   It is quite possible that some conflicts between groups cannot be resolved, because they are basic properties of social systems. Some conflict—oppression, inequity, and injustice—does seem to be traceable to systems themselves, whereas other conflict—such as physical violence between two people—is more individually determined.

One way that systems contribute to intergroup conflict is by design. One group may decide that it wants a resource controlled by another group and may try to gain control of that resource. Wars have been fought to gain or protect resources such as land, wealth, and slaves. Institutions "trade" with employees, trying to gain the greatest benefit at the lowest cost (employees often follow the same principle). The conflict that results may range from exploitation in the institution to global war. Humans are unique in using entire social systems to gain resources. Of course, not all social systems produce war or exploitation by design, but most seem to.

Systems sometimes contribute to conflict simply through their design. In countries having a free-enterprise system, people are motivated to get the highest price they can for the goods and services they offer. Not everyone can pay this high price, however. As a result, some goods and services are unevenly distributed. For instance, although the United States has a lawyer for every 500 residents—more than any other country—90% of the country's lawyers serve 10% of its people (Carter, J., 1978). Of New York City's 35,000 lawyers (one for every 200 people), only a handful serve its 1 million poor—one lawyer for every 5000 people (Tolchin, 1978). Psychologists, psychiatrists, and doctors are similarly distributed. In fact, the wealthy have more and better parks, playgrounds, theaters, stores, and schools. There is virtually no product or service that people do not have unequal access to. Unequal access means unequal benefit.

Sometimes systems contribute to conflict simply through their design. In countries having a free enterprise system, for example, many goods and services are unevenly distributed.

Unequal distribution of limited resources is far easier for a system to achieve than equal distribution. Such unequal distribution seems to be an important source of intergroup conflict. When water is scarce, groups may quarrel and feud over it (Hart, D. M., 1954). When gasoline is scarce and not evenly distributed, groups and individuals may come into conflict over that. When lollipops are unevenly distributed to a group of happy children, conflict may break out. The way a system distributes scarce, coveted resources plays an important role in whatever inter-group conflict—if any—occurs.

Systems may also contribute to conflict when they are disrupted. When a system becomes disorganized by the introduction of strangers or by the removal of its leaders, conflict may increase considerably (Scott, J. P., 1975). When a new baby is added to a family, there may be internal conflicts such as jealousy and sibling rivalry. When John Kennedy was assassinated, there were reports of a sudden increase in crime, symptomatic of the conflict that accompanies social disruption.

The economic aspects of a system seem to play a major role in the nature of the conflict in that system. For instance, children and the elderly in industrialized societies are often prohibited from working. When they do work, they are often given menial jobs. It seems plausible that such work rules are designed to protect scarce jobs for others. In nonindustrialized societies there is more work to do and less surplus wealth. Perhaps as a consequence, both children and the elderly find meaningful work and have many rights and responsibilities. (In industrialized societies, the children of *poor* families are permitted to work. Farm children shell peas at the age of 4 and drive tractors at 5 or 6. In the Middle Ages, the poor continued to treat their children as adults long after the wealthy had stopped doing so [Plumb, 1972]).

A similar line of reasoning may apply to the other targets of discrimination mentioned in this chapter. Women are encouraged not to work in industrialized societies, and both women and members of minority groups often must accept menial jobs when they do. Nonindustrialized societies need a larger labor pool, and both women and minority groups receive better treatment.

A similar argument has been advanced by Marxists, who have suggested that "prejudice is a social attitude propagated among the public by an exploiting class for the purpose of stigmatizing some group as inferior so that exploitation of either the group itself or its resources may both be justified" (Cox, O. C., 1948, p. 393).

There are some problems with this explanation, however. It does not explain why there is a prejudice against people (for example, Jews) who are typically not exploited or why there is not much prejudice against some groups that have been exploited (for example, poor immigrants from Northern Europe). Such weaknesses in the economic explanation do not mean that it is wrong, however. It is merely incomplete.

We are unaccustomed to thinking that the economy influences our thoughts, feelings, and behavior, and economic explanations of conflict are not often suggested. But they are worth considering more carefully, because like other explanations of intergroup conflict they are probably true as far as they go.

SOLUTIONS TO CONFLICT

Can we solve the intergroup conflicts we have discussed in this chapter? Optimists and pessimists are divided on the question. Social psychologists would probably answer that we understand how to reduce conflicts, and this understanding could be put to work for the good of society. In this final section we will review some of the plausible strategies we might employ to reduce intergroup conflict.

Solution: Increased Contact to Reduce Prejudice.   If you live in an urban area, it is likely that you pass many Blacks and Whites on the street every day. Are they segregated? Do the whites live in a nearly all-White neighborhood and the Blacks in a nearly all-Black neighborhood? How about friendships? How often do you see mixed-race groups walking down the sidewalk? How about marriages?

We are probably all aware of racial segregation in friendship groups, but we probably underestimate its extent. One study measured segregation in social interaction in an area that was 52% Black (Russell, Stok, & Stang, 1976). In that study 51 of 58 groups passing on the sidewalk were same-race groups, and only 7 were of mixed race (12%). If two-person groups were formed randomly, disregarding race, we would have expected about 50% of these groups to be of mixed race. Similarly, in a cafeteria that was 87% White these researchers found only one mixed-race group and 28 same-race groups. Thus the frequency of segregated groups was much higher than expected by chance. (See Interest Box 14-2.)

In most areas of this country, Blacks and Whites are so spatially separated that there is little interaction between them at home, in the neighborhood, in school, or in church (Bennett, 1973; Levine, Fiddmont, & New, 1971). Does such segregation affect our attitudes? Would there be less prejudice with more contact? Or suppose that you were going to learn a foreign language by studying it very intensely abroad as an exchange student. How would your attitudes toward people who spoke that language change? Research findings vary. Some studies have found that such attitudes become more positive with contact, others that they become more negative, and others that they do not seem to change at all (reviewed in Clement, Gardner, & Smythe, 1977).

Researchers have long been interested in the effects of contact between ethnic groups and attitudes. For instance, one researcher (Brophy, 1946) found

---

Interest Box 14-2.   Measuring Integration

It is an easy matter for you to measure integration at your school. Follow these steps.

1. As a pair of people passes a particular point along the sidewalk, place a tally in one of three columns as shown below. Do this for several dozen pairs of passersby.

Hypothetical Data

Black Pair	White Pair	Mixed Pair
15	29	2

2. Calculate what is expected by chance.
   a. Find the total number of Blacks: $(15 \times 2) + 2 = 32$
   b. Find the total number of Whites: $(29 \times 2) + 2 = 60$
   c. Find what percentage of the total group each of these numbers is:
   Total group $= (15 + 29 + 2) \times 2 = 92$
   Blacks $= {}^{32}/_{92} = .3478$
   White $= {}^{60}/_{92} = .6522$
   d. The chances of encountering one Black in this group are therefore .3478; the chances of encountering a second Black are .3478 (actually, a little less, because you just met one, and there are only 31 left). So the chance of forming a group of two—by chance alone—is $.3478 \times .3478 = .12$, or

12% of the time. Because there are 46 groups, 5.5 ($.12 \times 46$) would be all Black by chance.
   e. Similarly, if Whites formed pairs by chance, this would occur $.6522 \times .6522 = .43$, or 43% of the time. Because there are 46 groups, you would expect that nearly 20 of them ($.43 \times 46$) would be all White by chance.
   f. The number of mixed groups is found by assuming that, if the first to join the group is White, the second must be Black ($.6522 \times .3478$) or vice versa ($.3478 \times .6522$), so multiply this by two: $.3478 \times .6522 \times 2 = .4537$. About 45% of the groups would be mixed race if they formed at random, or nearly 21.
   g. Check your work: 45% + 43% + 12% = 100%. All expected groups accounted for.
   h. Compare your expectations with your observations: $5\frac{1}{2}$ Black pairs were expected by chance, and 15 were observed; 20 White pairs were expected and 29 observed; 21 mixed pairs were expected and 2 observed.

What have you learned about integration? How much of it is there where you live? Less than you thought?

less interracial prejudice among sailors who had had more interracial contact. Another study (Triandis & Vassiliou, 1967) found that Greek stereotypes of Americans became more favorable with more contact. Another study (Jahoda, M., & West, 1951) found that, the longer a person lived in an integrated neighborhood, the more friends of the other race he or she had.

But just as contact sometimes reduces prejudice, prejudice can sometimes reduce contact. After conflict between two members of different groups, the parties sometimes withdraw. Avoiding an unpleasant confrontation is an instance of the Pollyanna Principle and may be a short-run "solution." But avoidance does not lead to positive attitudes and does not permit the two parties to resolve the conflict or reduce their antagonism. In fact, in the absence of accurate information on the other, misconceptions and prejudice may mount.

The pattern of segregation is a vicious circle. With low contact with the outgroup, beliefs lose their accuracy; as these beliefs become increasingly inaccurate and negative, contact is further reduced, and the cycle continues. Prejudice increases segregation and segregation increases prejudice.

Because it is desirable to reduce prejudice, and because contact sometimes reduces and sometimes increases prejudice, it is important to know why contact has its effects. Research suggests that several conditions may be important.

When the contact is superficial and casual, little change in attitude occurs. When the contact is intimate, more attitude change may occur (Amir, 1969).

The nature of the context determines the effects of contact. For instance, when Whites see photos of Blacks in positive settings dressed as members of the clergy or office workers, repeated contact increases attraction. But the same people photographed in a negative context—as a prisoner or janitor—may be liked less with repeated contact (Perlman & Oskamp, 1971). Other features of the context also affect attitudes. Contact with those of equal status to our own who have positive qualities and who work with us cooperatively takes place in a positive context. Contact under these circumstances seems to lead to more positive attitudes (Amir, 1969; Cook, S. W., 1972). The role of intergroup cooperation in reducing prejudice will be discussed later.

When contact is voluntary, its effects are more positive. For instance, when people choose to live in integrated housing, they usually become less prejudiced (Deutsch & Collins, 1951; Grier & Grier, 1960). When people are forced to interact with others of a different race, they may become more prejudiced (Foley, 1976). Perhaps people who volunteer differ from those who don't. One study compared attitudes of English-speaking students who chose or did not choose to visit a French-Canadian city (Clement et al., 1977). Before the visit the attitudes toward the French were more positive for those choosing to go than for those not choosing. Or perhaps we all transfer our feelings about our situation to those with whom we make contact. Those who volunteer may like their situation and those they meet more than those who are forced into the situation.

When the prevailing norms favor interracial association and egalitarian attitudes, contact is more effective in reducing prejudice (Cook, S. W., 1972). If you move from a prejudiced, segregated neighborhood to an unprejudiced, integrated neighborhood, you will find less social support for your old prejudices and new support for unprejudiced attitudes. Such norms are important in changing and maintaining attitudes.

In order to study how norms affect our attitudes, Foley (1976) studied new inmates of a prison who had been assigned to various areas. After measuring the prejudices of old inmates in these areas, Foley measured the prejudices of the incoming inmates. Three weeks later, she again measured the prejudices of the new inmates. Foley found that, in general, prejudice decreased in the various areas. But how prejudice changed depended on the norms that prevailed in the living area. In highly prejudiced areas prejudice increased more often than decreased. In areas of less prejudice the prejudice of new inmates tended to decrease.

Another finding of this study was that personality variables predicted change in prejudice for people in relatively unprejudiced living areas. But when prejudice was very high, personality variables didn't matter. Some situations allow individual differences to affect behavior, and some situations don't.

This kind of research can be done by social psychologists in their laboratories and in field settings. It is important, because the problem of prejudice is important in society. Reducing prejudice will reduce discrimination and injustice. But we need to know how to do it. Research such as that described here can help by specifying conditions under which contact will be effective in reaching our goals. Without such research we cannot predict whether integration will have positive or negative effects on prejudice.

We should strongly favor integration, because *separate* has historically meant *unequal*. But if integration is to result in a reduction in racism, we must be especially careful that the conditions of this contact are favorable to the development of positive attitudes.

Solution: Intergroup Cooperation.   One of the conditions of contact which seems to reduce intergroup conflict is that of **cooperation.** Intergroup cooperation occurs when two groups are working toward a common goal—when a gain for one group means a gain for the other and a loss for one is a loss for the other. (**Competition** occurs when one group's gain is the other's loss.)

Cooperation seems to be a powerful positive force. Studies (reviewed in Worchel, S., 1979) find that cooperation can lead to more communication, trust, attraction, satisfaction, helpfulness, and so on. Such effects are remarkable in both their strength and diversity.

How can such varied effects be explained? Diffusion-of-affect theory might apply here, suggesting that the negative feelings produced by conflict might in turn spread and color attitudes and behaviors toward the other groups. These negative feelings may lead to avoidance, hostility, suspiciousness, and distrust. As long as the negative feelings persist, such negative behaviors may persist as well.

If the two groups can be induced to cooperate, then cooperation will have a chance to produce positive feelings, particularly if cooperation is successful in helping the two groups reach their goals. Such positive feelings, in turn, may give rise to varied positive attitudes and behaviors, including increased trust, satisfaction, attraction, and helpfulness. Further, positive moods usually result in more activity of any sort (see Chapter 5). Hence, cooperation may lead to more communication, more contact, and so on. Diffusion-of-affect theory suggests that it is not the cooperation per se but rather the good feelings generated by the cooperation that are responsible for reducing intergroup conflict.

If cooperation is so important, how can it be increased? How can cooperation be promoted between groups that may prefer to avoid each other and that feel hostility, suspiciousness, and distrust toward each other? Stephen Worchel (1979) has reviewed several approaches.

One way is for each group to show the other that its behavior is contingent on the behavior of the other. Any unconditional pacifist strategies (such as turning the other cheek and behaving cooperatively when the other party is behaving competitively) may meet with failure, because the "nice guy" is taken advantage of (Shure, Meeker, & Hansford, 1965; Solomon, 1960).

Secondly, cooperation will be most easily brought about when both groups are similar in their ability to threaten each other—and when their use of such threats is low. Any negotiation that involves the use of threats is not likely to lead to cooperation. Charles Osgood (1962) has suggested a **GRIT strategy** for accomplishing this. GRIT stands for graduated reciprocation in tension-reduction, and the idea is that one party makes a small reduction in its ability to threaten the other and makes this concession known to the other. The first party then invites the second to make a similar reduction. If this occurs, the first party makes a further reduction, and so on. The GRIT strategy was developed to deal with international conflict, and it is easy to imagine how it might work with such conflicts, where threat potential is clear. It may be more difficult to apply to smaller disputes, such as those involving a husband and wife or teachers and the school board.

Finally, communication is necessary but not sufficient for reducing intergroup conflict and developing intergroup cooperation. Without communication, no cooperation is possible. But what is communicated determines the effectiveness of the communication process. If communication is used to insult, deceive, or threaten, then it contributes to conflict rather than to cooperation (Siegel & Fouraker, 1960).

Solution: Income Transfer.   One of the best-known approaches to helping targets of prejudice is redistributing income. The poor in the United States have been offered assistance by a negative income tax (those with higher salaries pay proportionately higher taxes), by earnings supplements (those who have low salaries may receive additional income from the government), by children's allowances (the more children you have, the lower your taxes), and so on. Such assistance is usually monetary and is usually offered on the basis of income. Is this the best approach? Garfinkel, Haveman, and Betson (1977) suggest that it may not be.

For instance, evidence reviewed earlier in this chapter showed that the poor work as hard as the wealthy. But the poor have lower income capacities than the wealthy because of differences in educational level, geographic distribution, and so on. Social programs designed to end poverty, rather than simply make it acceptable, would be more effective if they increased the income capacity of the poor. In the long run, providing the poor with the same quality and amount of education as the wealthy would help break the cycle of poverty.

Solution: Equity-Based Penalties.   Many conflicts between people are "settled" by the justice system. The courts punish those who break the law, in the hope that the punishment will deter others from similar offenses. Offenders are also sen-

tenced in hopes of rehabilitating them and, in some cases, in an effort to remove them from society. As Philip Brickman (1977) has wisely pointed out, though, justice is not served by these purposes. To effectively deter, we must punish more severely than is just. To rehabilitate, we might require some program that does not even involve punishment. Justice is better served by a judicial system that operates on an "equity" basis—that is, a system whose purpose is to restore fairness.

In sports, where conflict is part of the game, equity-based principles work well (Brickman, 1977). Losing a stroke in golf, getting a free shot in basketball, and losing yardage on the football field are examples of such penalties. All restore fairness and regulate behavior. They are given immediately, are based on the consequences of the offense, and are in proportion to what was gained by the offense. Sports do have some deterrent-based penalties—to prevent hitting below the belt, moving your golf ball, and so on. In contrast to equity-based penalties, such penalties are designed to prevent deviance. They are given after some delay, are based on intentions, and are disproportionate to what was gained by the offense. The deterrent-based penalties of sports resemble the criminal justice system in many ways (Brickman, 1977).

One advantage of an equity-based system of justice is that victims of crimes would receive some compensation for their loss as well as gaining a sense that justice had been done. In the present deterrent-based system, if you are robbed, you will spend days in court, the robber may go to prison, and you will go home penniless. A civil suit against a robber is expensive and may be worthless. Victims of crimes end up resenting the justice system and the criminal. But an equity-based system could offer compensation and other help to victims and require those convicted of crimes to "work off" the costs of compensating victims and processing the matter in the court. There would be justice in such a system of justice. Readers interested in learning more about such a system should read Brickman's (1977) provocative article on the subject.

Solution: More Legislation against Discrimination.   Blacks work as hard as Whites but earn less. Much of this gap appears to result from discrimination in the labor market. Between 43% and 60% of the racial income gap for men is attributable to discrimination, and between 30% and 39% of the gap between Black and White families results from job-market discrimination (Garfinkel, Haveman, & Betson, 1977). The male/female income gap is similarly traceable, in part, to job-market discrimination. Legislation has recently played a role in reducing such discrimination. More legislation may be able to reduce it further.

Solution: Paralegal Action.   According to recent surveys (Law Enforcement Assistance Administration, 1978), 10% of city dwellers report feeling somewhat unsafe or very unsafe being alone in their neighborhoods during the day. At night, this percentage climbs to 45%. Most people (82%) think that the crime rate has been increasing nationally, especially for crimes of violence. These fears are not directly related to victimization rates. For instance, older women are much more fearful than young men, even though young men are much more likely to be assault victims.

When people become anxious or fearful, they may affiliate with others who feel the same. Such affiliation in itself may reduce tension. It may also lead to collective action that confronts and reduces the source of tension. When this happens, there is both perceived and real safety in numbers.

For many city dwellers street crime is a source of considerable fear and anxiety. These feelings have led to the creation of neighborhood block associations. Effective block associations share much with cohesive small groups: they promote interaction among members; they help develop an identification with the group and, by association, promote a sense of community in the neighborhood. Through discussion and opportunities for action they provide feelings of control and responsibility and reduce the fear of crime. In addition, they may actually reduce the incidence of crime. Muggers in such a neighborhood must contend with citizen patrols (Baumgold, 1973), alarm systems, and bystanders willing to become involved. One member of a citizen patrol summed it up this way:

> Before we had the civilian patrol, no one knew anyone else. . . . Now they're talking to each other, and there's the beginning of a community feeling. We started learning about safety. If someone was screaming, we'd go for help. I liked it. It was a great feeling. And I met people and it got me out of the house and onto the street. Best of all, we caught muggers left and right [Shephard, 1973, quoted in Huston & Korte, 1974, p. 42].

People trained in social psychology could do much to help start block associations, maintain them should they succeed in lowering the crime rate or fear of crime, and evaluate their effectiveness.

MORE WORK NEEDED

Social psychologists have indeed made progress in understanding conflict between groups, although not enough attention has been devoted to solutions. Political leaders do not seem to have benefited from the research of social scientists, nor have individuals, judging from the level of conflict present in society. This may be partly a result of little communication between social scientists and the public and partly because much more work is needed on conflict resolution. Violent conflict, whether interpersonal or international, is so expensive and harmful that almost any amount of work on conflict resolution would be cost-beneficial. Perhaps you will want to do research, writing, or teaching on conflict.

SUMMARY

Intergroup relations are those between two or more groups and their members. This chapter focused on the conflict in intergroup relations, especially on the problems of prejudice and discrimination.

The chapter opened with a survey of some common instances of prejudice and discrimination: discrimination against the young and old, against women, against Blacks, against the poor, against the unattractive, and against the overweight. Such prejudice and discrimination is so common in everyday life and so devastating in its effects that it demands explanations and solutions.

Some (unsatisfactory) explanations focus on characteristics of the target of prejudice, although there is usually little objective, rational basis for such explanations. For it is simply not true that Blacks are poor because they do not work as hard as Whites. On the contrary, the evidence suggests that they may be working harder.

Other explanations focus on characteristics of the prejudiced person. Prejudiced people have been described as having authoritarian personalities and as being ethnocentric. The amount of similarity between the source and target and the familiarity of the source with the target also seem to play a role in prejudice.

Social processes themselves often generate prejudice and discrimination. Labeling someone with a derogatory term (such as *delinquent*) may change his or her behavior in a direction that justifies the label as well as changing the behavior of others toward the person. Competition between groups is a common source of tension that often leads to prejudice. Cooperation between groups, in contrast, may reduce tension and reduce prejudice. The Robbers-Cave experiment demonstrated how this can take place.

Social systems may generate prejudice through their design or when they are disrupted. The economic aspects of a social system seem to be quite important in their influence on prejudice and discrimination.

How can intergroup conflict be reduced? A variety of solutions were presented. Increased contact between the two groups often seems to be quite effective when the contact is intimate and voluntary and occurs in a positive context in which norms favor egalitarian contact. Intergroup cooperation is another potentially useful means of conflict reduction, if it can be achieved. Other solutions that have been proposed include income transfer, equity-based penalties, more legislation against discrimination, and paralegal action.

More research, writing, and teaching on intergroup relations is needed.

GLOSSARY TERMS

Define these terms in your own words, then look them up in the glossary at the back of the book.

Body types	Ethnocentrism
Capacity utilization	GRIT strategy
Competition	In-group
Conflict	Intergroup relations
Cooperation	Labeling
Discrimination	Mesomorph
Earnings capacity	Out-group
Ectomorph	Prejudice
Endomorph	Recidivism

FURTHER READING

You might want to browse through past issues of these journals in your library: the *Journal of Conflict Resolution,* the *Journal of Peace Research,* and the *Journal of Social Issues.*

Allport, G. W. *The nature of prejudice.* Reading, Mass.: Addison-Wesley, 1954.

Austin, W. G., & Worchel, S. (Eds.). *The social psychology of intergroup relations.* Monterey, Calif.: Brooks/Cole, 1979.

Brickman, P. Crime and punishment in sports and society. *Journal of Social Issues,* 1977, *33,* 140–164.

Coser, L. *The functions of social conflict.* Glencoe, Ill.: Free Press, 1956.

Dahrendorf, R. *Class and class conflict in industrial society.* Stanford, Calif.: Stanford University Press, 1959.

Deutsch, M. *The resolution of conflict.* New Haven, Conn.: Yale University Press, 1973.

epilogue:

Employment as a Social Psychologist

JOB PROSPECTS

If you enjoyed this course and did well in it, you might consider becoming a social psychologist. Social psychologists typically have a Ph.D., which requires four or more years of graduate work. Some have master's degrees, and others work as researchers and research assistants in industry with a bachelor's degree.

Largely because undergraduate enrollment has been leveling off, the current need for social psychologists in academic settings is fairly low (Kessler, McKenna, Russell, Stang, & Sweet, 1976). This low demand is expected to continue, according to some sources (for example, see U.S. Department of Labor, 1976), causing a reduction in enrollments in graduate school, some underemployment (employment that does not use the full range of a person's training and that is not altogether satisfying), but little unemployment. Probably only one-fifth of this year's new Ph.D. social psychologists will work in academic settings. As V. L. Hamilton (1977) has concluded, "The future of the majority of psychologically trained social psychologists lies outside of psychology departments" (p. 4).

Although some academic social psychologists call themselves applied social psychologists, nearly all the nonacademically employed are involved in applying social psychology. They are applied social psychologists, applied psychologists, research scientists, research associates, directors of personnel, industrial psychologists, consulting psychologists, psychologists, and so on.

Applied social psychologists are needed for several reasons. One is that we are now aware of many limitations of our academic laboratory research. Researchers who restrict themselves to studying unacquainted sophomore psychology majors find themselves with problems. It may be difficult, we now know, to generalize from these subjects and settings to others. Applied social psychologists do research on more varied populations in more varied settings. Such research, when reported in psychology's journals, can be very valuable in establishing the generality of psychological principles and developing new ones. Although academics sometimes call their nonapplied research *pure research*, applied research can be just as pure and just as important in theory testing.

One measure of the need for more *applied* social psychologists is a survey of job-placement centers that psychologists use. In 1974 there were 2.4 applicants for every academic psychology job and 1.6 applicants for every clinical and counseling job. But there were only .9 applicants for every industrial and applied job advertised. More evidence comes from an analysis of starting salaries. In 1974, the median annual salary for a Ph.D. with no experience was $13,000 for academics, $15,000 for those starting in hospitals and clinics, and $15,400 for those starting in government. So nonacademic salaries are typically higher. Still more evidence comes from a study of job-market perceptions conducted by Stang, McKenna and Kessler (1978). Job applicants guessed that the average academic job opening received about 100 applications and that the average nonacademic opening received only 50.

Nonacademic jobs appear very desirable in several ways. Levy (1976) surveyed a large group of social psychologists and found nonacademic environments growing in importance as locations for social psychologists. Academic environments were relatively stable. The academic subgroups in Levy's sample believed that additional social psychologists would be "of little value" to them. But the nonacademics felt that additional social psychologists would contribute "a fair amount" to their settings. Both groups expressed equal subjective satisfaction with their present employment environment and were substantially secure in their employment. Nonacademics felt more strongly than academics that a change in employment would be unlikely. Surprisingly, nonacademic social psychologists indicated a greater ability to decide how to spend their professional time than did the academic sample. Further, although the nonacademic social psychologists averaged a 42-hour week, compared with 51 hours for their academic counterparts, nonacademics appeared to average about $3000 more a year in income.

In summary, there is probably a job for you in social psychology, applying your perspectives, knowledge, and research methods to dealing with important social problems. The job you take may be in a college or university but is more likely to be in a nonacademic setting. If you are like other social psychologists surveyed, you will be well satisfied with a career in social psychology.

AN EXPANDING PROFESSION

You have seen that social psychology can make an important contribution toward our understanding and solution of social problems. And it can help us to better understand ourselves and our world. The future of the profession seems bright, in part because of its usefulness and in part because it is growing and expanding into new, important areas. As the field continues to grow, new topics will be added, and the field will become broader and broader. The inevitable result will be a more comprehensive and balanced perspective on social behavior. Some likely new topics are the quality of life, technology and work, and the use of leisure. Some older topics may increase in importance as interests shift—the nature of culture, "culture" in animal societies, the self, cognitive organization, and social organization. Some interesting research methods may become more common, such as cross-cultural research, naturalistic studies, archival studies, and single-case designs. And some of the familiar topics may undergo change and growth as new perspectives are developed. For instance, our knowledge of physiology, cognition, and social development may influence traditional topics and approaches. Social psychology is a growing field. You can be a part of it.

But whether you join the profession and work in the field or choose another career and watch social psychology from a distance, individuals in society will benefit from the profession's activities. I hope you have benefited from this book.

FURTHER READING

Fretz, B., & Stang, D. J. *Preparing for graduate study in psychology: Not for seniors only!* Washington, D.C.: American Psychological Association, 1980.

Schultz, D. P. *The science of psychology: Critical reflections.* New York: Appleton-Century-Crofts, 1970.

Woods, P. *Career opportunities for psychologists: Expanding and emerging areas.* Washington, D.C.: American Psychological Association, 1976.

Glossary

acculturation The transmission of culture between generations of the same society.

achieved role Any social status (for example, physician, mother, Catholic, Republican) that is chosen or earned by the individual.

achievement motivation An internal drive (first measured by McClelland) that impels the individual to perform tasks as quickly and proficiently as possible.

acquiescent response set A tendency or predisposition to agree with statements, particularly in paper-and-pencil measures of opinions.

actor/observer divergent perspectives hypothesis The finding that actors consistently explain their own behaviors in terms of situations, whereas observers explain the same behaviors in terms of dispositions.

adaptation-level theory A statement of social-judgment processes, proposed by Helson, in which the individual sees his or her own characteristics as a reference point from which others are compared.

affiliation An internal drive that impels the individual to seek the company of others in order to obtain protection, emotional support, or social-comparison information.

aggression Intentional behavior that is directed toward the goal of bringing harm or injury to another person or object.

altruism Behavior that is directed toward helping others at cost to oneself or without commensurate reward. The behavioral definition focuses on the outcome of the behavior (behavior that produces help), while the motivational definition focuses on the intention behind the behavior (behavior intended to help).

androgens Male hormones that are believed to influence the development of greater musculature and aggressiveness in men than in women.

androgyny (psychological androgyny) A psychological characteristic (first measured by Sandra Bem) that empowers the individual to exhibit the desirable behaviors characteristic of both sexes.

anxiety A personality trait (first measured by Taylor) through which an individual experiences strong and undifferentiated feelings of dread and apprehension. As a state, anxiety is a more transitory emotional condition that is less likely to be determined by dispositional than by situational variables.

application rules Statements of limiting conditions that determine when a specific theory or hypothesis applies to the social behavior under investigation.

archival research Use of written records (vital statistics, diaries, newspapers and the like), for the formulation and testing of hypotheses and theories. Archival research is less reactive than experimental research, but it does not allow for the manipulation of independent variables.

arousal One's level of physiological activation. Schachter found that individuals identify emotional states through perceptions of situationally appropriate feelings and self-perception of their own arousal.

ascribed role Any social status (for example, woman, Hispanic, or appointed leader) that is neither chosen nor earned, but rather "given"—as a result of biological or social processes—to an individual.

assimilation Judging the attitude of another person whose position is close to one's own as even closer than it really is.

atmospheric ions Tiny air particles with positive or negative electric charges. Positive ions are assumed to cause "negative" behaviors, and vice versa.

attention The application of conscious awareness to a stimulus. Stimuli that are not attended to are unlikely to elicit social behavior.

attitude A relatively permanent tendency to respond to a specific object, person, or place with a positive or negative orientation. Fully developed attitudes consist of distinct cognitive, affective, and behavioral components.

attitude object A person, place, event, or thing toward which an attitude is directed. Presentation of the attitude object frequently serves as a stimulus in scientific studies of attitude organization and change.

attitude stability The extent to which an individual's attitude persists across time and different situations. Attitudes that fulfill important personality needs are the most resistant to change.

attractiveness Personal attributes that determine the extent to which others will feel attraction toward an individual. Some attributes (for example, physical attractiveness) appear to induce attraction immediately. Other attributes (for example, attitude similarity) emerge from preliminary social interaction.

attributional approach to social perception The view that observers ascribe personality traits to others by making inferences from observed behaviors to unobserved personal dispositions.

audience effects Characteristics of an audience (such as education, occupation, religion) that affect its responses to different types of persuasive communication.

authoritarian personality A related cluster of personality traits (measured by the California F Scale) that includes submission to authority; repression of sexual impulses; denial of feelings; an emphasis on power, status, and dominance in interpersonal relations; and other personal characteristics associated with a fascist political orientation.

autokinetic effect The apparent movement of a stationary point of light in a completely darkened room. Sherif found that individual judgments of autokinetic movement tend to converge around a group norm that emerges from social interaction.

availability (*see* **field of availables**)

balanced state A condition described by balance theory in which three or more unit relationships are consistent among themselves in terms of positive or negative values.

balance theory A statement of cognitive processes that assumes pressures toward balanced unit relationships among all of the individual's attitudes.

behavior intentions Subjects' intentions to behave in specific ways in the presence of specified stimuli. Intentions are usually measured by asking subjects to describe their anticipated behaviors, and these measures frequently substitute for the measurement of overt behavior in attitude research.

biased sample A sample that does not accurately represent the population from which it is supposed to be drawn. For example, subjects who volunteer for social-psychology experiments may differ from paid subjects, thus representing a biased sample of the population under study.

birth order Ordinal birth position. It has important influences on the development of the individual's personality and cognitive processes.

body-adjustment test A technique for the assessment of individual differences in field dependence. Subjects are required to raise their chairs to an upright position in a specially tilted room.

body language Nonverbal behaviors and cues that intentionally or unintentionally provide others with information about one's moods and feelings. An individual's body language may or may not be consistent with what he or she is expressing verbally.

body types Three distinct kinds of physique—ectomorph, mesomorph, and endomorph—first studied by Sheldon. Constitutional psychologists believe that an individual's personality is closely related to his or her body type.

boomerang effect A situation in which the recipients of a persuasive communication change their attitudes in a direction opposite to that intended by the communicator.

butterfly curve A diagrammatic representation of the finding that slight discrepancies from one's adaptation level are pleasant, whereas extreme discrepancies are unpleasant.

capacity utilization The extent to which an individual or family achieves its theoretically maximum income, based on age, sex, education, job opportunities, current salaries, and other factors.

carpentered world hypothesis The hypothesis that living in environments in which walls and ceilings meet at right angles gives rise to differing visual expectations (and optical illusions) than living in other, nonangular environments such as igloos or grass huts.

categorization The process in which people or objects are sorted into a smaller number of categories or sets on the basis of certain similarities and differences.

catharsis A hypothetical process in which people experience a reduction in tension, frustration, or anger by observing (or sometimes by engaging in) aggression.

cause A variable that is sufficient to determine a specifiable change in an individual's cognitions, feelings, or behaviors. The establishment of causality requires experimental manipulation of the variables under study.

centrality An individual's location in a communication structure. Central positions permit communication with most other members, but peripheral positions restrict communication with others.

centralization A measure of the number of two-way communication channels in an entire group. Compared to decentralized groups, centralized groups develop more rapidly, display more consensus, provide greater member satisfaction, and may be more efficient at problem solving.

central traits The trait dimensions that are most inportant for determining the individual's complete impressions of others. Central traits influence the perception of peripheral traits, and the warm/cold dimension appears to be the most central of all traits.

channels Open channels permit two-way communication between pairs of group members, and closed channels restrict communication. In natural settings status, proximity, and similarity are important determinants of channel openness between people.

check on the manipulation Any method by which an experimenter determines whether the **independent variable** (the "manipulation") was experienced by the subject, thus determining whether the independent variable could have affected the dependent variable(s).

coaction effects Changes in individual levels of task performance that result from the presence of coworkers. Coaction effects are produced by the mere presence of others engaged in the same task, not from communication, productivity norms, or other social processes.

coercive power Control over another person's behavior that results from the capacity to punish.

cognition A unit of knowledge, belief, or evaluation held by an individual about his or her environment, behavior, or self.

cognitive Resulting from brain activity; mental.

cognitive-dissonance theory A consistency theory of attitude organization and change proposed by Festinger. Dissonance results from an inconsistency between two or more cognitive elements, and Festinger's theory assumes that individuals will change their attitudes in order to alleviate dissonance and attain consonance.

cognitive theory of emotion A statement proposed by Schachter in which individuals define their emotions in terms of cognitive explanations of their situations and self-perceived levels of arousal.

cohesiveness The forces that increase and sustain group solidarity. Cohesive groups are more likely to provide their individual members with attractive interactions, inherent values, and opportunities to achieve many goals.

collative variables Conditions that derive their meaning from the comparison of two or more diverse experiences. Primary examples of collative variables include novelty, unexpectedness, uncertainty, conflict, and complexity.

collective behavior Actions of large aggregates of people that cannot be performed by individuals or very small groups. Wars and revolutions are examples of collective behavior.

commitment A personal decision to engage in a specific behavior. In cognitive-dissonance research, high levels of commitment to behaviors contrary to one's initial beliefs facilitate attitude change.

common sense Cultural knowledge that constitutes shared and standardized explanations and interpretations of social behavior. As such, common sense provides a useful beginning for scientific inquiry, but it lacks application rules that state the limiting conditions of proverbs and other cultural generalizations.

communication network The pattern of open channels in a small group or organization. Networks are also diagrammatic representations of these channels, and communication networks have been the subject of considerable research.

comparative appraisal An evaluation of one's own beliefs, emotions, or behaviors that results from comparison with the beliefs, emotions, or behaviors of others. A comparison group provides the opportunity for appraisal of one's characteristics from observation of several other people.

competition Contending against others in order to obtain scarce goals or rewards.

complementary needs A theory of interpersonal attraction and mate selection proposed by Winch. Complementarity occurs when each member of a dyad has needs that are expressed in behavior that is rewarding to the second member.

compliance A type of conforming or obedient behavior that results from the use of coercive power. Behaviors resulting from compliance thus tend to be unstable and limited to situations in which the person is under the surveillance of one who exercises power.

confederate A person used as an agent to serve specific purposes in a deception experiment. Most frequently, confederates pose as other experimental subjects, members of crowds, experimenter's assistants, or passersby.

confidentiality The assurance that embarrassing, immoral, illegal, and undesirable behaviors disclosed by an experimental subject will be treated as privileged communications. Because social psychologists are not legally entitled to privileged information, however, confidentiality cannot always be assured.

conflict Direct and conscious struggle between individuals or groups for the same scarce resources. At the intrapersonal level, conflict results when an individual must choose between two or more mutually incompatible alternatives.

conformity Behavior that is in accord with the expectations of a social group. Determinants of conformity involve some type of group pressure, and conformity based on compliance is most often viewed as a temporary change in behavior.

confounding A misleading experimental finding that results from the unanticipated correlation of the independent variables with genuinely causal variables. For example, fear-arousing appeals may fail to induce attitude change in persuasive communication, because they are confounded with the variable of message credibility.

connotative meaning Beliefs and feelings about a person, place, or object that are not included in its precise definition. For example, a wolf is a large wild dog, but the connotative meanings of *wolf* may include feelings of respect, fear, or hatred. Connotative meanings generally include our evaluation of an object's goodness, strength, and activity.

consensual validation A process by which individuals determine the validity of their ideas and feelings through comparison with the ideas and feelings of others.

consensus The identification of areas of agreement and common definitions of the situation by persons who are engaged in joint undertakings.

consistency A condition in which many different behaviors lead an observer to infer the existence of an enduring trait or disposition in the personality of the subject under investigation.

content analysis A procedure by which written and narrative materials are converted to numerical data for statistical analysis. Content analysis is reliable to the extent that its rules are clear and lead different raters to the same numerical data.

control Occurs when an experimenter can consistently cause the appearance of a response by the manipulation of specified stimulus conditions. Control is neither a necessary nor sufficient condition for prediction and understanding, and it is the principal goal of technological development rather than scientific research.

control system The description of social behaviors that occur in circular causal chains. For example, high levels of self-esteem may lead to improved task performance, which in turn leads to more stable feelings of self-esteem.

conventions Socially prescribed standards of behavior for which violators receive intermediate punishments. For example, public nudity is a more serious offense than jaywalking but a less serious one than murder.

cooperation The act of working together for mutual benefit. Cooperation is most frequently studied in mixed-motive games, interactions in which players choose either competitive or cooperative responses.

correction for incredulity The finding that large discrepancies between sources and messages reduce the impact of persuasive communications. For example, if it were said that the Pope endorsed Communism, the resulting incredibility might lead people to ignore both the source and the statement.

correlational method A relationship of two (or more) variables, such that an increase in one variable is consistently associated with an increase or decrease in the second variable. High correlations make it possible to predict the value of one variable from knowledge of the second variable. But the existence of correlation does not provide evidence for causal relationships among variables.

cost/benefit analysis The assumption that people make rational choices that simultaneously maximize rewards or benefits and minimize costs or risks. For example, a cost/benefit analysis of helping behavior suggests that people are most likely to act altruistically when they have much to gain and little to lose.

cover story The presentation of false, misleading, or incomplete information about the purpose of an experiment. Cover stories are used to control the potential effects of the subject's expectations, and they should be followed by careful debriefing.

crowd A temporary grouping of individuals with a common interest and physical proximity. Crowds are frequently classified as acting, casual, conventionalized, and expressive.

crowding The experience of restricted space and the motivation to alleviate such feelings. Crowding is an individual experience, whereas density is a physical variable that is a measure of people per unit of space.

Crutchfield apparatus A cluster of isolated booths that enables experimenters to study the conformity responses of several individuals at the same time. The apparatus is more efficient than the Asch-type procedure, in which several confederates are required in order to manipulate the social judgments of one naive subject.

cultural diffusion The processes by which two (or more) societies have an impact on each other. The present industrial development of the Third-World nations is an example of cultural diffusion.

culture The way of life of a social group, including all of the material and nonmaterial products of group life that are transmitted from one generation to the next. The most essential characteristics of culture are widely shared ideas and values.

culture shock The extreme stress experienced by members of one culture when they suddenly find themselves immersed in a different culture. Culture shock is especially likely to occur among immigrants, exchange students, and residents of occupied countries.

curvilinear relationship A description of a curved rather than linear relationship between two or more variables. For example, both extremely plausible and implausible sources may evoke less attitude change than persuasive communications emanating from somewhat plausible sources.

data reduction Procedures for the conversion of scientific information into manageable quantitative terms. Descriptive statistics prepare the data for summary presentation and for further statistical analysis.

decentralization The extent to which the communication channels in a small group are closed. Decentralized groups may be less satisfying and less efficient at solving problems.

deception Giving subjects incorrect or incomplete information about the method or purpose of an experiment. Cover stories, props, confederates, and false information are used to keep subjects unaware of the hypothesis under study. Use of deception presents serious ethical problems for experimenters in social psychology.

decode To transform information into more useful forms. In communication processes decoding occurs when incoming signals are transformed into meaningful messages.

deduction The process by which experimental hypotheses are derived from scientific theories or specific predictions or explanations are created from more general principles.

definition of the situation A process by which an individual examines and evaluates a situation in order to decide which attitudes and behaviors are appropriate. The individual's definition of any situation will be similar to the definitions of others who share common values and experiences.

deindividuation Any process by which individuals may assume reduced responsibility for their own behaviors. The most widely studied determinant of deindividuation is anonymity, and the most common outcome is antisocial behavior.

demand characteristics The characteristics of an experiment that convey to subjects the desired outcome of the research.

denotative meaning The formal definition of a word. It involves minimal affect and evaluation.

density The number of people who occupy a given area of space. Density, a physical measurement, is contrasted to crowding, which refers to psychological feelings of restraint.

dependent measure The method used by an experimenter to assess the dependent variable (see **dependent variable**).

dependent variable A variable that is expected to depend on or be affected by some prior causal variable (see **dependent measure**).

descriptive personal theory An individual's belief about the relationships among different personality traits in other people. For example, the belief that redheaded people are hot tempered is an example of a descriptive personal theory.

descriptive research Nonexperimental studies that are designed to provide the greatest possible information about a social behavior and its correlates. Descriptive research can be contrasted with experimental research, or efforts to test explanatory or causal theories and hypotheses about social behavior.

determinism The view that all human behavior is determined by antecedent causes. Determinism rejects the idea of free will, and different theories of social behavior embrace determinism to different degrees.

diffusion of affect The spread of emotions that have been caused by one event so that they influence contiguous thoughts, feelings, and behaviors. For example, individuals consistently show greater liking for strangers after pleasant rather than unpleasant experiences.

diffusion of responsibility The finding that individuals are less likely to take responsible action in larger groups of people.

diffusion-of-responsibility hypothesis Use of diffusion of responsibility to explain several different social behaviors, including the failure of bystanders to respond to emergencies and tendencies for groups to make riskier decisions than individuals.

discrimination The inequitable treatment of people who belong to a group that is considered to be inferior. Discrimination also refers to the process by which stimuli are identified as different from one another.

displacement A psychoanalytic defense mechanism through which negative feelings caused by one source are attributed to a second and inappropriate source. For example, an employee who has difficulties with his employer might direct his hostile feelings toward his wife.

dispositional approach The view that personality and other individual differences are the primary determinants of social behavior. The dispositional approach is frequently contrasted with the situational approach to social behavior.

dissonance A hypothetical cognitive tension state that may arise when a person becomes aware that he or she holds contradictory, incompatible thoughts or beliefs.

distinctiveness An aspect of an individual's behavior that enables observers to draw plausible inferences about the causes of that behavior.

division of labor An integrated system of occupational roles or specializations within a society. The individual's roles as a producer and consumer frequently have important implications for noneconomic aspects of social interaction.

dogmatism A personality characteristic (first measured by Rokeach) that involves closed-mindedness, rigid adherence to authoritarian beliefs, and intolerance. The dogmatism scale purports to measure general rather than right-wing authoritarianism.

drive A hypothetical construct that summarizes the variety of physiological states that motivate goal-directed behavior. Acquired drives have been learned through social interaction rather than physiological inheritance.

dyad A two-person group. Bridge partnerships and marriages are examples of dyadic social interactions.

dyadic effect The tendency to reciprocate self-disclosure in a dyad: The more you tell me about yourself, the more I'm likely to tell you about me.

dynamic The processes by which we form and reform our impressions of others whom we perceive in social interaction.

earnings capacity An individual's probable future income level. For example, a beginning physician may earn less than a construction worker, but his or her earnings capacity is greater.

ectomorph One of the three basic body types identified by Sheldon. Ectomorphs show a thin and angular appearance.

ego-defensive function An attitude function that serves as a defense mechanism.

encode To transform information from a form most suitable for understanding to forms most suitable for transmission and storage.

endomorph One of Sheldon's basic body types. Endomorphs are fat and corpulent.

endurance The extent to which individuals tolerate noxious environmental stimuli without deterioration of their cognitive, emotional, and behavioral processes.

estrogens Hormones that may be responsible for greater field dependency and other sex-linked behaviors characteristic of human females.

ethnocentrism An attitude that regards one's own culture or group as inherently superior to others in all respects. Ethnocentrism consistently leads the individual to rejection of those who are "different."

evaluation apprehension A concern one feels to receive a positive or favorable evaluation from others. Evaluation apprehension frequently leads subjects to engage in cooperative and helpful behavior in experimental settings.

exchanged power A capacity to control the behavior of others that emerges from the results of previous social interaction. For example, a group will transfer some decision-making power to its elected leaders.

experimental design The plan of an experiment. It specifies how subjects will be selected and assigned to various experimental conditions, how independent variables will be manipulated, how dependent variables will be measured, and how the data that are collected will be analyzed.

experimental realism The extent to which an experiment captures the subjects' attention and involvement.

experimenter-expectancy effects Any of the complex processes through which an experimenter's beliefs and expectations regarding the outcome of the experiment come to influence and bias that outcome; experimenter bias.

expert power Power or influence potential that derives from one's mastery of some relevant knowledge or skill.

explanatory personal theory An individual's beliefs concerning the causation of some event. For instance, believing that a person acted belligerently because he or she has red hair would be an explanatory personal theory (*see* **descriptive personal theory**).

explanatory research A type of research that seeks to understand why or how things happen (*see* **descriptive research).**

expressive function An attitude function in which an individual's identity is established and maintained through holding certain attitudes and expressing certain opinions.

external locus of control In Rotter's social-learning theory, the subjects' perceptions that their behaviors are governed by forces that lie beyond their personal control.

extreme response style Subjects' frequent endorsement of the most extreme responses on attitude and personality scales. Infrequent endorsement of neutral and moderate responses is a potential source of systematic bias in personality and attitude scales.

false-feedback studies Experiments in which subjects receive incorrect information about their own behavior, feelings, beliefs, or attitudes. False feedback is also used to provide subjects with incorrect information about the attitudes and behaviors of others.

favored descriptors The traits that an individual is most likely to use in thinking about and describing other people.

fear A strong emotion that is experienced by persons who are confronted with real, imagined, or expected danger or pain. Fear is characterized by physiological changes and a strong desire to withdraw from the fear-arousing situation.

fear of failure A motive that leads subjects to behaviors that minimize risks rather than maximize rewards. In research on achievement motivation, low-need achievers frequently choose impossibly difficult or extraordinarily easy tasks in order to minimize fear of failure.

fear of success Negative feelings that result from the expectation that assertive and successful behavior may not be consistent with one's ideal self-concept. For example, women may not pursue occupational success as avidly as men because of fears of decreased "femininity."

feedback A process in which knowledge of the results of past performance leads to modification of future performance. In social behavior one person may tell others how they are perceived, and this may affect the subsequent social behaviors of those persons.

feedback loop A communication pattern in which two (or more) people alternately respond to each other (or one another), providing ongoing feedback to each other (or one another).

field independence/dependence A personality characteristic (measured by Witkin) that involves perceptual and intellectual style. Field dependence is usually assessed with the rod-and-frame test, and field-independent people are those who are least influenced by the tilt of the frame. Field independence/dependence has been correlated with extroversion, creativity, and sex differences.

field of availables The total number of people with whom the individual might develop an intimate relationship. The processes of friendship and mate selection progressively narrow the field of availables until the individual establishes intimate relationships with only a few others.

filtering processes The steps by which a large field of availables is narrowed down to a smaller number of intimate relationships. Characteristics such as physical attractiveness, attitude similarity, and similar educational status serve as filters in the process of friendship and mate selection.

folkways Social norms, or standards of behavior, that are socially approved but not considered to be of moral significance.

foot-in-the-door technique A procedure by which the likelihood of people's assenting to a large request is increased by first manipulating them to agree to a smaller request. It is an extraordinarily effective method of inducing compliance, possibly because it provides people with opportunities to see themselves as helpful persons.

forced compliance An experimental procedure that requires subjects to behave in a manner contrary to their attitudes or beliefs. Attitude change is especially likely to follow acts of forced compliance for which the subjects perceive considerable choice.

formal research Research that uses established guidelines and rigorous procedures to carefully study some phenomenon; contrasted with **personal research.**

frustration Any condition that blocks or otherwise interferes with goal-directed behavior. The frustration/aggression hypothesis holds that violence and conflict are the probable results of individual frustration.

functionalism The analysis of personality and social behavior in terms of the needs that they fulfill in social interaction. For example, the functional theory of attitude organization ties an individual's beliefs to needs for ego defense and enhancement.

future shock A term (proposed by Toffler) for negative cognitive, emotional, and behavioral responses to rapid culture change.

gender One's perception and presentation of self as masculine or feminine. *Gender* is socially defined, whereas *sex* refers to the biological definition of the individual as male or female.

generalization A step in the process of scientific inquiry. Generalization is part of the continuous cycle of scientific induction, generalization, deduction, and observation.

grammar Rules that regulate how the words of a language are to be organized into meaningful communication.

GRIT strategy A procedure proposed by Osgood for reducing international tensions. GRIT is an acronym for graduated and reciprocated initiatives in tension-reduction. GRIT involves mutual deescalation of international conflict and violence.

group Two or more people engaged in social interaction. Members of groups frequently have a common identity, shared feelings of unity, and similar goals and norms.

group-maintenance role Behaviors that reduce tension and conflict in the group, prevent its dissolution, and maintain cohesiveness, morale, and interdependence. The individuals who assume group maintenance roles are frequently defined as social-emotional specialists.

group pressure The normative expectations of others about one's behavior, feelings, and beliefs. The social influence processes through which the individual complies with these expectations.

group roles Specializations of labor that provide different statuses to different group members. Task leadership and social/emotional leadership are the two roles that emerge most consistently in small-group interaction.

group structure The stable patterns of attraction, power, status, leadership, and communication that emerge from group interaction.

groupthink A loss of critical and independent thought that results from efforts to maintain group cohesiveness, stability, and consensus.

habit A learned response that is "automatically" repeated without apparent effort or thought.

habituate To reduce the strength or rate of a response through continual exposure to a stimulus.

halo effect A response bias by which raters make consistently favorable or unfavorable evaluations of others on the basis of initial impressions.

hedonic relevance A principle of social perception through which perceivers interpret the characteristics of the perceived person in terms of their own motivations for social interaction.

helping Any action that benefits another person, irrespective of its benefits to oneself. A behavioral definition of helping focuses on the outcome of the behavior (whether or not another is helped), whereas a motivational definition focuses on the intention (whether or not help was intended).

historical reconstructionism The view that social history and individual biography are continuously reinterpreted in order to meet the needs of the present time.

homeostasis Any stable state within an organism or between an organism and its environment.

hurdles Explanations of discrepancies between individual statements of intended behavior and actual behavior. Because verbal behavior is frequently less effortful or less costly than overt behavior, the former is characterized by lower hurdles.

hypothetical construct A concept developed to explain the occurrence of any social behavior. Most hypothetical constructs (for example, *attitude, self, trait*) used in social psychology are metaphorical, and they are unlikely to have measurable physical referents.

idiosyncrasy credit An entitlement that enables an individual to deviate, innovate, and assert influence because of previously demonstrated conformity or competence.

I-E scale The attitude measure developed by Julian Rotter (1966) to assess internal/external locus of control.

image storage The process by which individuals briefly retain meaningless likenesses of the stimuli to which they have been exposed.

imitation The process by which individuals copy the behavior of others. Internalization and identification are cognitive and emotional processes that may or may not accompany imitation.

implicit personality theory Private beliefs that perceivers use to infer the existence of certain traits from knowledge of other traits. For example, the belief that warm people are also likely to be generous is a case of stereotype formation from implicit personality theory.

impression formation The stage of social perception in which perceivers acquire initial information about people they do not know.

impression management A form of self-presentation through which individuals attempt to create and maintain certain identities in their interactions with others.

incest taboo The universal prohibition of sexual relations between certain blood kin. The universality of incest taboos makes them attractive targets of both psychological and sociological explanations.

incomplete information A technique of experimental deception that withholds the purposes of an investigation from the subjects who participate in it.

independent variable A treatment manipulated by an experimenter in order to account for a social behavior under study. Some independent variables involve the classification of subjects on dimensions (for example, age, sex, race) that are not amenable to experimental manipulation.

induction The cognitive process in which generalizations, hypotheses, and theories are inferred from specific observations, facts and information (see **deduction**).

infatuation Feelings of "love at first sight." Infatuation is not likely to attain stability unless the individual's initial feelings of love are quickly reciprocated.

informational social influence A process in which an individual uses information or expert opinion as a method for the description and control of reality.

informed consent Subjects' voluntary participation in an experiment with full information about what the experimenter will require of them.

The policy of informed consent has been advocated by many who are concerned with the ethical problems of social-psychological research.

ingratiation Tactics used to obtain the support and approval of others. Compliments, flattery, false agreement, and conformity are widely used tactics of ingratiation.

in-group A group of people who experience a sense of stability, cohesiveness, loyalty, and common identity.

integration (1) The unification of formerly separate groups into a single group with the obliteration of social characteristics such as race, religion, sex, age, and ethnicity. Integration may also refer to a more personal acceptance of individuals who are members of other groups. (2) The process in which new information, facts, beliefs, and opinions are combined with older ones to "fit together" in a person's cognitive organization.

intelligence A hypothetical construct that is used to account for consistent variations in the quality of intellectual processes. The IQ, or intelligence quotient, is the individual's mental age divided by his or her chronological age. The IQ is best understood as an estimate of intelligence for a limited number of specific ability factors.

intended meaning That which the speaker wants listeners to understand from his or her communication.

interaction The basic social processes represented in a mutual relationship between two or more individuals.

interaction-process analysis A method developed by Bales for the observation of communication among group members in a systematic and quantitative fashion.

interaction rates The number of interactions observed between two (or more) persons in a specified period.

Rates of interaction frequently serve as measures of channel openness and interpersonal attraction.

interdependence through a third party The induction of similar beliefs, feelings, or behaviors in two (or more) persons as a result of the common influence of a third person or agency. Mass-communications media exert such influence.

intergroup relations Interactions among different social groups. The term *intergroup relations* frequently refers to the study of contact, coexistence, or conflict among different ethnic, religious, or racial groups.

internal locus of control In Rotter's social-learning theory, people's perceptions that their behaviors are determined by forces that lie within their personal control.

interpersonal space The general distance limits used by individuals when interacting with others. Hall has identified four specific types of interpersonal space—intimate, personal, social, and public.

interrole conflict Strain that emerges from efforts to enact the inconsistent requirements of different roles.

intersubject communication A source of confounding that results when subjects in the same experiment talk with one another. Experimenters usually minimize it through restricting communication channels and using subjects who do not know one another.

intrarole conflict Strain that emerges from efforts to enact inconsistent behaviors demanded by the same role.

invariance The characteristics of a relationship or finding that remain the same across several different experiments and correlational studies.

isolate A group member who is infrequently chosen by other members on sociometric measures.

J-curve of conformity The description of a frequency distribution in which the incidence of deviant behavior declines sharply after the first class interval.

Johari window A 2×2 matrix that uses the variables of self-knowledge and knowledge of others to predict inconsistencies between one's opinion of oneself and other people's opinion of oneself.

kernel-of-truth hypothesis The belief or finding that certain stereotypes may be reasonably accurate. The hypothesis is most likely to apply to people with first-hand knowledge of the stereotyped group.

kinesics The study of body signals (as defined by Birdwhistell) such as posture, gestures, facial expressions, and movements involved in nonverbal communication.

knowledge function An attitude function in which specific attitudes serve to provide their holder with a sense of understanding.

labeling The process by which a group labels or names a deviant (such as "delinquent," "Goyim," or "Honkey"). In the view of labeling theorists, the process reflects group activity in both labeling the deviant and responding to the label in discriminating against the deviant.

laboratory group A number of strangers brought together in a controlled setting for experimental study of social interaction. Correlational research on social interaction is more likely to involve intact groups that occur in natural settings.

language A universal form of human behavior involving symbolic communication through an arbitrary and culturally determined system of sound patterns with loosely standardized meanings.

latitude of acceptance The range of attitude positions that are sufficiently close to the person's attitude that he or she responds favorably.

latitude of rejection The range of attitude positions that are sufficiently different from the person's attitude that he or she responds unfavorably.

leadership The consistent exercise of influence and authority within a group or other social relationship. Leadership roles typically carry more power and status than follower roles.

leadership style Any identifiable and consistent pattern of leadership behavior. The leadership styles that have been most frequently identified and studied are the authoritarian, democratic, and laissez faire.

learned helplessness Behaviors that involve a failure to exercise possible control over a threatening environment.

legitimate power The capacity to control another individual's behavior through his or her own consent. Legitimate power is frequently defined as authority.

leniency effect A systematic bias toward highly favorable ratings of one's self and others. Most people show a leniency effect in their evaluations of others in natural settings.

leveling The process by which the recall and transmission of information becomes more consistent, regular, congruous, or symmetrical than the original data.

lexicon The pronunciations and definitions of the words of a language.

limiting conditions Statements of the circumstances under which a hypothesis or generalization does and does not apply to the social behavior under study. Considerable research in social psychology is devoted toward the identification of limiting conditions for basic hypotheses and empirical generalizations.

line The complete pattern of verbal and nonverbal behaviors that an individual brings to social interaction.

linguistics Comparative study of the structures and functions of languages. Although linguistics is classified as a branch of anthropology, social psychologists have grown increasingly interested in the relationships between language and social interaction.

logical error A perceptual bias in which the implicit personality theory of the perceiver leads to misperception of the perceived person. For example, if Mary believes that aggressive people are usually competent, she may conclude that Jim is competent solely on the basis of his observed aggressiveness.

love Strong feelings of attraction, trust, involvement, commitment, concern, and understanding for another person. Behavioral concomitants of love include frequent, intense, and personal interaction.

Machiavellianism The extent to which an individual is motivated to successfully manipulate others in order to gain his or her own ends.

Mach scale A personality measure of Machiavellianism, first developed by Christie. The most widely used scale is the Mach V, a forced-choice instrument which measures cynical beliefs about human nature, tactics for the manipulation of others, and values. The Kiddie-Mach is the form administered to children.

manipulation Systematic control of the independent variables of a social-psychology experiment. Manipulation enables the independent variable to assume one of several predetermined levels. For example, subjects might receive strong, medium, or mild shocks in an experiment on aggressive behavior.

member selection The process by which groups solicit or accept new entrants.

membership group Any group to which one belongs, such as a family or club (*see* **reference group**).

mere thought The idea that the continued repetition of any thought changes and strengthens the individual's basic attitudes.

mesomorph A basic body type identified by Sheldon. Mesomorphs have strong and muscular physiques.

message In persuasive communication, the statement that is made by the source and presented to the audience. Widely studied message variables include ordering of arguments, one- versus two-sided communication, and level of threat.

methodologists Investigators who study and seek to develop techniques for the conduct of experimental and correlational research in social psychology.

misinformation The provision of subjects with false explanations about the purposes of an experiment. Misinformation is an important technique of deception.

model A physical analogy or a conceptual metaphor developed to understand specific social behaviors. Models are used to suggest hypotheses and frequently to provide explanations of the less familiar in terms of the more familiar; also, any person, such as a parent, teacher, or peer, who is imitated by another.

modeling Learning the behavior of a person whom one has observed.

model of social influence An abstract representation of the most important processes by which one individual affects the behavior, feelings, or beliefs of another person.

mores The social norms that provide the moral standards of behavior for a group or society. They are viewed by a social group as important to its survival.

motive A hypothetical internal state that directs and energizes behavior, usually in order to satisfy some hypothesized need.

motive to avoid success A construct used to account for failure or to explain why individuals with comparable ability may substantially differ in their achievements (*see* **fear of success**).

multiple causation The process in which two or more causal factors jointly influence some outcome.

mundane realism The quality of resembling real-world situations of interest; a desirable quality of all laboratory research.

nature A term used to summarize all nonexperiential influences on the organism, particularly inherited influences.

need A hypothetical internal state of actual or felt deprivation. The need for approval and the need for achievement are common needs experienced and studied by social psychologists.

need for achievement A persistent drive to excel and achieve recognition for one's accomplishments.

need for information Motivation that leads individuals to seek additional knowledge about the subjective social realities of other people. It frequently leads to social-comparison processes.

negative correlation A relationship in which increases in one variable are consistently accompanied by decreases in a second variable. For example, the level of individual income is negatively correlated with the likelihood of suffering malnutrition.

noise In information theory, any interference with the transmission of a message between two people. Noise makes understanding more difficult, less accurate.

nonverbal communication Any personal means of interaction other than the grammatical aspects of speech or writing. Vocal characteristics and body movements are the principal forms of nonverbal communication.

norm An implicit agreement by group members that defines the limits of acceptable, appropriate behavior.

normative behavior Behavior that is consistent with prevailing group norms and standards. Normative behaviors may differ across societies, groups, and social contexts. Nonconformity and deviance are examples of counternormative behaviors.

normative control The influencing of individual behavior with rewards and punishments that are clearly related to stable group norms. Normative control reduces the need for constant bargaining, social influence, and power struggles in the regulation of the individual's behaviors, feelings, and beliefs. Reference groups are an important source of normative control.

normative expectations Shared assumptions and agreements concerning how a group member should behave.

normative social influence Control of the individual's behaviors, feelings, and beliefs through the invocation of group standards.

norm of reciprocity The expectation that a person will behave toward another as that person has behaved toward him or her. Exchanges of compliments or "an eye for an eye, a tooth for a tooth" exemplify this norm.

novelty The lack of (recent) experience with a stimulus. Novel stimuli frequently evoke responses of curiosity and interest. A *collative variable*.

nurture The role of the environment in shaping an individual's personality and social behavior. Nurture refers to environmental influences on individual development, and nature refers to inherited influences.

obedience Submissive responses to the demands of authority, laws, or norms. Obedience and conformity may result from the processes of compliance, identification, or internalization.

observation Careful and systematic attention to a social behavior, frequently accompanied by the measurement and recording of what has been observed.

one-sided communication A persuasive message that is limited to arguments favoring the proposed attitude position. Two-sided communications present both arguments and counterarguments for a given attitude position, and they are more likely to be effective with better-educated audiences.

one-way mirror A glass partition that permits experimenters in one room to observe subjects in a second room, but not vice versa.

operational definition A definition that provides empirical meaning to a construct or variable by specifying the operations or methods used to measure or manipulate it. A concept must be operationalized if it is to be measured.

opinion A conscious judgment, conviction, view, or belief held by an individual toward a specific attitude object.

optimal level of arousal A level of physiological activation that is comfortable for the individual. Boredom is the result of too little arousal; stress is the result of too much arousal.

other-variables approach An explanation for the absence of any straightforward relationship between individual attitudes and subsequent behavior. Ajzen and Fishbein have developed the concept of behavioral intentions as an example of an other-variables approach.

out-group From the perspective of in-group members, a group with distinctive characteristics that set it apart from the in-group. Out-groups are frequently regarded with hostility, fear, and contempt.

overachiever An individual who performs better than would be expected from knowledge of his or her abilities.

overdetermination The phenomenon in which increases in causal force are not accompanied by increases in the causal outcome. For instance, if a person performs a task exactly the same, whether motivated by $50 or $500, we might say that, in the $500 situation, performance has been overdetermined; that is, more cause was present than necessary to produce the behavior.

paralanguage The nongrammatical aspects of speech, such as intonation, pauses, and pronunciation.

participant observation A research technique that requires investigators to participate in the activities of a group in order to make detailed observations. It is intended to minimize the reactive effects of measurement and to provide information that would otherwise be difficult to observe.

passionate love Powerful feelings of attachment, intimacy, and caring for another person. It is frequently distinguished by a major erotic component.

pattern matching A process by which present observations are systematically compared to previous observations on specific measures of similarity.

perceived meaning The listener's understanding of the intention and significance of the verbal communications perceived from other people.

perception The cognitive processes through which sensory experience is organized and provided with meaning or significance.

perceptual bias Any systematic distortion in the individual's perception of other persons or objects. Halo effects, hedonic relevance, dispositional inference, and perceptual defense are frequently studied examples of such biases.

perceptual defense The process through which individuals often perceive unpleasant and threatening stimulus materials more slowly and less accurately than pleasant materials. There is considerable controversy about the conditions under which perceptual defense occurs.

perceptual vigilance The process by which individuals show increased abilities to recognize stimulus materials that are related to their needs or alert them to danger. Evidence for the occurrence of perceptual vigilance and accentuation is more conclusive than evidence for perceptual defense.

personal explanation A form of explanation that locates the determinants of social behavior in the personality characteristics ascribed to another person.

personalism The extent to which the actions of others have emotional or behavioral consequences for ourselves.

personality psychologist A scientist who studies and measures consistent individual differences in behavior, feeling, and cognition. Because many of the individual differences studied by personality psychology are determined by social processes, it is often viewed as closely related to social psychology.

personal research Informal or casual observations made by people in everyday life to answer questions that arise. Personal research is sometimes followed by **formal research**.

personal space An area surrounding the individual's body into which intruders may not enter. Personal space does not extend equally in all directions, and the size of the protected area changes with different types of social interaction.

personologist A psychologist who studies the characteristics of other people in terms of person concepts that describe basic dispositions. A personality psychologist.

persuasibility A readiness or disposition to be persuaded or to accept persuasive communications. Individual and group differences in persuasibility are important audience variables in the study of persuasive communication.

phonology The linguistic rules of sound patterning. It involves the study of phonetics—the description of sounds in speech—and phonemics—the description of a language's smallest units of speech sound.

pilot study A small-scale exploratory investigation that is conducted before more extensive research. It is frequently used to assess the clarity of experimental instructions, the impact of manipulations, and the variability of dependent measures. It can also be any form of experimental pretesting.

placebo An inert control treatment administered to patients or to control subjects. It may be administered because genuine treatment is unavailable, but its scientific use is to establish the effects of suggestion on behavior. Thus, it is administered to subjects under the same conditions as an experimental treatment, and the *placebo effect* refers to changes attributed to the effects of suggestion.

pluralistic ignorance A situation in which individual members of a group believe incorrectly that they are the only deviants from group values. But because the majority no longer accepts the traditional behaviors or beliefs, the sudden exposure of pluralistic ignorance can lead to rapid changes in social behavior.

Pollyanna Principle The finding that pleasant material seems to predominate over unpleasant material in the processes of thought, learning, memory, and speech. For example, pleasant information is consistently easier to learn and easier to remember than unpleasant information.

population A group of people from which a **sample** may be drawn; the researcher may then wish to draw conclusions about the population based on data obtained from the sample.

positive correlation A relationship in which increases in one variable are consistently accompanied by increases in a second variable. For example, there is a positive correlation between family income and the likelihood of regular dental examinations.

positivity bias The tendency to evaluate in a positive way, rating bad things as less bad and good things as better than is objectively appropriate.

posttest-only, control-group design A **posttest-only design** that includes a control group for comparison purposes. The experimental or treatment condition receives the treatment, then both conditions are measured (the posttest). The design is superior to the posttest-only design.

posttest-only design An experimental procedure that does not require pretest measures or a control group. Subjects are randomly assigned to two or more conditions, and the dependent variable is measured one time only for the experimental groups (and any available control groups). Posttest-only designs do not rule out the possibility that different groups showed different pretest measures; hence, they provide only weak evidence for the drawing of causal inferences.

power Social power is the capacity to control the behavior of another person. French and Raven have identified six types of social power: reward, coercive, expert, information, referent, and legitimate.

prediction The forecasting of any social behavior. In social psychology, predictions are based on hypotheses that relate the occurrence of specific social behaviors to specific stimulus conditions. Prediction thus serves as a check on scientific understanding, but it has little scientific value in its own right.

predictive personal theory An individual's theory about how other people and objects are likely to respond to specific stimulus conditions. For example, the view that hungry dogs will bite can be used to predict biting if the person knows the dog is hungry.

prejudice An attitude that predisposes a person to behave, feel, and think in consistently favorable or unfavorable ways toward members of a specific group.

prescriptive personal theory An individual's beliefs about how other people should behave. Examples of prescriptive personal theories are "look before you leap" or "plan ahead"— expressions that encourage people to anticipate the consequences of their actions.

prestige suggestion Social influence that obtains its effectiveness because of its origination in highly trustworthy and expert sources.

pretest/posttest, control-group design An experimental plan in which both a control condition and one or more treatment conditions are pretested and then tested again later. In the interim between these two measurements, the treatment conditions experience some independent variable.

pretest/posttest design An experiment in which one or more experimental groups are measured on the dependent variable before and after the administration of the independent variables. It provides direct assessment of the amount of change induced by an experimental manipulation.

primacy effect The concept in impression formation or persuasive communication that refers to the tendency for material that appears early in a sequence to have a greater effect than material that appears at the middle or end of a sequence.

primary group A small, intimate group in which members attempt to satisfy one another's emotional needs.

prior-entry effect The concept in social categorization that refers to the error that occurs when early information contributes to the formation of a category more than later information will contribute to change in the category.

private acceptance A case in which individuals experience attitude change but do not necessarily act or publicly acknowledge their changed attitudes (contrasts with **public compliance**).

probability level The chance that observed differences in social behavior have occurred as a result of random variation. A probability level of .05 states a 5 in 100 chance that the difference resulted from random variations (Type I error), and a .01 probability level reduces the likelihood of a false inference to 1 chance in 100.

projection A psychological process in which an individual unconsciously attributes his or her own unacceptable thoughts, feelings, and behaviors to other people or objects. Projection is usually regarded as a type of ego-defense mechanism.

projective test A paper-and-pencil measure that invites open-ended, unstructured responses to somewhat ambiguous stimuli—that is, pictures, inkblots, or brief stories. The responses—called *protocols*—are then scored for various themes or for particular content.

proscriptive personal theory An individual's theory about how other people should *not* behave. An example is the commandment "Thou shalt not kill."

protocol A complete and verbatim statement of an individual's verbal or overt behavior. Written protocols are frequently used to assess individual responses to projective personality devices.

proximity A relationship in which two or more persons or objects are physically near. Proximity frequently refers to physical opportunities for social interaction, whereas propinquity refers to socially structured opportunities for interaction.

psychogenic need Psychological motivations that lead an individual to a unique and consistent configuration of personality traits. According to Murray, nurturance, sex, affiliation, and achievement are examples of psychogenic needs.

psychological androgyny (see **androgyny**)

psychological distance An individual's cognitive, emotional, or behavioral detachment from a specific person or object. Psychological-distance and social-distance scales are especially useful in the assessment of attitudes toward members of out-groups.

psychological reactance An unpleasant motivational state resulting from a reduction, or threatened reduction, in the freedom to act. In Brehm's (1966) theory of psychological reactance, this motivational state is hypothesized to give rise to behavior that reestablishes the lost freedom.

psychosocial death Death that results from excessive psychologically or socially induced stress.

public compliance A condition in which an individual's statements and behaviors are enacted in the presence of other people. Public acts of compliance are more likely to cause and maintain attitude change than are private behaviors.

random assignment The allocation of subjects among different experimental treatments on the basis of chance. It increases the probability that subjects in different conditions will be similar at the beginning of an experiment, thus reducing the likelihood that posttest differences have resulted from any systematic pretest differences.

random sample Individuals selected for a study from a larger set of people on the basis of chance alone. When those selected have the same chance of inclusion as those not selected, the sample is random. Such a procedure assures that the sample is representative of the larger group.

reactance (see **psychological reactance**)

reasons The explanations people offer to account for their own behavior. Reasons differ from causes in that the former are guesses and constructions, usually made after the fact, and often more logical and self-serving than causes.

recency effect The concept in impression formation or persuasive communication that refers to the tendency of material received most recently to be predominant in forming judgments or opinions about persons, objects or issues.

reciprocal influence The quality of a system pertaining to mutual action and change, where one component affects another, and vice versa.

reciprocity A form of reciprocal influence in which the effects or actions are of the same nature (*see* **norm of reciprocity**).

redundancy In communication, the repetition of information that serves to ensure that the message will be received accurately.

reference group A group that individuals use as a standard for evaluating their own beliefs, feelings, and behaviors.

referent power Social power or influence that results from being identified with and respected.

reflexive thinking Cognitive activities in which individuals view themselves as both agents and objects of social interaction.

rehearse To engage in symbolic activities that enable one to practice techniques of impression management.

reinforcement Any stimulus that changes the probability of the response that it follows. Reinforcers may be either positive or negative, and they may be either applied or withdrawn following a specific response. Presentation of a positive reinforcer and withdrawal of a negative reinforcer are rewards that increase the probability of a response. Application of a negative reinforcer and withdrawal of a positive reinforcer are punishments that decrease the probability of a response.

reinforcement system A form of reciprocal influence in which each organism in the system rewards or punishes the others for certain actions.

rejection The act of depriving an individual of appropriate and normal social interaction. Rejection may involve personal exclusion from a primary relationship or institutional exclusion from an appropriate social role.

responsive Showing significant and appropriate variation in feelings and behavior as a function of the variation in the feelings and behaviors of others.

reward power Social power or influence that results from being able to benefit or help others.

Ringleman effect The finding that the combined efforts of two (or more) individuals are less than the sum of the effort put forth by separate individuals.

rod-and-frame test A measure of field dependence in which an individual is required to make vertical a rod enclosed within a tilted frame.

role A pattern of behavior structured around specific rights and duties and associated with a particular status position in a group or society. Roles may be achieved or ascribed, formal or informal, and universalistic or particularistic. Role enactment may be either perfunctory or involving. Many social psychologists also find it useful to make distinctions between prescribed, perceived, and performed roles.

role conflict Strain experienced when two or more roles with incompatible behaviors are held by an individual at the same time.

role distance A process by which individuals attempt to deny or limit their responsibility for their own actions. For example, a physician's efforts to save a dying patient may be accompanied by nonverbal behaviors that deny personal responsibility for the death.

rumor An unverified account of an event that is spread by word of mouth and frequently changes during transmission.

sample A limited number of cases selected for study from a specific population. Because inferences are made from samples to populations, it is important that the sample be representative of its underlying population. Random selection is the most widely used technique for assuring representative samples.

satiation Sufficient exposure to a reinforcer or other stimulus to lead to reductions in the reinforcer's effectiveness and pleasantness.

science Attempts to obtain knowledge by the development of general principles that are subject to control and systematic observation. Scientific knowledge is based on the assumption that it is possible to derive objective knowledge of the world through the senses and that the truth of knowledge is verified by controlled observations.

scientific explanation An interpretation of observed facts and relationships in terms of theories and hypotheses that are subject to empirical verification. Scientific explanation is more provisional and tentative than other forms of explanation, and it may be sharply revised when new facts and findings are uncovered.

secondary group A small group whose members lack intimate, personal ties, such as the relationship between a radio announcer and the audience or between a store clerk and a customer.

selectivity The principle that an individual's social perception and attention are focused on limited aspects of a specific stimulus. The selectiveness of social perception results from such processes as hedonic relevance, first impressions, and attribution of dispositional traits to other persons.

self-fulfilling prophecy The occurrence of a predicted outcome that is at least partially caused by the prediction itself. For example, government predictions of increased inflation in the future may lead individuals to spend more and save less, thus increasing the actual rate of inflation.

self-monitoring The extent to which individuals are aware of their own verbal and nonverbal behaviors in social interaction. For example, persons scoring high in self-monitoring

are more effective liars than low-scoring persons.

self-perception The process by which individuals infer their own attitudes, emotions, and other internal states from observation of their own behavior and the circumstances under which it occurs. According to Daryl Bem, individuals' perceptions and interpretations of their own internal states result from the same processes that are used to infer these states in other people.

self-presentation Behaving in a fashion that serves to guide and control the impressions that other people form of oneself. Self-presentation in natural settings has been intensively studied by Goffman.

self-selection The process by which individuals choose their situations, usually resulting in more congruence between personality and situation than would occur by chance; a process by which experimental or correlational findings may be confounded by the variable of individual choice. For example, subjects who choose to submit to an interview about their sexual behavior may be quite different from those who refuse participation.

sensation seeking A personality characteristic that leads individuals to consistently pursue new experiences and feelings in their everyday behaviors.

sensory deprivation The artificial restriction of variation in an individual's sensory input. Laboratory studies involve exposure of individuals to sustained levels of sensory deprivation, and the most frequent result is a marked deterioration in the individual's cognitive and motor performances.

sensory overload An excessive variation in an individual's sensory input. It is the opposite of sensory deprivation, but it frequently has similar effects on the individual's thoughts, feelings, and behavior.

sensory restriction A condition in which individuals are somewhat deprived of environmental stimulation, often with negative psychological consequences.

serial-position effect The finding that the first and last parts of verbal communications are the most easily learned and recalled. Serial-position effects may also occur in impression formation and persuasive communication.

sex The biological characteristics that differentiate men and women (see **gender**).

sex role The specific rights, obligations, and expectations that surround the social status of "male" and "female." The specific content of sex-role expectations differs across societies, subcultures, and groups.

sex-role socialization The social processes through which individuals learn the behaviors, feelings, and beliefs that are viewed as desirable for men or women.

sharpening The cognitive process in which certain details of an event are emphasized—in recalling and recounting it—to the exclusion of other details.

short-term storage A hypothetical stage in learning or perception in which small quantities of information are briefly retained before being forgotten or passed on to long-term (permanent) storage.

similarity The extent to which likeness appears in the physical characteristics, behavior, feelings, or beliefs of two or more people. Similarities are important determinants of friendship and mate selection, and attitude similarity appears to be the most important single cause of interpersonal attraction.

situational approach A view that individual social behavior is primarily determined by environmental rather than personality variables.

small group A social group in which each member may interact freely with all others face-to-face, thus restricting the size of the group to only a few members (perhaps ten or fewer).

small-group confinement An experimental procedure in which two or more subjects are placed in a small room, isolated from others, and carefully observed over a period of time.

social-comparison theory A statement (proposed by Festinger) that assumes that individuals use others as sources of information for evaluating their own attitudes and abilities. According to social-comparison theory, it is extraordinarily difficult to make judgments of one's own feelings, beliefs, abilities, and attitudes without knowledge of these characteristics of others.

social construction of reality The social processes (described by Berger and Luckmann) by which individuals negotiate agreements about the nature of the world and knowledge, thus establishing a shared social reality. Sociology of knowledge attempts to explain the social constructions of subjective and objective reality.

social contract An unwritten pact, rule, expectation, or norm shared by two or more people. The doctrine that government should depend on the consent of the governed is an example of a social contract.

social costs The frustrations and negative feelings that frequently arise from social interaction. Social costs may also refer to punishments that result when rewards are withdrawn or withheld.

social desirability A response bias in which subjects endorse statements that are socially acceptable or valued. According to Edwards, subjects' responses to many attitude and personality scales are contaminated by a social-desirability response set; also, qualities of others, such as similarity, competence, attractiveness, health, wealth, power, and intelligence, that make them valuable to us as associates, friends, and lovers.

social/emotional specialist A role that often emerges in small groups. The social/emotional specialist is concerned with the feelings of other members, works to reduce tensions, and tries to maintain a cordial, cooperative atmosphere.

social facilitation The stimulating effect of the presence of other people on an individual's motivation or performance. Coaction effects may be either facilitating or inhibiting.

social-impact theory The hypothesis that larger numbers of people exert greater social influence on the individual than do smaller groups.

social interference Decreases in the strength or frequency of some behavior due to the presence or coaction of others.

social isolation Deprivation from contact with others, such as occurs in solitary confinement.

socialization The basic processes through which an individual becomes integrated into a social group by learning the culture and roles of that group. Its principal mechanisms are internalization, reinforcement, and imitation, and the socialization process continues throughout the life cycle.

social-penetration theory A hypothesis by Altman and Taylor that views gradually escalating levels of mutual self-disclosure as a major determinant of interpersonal attraction.

social perception The entire process by which an individual comes to know and evaluate other persons. The principal determinants of the outcomes of social perception are the setting of observation, the actions of the

observed, and the nature of the observer.

social psychology A branch of psychology and sociology that studies individual behavior in terms of social factors and group structures in terms of individual behaviors.

social rewards The satisfactions and positive feelings that arise from social interaction.

sociogram A graphic representation of patterns of attraction and exclusion within a small group.

sociometry A method for studying emergent structures based on affection or attraction. The resulting sociograms provide information about the emotional structure and cohesiveness of a group.

source In persuasive communication, the origin that is attributed to a message intended to evoke attitude change. Perceptions of trustworthiness and expertise are the two principal determinants of source credibility, and credible sources consistently evoke more initial attitude change than incredible sources.

star In sociometry, a very frequently chosen member of a group. The characteristics of sociometric stars are usually specific to the groups under study.

state An internal condition that is less stable than a trait. For example, feelings of self-confidence are states, and measures of self-esteem refer to traits.

state of readiness An individual's predisposition to respond to a specific stimulus with a certain behavior.

static view A result of social perception that stems from immediate impressions of other people under conditions of limited social interaction.

statistical significance The probability that observed differences in the dependent measures could have occurred on the basis of chance variations in sampling. The assumption of a difference that does not exist is a Type I error, and the probability level is the likelihood of such an error's occurring on the basis of chance.

status The worth of an individual as estimated by other persons. A status may also be a defined position in the social structure of a group, and higher status is usually accompanied by greater prestige and power.

stereotype A set of biased and widely shared generalizations about a group or category of people that is usually unfavorable, exaggerated, and oversimplified. Even when stereotypes possess elements of truth, they eliminate the possibility of individual differences within the categorized group.

stereotype accuracy A process in which an individual's perceptions of others attain greater accuracy than would be expected by chance due to the use of partially accurate stereotypes.

stimulus Any change or event in the environment that elicits a behavioral, emotional, or cognitive response in an individual.

store To hold images and information in the individual's memory for retrieval at a later time. Storage may involve short- or long-term memory.

strain toward symmetry A tendency toward consistency in one's attitude toward oneself and the attitudes of other people toward one.

stress Any unpleasant and disturbing emotional experience that results from frustration or interference with an individual's customary pattern of behavior.

stressor Any unpleasant, disruptive event or situation that produces **stress**.

system of explanation An integrated set of personal theories that support each other and together combine to provide a general understanding of the world.

taboo A traditional prohibition against some behavior, such as an incest taboo.

task specialist A leadership role that often emerges in small groups. The task specialist concentrates on guiding discussion, improving group performance, and moving the group toward its goals.

testosterone A male hormone produced in the testes that contributes to secondary sexual characteristics associated with males, such as a deep voice, large muscles, and body and facial hair.

thematic apperception test A projective technique for the study of personality in which an individual is asked to respond to a series of ambiguous pictures by telling stories about each of them. The TAT is used to measure such personality characteristics as achievement motivation and fear of success.

threshold A level at which stimuli of specified intensity evoke a response one-half of the time. Stimuli above the threshold consistently elicit responses, and stimuli below it consistently fail to do so; also a hypothetical level of causal force that must be exceeded for an effect to occur.

tradition Prescribed, valued, situation-specific behavior patterns that are transmitted across generations.

trait A relatively consistent and enduring pattern or other aspect of an individual's behavior, feelings, or beliefs. A trait appears in many different situations, and it can be used to differentiate one individual from another.

triad A three-person group.

truncated law of effect A form of reinforcement theory, proposed by Thorndike, that emphasizes the effects of delivering or withdrawing rewards.

two-sided communication A persuasive appeal that appears to present both sides of the issue, with emphasis (often subtle) on the side advocated by the source.

unbalanced The condition in which one person's (A's) feelings toward another (B), A's feelings toward some attitude object (C), and B's feelings toward C include either one or three negative feelings. In this case, A may experience some unpleasant tension.

underachiever An individual who performs more poorly than would be expected from knowledge of his or her abilities.

underdetermination The finding that all stimuli below individual threshold levels fail to elicit responses. Underdetermination results whether the stimulus is only slightly below or far below threshold.

uniformity Behaviors, feelings, and beliefs that are widely shared within a group or society. Uniformities often result from social processes that induce conformity.

unresponsive Insensitive to variations in the behaviors of other people and different social situations.

usages Standards of behavioral uniformity that do not ordinarily lead to punishment when they are violated.

utilitarian adaptive function The finding that specific attitudes may help the individual to function and cope with specific situations. For example, high-ranking military officers are likely to advocate increased defense spending.

variable Any characteristic of social behavior that is amenable to observations that assume different values. Independent and dependent variables are the principal inputs and outputs of social-psychology experiments.

verbal communication Meanings conveyed by the grammatical aspects of spoken or written language.

violence Physical force with the potential of injuring property or other persons.

viscerogenic need A need of the body that must be fulfilled in order to assure survival. According to Murray, food, water, and sleep are examples of viscerogenic needs.

wishful thinking A cognitive process in which expectations of the future are biased by wishes and desires, usually without awareness of these biases.

References

Abelson, R. P., & Miller, J. Negative persuasion via personal insult. *Journal of Experimental Social Psychology*, 1967, *3*, 321–333.

Abelson, R. P., & Rosenberg, M. J. Symbolic psycho-logic: A model of attitudinal cognition. *Behavioral Science*, 1958, *3*, 1–13.

Abney, F. G., & Hill, L. B. Natural disasters as a political variable: The effect of a hurricane on an urban election. *American Political Science Review*, 1966, *60*, 974–981.

Abramowitz, S. I., Abramowitz, C. V., Jackson, C., & Gomes, B. The politics of clinical judgment: What nonliberal examiners infer about women who don't stifle themselves. *Journal of Consulting and Clinical Psychology*, 1973, *41*, 385–391.

Adams, B. N. *The American family.* Chicago: Markham, 1971.

Adams, G. R., & Huston, T. L. Social perception of middle-aged persons varying in physical attractiveness. *Developmental Psychology*, 1975, *11*, 657–658.

Adams, H. E., & Berg, I. A. Affective tone of test option choice as a deviant response. *Psychological Reports*, 1961, *8*, 79–85.

Adamson, J., & Schmale, A. Object loss, giving up, and the onset of psychiatric disease. *Psychosomatic Medicine*, 1965, *27*, 557–576.

Ader, R., Kreutner, A., Jr., & Jacobs, H. L. Social environment, emotionality and alloxon diabetes in the rat. *Psychosomatic Medicine*, 1963, *25*, 60.

Aderman, D. Elation, depression, and helping behavior. *Journal of Personality and Social Psychology*, 1972, *24*, 91–101.

Aderman, D., & Berkowitz, L. Observational set, empathy, and helping. *Journal of Personality and Social Psychology*, 1970, *14*, 141–148.

Adler, L. L., & Iverson, M. A. Interpersonal distance as a function of task difficulty, praise, status orientation and sex of partner. *Perceptual and Motor Skills*, 1974, *39*, 683–692.

Adorno, T. W., Frenkel-Brunswick, E., Levinson, D. J., & Sanford, R. N. *The authoritarian personality.* New York: Harper, 1950.

Agranoff, R. *The new style in election campaigns.* Boston: Holbrook Press, 1972.

Aiello, J. R., & Aiello, T. D. The development of personal space: Proxemic behavior of children 6 through 16. *Human Ecology*, 1974, *2*, 177–189.

Aiello, J. R., & Cooper, R. E. The use of personal space as a function of social affect. *Proceedings of the 80th Annual Convention of the American Psychology Association*, 1972, *7*, 207–208. (Summary)

Aiello, J. R., & Jones, S. E. Field study of the proxemic behavior of young children in three subcultural groups. *Journal of Social Psychology*, 1971, *19*, 351–356.

Ajzen, I. Attitudinal vs. normative messages: An investigation of the differential effects of persuasive communications on behavior. *Sociometry*, 1971, *34*, 263–280.

Ajzen, I. Intuitive theories of events and the effects of base-rate information on prediction. *Journal of Personality and Social Psychology*, 1977, *35*(5), 303–314.

Ajzen, I., Darroch, R. K., Fishbein, M., & Hornik, J. A. Looking backward revisited: A reply to Deutscher. *American Sociologist*, 1970, *5*, 267–273.

Ajzen, I., & Fishbein, M. Attitudinal and normative variables as predictors of specific behaviors. *Journal of Personality and Social Psychology*, 1973, *27*, 41–57.

Ajzen, I., & Fishbein, M. A Bayesian analysis of attribution processes. *Psychological Bulletin*, 1975, *82*, 261–277.

Ajzen, I., & Fishbein, M. Attitude-behavior relations: A theoretical analysis and review of empirical research. *Psychological Bulletin*, 1977, *84*, 888–918.

Albrecht, S. L., & Carpenter, K. E. Attitudes as predictors of behavior versus behavior intentions: A convergence of research traditions. *Sociometry*, 1976, *39*, 1–10.

Allen, V. L. Situational factors in conformity. In L. Berkowitz (Ed.), *Advances in experimental social psychology* (Vol. 2). New York: Academic Press, 1970.

Allgeier, A. R., & Byrne, D. Attraction toward the opposite sex as a determinant of physical proximity. *Journal of Social Psychology*, 1973, *90*, 213–219.

Allport, F. H. The influence of the group upon association and thought. *Journal of Experimental Psychology*, 1920, *3*, 159–182.

Allport, F. H. *Social psychology.* Boston: Houghton Mifflin, 1924.

Allport, F. H. The J-curve hypothesis of conforming behavior. *Journal of Social Psychology*, 1934, *5*, 141–183.

Allport, G. W. Attitudes. In C. Murchison (Ed.), *Handbook of social psychology*. Worcester, Mass.: Clark University Press, 1935, 798–884.

Allport, G. W. The historical background of modern social psychology. In G. Lindzey (Ed.), *Handbook of social psychology* (Vol. 1). Cambridge, Mass.: Addison-Wesley, 1954. (a)

Allport, G. W. *The nature of prejudice.* Cambridge, Mass.: Addison-Wesley, 1954. (b)

Allport, G. W. The historical background of modern social psychology. In G. Lindzey & E. Aronson (Eds.), *Handbook of social psychology* (Vol. 1, 2nd ed.). Reading, Mass.: Addison-Wesley, 1968.

Allport, G. W., & Odbert, H. S. Trait-names: A psycho-lexical study. *Psychological Monographs*, 1936, *47* (Whole No. 211).

Allport, G. W., & Postman, L. J. The basic psychology of rumor. In E. E. Maccoby, T. M. Newcomb, & E. L. Hartley (Eds.), *Readings in social psychology* (3rd ed.). New York: Holt, Rinehart & Winston, 1958.

Allport, G. W., & Ross, J. Personal religious orientation and prejudice. *Journal of Personality and Social Psychology*, 1967, *5*, 432–443.

Alluisi, E. A., Chiles, W. D., Hall, T. J., & Hawkes, G. R. *Human group performance during confinement*. Tech. Report No. AMRL-TDR-63-87. (Contract No. AF 33 (616)-7607), Wright-Patterson AFB, Ohio. Lockheed Air Craft Corp., Georgia, November, 1963.

Alper, T. G. The relationship between role orientation and achievement motivation in college women. *Journal of Personality*, 1973, *41*, 9–31.

Alper, T. G. Achievement motivation in college women: A now-you-see-it—now-you-don't phenomenon. *American Psychologist*, 1974, *29*, 194–203.

Altman, I. The communication of interpersonal attitudes: An ecological approach. In T. L. Huston (Ed.), *Foundations of interpersonal attraction*. New York: Academic Press, 1974.

Altman, I. *The environment and social behavior: Privacy, personal space, territory, and crowding*. Monterey, Calif.: Brooks/Cole, 1975.

Altman, I., & Haythorn, W. W. Interpersonal exchange in isolation. *Sociometry*, 1965, *28*, 411–426.

Altman, I, & Haythorn, W. W. The effects of social isolation and group composition on performance. *Human Relations*, 1967, *20*, 313–340.

Altman, I., & Taylor, D. A. *Social penetration: The development of interpersonal relations*. New York: Holt, 1973.

Altus, W. D. Birth order and academic primogeniture. *Journal of Personality and Social Psychology*, 1965, *2*, 872–876.

American Psychological Association. *Ethical principles in the conduct of research with human participants*. Washington, D. C.: Author, 1973.

American Psychological Association. *Publication manual* (2nd ed.). Washington, D. C.: Author, 1974.

Amir, Y. Contact hypothesis in ethnic relations. *Psychological Bulletin*, 1969, *71*, 319–342.

Anderson, J. P., & Perlman, D. Effects of an adult's preaching and responsibility for hypocritical behavior on children's altruism. *Proceedings of the 81st Annual Convention of the American Psychological Association*, 1973, *8*, 291–292. (Summary)

Anderson, L., & Fishbein, N. Prediction of attitude from the number, strength, and evaluative aspects of beliefs about the attitude object. *Journal of Personality and Social Psychology*, 1965, *2*, 437–443.

Anderson, L. R., & McGuire, W. J. Prior reassurance of group consensus as a factor in producing resistance to persuasion. *Sociometry*, 1965, *28*, 44–56.

Anderson, N. Test of a model for opinion change. *Journal of Abnormal and Social Psychology*, 1959, *59*, 371–381.

Anderson, N., & Hovland, C. The representation of order effects in communication research. In C. Hovland et al. (Eds.), *The order of presentation in persuasion*. New Haven, Conn.: Yale University Press, 1957.

Anderson, N. H. Application of an additive model to impression formation. *Science*, 1962, *138*, 817–818.

Anderson, N. H. Averaging versus adding as a stimulus-combination rule in impression formation. *Journal of Experimental Psychology*, 1965, *70*, 394–400.

Anderson, N. H. Cognitive algebra: Integration theory applied to social attribution. In L. Berkowitz (Ed.), *Advances in experimental social psychology* (Vol. 7). New York: Academic Press, 1974.

Anderson, N. H., & Alexander, G. R. Choice test of the averaging hypothesis for information integration. *Cognitive Psychology*, 1971, *2*, 313–324.

Andrew, R. J. Evolution of facial expression. *Science*, 1963, *142*, 1034–1041.

Ardrey, R. *African genesis*. New York: Delta Books, 1961.

Ardrey, R. *The territorial imperative*. New York: Atheneum, 1966.

Ardrey, R. *The social contract*. New York: Atheneum, 1970.

Argyle, M., & Dean, J. Eye contact, distance, and affiliation. *Sociometry*, 1965, *28*, 289–304.

Argyle, M., & Ingham, R. Gaze, mutual gaze, and proximity. *Semiotica*, 1972, *6*(2), 32–50.

Aries, P. *Centuries of childhood: A social history of family life*. New York: Knopf, 1962.

Aronoff, J., & Crano, W. D. A re-examination of the cross-cultural principles of task segregation and sex role differentiation in the family. *American Sociological Review*, 1975, *40*, 12–20.

Aronson, E. Dissonance theory: Progress and problems. In R. P. Abelson, E. Aronson, W. J. McGuire, P. M. Newcomb, M. J. Rosenberg, & P. H. Tannenbaum (Eds.), *Theories of cognitive consistency: A sourcebook*. Skokie, Ill.: Rand McNally, 1968.

Aronson, E. The rationalizing animal. *Psychology Today*, May 1973, 222–226.

Aronson, E. & Carlsmith, J. M. Experimentation in social psychology. In G. Lindzey & E. Aronson (Eds.), *Handbook of social psychology* (Vol. 1, 2nd ed.). Reading, Mass.: Addison-Wesley, 1968.

Aronson, E., & Golden, B. The effect of relevant and irrelevant aspects of communicator credibility on opinion change. *Journal of Personality*, 1962, *30*, 135–146.

Aronson, E., & Linder, D. Gain and loss of esteem as determinants of interpersonal attractiveness. *Journal of Experimental Social Psychology*, 1965, *1*, 156–171.

Aronson, E., & Mills, J. The effect of severity of initiation on liking for a group. *Journal of Abnormal and Social Psychology*, 1959, *59*, 177–181.

Aronson, E., Willerman, B., & Floyd, J. The effect of a pratfall on increasing interpersonal attractiveness. *Psychonomic Science*, 1966, *4*, 157–158.

Asberg, M., Thoren, P., & Traskman, L. Serotonin depression—A biochemical subgroup within the affective disorders? *Science*, 1976, *191*, 478–480.

Asch, S. E. Studies in the principles of judgments and attitudes, II. Determination of judgments by groups and ego standards. *Journal of Social Psychology*, 1940, *12*, 433–465.

Asch, S. E. Forming impressions of personality. *Journal of Abnormal and Social Psychology*, 1946, *41*, 258–290.

Asch, S. E. The doctrine of suggestion, prestige, and imitation in social psychology. *Psychological Review*, 1948, *55*, 250–276.

Asch, S. E. *Social psychology*. Englewood Cliffs, N.J.: Prentice-Hall, 1952.

Asch, S. E. Opinions and social pressure. *Scientific American*, 1955, *193*, 31–35.

Asch, S. E. Effects of group pressure upon modification and

distortion of judgments. In E. E. Maccoby, T. M. Newcomb, & E. L. Hartley (Eds.), *Readings in social psychology* (3rd ed.). New York: Holt, 1958.

Asher, S., & Allen, V. Racial preference and social comparison processes. *Journal of Social Issues,* 1969, *25,* 157–165.

Assael, M., Pfeifer, Y., & Sulman, F. G. Influence of artificial air ionization on the human electroencephalogram. *International Journal of Biometeorology,* 1974, *18,* 306–312.

Astin, H. S. *The woman doctorate in America.* New York: Sage, 1969.

Astin, H. S. Employment and career status of women psychologists. *American Psychologist,* May 1972, 371–381.

Astin, H. S., & Boyer, A. E. Sex discrimination in academe. *Educational Record,* 1972, *53,* 101–118.

Athanasiou, R., & Yoshioka, G. The spatial character of friendship formation. *Environment and Behavior,* 1973, *5,* 43–65.

Atkinson, J. W. Motivational determinants of risk-taking behavior. *Psychological Review,* 1957, *64,* 359–372.

Atkinson, J. W. (Ed.). *Motives in fantasy, action, and society.* Princeton, N.J.: Van Nostrand, 1958.

Atkinson, J. W., & Litwin, G. H. Achievement motive and test anxiety conceived as motive to approach success and motive to avoid failure. *Journal of Abnormal and Social Psychology,* 1960, *60,* 52–63.

Aveni, A. F. The not-so-lonely crowd: Friendship groups in collective behavior. *Sociometry,* 1977, *40,* 96–99.

Ax, A. F. The physiological differentiation of emotional states. *Psychosomatic Medicine,* 1953, *15,* 433–442.

Azrin, N. H., Hutchinson, R. R., & Hake, D. F. Pain-induced fighting in the squirrel monkey. *Journal of the Experimental Analysis of Behavior,* 1963, *6,* 620.

Azrin, N. H., Hutchinson, R. R., & Hake, D. F. Attack, avoidance, and escape reactions to aversive shock. *Journal of the Experimental Analysis of Behavior,* 1967, *10,* 131–148.

Azrin, N. H., Hutchinson, R. R., & Sallery, R. D. Pain-induced aggression toward inanimate objects. *Journal of the Experimental Analysis of Behavior,* 1964, *7,* 223–228.

Azrin, N. H., Rubin, H. B., & Hutchinson, R. R. Biting attack by rats in response to aversive shock. *Journal of the Experimental Analysis of Behavior,* 1968, *11,* 633–639.

Babchuk, N., & Bates, A. Professor or producer: The two faces of academic man. *Social Forces,* 1962, *40,* 341–344.

Bach, G. R., & Wyden, P. *The intimate enemy: How to fight fair in love and marriage.* New York: Avon Books, 1968.

Back, K. W. Influence through social communication. *Journal of Abnormal and Social Psychology,* 1951, *46,* 9–23.

Back, K. W., & Davis, K. E. Some personal and situational factors relevant to the consistency and prediction of conforming behavior. *Sociometry,* 1965, *28,* 227–240.

Backman, C. W., & Secord, P. F. The effect of perceived liking on interpersonal attraction. *Human Relations,* 1959, *12,* 379–384.

Backman, C. W., & Secord, P. F. *A social psychological view of education.* New York: Harcourt Brace Jovanovich, 1968.

Baddeley, A. D. *The psychology of memory.* New York: Basic Books, 1976.

Bales, R. F. *Interaction process analysis, a method for the study of small groups.* Reading, Mass.: Addison-Wesley, 1950. (a)

Bales, R. F. A set of categories for the analysis of small group interaction. *American Sociological Review,* 1950, *15*(2), 257–263. (b)

Bales, R. F. The equilibrium problem in small groups. In T. Parsons, R. F. Bales, & E. A. Shils (Eds.), *Working papers in the theory of action.* Glencoe, Ill.: Free Press, 1953.

Bales, R. F. Task roles and social roles in problem-solving groups. In E. E. Maccoby, T. M. Newcomb, & F. L. Hartley (Eds.), *Readings in social psychology* (3rd ed.). New York: Holt, 1958.

Bales, R. F. *Personality and interpersonal behavior.* New York: Holt, Rinehart & Winston, 1970.

Bales, R. F., & Borgatta, E. F. Size of group as a factor in the interaction profile. In A. P. Hare, E. F. Borgatta, & R. F. Bales (Eds.), *Small groups.* New York: Knopf, 1955.

Bales, R. F., & Gerbrands, H. The interaction recorder, an apparatus and check list for sequential content analysis of social interaction. *Human Relations,* 1943, *1*(4).

Bales, R. F., & Hare, A. P. Diagnostic use of the interaction profile. *Journal of Social Psychology,* 1965, *59,* 239–258.

Balswick, J., & Avertt, C. P. Differences in expressiveness: Gender, interpersonal orientation, and perceived parental expressiveness as contributing factors. *Journal of Marriage and the Family,* February 1977, 121–127.

Bandler, R. J., Madaras, G. R., & Bem, D. J. Self-observation as a source of pain perception. *Journal of Personality and Social Psychology,* 1968, *9,* 205–209.

Bandura, A. Influence of model's reinforcement contingencies on the acquisition of imitative responses. *Journal of Personality and Social Psychology,* 1965, *1,* 589–595.

Bandura, A. *Aggression: A social learning analysis.* Englewood Cliffs, N.J.: Prentice-Hall, 1973.

Bandura, A. The self-system in reciprocal determinism. *American Psychologist,* 1978, *33,* 344–358.

Bandura, A., Ross., D., & Ross, S. A. Transmission of aggression through imitation of aggressive models. *Journal of Abnormal and Social Psychology,* 1961, *63,* 575–582.

Bandura, A., Ross, D., & Ross, S. A. Imitation of film-mediated aggressive models. *Journal of Abnormal and Social Psychology,* 1963, *66,* 3–11. (a)

Bandura, A., Ross, D., & Ross, S. A. Vicarious reinforcement and imitative learning. *Journal of Abnormal and Social Psychology,* 1963, *67,* 601–607. (b)

Banks, W. C. The effects of perceived similarity upon the use of reward and punishment. *Journal of Experimental Social Psychology,* 1976, *12,* 131–138.

Barch, A. M., Trumbo, D., & Nangle, J. Social setting and conformity to a legal requirement. *Journal of Abnormal and Social Psychology,* 1957, *55,* 396–398.

Barchas, J. D., Akil, H., Elliot, G. R., Holman, R. B., & Watson, S. J. Behavioral neurochemistry: Neuroregulators and behavioral states. *Science,* 1978, *200,* 964–973.

Bard, C. The relation between perceptual style and physical activities. *International Journal of Sports Psychology,* 1972, *3,* 107–113.

Bardwick, J. M. *Psychology of women.* New York: Harper & Row, 1971.

Bardwick, J. M., & Douvan, E. Ambivalence: The socialization of women. In V. Gornick & B. K. Moran (Eds.), *Women in sexist society.* New York: New American Library, 1971.

Barefoot, J. C., Hoople, M., & McClay, D. Avoidance of an act which would violate personal space. *Psychonomic Science,* 1972, *28,* 205–206.

Barker, R. *Ecological psychology.* Palo Alto, Calif.: Stanford University Press, 1967.

Barker, R. G. (Ed.). *The stream of behavior.* New York: Appleton-Century-Crofts, 1963.

Barker, R. G., & Wright, H. F. *Midwest and its children.* Evanston, Ill.: Row, Peterson, 1954.

Barocas, R., & Gorlow, L. Self-report personality measurement and conformity behavior. *Journal of Social Psychology,* 1967, *71,* 227–234.

Baron, R. A. Effects of magnitude of model's apparent pain on observer reaction time. *Psychonomic Science,* 1970, *20,* 229–231.

Baron, R. A. Behavioral effects of interpersonal attraction: Compliance with requests from liked and disliked others. *Psychonomic Science,* 1971, *25,* 325–346. (a)

Baron, R. A. Exposure to an aggressive model and apparent probability of retroaction from the victim as determinants of adult aggressive behavior. *Journal of Experimental Social Psychology,* 1971, *7,* 343–355. (b)

Baron, R. A. Aggression as a function of ambient temperature and prior anger arousal. *Journal of Personality and Social Psychology,* 1972, *21,* 183–189.

Baron, R. A., & Bell, P. A. Aggression and heat: Mediating effects of prior provocation and exposure to an aggressive model. *Journal of Personality and Social Psychology,* 1975, *31,* 825–832.

Baron, R. A., & Bell, P. A. Aggression and heat: The influence of ambient temperature, negative affect, and a cooling drink on physical aggression. *Journal of Personality and Social Psychology,* 1976, *33,* 245–255.

Baron, R. A., & Byrne, D. *Social psychology* (2nd ed.). Boston: Allyn & Bacon, 1977.

Baron, R. A., Byrne, D., & Griffitt, W. *Social psychology.* Boston: Allyn & Bacon, 1974.

Baron, R. A., & Ransberger, V. M. Ambient temperature and the occurrence of collective violence: The "long, hot summer" revisited. *Journal of Personality and Social Psychology,* 1978, *36,* 351–360.

Baron, R. M., Mandel, D. R., Adams, C. A., & Griffin, L. M. *Effects of social density in university residential environments.* Unpublished manuscript, University of Connecticut, 1975.

Baron, R. S., Baron, P. H., & Miller, N. The relation between distraction and persuasion. *Psychological Bulletin,* 1973, *80,* 310–323.

Barron, F. Some personality correlates of independence of judgment. *Journal of Personality,* 1953, *21,* 287–297.

Barry, H., III, Bacon, M. K., & Child, I. L. A cross-cultural survey of some sex differences in socialization. *Journal of Abnormal and Social Psychology,* 1957, *55,* 327–332.

Bar-Tal, D., & Frieze, I. *Achievement motivation and gender as determinants of attributions for success and failure.* Unpublished manuscript, University of Pittsburgh, 1974.

Bar-Tal, D., & Saxe, L. Perceptions of similarly attractive couples and individuals. *Journal of Personality and Social Psychology,* 1976, *33,* 772–781.

Bartol, K. M., & Wortman, M. S. Sex effects in leader behav-

ior: Self-descriptions and job satisfaction. *Journal of Psychology,* 1976, *94,* 177–183.

Bass, B. M. An analysis of leaderless group discussion. *Journal of Applied Psychology,* 1949, *33,* 527–533.

Bass, B. M. The leaderless group discussion. *Psychological Bulletin,* 1954, *51,* 465–492.

Bass, B. M. Authoritarianism or acquiescence? *Journal of Abnormal and Social Psychology,* 1955, *51,* 616–623.

Bass, B. M. Conformity, deviation, and a general theory of interpersonal behavior. In B. A. Berg & B. M. Bass (Eds.), *Conformity and deviation.* New York: Harper, 1961.

Bass, B. M. *Organizational psychology.* Boston: Allyn & Bacon, 1965.

Bass, B. M., & Klubeck, S. Effects of seating arrangement on leaderless group discussions. *Journal of Abnormal and Social Psychology,* 1952, *47,* 724–727.

Bass, B. M., & Wurster, C. R. Effects of company rank on LGD performance of oil refinery supervisors. *Journal of Applied Psychology,* 1953, *37,* 100–104. (a)

Bass, B. M., & Wurster, C. R. Effects of the nature of the problem on LGD performance. *Journal of Applied Psychology,* 1953, *37,* 96–99. (b)

Bassett, R. L., & Latané, B. *Social influence and news stories.* Unpublished manuscript, Ohio State University, Columbus, 1976.

Batson, D. Moon madness: Greed or creed? *APA Monitor,* June 1976.

Baum, A., & Valins, S. Residential environments, group size and crowding. *Proceedings of the 81st Annual Convention of the American Psychological Association,* 1973, *8,* 211–221. (Summary)

Baumgold, J. The new community of victims. *New York,* September 1973, p. 54.

Baumrind, D. Some thoughts on ethics of research: After reading Milgram's behavioral study of obedience. *American Psychologist,* 1964, *19,* 421–423.

Bavelas, A. Communication patterns in task-oriented groups. In D. Cartwright & A. Zander (Eds.), *Group dynamics.* Evanston, Ill.: Row, Peterson, 1953.

Bavelas, A., Hastorf, A. H., Gross, A. E., & Kite, W. R. Experiments in the alteration of group structure. *Journal of Experimental Social Psychology,* 1965, *1,* 55–71.

Baxter, J. C. Interpersonal spacing in natural settings. *Sociometry,* 1970, *33,* 444–456.

Baxter, J. C., & Deanovich, B. S. Anxiety arousing effects of inappropriate crowding. *Journal of Consulting and Clinical Psychology,* 1970, *35,* 174–178.

Baxter, J. C., & Rozelle, R. M. Nonverbal expression as a function of crowding during a simulated police-citizen encounter. *Journal of Personality and Social Psychology,* 1975, *32,* 40–54.

Bayer, E. *Zeitschrift für Psychologie,* 1929, *112,* 1.

Beattie, R. H., & Kenney, J. P. Aggressive crimes. *Annals of the American Academy of Political and Social Science,* 1966, *364,* 73–85.

Beck, A. T., & Lester, D. Attempted suicide and month of birth. *Psychological Reports,* 1973, *33,* 506.

Becker, G. Affiliate perception and the arousal of the participation-affiliation motive. *Perceptual and Motor Skills,* 1967, *24,* 991–997.

Becker, G., & McClintock, C. G. Scientific theory and social psychology. In C. G. McClintock (Ed.), *Experimental social psychology*. New York: Holt, Rinehart & Winston, 1972.

Bee, H., Broverman, D. M., Broverman, I., Rosenkrantz, P., & Vogel, S. Sex-role stereotypes and self-concepts in college students. *Journal of Consulting and Clinical Psychology*, 1968, *52*, 287–295.

Bell, P. A., & Baron, R. A. Environmental influences on attraction: Effects of heat, attitude similarity, and personal evaluations. *Bulletin of the Psychonomic Society*, 1974, *4*, 479–481.

Bell, P. A., & Baron, R. A. Aggression and heat: The mediating role of negative affect. *Journal of Applied Social Psychology*, 1976, *6*, 18–30.

Bell, R. Q. A reinterpretation of the direction of effects in studies of socialization. *Psychological Review*, 1968, *75*, 81–95.

Bell, R. Q. Stimulus control of parent or caretaker behavior by offspring. *Developmental Psychology*, 1971, *4*, 63–72.

Bell-Rowbotham, B., & Boydell, C. Crime in Canada: A distributional analysis. In C. Boydell, C. Grindstaff, & P. Whitehead (Eds.), *Deviant behavior and societal reaction*. Toronto: Holt, 1972.

Belmont, L., & Marolla, F. A. Birth order, family size, and intelligence. *Science*, 1973, *182*, 1096–1101.

Beloff, H. Two forms of social conformity: Acquiescence and conventionality. *Journal of Abnormal and Social Psychology*, 1958, *56*, 99–103.

Bem, D. J. An experimental analysis of self-persuasion. *Journal of Personality and Social Psychology*, 1965, *1*, 199–218.

Bem, D. J. Inducing belief in false confessions. *Journal of Personality and Social Psychology*, 1966, *3*, 707–710.

Bem, D. J. Self-perception: An alternative interpretation of cognitive dissonance phenomena. *Psychological Review*, 1967, *74*, 183–200.

Bem, D. J. *Beliefs, attitudes, and human affairs*. Monterey, Calif.: Brooks/Cole, 1970.

Bem, D. J. Self-perception theory. In L. Berkowitz (Ed.), *Advances in experimental social psychology* (Vol. 6). New York: Academic Press, 1972.

Bem, D. J., & Allen, A. On predicting some of the people some of the time: The search for cross-situational consistencies in behavior. *Psychological Review*, 1974, *81*, 506–520.

Bem, S. L. The measurement of psychological androgyny. *Journal of Consulting and Clinical Psychology*, 1974, *42*, 155–162.

Bem, S. L. Sex role adaptability: One consequence of psychological androgyny. *Journal of Personality and Social Psychology*, 1975, *31*, 634–643.

Bem, S. L. Probing the promise of androgyny. In A. G. Kaplan & J. P. Bean (Eds.), *Beyond sex-role stereotypes: Readings toward a psychology of androgyny*. Boston: Little, Brown, 1976.

Bem, S. L. Beyond androgyny: Some presumptuous prescriptions for a liberated sexual identity. In J. Sherman & F. Denmark (Eds.), *Psychology of women: Future directions of research*. New York: Psychological Dimensions, in press.

Bender, L. *Child psychiatric techniques*. Springfield, Ill.: Charles C Thomas, 1952.

Bennett, D. C. Segregation and racial integration. *Annals of the Association of American Geographers*, 1973, *63*, 48–57.

Bennett, D. C. Interracial ratios and proximity in dormitories: Attitudes of university students. *Environment & Behavior*, 1974, *6*(2), 212–232.

Bennis, W. G., Berkowitz, M., Affinito, M., & Malone, M. Authority, power, and the ability to influence. *Human Relations*, 1958, *11*, 143–155.

Benson, P. L., Karabenick, S. A., & Lerner, R. M. *Pretty pleases: The effects of physical attractiveness, race and sex on receiving help*. Paper presented at the meeting of the Midwestern Psychological Association, Chicago, May 1975.

Bentham, J. An introduction to the principles of morals and legislation. Oxford: Clarendon Press, 1879. (Quoted in G. W. Allport, 1954a.)

Berdie, R. F. Playing the dozens. *Journal of Abnormal and Social Psychology*, 1947, *42*, 120–121.

Berg, I. A., & Collier, J. S. Personality and group differences in extreme response sets. *Educational and Psychological Measurement*, 1953, *13*, 164–169.

Berg, K. E. Ethnic attitudes and agreement with a Negro person. *Journal of Personality and Social Psychology*, 1966, *4*, 215–220.

Berkowitz, L. Sharing leadership in small, decision-making groups. *Journal of Abnormal and Social Psychology*, 1953, *48*, 231–238.

Berkowitz, L. Group standards, cohesiveness, and productivity. *Human Relations*, 1954, *7*, 509–519.

Berkowitz, L. Liking for the group and the perceived merit of the group's behavior. *Journal of Abnormal and Social Psychology*, 1957, *54*, 353–357.

Berkowitz, L. Some factors affecting the reduction of overt hostility. *Journal of Abnormal and Social Psychology*, 1960, *60*, 14–21.

Berkowitz, L. The contagion of violence: An S-R mediational analysis of some effects of observed aggression. In *Nebraska Symposium on Motivation*. Lincoln: University of Nebraska Press, 1970.

Berkowitz, L. Social norms, feelings, and other factors affecting helping and altruism. In L. Berkowitz (Ed.), *Advances in experimental social psychology* (Vol. 6). New York: Academic Press, 1972.

Berkowitz, L. Reactance and the unwillingness to help others. *Psychological Bulletin*, 1973, *79*, 310–337.

Berkowitz, L. *A survey of social psychology*. Hinsdale, Ill.: Dryden Press, 1975.

Berkowitz, L., Corwin, R., & Hieronimus, M. Film violence and subsequent aggressive tendencies. *Public Opinion Quarterly*, 1963, *27*, 217–229.

Berkowitz, L., & Cottingham, D. R. The interest value and relevance of fear-arousing communications. *Journal of Abnormal and Social Psychology*, 1960, *60*, 37–43.

Berkowitz, L., & Geen, R. G. Film violence and the cue properties of available targets. *Journal of Personality and Social Psychology*, 1966, *3*, 525–530.

Berkowitz, L., & Lundy, R. M. Personality characteristics related to susceptibility to influence by peers or authority figures. *Journal of Personality*, 1957, *25*, 306–316.

Berkowitz, L., & Macaulay, J. R. Some effects of differences in status level and status stability. *Human Relations*, 1961, *14*, 135–148.

Berkowitz, L., & Rawlings, E. Effects of film violence in inhibitions against subsequent aggression. *Journal of Abnormal and Social Psychology*, 1963, *66*, 405–412.

Berkowitz, M. I. *An experimental study of the relation between group size and social organization.* Unpublished doctoral dissertation, Yale University. (Summarized in E. J. Thomas & C. F. Fink, 1963.)

Berkowitz, N. H., & Wolkon, G. H. A forced choice form of the F scale free of acquiescent response set. *Sociometry*, 1964, *27*, 54–65.

Berkowitz, W. R., Nebel, J. C., & Reitman, J. W. *Height and interpersonal attraction: The 1969 mayoral election in New York City.* Paper presented at the 79th Annual Convention of the American Psychological Association, Washington, D. C., September 1971.

Bernard, J. *Academic women.* University Park: Pennsylvania State University Press, 1964.

Bernstein, D. A., & Allen, G. J. Fear survey schedule (II): Normative data and factor analysis based upon a large college sample. *Behavior Research and Therapy*, 1969, *7*, 403–408.

Berry, J. W. Independence and conformity in subsistence-level societies. *Journal of Personality and Social Psychology*, 1967, *7*, 415–418.

Berry, J. W. Ecological and cultural factors in spatial perceptual development. *Canadian Journal of Behavioral Science*, 1971, *3*, 324–336.

Berry, J. W. *Human ecology and cognitive style: Comparative studies in cultural and psychological adaptation.* New York: Wiley, 1976.

Berscheid, E. Opinion change and communicator-communicatee similarity and dissimilarity. *Journal of Personality and Social Psychology*, 1966, *4*, 670–680.

Berscheid, E., Dion, K., Walster, E., & Walster, G. W. Physical attractiveness and dating choice: A test of the matching hypothesis. *Journal of Experimental Social Psychology*, 1971, *7*, 173–189.

Berscheid, E., & Walster, E. When does a harm-doer compensate a victim? *Journal of Personality and Social Psychology*, 1967, *6*, 435–441.

Berscheid, E., & Walster, E. *Interpersonal attraction.* Reading, Mass.: Addison-Wesley, 1969. (2nd ed. 1978.)

Berscheid, E., & Walster, E. A little bit about love. In T. L. Huston (Ed.), *Foundations of interpersonal attraction.* New York: Academic Press, 1974.

Berschied, E., Walster, E., & Barclay, A. The effect of time on the tendency to compensate a victim. *Psychological Reports*, 1969, *25*, 431–436.

Bevan, W. The sound of the wind that's blowing. *American Psychologist*, 1976, *31*, 481–491.

Biase, D. V., & Zuckerman, M. Sex differences in stress responses to total and partial sensory deprivation. *Psychosomatic Medicine*, 1967, *29*, 380–390.

Bickman, L. *The effect of the presence of others on bystander intervention in an emergency.* Unpublished doctoral dissertation, City University of New York, 1969.

Bickman, L. The effect of another bystander's ability to help on bystander intervention in an emergency. *Journal of Experimental Social Psychology*, 1971, *7*, 367–379. (a)

Bickman, L. The effect of social status on the honesty of others. *Journal of Social Psychology*, 1971, *85*, 87–92. (b)

Bickman, L. Social influence and diffusion of responsibility in an emergency. *Journal of Experimental Social Psychology*, 1972, *8*, 438–445.

Biddle, B. J., & Thomas, E. J. (Eds.). *Role theory: Concepts and research.* New York: Wiley, 1966.

Bieliauskas, V., Miranda, S. B., & Lansky, L. M. Obviousness of two masculinity-femininity tests. *Journal of Consulting and Clinical Psychology*, 1968, *32*, 314–318.

Bierhoff-Alfermann, D., & Bierhoff, H. W. *Social interaction and the use of psychological theories by "naive" judges.* Paper presented at the 21st International Congress in Psychology, Paris, 1976.

Bierhoff, H. W., & Bierhoff-Alfermann, D. The use of psychological theories by "naive" judges: A study in implicit personality theory. *European Journal of Social Psychology*, 1976, *6*(14), 429–445.

Bindra, D. *Motivation: A systematic reinterpretation.* New York: Ronald Press, 1959.

Birmingham, D. L. Situational and personality factors in conformity (Doctoral dissertation, St. Louis University, 1974). *Dissertation Abstracts International*, 1974, *35*, 2421B. (University Microfilms No. 74–24,042)

Bixenstine, V. E., DeCorte, M. S., & Bixenstine, B. A. Conformity to peer-sponsored misconduct at four grade levels. *Developmental Psychology*, 1976, *12*, 226–236.

Bjerstedt, A. Preparation, process, and product in small group interaction. *Human Relations*, 1961, *14*, 183–189.

Blake, R. R., Helson, H., & Mouton, J. S. The generality of conformity behavior as a function of factual anchorage, difficulty of task, and amount of social pressure. *Journal of Personality*, 1957, *25*, 294–305.

Blake, R. R., & Mouton, J. S. *Group dynamics: Key to decision making.* Houston: Gulf, 1961.

Blake, R. R., Rhead, C. C., Wedge, B., & Mouton, J. S. Housing architecture and social interaction. *Sociometry*, 1956, *19*, 133–139.

Blau, P. *Exchange and power in social life.* New York: Wiley, 1964.

Bleda, P. R. *Sex differences in the conditioning of attraction.* Unpublished manuscript, U.S. Army Research Institute, undated.

Blood, R. O., Jr., & Wolfe, D. M. *Husbands and wives: The dynamics of married living.* New York: Free Press, 1960.

Blum, G. S. *Psychodynamics: The science of unconscious mental forces.* Belmont, Calif.: Brooks/Cole, 1966.

Blumer, H. Collective behavior. In J. Gould & W. L. Kolb (Eds.), *Dictionary of the social sciences.* New York: Free Press, 1964.

Blurton Jones, N. G. Criteria for use in describing facial expressions of children. *Human Biology*, 1971, *43*, 365–413.

Boas, F. (Ed.). *General anthropology.* Boston: Heath, 1938.

Bock, R. D. Multivariate analysis of variance of repeated measurements. In C. W. Harris (Ed.), *Problems in measuring change.* Madison: University of Wisconsin Press, 1963.

Bogardus, E. S. *Fundamentals of social psychology* (2nd ed.). New York: Century, 1931.

Bolwig, N. Facial expression in primates with remarks on parallel development in certain carnivores. *Behavior*, 1964, *22*, 167–192.

Boneau, A. Psychology's manpower: Report on the 1966 national register of scientific and technical personnel. *American Psychologist*, 1968, *23*, 325–334.

Boomer, D. S. Subjective certainty and resistance to change. *Journal of Abnormal and Social Psychology*, 1959, *58*, 323–328.

Borden, R. J., Bowen, R., & Taylor, S. P. Shock setting behavior as a function of physical attack and extrinsic reward. *Perceptual and Motor Skills*, 1971, *33*, 563–568.

Borgatta, E. F. Analysis of social interaction and sociometric perception. *Sociometry*, 1954, *17*, 7–32.

Borgatta, E. F., & Bales, R. F. Sociometric status patterns and characteristics of interaction. *Journal of Abnormal and Social Psychology*, 1956, *43*, 289–297.

Borgatta, E. F., Couch, A. S., & Bales, R. F. Some findings relevant to the great man theory of leadership. *American Sociological Review*, 1954, *19*, 755–759.

Borgatta, E. F., & Glass, D. C. Personality concomitants of extreme response sets (ERS). *Journal of Social Psychology*, 1961, *55*, 213–221.

Borgatta, E. F., & Stimson, J. Sex differences in interaction characteristics. *Journal of Social Psychology*, 1963, *60*, 89–100.

Bose, C. E. *Jobs and gender: Sex and occupational prestige*. Baltimore, Md.: Center for Metropolitan Planning and Research, Johns Hopkins University, August 1973.

Bossard, J. H. S. Residential propinquity as a factor in mate selection. *American Journal of Sociology*, 1932, *38*, 219–224.

Bouchard, T. J. Personality, problem-solving procedure, and performance in small groups. *Journal of Applied Psychology Monograph*, 1969, *53*.

Bouchard, T. J., & Hare, M. Size, performance, and potential in brainstorming groups. *Journal of Applied Psychology*, 1970, *54*, 51–55.

Bovard, E. W. Group structure and perception. *Journal of Abnormal and Social Psychology*, 1951, *46*, 398–405.

Bovard, E. W. *Psychological Review*, 1959, *66*, 267.

Bowerman, C. E. Age relationships at marriage, by marital status and age at marriage. *Marriage and Family Living*, 1956, *18*, 231–233.

Bradburn, N. M. *The structure of psychological well-being*. Chicago: Aldine, 1968.

Braginsky, D. Machiavellianism and manipulative interpersonal behavior in children. *Journal of Experimental Social Psychology*, 1970, *6*, 77–99.

Brannigan, C. R., & Humphries, D. A. Human nonverbal behavior, a means of communication. In N. G. Blurton Jones, *Ethological studies of child behavior*. Cambridge, England: Cambridge University Press, 1972.

Brannon, R. C. Predicting behavior from verbal attitude expression. *Dissertation Abstracts International;* 1975, *36* (3–B), 1497.

Brehm, J. W. *A theory of psychological reactance*. New York: Academic Press, 1966.

Brehm. J. W. *Responses to loss of freedom: A theory of psychological reactance*. Morristown, N.J.: General Learning Press, 1972.

Brehm, J. W., & Cohen, A. R. *Explorations in cognitive dissonance*. New York: Wiley, 1962.

Brehm, J. W., & Mann, M. Effect of importance of freedom and attraction to group members on influence produced by group pressure. *Journal of Personality and Social Psychology*, 1975, *31*, 816–824.

Brewer, E., & Tomlinson, J. W. C. The manager's working day. *Journal of Industrial Economics*, 1963–1964, *12*, 191–197.

Brewer, M. B. Averaging versus summation in composite ratings of complex social stimuli. *Journal of Personality and Social Psychology*, 1968, *8*, 20–26.

Brewer, M. B. The role of ethnocentrism in intergroup conflict. In W. G. Austin & S. Worchel (Eds.), *The social psychology of intergroup relations*. Monterey, Calif.: Brooks/Cole, 1979.

Brickman, P. Crime and punishment in sports and society. *Journal of Social Issues*, 1977, *33*, 140–164.

Brigham, J. C. Ethnic stereotypes. *Psychological Bulletin*, 1971, *76*, 15–38.

Brislin, R. W., & Lewis, S. A. Dating and physical attractiveness: Replication. *Psychological Reports*, 1968, *22*, 976.

Brislin, R. W., & Olmstead, K. H. An examination of two models designed to predict behavior from attitude and other verbal measures. *Proceedings of the 81st Annual Convention of the American Psychological Association*, 1973, pp. 259–260. (Summary)

Brock, T. Communicator-recipient similarity and decision-change. *Journal of Personality and Social Psychology*, 1965, *1*, 650–654.

Brock, T. C., & Becker, L. A. Ineffectiveness of "overheard" counterpropaganda. *Journal of Personality and Social Psychology*, 1965, *2*, 654–660.

Brockner, J., & Swap, W. C. Effects of repeated exposure and attitudinal similarity on self-disclosure and interpersonal attraction. *Journal of Personality and Social Psychology*, 1976, *33*, 531–540.

Brookover, W. B., & Holland, J. B. An inquiry into the meaning of minority group attitude expressions. *American Sociological Review*, 1952, *17*, 196–202.

Brookover, W. B., Thomas, S., & Peterson, A. Self-concept of ability and school performance. *Sociology of Education*, 1964, *37* (Spring), 271–278.

Brophy, I. N. The luxury of anti-Negro prejudice. *Public Opinion Quarterly*, 1946, *9*, 456–466.

Broverman, I. K., Broverman, D. M., Clarkson, F. E., Rosenkrantz, P. S., & Vogel, S. R. Sex-role stereotypes and clinical judgments of mental health. *Journal of Consulting Psychology*, 1972, *34*, 1–7.

Brown, M., Jennings, J., & Vanik, V. The motive to avoid success: A further examination. *Journal of Experimental Research in Personality*, 1974, *8*, 172–176.

Brown, P., & Elliot, R. Control of aggression in a nursery school class. *Journal of Experimental Child Psychology*, 1965, *2*, 103–107.

Brown, R. *Social psychology*. New York: Free Press, 1965.

Brown, R. W., Black, A. H., & Horowitz, A. E. Phonetic symbolism in natural languages. *Journal of Abnormal and Social Psychology*, 1955, *50*, 388–393.

Brown, R. W., & Lenneberg, E. H. A study in language and cognition. *Journal of Applied Social Psychology*, 1954, *49*, 454–462.

Browne, J. The used car game. In M. P. Golden (Ed.), *The research experience*. Itasca, Ill.: Peacock, 1976.

Bruner, J. S., Oliver, R. R., Greenfield, P. M., et al. *Studies in cognitive growth: A collaboration at the Center for Cognitive Studies*. New York: Wiley, 1966.

Bruner, J. S., & Tagiuri, R. Person perception. In G. Lindzey

(Ed.), *Handbook of Social Psychology* (Vol. 2). Reading, Mass.: Addison-Wesley, 1954.

Bryan, A. I., & Boring, E. G. Women in academic psychology: Factors affecting their professional careers. *American Psychologist*, 1947, *2*, 3–20.

Bryan, J. H. Why children help: A review. *Journal of Social Issues*, 1972, *28*, 87–104.

Bryan, J. H., & London, P. Altruistic behavior by children. *Psychological Bulletin*, 1970, *73*, 200–211.

Bryan, J. H., & Schwartz, T. H. The effects of film material upon children's behavior. *Psychological Bulletin*, 1971, *75*, 50–59.

Bryan, J. H., & Test, M. A. Models and helping: Naturalistic studies in aiding behavior. *Journal of Personality and Social Psychology*, 1967, *6*, 400–407.

Bryan, J. H., & Walbeck, N. The impact of words and deeds concerning altruism upon children. *Child Development*, 1970, *41*, 747–757. (a)

Bryan, J. H., & Walbeck, N. Preaching and practicing self sacrifice: Children's actions and reactions. *Child Development*, 1970, *41*, 329–353. (b)

Buchanan, D. R., Juhnke, R., & Goldman, M. Violation of personal space as a function of sex. *Journal of Social Psychology*, 1976, *99*, 187–192.

Buck, R. W., Miller, R. E., & Caul, W. F. Sex, personality, and physiological variables in the communication of affect via facial expression. *Journal of Personality and Social Psychology*, 1974, *30*, 587–596.

Buck, R. W., & Parke, R. D. Behavioral and physiological response to the presence of a friendly or neutral person in two types of stressful situations. *Journal of Personality and Social Psychology*, 1972, *24*, 362–371.

Buck, R. W., Savin, V. J., Miller, R. E., & Caul, W. F. Communication of affect through facial expressions in humans. *Journal of Personality and Social Psychology*, 1972, *23*, 362–371.

Buckhout, R., Alper, A., Chern, S., Silverberg, G., & Slomovits, M. Determinants of eyewitness performance on a lineup. *Bulletin of the Psychonomic Society*, 1974, *4*, 191–192.

Buckhout, R., Figueroa, D., & Proff, E. *Eyewitness identification: Effects of suggestion and bias in identifications from photographs* (Report No. CR–11). Brooklyn, N.Y.: Brooklyn College, Center for Responsive Psychology, 1974.

Buikhuisen, W., Buikhuisen, F., & Dijksterhuis, P. H. Delinquency and stigmatization. *British Journal of Sociology*, 1971, *11*, 185–187.

Bullitt, S. *To be a politician*. Garden City, N.Y.: Doubleday, 1961.

Bumpass, L. The trend of interfaith marriage in the United States. *Social Biology*, 1970, *3*, 253–259.

Bunge, M. Culture as a subsystem of society: Culture change as an aspect of social change. In *Reconstructing a Culture*. Symposium presented at the meeting of the American Association for the Advancement of Science, Boston, February 1976.

Burgess, R. L. The withering away of social psychology. *American Sociologist*, 1977, *12*, 12–14.

Burke, P. J. Role differentiation and the legitimation of task activity. *Sociometry*, 1968, *31*, 404–411.

Burke, P. J. Participation and leadership in small groups. *American Sociological Review*, 1974, *39*, 832–843.

Burns, T. The directions of activity and communication in a departmental executive group. *Human Relations*, 1954, *7*, 73–97.

Buss, A. *The psychology of aggression*. New York: Wiley, 1961.

Buss, A. Instrumentality of aggression, feedback, and frustration as determinants of physical aggression. *Journal of Personality and Social Psychology*, 1966, *3*, 153–162.

Byrne, D. The influence of propinquity and opportunities for interaction on classroom relationships. *Human Relations*, 1961, *14*, 63–69.

Byrne, D. Attitudes and attraction. In L. Berkowitz (Ed.), *Advances in experimental social psychology* (Vol. 4). New York: Academic Press, 1969.

Byrne, D. *The attraction paradigm*. New York: Academic Press, 1971.

Byrne, D., & Buehler, J. A. A note on the influence of propinquity upon acquaintanceships. *Journal of Abnormal and Social Psychology*, 1955, *51*, 147–148.

Byrne, D., Clore, G., & Worchel, P. The effect of economic similarity-dissimilarity on interpersonal attraction. *Journal of Personality and Social Psychology*, 1966, *4*, 220–224.

Byrne, D., Ervin, C. R., & Lamberth, J. Continuity between the experimental study of attraction and real-life computer dating. *Journal of Personality and Social Psychology*, 1970, *16*, 157–165.

Byrne, D., Golightly, C., & Capaldi, E. J. Construction and validation of the food attitude scale. *Journal of Consulting Psychology*, 1963, *27*, 215–222.

Byrne, D., London, O., & Reeves, K. The effects of physical attractiveness, sex, and attitude similarity on interpersonal attraction. *Journal of Personality*, 1968, *36*, 259–276.

Byrne, D., & Nelson, D. Attraction as a function of attitude similarity-dissimilarity: The effect of topic importance. *Psychonomic Science*, 1964, *1*, 93–94.

Byrne, D., & Nelson, D. Attraction as a linear function of proportion of positive reinforcements. *Journal of Personality and Social Psychology*, 1965, *1*, 659–663.

Byrne, D., Nelson, D., & Reeves, K. Effects of consensual validation and invalidation on attraction as a function of verifiability. *Journal of Experimental Social Psychology*, 1966, *2*, 98–107.

Caballero, C. M., Giles, P., & Shaver, P. Sex role traditionalism and fear of success. *Sex Roles*, 1975, *1*(4), 319–326.

Cahnman, W. J. The stigma of obesity. *Sociological Quarterly*, 1968, *9*, 283–299.

Cairns, L. G., & Bochner, S. Measuring sympathy toward handicapped children with the "lost-letter" technique. *Australian Journal of Psychology*, 1974, *26*, 89–91.

Cairns, R. B., & Nakelski, J. S. On fighting in mice: Situational determinants of intragroup dyadic stimulation. *Psychonomic Science*, 1970, *18*(1), 16–17.

Calder, B. J., & Ross, M. *Attitudes and behavior*. Morristown, N.J.: General Learning Press, 1973.

Calvin, A. Social reinforcement. *Journal of Social Psychology*, 1962, *56*, 15–19.

Campbell, A., Converse, P., Miller, W., & Stokes, D. *The American voter*. New York: Wiley, 1960.

Campbell, D. T. *The generality of social attitudes*. Unpublished doctoral dissertation, University of California, Berkeley, 1947.

Campbell, D. T. The indirect assessment of social attitudes. *Psy-*

chological Bulletin, 1950, *47*, 15–38.

Campbell, D. T. Social attitudes and other acquired behavioral dispositions. In S. Koch (Ed.), *Psychology: A study of a science* (Vol. 6). New York: McGraw-Hill, 1963.

Campbell, D. T. Distinguishing differences of perception from failures of communication in cross-cultural studies. In F. C. S. Northrop & H. H. Livingston (Eds.), *Cross-cultural understanding: Epistemology in anthropology*. New York: Harper & Row, 1964.

Campbell, D. T., & McCandless, B. R. Ethnocentrism, xenophobia, and personality. *Human Relations*, 1951, *4*, 185–192.

Campbell, D. T., Siegman, C., & Rees, M. B. Direction-of-wording effects in the relationships between scales. *Psychological Bulletin*, 1967, *68*, 293–303.

Campus, N. *Convergence between different measures of trans-situational consistency*. Paper presented at the 81st Annual Convention of the American Psychological Association, September 1973.

Campus, N. Trans-situational consistency as a dimension of personality. *Journal of Personality and Social Psychology*, 1974, *29*, 593–600.

Cancro, R. Genetic considerations in the etiology and prevention of schizophrenia. In G. Usdin (Ed.), *Schizophrenia: Biological and psychological perspectives*. New York: Brunner-Mazel, 1975.

Cannavale, F. J., Scarr, H. A., & Pepitone, A. Deindividuation in the small group: Further evidence. *Journal of Personality and Social Psychology*, 1970, *16*, 141–147.

Cantril, H. Attitudes in the making. *Understanding the Child*, 1934, *4*, 13–15.

Cantril, H. *The invasion from Mars. A study in the psychology of panic*. Princeton, N.J.: Princeton University Press, 1940.

Cantril, H. The intensity of an attitude. *Journal of Abnormal and Social Psychology*, 1946, *41*, 129–135.

Cantril, H. *The pattern of human concerns*. New Brunswick, N.J.: Rutgers University Press, 1965.

Caplow, T., & Forman, R. Neighborhood interaction in a homogeneous community. *American Sociological Review*, 1950, *15*, 357–366.

Carlson, E., & Carlson, R. Male and female subjects in personality research. *Journal of Personality and Social Psychology*, 1960, *61*, 482–483.

Carlson, S. *Executive behavior*. Stockholm: Strombergs, 1951.

Carment, D. W. Rate of simple motor responding as a function of coaction, competition, and sex of the participants. *Psychonomic Science*, 1970, *19*, 342–343.

Carr, S. J., & Dabbs, J. M., Jr. The effects of lighting, distance, and intimacy of topic on verbal and visual behavior. *Sociometry*, 1974, 592–600.

Carter, L. F., Haythorn, W., & Howell, M. A further investigation of the criteria of leadership. *Journal of Abnormal and Social Psychology*, 1950, *45*, 350–358.

Carter, L. F., Haythorn, W., Shriver, B., & Lanzetta, J. The behavior of leaders and other group members. *Journal of Abnormal and Social Psychology*, 1951, *46*, 589–595.

Cartwright, D., & Harary, F. Structural balance: A generalization of Heider's theory. *Psychological Review*, 1956, *63*, 277–293.

Carver, C. S. Physical aggression and attitudes toward punish-

ment. *Journal of Experimental Social Psychology*, 1975, *11*(6), 510–519.

Castell, P. J., & Goldstein, J. H. Social occasions for joking: A cross-cultural study. In A. J. Chapman & H. C. Foot (Eds.), *It's a funny thing, humour*. Oxford: Pergamon Press, 1977.

Castell, P. J., & Taylor, D. A. *Effects of disclosure style on resistance to disclosure and liking*. Paper presented at the 48th Annual Meeting of the Eastern Psychological Association, Boston, Massachusetts, 1977.

Cates, J. Psychology's manpower: Report on the 1968 National Register of Scientific and Technical Personnel. *American Psychologist*, 1970, *25*, 254–263.

Cattell, R. B. New concepts for measuring leadership in terms of group syntality. *Human Relations*, 1951, *4*, 161–184.

Cerbus, G. Seasonal variation in some mental health statistics: Suicides, homicides, psychiatric admissions, and institutional placement of the retarded. *Journal of Clinical Psychology*, 1970, *26*, 61–63.

Cerbus, G., & Dallara, R. F. Seasonal differences of depression in mental hospital admissions as measured by the MMPI. *Psychological Reports*, 1975, *36*, 737–738.

Chafetz, J. S. *Masculine/feminine or human*. Itasca, Ill.: Peacock, 1974.

Chapanis, N. P., & Chapanis, A. Cognitive dissonance: Five years later. *Psychological Bulletin*, 1964, *61*, 1–22.

Chapko, M. K., & Revers, R. R. Contagion in a crowd: The effects of crowd size and initial discrepancy from unanimity. *Journal of Personality and Social Psychology*, 1976, *33*, 382–386.

Chapko, M. K., & Solomon, H. Air pollution and recreational behavior. *Journal of Social Psychology*, 1976, *100*, 149–150.

Chapman, A. J. Eye contact, physical proximity and laughter: A re-examination of the equilibrium model of social intimacy. *Social Behavior and Personality*, 1975, *3*, 143–155.

Charry, J. M. *Meteorology and behavior: The effects of positive air ions on human performance, physiology and mood*. Unpublished doctoral dissertation, New York University, 1976.

Charry, J. M., & Hawkinshire, F. B. W. *Biologically mediated behavior in response to meteorological conditions*. Paper presented at 84th Annual Convention of the American Psychological Association, Washington, D.C., September 1976.

Chase, J. Inside HEW: Women protest sex discrimination. *Science*, 1971, *174*, 270–274.

Chein, I. The problems of inconsistency: A restatement. *Journal of Social Issues*, 1949, *5*, 52–61.

Chein, I. Notes on a framework for the measurement of discrimination and prejudice. In M. Jahoda, M. Deutsch, & S. W. Cook (Eds.), *Research methods in social relations*. New York: Dryden Press, 1951.

Chen, S. C. Social modification of the activity of ants in nest building. *Physiological Zoology*, 1938, *10*, 420–436.

Child, I. L., Potter, E. H., & Levine, E. M. Children's textbooks and personality development: An exploration in the social psychology of education. *Psychological Monographs*, 1946, *60*, No. 3.

Child, I. L., Storm, T., & Veroff, J. Achievement themes in folk tales related to socialization practice. In J. W. Atkinson (Ed.), *Motives in fantasy, action and society*. Princeton, N.J.: Van Nostrand, 1958.

Chittenden, E. A., Foan, W., Zweil, D. M., & Smith, J. R. *Child Development*, 1968, *39*, 1223.

Chodoff, P., & Carpenter, W. T. Psychogenic theories of schizophrenia. In G. Usdin (Ed.), *Schizophrenia: Biological and psychological perspectives.* New York: Brunner-Mazel, 1975.

Choo, T. Communicator credibility and communication discrepancy as determinants of opinion change. *Journal of Social Psychology*, 1964, *64*, 1–20.

Christian, J. J. The adreno-pituitary system and population cycles in mammals. *Journal of Mammalogy*, 1950, *31*, 247–259.

Christian, J. J. Effect of population size on the adrenal glands and reproductive organs of male white mice. *American Journal of Physiology*, 1955, *181*, 477–480.

Christian, J. J. The role of endocrine and behavioral factors in the growth of mammalian populations. In Gorbman (Ed.), *Comparative endocrinology.* New York: Wiley, 1959.

Christian, J. J. Endocrine adaptive mechanisms and the physiologic regulation of population growth. In Mayer & Van Gelder (Eds.), *Physiological mammalogy.* New York: Academic Press, 1963.

Christian, J. J., Flyger, V., & Davis, D. C. Factors in the mass mortality of a herd of sitka deer, *Cervus nippon. Chesapeake Science*, 1960, *1*, 79–95.

Christian, J. J., Lloyd, J. A., & Davis, D. E. The role of endocrines in the self-regulation of mammalian populations. *Recent Progress in Hormone Research*, 1965, *21*, 501–578.

Christie, L. S., Luce, R. D., & Macy, J., Jr. *Communication and learning in task-oriented groups* (Tech. Rep. W231). Cambridge, Mass.: Massachusetts Institute of Technology, Research Laboratory of Electronics, 1952.

Christie, R., & Geis, F. Some consequences of taking Machiavelli seriously. In E. F. Borgatta & W. W. Lambert (Eds.), *Handbook of personality theory and research.* Chicago: Rand McNally, 1968.

Christie, R., & Geis, F. (Eds.). *Studies in Machiavellianism.* New York: Academic Press, 1970. (a)

Christie, R., & Geis, F. The ten dollar game. In R. Christie & F. Geis (Eds.), *Studies in Machiavellianism.* New York: Academic Press, 1970. (b)

Christie, R., & Jahoda, M. (Eds.). *Studies in the scope and method of the authoritarian personality.* New York: Free Press, 1954.

Cialdini, R. B., Darby, B. L., & Vincent, J. E. Transgression and altruism: A case for hedonism. *Journal of Experimental Social Psychology*, 1973, *9*, 502–516.

Cicourel, A. *Method and measurement in sociology.* New York: Free Press, 1964.

Clancy, K., & Gove, W. Sex differences in mental illness: An analysis of response bias in self-reports. *American Journal of Sociology*, 1974, *80*, 205–216.

Claridge, G. S. *Personality and arousal.* Oxford: Pergamon Press, 1967.

Clark, K., & Clark, M. Racial identification and preference in Negro children. In T. Newcomb & E. Hartley (Eds.), *Readings in social psychology.* New York: Holt, 1947.

Clark, M. S., Gotay, C. C., & Mills, J. Acceptance of help as a function of similarity of the potential helper and opportunity to repay. *Journal of Applied Social Psychology*, 1974, *4*, 224–229.

Clark, R. D., III, & Word, L. E. Why don't bystanders help? Because of ambiguity? *Journal of Personality and Social Psychology*, 1972, *24*, 392–400.

Clark, R. D., III, & Word, L. E. Where is the apathetic bystander? Situational characteristics of the emergency. *Journal of Personality and Social Psychology*, 1974, *29*, 279–287.

Clement, R., Gardner, R. C., & Smythe, P. C. Inter-ethnic contact: Attitudinal consequences. *Canadian Journal of Behavioral Sciences*, 1977, *9*, 205–215.

Clemente, F. Age and academic mobility. *Gerontologist*, 1973, *13*, 180–185. (a)

Clemente, F. Early career determinants of research productivity. *American Journal of Sociology*, 1973, *79*, 409–419. (b)

Clemente, F., & Hendricks, J. A further look at the relationship between age and productivity. *Gerontologist*, 1973, *13*, 106–110.

Clifford, M. M., & Walster, E. The effect of physical attractiveness on teacher expectation. *Sociology of Education*, 1973, *46*, 248–258.

Clifton, A. K., & Lee, D. E. Self-destructive consequences of sex-role socialization. *Suicide and Life-Threatening Behavior*, 1976, *6*(1), 11–22.

Clinard, M. *The black market.* New York: Rinehart, 1952.

Cline, M. The influence of social context on the perception of faces. *Journal of Personality*, 1956, *25*, 142–158.

Clore, G. L. *Interpersonal attraction: An overview.* Morristown, N.J.: General Learning Press, 1975.

Clore, G. L., & Byrne, D. A reinforcement-affect model of attraction. In T. L. Huston (Ed.), *Foundations of interpersonal attraction.* New York: Academic Press, 1974.

Clore, G. L., & Jeffrey, K. M. *Emotional role playing, attitude change and attraction toward a disabled person.* Unpublished manuscript, University of Illinois, 1971.

Clore, G. L., Wiggins, N. H., & Itkin, S. Gain and loss in attraction: Attributions from nonverbal behavior. *Journal of Personality and Social Psychology*, 1975, *31*, 706–712.

Coates, S., Lord, M., & Jakobovics, E. Field dependence-independence, social-non-social play and sex differences in preschool children. *Perceptual and Motor Skills*, 1975, *40*, 195–202.

Coch, L., & French, J. R. P., Jr. Overcoming resistance to change. *Human Relations*, 1948, *1*, 512–532.

Cohen, A. M., Bennis, W. G., & Wolkon, G. H. The effects of changes in communication networks on the behaviors of problem-solving groups. *Sociometry*, 1962, *25*, 177–196.

Cohen, A. M., & Mennic, W. G. The effects of continual practice on the behavior of problem-solving groups. *Sociometry*, 1961, *24*, 416–431.

Cohen, A. R. Upward communication in experimentally-created hierarchies. *Human Relations*, 1958, *11*, 41–53.

Cohen, A. R. Some implications of self-esteem for social influence. In C. I. Hovland & I. L. Janis (Eds.), *Personality and persuasibility.* New Haven, Conn.: Yale University Press, 1959.

Cohen, A. R. *Attitude change and social influence.* New York: Basic Books, 1964.

Coleman, A. D. Territoriality in man: A comparison of behavior in home and hospital. *American Journal of Orthopsychiatry*, 1968, *38*, 464–468.

Coleman, J. F., Blake, R. R., & Mouton, J. S. Task difficulty and conformity pressures. *Journal of Abnormal and Social Psychology*, 1958, *57*, 120–122.

Collins, B. E. *Public and private conformity: Competing explanations by improvisation, cognitive dissonance, and attribution theories.* New York: Warner Modular Publications, 1973.

Collins, B. E., & Raven, B. H. Group structure: Attraction, coalitions, communication, and power. In G. Lindzey & E. Aronson (Eds.), *The handbook of social psychology* (Vol. 4, 2nd ed.). Reading, Mass.: Addison-Wesley, 1969.

Colson, W. N. *Self-disclosure as a function of social approval.* Unpublished master's thesis, Howard University, 1968.

Conrad, R. The effect of vocalizing on comprehension in the profoundly deaf. *British Journal of Psychology*, 1971, *62*(2), 147–150.

Constantinople, A. Masculinity: An exception to a famous dictum? *Psychological Bulletin*, 1973, *80*, 389–407.

Cook, A. Fat pride. *Washington Post Magazine*, May 14, 1978, 25; 27; 28.

Cook, S. W. Desegregation: A psychological analysis. *American Psychologist*, 1957, *12*, 1–13.

Cook, S. W. Motives in a conceptual analysis of attitude-related behavior. In J. Brigham & T. Weissbach (Eds.), *Racial attitudes in America: Analyses and findings of social psychology.* New York: Harper & Row, 1972.

Cook, S. W., & Sellitz, C. A. A multiple-indicator approach to attitude measurement. *Psychological Bulletin*, 1964, *62*, 36–55.

Cooley, C. H. *Social organization.* New York: Scribner's, 1909.

Coopersmith, S. *The antecedents of self-esteem.* San Francisco: Freeman, 1967.

Coppen, A. Role of serotonin in affective disorders. In J. Barchas & G. Usdin (Eds.), *Serotonin and behavior.* New York: Academic Press, 1973.

Cortes, J. B., & Gatti, F. M. *Delinquency and crime: A biopsychosocial approach.* New York: Seminar Press, 1972.

Costanzo, P. R., Reitan, H. T., & Shaw, M. E. Conformity as a function of experimentally induced minority and majority competence. *Bulletin of the Psychonomic Society*, 1968, *10*, 329–330.

Cottrell, N. B., Wack, D. L., Sekerak, G. J., & Rittle, R. H. Social facilitation of dominant response by the presence of an audience and the mere presence of others. *Journal of Personality and Social Psychology*, 1968, *9*, 245–250.

Couch, A., & Keniston, K. Yeasayers and naysayers: Agreeing response set as a personality variable. *Journal of Abnormal and Social Psychology*, 1960, *60*, 151–174.

Couch, A., & Keniston, K. Agreeing response set and social desirability. *Journal of Abnormal and Social Psychology*, 1961, *62*, 175–179.

Coutts, L. M., & Ledden, M. Nonverbal compensatory reactions to changes in interpersonal proximity. *Journal of Social Psychology*, in press.

Coutts, L. M., & Schneider, F. W. Visual behavior in an unfocused interaction as a function of sex and distance. *Journal of Experimental Social Psychology*, 1975, *11*, 64–77.

Coutts, L. M., & Schneider, F. W. Affiliative conflict theory: An investigation of the intimacy equilibrium and compensation

hypothesis. *Journal of Personality and Social Psychology*, 1976, *34*, 1135–1142.

Cowan, T. A., & Strickland, D. A. *The legal structure of a confined microsociety* (A report on the cases of Penthouse I and III). Internal working paper No. 34, Space Sciences Laboratory, Social Sciences Project, University of California, Berkeley, August 1965.

Cowen, E. L., Landes, J., & Schaet, D. E. The effects of mild frustration on the expression of prejudiced attitudes. *Journal of Abnormal and Social Psychology*, 1958, *58*, 33–38.

Cowley, W. H. Traits of face-to-face leaders. *Journal of Abnormal and Social Psychology*, 1931, *5*, 304–313.

Cox, D. F., & Bauer, R. A. Self-confidence and persuasibility in women. *Public Opinion Quarterly*, 1964, *28*, 453–466.

Cox, O. C. *Caste, class and race.* New York: Doubleday, 1948.

Cozby, P. C. Self-disclosure: A literature review. *Psychological Bulletin*, 1973, *79*, 73–91.

Cramer, E. H., & Flinn, D. E. *Psychiatric aspects of the SAM two-man space cabin simulator.* Tech. Report No. SAM-TDR-63-27, USAF School of Aerospace Medicine, Brooks AFB, Texas, September 1963.

Crandall, J. E. Some relationships among sex, anxiety, and conservatism of judgment. *Journal of Personality*, 1965, *33*, 99–107.

Crandall, J. E. Sex differences in extreme response style: Differences in frequency of use of extreme positive and negative ratings. *Journal of Social Psychology*, 1973, *89*, 281–293.

Crandall, J. E., & Rasmussen, R. D. Purpose in life as related to specific values. *Journal of Clinical Psychology*, 1975, *31*(3), 483–485.

Crandall, R. The assimilation of newcomers into groups. *Small Group Behavior*, in press.

Crandall, R., & Moreland, R. *Social categorization by "new" group members.* Unpublished manuscript, Texas Christian University, 1978.

Crane, D. Scientists at major and minor universities: A study of productivity and recognition. *American Sociological Review*, 1965, *30*, 699–714.

Crano, W. D. *Order effects in recall of counterattitudinal information.* Paper presented at the meeting of the Midwestern Psychological Association, Chicago, May 1973.

Cromwell, H. The relative effect on audience attitude of the first versus the second argumentative speech of a series. *Speech Monographs*, 1950, *17*, 105–122.

Cromwell, H., & Kuchel, R. An experimental study of the effect on attitude of listeners of repeating the same oral propaganda. *Journal of Social Psychology*, 1952, *35*, 175–184.

Cronbach, L. J. Processes affecting scores on "understanding others" and "assumed similarity." *Psychological Bulletin*, 1955, *52*, 177–193.

Cronbach, L. J. Proposals leading to analytic treatment of social perception scores. In R. Tagiuri & L. Petrullo (Eds.), *Person perception and interpersonal behavior.* Stanford, Calif.: Stanford University Press, 1958.

Croner, M. D., & Willis, R. H. Perceived differences in task competence and asymmetry of dyadic influence. *Journal of Abnormal and Social Psychology*, 1961, *62*, 705–708.

Crosbie, P. V. Social exchange and power compliance: A test of Homan's proposition. *Sociometry*, 1972, *35*, 203–222.

Crow, W. J. The effect of training upon accuracy and variability in interpersonal perception. *Journal of Abnormal and Social Psychology*, 1957, *55*, 355–359.

Crown, S. On being sane in insane places: A comment from England. *Journal of Abnormal Psychology*, 1975, *84*, 453–455.

Crowne, D. P., & Marlowe, D. *The approval motive: Studies in evaluative dependence.* New York: Wiley, 1964.

Crutchfield, R. S. Conformity and character. *American Psychologist*, 1955, *10*, 191–198.

Curran, J. P., & Lippold, S. The effects of physical attraction and attitude similarity on attraction in dating dyads. *Journal of Personality*, 1975, *43*, 528–539.

Dabbs, J. M., Jr., & Leventhal, H. Effects of varying the recommendations in fear-arousing communication. *Journal of Personality and Social Psychology*, 1966, *4*, 525–531.

Dahl, R. A. The analysis of influence in local communities. In C. A. Adrian (Ed.), *Social science and community action.* East Lansing, Mich.: 1960. (Cited in M. Hamilton, 1977.)

Dahl, R. A. *Who governs?* New Haven, Conn.: Yale University Press, 1961.

D'Andrade, R. Sex differences and cultural institutions. In E. Maccoby (Ed.), *The development of sex differences.* Stanford, Calif.: Stanford University Press, 1966.

Daniels, J. *Ordeal of ambition: Jefferson, Hamilton, Burr.* Garden City, N.Y.: Doubleday, 1970.

Daniels, L. R., & Berkowitz, L. Liking and response to dependency relationships. *Human Relations*, 1963, *16*, 141–148.

Dannenmaier, W. D., & Thumain, F. J. Authority status as a factor in perceptual distortion of size. *Journal of Social Psychology*, 1964, *63*, 361–365.

Darley, J. M. Fear and social comparison as determinants of conformity behavior. *Journal of Personality and Social Psychology*, 1966, *4*, 73–78.

Darley, J. M., & Aronson, E. Self-evaluation vs. direct anxiety reduction as determinants of the fear-affiliation relationship. *Journal of Experimental Social Psychology Monograph*, 1966.

Darley, J. M., & Batson, C. "From Jerusalem to Jericho": A study of situational and dispositional variables in helping behavior. *Journal of Personality and Social Psychology*, 1973, *27*, 100–108.

Darley, J. M., & Berscheid, E. Increased liking as a result of the anticipation of personal contact. *Human Relations*, 1967, *20*, 29–39.

Darley, J. M., & Latané, B. Bystander intervention in emergencies: Diffusion of responsibility. *Journal of Personality and Social Psychology*, 1968, *8*, 377–383. (a)

Darley, J. M., & Latané, B. When will people help in a crisis? *Psychology Today*, 1968, *2*(7), 54–57; 70–71. (b)

Darwin, C. *The expression of emotions in man and animals.* London: Murray, 1872.

Das, J. Prestige effects in body-sway suggestibility. *Journal of Abnormal Social Psychology*, 1960, *61*, 487–488.

Dashiell, J. F. Experimental studies of the influence of social situations on the behavior of individual human adults. In C. Murchison (Ed.), *Handbook of Social Psychology.* Worcester, Mass.: Clark University Press, 1935.

David, H. M. Prolonged space flight poses monotony problem. *Missiles & Rockets*, November 1963, 31–32.

Davis, A. E. Women as a minority group in higher academics. *American Sociologist*, 1969, *4*, 95–99.

Davis, D. A. On being *detectably* sane in insane places: Base rates and psychodiagnosis. *Journal of Abnormal Psychology*, 1976, *85*, 416–422.

Davis, J. A. Compositional effects, role systems, and the survival of small discussion groups. *Public Opinion Quarterly*, 1961, *25*, 578–584.

Davis, J. D. Self-disclosure in an acquaintance exercise: Responsibility for level of intimacy. *Journal of Personality and Social Psychology*, 1976, *33*, 787–792.

Davis, J. H., & Hornseth, J. Discussion patterns and word problems. *Sociometry*, 1967, *30*(1), 91–103.

Davis, J. H., Laughlin, P. R., & Komorita, S. S. The social psychology of small groups: Cooperative and mixed-motive interaction. *Annual Review of Psychology*, 1976, *27*, 501–541.

Davis, J. H., & Restle, F. The analysis of problems and prediction of group problem solving. *Journal of Abnormal and Social Psychology*, 1963, *66*, 103–116.

Davis, J. M., McCourt, W. F., Courtney, J., & Solomon, P. Sensory deprivation, the role of social isolation. *Archives of General Psychiatry*, 1961, *5*, 84–90.

Davis, K., & Moore, W. E. Some principles of stratification. *American Sociological Review*, 1945, *10*, 242–249.

Davis, W. L., & Davis, D. E. Internal-external control and attribution of responsibility for success and failure. *Journal of Personality*, 1972, *40*(1), 123–136.

Davison, G. D., & Valins, S. Maintenance of self-attributed and drug-attributed behavior change. *Journal of Personality and Social Psychology*, 1969, *11*, 25–33.

Davitz, J. R., & Mason, D. J. Socially facilitated redirection of a fear response in rats. *Journal of Comparative and Physiological Psychology*, 1955, *48*, 149–151.

Dawson, J. L. M. Cultural and physiological influences upon spatial-perceptual processes in West Africa—Part I. *International Journal of Psychology*, 1967, *2*, 115–128. (a)

Dawson, J. L. M. Cultural and physiological influences upon spatial-perceptual processes in West Africa—Part II. *International Journal of Psychology*, 1967, *2*, 171–185. (b)

Deaux, K. *The behavior of women and men.* Monterey, Calif.: Brooks/Cole, 1976.

Deaux, K., & Emswiller, T. Explanation of successful performance on sex-linked tasks: What is skill for the male is luck for the female. *Journal of Personality and Social Psychology*, 1974, *29*, 80–85.

Deaux, K., & Farris, E. *Attributing causes for one's own performance: The effects of sex, norms and outcomes.* Unpublished manuscript, Purdue University, 1974.

Deaux, K., & Farris, E. Complexity, extremity, and affect in male and female judgments. *Journal of Personality*, 1975, *43*, 379–389.

Deaux, K., & Taynor, J. Evaluation of male and female ability: Bias works two ways. *Psychological Reports*, 1973, *32*, 261–262.

Deaux, K., White, L., & Farris, E. Skill versus luck: Field and laboratory studies of male and female preferences. *Journal of Personality and Social Psychology*, 1975, *32*, 629–636.

DeFleur, M. L., & Westie, F. R. Verbal attitudes and overt acts: An experiment on the salience of attitudes. *American Sociological Review*, 1958, *23*, 667–673.

DeFleur, M. L., & Westie, F. R. Attitude as a scientific concept. *Social Forces*, 1963, *42*, 17–31.

Dement, W. C. A new look at the third state of existence. *Stanford M.D.*, 1969, *8*, 2–8.

Depner, C. E., & O'Leary, V. E. Understanding female careerism: Fear of success and new directions. *Sex Roles*, 1976, *2*(3), 259–268.

Derogatis, L. R., Covi, L., Lipman, K. S., Davis, D. M., & Rickels, K. Social class and race as mediator variables in neurotic symptomatology. *Archives of General Psychiatry*, 1971, *25*, 31–40.

Deutsch, M. The directions of behavior: A field-theoretical approach to the understanding of inconsistencies. *Journal of Social Issues*, 1949, *5*, 43–49.

Deutsch, M., & Collins, B. E. *Interracial housing: A psychological evaluation of a social experiment.* Minneapolis: University of Minnesota Press, 1951.

Deutsch, M., & Gerard, H. B. A study of normative and informational social influences upon individual judgment. *Journal of Abnormal and Social Psychology*, 1955, *51*, 629–636.

Deutsch, M., & Krauss, R. M. Studies of interpersonal bargaining. *Journal of Conflict Resolution*, 1962, *6*, 52–76.

Deutscher, I. Words and deeds: Social science and social policy. *Social Problems*, 1965, *13*, 233–254.

DeWolfe, A. S., & Governale, C. N. Fear and attitude change. *Journal of Abnormal and Social Psychology*, 1964, *69*, 119–123.

Diener, E., & Crandall, R. *Ethics in social and behavioral research.* Chicago: University of Chicago Press, 1978.

Dillehay, R. C. On the irrelevance of the classical negative evidence concerning the effect of attitudes on behavior. *American Psychologist*, 1973, *28*, 887–891.

Diller, P. *Phyllis Diller's housekeeping hints.* Garden City, N.Y.: Doubleday, 1966.

Dinerman, B. Sex differences in academia. *Journal of Higher Education*, 1971, *42*, 253–264.

Dinitz, S., Banks, F., & Pasamanick, B. Mate selection and social class: Changes during the past quarter century. *Marriage and Family Living*, 1960, *22*, 348–351.

Dion, K. K. Physical attractiveness and evaluation of children's transgressions. *Journal of Personality and Social Psychology*, 1972, *24*, 207–213.

Dion, K. K. Children's physical attractiveness and sex as determinants of adult punitiveness. *Developmental Psychology*, 1974, *10*, 772–778.

Dion, K. K., & Berscheid, E. *Physical attractiveness and sociometric choice in young children.* Unpublished manuscript, University of Minnesota, 1971.

Dion, K. K., Berscheid, E., & Walster, E. What is beautiful is good. *Journal of Personality and Social Psychology*, 1972, *24*, 285–290.

Dion, K. K., & Dion, K. L. Self-esteem and romantic love. *Journal of Personality*, 1975, *43*, 39–57.

Dion, K. L., & Dion, K. K. Correlates of romantic love. *Journal of Consulting and Clinical Psychology*, 1973, *41*, 51–56.

Dipboye, R. L., Fromkin, H. L., & Wiback, K. Relative importance of applicant sex, attractiveness, and scholastic standing in evaluation of job applicant resumes. *Journal of Applied Psychology*, 1975, *60*, 39–45.

Dittes, J. E., & Kelley, H. H. Effects of different conditions of acceptance upon conformity to group norms. *Journal of Abnormal and Social Psychology*, 1956, *53*, 100–107.

DiVesta, F. J., & Cox, L. Some dispositional correlates of conformity behavior. *Journal of Social Psychology*, 1960, *52*, 259–268.

Dohrenwend, B. P., & Dohrenwend, B. S. *Social status and psychological disorder.* New York: Wiley-Interscience, 1969.

Dollard, J. Under what conditions do opinions predict behavior? *Public Opinion Quarterly*, 1949, *12*, 623–632.

Dollard, J., Doob, L. W., Miller, N. E., Mowrer, O. H., & Sears, R. R. *Frustration and aggression.* New Haven, Conn.: Yale University Press, 1939.

Donnerstein, E., & Donnerstein, M. The effect of attitudinal similarity on interracial aggression. *Journal of Personality*, 1975, *43*, 485–502.

Donnerstein, E., Donnerstein, M., & Barrett, G. Where is the facilitation of media violence: The effects of nonexposure and placement of anger arousal. *Journal of Research in Personality*, in press.

Doob, A. N., Carlsmith, J., Freedman, J., Landover, T., & Tom, S. Effects of initial selling price on subsequent sales. *Journal of Personality and Social Psychology*, 1969, *11*, 345–350.

Doob, A. N., & Ecker, B. P. Stigma and compliance. *Journal of Personality and Social Psychology*, 1970, *14*, 302–304.

Doob, A. N., & Gross, A. E. Status of frustrator as an inhibitor of horn-honking responses. *Journal of Social Psychology*, 1968, *76*, 213–218.

Doob, L. W. The behavior of attitudes. *Psychological Review*, 1947, *54*, 135–156.

Dosey, M. A., & Meisels, M. Personal space and self-protection. *Journal of Personality and Social Psychology*, 1969, *11*, 93–97.

Douglass, C. D., & James, J. C. Support of new principal investigators by NIH: 1966 to 1972. *Science*, 1973, *181*, 241–244.

Dreger, R. M., & Miller, K. S. Comparative psychological studies of Negroes and Whites in the United States: 1959–1965. *Psychological Bulletin Monograph*, 1968, *70*(3, Pt. 2).

Dreyer, A. S., Dreyer, C. A., & Nebelkopf, E. B. Portable rod-and-frame test as a measure of cognitive style in kindergarten children. *Perceptual and Motor Skills*, 1971, *33*, 775–781.

Druckman, D. Dogmatism, prenegotiation experience, and simulated group representation as determinants of dyadic behavior in a bargaining situation. *Journal of Personality and Social Psychology*, 1967, *6*, 279–290.

Dubin, R. Business behavior behaviorally viewed. In G. B. Strother (Ed.), *Social science approaches to business behavior.* Homewood, Ill.: Dorsey Press, 1962.

Dubin, R., & Spray, S. L. Executive behavior and interaction. *Industrial Relations*, 1964, *3*(2), 99–108.

Duck, S. W. *The study of acquaintance.* London: Tweakfields, 1977. (a)

Duck, S. W. (Ed.). *Theory and practice in interpersonal attraction.*

New York: Academic Press, 1977. (b)

Duck, S. W. This is what friends are for. *Psychology Today* (British Ed.), 1977, *3*(3), 37–41. (c)

Duffy, E. The conceptual categories of psychology: A suggestion for revision. *Psychological Review*, 1941, *48*, 177–203.

Duffy, E. The concept of energy mobilization. *Psychological Review*, 1951, *58*, 30–40.

Duffy, E. *Activation and behavior.* New York: Wiley, 1962.

Duffy, E. Activation. In N. S. Greenfield & R. A. Sternbach (Eds.), *Handbook of psychophysiology.* New York: Holt, Rinehart & Winston, 1972.

Duncan, O. D., & Duncan, B. Residential distribution and occupational stratification. *American Journal of Sociology*, 1960, *60*, 493–503.

Duncker, K. Experimental modification of children's food preferences through social suggestion. *Journal of Abnormal and Social Psychology*, 1938, *33*, 489–507.

Dunnette, M. D., Campbell, J., & Jaastad, K. The effects of group participation on brainstorming effectiveness for two industrial samples. *Journal of Applied Psychology*, 1963, *47*, 30–37.

Durkheim, E. *Division of labor.* Glencoe, Ill.: Free Press, 1947.

Durkheim, E. *Suicide* (J. A. Spaulding & G. Simpson, trans.). New York: Free Press, 1951. (Originally published, 1897.)

Dutton, D. G., & Aron, A. P. Some evidence for heightened sexual attraction under conditions of high anxiety. *Journal of Personality and Social Psychology*, 1974, *30*, 510–517.

Dweck, C. S. The role of expectations and attributions on the alleviation of learned helplessness. *Journal of Personality and Social Psychology*, 1975, *31*, 674–685.

Dweck, C. S., & Repucci, N. D. Learned helplessness and reinforcement responsibility in children. *Journal of Personality and Social Psychology*, 1973, *25*, 109–116.

Eagle, M., Goldberger, L., & Breitman, M. Field dependence and memory for social vs neutral and relevant vs irrelevant incidental stimuli. *Perceptual and Motor Skills*, 1969, *29*, 903–910.

Eagly, A. H. Sex differences in influenceability. *Psychological Bulletin*, 1978, *85*, 86–116.

Easterlin, R. A. Does economic growth improve the human lot? Some empirical evidence. In P. A. David & M. W. Reder (Eds.), *Nations and households in economic growth.* Stanford, Calif.: Stanford University Press, 1973.

Eberts, E. H., & Lepper, M. R. Individual consistency in the proxemic behavior of preschool children. *Journal of Personality and Social Psychology*, 1975, *32*, 841–849.

Edney, J. J., Walker, C. A., & Jordan, N. L. Is there reactance in personal space? *Journal of Social Psychology*, 1976, *100*, 207–217.

Edsell, R. D. Noise and social interaction as simultaneous stressors. *Perceptual and Motor Skills*, 1976, *42*, 1123–1129.

Edwards, A. L. *Techniques of attitude scale construction.* New York: Appleton-Century-Crofts, 1957.

Edwards, A. L., & Walker, J. N. A note on the Couch and Keniston measure of agreement response set. *Journal of Abnormal and Social Psychology*, 1961, *62*, 173–174.

Edwards, D. J. A. Approaching the unfamiliar: A study of human interaction distances. *Journal of Behavioral Sciences*,

1972, *1*(4), 249–250.

Efran, M. G. *Visual interaction and interpersonal attraction.* Unpublished doctoral dissertation, University of Texas, 1969.

Efran, M. G. The effect of physical appearance on the judgment of guilt, interpersonal attraction, and severity of recommended punishment in a simulated jury task. *Journal of Research in Personality*, 1974, *8*, 45–54.

Efran, M. G., & Patterson, E. W. J. Voters vote beautiful: The effect of physical appearance on a national election. *Canadian Journal of Behavioral Science*, 1974, *6*, 352–356.

Ehrlich, D., Guttman, I., Schönbach, P., & Mills, J. Postdecision exposure to relevant information. *Journal of Abnormal and Social Psychology*, 1957, *54*, 98–102.

Ehrlich, H. J. Attitudes, behavior, and the intervening variables. *American Sociologist*, 1969, *4*, 29–34.

Ekman, P., & Friesen, W. V. Constants across cultures in the face and emotion. *Journal of Personality and Social Psychology*, 1971, *17*, 124–129.

Elder, G. H. Appearance and education in marriage mobility. *American Sociological Review*, 1969, *34*, 519–533.

Eldersveld, S. J., & Dodge, R. W. Personal contact or mail propaganda? An experiment in voting turnout and attitude change. In D. Katz, D. Cartwright, S. Eldersveld, & A. McC. Lee (Eds.), *Public opinion and propaganda.* New York: Dryden Press, 1954.

Ellis, L. J., & Bentler, P. M. Traditional sex-determined role standards and sex stereotypes. *Journal of Personality and Social Psychology*, 1973, *25*, 28–34.

Ellsworth, P. C., & Carlsmith, J. M. Effects of eye contact and verbal content on affective response to a dyadic interaction. *Journal of Personality and Social Psychology*, 1968, *10*, 15–20.

Ellsworth, P. C., & Carlsmith, J. M. Eye contact and gaze aversion in an aggressive encounter. *Journal of Personality and Social Psychology*, 1973, *28*, 280–292.

Ellsworth, P. C., & Ross, L. Intimacy in response to direct gaze. *Journal of Experimental Social Psychology*, 1975, *11*, 592–613.

Elman, J. B., Press, A., & Rosenkrantz, P. S. *Sex-roles and self-concepts: Real and ideal.* Paper presented at the 78th Annual Convention of the American Psychological Association, Miami, August 1970.

Elms, A. C. Acts of submission. In A. C. Elms (Ed.), *Social Psychology and Social Relevance.* Boston: Little, Brown, 1972.

Elzinga, R. H. Nonverbal communication: Body accessibility among Japanese. *Psychologia*, 1975, *18*, 205–211.

Emerson, R. M. Deviation and rejection: An experimental replication. *American Sociological Review*, 1954, *19*, 688–693.

Emerson, R. M. Social exchange theory. *Annual Review of Sociology*, 1976, *2*, 335–362.

Emswiller, T., Deaux, K., & Willits, J. E. Similarity, sex, and requests for small favors. *Journal of Applied Social Psychology*, 1971, *1*, 284–291.

Endler, N. S. The case for person-situation interactions. *Canadian Psychological Review*, 1975, *16*, 12–21.

Endler, N. S., Coward, T. R., & Wiesenthal, D. L. The effects of prior experience with a task on subsequent conformity to a different task. *Journal of Social Psychology*, 1975, *95*, 207–219.

Endler, N. S., & Hunt, J. McV. Sources of behavioral variance as measured by the S-R inventory of anxiousness. *Psychological Bulletin*, 1966, *65*, 336–346.

Endler, N. S., Wiesenthal, D. L., & Geller, S. H. The generalization of the effects of agreement and correctness on relative competence mediating conformity. *Canadian Journal of Behavioral Science*, 1972, *4*, 322–329.

Entwisle, D. R., & Webster, M. Expectations in mixed racial groups. *Sociology of Education*, 1974, *47*, 301–318.

Epstein, C. F. Encountering the male establishment: Sex-status limits on women's careers in the professions. *American Journal of Sociology*, 1970, *75*, 965–982.

Epstein, R., & Komorita, S. Childhood prejudice as a function of parental ethnocentrism, punitiveness, and outgroup characteristics. *Journal of Personality and Social Psychology*, 1966, *3*, 259–264.

Epstein, Y. N., & Hornstein, H. A. Penalty and interpersonal attraction as factors influencing the decision to help another person. *Journal of Experimental Social Psychology*, 1969, *5*, 272–282.

Eskilson, A., & Wiley, M. G. Sex composition and leadership in small groups. *Sociometry*, 1976, *39*, 183–194.

Esser, A. H., Chamberlain, A. S., Chappel, E. D., & Kline, N. S. Territoriality of patients on a research ward. In A. H. Esser (Ed.), *Recent advances in biological psychiatry* (Vol. 7). New York: Plenum Press, 1965.

Ettinger, R. F., Marino, C. J., Endler, N. S., Geller, S. H., & Natziuk, T. Effects of agreement and correctness on relative competence and conformity. *Journal of Personality and Social Psychology*, 1971, *19*, 204–212.

Etzioni, A. Human beings are not very easy to change after all. *Saturday Review*, June 3, 1972.

Etzioni, A. Social science in the jury box. *Cleveland Plain Dealer*, June 7, 1974, p. 5B; June 8, 1974, p. 5B.

Evans, G., & Howard, R. B. Personal space. *Psychological Bulletin*, 1973, *80*, 334–344.

Evans, R. I., Rozelle, R. M., Lasater, T. M., Dembroski, T. M., & Allen, B. P. Fear arousal, persuasion, and actual vs. implied behavioral change: New perspective utilizing a real-life dental hygiene program. *Journal of Personality and Social Psychology*, 1970, *16*, 220–227.

Exline, R. V. Visual interaction: The glances of power and preference. In J. Cole (Ed.), *Nebraska Symposium on Motivation* (Vol. 19). Lincoln: University of Nebraska Press, 1972.

Exline, R. V., Gray, D., & Schuette, D. Visual behavior in a dyad as affected by interview content and sex of respondent. *Journal of Personality and Social Psychology*, 1965, *1*, 201–209.

Exline, R. V., & Yellin, A. M. *Eye contact as a sign between man and monkey*. Paper presented at the 19th International Congress of Psychology, London, 1969.

Fagen, S. A. *Conformity and the relations between others' competence and own competence* (Doctoral dissertation, University of Pennsylvania, 1963). (University Microfilms No. 63–7037.)

Faley, T. E., & Tedeschi, J. T. Status and reactions to threats. *Journal of Personality and Social Psychology*, 1971, *17*, 192–199.

Farber, I. E. Sane and insane: Constructions and misconstructions. *Journal of Abnormal Psychology*, 1975, *84*, 589–620.

Farina, A., Chapnick, M., Simon, S., & Ditrichs, C. Variables in interracial aggression: Anonymity, expected retaliation, and a riot. *Journal of Personality and Social Psychology*, 1972, *22*, 273–278.

Farina, A., Fischer, E. H., Sherman, S., Smith, W. T., Groh, T., & Mermin, P. Physical attractiveness and mental illness. *Journal of Abnormal Psychology*, 1977, *86*(5), 510–517.

Farnsworth, P., & Misumi, I. Further data on suggestion in pictures. *Journal of Abnormal and Social Psychology*, 1931, *43*, 632.

Farrell, R. J., & Smith, S. *Behavior of five men confined for 30 days: Psychological assessment during project MESA*. Contract No. NASW-658, The Boeing Co., Seattle, Wash., No. D2-90586, 1964.

Farris, G. F., & Lim, F., Jr. Effects of performance on leadership, cohesiveness, influence, satisfaction, and subsequent performance. *Journal of Applied Psychology*, 1969, *53*(6), 490–497.

Faust, W. L. Group versus individual problem solving. *Journal of Abnormal and Social Psychology*, 1959, *59*, 68–72.

Feather, N. T. A structural balance model of communication effects. *Psychological Review*, 1964, *71*, 291–313.

Feather, N. T. Effects of prior success and failure on expectations of success and subsequent performance. *Journal of Personality and Social Psychology*, 1966, *3*, 287–298.

Feather, N. T. Attribution of responsibility and valence of success and failure in relation to initial confidence and task performance. *Journal of Personality and Social Psychology*, 1969, *13*, 129–144.

Feldman, R. A. An experimental study of conformity behavior as a small group phenomenon. *Small Group Behavior*, 1974, *5*(4), 404–426.

Feldman, R. H. L. Changes in nutrition attitudes and knowledge as a function of similar and expert communication sources among the Gusii of Kenya (Doctoral dissertation, Syracuse University, 1974). *Dissertation Abstracts International*, 1975, *35*, 5694B. (University Microfilms No. 75–10,539.)

Felipe, N. J., & Sommer, R. Invasions of personal space. *Social Problems*, 1966, *14*(2), 206–214.

Fendrich, J. M. A study of the association among verbal attitudes, commitment, and overt behavior in different experimental situations. *Social Forces*, 1967, *45*, 347–355.

Ferguson, L. W. Primary social attitudes. *Journal of Psychology*, 1939, *8*, 217–223.

Fernberger, S. W. A figural aftereffect in the third dimension of visual space. *American Journal of Psychology*, 1948, *61*, 291–293.

Ferri, E. *Criminal sociology* (J. I. Kelly & J. Lisle, trans.). New York: Agathon Press, 1967. (Originally published, 1917.)

Feshbach, N., & Sones, G. Sex differencces in adolescent reactions toward newcomers. *Developmental Psychology*, 1971, *4*, 381–386.

Feshbach, S. The drive-reducing function of fantasy behavior. *Journal of Abnormal and Social Psychology*, 1955, *50*, 3–11.

Feshbach, S. The catharsis hypothesis and some consequences of interaction with aggressive and neutral play objects. *Journal of Personality*, 1956, *24*, 449–462.

Feshbach, S. *Film violence and its effects on children: Some comments on the implications of research for public policy*. Paper presented at the 77th Annual Convention of the American Psychological Association, Washington, D.C., September 1969.

Feshbach, S. Aggression. In P. H. Mussen (Ed.), *Carmichael's man-*

ual of child psychology (Vol. 2). New York: Wiley, 1970.

Feshbach, S., & Singer, R. D. *Television and aggression*. San Francisco: Jossey-Bass, 1970.

Festinger, L. Informal social communication. *Psychological Review*, 1950, *57*, 271–282.

Festinger, L. An analysis of compliant behavior. In M. Sherif & M. O. Wilson (Eds.), *Group relations at the crossroads*. New York: Harper, 1953.

Festinger, L. A theory of social comparison processes. *Human Relations*, 1954, *7*, 117–140.

Festinger, L. *A theory of cognitive dissonance*. Stanford, Calif.: Stanford University Press, 1957.

Festinger, L. Cognitive dissonance. Scientific offprint No. 472, p. 6. (Originally published in *Scientific American*, 1962, *207*(4), 93–102.)

Festinger, L. Behavioral support for opinion change. *Public Opinion Quarterly*, 1964, *28*, 404–417. (a)

Festinger, L. *Conflict, decision, and dissonance*. Stanford, Calif.: Stanford University Press, 1964. (b)

Festinger, L., & Carlsmith, J. M. Cognitive consequences of forced compliance. *Journal of Abnormal and Social Psychology*, 1959, *58*, 203–210.

Festinger, L., Gerard, H. B., Hymovitch, B., Kelley, H. B., & Raven, B. The influence process in the presence of extreme deviants. *Human Relations*, 1952, *5*, 327–346.

Festinger, L., Pepitone, A., & Newcomb, T. Some consequences of de-individuation in a group. *Journal of Abnormal and Social Psychology*, 1952, *47*, 382–389.

Festinger, L., Schachter, S., & Back, K. *Social pressures in informal groups: A study of human factors in housing*. New York: Harper & Row, 1950.

Festinger, L., & Thibaut, J. Interpersonal communications in small groups. *Journal of Abnormal and Social Psychology*, 1951, *46*, 92–100.

Fidell, L. S. Empirical verification of sex discrimination in hiring practices in psychology. *American Psychologist*, 1970, *25*, 1094–1098.

Fiedler, F. E., Blaisdell, F. J., & Warrington, W. G. Unconscious attitudes as correlates of sociometric choice in a social group. *Journal of Abnormal and Social Psychology*, 1952, *4*, 790–796.

Fields, R. M. The status of women in psychology: How many and how come? *International Journal of Group Tensions*, 1974, *4*, 93–121.

Fine, G. A. *Social psychology, naive psychology and folklore: All together now?* Paper presented at the 83rd Annual Convention of the American Psychological Association, August 1975.

Fine, G. A. *The role of folklore and naive psychology in contemporary psychological research*. In preparation, 1980.

Finifter, A. W., & Abramson, P. R. City size and feelings of political competence. *Public Opinion Quarterly*, 1975, *39*, 189–198.

Firestone, I. J., Kaplan, K. J., & Russell, J. C. Anxiety, fear, and affiliation with similar-state versus dissimilar-state others: Misery sometimes loves nonmiserable company. *Journal of Personality and Social Psychology*, 1973, *26*, 409–414.

Fischer, E. H., & Winer, D. Participation in psychological research: Relation to birth order and demographic factors. *Journal of Consulting and Clinical Psychology*, 1969, *33*, 610–613.

Fishbein, M. Attitude and the prediction of behavior. In M.

Fishbein (Ed.), *Readings in attitude theory and measurement*. New York: Wiley, 1967.

Fishbein, M. The prediction of behavior from attitudinal variables. in C. D. Mortensen & K. K. Sereno (Eds.), *Advances in communication research*. New York: Harper & Row, 1973.

Fishbein, M., & Ajzen, I. Attitudes and opinions. *Annual Review of Psychology*, 1972, *23*, 487–544.

Fishbein, M., & Ajzen, I. Attitudes toward objects as predictors of single and multiple behavioral criteria. *Psychological Review*, 1974, *81*, 59–74.

Fishbein, M., & Ajzen, I. *Belief, attitude, intention, and behavior: An introduction to theory and research*. Reading, Mass.: Addison-Wesley, 1975.

Fishbein, M., & Hunter, R. Summation versus balance in attitude organization and change. *Journal of Abnormal and Social Psychology*, 1964, *69*, 505–510.

Fisher, A. Effects of stimulus variation on sexual satiation in the male rat. *Journal of Comparative and Physiological Psychology*, 1962, *55*(4), 614–620.

Fisher, J. D. *Attitude similarity as a determinant of perceived crowdedness and perceived environmental quality: Support for an interactive model for prediction of the behavioral effects of density and other environmental stimuli*. Unpublished master's thesis, Purdue University, 1973.

Fisher, J. D. Situation-specific variables as determinants of perceived environmental esthetic quality and perceived crowdedness. *Journal of Research in Personality*, 1974, *8*, 177–188.

Fisher, J. D., Rytting, M., & Heslin, R. *Hands touching hands: Affective and evaluative effects of an interpersonal touch*. Paper presented at the meeting of the Midwestern Psychological Association, Chicago, May 1975.

Fisher, J. M., & Harris, M. B. *Models, arousal and aggression*. Paper presented at the convention of the Rocky Mountain Educational Research Association, 1973.

Fisher, S., & Lubin, A. Distance as a determinant of influence in a two-person serial interaction situation. *Journal of Abnormal and Social Psychology*, 1958, *56*, 230–238.

Fisher, S., Rubinstein, I., & Freeman, R. W. Inter-trial effects of immediate self-committal in a continuous social influence situation. *Journal of Abnormal and Social Psychology*, 1956, *52*, 200–207.

Fitzgibbons, D. J., & Goldberger, L. Task and social orientation: A study of field dependence, "arousal," and memory for incidental material. *Perceptual and Motor Skills*, 1971, *32*, 167–174.

Fleishman, E., Harris, E., & Burtt, H. *Leadership and supervision in industry: An evaluation of a supervisory training program*. Columbus, Ohio: Ohio State University, Bureau of Educational Research, 1955. (Cited in L. Festinger, 1964.)

Flerx, V. C., & Rogers, R. W. *Sex-role stereotypes: Developmental aspects and early intervention*. Unpublished manuscript, University of South Carolina, 1975.

Foa, U. G. Interpersonal and economic resources. *Science*, 1971, *171*, 345–351.

Foley, L. A. Personality and situational influences on changes in prejudice: A replication of Cook's railroad game in a prison setting. *Journal of Personality and Social Psychology*, 1976, *34*, 846–856.

Ford, C. S., & Beach, F. A. *Patterns of sexual behavior.* New York: Harper, 1951.

Form, W. H., & Nosow, S. *Community in disaster.* New York: Harper, 1958.

Fortuno, R. F. Arapesh warfare. *American Anthropologist,* 1939, *41,* 28.

Fox, D. J., & Lorge, I. The relative quality of decisions written by individuals and by groups as the available time for problem solving is increased. *Journal of Social Psychology,* 1962, *57,* 227–242.

Francis, R. D. The effect of prior instructions and time knowledge on the tolerance of sensory isolation. *Journal of Nervous and Mental Disorders,* 1964, *139,* 182–185.

Frank, F., & Anderson, L. R. Effects of task and group size upon group productivity and member satisfaction. *Sociometry,* 1971, *34*(1), 135–149.

Frankfurt, L. P. *The role of some individual and interpersonal factors in the acquaintance process.* Unpublished doctoral dissertation, American University, 1965.

Freedman, J. L. *Crowding and behavior.* New York: Freeman, 1975.

Freedman, J. L., & Fraser, S. C. Compliance without pressure: The foot-in-the-door technique. *Journal of Personality and Social Psychology,* 1966, *4,* 195–202.

Freedman, J. L., Heshka, S., & Levy, A. *Population density and crime in metropolitan U.S. areas.* Unpublished manuscript, 1973.

Freedman, J. L., Heshka, S., & Levy, A. Population density and pathology: Is there a relationship? *Journal of Experimental Social Psychology,* 1974.

Freedman, J. L., Klevansky, S., & Ehrlich, P. I. The effect of crowding on human task performance. *Journal of Applied Social Psychology,* 1971, *1,* 7–26.

Freedman, J. L., Levy, A. S., Buchanan, R. W., & Price, J. Crowding and human aggressiveness. *Journal of Experimental Social Psychology,* 1972, *8,* 528–548.

Freeman, G. L. *The energetics of human behavior.* Ithaca, N.Y.: Cornell University Press, 1948.

Freeman, L. Homogamy in interethnic mate selection. *Sociology and Social Research,* 1955, *39,* 369–377.

French, J. R. P., Jr. The disruption and cohesion of groups. *Journal of Abnormal and Social Psychology,* 1941, *36,* 361–377.

French, J. R. P., Jr., & Raven, B. The bases of social power. In D. Cartwright (Ed.), *Studies in social power.* Ann Arbor: University of Michigan Press, 1959.

French, J. R. P., Jr., & Snyder, R. Leadership and interpersonal power. In D. Cartwright (Ed.), *Studies in social power.* Ann Arbor: University of Michigan Press, 1959.

Freud, E. L. (Ed.). *Letters to Sigmund Freud.* New York: Basic Books, 1960.

Freud, S. *Civilization and its discontents.* London: Hogarth Press, 1930.

Frieze, I. H. *Changing self-images and sex-role stereotypes in college women.* Paper presented at the 82nd Annual Convention of the American Psychological Association, New Orleans, August 1974.

Fromkin, H. L. Feelings of interpersonal undistinctiveness: An unpleasant affective state. *Journal of Experimental Research in Personality,* 1972, *6,* 178–185.

Fromkin, H. L., Dipboye, R. L., & Pyle, M. *Reversal of the attitude similarity-attraction effect by uniqueness deprivation* (Paper No. 344). Lafayette, Ind.: Purdue University, Institute for Research in the Behavioral, Economic, and Management Sciences, 1972.

Furth, H. G. Linguistic deficiency and thinking: Research with deaf subjects 1964–1969. *Psychological Bulletin,* 1971, *76* (1), 58–72.

Gaebelein, J. W. Instigative aggression in females. *Psychological Reports,* 1973, *33,* 619–622.

Gaebelein, J. W. Sex differences in instigative aggression. *Journal of Research in Personality,* 1977, *11,* 466–474.

Gaertner, S. L. Situational determinants of hurting and helping behavior. In R. Seidenberg & A. Snadowsky (Eds.), *Social psychology: An introduction.* New York: Free Press, 1976.

Gage, N. L. Judging interests from expressive behavior. *Psychological Monographs,* 1952, *66* (18, Whole No. 350).

Gage, N. L., & Cronbach, L. J. Conceptual and methodological problems in interpersonal perception. *Psychological Review,* 1955, *62,* 411–422.

Galle, O. R., Gove, W. R., & McPherson, J. M. Population density and pathology: What are the relations for man? *Science,* 1972, *176,* 23–30.

Galtung, J. Violence, peace, and peace research. *Journal of Peace Research,* 1969, *3,* 167–193.

Gans, H. *Urban villagers.* New York: Free Press, 1962.

Gardner, R. C., Wonnacott, E. J., & Taylor, D. M. Ethnic stereotypes: A factor analytic investigation. *Canadian Journal of Psychology,* 1968, *22,* 35–44.

Garfinkel, H. Studies of the routine grounds of everyday activities. *Social Problems,* 1964, *2,* 225–250.

Garfinkel, I., Haveman, R., & Betson, D. *Earnings capacity, poverty, and inequality.* New York: Academic Press, 1977.

Garland, H., & Brown, B. R. Face-saving as affected by subjects' sex, audiences' sex, and audience expertise. *Sociometry,* 1972, *35,* 280–289.

Gates, M. J., & Allee, W. C. Conditioned behavior of isolated and grouped cockroaches on a simple maze. *Journal of Comparative Psychology,* 1933, *15,* 331–358.

Geen, R. G. *Aggression.* Morristown, N.J.: General Learning Press, 1972. (Module No. 4039 V00)

Geen, R. G. Some effects of observing violence upon the behavior of the observer. In B. Maher (Ed.), *Progress in experimental personality research* (Vol. 8). New York: Academic Press, in press.

Geen, R. G., & O'Neal, E. C. Activation of cue-elicited aggression by general arousal. *Journal of Personality and Social Psychology,* 1969, *11,* 289–292.

Geen, R. G., & Pigg, R. Acquisition of an aggressive response and its generalization to verbal behavior. *Journal of Personality and Social Psychology,* 1970, *15,* 165–170.

Geen, R. G., & Stonner, D. Effects of aggressiveness habit strength on behavior in the presence of aggression-related stimuli. *Journal of Personality and Social Psychology,* 1971, *17,* 149–153.

Geer, J., Davison, G., & Gatchel, R. Reduction of stress in humans through nonveridical perceived control of aversive stimulation. *Journal of Personality and Social Psychology,* 1970, *16,* 731–738.

Geer, J. H., & Jarmecky, L. The effect of being responsible for reducing another's pain on subject's response and arousal. *Journal of Personality and Social Psychology*, 1973, *26*, 232–237.

Geis, F. L. The con game. In R. Christie & F. L. Geis (Eds.), *Studies in Machiavellianism*. New York: Academic Press, 1970.

Geis, F. L., Krupat, E., & Berger, D. *Taking over in group discussion*. Unpublished manuscript, New York University, 1965. (Cited in R. L. Christie & F. L. Geis [Eds.], *Studies in Machiavellianism*. New York: Academic Press, 1970.)

Gelfand, D. M. The influence of self-esteem on the rate of verbal conditioning and social matching behavior. *Journal of Abnormal and Social Psychology*, 1962, *65*, 259–265.

Gelfand, D. M., Hartmann, D. P., Walder, P., & Page, B. Who reports shoplifters? A field-experimental study. *Journal of Personality and Social Psychology*, 1973, *25*, 276–285.

Geller, S. H., Endler, N. S., & Wiesenthal, D. L. Conformity as a function of task generalization and relative competence. *European Journal of Social Psychology*, 1973, *3*, 53–62.

Genschaft, J. L., & Hirt, M. Language differences between black and white children. *Developmental Psychology*, 1974, *10*(3), 451–456.

Gerard, H. B. The effect of different dimensions of disagreement on the communication process in small groups. *Human Relations*, 1953, *6*, 249–272.

Gerard, H. B. The anchorage of opinions in face-to-face groups. *Human Relations*, 1954, *7*, 313–326.

Gerard, H. B. Disagreement with others, their credibility, and experienced stress. *Journal of Abnormal and Social Psychology*, 1961, *62*, 559–564.

Gerard, H. B., & Mathewson, G. C. The effect of severity of initiation on liking for a group: A replication. *Journal of Experimental Social Psychology*, 1966, *2*, 278–287.

Gerard, H. B., & Rabbie, J. M. Fear and social comparison. *Journal of Abnormal and Social Psychology*, 1961, *62*, 586–592.

Gergen, K. Interaction goals and personalistic feedback as factors affecting the presentation of self. *Journal of Personality and Social Psychology*, 1965, *1*, 413–424.

Gergen, K. J. *Experimentation in social psychology: A reappraisal*. Address presented to the 83rd Annual Convention of the American Psychological Association, Chicago, August, 1975.

Gibb, C. A. The sociometry of leadership in temporary groups. *Sociometry*, 1950, *13*, 226–243.

Gibb, C. A. Leadership. In G. Lindzey & E. Aronson (Eds.), *The handbook of social psychology* (Vol. 4, 2nd ed.). Reading, Mass.: Addison-Wesley, 1969.

Gibb, J. R. The effects of group size and of threat reduction upon creativity in a problem-solving situation. *American Psychologist*, 1951, *6*, 324. (Abstract)

Gilbert, G. O. Effect of negative air ions upon emotionality and brain serotonin levels in isolated rats. *International Journal of Biometeorology*, 1973, *17*(3), 267–275.

Gilmor, T. M., & Minton, H. L. Internal versus external attribution of task performance as a function of locus of control, initial confidence and success-failure outcome. *Journal of Personality*, 1974, *42*, 159–173.

Ginter, G., & Lindskold, S. Rate of participation and expertise as factors influencing leader choice. *Journal of Personality and Social Psychology*, 1975, *32*, 1085–1089.

Glanzer, M. R., & Glaser, R. Techniques for the study of group structure and behavior: I. Analyses of structure. *Psychological Bulletin*, 1959, *56*, 317–332.

Glanzer, M. R., & Glaser, R. Techniques for the study of group structure and behavior: II. Empirical studies of the effects of structure in small groups. *Quarterly Bulletin*, 1961, *58*, 1–27.

Glass, D. C., Cohen, S., & Singer, J. Urban din fogs the brain. *Psychology Today*, 1973, *6*(12), 94–99.

Glass, D. C., & Singer, J. E. *Urban stress*. New York: Academic Press, 1972.

Glass, D. C., & Singer, J. E. Experimental studies of uncontrollable and unpredictable noise. *Representative Research in Social Psychology*, 1973, *4*, 165–183.

Glass, D. C., Singer, J. E., & Friedman, L. N. Psychic cost of adaptation to an environmental stressor. *Journal of Personality and Social Psychology*, 1969, *12*, 200–210.

Glasser, J. *Nonverbal clues to deception*. Paper presented at the meeting of the District of Columbia Psychological Association, Washington, D.C., November 1977.

Glick, P. C. Intermarriage and fertility patterns among persons in major religious groups. *Eugenics Quarterly*, 1960, *7*, 31–38.

Glock, C. Y., & Stark, R. *Christian belief and anti-Semitism*. New York: Harper, 1966.

Goethals, G. R. Consensus and modality in the attribution process: The role of similarity and information. *Journal of Personality and Social Psychology*, 1972, *21*, 84–92.

Goffman, E. On face-work. *Psychiatry*, 1955, *18*, 213–231.

Goffman, E. *The presentation of self in everyday life*. Garden City, N.Y.: Doubleday/Anchor, 1959.

Goffman, E. *Behavior in public places: Notes on the social organization of gatherings*. New York: Free Press, 1966.

Gold, S. S. Alternative national goals and women's employment. *Science*, 1973, *179*, 656–660.

Goldberg, H., & Iverson, M. Inconsistency in attitude of high status persons and loss of influence: An experimental study. *Psychological Reports*, 1965, *16*, 673–683.

Goldberg, L. R., & Rorer, L. G. Use of two different response modes and repeated testings to predict social conformity. *Journal of Abnormal and Social Psychology*, 1966, *3*, 28–37.

Goldberg, S. *The inevitability of patriarchy*. New York: Morrow, 1973.

Goldberg, S. C. Three situational determinants of conformity to social norms. *Journal of Abnormal and Social Psychology*, 1954, *49*, 325–329.

Goldberg, S. C. Influence and leadership as a function of group structure. *Journal of Abnormal and Social Psychology*, 1955, *51*, 119–122.

Goldberg, S. C., & Lubin, A. Influence as a function of perceived judgment error. *Human Relations*, 1958, *11*, 275–280.

Goldberger, L., & Holt, R. R. Experimental interference with reality contact (perceptual isolation): I. Method and group results. *Journal of Nervous and Mental Disorders*, 1958, *127*, 99–112.

Goldsen, R., Rosenberg, M., Williams, R., & Suchman, E. *What college students think.* Princeton, N.J.: Van Nostrand, 1960.

Goldstein, J. H., & Arms, R. L. Effects of observing athletic contests on hostility. *Sociometry*, 1971, *34*, 83–90.

Gonos, G., Mulkern, V., & Poushinsky, N. Anonymous expression: A structural view of graffiti. *Journal of American Folklore*, 1976, *89*, 40–48.

Goode, W. J. The theoretical importance of love. *American Sociological Review*, 1959, *24*, 38–47.

Goodenough, D. R., & Witkin, H. A. *Origins of the field-dependent and field-independent cognitive styles* (ETS #RB-77-9). Princeton, N.J.: Educational Testing Service, 1977.

Goodenough, F. L. Interrelationships in the behavior of young children. *Child Development*, 1930, *1*, 29–48.

Goodnow, J. J. Cultural variations in cognitive skills. *Cognitive Studies*, 1970, *1*, 242–257.

Goranson, R. E. Media violence and aggressive behavior: A review of experimental research. In L. Berkowitz (Ed.), *Advances in experimental social psychology* (Vol. 5). New York: Academic Press, 1970.

Goranson, R. E., & Berkowitz, L. Reciprocity and responsibility reactions to prior help. *Journal of Personality and Social Psychology*, 1966, *3*, 227–232.

Goranson, R. E., & King, D. *Rioting and daily temperature: Analysis of the U.S. riots in 1967.* Unpublished manuscript, York University, Toronto, 1970.

Gorden, C., & Gergen, K. J. (Eds.). *The self in social interaction* (Vol. 1): *Classic and contemporary perspectives.* New York: Wiley, 1968.

Gordon, K. A study of esthetic judgments. *Journal of Experimental Psychology*, 1923, *6*, 36–43.

Gordon, K. Group judgments in the field of lifted weights. *Journal of Experimental Psychology*, 1924, *7*, 398–400.

Gorer, G. Man has no "killer" instinct. In M. F. A. Montagu (Ed.), *Man and aggression.* New York: Oxford University Press, 1968.

Gouaux, C. Induced affective states and interpersonal attraction. *Journal of Personality and Social Psychology*, 1971, *20*, 37–43.

Gough, H. G. *The adjective check list.* Palo Alto, Calif.: Consulting Psychologists Press, 1952.

Gould, R. Adult life stages: Growth toward self-tolerance. *Psychology Today*, February, 1975.

Gouldner, A. W. The norm of reciprocity: A preliminary statement. *American Sociological Review*, 1960, *25*, 161–178.

Gove, W. R., & Tudor, J. F. Adult sex roles and mental illness. *American Journal of Sociology*, 1973, *78*, 812–835.

Gowin, E. B. *The executive and his control of men.* New York: Macmillan, 1915.

Granberg, D. *Statistical analysis of the House Judiciary Committee's recommendation to impeach Richard Nixon.* Columbia, Mo.: University of Missouri, Center for Research in Social Behavior, 1975.

Greene, C. N. The reciprocal nature of influence between leader and subordinate. *Journal of Applied Psychology*, 1975, *60*, 187–193.

Greene, S. Attitudes toward working women have a "long way to go." *Gallup Opinion Index*, March 1976, 32–45 (Report No. 128).

Greenstein, T. N. Behavior change through value self-confrontation: A field experiment. *Journal of Personality and Social Psychology*, 1976, *34*, 254–262.

Greenwald, A. G. Behavior change following a persuasive communication. *Journal of Personality*, 1965, *33*, 370–391.

Greenwald, A. G. Effects of prior commitment on behavior change after a persuasive communication. *Public Opinion Quarterly*, 1966, *29*(4), 595–601.

Greenwald, A. G., & Ronis, D. L. Twenty years of cognitive dissonance: Case study of the evolution of a theory. *Psychological Review*, 1978, *85*, 53–57.

Grier, E., & Grier, G. *Privately developed interracial housing.* Berkeley: University of California Press, 1960.

Griffitt, W. B. Attraction toward a stranger as a function of direct and associated reinforcement. *Psychonomic Science*, 1968, *11*, 147–148.

Griffitt, W. B. Environmental effects on interpersonal affective behavior: Ambient effective temperature and attraction. *Journal of Personality and Social Psychology*, 1970, *15*, 240–244.

Griffitt, W. B. Attitude similarity and attraction. In T. L. Huston (Ed.), *Foundations of interpersonal attraction.* New York: Academic Press, 1974.

Griffitt, W. B., & Jackson, T. The influence of ability and non-ability information on personnel selection decisions. *Psychological Reports*, 1970, *27*, 959–962.

Griffitt, W. B., & Jackson, T. Simulated jury decisions: The influence of jury-defendant attitude similarity-dissimilarity. *Social Behavior and Personality: An International Journal*, 1973, *1*, 1–7.

Griffitt, W. B., & Veitch, R. Hot and crowded: Influences of population density and temperature on interpersonal affective behavior. *Journal of Personality and Social Psychology*, 1971, *17*, 92–98.

Griffitt, W. B., & Veitch, R. Preacquaintance attitude similarity and attraction revisited: Ten days in a fall-out shelter. *Sociometry*, 1974, *37*, 163–173.

Gross, A. E., Wallston, B. S., & Piliavin, I. M. Beneficiary attractiveness and cost as determinants of responses to routine requests for help. *Sociometry*, 1975, *38*, 131–140.

Gruder, C. L., & Cook, T. D. Sex, dependency, and helping. *Journal of Personality and Social Psychology*, 1971, *19*, 290–294.

Grusec, J. E., & Skubiski, S. L. Model nurturance, demand characteristics of the modeling experiment, and altruism. *Journal of Personality and Social Psychology*, 1970, *14*, 352–359.

Grush, J. E. *The impact of candidate expenditures, regionality, and prior outcomes on the 1976 Democratic presidential primaries.* Unpublished manuscript, University of Northern Illinois, 1978.

Grush, J. E., McKeough, K. L., & Ahlering, R. F. Extrapolating laboratory exposure research to actual political elections. *Journal of Personality and Social Psychology*, 1978, *36*, 257–270.

Guest, R. H. Of time and the foreman. *Personnel*, 1955–1956, *32*, 478–486.

Guetzkow, H., & Dill, W. R. Factors in the organizational development of task-oriented groups. *Sociometry*, 1957, *20*, 175–204.

Guetzkow, H., & Simon, H. The impact of certain communication nets in task-oriented groups. *Management Science*, 1955, *1*, 233–250.

Gullahorn, J. T. Distance and friendship as factors in the gross interaction matrix. *Sociometry*, 1952, *15*, 123–134.

Gurr, T. R. *Why men rebel*. Princeton, N.J.: Princeton University Press, 1970.

Gutmann, D. Men, women, and the parental imperative. *Commentary*, 1973, *56*(6), 59–64.

Guyer, L., & Fidell, L. Publications of men and women psychologists: Do women publish less? *American Psychologist*, February 1973, 157–160.

Haber, R. N. Discrepancy from adaptation-level as a source of affect. *Journal of Experimental Psychology*, 1958, *56*, 370–375.

Hackman, J. R., & Vidmar, N. Effects of size and task type on group performance and member reactions. *Sociometry*, 1970, *33*(1), 37–54.

Hadden, J. K. *A house divided*. Garden City, N.Y.: Doubleday, 1969.

Haeberlein, T. A., & Black, J. S. Attitudinal specificity and the prediction of behavior in a field setting. *Journal of Personality and Social Psychology*, 1976, *33*, 474–479.

Haefner, D. P. Some effects of guilt-arousing and fear-arousing persuasive communications on opinion change. *American Psychologist*, 1956, *11*, 359. (Abstract)

Hagen, R. L., & Kahn, A. Discrimination against competent women. *Journal of Applied Social Psychology*, 1975, *5*(4), 362–376.

Halcomb, C. G., & Kirk, R. E. Effects of air ionization upon the performance of a vigilance task. *Journal of Engineering Psychology*, 1965, *4*(4), 120–126.

Hall, E. T. *The silent language*. Garden City, N.Y.: Doubleday, 1959.

Hall, E. T. A system for the notation of proxemic behavior. *American Anthropologist*, 1963, *65*, 1003–1026.

Hall, E. T. *The hidden dimension*. Garden City, N.Y.: Anchor Books, 1966.

Hamilton, D. C., & Huffman, L. J. Generality of impression-formation processes for evaluative and nonevaluative judgments. *Journal of Personality and Social Psychology*, 1971, *20*, 200–207.

Hamilton, M. An analysis and typology of social power (Part II). *Philosophy of the Social Sciences*, 1977, *7*, 51–65.

Hamilton, V. L. *Applied social psychology: Response to crisis*. Paper delivered at the 85th Annual Convention of the American Psychological Association, San Francisco, August 1977.

Hammes, J. A. *Shelter occupancy studies at the University of Georgia*. Final report, Civil Defense Research, Athens, Ga., 1964.

Hare, A. P. A study of interaction and consensus in different sized groups. *American Sociological Review*, 1952, *17*(3), 261–267.

Hare, A. P., & Bales, R. F. Seating position and small group interaction. *Sociometry*, 1963, *26*, 480–486.

Hare, A. P., Borgatta, E. F., & Bales, R. F. (Eds.). *Small groups: Studies in social interaction*. New York: Knopf, 1965.

Harlow, H. F. *Journal of Genetic Psychology*, 1932, *43*, 211.

Harper, F. B. W., & Tuddenham, R. D. The sociometric composition of the group as a determinant of yielding to a distorted norm. *Journal of Psychology*, 1964, *58*, 307–311.

Harré, R., & Secord, P. F. *The explanation of social behavior*. New York: Littlefield, Adams, 1973.

Harris, D. V. Physical sex differences: A matter of degree. *Counseling Psychologist*, 1976, *6*(2), 9–11.

Harris, M. B. Reciprocity and generosity: Some determinants of sharing in children. *Child Development*, 1970, *41*, 313–328.

Harris, M. B. Models, norms and sharing. *Psychological Reports*, 1971, *29*, 147–153.

Harris, M. B. Field studies of modeled aggression. *Journal of Social Psychology*, 1973, *89*, 131–139.

Harris, M. B., & Samerotte, G. The effects of aggressive and altruistic modeling on subsequent behavior. *Journal of Social Psychology*, 1975, *95*, 173–182.

Harris, M. B., & Siebel, C. E. Affect, aggression, and altruism. *Developmental Psychology*, 1975, *11*, 623–627.

Harris, T. G. The scarlet letters: FAT. *Washington Post Magazine*, May 14, 1978, pp. 24; 27.

Harris, T. M. *Machiavellianism, judgment, independence, and attitudes toward teammate in a cooperative judgment task*. Unpublished doctoral dissertation, Columbia University, 1966. (Cited in R. Christie & F. L. Geis [Eds.], *Studies in Machiavellianism*. New York: Academic Press, 1970.)

Harrison, A. A. Exposure and popularity. *Journal of Personality*, 1969, *37*, 359–377.

Harrison, A. A. *Individuals and groups*. Monterey, Calif.: Brooks/Cole, 1976.

Hart, D. M. An ethnographic survey of the Riffian tribe of Aith Wuryāghil. *Tamuda* (Tetuan, Morocco), 1954, *2*, 51–86.

Hart, H. L. A., & Honore, A. M. *Causation in the law*. Oxford: Oxford University Press, 1959.

Hartley, E. L., & Hartley, R. E. *Fundamentals of social psychology*. New York: Knopf, 1952.

Hartnett, J. J., Bailey, K. G., & Gibson, F. W., Jr. Personal space as influenced by sex and type of movement. *Journal of Psychology*, 1970, *76*, 139–144.

Hartnett, J. J., & Elder, D. The princess and the nice frog: Study in person perception. *Perceptual and Motor Skills*, 1973, *37*, 863–866.

Hartnett, J. J., Gottlieb, J., & Hayes, R. L. Social facilitation theory and experimenter attractiveness. *Journal of Social Psychology*, 1976, *99*, 293–294.

Hartup, W. W. Peer interaction and social organization. In P. H. Mussen (Ed.), *Manual of Child Psychology* (Vol. 2). New York: Wiley, 1970.

Harvey, J. H., Arkin, R. M., Gleason, J. M., & Johnston, S. Effect of expected and observed outcome of an action on the differential causal attributions of actor and observer. *Journal of Personality*, 1974, *42*, 62–77.

Harvey, J. H., & Hays, D. G. Effect of dogmatism and authority of the source of communication upon persuasion. *Psychological Reports*, 1972, *30*, 119–122.

Harvey, O. J., & Consalvi, C. Status and conformity to pressures in informal groups. *Journal of Abnormal and Social Psychology*, 1960, *60*, 182–187.

Hastorf, A. H., & Piper, G. A note on the effect of explicit instructions on prestige suggestion. *Journal of Social Psychology*, 1951, *33*, 289–293.

Hastorf, A. H., Schneider, D. J., & Polefka, J. *Person perception*. Reading, Mass.: Addison-Wesley, 1970.

Havighurst, R. J., & Taba, H. *Adolescent character and personality*. New York: Wiley, 1949.

Haythorn, W. W., & Altman, I. Personality factors in isolated environments. In M. H. Appley & R. Trumbull (Eds.), *Psychological stress*. New York: Appleton-Century-Crofts, 1967. (a)

Haythorn, W. W., & Altman, I. Together in isolation. *Transaction*, 1967, *4*, 18–23. (b)

Haythorn, W. W., Altman, I., & Myers, T. I. Emotional symptomatology and subjective stress in isolated pairs of men. *Journal of Experimental Research in Personality*, 1966, *1*, 290–305.

Hearn, G. Leadership and the spatial factor in small groups. *Journal of Abnormal and Social Psychology*, 1957, *54*, 269–272.

Hebb, D. O. Drives and the CNS (conceptual nervous system). *Psychological Review*, 1955, *62*, 243–254.

Heider, F. Social perception and phenomenal causality. *Psychological Review*, 1944, *51*, 358–374.

Heider, F. Attitudes and cognitive organization. *Journal of Psychology*, 1946, *21*, 107–112.

Heider, F. *The psychology of interpersonal relations*. New York: Wiley, 1958.

Heilbrun, A. B. Sex role, instrumental-expressive behavior, and psychopathology in females. *Journal of Abnormal Psychology*, 1968, *73*, 131–136.

Heilbrun, A. B. Measurement of masculine and feminine sex role identities as independent dimensions. *Journal of Consulting and Clinical Psychology*, 1976, *44*(2), 183–190.

Heinemann, P. O., & Zax, M. Extremeness in evaluative responses to clinical test materials. *Journal of Social Psychology*, 1968, *75*, 175–183.

Heise, G. A., & Miller, G. A. Problem solving by small groups using various communication nets. *Journal of Abnormal Sociology Quarterly*, 1951, *46*, 327–335.

Heiss, J. S. Premarital characteristics of the religiously intermarried in an urban area. *American Sociological Review*, 1960, *25*, 47–55.

Heiss, J. S. Degree of intimacy and male-female interaction. *Sociometry*, 1962, *25*, 197–208.

Helmreich, R. L., & Collins, B. E. Situational determinants of affiliative preference under stress. *Journal of Personality and Social Psychology*, 1967, *6*, 79–85.

Helson, H. Adaptation-level as a basis for a quantitative theory of frames of reference. *Psychological Review*, 1948, *55*, 297–313.

Helson, H. Adaptation-level theory. In S. Koch (Ed.), *Psychology: A study of a science* (Vol. 1). New York: McGraw-Hill, 1959.

Helson, H. *Adaptation-level theory*. New York: Harper & Row, 1964.

Helson, H., Blake, R. R., & Mouton, J. S. Petition-signing as adjustment to situational and personal factors. *Journal of Social Psychology*, 1958, *48*, 3–10.

Henchy, T., & Glass, D. C. Evaluation apprehension and the social facilitation of dominant and subordinate responses. *Journal of Personality and Social Psychology*, 1968, *10*, 446–454.

Hendrick, C. Averaging versus summation in impression formation. *Perceptual and Motor Skills*, 1968, *27*, 443–446.

Hendrick, C., Bixenstine, V., & Hawkins, G. Race versus belief similarity as determinants of attraction. A search for a fair test. *Journal of Personality and Social Psychology*, 1971, *17*, 250–258.

Hendrick, C., & Giesen, M. Self-attribution of attitude as a function of belief feedback. *Memory and Cognition*, 1976, *4*, 150–155.

Hendrick, C., Giesen, M., & Borden, R. False physiological feedback and persuasion: Effect of fear arousal vs. fear reduction on attitude change. *Journal of Personality*, 1975, *43*, 196–214.

Hendrick, C., & Shaffer, D. R. Effect of pleading the Fifth Amendment on perceptions of guilt and morality. *Bulletin of the Psychonomic Society*, 1975, *6*(5), 449–452. (a)

Hendrick, C., & Shaffer, D. R. Murder: Effects of number of killers and victim mutilation on simulated jurors' judgments. *Bulletin of the Psychonomic Society*, 1975, *6*(3), 313–316. (b)

Herman, C. P. External and internal cues as determinants of the smoking behavior of light and heavy smokers. *Journal of Personality and Social Psychology*, 1974, *30*, 664–672.

Heshka, S., & Nelson, Y. Interpersonal speaking distance as a function of age, sex and relationship. *Sociometry*, 1972, *35*, 491–498.

Hess, R., & Torney, J. *The development of political attitudes in children*. Chicago: Aldine, 1967.

Hiebert, R., Jones, R., Lotito, E., & Lorenz, J. (Eds.). *The political image merchants*. Washington, D.C.: Acropolis Books, 1971.

Higbee, K. L. Fifteen years of fear arousal: Research on threat appeals: 1953–1968. *Psychological Bulletin*, 1969, *72*, 426–444.

Hill, R. C. Unionization and racial income inequality in the metropolis. *American Sociological Review*, 1974, *39*, 507–522.

Hill, W. A. Leadership style: Rigid or flexible. *Organizational Behavior and Human Performance*, 1973, *9*(1), 35–47.

Hill, W. A., & Hughes, D. Variations in leader behavior as a function of task type. *Organizational Behavior and Human Performance*, 1974, *11*, 83–86.

Hiller, E. T. *Principles of sociology.* New York: Harper, 1933.

Hilton, I. Differences in the behavior of mothers toward first- and later-born children. *Journal of Personality and Social Psychology,* 1967, *7,* 282–290.

Hineline, P. N., & Harrison, J. F. Lever biting as an avoidance response. *Bulletin of the Psychonomic Society,* 1978, *11*(4), 223–226.

Hiroto, D. S. Locus of control and learned helplessness. *Journal of Experimental Psychology,* 1974, *102,* 187–193.

Hirsig, R. [A computer simulation of conformity behavior.] Basel: Birkhäuser-Verlag, 1974. (Reviewed in R. DeRidder, *European Journal of Social Psychology,* 1974, *6,* 125–128.

Hochbaum, G. M. The relation between group members' self-confidence and their reactions to group pressures to uniformity. *American Sociological Review,* 1954, *19,* 678–687.

Hodge, R. W., Siegel, P. M., & Rossi, P. H. Occupational prestige in the United States: 1925–1963. In R. Bendix & S. M. Lipset (Eds.), *Class, status and power* (2nd ed.). New York: Free Press, 1966.

Hodge, R. W., Treiman, D. J., & Rossi, P. H. A comparative study of occupational prestige. In R. Bendix & S. M. Lipset (Eds.), *Class, status and power* (2nd ed.). New York: Free Press, 1966.

Hodgson, S. A., Hornstein, H. A., & LaKind, E. Socially mediated Zeigarnik effects as a function of sentiment, violence and desire for goal attainment. *Journal of Experimental Social Psychology,* 1972, *8,* 446–456.

Hoffman, C., & Kagan, S. Field dependence and facial recognition. *Perceptual and Motor Skills,* 1977, *44,* 119–124.

Hoffman, L. R., Burke, R. J., & Maier, N. R. F. Participation, influence, and satisfaction among members of problem-solving groups. *Psychological Reports,* 1965, *16,* 661–667.

Hoffman, L. W. Fear of success in males and females: 1965–1971. *Journal of Consulting and Clinical Psychology,* 1974, *42,* 353–358.

Hofling, C. K., Brotzman, E., Dalrymple, S., Graves, N., & Pierce, C. M. An experimental study in nurse-physician relationships. *Journal of Nervous and Mental Disease,* 1966, *143,* 171–180.

Hoiberg, B. C., & Stires, L. K. The effect of several types of pretrial publicity on the guilt attributions of simulated jurors. *Journal of Applied Social Psychology,* 1973, *3,* 267–275.

Hokanson, J. E. The effects of frustration and anxiety on overt aggression. *Journal of Abnormal and Social Psychology,* 1961, *62,* 346–351.

Holden, C. Women in Michigan: Academic sexism under siege. *Science,* 1972, *178,* 841–844.

Hollander, E. P. Conformity, status and idiosyncrasy credit. *Psychological Review,* 1958, *65,* 117–127.

Hollander, E. P. Competence and conformity in the acceptance of influence. *Journal of Abnormal and Social Psychology,* 1960, *61,* 365–369.

Hollander, E. P. *Leaders, groups and influence.* New York: Oxford University Press, 1964.

Hollander, E. P. *Principles and methods of social psychology.* New York: Oxford University Press, 1971.

Hollander, E. P. Independence, conformity, and civil liberties: Some implications from social psychological research. *Journal of Social Issues,* 1975, *31*(2), 55–67.

Hollander, E. P., & Julian, J. W. Studies in leader legitimacy, influence, and innovation. In L. Berkowitz (Ed.), *Advances in experimental social psychology* (Vol. 5). New York: Academic Press, 1970.

Hollander, E. P., & Webb, W. B. Leadership, followership, and friendship: An analysis of peer nominations. *Journal of Abnormal and Social Psychology,* 1955, *50,* 163–167.

Holley, M. Field dependence-independence, sophistication-of-body concept, and social distance selection (Doctoral dissertation, New York University, 1972). *Dissertation Abstracts International,* 1972, *33,* 296B. (University Microfilms No. 72–20,635.)

Hollingshead, A. B. Age relationships and marriage. *American Sociological Review,* 1951, *16,* 492–499.

Holmes, D. S., & Jorgenson, B. W. Do personality and social psychologists study men more than women? *Representative Research in Social Psychology,* 1971, *2,* 71–76.

Holzman, P. On hearing one's own voice. *Psychology Today,* 1971, *5*(6), 67–69; 98.

Homans, G. C. *The human group.* New York: Harcourt, 1950.

Homans, G. C. Social behavior as exchange. *American Journal of Sociology,* 1956, *63,* 597–606.

Homans, G. C. *Social behavior: Its elementary forms.* New York: Harcourt, 1961.

Homans, G. C. *Social behavior* (Rev. ed.). New York: Harcourt, Brace, 1974.

Honigann, J. J. *Culture and personality.* New York: Harper, 1954.

Horai, J., & Tedeschi, J. T. The effects of threat credibility and magnitude of punishment upon compliance. *Journal of Personality and Social Psychology,* 1969, *12,* 164–169.

Horn, P. The effects of crowding on children, adults and !Kung. *Psychology Today,* April 1974.

Horne, J. H., & Lupton, T. The work activities of "middle" managers—An exploratory study. *Journal of Management Studies,* 1965, *2*(1), 14–33.

Horner, M. S. *Sex differences in achievement motivation and performance in competitive and non-competitive situations.* Unpublished doctoral dissertation, University of Michigan, 1968.

Horner, M. S. Fail: Bright woman. *Psychology Today,* 1969, *3,* 36–38; 62.

Horner, M. S. The motive to avoid success and changing aspirations of college women. In J. M. Bardwick (Ed.), *Readings on the psychology of women.* New York: Harper & Row, 1972. (a)

Horner, M. S. Toward an understanding of achievement-related conflicts in women. *Journal of Social Issues,* 1972, *28*(2), 157–176. (b)

Hornstein, H. A. Social models and helping. In J. Macaulay & L. Berkowitz (Eds.), *Altruism and helping behavior.* New York: Academic Press, 1970.

Hornstein, H. A., Fisch, E., & Holmes, M. Influence of a model's feeling about his behavior and his relevance as a comparison other on observers' helping behavior. *Journal of Personality and Social Psychology*, 1968, *10*, 222–226.

Hornstein, H. A., Masor, H. N., Sole, K., & Heilman, M. Effects of sentiment and completion of a helping act on observer helping: A case for socially mediated Zeigarnik effects. *Journal of Personality and Social Psychology*, 1971, *17*, 107–112.

Horowitz, E., & Horowitz, R. Development of social attitudes in children. *Sociometry*, 1938, *1*, 301–338.

Horowitz, I. The effect of group norms on bystander intervention. *Journal of Social Psychology*, 1971, *83*, 265–273.

Horowitz, M. J. Human spatial behavior. *American Journal of Psychology*, 1965, *19*, 20–28.

Horowitz, M. J., Duff, D. F., & Stratton, L. O. Personal space and the body buffer zone. In H. Proshansky, W. Ittelson, & L. Rivlin (Eds.), *Environmental psychology: Man and his physical setting*. New York: Holt, Rinehart & Winston, 1970.

Horowitz, M. W. *The future of social psychology*. Paper presented to the meeting of the New York State Psychological Association, Kiamesha Lake, N.Y., April 1975.

Hovland, C. I. Reconciling conflicting results derived from experimental and survey studies of attitude change. *American Psychologist*, 1959, *14*, 8–17.

Hovland, C. I., Harvey, O. J., & Sherif, M. Assimilation and contrast effects in reactions to communication and attitude change. *Journal of Abnormal and Social Psychology*, 1957, *55*, 244–252.

Hovland, C. I., Janis, I. L., & Kelley, H. H. *Communication and persuasion*. New Haven, Conn.: Yale University Press, 1953.

Hovland, C. I., Lumsdaine, A. A., & Sheffield, F. D. *Experiments on mass communication*. Princeton, N.J.: Princeton University Press, 1949.

Hovland, C. I., & Mandell, W. An experimental comparison of conclusion drawing by the communicator and by the audience. *Journal of Abnormal and Social Psychology*, 1952, *47*, 581–588.

Hovland, C. I., & Mandell, W. Is there a "law of primacy in persuasion"? In C. Hovland et al. (Eds.), *The order of presentation in persuasion*. New Haven, Conn.: Yale University Press, 1957.

Hovland, C. I., & Pritzker, H. A. Extent of opinion change as a function of amount of change advocated. *Journal of Abnormal and Social Psychology*, 1957, *54*, 257–261.

Hovland, C. I., & Weiss, W. The influence of source credibility on communication effectiveness. *Public Opinion Quarterly*, 1951, *15*, 635–650.

Howells, L. T., & Becker, S. W. Seating arrangement and leadership emergence. *Journal of Abnormal and Social Psychology*, 1962, *64*(2), 148–150.

Hoyt, M. F., & Raven, B. H. Birth order, internal-external control, and the 1971 Los Angeles earthquake. *Journal of Personality and Social Psychology*, 28, 123–128.

Hrycenko, I., & Minton, H. L. Internal-external control, power position, and satisfaction in task-oriented groups. *Journal of Personality and Social Psychology*, 1974, *30*, 871–878.

Huang, L. C., & Harris, M. B. Altruism and imitation in Chinese and Americans: A cross-cultural experiment. *Journal of Social Psychology*, 1974, *93*, 193–195.

Huber, J. Review of *The inevitability of patriarchy* by S. Goldberg. *American Journal of Sociology*, 1974, *80*, 567–568.

Hughes, E., Becker, H., & Geer, B. Student culture and academic effort. In Nevitt Sanford (Ed.), *The American college: A psychological and social interpretation of higher learning*. New York: Wiley, 1962.

Humphreys, L. *Tearoom trade: Impersonal sex in public places*. Chicago: Aldine, 1970.

Hunt, J. McV. Traditional personality theory in the light of recent evidence. *American Scientist*, 1965, *53*, 80–96.

Hunter, F. M. Letter to the editor. *Science*, 1973, *180*, 361.

Hunter, J. R. Communication of velocity changes in jack mackerel (*Trachurus symmetricus*) schools. *Animal Behavior*, 1969, *17*, 507–514.

Hurwitz, J. I., Zander, A. F., & Hymovitch, B. Some effects of power on the relations among group members. In D. Cartwright & A. Zander (Eds.), *Group dynamics: Research and theory*. Evanston, Ill.: Row, Peterson, 1953.

Huston, T. L. Ambiguity of acceptance, social desirability, and dating choice. *Journal of Experimental Social Psychology*, 1973, *9*, 32–42.

Huston, T. L., & Korte, C. *The responsive bystander: Why he helps*. Unpublished manuscript, Pennsylvania State University, 1974. (A condensed version appears as Huston & Korte, 1975.)

Huston, T. L., & Korte, C. The responsive bystander: Why he helps. In T. Lickona (Ed.), *Morality: Theory, research, and social issues*. New York: Holt, Rinehart & Winston, 1975.

Huston, T. L., & Levinger, G. Interpersonal attraction and relationships. *Annual Review of Psychology*, 1978, *29*, 115–156.

Hutchinson, R. R., Azrin, N. H., & Hake, D. F. An automatic method for the study of aggression in squirrel monkeys. *Journal of the Experimental Analysis of Behavior*, 1966, *9*, 233–237.

Hutt, C., & Vaizey, M. J. Differential effects of group density on social behavior. *Nature*, 1966, *209*, 1371–1372.

Huxley, A. *Brave new world*. Garden City, N.Y.: Garden City Publishing, 1933.

Hyman, H. Inconsistencies as a problem in attitude measurement. *Journal of Social Issues*, 1949, *5*, 38–42.

Ickes, W., & Barnes, R. D. The role of sex and self-monitoring in unstructured dyadic interactions. *Journal of Personality and Social Psychology*, 1977, *35*, 315–330.

Indik, B. P. Some effects of organization size on member attitudes and behavior. *Human Relations*, 1963, *16*, 369–384.

Ingham, A. C., Levinger, G., Graves, J., & Peckham, V. The Ringleman effect: Studies of group size and group performance. *Journal of Experimental Social Psychology*, 1974, *10*, 371–384.

Inkeles, A. Industrial man: The relation of status to experience, perception and value. *American Journal of Sociology*, 1960, *66*, 1–31.

Insko, C. A. Primacy versus recency in persuasion as a function of timing of arguments and measures. *Journal of Abnormal and Social Psychology*, 1964, *69*, 381–391.

Insko, C. A. Verbal reinforcement of attitude. *Journal of Personality and Social Psychology*, 1965, *2*, 621–623.

Insko, C. A. *Theories of attitude change.* New York: Appleton-Century-Crofts, 1967.

Insko, C. A., Arkoff, A., & Insko, V. M. Effects of high and low fear-arousing communications upon opinions toward smoking. *Journal of Experimental Social Psychology*, 1965, *1*, 256–266.

Insko, C. A., & Schopler, J. *Experimental social psychology.* New York: Academic Press, 1972.

Insko, C. A., Thompson, V. D., Stroebe, W., Shaud, K. F., Pinner, E. E., & Layton, B. D. Implied evaluation and the similarity-attraction effect. *Journal of Personality and Social Psychology*, 1973, *25*, 297–308.

Isen, A. M. Success, failure, attention and reactions to others: The warm glow of success. *Journal of Personality and Social Psychology*, 1970, *15*, 294–301.

Isen, A. M., Clark, M., & Schwartz, M. F. Duration of the effect of good mood on helping: "Footprints on the sands of time." *Journal of Personality and Social Psychology*, 1976, *34*, 385–393.

Isen, A. M., Horn, N., & Rosenhan, D. L. Effects of success and failure on children's generosity. *Journal of Personality and Social Psychology*, 1973, *27*, 239–247.

Isen, A. M., & Levin, P. F. Effect of feeling good on helping: Cookies and kindness. *Journal of Personality and Social Psychology*, 1972, *21*, 384–388.

Isen, A. M., Shalker, T. E., Clark, M., & Karp, L. Affect, accessibility of material in memory, and behavior: A cognitive loop? *Journal of Personality and Social Psychology*, 1978, *36*, 1–12.

Iverson, M. A. Personality impressions of punitive stimulus persons of differential status. *Journal of Abnormal and Social Psychology*, 1964, *68*, 617–626.

Iverson, M. A. Attraction toward flatterers of different statuses. *Journal of Social Psychology*, 1968, *74*, 181–187.

Ivey, M. E., & Bardwick, J. M. Patterns of affective fluctuation in the menstrual cycle. *Psychosomatic Medicine*, 1968, *30*, 336–345.

Jacklin, C. N. *As the twig is bent: Sex role stereotyping in early readers.* Unpublished manuscript, Stanford University, 1973. (Cited in Manes & Melnyk, 1974.)

Jacobs, R. C., & Campbell, D. T. The perpetuation of an arbitrary tradition through several generations of a laboratory microculture. *Journal of Abnormal and Social Psychology*, 1961, *62*, 649–658.

Jacobson, C. J. Women workers: Profile of a growing force. *New York Teacher Magazine*, September 15, 1974.

Jacobson, G. C. The impact of broadcast campaigning on electoral outcomes. *Journal of Politics*, 1975, *37*, 769–793.

Jaeger, G., & Selznick, P. A normative theory of culture. *American Sociological Review*, 1964, *29*, 653–669.

Jaffee, C. L., & Lucas, R. M. Effects of rates of talking and correctness of decision on leader choice in small groups. *Journal of Social Psychology*, 1969, *79*, 247–254.

Jahoda, G. Geometric illusions and environment: A study in Ghana. *British Journal of Psychology*, 1966, *57*, 193–199.

Jahoda, M., & West, P. Race relations in public housing. *Journal of Social Issues*, 1951, *7*, 132–139.

James, W. H., Woodruff, A. B., & Werner, W. Effect of internal and external control upon changes in smoking behavior. *Journal of Consulting Psychology*, 1965, *29*, 184–186.

Janis, I. L. Personality correlates of susceptibility to persuasion. *Journal of Personality*, 1954, *22*, 504–518.

Janis, I. L. Anxiety indices related to susceptibility to persuasion. *Journal of Abnormal and Social Psychology*, 1955, *51*, 663–667.

Janis, I. L. *Psychological stress.* New York: Wiley, 1958.

Janis, I. L. Groupthink. *Psychology Today*, 1971, *5*(6), 43–46.

Janis, I. L. *Victims of groupthink.* Boston: Houghton Mifflin, 1974.

Janis, I. L., & Feshbach, S. Effects of fear-arousing communications. *Journal of Abnormal and Social Psychology*, 1953, *48*, 78–92.

Janis, I. L., & Field, P. B. Sex differences and personality factors related to persuasibility. In C. I. Hovland & I. L. Janis (Eds.), *Personality and persuasibility.* New Haven, Conn.: Yale University Press, 1959.

Janis, I. L., & Hoffman, D. Facilitating effects of daily contact between partners who make a decision to cut down on smoking. *Journal of Personality and Social Psychology*, 1971, *17*, 25–35.

Janis, I. L., & Rife, D. Personality and emotional disorder. In C. I. Hovland & I. L. Janis (Eds.), *Personality and persuasibility.* New Haven, Conn.: Yale University Press, 1959.

Janov, A. *The primal scream.* New York: Putnam's, 1970.

Jenkin, N. & Vroegh, K. Contemporary concepts of masculinity and femininity. *Psychological Reports*, 1969, *25*(3), 679–697.

Jennings, M., & Niemi, R. The transmission of political values from parent to child. *American Political Science Review*, 1968, *62*, 169–184.

Jensen, A. R. How much can we boost IQ and scholastic achievement? *Harvard Educational Review*, 1969, *39*, 1–123.

Joffe, J. M., Rawson, R. A., & Mulick, J. A. Control of their environment reduces emotionality in rats. *Science*, 1973, *180*, 1383–1384.

Johnson, J., Gormly, J., & Gormly, A. Disagreements and self-esteem: Support for the competence-reinforcement models of attraction. *Journal of Research in Personality*, 1973, *7*, 165–172.

Jones, E. E. *Ingratiation.* New York: Appleton-Century-Crofts, 1964.

Jones, E. E., & Davis, K. E. From acts to dispositions: The attribution process in person perception. In L. Berkowitz (Ed.), *Advances in experimental social psychology* (Vol. 2). New York: Academic Press, 1965.

Jones, E. E., & Gerard, H. B. *Foundations of social psychology.* New York: Wiley, 1967.

Jones, E. E., & Harris, V. A. The attribution of attitudes.

Journal of Experimental Social Psychology, 1967, *3*, 1–24.

Jones, E. E., & Nisbett, R. E. *The actor and the observer: Divergent perceptions of the causes of behavior.* Morristown, N.J.: General Learning Press, 1971.

Jones, S. C., & Shrauger, J. S. Reputation and self-evaluation as determinants of attractiveness. *Sociometry*, 1970, *33*(3), 276–286.

Jourard, S. Body accessibility. *British Journal of Social and Clinical Psychology*, 1966, *5*, 221–231.

Jourard, S. M. *The transparent self: Self-disclosure and well-being.* Princeton, N.J.: Van Nostrand, 1964.

Jourard, S. M. *Self-disclosure: An experimental analysis of the transparent self.* New York: Wiley, 1971.

Jourard, S. M., & Lasakow, P. Some factors in self-disclosure. *Journal of Abnormal and Social Psychology*, 1958, *56*, 91–98.

Jouvet, M. Biogenic amines and stages of sleep. *Science*, 1969, *163*, 32–41.

Joysen, R. B. *Psychology and common sense.* London: Routledge, 1974.

Judd, N., Bull, R. H. C., & Gahagan, D. The effects of clothing style upon the reactions of a stranger. *Social Behavior and Personality*, 1975, *3*, 225–227.

Julian, J. W., Regula, C. R., & Hollander, E. P. Effects of prior agreement by others on task confidence and conformity. *Journal of Personality and Social Psychology*, 1968, *9*(2), 171–178.

Julian, J. W., & Steiner, I. D. Perceived acceptance as a determinant of conformity behavior. *Journal of Social Psychology*, 1961, *55*, 191–198.

Justice, M. T. Field dependency, intimacy of topic and interpersonal distance (Doctoral dissertation, University of Florida, 1969). *Dissertation Abstracts International*, 1970, *31*, 395B-396B. (University Microfilms No. 70– 12,243.)

Kahn, A., Hottes, J., & Davis, W. L. Cooperation and optimal responding in the Prisoner's Dilemma Game: Effects of sex and physical attractiveness. *Journal of Personality and Social Psychology*, 1971, *17*, 267–279.

Kahn, L. A. The organization of attitudes toward the Negro as a function of education. *Psychological Monographs*, 1951, *65*(13, Whole No. 330).

Kaheman, D. *Attention and effort.* Englewood Cliffs, N.J.: Prentice-Hall, 1973.

Kandel, D. Adolescent marijuana use: Role of parents and peers. *Science*, 1973, *181*, 1067–1069.

Kanouse, D. E. Language, labeling, and attribution. In E. E. Jones, D. Kanouse, H. H. Kelley, R. E. Nisbett, S. Valins, & B. Weiner (Eds.), *Attribution: Perceiving the causes of behavior.* Morristown, N.J.: General Learning Press, 1972.

Kaplan, M. F. Interpersonal attraction as a function of relatedness of similar and dissimilar attitudes. *Journal of Experimental Research in Personality*, 1972, *6*, 17–21.

Karabenick, S. A., Lerner, R. M., & Breecher, M. D. Relation of political affiliation to helping behavior on election day, November 7, 1972. *Journal of Social Psychology*, 1973, *91*, 223–227.

Karlins, M., & Abelson, H. I. *How opinions and attitudes are changed* (2nd ed.). New York: Springer, 1970.

Kassarjian, H. H. Voting intention and political perception. *Journal of Psychology*, 1963, *56*, 85–88.

Katkin, E. S., & Hoffman, L. S. Sex differences and self report of fear: A psychophysiological assessment. *Journal of Abnormal Psychology*, 1976, *85*, 607–610.

Katz, A. M., & Hill, R. Residential propinquity and marital selection: A review of theory, method, and fact. *Marriage and Family Living*, 1958, *20*, 27–35.

Katz, D. *Animals and men.* New York: Longmans, Green, 1937.

Katz, D. The functional approach to the study of attitudes. *Public Opinion Quarterly*, 1960, *24*, 163–204.

Katz, D. Consistency for what? The functional approach. In R. P. Abelson, E. Aronson, W. J. McGuire, T. M. Newcomb, M. J. Rosenberg, & P. H. Tannenbaum (Eds.), *Theories of cognitive consistency: A sourcebook.* Chicago: Rand McNally, 1968.

Katz, D., & Stotland, E. A preliminary statement to a theory of attitude structure and change. In S. Koch (Ed.), *Psychology: A study of a science* (Vol. 3). New York: McGraw-Hill, 1959.

Katz, I. Experimental studies of Negro-white relationships. In L. Berkowitz (Ed.), *Advances in experimental social psychology* (Vol. 5). New York: Academic Press, 1970.

Katz, I., & Cohen, M. The effects of training Negroes upon cooperative problem solving in biracial teams. *Journal of Abnormal and Social Psychology*, 1962, *64*, 319–325.

Katz, J. M. *Experimentation with human beings: The authority of the investigator, subject, professions, and state in the human experimentation process.* New York: Sage, 1972.

Katzenbach, N. *The challenge of crime in a free society: A report by the President's Commission on Law Enforcement and Administration of Justice.* New York: Avon, 1968.

Kazdin, A. E., & Bryan, J. H. Competence and volunteering. *Journal of Experimental Social Psychology*, 1971, *7*, 87–97.

Keasey, C., & Tomlinson-Keasey, C. Petition signing in a naturalistic setting. *Journal of Social Psychology*, 1973, *89*, 313–314.

Keating, C. F., Mazur, A., & Segall, M. H. Facial gestures which influence the perception of status. *Sociometry*, 1977, *40*, 374–378.

Kelley, H. H. Communication in experimentally created hierarchies. *Human Relations*, 1951, *4*, 39–56.

Kelley, H. H. The two functions of reference groups. In G. E. Swanson, T. M. Newcomb, & E. L. Hartley (Eds.), *Readings in social psychology.* New York: Holt, 1952.

Kelley, H. H. Attribution theory in social psychology. In D. Levine (Ed.), *Nebraska Symposium on Motivation* (Vol. 15). Lincoln: University of Nebraska Press, 1967, 192–238.

Kelley, H. H. *Attribution in social interaction.* Morristown, N.J.: General Learning Press, 1971.

Kelley, H. H. *Causal schemata and the attribution process.* Morristown, N.J.: General Learning Press, 1972.

Kelley, H. H. The processes of causal attribution. *American Psychologist*, 1973, *28*, 107–128.

Kelley, H. H., Condry, J. C., Dahlke, A. E., & Hill, A. H. Collective behavior in a simulated panic situation. *Journal of Experimental Social Psychology*, 1965, *1*, 20–54.

Kelley, H. H., & Shapiro, M. M. An experiment on conformity to group norms where conformity is detrimental to group achievement. *American Sociological Review*, 1954, *19*, 667–677.

Kelley, H. H., & Thibaut, J. W. Group problem solving. In G. Lindzey & E. Aronson (Eds.), *Handbook of social psychology* (Vol. 4, 2nd ed.). Reading, Mass.: Addison-Wesley, 1969.

Kelly, G. A. *The psychology of personal constructs: A theory of personality* (Vol. 1). New York: Norton, 1955.

Kelly, G. A. *A theory of personality: The psychology of personal constructs.* New York: Norton, 1963.

Kelman, H. C. Effects of success and failure on "suggestibility" in the autokinetic situation. *Journal of Abnormal Social Psychology*, 1950, *45*, 267–285.

Kelman, H. C. Compliance, identification and internalization: Three processes of attitude change. *Journal of Conflict Resolution*, 1958, *2*, 51–60.

Kelman, H. C. Human use of human subjects: The problem of deception in social psychological experiments. *Psychological Bulletin*, 1967, *67*, 1–11.

Kelman, H. C. Attitudes are alive and well and gainfully employed in the sphere of action. *American Psychologist*, 1974, *29*, 310–324.

Kelman, H. C., & Hovland, C. "Reinstatement" of the communicator in delayed measurement of opinion change. *Journal of Abnormal and Social Psychology*, 1953, *48*, 327–335.

Kelman, H. C., & Lawrence, L. H. Assignment of responsibility in the case of Lt. Calley: Preliminary report on a national survey. *Journal of Social Issues*, 1972, *28*(1), 177–212.

Kendler, H. H., & Kendler, T. S. A methodological analysis of the research area of inconsistent behavior. *Journal of Social Issues*, 1949, *5*, 27–31.

Keniston, K. Do Americans *really* like children? *Today's Education*, journal of the National Education Association, November/December 1975.

Kenkel, W. F. Differentiation in family decision making. *Sociology and Social Research*, 1957, *42*, 18–25.

Kennedy, J. F. *Profiles in courage.* New York: Harper, 1956.

Kerckhoff, A. C. Patterns of homogamy and the field of eligibles. *Social Forces*, 1964, *42*, 289–297.

Kerckhoff, A. C., Back, K. W., & Miller, N. Sociometric patterns in hysterical contagion. *Sociometry*, 1965, *28*(1), 2–15.

Kerrick, J. The effect of relevant and non-relevant sources on attitude change. *Journal of Social Psychology*, 1958, *47*, 15–20.

Kerrick, J. The effects of instructional set on the measurement of attitude change through communications. *Journal of Social Psychology*, 1961, *53*, 113–120.

Kessler, S., McKenna, W., Russell, V., Stang, D. J., & Sweet, S. The job market in psychology: A survey of despair. *Personality and Social Psychology Bulletin*, 1976, *2*(1). (An earlier version appeared in *SPAA* Newsletter [State Psychological Association Affairs, Division 31, APA, 1975, 7(1), 7].)

Kidder, L. H., Bellettirie, G., & Cohn, E. S. Secret ambitions and public performances. The effects of anonymity on reward allocations made by men and women. *Journal of Experimental Social Psychology*, 1977, *13*, 70–80.

Kilham, W., & Mann, L. Level of destructive obedience as a function of transmitter and executant roles in the Milgram obedience paradigm. *Journal of Personality and Social Psychology*, 1974, *29*, 696–702.

Kimmel, E. Status of women in the psychological community in the southeast: A case study. *American Psychologist*, July 1974, 519–520; 536–539.

Kinch, J. W. *Social psychology.* New York: McGraw-Hill, 1973.

King, M. G. Interpersonal relations in preschool children and average approach distance. *Journal of Genetic Psychology*, 1966, *108*, 109–110.

Kinsey, A. C., Pomeroy, W. B., & Martin, C. E. *Sexual behavior in the human male.* Philadelphia: Saunders, 1948.

Kinsey, A. C., Pomeroy, W. B., Martin, C. E., & Gebhard, P. H. *Sexual behavior in the human female.* Philadelphia: Saunders, 1953.

Kipnis, D. M. Interaction between members of bomber crews as a determinant of sociometric choice. *Human Relations*, 1957, *10*, 263–270.

Kirkendall, L. A., & Rubin, I. Sexuality and the life cycle (SIECUS Study Guide No. 8). From *Sexuality and man.* New York: SIECUS and Scribner's, 1970.

Kirkpatrick, C., & Cotton, J. Physical attractiveness, age, and marital adjustment. *American Sociological Review*, 1961, *16*, 81–86.

Kirscht, J. B., Lodahl, T. M., & Haire, M. Some factors in the selection of leaders by members of small groups. *Journal of Abnormal and Social Psychology*, 1959, *58*, 406–408.

Kistiakowsky, V. *Two hundred years of American women scientists.* Paper presented at the annual meeting of the American Association for the Advancement of Science, February 1976.

Klapper, J. T. *Effects of mass communication.* Glencoe, Ill.: Free Press, 1961.

Kleck, R. E., & Rubenstein, C. Physical attractiveness, perceived attitude similarity, and interpersonal attraction in an opposite-sex encounter. *Journal of Personality and Social Psychology*, 1975, *31*, 107–114.

Klein, M. W. Labeling, deterrence, and recidivism: A study of police dispositions of juvenile offenders. *Social Problems*, 1974, *22*, 292–300.

Kleinke, C. L., Bustos, A. A., Meeker, F. B., & Staneski, R. A. Effects of self-attributed and other-attributed gaze on interpersonal evaluations between males and females. *Journal of Experimental Social Psychology*, 1973, *9*, 154–163.

Kleinke, C. L., Kahn, M. L., & Tully, T. B. *First impressions of talking rates in opposite-sex and same-sex interactions.* Unpublished manuscript, Wheaton College, undated.

Kleinke, C. L., Staneski, R. A., & Pipp, S. L. Effects of gaze, distance, and attractiveness on males' first impressions of females. *Representative Research in Social Psychology*, 1975, *6*, 7–12.

Klugman, S. F. Cooperative versus individual efficiency in

problem solving. *Journal of Educational Psychology*, 1944, *35*, 91–100.

Knapp, M. L. *Nonverbal communication in human interaction.* New York: Holt, Rinehart & Winston, 1972.

Knower, R. Experimental studies of changes in attitude: II. A study of the effect of printed argument on changes in attitude. *Journal of Abnormal Social Psychology*, 1936, *30*, 522–532.

Knox, R. E., & Inkster, J. A. Postdecision dissonance at post time. *Journal of Personality and Social Psychology*, 1968, *8*, 319–323.

Kohn, M. L. *Class and conformity.* Homewood, Ill.: Dorsey Press, 1969.

Kohn, M. L., & Schooler, C. Occupational experience and psychological functioning: An assessment of reciprocal effects. *American Sociological Review*, 1973, *38*, 97–118.

Kolko, G. *Wealth and power in America.* New York: Praeger, 1962.

Konečni, V. J. Some effects of guilt on compliance: A field replication. *Journal of Personality and Social Psychology*, 1972, *23*, 30–32.

Konečni, V. J. Annoyance, type and duration of postannoyance activity, and aggression: The "cathartic" effect. *Journal of Experimental Psychology: General*, 1975, 104.

Konečni, V. J. The role of aversive events in the development of intergroup conflict. In W. G. Austin & S. Worchel (Eds.), *The social psychology of intergroup relations.* Monterey, Calif.: Brooks/Cole, 1979.

Konečni, V. J., Libuser, L., Morton, H., & Ebbesen, E. B. Effects of a violation of personal space on escape and helping responses. *Journal of Experimental Social Psychology*, 1975, *11*, 288–299.

Konopasky, R. J., & Telegdy, G. A. Conformity in the rat: A leader's selection of door color versus a learned door-color discrimination. *Perceptual and Motor Skills*, 1977, *44*, 31–37.

Korte, C. Group effects on help giving in an emergency. *Proceedings of the 77th Annual Convention of the American Psychological Association.* Washington, D.C.: American Psychological Association, 1969.

Korte, C., & Kerr, N. Response to altruistic opportunities in urban and nonurban settings. *Journal of Social Psychology*, 1975, *95*, 183–184.

Koulack, D., & Tuthill, J. A. Height perception: A function of social distance. *Canadian Journal of Behavioral Science*, 1972, *4*, 50–53.

Kozlowski, L. T., & Schachter, S. Effects of cue prominence and palatability on the drinking behavior of obese and normal humans. *Journal of Personality and Social Psychology*, 1975, *32*, 1055–1059.

Kramer, C. Women's speech: Separate but unequal? *Quarterly Journal of Speech*, February 1974, 14–24.

Kramer, E. Judgment of personal characteristics and emotions from nonverbal properties of speech. *Psychological Bulletin*, 1963, *60*, 408–420.

Krames, L. *Sexual responses of polygamous female and monogamous male rats to novel partners after sexual cessation.* Un-published manuscript, University of Toronto, Erindale College, July 1970.

Krantz, D. S. The social context of obesity research: Another perspective on its place in the field of social psychology. *Personality and Social Psychology Bulletin*, 1977.

Krantz, D. S., Glass, D. C., & Snyder, M. L. Helplessness, stress level, and the coronary prone behavior pattern. *Journal of Experimental Social Psychology*, 1974, *10*, 284–300.

Kranz, P. L., & Ostler, R. Adult expectations of children—Do as I say, not as I do. *Young Children*, July 1974, 277–279.

Kraus, S., El-Assal, E., & DeFleur, M. L. Fear-threat appeals in mass communications: An apparent contradiction. *Speech Monographs*, 1966, *33*, 23–29.

Krebs, D. L. Altruism—An examination of the concept and a review of the literature. *Psychological Bulletin*, 1970, *73*, 258–302.

Krech, D., & Crutchfield, R. S. *Theory and problems in social psychology.* New York: McGraw-Hill, 1948.

Krech, D., Crutchfield, R., & Ballachey, E. *Individual in society.* New York: McGraw-Hill, 1962.

Krovetz, M. L. Explaining success or failure as a function of one's locus of control. *Journal of Personality*, 1974, *42*, 175–189.

Krueger, A. P., & Kotaka, S. The effects of air ions on brain levels of serotonin in mice. *International Journal of Biometeorology*, 1969, *13*(1), 25–38.

Krueger, A. P., & Reed, E. J. Biological impact of small air ions. *Science*, 1976, *193*, 1209–1213.

Krueger, E. T., & Reckless, W. C. *Social psychology.* New York: Longmans, Green, 1931.

Kruglanski, A. W. Incentives in interdependent escape as affecting the degree of group incoordination. *Journal of Experimental Social Psychology*, 1969, *5*, 454–467.

Krupat, E., & Coury, M. *The lost letter technique and helping: An urban-nonurban comparison.* Paper presented at the 83rd Annual Convention of the American Psychological Association, Chicago, August–September 1975.

Kryter, K. D. *The effects of noise on man.* New York: Academic Press, 1970.

Kuhn, D. Z., Madsen, C. H., Jr., & Becker, W. C. Effects of exposure to an aggressive model and frustration on children's aggressive behavior. *Child Development*, 1967, *38*, 739–746.

Kurtzberg, R. L., Safar, H., & Cavior, N. Survival and social rehabilitation of adult offenders. *Proceedings of the 76th Annual Convention of the American Psychological Association*, 1968, *3*, 649–650. (Summary)

Kutner, B., Wilkins, C., & Yarrow, P. R. Verbal attitudes and overt behavior involving racial prejudice. *Journal of Abnormal and Social Psychology*, 1952, *47*, 649–652.

Kymissis, E. P., & Stang, D. J. Leadership: An index to references in thirty-six social psychology texts. JSAS *Catalog of Selected Documents in Psychology*, 1975, *5*, 22.

Kyucharyants, V. Will the human life-span reach one hundred? *Gerontologist*, October 1974, 377–380.

Lacey, J. I. The evaluation of autonomic responses: Toward

a general solution. *Annals of the New York Academy of Sciences*, 1956, *67*, 123–164.

Lacey, J. I. Somatic response patterning and stress: Some revisions of activation theory. In M. H. Appley & R. Trumbull (Eds.), *Psychological stress*. New York: Appleton-Century-Crofts, 1967.

Lambert, W. E., & Lowy, F. H. Effects of the presence and discussion of others on expressed attitudes. *Canadian Journal of Psychology*, 1957, *11*, 151–156.

Lana, R. Controversy of the topic and order of presentation in persuasive communications. *Psychological Reports*, 1963, *12*, 163–170. (a)

Lana, R. Interest, media, and order effects in persuasive communications. *Journal of Psychology*, 1963, *56*, 9–13. (b)

Lana, R. The influence of the pretest on order effects in persuasive communications. *Journal of Abnormal and Social Psychology*, 1964, *69*, 337–341. (a)

Lana, R. Three theoretical interpretations of order effects in persuasive communications. *Psychological Bulletin*, 1964, *61*, 314–320. (b)

Lander, B. *Toward an understanding of juvenile delinquency*. New York: Columbia University Press, 1954.

Lando, H. A. On being sane in insane places: A supplemental report. *Professional Psychology*, February 1976, 47–52.

Landy, D., & Sigall, H. Beauty is talent: Task evaluation as a function of the performer's physical attractiveness. *Journal of Personality and Social Psychology*, 1974, *29*, 299–304.

Langer, E. J. The illusion of control. *Journal of Personality and Social Psychology*, 1975, *32*, 311–328.

Langer, E. J., & Abelson, R. P. A patient by any other name . . .! Clinician group differences in labeling bias. *Journal of Consulting and Clinical Psychology*, 1974, *42*, 4–9.

Langer, E. J., & Rodin, J. The effects of choice and enhanced personal responsibility for the aged: A field experiment in an institutional setting. *Journal of Personality and Social Psychology*, 1976, *34*, 191–198.

Langman, B., & Cockburn, A. Sirhan's gun. *Harper's*, January 1975, 16–27.

Lanzetta, J. T. Group behavior under stress. *Human Relations*, 1955, *8*, 29–53.

LaPiere, R. T. Attitudes vs. action. *Social Forces*, 1934, *13*, 230–237.

LaPiere, R. T. Type-rationalizations of group anti-play. *Social Forces*, 1936, *15*, 232–237.

Lasswell, H. D., & Kaplan, A. *Power and society*. New Haven, Conn.: Yale University Press, 1950.

Latané, B. *Theory of social impact*. Paper presented at the annual meeting of the Psychonomic Society, St. Louis, 1973.

Latané, B., & Dabbs, J. M., Jr. Sex, group size, and helping in three cities. *Sociometry*, 1975, *38*, 180–194.

Latané, B., & Darley, J. M. Group inhibition of bystander intervention in emergencies. *Journal of Personality and Social Psychology*, 1968, *10*, 215–221.

Latané, B., & Darley, J. M. *The unresponsive bystander: Why doesn't he help?* New York: Appleton-Century-Crofts, 1970.

Latané, B., & Rodin, J. A lady in distress: Inhibiting effects of friends and strangers on bystander intervention. *Journal of Experimental and Social Psychology*, 1969, *5*, 189–202.

Latham, G. P., & Yukl, G. A. Effects of assigned and participative goal setting on performance and job satisfaction. *Journal of Applied Psychology*, 1976, *61*, 166–171.

Laucken, U. *Naive Verhaltenstheorie*. Stuttgart, Germany: Klett, 1974.

Laumann, E. O. Friends of urban men: An assessment of accuracy in reporting their socioeconomic attributes, mutual choice, and attitude agreement. *Sociometry*, 1969, *32*, 54–70.

Law Enforcement Assistance Administration. Fear of crime varies slightly. *LEAA Newsletter*, 1978, *7*, 3; 9.

Layzer, D. Heritability analyses of I.Q. scores: Science or numerology? *Science*, 1974, *183*, 1259–1266.

Lazarsfeld, P. F. The American soldier—An expository review. *Public Opinion Quarterly*, 1949, *13*, 377–404.

Lazarsfeld, P. F., Berelson, B., & Gaudet, H. *The people's choice*. New York: Columbia University Press, 1948.

League, B. J., & Jackson, D. N. Conformity, veridicality, and self-esteem. *Journal of Abnormal and Social Psychology*, 1964, *68*(1), 113–115.

Leavitt, H. Some effects of certain communication patterns on group performance. In G. Swanson, T. Newcomb, & E. Hartley (Eds.), *Readings in social psychology*. New York: Holt, 1952.

Lefcourt, H. M. Internal vs. external control of reinforcements: A review. *Psychological Bulletin*, 1966, *65*, 206–220.

Lefcourt, H. M. Recent developments in the study of locus of control. In B. A. Maher (Ed.), *Progress in experimental personality research* (Vol. 6). New York: Academic Press, 1972.

Lefcourt, H. M. The function of the illusion of control and freedom. *American Psychologist*, 1973, *28*, 417–425.

Lefcourt, H. M., Hogg, E., Struthers, S., & Holmes, C. Causal attributions as a function of locus of control, initial confidence, and performance outcomes. *Journal of Personality and Social Psychology*, 1975, *32*, 391–397.

Lefkowitz, M., Blake, R. R., & Mouton, J. S. Status factors in pedestrian violation of traffic signals. *Journal of Abnormal and Social Psychology*, 1955, *51*, 704–706.

Leginski, W., & Izzett, R. R. The selection and evaluation of interpersonal distances as a function of linguistic styles. *Journal of Social Psychology*, 1976, *99*, 125–137.

Leiderman, P. H. Imagery and sensory deprivation, an experimental study. *Tech. Report*, MRL-TDR-62-28. (Contract No. AF 33 (616)-6110), Wright-Patterson AFB, Ohio, May 1962.

Leipold, W. D. *Psychological distance in a dyadic interview as a function of introversion-extroversion, anxiety, social desirability, and stress*. Unpublished doctoral dissertation, University of North Dakota. (Cited in H. Patterson, 1968.)

Lemert, E. M. *Human deviance, social problems and social control*. Englewood Cliffs, N.J.: Prentice-Hall, 1967.

Lemon, N. *Attitudes and their measurement.* New York: Wiley, 1973.

Lenneberg, E. H. *Biological foundations of language.* New York: Wiley, 1967.

Lerner, M. J. *Conditions eliciting acceptance or rejection of a martyr.* Unpublished manuscript, University of Kentucky, 1968.

Lerner, M. J., & Agar, E. The consequences of perceived similarity: Attraction and rejection, approach and avoidance. *Journal of Experimental Research in Personality,* 1972, *6,* 69–75.

Lerner, M. J., & Matthews, G. Reactions to suffering of others under conditions of indirect responsibility. *Journal of Personality and Social Psychology,* 1967, *5,* 319–325.

Lerner, R. M. The development of stereotyped expectations of body build-behavior relations. *Child Development,* 1969, *40,* 137–141.

Lerner, R. M., & Gellert, E. Body build identification, preference, and aversion in children. *Developmental Psychology,* 1969, *1,* 456–462.

Lesko, W. A. Psychological distance, mutual gaze, and the affiliative-conflict theory. *Journal of Social Psychology,* 1977, *103,* 311–312.

Lesser, G. S., & Abelson, R. P. Personality correlates of persuasibility in children. In C. I. Hovland & I. L. Janis (Eds.), *Personality and persuasibility.* New Haven, Conn.: Yale University Press, 1959.

Leventhal, H. Findings and theory in the study of fear communications. In L. Berkowitz, (Ed.), *Advances in experimental social psychology* (Vol. 5). New York: Academic Press, 1970.

Leventhal, H., Singer, R. P., & Jones, S. Effects of fear and specificity of recommendation upon attitudes and behavior. *Journal of Personality and Social Psychology,* 1965, *2,* 20–29.

Leventhal, H., Watts, J. C., & Pagano, F. Effects of fear and instructions on how to cope with danger. *Journal of Personality and Social Psychology,* 1967, *6,* 313–321.

Levin, H. Audience stress, personality, and speech. *Journal of Abnormal and Social Psychology,* 1960, *61,* 469–473.

Levin, P. F., & Isen, A. M. Further studies on the effect of feeling good on helping. *Sociometry,* 1975, *38,* 141–147.

Levine, A. S. Prolonged isolation and confinement. A problem for naval medical research. *Navy Magazine,* January 1965, 26–28.

Levine, D., Fiddmont, N., & New, J. Interracial attitudes and contacts. *Urban Education,* 1971, *5,* 309–327.

Levine, E. L., & Katzell, R. A. Effects of variations in control structure on group performance and satisfaction: A laboratory study. *Proceedings of the 79th Annual Convention of the American Psychological Association,* 1971, 475–476. (Summary)

Levine, J. M., Saxe, L., & Harris, H. J. *Reaction to attitudinal deviance: Impact of deviate's direction and distance of movement.* Paper presented at the meeting of the Midwestern Psychological Association, Chicago, May 1974.

Levine, R. A. Cross-cultural study in child psychology. In P. H. Mussen (Ed.), *Carmichael's manual of child psychology* (Vol. 2, 3rd ed.). New York: Wiley, 1970.

Levinger, G., & Breedlove, J. Interpersonal attraction and agreement: A study of marriage partners. *Journal of Personality and Social Psychology,* 1966, *3,* 367–372.

Levonian, E. Student personality and academic achievement. *Personality,* 1970, *1,* 25–29.

Levy, S. G. The employment environment for social psychologists. In P. J. Woods (Ed.), *Career opportunities for psychologists.* Washington, D.C.: American Psychological Association, 1976.

Lewin, K. Psycho-sociological problems of a minority group. *Character and Personality,* 1935, *3,* 175–187.

Lewin, K. *Principles of topological psychology.* New York: McGraw-Hill, 1936.

Lewin, K. The conceptual representation and the measurement of psychological forces. In *Contributions to psychological theory.* Durham, N.C.: Duke University Press, 1938.

Lewin, K. Self-hatred among Jews. *Contemporary Jewish Record,* 1941, *4,* 219–232.

Lewin, K. *Field theory in social science.* New York: Harper and Brothers, 1951.

Lewis, J., Baddeley, A. D., Bonham, K. G., & Lovett, D. Traffic pollution and mental efficiency. *Nature,* 1970, *225,* 96.

Lewis, M. Culture and gender roles: There's no unisex in the nursery. *Psychology Today,* May 1972, 54–57.

Lewis, W. H. Feuding and social change in Morocco. *Journal of Conflict Resolution,* 1961, *5,* 43–54.

Leyens, J. P., Camino, L., Parke, R. D., & Berkowitz, L. Effects of movie violence on aggression in a field setting as a function of group dominance and cohesion. *Journal of Personality and Social Psychology,* 1975, *32,* 346–360.

Libo, L. M. *Measuring group cohesiveness.* Ann Arbor: University of Michigan Institute for Social Research, 1953.

Lieberman, M. A., Yalom, I. D., & Miles, M. B. *Encounter groups: First facts.* New York: Basic Books, 1973.

Lieberson, S. *Ethnic patterns in American cities.* New York: Free Press, 1963.

Liebert, R. M., Neale, J. M., & Davidson, E. S. *The early window: Effects of television on children and youth.* New York: Pergamon Press, 1973.

Liebman, M. The effects of sex and race norms on personal space. *Environment and Behavior,* 1970, *2,* 208–246.

Likert, R. A technique for the measurement of attitudes. *Archives of Psychology,* 1932, *22,* 1–55.

Liktorius, A., & Stang, D. J. Altruism, bystander intervention, and helping behavior: A bibliography. JSAS *Catalog of Selected Documents in Psychology,* 1975, *5,* 326. (Ms. No. 1096)

Linde, T. F., & Patterson, C. H. Influence of orthopedic disability on conforming behavior. *Journal of Abnormal and Social Psychology,* 1964, *68,* 115–118.

Lindsay, J. *The writing on the wall.* London: Muller, 1960.

Lindskold, S., & Tedeschi, J. T. Reward power and attraction in interpersonal conflict. *Psychonomic Science,* 1971, *22,* 211–213. (a)

Lindskold, S., & Tedeschi, J. T. Self-esteem and sex as factors affecting influenceability. *British Journal of Social and Clinical Psychology,* 1971, *10,* 114–122. (b)

Lindsley, D. B. Common factors in sensory deprivation, sensory distortion, and sensory overload. In P. Solomon, P. E. Kubansky, P. H. Leiderman, J. H. Mendelson, R. Trumbull, & D. Wexler (Eds.), *Sensory deprivation*. Cambridge, Mass.: Harvard University Press, 1961.

Linton, H. B. Dependence on external influence: Correlates in perception, attitudes, and judgment. *Journal of Abnormal and Social Psychology*, 1955, *51*, 502–507.

Linton, H. B., & Graham, E. Personality correlates of persuasibility. In C. I. Hovland & I. L. Janis (Eds.), *Personality and persuasibility*. New Haven, Conn.: Yale University Press, 1959.

Linton, R. Culture, society and the individual. *Journal of Abnormal and Social Psychology*, 1938, *33*, 425–436.

Linton, R. *The cultural background of personality*. New York: Appleton-Century, 1945.

Lippa, R. Expressive control and the leakage of dispositional introversion-extraversion during role-played teaching. *Journal of Personality*, 1976, *44*, 541–559.

Lipset, S. M. Social class. In D. L. Sills (Ed.), *International encyclopedia of the social sciences* (Vol. 15). New York: Macmillan, 1968.

Liska, A. E. Emergent issues in the attitude-behavior consistency controversy. *American Sociological Review*, 1974, *39*, 262–272.

Little, K. B. Personal space. *Journal of Experimental Sociology*, 1965, *1*, 237–247.

Little, K. B. Cultural variations in social schemata. *Journal of Personality and Social Psychology*, 1968, *10*, 1–7.

Lockard, J. S., McVittie, R. I., & Isaac, L. M. Functional significance of the affiliative smile. *Bulletin of the Psychonomic Society*, 1977, *9*, 367–370.

Loflin, M. D., & Winogrond, I. R. *A culture as a set of shared beliefs*. Paper presented at the annual meeting of the American Association for the Advancement of Science, Boston, February 1976.

Loftus, E. F. Reconstructing memory: The incredible eyewitness. *Psychology Today*, 1974, *8*(7), 116–119.

Loftus, E. F., & Palmer, J. C. Reconstruction of automobile destruction: An example of the interaction between language and memory. *Journal of Verbal Learning and Verbal Behavior*, 1974, *11*, 585–589.

Lomas, H. D. Graffiti: Some observations and speculations. *Psychoanalytic Review*, 1973, *60*(1).

Lombroso, C. *Crime: Its causes and remedies* (H. P. Horton, trans.). Boston: Little, Brown, 1918.

London, P. The rescuers: Motivational hypotheses about Christians who saved Jews from the Nazis. In J. Macaulay & L. Berkowitz (Eds.), *Altruism and helping behavior*. New York: Academic Press, 1970.

London, P., & Lim, H. Yielding reason to social pressure: Task complexity and expectation in conformity. *Journal of Personality*, 1964, *32*, 75–89.

Long, G. T., Calhoun, L. G., & Selby, J. W. Personality characteristics related to cross-situational consistency of interpersonal distance. *Journal of Personality Assessment*, 1977, *41*, 274–278.

Loo, C. M. The effects of spatial density on the social behavior of children. *Journal of Applied Social Psychology*, 1972, *2*, 372–381.

Lorge, I. Prestige suggestion and attitude. *Journal of Social Psychology*, 1936, *7*, 386–402.

Lorge, I., Fox, D., Davitz, J., & Brenner, M. A survey of studies contrasting the quality of group performance and individual performance: 1920–1957. *Psychological Bulletin*, 1958, *55*, 337–372.

Lott, A. J., & Lott, B. E. Group cohesiveness, communication level, and conformity. *Journal of Abnormal and Social Psychology*, 1961, *62*, 408–412.

Lott, A. J., & Lott, B. E. Group cohesiveness as interpersonal attraction: A review of relationships with antecedent and consequent variables. *Psychological Bulletin*, 1965, *64*, 259–309.

Lott, A. J., & Lott, B. E. The role of reward in the formation of positive interpersonal attitudes. In T. L. Huston (Ed.), *Foundations of interpersonal attraction*. New York: Academic Press, 1974.

Lott, D. F., & Sommer, R. Seating arrangements and status. *Journal of Personality and Social Psychology*, 1967, *7*, 90–95.

Lottier, S. Distribution of criminal offenses in metropolitan regions. *Journal of Criminal Law and Criminology*, 1938, *29*, 39–45.

Lowin, A., & Craig, J. R. The influence of level of performance on managerial style: An experimental object lesson in the ambiguity of correlational data. *Organizational Behavior and Human Performance*, 1968, *3*, 440–458.

Luchins, A. S. Social influences on perception of complex drawings. *Journal of Social Psychology*, 1945, *21*, 257–273.

Luchins, A. S. Primacy-recency in impression formation. In C. I. Hovland (Ed.), *The order of presentation in persuasion*. New Haven, Conn.: Yale University Press, 1957.

Luchins, A. S. Definitiveness of impression and primacy-recency in communications. *Journal of Social Psychology*, 1958, *48*, 275–290.

Luchins, A. S., & Luchins, E. H. Previous experience with ambiguous and non-ambiguous perceptual stimuli under various social influences. *Journal of Social Psychology*, 1955, *42*, 249–270.

Luchins, A. S., & Luchins, E. H. On conformity with judgments of a majority or an authority. *Journal of Social Psychology*, 1961, *53*, 303–316.

Luchins, A. S., & Luchins, E. H. Focusing on the object of judgment in the social situation. *Journal of Social Psychology*, 1963, *60*, 273–287.

Luft, J. On nonverbal interaction. *Journal of Psychology*, 1966, *63*, 261–268.

Luft, J., & Ingham, H. The Johari window: A graphic model of interpersonal awareness. *Proceedings of the Western Training Laboratory in Group Development of the UCLA Extension Office*, Los Angeles, August 1955.

Lund, F. The psychology of belief. IV. The law of primacy in persuasion. *Journal of Abnormal and Social Psychology*, 1925, *20*, 183–191.

Lundgren, D. C., & Bogart, D. H. Group size, member dissatisfaction, and group radicalism. *Human Relations*, 1974, *27*(4), 339–355.

Lunneborg, P. W. Stereotypic aspect in masculinity-femininity measurement. *Journal of Consulting and Clinical Psychology*,

1970, *34*, 113–118.

Macaulay, J. A shill for charity. In J. Macaulay & L. Berkowitz (Eds.), *Altruism and helping behavior.* New York: Academic Press, 1970.

Macaulay, J. Familiarity, attraction, and charity. *Journal of Social Psychology,* 1975, *95*, 27–37.

Macaulay, J., & Berkowitz, L. (Eds.). *Altruism and helping behavior.* New York: Academic Press, 1970.

Maccoby, E. E. Sex differences in intellectual functioning. In E. E. Maccoby (Ed.), *The development of sex differences.* Stanford, Calif.: Stanford University Press, 1966.

Maccoby, E. E., & Jacklin, C. N. *The psychology of sex differences.* Stanford, Calif.: Stanford University Press, 1974. (a)

Maccoby, E. E., & Jacklin, C. N. What we know and don't know about sex differences. *Psychology Today,* 1974, *8*(7), 109–112. (b)

Maccoby, E. E., Maccoby, N., Romney, A. K., & Adams, J. S. Social reinforcement in attitude change. *Journal of Abnormal and Social Psychology,* 1961, *63*, 109–115.

Maccoby, N., Romney, A. K., Adams, J. S., & Maccoby, E. E. *Critical periods in seeking and accepting information.* Stanford, Calif.: Paris-Stanford Studies in Communication, Institute for Communication Research, 1962. (Cited in L. Festinger, 1964.)

MacDonald, A. P., Jr. Anxiety, affiliation, and social isolation. *Developmental Psychology,* 1970, *3*, 242–254.

MacKenzie, B. K. The importance of contact in determining attitudes toward Negroes. *Journal of Abnormal and Social Psychology,* 1948, *43*, 417–441.

MacKinnon, D. W. The personality correlates of creativity: A study of American architects. In G. Nielson (Ed.), *Proceedings of the 14th International Congress of Applied Psychology* (Vol. 2). Copenhagen, Denmark: Munksgaard, 1962.

MacNeil, R. *The people machine: The influence of television on American politics.* New York: Harper & Row, 1968.

Macy, J., Jr., Christie, L. S., & Luce, R. D. Coding noise in a task-oriented group. *Journal of Abnormal and Social Psychology,* 1953, *48*, 401–409.

Malinowski, B. Social anthropology. In *Encyclopaedia Brittanica* (Vol. 20). 1944, *20*, 862–870.

Maliver, B. Anti-Negro bias among Negro college students. *Journal of Personality and Social Psychology,* 1965, *2*, 770–775.

Mallick, S. K., & McCandless, B. R. A study of catharsis of aggression. *Journal of Personality and Social Psychology,* 1966, *4*, 591–596.

Malmo, R. B. Activation: A neurophysiological dimension. *Psychological Review,* 1959, *66*, 367–386.

Manes, A. L., & Melnyk, P. Televised models of female achievement. *Journal of Applied Social Psychology,* 1974, *4*(4), 365–374.

Mann, R. D. A review of the relationship between personality and performance in small groups. *Psychological Bulletin,* 1959, *56*, 241–270.

Mantell, D. M. The potential for violence in Germany. *Journal of Social Issues,* 1971, *27*, 101–112.

Manz, W., & Lueck, H. E. Influence of wearing glasses on personality ratings: Crosscultural validation of an old experiment. *Perceptual and Motor Skills,* 1968, *27*(3, part 1), 704.

Marecek, J. *When stereotypes hurt: Responses to dependent and aggressive communications.* Paper presented at the meeting of the Eastern Psychological Association, 1974.

Margolis, C. The black student in political strife. *Proceedings of the 79th Annual Convention of the American Psychological Association,* 1971, *6*, 395–396. (Summary)

Marlowe, D., & Gergen, K. J. Personality and social interaction. In G. Lindzey & E. Aronson (Eds.), *Handbook of social psychology* (Vol. 3, 2nd ed.). Reading, Mass.: Addison-Wesley, 1969.

Marquis, D. C., Guetzkow, H., & Heyns, R. W. A social psychological study of the decision-making conference. In H. Guetzkow (Ed.), *Groups, leadership, and men.* Pittsburgh: Carnegie Press, 1951.

Marriott, R. Size of working group and output. *Occupational Psychology,* 1949, *23*, 47–57.

Marsella, A. J., Escudero, M., & Gordon, P. The effects of dwelling density on mental disorders in Filipino men. *Journal of Health and Social Behavior,* 1970, *11*, 288–294.

Martindale, D. A. Territorial dominance behavior in dyadic verbal interactions. *Proceedings of the 79th Annual Convention of the American Psychological Association,* 1971, *6*, 305–306. (Summary)

Maruyama, G., & Miller, N. *Physical attractiveness and classroom acceptance* (Social Science Research Institute Report 75-2). Los Angeles: University of Southern California, 1975.

Marwit, S. J., & Neumann, G. Black and white children's comprehension of standard and nonstandard English passages. *Journal of Educational Psychology,* 1974, *66*(3), 329–332.

Marx, M. H., & Marx, K. Affective transfer as a function of reward and sex of subject. *Bulletin of the Psychonomic Society,* 1978, *12*(2), 159–161.

Masserman, J. Debatable conclusions. *International Journal of Psychiatry,* 1968, *6*, 181–182.

Matarazzo, J. D., & Wiens, A. N. Interviewer influence on durations of interviewee silence. *Journal of Experimental Research in Personality,* 1967, *2*, 59–69.

Matarazzo, J. D., Wiens, A. A., Saslow, G., Dunham, R. M., & Voss, R. B. Speech durations of astronaut and ground communication. *Science,* 1964, *143*, 148–150.

Matlin, M. W., & Stang, D. J. Some determinants of word frequency estimates. *Perceptual and Motor Skills,* 1975, *40*, 923–929.

Matlin, M. W., & Stang, D. J. *The Pollyanna Principle: Selectivity in language, memory, and cognition.* Cambridge, Mass.: Schenkman, 1978. (a)

Matlin, M. W., & Stang, D. J. The Pollyanna Principle. *Psychology Today,* March 1978, 56; 59; 100. (b)

Matthews, K. E., & Cannon, L. K. Environmental noise level as a determinant of helping behavior. *Journal of Personality and Social Psychology,* 1975, *32*, 571–577.

Mausner, B. Studies in social interaction: III. Effect of variation in one partner's prestige on the interaction of observer pairs. *Journal of Applied Psychology*, 1953, *37*, 391–393.

Mausner, B. The effect of prior reinforcement on the interaction of observer pairs. *Journal of Abnormal and Social Psychology*, 1954, *49*, 65–68. (a)

Mausner, B. The effect of one partner's success in a relevant task on the interaction of observer pairs. *Journal of Abnormal and Social Psychology*, 1954, *49*, 557–560. (b)

Mayo, C. W., & Crockett, W. H. Cognitive complexity and primacy-recency effects in impression formation. *Journal of Abnormal and Social Psychology*, 1964, *68*, 335–338.

McArthur, L. Z., & Resko, B. G. The portrayal of men and women in American television commercials. *Journal of Social Psychology*, in press.

McBride, G., King, M. G., & James, J. W. Social proximity effects on galvanic skin responses in adult humans. *Journal of Psychology*, 1965, *61*, 153–157.

McCall, M. W., Jr. *Leaders and leadership: Of substance and shadow* (Tech. Rep. 2). Center for Creative Leadership, 1977.

McClelland, D., Atkinson, J. W., Clark, R. A., & Lowell, E. L. *The achievement motive.* New York: Appleton-Century-Crofts, 1953.

McClelland, L. Interaction level and acquaintance as mediators of density effects. *Personality and Social Psychology Bulletin*, 1976, *2*, 175–178.

McClintock, C. G., Spaulding, C. B., & Turner, H. A. Political orientations of academically affiliated psychologists. *American Psychologist*, 1965, *20*, 211–221.

McColley, S. H., & Thelen, M. H. Imitation and locus of control. *Journal of Research in Personality*, 1975, *9*, 211–216.

McCullough, J. L., & Ostrom, T. M. Repetition of highly similar messages and attitude change. *Journal of Applied Psychology*, 1974, *59*, 395–397.

McCutcheon, L. E. Dumber by the dozen? Not necessarily! *Psychological Reports*, 1977, *40*, 109–110.

McDougall, W. *Introduction to social psychology.* London: Methuen, 1908.

McGinley, H., McGinley, P., & Nicholas, K. Smiling, body position and interpersonal attraction. *Bulletin of the Psychonomic Society*, 1978, *12*(1), 21–24.

McGinnies, E., Nordholm, L. A., Ward, C. D., & Bhanthumnavin, D. L. Sex and cultural differences in perceived locus of control among students in five countries. *Journal of Consulting and Clinical Psychology*, 1974, *42*, 451–455.

McGinnies, E., & Ward, C. D. Persuasibility as a function of source credibility and locus of control: Five cross cultural experiments. *Journal of Personality*, 1974, *42*, 360–371.

McGinnis, J. *The selling of the president.* New York: Trident Press, 1968.

McGovern, L. P., Ditzian, J. L., & Taylor, S. P. The effect of one positive reinforcement on helping with cost. *Bulletin of the Psychonomic Society*, 1975, *5*, 421–423. (a)

McGovern, L. P., Ditzian, J. L., & Taylor, S. P. Sex and perceptions of dependency in a helping situation. *Bulletin of the Psychonomic Society*, 1975, *5*. (b)

McGrath, J. E. *Social psychology: A brief introduction.* New York: Holt, Rinehart & Winston, 1964.

McGrew, P. Social and spacing density effects on spacing density in preschool children. *Journal of Child Psychology and Psychiatry*, 1970, *11*, 197–205.

McGuire, W. J. A syllogistic analysis of cognitive relationships. In C. Hovland & M. Rosenberg (Eds.), *Attitude organization and change.* New Haven, Conn.: Yale University Press, 1960, 65–111. (a)

McGuire, W. J. Cognitive consistency and attitude change. *Journal of Abnormal and Social Psychology*, 1960, *60*, 345–353. (b)

McGuire, W. J. Direct and indirect effects of dissonance-producing messages. *Journal of Abnormal and Social Psychology*, 1960, *60*, 354–358. (c)

McGuire, W. J. The effectiveness of supportive and refutational defenses in immunizing and restoring beliefs against persuasion. *Sociometry*, 1961, *24*, 184–197.

McGuire, W. J. Inducing resistance to persuasion: Some contemporary approaches. In L. Berkowitz (Ed.), *Advances in experimental social psychology.* New York: Academic Press, 1964.

McGuire, W. J. Personality and susceptibility to social influence. In E. F. Borgatta & W. W. Lambert (Eds.), *Handbook of personality theory and research.* Chicago: Rand McNally, 1967.

McGuire, W. J. Personality and attitude change: A theoretical housing. In A. G. Greenwald, T. C. Brock, & T. M. Ostrom (Eds.), *Psychological foundations of attitudes.* New York: Academic Press, 1968, 171–196.

McGuire, W. J. The nature of attitudes and attitude change. In G. Lindzey & E. Aronson (Eds.), *Handbook of social psychology* (Vol. 3, 2nd ed.). Reading, Mass.: Addison-Wesley, 1969, 136–314.

McGuire, W. J. Attitude change: The information-processing paradigm. In C. G. McClintock (Ed.), *Experimental social psychology.* New York: Holt, Rinehart & Winston, 1972.

McGuire, W. J., & Papageorgis, D. The relative efficacy of various types of prior belief-defense in producing immunity against persuasion. *Journal of Abnormal and Social Psychology*, 1961, *62*, 327–337.

McKee, J. P., & Sherriffs, A. C. The differential evaluation of males and females. *Journal of Personality*, 1957, *25*, 356–371.

McKenna, W., & Kessler, S. J. Experimental design as a source of sex bias in social psychology. *Sex Roles*, 1977, *3*(2), 117–128.

McMahon, A., & Rhudick, P. Reminiscing: Adaptational significance in the aged. *Archives of General Psychiatry*, 1964, *10*, 292–298.

McMillen, D. L. Transgression, self-image, and compliant behavior. *Journal of Personality and Social Psychology*, 1971, *20*, 176–179.

McNamee, S. Relation of moral behavior to moral development. In L. Kohlberg (Ed.), *Recent research in moral development.* New York: Holt, Rinehart & Winston, 1974.

McNeil, K., Nevin, J., Trubek, D., & Edelman, L. *Bargaining power and consumer protection.* Madison: University of Wisconsin, Institute for Research on Poverty, 1978.

McNeill, D. Developmental psycholinguistics. In F. Smith & G. A. Miller (Eds.), *The genesis of language: A psycholinguistic approach.* Cambridge, Mass.: M.I.T. Press, 1966.

McNemar, Q. Opinion-attitude methodology. *Psychological Bulletin,* 1946, *43,* 289–374.

Mead, G. H. *Mind, self, and society.* Chicago: University of Chicago Press, 1934.

Mead, M. *Sex and temperament in three primitive societies.* New York: Morrow, 1935.

Meglino, B. M. The effect of evaluation on dominance characteristics: An extension of social facilitation theory. *Journal of Psychology,* 1976, *92,* 167–172.

Mehrabian, A. Inference of attitude from the posture, orientation, and distance of a communicator. *Journal of Consulting and Clinical Psychology,* 1968, *32,* 296–308. (a)

Mehrabian, A. Relationship of attitude to seated posture, orientation, and distance. *Journal of Personality and Social Psychology,* 1968, *10,* 26–30. (b)

Mehrabian, A. Some referents and measures of nonverbal behavior. *Behavior Research Methods and Instrumentation,* 1969, *1,* 203–207.

Mehrabian, A., & Friar, J. T. Encoding of attitude by a seated communicator via posture and position cues. *Journal of Consulting and Clinical Psychology,* 1969, *33,* 330–336.

Mendelsohn, J., Kubzansky, P. E., Leiderman, P. H., Wexler, D., Dutoit, D., & Solomon, P. Catecholamine excretion and behavior during sensory deprivation. *Archives of General Psychiatry,* 1960, *2,* 147–155.

Merton, R. K. The social psychology of housing. In W. Dennis (Ed.), *Current trends in social psychology.* Pittsburgh: University of Pittsburgh Press, 1947.

Merton, R. K. The social nature of leadership. *American Journal of Nursing,* 1969, *69*(12), 2614–2618.

Meunier, C., & Rule, B. G. Anxiety, confidence, and conformity. *Journal of Personality,* 1967, *35,* 498–504.

Meyer, P. If Hitler asked you to electrocute a stranger, would you? Probably. *Esquire,* 1970.

Michelini, R. L., Passalacqua, R., & Cusimano, J. Effects of seating arrangement on group participation. *Journal of Social Psychology,* 1976, *99,* 179–186.

Midlarsky, E. Aiding responses: An analysis and review. *Merrill-Palmer Quarterly,* 1968, *14,* 229–260.

Midlarsky, E., & Bryan, J. H. Affect expressions and children's imitative altruism. *Journal of Experimental Research in Personality,* 1972, *6,* 195–203.

Midlarsky, E., & Midlarsky, M. Some determinants of aiding under experimentally induced stress. *Journal of Personality,* 1973, *41,* 305–327.

Milgram, S. Behavioral study of obedience. *Journal of Abnormal and Social Psychology,* 1963, *67,* 371–378.

Milgram, S. *Obedience* (film). New York University Film Library, 1965.

Milgram, S. The small world problem. *Psychology Today,* 1967, *1,* 61–67.

Milgram, S. The experience of living in cities. *Science,* 1970, *167,* 1461–1468.

Milgram, S. *Obedience to authority: An experimental view.* New York: Harper & Row, 1974.

Milgram, S., & Toch, H. Collective behavior: Crowds and social movements. In G. Lindzey & E. Aronson (Eds.), *Handbook of social psychology* (Vol. 4, 2nd ed.). Reading, Mass.: Addison-Wesley, 1969.

Miller, G. A. The magical number seven, plus or minus two: Some limits on our capacity for processing information. *Psychological Review,* 1956, *63,* 81–97.

Miller, G. A. Psychology as a means of promoting human welfare. *American Psychologist,* 1969, *24,* 1063–1075.

Miller, K. S., & Dreger, R. M. (Eds.). *Comparative studies of blacks and whites in the United States: Psychological, social, physiological.* New York: Seminar Press, 1973.

Miller, N., & Campbell, D. Recency and primacy in persuasion as a function of the timing of speeches and measurements. *Journal of Abnormal and Social Psychology,* 1959, *54,* 1–9.

Miller, N., & Zimbardo, P. G. Motives for fear-induced affiliation: Emotional comparison or interpersonal similarity? *Journal of Personality,* 1966, *34,* 481–503.

Miller, N. E. The frustration-aggression hypothesis. *Psychological Review,* 1941, *48,* 337–342.

Miller, N. E., & Bugelski, R. Minor studies of aggression: II. The influence of frustrations imposed by the in-group on attitudes expressed toward out-groups. *Journal of Psychology,* 1948, *25,* 437–442.

Miller, N. E., Jr. *The effect of group size on decision-making discussions* (Unpublished doctoral dissertation, University of Michigan, 1952).

Millon, T. Reflections on Rosenhan's "On being sane in insane places." *Journal of Abnormal Psychology,* 1975, *84,* 456–461.

Mills, J., & Aronson, E. Opinion change as a function of communicator's attractiveness and desire to influence. *Journal of Personality and Social Psychology,* 1965, *1,* 173–177.

Mills, T. M. Power relations in three-person groups. *American Sociological Review,* 1953, *18,* 351–357.

Minahan, N. *Self-concept and somatic preference in adolescent girls.* Unpublished doctoral dissertation, University of Illinois, 1971.

Minard, R. D. Race relationships in the Pocahontas coal field. *Journal of Social Issues,* 1952, *8,* 29–44.

Minturn, L., & Lambert, W. W. *Mothers of six cultures.* New York: Wiley, 1964.

Mintz, A. Non-adaptive group behavior. *Journal of Abnormal and Social Psychology,* 1951, *46,* 150–159.

Mintzberg, H. *The nature of managerial work.* New York: Harper & Row, 1973.

Mintzberg, H. The manager's job: Folklore and fact. *Harvard Business Review,* 1975, *53*(4), 49–61.

Mischel, W. *Personality and assessment.* New York: Wiley, 1968.

Mischel, W., Coates, B., & Rastoff, A. Effects of success and failure on self-gratification. *Journal of Personality and Social Psychology,* 1968, *10,* 381–390.

Mischel, W., Ebbesen, E., & Zeiss, A. Selective attention to the self: Situational and dispositional determinants. *Journal of Personality and Social Psychology,* 1973, *27,* 129–142.

Mitchell, H. E., & Byrne, D. The defendant's dilemma: Effects of jurors' attitudes and authoritarianism on judicial decisions. *Journal of Personality and Social Psychology*, 1973, *25*, 123–129.

Mitnick, L., & McGinnies, E. Influencing ethnocentrism in small discussion groups through a film communication. *Journal of Abnormal and Social Psychology*, 1958, *56*, 82–90.

Miyamoto, S., & Dornbusch, S. A test of interactionist hypotheses of self conception. *American Journal of Sociology*, 1956, *61*, 399–403.

Moede, W. Die Richtlinien der Leistungspsychologie. *Industrielle Psychotechnik*, 1927, *4*, 193–209.

Monahan, L., Kuhn, D., & Shaver, P. Intrapsychic versus cultural explanations of the "fear of success" motive. *Journal of Personality and Social Psychology*, 1974, *29*(1), 60–64.

Money, J., & Erhardt, A. A. *Man and woman; boy and girl.* Baltimore: Johns Hopkins University Press, 1972.

Montgomery, C. L., & Burgoon, M. An experimental study of the interactive effects of sex and androgyny on attitude change. *Communication Monographs*, 1977, *44*, 130–135.

Montmayor, R. Men and their bodies: The relationship between body type and behavior. *Journal of Social Issues*, 1978, *34*(1), 48–64.

Moore, B. S., Underwood, B., & Rosenhan, D. L. Affect and altruism. *Developmental Psychology*, 1973, *8*, 99–104.

Moreland, R. L., & Zajonc, R. B. A strong test of exposure effects. *Journal of Experimental Social Psychology*, 1976, *12*, 170–179.

Morgenstern, R. D., Groszko, M., & Friedman, L. S. *Fear of success in the classroom: How it affects responses to evaluation questionnaires.* Unpublished manuscript, Queens College, 1974.

Moriarty, T. Crime, commitment and the responsive bystander: Two field experiments. *Journal of Personality and Social Psychology*, 1975, *31*, 370–376.

Morland, J. A comparison of race awareness in Northern and Southern children. In M. Gold-Schmid (Ed.), *Black Americans and White racism: Theory and research.* New York: Holt, Rinehart & Winston, 1970.

Morris, C. G., & Hackman, J. R. Behavioral correlates of perceived leadership. *Journal of Personality and Social Psychology*, 1969, *13*, 350–361.

Morris, W. N., Worchel, S., Bois, J. L., Pearson, J. A., Rountree, C. A., Samaha, G. M., Wachtler, J., & Wright, S. L. Collective coping with stress: Group reactions to fear, anxiety, and ambiguity. *Journal of Personality and Social Psychology*, 1976, *33*, 674–679.

Morrison, B. J., & Thatcher, R. Overpopulation effects on social reduction of emotionality in the albino rat. *Journal of Comparative and Physiological Psychology*, 1969, *69*, 658–662.

Morrison, T. L., & Thomas, M. D. Self-esteem and classroom participation. *Journal of Educational Research*, 1975, *68*(10), 374–378.

Morselli, E. A. *Suicide: An essay on comparative moral statistics.* New York: Appleton, 1882.

Moss, M. K., & Page, R. A. Reinforcement and helping behavior. *Journal of Applied Social Psychology*, 1972, *2*, 360–371.

Muecher, H., & Ungeheuer, H. Meteorological influence on reaction time, flicker-fusion frequency, job accidents, and medical treatment. *Perceptual and Motor Skills*, 1961, *12*, 163–168.

Mulder, M., & Stemerding, A. Threat, attraction to group, and need for strong leadership. *Human Relations*, 1963, *16*, 317–334.

Mulvihill, D. J., & Tumin, M. M. *Crimes of violence* (Staff report to the National Commission on the Causes and Prevention of Violence, Vol. 11). Washington, D.C.: U.S. Government Printing Office, 1969.

Murdock, G. P. *Social structure.* New York: Macmillan, 1949.

Murdock, G. P. Family stability in non-European cultures. *Annals of the American Academy of Political and Social Science*, 1950, *22*, 195–201.

Murphy, G., Murphy, L. B., & Newcomb, T. M. *Experimental social psychology.* New York: Harper, 1937.

Murray, H. A. *Explorations in personality.* New York: Science Editions, 1962. (Originally published, 1938.)

Murstein, B. I. Physical attractiveness and marital choice. *Journal of Personality and Social Psychology*, 1972, *22*, 8–12.

Mussen, P. H., Conger, J. J., & Kagan, J. *Child development and personality.* New York: Harper & Row, 1969.

Nadler, A., Jazwinski, C., & Lau, S. *The cold glow of success: Effects of the interpersonal success of a similar or a dissimilar other on the observer's self and other perceptions.* Unpublished manuscript, Purdue University, 1976.

Nadler, E. *The ideological correlates of conformity.* Unpublished doctoral dissertation, Western Reserve University, 1956.

Nahemow, L., & Lawton, M. P. Similarity and propinquity in friendship formation. *Journal of Personality and Social Psychology*, 1975, *32*, 205–213.

Nardini, J. E., Herman, R. S., & Rasmussen, J. E. Navy psychiatric assessment program in the Antarctic. *American Journal of Psychiatry*, 1962, *119*, 97–105.

Nash, D. J., & Heiss, J. Sources of anxiety in laboratory strangers. *Sociological Quarterly*, 1967, *8*, 215–221.

Nash, D. J., & Wolfe, A. W. The stranger in laboratory culture. *American Sociological Review*, 1957, *22*, 400–405.

National Commission on the Causes and Prevention of Violence. *To establish justice, to insure domestic tranquility.* New York: Award Books, 1969.

Nelson, D. A. *The effect of differential magnitude of reinforcement on interpersonal attraction.* Unpublished doctoral dissertation, University of Texas, 1965.

Nemeth, C. Effects of free versus constrained behavior on attraction between people. *Journal of Personality and Social Psychology*, 1970, *15*, 302–311.

Nesbitt, P. The effectiveness of student canvassers. *Journal of Applied Social Psychology*, 1972, *2*, 252–258.

Newcomb, T. M. *Personality and social change.* New York: Dryden Press, 1943.

Newcomb, T. M. An approach to the study of communicative acts. *Psychological Review*, 1953, *60*, 393–404.

Newcomb, T. M. The prediction of interpersonal attraction.

American Psychologist, 1956, *11*, 575–586.

Newcomb, T. M. Individual systems of orientation. In S. Koch (Ed.), *Psychology: A study of a science* (Vol. 3). New York: McGraw-Hill, 1959, 384–422.

Newcomb, T. M. *The acquaintance process.* New York: Holt, Rinehart & Winston, 1961.

Newcomb, T. M. Stabilities underlying changes in interpersonal attraction. *Journal of Abnormal and Social Psychology*, 1963, *66*, 376–386.

Newcomb, T. M. Dyadic balance as a source of clues about interpersonal attraction. In B. I. Murstein (Ed.), *Theories of attraction and love.* New York: Springer, 1971.

Newcomb, T. M., Koenig, K., Flacks, R., & Warwick, D. *Persistence and change: Bennington College and its students after 25 years.* New York: Wiley, 1967.

Newcomb, T. M., Turner, R. H., & Converse, P. E. *Social psychology: The study of human interaction.* New York: Holt, 1965.

Newman, O. *Defensible space.* New York: Macmillan, 1973.

Newton, R. R., & Schulman, G. I. Sex and conformity: A new view. *Sex Roles*, 1977, *3*(6), 511–521.

New York Times Encyclopedic Almanac. New York: New York Times, 1969.

Nicosia, G. J., & Aiello, J. R. *Effects of bodily contact on reactions to crowding.* Paper presented at the 84th Annual Convention of the American Psychological Association, Washington, D.C., August 1976.

Nielsen, A. C. Television audience. In The Corporation for Public Broadcasting's *News Briefs*, *1*(3), October 14, 1977, Office of Communication Research.

Nisbett, R. E., Caputo, C., Legant, P., & Maracek, J. Behavior as seen by the actor and as seen by the observer. *Journal of Personality and Social Psychology*, 1973, *27*, 154–164.

Nisbett, R. E., & Schachter, S. Cognitive manipulation of pain. *Journal of Experimental Social Psychology*, 1966, *7*, 227–236.

Nisbett, R. E., & Temoshok, L. Is there an "external" cognitive style? *Journal of Personality and Social Psychology*, 1976, *33*, 36–47.

Nisbett, R. E., & Wilson, T. D. The halo effect: Evidence for unconscious alteration of judgments. *Journal of Personality and Social Psychology*, 1977, *35*, 250–256.

Nord, W. R. Social exchange theory: An integrative approach to social conformity. *Psychological Bulletin*, 1969, *71*(3), 174–208.

Nordholm, L. A. Effects of group size and stimulus ambiguity on conformity. *Journal of Social Psychology*, 1975, *97*, 123–130.

Norfleet, B. Interpersonal relations and group productivity. *Journal of Social Issues*, 1948, *4*(2), 66–69.

Norman, R. Affective-cognitive consistency, attitudes, conformity, and behavior. *Journal of Personality and Social Psychology*, 1975, *32*(1), 83–91.

Nowicki, S., & Blumberg, N. The role of locus of control of reinforcement in interpersonal attraction. *Journal of Research in Personality*, 1975, *9*(1), 48–56.

O'Connor, Gerald G. The impact of initial detention upon male delinquents. *Social Problems*, 1970, *18*, 194–199.

O'Dell, J. W. Group size and emotional interaction. *Journal of Personality and Social Psychology*, 1968, *8*(1), 75–78.

Oelsner, L. High court rules pupil spankings are permissible. *New York Times*, October 21, 1975, 1.

Olds, B. On the mathematics of committees, boards and panels. *Scientific Monthly*, August 1946.

O'Leary, M. R., & Dengerink, H. A. Aggression as a function of the intensity and pattern of attack. *Journal of Experimental Research in Personality*, 1973, 7, 61–70.

O'Leary, V. E. Some attitudinal barriers to occupational aspirations in women. *Psychological Bulletin*, 1974, *81*(11), 809–826.

O'Leary, V. E. *Sex role development.* Unpublished manuscript, Oakland University, 1975.

O'Leary, V. E., & Depner, C. E. College males' ideal female: Changes in sex-role stereotypes. *Journal of Social Psychology*, 1975, *95*, 139–140.

O'Leary, V. E., & Hammack, B. Sex role orientation and achievement context as determinants of the motive to avoid success. *Sex Roles*, 1975, *1*(3), 225–233.

O'Leary, V. E., & Harrison, A. O. *Sex role stereotypes as a function of race and sex.* Paper presented at the 83rd Annual Convention of the American Psychological Association, Chicago, September 1975.

Olmsted, M. S. *The small group.* New York: Random House, 1959.

Oltman, P. K., Goodenough, D. R., Witkin, H. A., Freedman, N., & Friedman, F. Psychological differentiation as a factor in conflict resolution. *Journal of Personality and Social Psychology*, 1975, *32*, 730–736.

Oppenheimer, R. Analogy in science. *American Psychologist*, 1956, *11*, 127–136.

Orne, M. T. On the social psychology of the psychological experiment: With particular reference to demand characteristics and their implications. *American Psychologist*, 1962, *17*, 776–783.

Orne, M. T., & Holland, C. H. On the ecological validity of laboratory deceptions. *International Journal of Psychiatry*, 1968, *6*, 282–293.

Ornstein, R. E. *Common knowledge, or foot powder elected mayor of Ecuadorian town.* New York: Viking Compass, undated.

Osborn, R. N., & Hunt, J. G. Relations between leadership, size, and subordinate satisfaction in a voluntary organization. *Journal of Applied Psychology*, 1975, *60*, 730–735.

Osgood, C. E. *An alternative to war or surrender.* Urbana: University of Illinois Press, 1962.

Osgood, C. E., Suci, G. J., & Tannenbaum, P. H. *The measurement of meaning.* Urbana: University of Illinois Press, 1957.

Osgood, C. E., & Tannenbaum, P. H. The principle of congruity in the prediction of attitude change. *Psychological Review*, 1955, *62*, 42–55.

Oshofsky, J. D., & O'Connell, E. J. Parent-child interaction: Daughters' effects upon mothers' and fathers' behaviors. *Developmental Psychology*, 1972, *7*, 157–168.

Ostrom, T. M. The relationship between the affective, behavioral, and cognitive components of attitude. *Journal of Experimental Social Psychology*, 1969, *5*, 12–30.

Overmier, J. P., & Seligman, M. Effects of inescapable shock on subsequent escape and avoidance responding. *Journal of Comparative and Physiological Psychology*, 1967, *63*, 28–33.

Packwood, W. T. Loudness as a variable in persuasion. *Journal of Counseling Psychology*, 1974, *21*, 1–2.

Page, J. *Social penetration processes. The effects of interpersonal reward and cost factors on the stability of dyadic relationships.* Unpublished doctoral dissertation, American University, 1968.

Page, M. M., & Roy, R. E. Internal-external control and independence of judgment in course evaluations among college students. *Personality and Social Psychology Bulletin*, 1975, *1*, 509–512.

Painter, J. J. *An investigation of the relationship between self-confidence, persuasibility and related behavior among males* (Doctoral dissertation, University of Texas at Austin, 1968.) (University Microfilms No. 68-10,877)

Pandey, J., & Griffitt, W. Attraction and helping. *Bulletin of the Psychonomic Society*, 1974, *3*, 123–124.

Panek, P. E., Rush, M. C., & Greenawalt, J. P. Current sex stereotypes of 25 occupations. *Psychological Reports*, 1977, *40*, 212–214.

Papageorgis, D., & McGuire, W. J. The generality of immunity to persuasion produced by pre-exposure to weakened counterarguments. *Journal of Abnormal and Social Psychology*, 1961, *62*, 475–481.

Parke, R. D., Berkowitz, L., Leyens, J.-P., & Sebastian, R. The effects of repeated exposure to movie violence on aggressive behavior in juvenile delinquent boys: Field experimental studies. In L. Berkowitz (Ed.), *Advances in experimental social psychology* (Vol. 9). New York: Academic Press, in press.

Parkinson, C. N. *Parkinson's Law, and other studies in administration.* Boston: Houghton Mifflin, 1957.

Parlee, M. B. The premenstrual syndrome. *Psychological Bulletin*, 1973, *80*, 454–465.

Parsons, T., & Bales, R. *Family, socialization and interaction process.* Glencoe, Ill.: Free Press, 1955.

Partridge, E. D. Leadership among adolescent boys. *Teach. Coll. Contr. Educ.*, No. 608, 1934.

Pastore, N., & Horowitz, M. The influence of attributed motive on the acceptance of statement. *Journal of Abnormal and Social Psychology*, 1955, *51*, 331–332.

Patterson, H. Spatial factors in social interactions. *Human Relations*, 1968, *21*(4), 350–361.

Patterson, M. L. Compensation in nonverbal immediacy behaviors: A review. *Sociometry*, 1973, *36*, 237–252. (a)

Patterson, M. L. Stability of nonverbal immediacy behaviors. *Journal of Experimental Social Psychology*, 1973, *9*, 97–109. (b)

Patterson, M. L., & Sechrest, L. B. Interpersonal distance and impression formation. *Journal of Personality*, 1970, *38*, 161–166.

Patterson, T. T., & Willett, E. J. An anthropological experiment in a British colliery. *Human Organization*, 1951, *10*, 19–23.

Paulus, P. B., Aunis, A. B., Seta, J. J., Schkade, J. K., & Matthews, R. W. Crowding does affect task performance. *Journal of Personality and Social Psychology*, 1976, *34*, 248–253.

Pear, J. J., Moody, J. E., & Persinger, M. A. Lever attacking by rats during free-operant avoidance. *Journal of the Experimental Analysis of Behavior*, 1972, *18*, 517–523.

Pearlstein, L. S. *The relationships between intelligence and cognitive style and the creative ability of kindergarten age children.* Unpublished master's thesis, University of Connecticut, 1971.

Pearson, K., & Lee, A. On the laws of inheritance in man: I. Inheritance of physical characteristics. *Biometrika*, 1903, *2*, 357–462.

Pedersen, D. M., & Heaston, A. B. The effects of sex of subject, sex of approaching person, and angle of approach upon personal space. *Journal of Psychology*, 1972, *82*, 277–286.

Penman, K. A., Hastad, D. N., & Cords, W. L. Success of the authoritarian coach. *Journal of Social Psychology*, 1974, *92*, 155–156.

Perlman, D., & Oskamp, S. The effects of picture content and exposure frequency on evaluations of Negroes and Whites. *Journal of Experimental Social Psychology*, 1971, *7*, 503–515.

Perlmutter, H. V. Group memory of meaningful material. *Journal of Psychology*, 1953, *35*, 361–370.

Perlmutter, H. V., & de Montmollin, G. Group learning of nonsense syllables. *Journal of Abnormal and Social Psychology*, 1952, *47*, 762–769.

Perry, R. W., Gillespie, D. F., & Lotz, R. E. Attitudinal variables as estimates of behavior: A theoretical examination of the attitude-action controversy. *European Journal of Social Psychology*, 1976, *6*, 227–243.

Pervin, L. The need to predict and control under conditions of threat. *Journal of Personality*, 1963, *31*, 570–585.

Peterson, K. K., & Dutton, J. E. Centrality, extremity, intensity: Neglected variables in research on attitude-behavior consistency. *Social Forces*, 1975, *54*, 393–414.

Phares, E. J. Locus of control. In H. London & J. Exner (Eds.), *Dimensions of personality.* New York: Wiley-Interscience, 1976. (a)

Phares, E. J. *Locus of control in personality.* Morristown, N.J.: General Learning Press, 1976. (b)

Piccolino, E. B. *Depicted threat, realism, and specificity, variables governing safety poster effectiveness.* Unpublished doctoral dissertation, Illinois Institute of Technology, 1966.

Pigors, P. *Leadership or domination.* London: Harrap, 1935.

Piliavin, I. M., Rodin, J., & Piliavin, J. A. Good samaritanism: An underground phenomenon? *Journal of Personality and Social Psychology*, 1969, *13*, 289–299.

Piliavin, J. A., & Piliavin, I. M. Effect of blood on reaction to a victim. *Journal of Personality and Social Psychology*, 1972, *23*, 353–361.

Piliavin, J. A., & Piliavin, I. M. *The good samaritan: Why does he help?* New York: MSS Publications, 1975.

Pliner, P. L. Effects of cue salience on the behavior of obese and normal subjects. *Journal of Abnormal Psychology*, 1973, *82*, 226–232. (a)

Pliner, P. L. Effect of external cues on the thinking behavior of obese and normal subjects. *Journal of Abnormal Psychology*, 1973, *82*, 233–238. (b)

Pliner, P. L. Effects of auditory cues on time estimation judgments of obese and normals. In S. Schachter & J. Rodin (Eds.), *Obese humans and rats*. Potomac, Md.: Erlbaum, 1974.

Pliner, P. L., Hart, H., Kuhl, J., & Saari, D. Compliance without pressure: Some further data on the foot-in-the-door technique. *Journal of Experimental Social Psychology*, 1974, *10*, 17–22.

Plumb, J. H. Children: The victims of time. In J. H. Plumb (Ed.), *The light of history*. London: Lane, 1972.

Plutchik, R., & Bender, H. Electrocutaneous pain thresholds in humans to low frequency square-wave pulses. *Journal of Psychology*, 1966, *62*, 151–154.

Pocs, O., Godow, A., Tolone, W. L., & Walsh, R. H. Is there sex after 40? *Psychology Today*, 1977, *4*(1), 54–56; 87.

Pollis, N. P., Montgomery, R. L., & Smith, T. G. Autokinetic paradigms: A reply to Alexander, Zucker, and Brody. *Sociometry*, 1975, *38*, 358–373.

Poloma, M. T., & Garland, T. N. *The myth of the egalitarian family: Familial roles and the professionally employed wife*. Paper presented at the annual meeting of the American Sociological Association, September 1970.

Pomazal, R. J., & Clore, G. L. Helping on the highway: The effects of dependency and sex. *Journal of Applied Social Psychology*, 1973, *3*, 150–164.

Pomazal, R. J., & Jaccard, J. J. An informational approach to altruistic behavior. *Journal of Personality and Social Psychology*, 1976, *33*, 317–326.

Poor vs. rich: A new global conflict. *Time*, December 22, 1975, 34–42.

Porier, G., & Lott, A. Galvanic skin responses and prejudice. *Journal of Personality and Social Psychology*, 1967, *5*, 253–259.

Premack, A. J., & Premack, D. Teaching language to an ape. *Scientific American*, 1972, *227*, 92–99.

Prescott, J. W. Child abuse in America: Slaughter of the innocents. *Hustler*, October 1977, 97–102.

Pressman, I., & Carol, A. Crime as a diseconomy of scale. *Review of Social Economy*, 1971, *29*, 227–236.

Price, J. *The effects of crowding on the social behavior of children*. Unpublished doctoral dissertation, Columbia University, 1971.

Prociuk, T. J., & Lussier, R. J. Internal-external locus of control: An analysis and bibliography of two years of research (1973–1974). *Psychological Reports*, 1975, *37*, 1323–1327.

Prokupek, J. Seasonal occurrence of suicide. *Czechoslovakia Psychiatry*, 1968, *64*, 13–20. (Abstract)

Proshansky, H., & Seidenberg, B. *Basic studies in social psychology*. New York: Holt, Rinehart & Winston, 1965.

Quereshi, M. Y., Leggio, A. H., & Widlak, F. W. Some biosocial determinants of interpersonal perception. *Journal of Social Psychology*, 1974, *93*, 229–244.

Quinlan, D. M., & Blatt, S. J. Field articulation and performance under stress: Differential predictions in surgical and psychiatric nursing training. *Journal of Consulting and Clinical Psychology*, 1972, *39*, 517.

Rabbie, J. M. Differential preference for companionship under threat. *Journal of Abnormal and Social Psychology*, 1963, *67*, 643–648.

Rabichow, H. G., & Pharis, M. E. *Rosenhan was wrong: The staff was lousy*. Unpublished manuscript, 1975.

Radloff, R., & Helmreich, R. *Groups under stress: Psychological research in SEALAB II*. New York: Appleton-Century-Crofts, 1968.

Rainwater, L. Marital sexuality in four "cultures of poverty." In D. S. Marshall & R. C. Suggs (Eds.), *Human sexual behavior*. New York: Basic Books, 1971.

Rajecki, D. W., Kidd, R. F., Wilder, D. A., & Jaeger, J. Social factors in the facilitation of feeding in chickens: Effects of imitation, arousal, or disinhibition? *Journal of Personality and Social Psychology*, 1975, *32*, 510–518.

Rarick, D. L., Soldow, G. F., & Geizer, R. S. Self-monitoring as a mediator of conformity. *Central States Speech Journal*, 1976, *27*, 267–271.

Raven, B. H. *A bibliography of publications relating to the small group*. (Supplement to Tech. Rep. 24, Contract Nonr-233[54].) Los Angeles: University of California, Los Angeles, 1969.

Raven, B. H., & Rubin, J. Z. *Social psychology: People in groups*. New York: Wiley, 1976.

Rawls, J. R., Trego, R. E., McGaffey, C. N., & Rawls, D. J. Personal space as a predictor of performance under close working conditions. *Journal of Social Psychology*, 1972, *86*, 261–267.

Reagor, P. A., & Clore, G. L. Attraction, test anxiety, and similarity-dissimilarity of test performance. *Psychonomic Science*, 1970, *18*, 219–220.

Redlich, F. C., & Freedman, D. X. *The theory and practice of psychiatry*. New York: Basic Books, 1966.

Reeder, L., Donohue, G., & Biblarz, A. Conceptions of self and others. *American Journal of Sociology*, 1960, *66*, 153–159.

Regan, D. T., & Fazio, R. On the consistency between attitudes and behavior: Look to the method of attitude formation. *Journal of Experimental Social Psychology*, 1977, *13*, 28–45.

Reilly, R. R. *A study of the effects of task-irrelevant factors on leader selection* (Doctoral dissertation, University of Tennessee, 1969). (University Microfilms No. 70-2134)

Reis, H. T., Earing, B., Kent, A., & Nezlek, J. The tyranny of numbers: Does group size affect petition signing? *Journal of Applied Psychology*, 1976, *6*, 228–234.

Rensberger, B. Computer helps chimpanzees learn to read, write and "talk" to humans. *New York Times*, May 29, 1974, 43; 52.

Renzulli, J. S., Owen, S. V., & Callahan, C. M. Fluency, flexibility, and originality as a function of group size. *Journal of Creative Behavior*, 1971, *8*(2), 107–113.

Report of the National Advisory Commission on Civil Disorders. New York: Bantam Books, 1968.

Reynolds, G. *A primer of operant conditioning*. Glenview, Ill.: Scott, Foresman, 1968.

Rhine, W. R. Birth order differences in conformity and level of achievement arousal. *Child Development*, 1968, *39*, 987–996.

Rice, M. E., & Grusec, J. E. Saying and doing: Effects on observer performance. *Journal of Personality and Social Psychology*, 1975, *32*, 584–593.

Richardson, H. Studies of mental resemblance between husbands and wives and between friends. *Psychological Bulletin*, 1939, *36*, 104–120.

Richardson, L. F. Statistics of deadly quarrels. In T. H. Pear (Ed.), *Psychological factors of peace and war*. New York: Philosophical Library, 1950.

Richardson, S. A., Goodman, N., Hastorf, A. H., & Dornbusch, S. M. Cultural uniformity in reactions to physical disabilities. *American Sociological Review*, 1961, *26*, 241–247.

Richter, C. On the phenomenon of sudden death in animals and man. *Psychosomatic Medicine*, 1957, *19*, 191–198.

Rickfelder, A. R. *Nonparticipation and alienation in the college classroom* (Doctoral dissertation, University of Michigan, 1970). (University Microfilms No. 71-15,280)

Riecken, H. W. The effect of talkativeness on ability to influence group solutions of problems. *Sociometry*, 1958, *21*(4), 309–321.

Riley, M., Cohn, W. R., Toby, J., & Riley, R. W., Jr. Interpersonal orientations in small groups: A consideration of the questionnaire approach. *American Sociological Review*, 1954, *19*, 715–724.

Rim, Y. Machiavellianism and decisions involving risks. *British Journal of Social and Clinical Psychology*, 1966, *5*, 36–50.

Ring, K., Lipinski, C. E., & Braginsky, D. The relationship of birth order to self-evaluation, anxiety reduction, and susceptibility to emotional contagion. *Psychological Monographs*, 1965, *79*(10, Whole No. 603).

Ring, K., Wallston, K., & Corey, M. Mode of debriefing as a factor affecting subjective reaction to a Milgram-type obedience experiment: An ethical inquiry. *Representative Research in Social Psychology*, 1970, *1*, 67–88.

Ritchie, E., & Phares, E. J. Attitude change as a function of internal-external control and communicator status. *Journal of Personality*, 1969, *37*, 429–443.

Rittle, R. H., & Cottrell, N. B. Cognitive bias in the perception of interpersonal relations. *Psychonomic Science*, 1967, *9*, 551–552.

Rivers, W. H. R. Vision. In A. C. Haddon (Ed.), *Reports of the Cambridge anthropological expedition to the Torres Straits* (Vol. 2). Cambridge, England: Cambridge University Press, 1901.

Rivers, W. H. R. Observations on the senses of the Todas. *British Journal of Psychology*, 1905, *1*, 321–396.

Rodin, J. Effects of distraction on performance of obese and normal subjects. *Journal of Comparative and Physiological Psychology*, 1973, *83*, 68–75.

Rodin, J. Research on eating behavior and obesity: Where does it fit in personality and social psychology? *Personality and Social Psychology Bulletin*, 1977.

Rodin, J., & Langer, E. J. Long-term effects of a control-relevant intervention with the institutionalized aged.

Journal of Personality and Social Psychology, 1977, *35*(12), 897–902.

Roethlisberger, F. J., & Dickson, W. J. *Management and the worker*. Cambridge, Mass.: Harvard University Press, 1947.

Rogers, C. R. A note on the "nature of man." *Journal of Counseling Psychology*, 1957, *4*, 199–203.

Rogers, R. W., & Thistlethwaite, D. L. Effects of fear arousal and reassurance on attitude change. *Journal of Personality and Social Psychology*, 1970, *15*, 227–233.

Rohe, W., & Patterson, A. H. *The effects of varied levels of resources and density on behavior in a day care center*. Paper presented at the meeting of the Environmental Design Research Association, Milwaukee, 1974.

Rohrer, J. H., Baron, S. H., Hoffman, E. L., & Swander, D. V. The stability of autokinetic judgments. *Journal of Abnormal and Social Psychology*, 1954, *49*, 595–597.

Rokeach, M. *The open and closed mind: Investigations into the nature of belief systems and personality systems*. New York: Basic Books, 1960.

Rokeach, M. The double agreement phenomenon: Three hypotheses. *Psychological Review*, 1963, *70*, 304–309.

Rokeach, M. Attitude change and behavior change. *Public Opinion Quarterly*, 1967, *30*, 529–550.

Rokeach, M. *The nature of human values*. New York: Free Press, 1973.

Rokeach, M., & McLellan, D. D. Feedback of information about the values and attitudes of self and others as determinants of long-term cognitive and behavioral change. *Journal of Applied Social Psychology*, 1972, *2*, 236–251.

Rokeach, M., & Mezei, L. Race and shared belief as factors in social choice. *Science*, 1966, *151*, 167–172.

Rokeach, M., & Vidmar, N. Testimony concerning possible jury bias in a Black Panther murder trial. *Journal of Applied Social Psychology*, 1973, *3*, 19–29.

Romer, N. The motive to avoid success and its effects on performance in school-age males and females. *Developmental Psychology*, 1975, *11*, 689–699.

Ronis, D. L., Baumgardner, M. H., Leippe, M. R., Cacioppo, J. T., & Greenwald, A. G. In search of reliable persuasion effects: I. A computer controlled procedure for studying persuasion. *Journal of Personality and Social Psychology*, 1977, *35*(8), 548–569.

Rorer, L. G. The great response-style myth. *Psychological Bulletin*, 1965, *63*, 129–156.

Rose, A. M. The ecological influential: A leadership type. *Sociology and Social Research*, 1968, *52*(2), 185–192.

Rose, H. M. The development of an urban subsystem: The case of the Negro ghetto. *Annals of the Association of American Geographers*, 1970, *60*, 1–17.

Rose, P. Student opinion on the 1956 presidential election. *Public Opinion Quarterly*, 1957, *21*, 371–376.

Rosen, B., & Jerdee, T. H. Effects of applicant's sex and difficulty of job on evaluations of candidates for managerial positions. *Journal of Applied Psychology*, 1974, *59*, 511–512. (a)

Rosen, B., & Jerdee, T. H. Influence of sex role stereotypes on personal decisions. *Journal of Applied Psychology*, 1974, *59*, 9–14. (b)

Rosen, B. C. Family structure and achievement motivation. *American Sociological Review*, 1961, *26*, 574–585.

Rosen, B. C., & D'Andrade, R. G. The psychosocial origin of achievement motivation. *Sociometry*, 1959, *22*, 185–218.

Rosen, S., & Tesser, A. On reluctance to communicate undesirable information: The MUM effect. *Sociometry*, 1970, *33*, 253–263.

Rosenberg, M. Cognitive structure and attitudinal affect. *Journal of Abnormal and Social Psychology*, 1956, *53*, 367–372.

Rosenberg, M. Psychological selectivity in self-esteem formation. in C. Gordon & K. Gergen (Eds.), *The self in social interaction*. New York: Wiley, 1968.

Rosenberg, S., Nelson, C., & Vivekananthan, P. S. A multidimensional approach to the structure of personality impressions. *Journal of Personality and Social Psychology*, 1968, *9*, 283–294.

Rosenblatt, P. C. Cross-cultural perspective on attraction. In T. L. Huston (Ed.), *Foundations of interpersonal attraction*. New York: Academic Press, 1974.

Rosenblatt, P. C., & Cozby, P. C. Courtship patterns associated with freedom of choice of spouse. *Journal of Marriage and the Family*, 1972, *34*, 689–695.

Rosenfeld, H. M. Effect of an approval-seeking induction on interpersonal proximity. *Psychological Reports*, 1965, *17*, 120–122.

Rosenfeld, H. M. Approval-seeking and approval-inducing functions of verbal and nonverbal responses in the dyad. *Journal of Personality and Social Psychology*, 1966, *4*, 597–605.

Rosenfeld, L. B., & Christie, V. R. Sex and persuasibility revisited. *Western Speech*, 1974, *38*, 244–253.

Rosenhan, D. The natural socialization of altruistic autonomy. In J. Macaulay & L. Berkowitz (Eds.), *Altruism and helping behavior*. New York: Academic Press, 1970.

Rosenhan, D. L. On being sane in insane places. *Science*, 1973, *179*, 250–258. (a)

Rosenhan, D. L. Letters to the editor. *Science*, 1973, *180*, 365–369. (b)

Rosenhan, D. L. Letters to the editor. *Journal of the American Medical Association*, 1973, *224*, 1646–1647. (c)

Rosenhan, D. L. The contextual nature of psychiatric diagnosis. *Journal of Abnormal Psychology*, 1975, *84*(5), 462–474.

Rosenkrantz, P. S., & Crockett, W. H. Some factors influencing the assimilation of disparate information in impression formation. *Journal of Personality and Social Psychology*, 1965, *2*, 397–402.

Rosenkrantz, P. S., Vogel, S. R., Bee, H., Broverman, I. K., & Broverman, D. M. Sex-role stereotypes and self-concepts in college students. *Journal of Consulting and Clinical Psychology*, 1968, *32*, 287–295.

Rosenthal, A. *Thirty-eight witnesses*. New York: McGraw-Hill, 1964.

Rosenthal, R. Experimenter outcome-orientation and the results of the psychological experiment. *Psychological Bulletin*, 1964, *61*, 405–412.

Rosenthal, R. *Experimenter effects in behavioral research*. New York: Appleton-Century-Crofts, 1966.

Rosenthal, R., Archer, D., DiMatteo, M. R., Koivumaki, J. H., & Rogers, P. L. Body talk and tone of voice: The language without words. *Psychology Today*, September 1974, 64–68.

Rosenthal, R., & Jacobson, L. *Pygmalion in the classroom: Teacher expectation and pupils' intellectual development*. New York: Holt, Rinehart & Winston, 1968.

Rosenthal, R., & Rosnow, R. L. The volunteer subject. In R. Rosenthal & R. L. Rosnow (Eds.), *Artifact in behavioral research*. New York: Academic Press, 1969.

Rosenwein, R. E. *Determinants of low verbal activity rates in small groups: A study of the silent person* (Doctoral dissertation, University of Michigan, 1970). (University Microfilms No. 71-15,284).

Roshwald, I. The voting studies and consumer decisions. In E. Burdick & A. J. Brodbeck (Eds.), *American voting behavior*. Glencoe, Ill.: Free Press, 1957.

Rosnow, R. L. Whatever happened to the "law of primacy"? *Journal of Communication*, 1966, *16*, 10–31.

Rosnow, R. L., & Arms, R. L. Adding versus averaging as a stimulus-combination rule in forming impressions of groups. *Journal of Personality and Social Psychology*, 1968, *10*, 363–369.

Rosnow, R. L., & Robinson, E. (Eds.). *Experiments in persuasion*. New York: Academic Press, 1967.

Rosow, I. The social effects of the physical environment. *Journal of the American Institute of Planners*, 1961, *27*, 127–133.

Ross, A. S. Effect of increased responsibility on bystander intervention: The presence of children. *Journal of Personality and Social Psychology*, 1971, *19*, 306–310.

Ross, A. S., & Braband, J. Effect of increased responsibility on bystander intervention: II. The cue value of a blind person. *Journal of Personality and Social Psychology*, 1973, *25*, 254–258.

Ross, A. S., & Burke, H. *Effect of visibility of the victim on bystander intervention*. Unpublished manuscript, University of Toronto, Scarborough College, undated.

Ross, E. A. *Social psychology*. New York: Macmillan, 1908.

Ross, L., Bierbrauer, G., & Hoffman, S. The role of attribution processes in conformity and dissent. *American Psychologist*, 1976, *31*, 148–157.

Ross, M., Layton, B., Erickson, B., & Schopler, J. Affect, facial regard, and reactions to crowding. *Journal of Personality and Social Psychology*, 1973, *28*, 69–76.

Rossi, A. S. Status of women in graduate departments of sociology: 1968–1969. *American Sociologist*, 1970, *5*, 1–12.

Rossi, R. [Psychogenic aspects in the psychology of immigration.] *Archivio di Psicologia, Neurologia e Psichiatria*, 1971, *32*, 103–115.

Rotter, J. B. Generalized expectancies for internal versus external control of reinforcement. *Psychological Monographs*, 1966, *80*(1), (Whole No. 609).

Rotter, J. B., Liverant, S., & Seeman, M. Internal-external control of reinforcement: A major variable in behavior theory. In N. Washburne (Ed.), *Decisions, values and groups* (Vol. 2). London: Pergamon Press, 1962.

Rotter, J., & Stein, D. Public attitudes toward the trustworthiness, competence, and altruism of twenty selected occupations. *Journal of Applied Social Psychology*, 1971, *1*, 334–343.

Rotton, J., Barry, T., Frey, J., & Soler, E. *Air pollution and interpersonal attraction.* Unpublished manuscript, University of Dayton, 1976.

Rowland, K. F. Environmental events predicting death for the elderly. *Psychological Bulletin*, 1977, *84*, 349–372.

Rozelle, R. M., & Baxter, J. C. Impression formation and danger recognition in experienced police officers. *Journal of Social Psychology*, in press.

Rubin, J. A., Provenzano, F. J., & Luria, Z. The eye of the beholder: Parents' views on sex of newborns. *American Journal of Orthopsychiatry*, 1974, *44*, 512–519.

Rubin, Z. Measurement of romantic love. *Journal of Personality and Social Psychology*, 1970, *16*, 265–273.

Rubin, Z. *Liking and loving: An invitation to social psychology.* New York: Holt, Rinehart & Winston, 1973.

Rubin, Z. From liking to loving: Patterns of attraction in dating relationships. In T. L. Huston (Ed.), *Foundations of interpersonal attraction.* New York: Academic Press, 1974.

Rubin, Z. Disclosing oneself to a stranger: Reciprocity and its limits. *Journal of Experimental Social Psychology*, 1975, *11*, 233–260.

Ruble, D. N., & Nakamura, C. Y. Task orientation versus social orientation in young children and their attention to relevant social cues. *Child Development*, 1972, *43*, 471–480.

Russell, V., Stok, K., & Stang, D. J. *Segregation in aggregation: Two field studies.* Queens College, N.Y.: Unpublished manuscript, 1976.

Saadi, M., & Farnsworth, P. The degree of acceptance of dogmatic statements and preferences for their supposed makers. *Journal of Abnormal and Social Psychology*, 1934, *29*, 143–150.

Sabath, G. The effect of disruption and individual status on person perception and group attraction. *Journal of Social Psychology*, 1964, *64*, 119–130.

Saegert, S. C., Swap, W., & Zajonc, R. B. Exposure, context, and interpersonal attraction. *Journal of Personality and Social Psychology*, 1973, *25*, 234–242.

Saenger, G., & Gilbert, E. Customer reactions to the integration of Negro sales personnel. *International Journal of Opinion and Attitude Research*, 1950, *4*, 57–76.

Sage, W. Violence in the children's room. *Human Behavior*, July 1975.

Sagi, P. C., Olmstead, D. W., & Atelsek, F. Predicting maintenance of membership in small groups. *Journal of Abnormal and Social Psychology*, 1955, *51*, 308–311.

Samelson, F. The relation of achievement and affiliation motives to conforming behavior in two conditions of conflict with a majority. In J. W. Atkinson (Ed.), *Motives in fantasy, action and society.* New York: Van Nostrand, 1958.

Samerotte, G. C., & Harris, M. B. Some factors influencing helping: The effects of a handicap, responsibility and requesting help. *Journal of Social Psychology*, in press.

Sample, J., & Warland, R. Attitude and prediction of behavior. *Social Forces*, 1973, *51*, 292–304.

Sampson, E. E. Birth order, need achievement and conformity. *Journal of Abnormal and Social Psychology*, 1962, *64*, 155–159.

Sanford, F. H. *Authoritarianism and leadership.* Philadelphia: Institute for Research in Human Relations, 1950.

Sapir, E. The status of linguistics as a science. *Language*, 1929, *5*, 207–214.

Sarnoff, I. *Identification with the aggressor: Some personality correlates of anti-Semitism among Jews.* Unpublished doctoral dissertation, University of Michigan, 1951.

Sarnoff, I. Psychoanalytic theory and social attitudes. *Public Opinion Quarterly*, 1960, *24*, 251–279.

Sarnoff, I., & Zimbardo, P. G. Anxiety, fear, and social affiliation. *Journal of Abnormal and Social Psychology*, 1961, *62*, 356–363.

Saville, M. R. Individual and group risk taking: A cross-cultural study. *Dissertation Abstracts International*, 1971, *31*(8-A), 4268.

Schachter, S. Deviation, rejection, and communication. *Journal of Abnormal and Social Psychology*, 1951, *46*, 190–207.

Schachter, S. *The psychology of affiliation.* Stanford, Calif.: Stanford University Press, 1959.

Schachter, S. Birth order, eminence and higher education. *American Sociological Review*, 1963, *28*(5), 757–768.

Schachter, S. The interaction of cognitive and physiological determinants of emotional state. In L. Berkowitz (Ed.), *Advances in experimental social psychology* (Vol. 1). New York: Academic Press, 1964.

Schachter, S. Obesity and eating. *Science*, 1968, *161*, 751–756.

Schachter, S., Ellertson, N., McBride, D., & Gregory, D. An experimental study of cohesiveness and productivity. *Human Relations*, 1951, *4*, 229–238.

Schachter, S., & Gross, L. P. Manipulated time and eating behavior. *Journal of Personality and Social Psychology*, 1968, *10*, 98–106.

Schachter, S., & Singer, J. Cognitive, social, and physiological determinants of emotional state. *Psychological Review*, 1962, *69*, 379–399.

Schachter, S., & Wheeler, L. Epinephrine, chlorpromazine, and amusement. *Journal of Abnormal and Social Psychology*, 1962, *65*, 121–128.

Schaffer, H. Behavior under stress: A neurophysiological hypothesis. *Psychological Review*, 1954, *61*, 323–331.

Schaffner, P., Wandersman, A., & Stang, D. *Name exposure and voting behavior.* Unpublished manuscript, Cornell University, 1978.

Schanck, R. L. A study of a community and its groups and institutions conceived of as behaviors of individuals. *Psychological Monographs*, 1932, *43*.

Schellenberg, J. A., & Blevins, G. A. Feeling good and helping: How quickly does the smile of Dame Fortune fade? *Psychological Reports*, 1973, *33*, 72–74.

Scherer, S. E. Proxemic behavior of primary school children as a function of their socioeconomic class and subculture. *Journal of Personality and Social Psychology*, 1974, *29*, 800–805.

Schettino, A. P., & Borden, R. J. Sex differences in response to naturalistic crowding: Affective reactions to group size and group density. *Personality and Social Psychology Bulletin*, 1976, *2*, 67–70.

Schiffenbauer, A., & Schiavo, S. R. Physical distance and attraction: An intensification effect. *Journal of Experimental Social Psychology*, 1976, *12*, 274–282.

Schilder, P. *The image and appearance of the body.* New York: International University Press, 1950.

Schiller, B. A quantitative analysis of marriage selection in a small group. *Journal of Social Psychology*, 1932, *3*, 297–319.

Schiller, J. C. F. *Essays, esthetical and philosophical, including the dissertation on the "Connexions between the animal and the spiritual in man."* London: Bell, 1882.

Schlosberg, H. Three dimensions of emotion. *Psychological Review*, 1954, *61*, 81–88. (a)

Schlosberg, H. *Fatigue, effort and work output.* Presidential address at the meeting of the Eastern Psychological Association, May 1954. (b)

Schmale, A. Relationships of separation and depression to disease. I.: A report on a hospitalized medical population. *Psychosomatic Medicine*, 1958, *20*, 259–277.

Schmale, A., & Iker, H. The psychological setting of uterine cervical cancer. *Annals of the New York Academy of Sciences*, 1966, *125*, 807–813.

Schmid, C. Urban crime areas: Part I. *American Sociological Review*, 1969, *25*, 527–542.

Schmid, C. Urban crime areas: Part II. *American Sociological Review*, 1970, *25*, 655–678.

Schmitt, R. C. Density, delinquency and crime in Honolulu. *Sociology and Social Research*, 1957, *41*, 274–276.

Schmitt, R. C. Recent trends in Hawaiian interracial marriage rates by occupation. *Journal of Marriage and the Family*, 1971, *33*, 373–374.

Schneider, D. J. Implicit personality theory: A review. *Psychological Bulletin*, 1973, *79*, 294–309.

Schneider, F. W., & Mockus, Z. Failure to find a rural-urban difference in incidence of altruistic behavior. *Psychological Reports*, 1974, *35*, 294.

Schorr, A. L. *Slums and social insecurity* (Report No. 1). Washington, D.C.: U.S. Department of Health, Education and Welfare, Social Security Administration, Division of Research and Statistics Research, 1963.

Schroeder, F. de N. *Anatomy for interior designers.* New York: Whitney Publications, undated. (Cited in Sommer, 1961.)

Schuckman, H. *Tutoring psychology today: A handbook for beginners.* Unpublished manuscript, Queens College, 1972.

Schuckman, H. *Criteria for evaluating answers to honors questions.* Unpublished manuscript, Queens College, undated.

Schuetz, A. The stranger: An essay in social psychology. *American Journal of Sociology*, 1944, *49*, 499–507.

Schulman, G. I. Asch conformity studies: Conformity to the experimenter and/or to the group? *Sociometry*, 1967, *30*, 26–40.

Schultz, B. Characteristics of emergent leaders of continuing problem-solving groups. *Journal of Psychology*, 1974, *88*, 167–173.

Schultz, D. P. The human subject in psychological research. *Psychological Bulletin*, 1969, *72*, 214–228.

Schuman, H. Social change and the validity of regional stereotypes in East Pakistan. *Sociometry*, 1966, *29*, 428–440.

Schwartz, B., & Barsky, S. F. The home advantage. *Social Forces*, 1977, *55*, 641–661.

Schwartz, M. S. *Effectance motivation and interpersonal attraction: Individual differences and personality correlates.* Unpublished doctoral dissertation, University of Texas, 1966.

Schwartz, R. D., & Skolnick, J. H. Two studies of legal stigma. In Howard S. Becker (Ed.), *The other side: Perspectives on deviance.* Glencoe, Ill.: Free Press, 1964.

Schwitzgebel, R., & Kolb, D. A. Inducing behavior change in adolescent delinquents. *Behavior Research and Therapy*, 1964, *1*, 297–304.

Scott, J. P. *Aggression* (2nd ed.). Chicago: University of Chicago Press, 1975.

Scott, J. P. Agonistic behavior: Function and dysfunction in social conflict. *Journal of Social Issues*, 1977, *33*(1), 9–21.

Scott, W. A. Attitude measurement. In G. Lindzey & E. Aronson (Eds.), *Handbook of social psychology* (Vol. 2, 2nd ed.). Reading, Mass.: Addison-Wesley, 1969.

Sears, D. O. Political behavior. In G. Lindzey & E. Aronson (Eds.), *Handbook of social psychology* (Vol. 5, 2nd ed.). Reading, Mass.: Addison-Wesley, 1969.

Sears, R. R., Maccoby, E. E., & Levin, H. *Patterns of child rearing.* New York: Harper & Row, 1957.

Seashore, S. E. *Group cohesiveness in the industrial work group.* Ann Arbor: University of Michigan Press, 1954.

Seeman, M. Alienation and social learning in a reformatory. *American Journal of Sociology*, 1963, *69*, 270–284.

Seeman, M. The urban alienations: Some dubious theses from Marx to Marcuse. *Journal of Personality and Social Psychology*, 1971, *19*, 135–143.

Segall, M. H., Campbell, D. T., & Herskovits, M. J. Cultural differences in the perception of geometrical illusions. *Science*, 1963, *139*, 769–771.

Segall, M. H., Campbell, D. T., & Herskovits, M. J. *The influence of culture on visual perception.* Indianapolis: Bobbs-Merrill, 1966.

Seiler, L. H., & Hough, R. L. Empirical comparisons of the Thurstone and Likert techniques. In G. F. Summers (Ed.), *Attitude measurement.* Chicago: Rand McNally, 1970.

Seiler, L. H., & Stang, D. J. Student ratings of college course and instructor. In *Improving College and University Teaching Yearbook*, 1977, 37–43. (a)

Seiler, L. H., & Stang, D. J. Student ratings of college course and instructor: A selected bibliography. In *Improving College and University Teaching Yearbook*, 1977, 45–51. (b)

Seligman, C., Paschall, N., & Takata, G. Effects of physical attractiveness on attribution of responsibility. *Canadian Journal of Behavioral Science*, 1974, *6*, 290–296.

Seligman, M. *Depression and learned helplessness.* Paper presented at the 80th Annual Convention of the American Psychological Association, Honolulu, September 1972.

Seligman, M. *Helplessness.* San Francisco: Freeman, 1975.

Seligman, M., & Maier, S. F. Failure to escape traumatic

shock. *Journal of Experimental Psychology*, 1967, *74*, 1–9.

Seligman, S. R., & Stang, D. J. SUBSIM: A subject simulation program for on-line conformity research. *Behavior Research Methods and Instrumentation*, 1975, 7(6), 576.

Senn, D. J. Attraction as a function of similarity-dissimilarity in task performance. *Journal of Personality and Social Psychology*, 1971, *18*, 120–123.

Sensenig, J., & Brehm, J. W. Attitude change from an implied threat to attitudinal freedom. *Journal of Personality and Social Psychology*, 1968, *8*, 324–330.

Sewell, W. H., & Haller, A. O. Social status and the personality adjustment of the child. *Sociometry*, 1956, *19*, 114–125.

Shaffer, D. R., & Wegley, C. Success orientation and sex-role congruence as determinants of the attractiveness of competent women. *Journal of Personality*, 1974, *42*, 586–600.

Shanab, M. E., & Yahya, K. A. A behavioral study of obedience in children. *Journal of Personality and Social Psychology*, 1977, *35*, 530–536.

Shanab, M. E., & Yahya, K. A. A cross-cultural study of obedience. *Bulletin of the Psychonomic Society*, 1978, *11*(4), 267–269.

Shapiro, D., & Crider, A. Psychophysiological approaches in social psychology. In G. Lindzey & E. Aronson (Eds.), *Handbook of social psychology* (Vol. 3, 2nd ed.). Reading, Mass.: Addison-Wesley, 1968.

Shartle, C. L. Leadership and executive performance. *Personnel*, March 1949, 370–380.

Shaver, K. G. *An introduction to attribution processes.* Cambridge, Mass.: Winthrop, 1975.

Shaw, J. Reactions to victims and defendants of varying degrees of attractiveness. *Psychonomic Science*, 1972, *27*, 329–330.

Shaw, M. E. Some effects of problem complexity upon problem solution efficiency in different communication nets. *Journal of Experimental Psychology*, 1954, *48*, 211–217. (a)

Shaw, M. E. Some effects of unequal distribution of information upon group performance in various communication nets. *Journal of Abnormal Sociology Quarterly*, 1954, *49*, 547–553. (b)

Shaw, M. E. A comparison of two types of leadership in various communication networks. *Journal of Abnormal Sociology Quarterly*, 1955, *50*, 127–134.

Shaw, M. E. Some motivational factors in cooperation and competition. *Journal of Personality*, 1958, *26*, 155–169.

Shaw, M. E., & Gilchrist, J. C. Intra-group communication and leader choice. *Journal of Social Psychology*, 1956, *43*, 133–138.

Shaw, M. E., Rothschild, G. H., & Strickland, J. F. Decision processes in communication nets. *Journal of Abnormal and Social Psychology*, 1957, *54*, 323–330.

Shaw, M. E., & Sadler, O. W. Interaction patterns in heterosexual dyads varying in degree of intimacy. *Journal of Social Psychology*, 1965, *66*, 345–351.

Sheehy, G. *Passages.* New York: Dutton, 1974.

Sheldon, W. H. *The varieties of human physique.* New York: Harper, 1940.

Sheldon, W. H. *The varieties of temperament.* New York: Harper, 1942.

Sheldon, W. H. *Varieties of delinquent youth.* New York: Harper, 1949.

Sheldon, W. H. *Atlas of men.* New York: Harper, 1954.

Shepherd, J. West Side report. *New York*, September 1973, *6*, 56–59.

Sheridan, C. L., & King, K. G. Obedience to authority with an authentic victim. *Proceedings of the 80th Annual Convention of the American Psychological Association*, 1972, *7*, 165–166. (Summary)

Sherif, C. W., Sherif, M., & Nebergall, R. E. *Attitude and attitude change: The social judgment approach.* Philadelphia: Saunders, 1965.

Sherif, M. A study of some social factors in perception. *Archives of Psychology*, 1935, No. 187.

Sherif, M., & Harvey, O. J. A study in ego-functioning: Elimination of stable anchorages in individual and group situations. *Sociometry*, 1952, *15*, 272–305.

Sherif, M., Harvey, O. J., White, B. J., Hood, W. R., & Sherif, C. W. *Intergroup cooperation and competition: The Robbers Cave experiment.* Norman, Okla.: University Book Exchange, 1961.

Sherif, M., & Hovland, C. *Social judgment.* New Haven, Conn.: Yale University Press, 1961.

Sherif, M., & Sherif, C. W. *Groups in harmony and tension.* New York: Harper, 1953.

Sherif, M., & Sherif, C. W. *Social psychology.* New York: Harper & Row, 1969.

Sherif, M., White, B. J., & Harvey, O. J. Status in experimentally produced groups. *American Journal of Sociology*, 1955, *60*, 370–379.

Sherriffs, A. C., & Jarret, R. F. Sex differences in attitudes about sex differences. *Journal of Psychology*, 1953, *35*, 161–168.

Sherriffs, A. C., & McKee, J. P. Qualitative aspects of beliefs about men and women. *Journal of Personality*, 1957, *25*, 451–464.

Sherrod, D. R., & Downs, R. Environmental determinants of altruism: The effects of stimulus overload and perceived control on helping. *Journal of Experimental Social Psychology*, 1974, *10*, 468–479.

Shils, E. A. Primary groups in the American army, continuities in social research. In R. Merton & P. Lazarsfeld (Eds.), *Studies in the scope and method of the American soldier.* Glencoe, Ill.: Free Press, 1950.

Shotland, L., & Johnson, M. *Bystander intervention: Victim and incident characteristics.* Unpublished manuscript, Pennsylvania State University, 1974.

Shure, G. H., Meeker, L. J., & Hansford, E. A. The effectiveness of pacifist strategies in bargaining games. *Journal of Conflict Resolution*, 1965, *9*, 106–117.

Shurley, J. T. Stress and adaptation as related to sensory/perceptual isolation research. *Military Medicine*, 1966, *131*, 254–258.

Siegel, S., & Fouraker, L. E. *Bargaining and group decision making.* New York: McGraw-Hill, 1960.

Sigall, H., & Aronson, E. Liking for an evaluator as a function of her physical attractiveness and nature of the evaluations. *Journal of Experimental Social Psychology*, 1969, *5*, 93–100.

Sigall, H., & Landy, D. Radiating beauty: Effects of having a physically attractive partner on person perception. *Journal of Personality and Social Psychology*, 1973, *28*, 218–224.

Sigall, H., & Ostrove, N. Beautiful but dangerous: Effects of offender attractiveness and nature of the crime on juridic judgment. *Journal of Personality and Social Psychology*, 1975, *31*, 410–414.

Sigall, H., Page, R., & Brown, A. Effort expenditure as a function of evaluation and evaluator attractiveness. *Representative Research in Social Psychology*, 1971, *2*, 19–25.

Silverman, D., & Kornblueh, I. H. Effect of artificial ionization of the air on electroencephalogram. *American Journal of Medicine*, 1957, *36*, 352–358.

Silverman, I. Differential effects of ego threat upon persuasibility for high and low self-esteem subjects. *Journal of Abnormal and Social Psychology*, 1964, *69*, 567–572.

Silverstein, C. H., & Stang, D. J. Seating position and interaction in triads: A field study. *Sociometry*, 1976, *39*(2), 166–170.

Simmel, G. The number of members as determining the sociological form of the group. *American Journal of Sociology*, 1902, *8*, 158–196.

Simon, R. J., Clark, S. M., & Galway, K. The woman Ph.D.: A recent profile. *Social Problems*, 1967, *15*, 221–236.

Simons, H. W. Authoritarianism and social perceptiveness. *Journal of Social Psychology*, 1966, *68*, 291–297.

Simonson, N. *Self-disclosure and psychotherapy*. Amherst, Mass.: Department of Psychology, University of Massachusetts, 1973.

Singer, J., Brush, C., & Lublin, S. Some aspects of deindividuation: Identification and conformity. *Journal of Experimental Social Psychology*, 1965, *1*, 356–378.

Skidmore, F. The used car rip-off. *Focus*, 1978, *2*(3), 1–2; 6. (Newsletter of the Institute for Research on Poverty, University of Wisconsin.)

Skotko, V., Langmeyer, D., & Lundgren, D. Sex differences as artifacts in the prisoner's dilemma game. *Journal of Conflict Resolution*, 1974, *18*, 707–713.

Slater, P. E. Role differentiation in small groups. *American Sociological Review*, 1955, *20*, 300–310.

Slater, P. E. Contrasting correlates of group size. *Sociometry*, 1958, *21*, 129–139.

Slote, L. An experimental evaluation of man's reaction to an ionized air environment. *Proceedings of the International Conference on the Ionization of the Air*, Philadelphia, 1962.

Smith, E. E. *Methods for changing consumer attitudes: A report of three experiments*. Project report, Quartermaster Food and Container Institute for the Armed Forces (PRA Report 61–2), 1961.

Smith, M. B., Bruner, J. S., & White, R. W. *Opinions and personality*. New York: Wiley, 1956.

Smith, R. E., Meadow, B. L., & Sisk, T. K. Attitude similarity, interpersonal attraction, and evaluative social perception. *Psychonomic Science*, 1970, *18*, 226–227.

Smith, S. Studies of small groups in confinement. In J. P. Zubek (Ed.), *Sensory deprivation: Fifteen years of research*. New York: Appleton-Century-Crofts, 1969.

Smith, T. I., & Suinn, R. M. A note on identification, self-

esteem, anxiety and conformity. *Journal of Clinical Psychology*, 1965, *21*(3), 286.

Smith, W. I., Powell, E. K., & Ross, S. Food aversions: Some additional personality correlates. *Journal of Consulting Psychology*, 1955, *19*, 145–149. (a)

Smith, W. I., Powell, E. K., & Ross, S. Manifest anxiety and food aversions. *Journal of Abnormal and Social Psychology*, 1955, *50*, 101–104. (b)

Smith, W. M. Observations over the lifetime of a small isolated group: Structure, danger, boredom, and vision. *Psychological Reports*, 1966, *19*, 475–514.

Snow, R. E. Review of *Pygmalion in the classroom* by R. Rosenthal & L. Jacobson. *Contemporary Psychology*, 1969, *14*, 197–199.

Snyder, M. The self-monitoring of expressive behavior. *Journal of Personality and Social Psychology*, 1974, *30*, 526–537.

Snyder, M. Impression management. In L. S. Wrightsman, *Social psychology* (2nd ed.). Monterey, Calif.: Brooks/Cole, 1977.

Snyder, M., & Cunningham, M. R. To comply or not comply: Testing the self-perception explanation of the "foot-in-the-door" phenomenon. *Journal of Personality and Social Psychology*, in press.

Snyder, M., Grether, J., & Keller, K. Staring and compliance: A field experiment on hitchhiking. *Journal of Applied Social Psychology*, 1974, *4*, 165–170.

Snyder, M., & Monson, T. C. Persons, situations, and the control of social behavior. *Journal of Personality and Social Psychology*, 1975, *32*, 637–644.

Snyder, M., & Rothbart, M. Communicator attractiveness and opinion change. *Canadian Journal of Behavioral Science*, 1971, *3*, 377–387.

Snyder, M., & Swann, W. B., Jr. When actions reflect attitudes: The politics of impression management. *Journal of Personality and Social Psychology*, 1976, *34*, 1034–1042.

Snyder, M., & Tanke, E. D. Behavior and attitude: Some people are more consistent than others. *Journal of Personality*, 1976, *44*, 501–517.

Snyder, M., Tanke, E. D., & Berscheid, E. Social perception and interpersonal behavior: On the self-fulfilling nature of social stereotypes. *Journal of Personality and Social Psychology*, 1977, *35*, 656–666.

Socialism: Trials and errors. *Time*, March 13, 1978, 24–27, 29–30, 35–36.

Sole, K., Marton, J., & Hornstein, H. A. Opinion similarity and helping: Three field experiments investigating the bases of promotive tension. *Journal of Experimental Social Psychology*, 1975, *11*, 1–13.

Solomon, L. The influence of some types of power relationships and game strategies upon the development of interpersonal trust. *Journal of Abnormal and Social Psychology*, 1960, *61*, 223–230.

Sommer, R. Studies in personal space. *Sociometry*, 1959, *22*, 247–260.

Sommer, R. Leadership and group geography. *Sociometry*, 1961, *24*, 99–110.

Sommer, R. The distance for comfortable conversation: A further study. *Sociometry*, 1962, *25*, 111–116.

Sommer, R. Further studies of small group ecology. *Sociom-*

etry, 1965, *28*(4), 337–348.

Sommer, R. Classroom ecology. *Journal of Applied Behavioral Science*, 1967, *3*(4), 489–502.

Songer-Nocks, E. Situational factors affecting the weighting of predictor components in the Fishbein model. *Journal of Experimental Social Psychology*, 1976, *12*, 56–69.

Sophie, J. Women as scholars. *American Psychologist*, July 1974, 529–532.

Sosis, R. H. Internal-external control and the perception of responsibility of another for an accident. *Journal of Personality and Social Psychology*, 1974, *30*, 393–399.

Soueif, M. I. Extreme response sets as a measure of intolerance of ambiguity. *British Journal of Psychology*, 1958, *49*, 329–334.

Southam, A. L., & Gonzaga, G. P. Systemic changes during the menstrual cycle. *American Journal of Obstetrics and Gynecology*, 1965, *91*, 142–157.

Spence, J. T. The thematic apperception test and attitudes toward achievement in women: A new look at the motive to avoid success and a new method of measurement. *Journal of Consulting and Clinical Psychology*, 1974, *42*, 427–437.

Spence, J. T., & Helmreich, R. Who likes competent women? Competence, sex-role congruence of interests, and subjects' attitudes toward women as determinants of interpersonal attraction. *Journal of Applied Social Psychology*, 1972, *3*, 197–213.

Spence, J. T., Helmreich, R., & Stapp, J. Ratings of self and peers on sex-role attributes and their relation to self-esteem and conceptions of masculinity and femininity. *Journal of Personality and Social Psychology*, 1975, *32*, 29–39.

Spiro, M. E. *Children of the kibbutz*. Cambridge, Mass.: Harvard University Press, 1958.

Spitzer, R. L. On pseudoscience in science, logic in remission, and psychiatric diagnoses: A critique of Rosenhan's "On being sane in insane places." *Journal of Abnormal Psychology*, 1975, *84*, 442–452.

Srole, L., Langner, T. S., Michael, S. T., Opler, M. K., & Rennie, T. A. C. *Mental health in the metropolis*. New York: McGraw-Hill, 1962.

Staats, A. W. Experimental demand characteristics and the classical conditioning of attitudes. *Journal of Personality and Social Psychology*, 1969, *11*, 187–192.

Staats, A. W., & Staats, C. K. Attitudes established by classical conditioning. *Journal of Abnormal and Social Psychology*, 1958, *57*, 37–40.

Stachowiak, J., & Moss, C. Hypnotic alterations of social attitudes. *Journal of Personality and Social Psychology*, 1965, *2*, 77–83.

Stalling, R. B. Personality similarity and evaluation meaning as conditioners of attraction. *Journal of Personality and Social Psychology*, 1970, *14*, 77–81.

Stang, D. J. Conformity, ability, and self-esteem. *Representative Research in Social Psychology*, 1972, *3*(2), 97–103.

Stang, D. J. The effect of interaction rate on ratings of leadership and liking. *Journal of Personality and Social Psychology*, 1973, *27*(3), 405–408.

Stang, D. J. Intuition as artifact in mere exposure studies.

Journal of Personality and Social Psychology, 1974, *30*, 647–653. (a)

Stang, D. J. Methodological factors in mere exposure research. *Psychological Bulletin*, 1974, *81*, 1014–1025. (b)

Stang, D. J. Research in conformity: A bibliography. *JSAS Catalog of Selected Documents in Psychology*, 1974, *4*, 77. (c)

Stang, D. J. Effects of "mere exposure" on learning and affect. *Journal of Personality and Social Psychology*, 1975, *31*(1), 7–12. (a)

Stang, D. J. When familiarity breeds contempt, absence makes the heart grow fonder: Effects of exposure and delay on taste pleasantness ratings. *Bulletin of the Psychonomic Society*, 1975, *6*(3), 273–275. (b)

Stang, D. J. Student evaluations of 28 social psychology texts. *Teaching of Psychology*, 1975, *2*(1), 12–15. (c)

Stang, D. J. A critical examination of the response competition hypothesis. *Bulletin of the Psychonomic Society*, 1976, *7*(6), 530–532. (a)

Stang, D. J. Group size effects on conformity. *Journal of Social Psychology*, 1976, *98*, 175–181. (b)

Stang, D. J. Ineffective deception in conformity research: Some causes and consequences. *European Journal of Social Psychology*, 1976, *6*(3), 353–367. (c)

Stang, D. J. Exposure, recall, judged favorability and sales: "Mere exposure" and consumer behavior. *Social Behavior and Personality*, 1977, *5*(2), 329–335.(a)

Stang, D. J. On the relationship between novelty and complexity. *Journal of Social Psychology*, 1977, *95*, 317–323. (b)

Stang, D. J. *Group size and member satisfaction*. Paper presented at the annual meeting of the Eastern Psychological Association, Washington, D.C., May 1978. (a)

Stang, D. J. *Sex differences in salaries of graduate faculty in psychology, 1977–1978*. Unpublished manuscript, May 3, 1978. (b)

Stang, D. J. *No effect of thought on attitude polarization; Effect of attitude on thought: Evidence for selective rehearsal*. Unpublished manuscript, American Psychological Association, 1978. (c)

Stang, D. J. *Social research methods*. Monterey, Calif.: Brooks/Cole, in preparation.

Stang, D. J., Campus, N., & Wallach, C. Exposure duration as a confounding methodological factor in projective testing. *Journal of Personality Assessment*, 1975, *39*(6), 583–586.

Stang, D. J., Castellanetta, J. A., Constantinidis, G., & Fortuno, C. R. Actual vs. perceived talkativeness as determinants of judged leadership, popularity and likeableness. *Bulletin of the Psychonomic Society*, 1976, *8*(1), 44–46.

Stang, D. J., & Crandall, R. Familiarity and interpersonal attraction. In T. Steinfatt (Ed.), *Readings in human communication: An interpersonal introduction*. Indianapolis: Bobbs-Merrill, 1977, 279–287.

Stang, D. J., & Matlin, M. W. Effect of meaningfulness and instructions on frequency estimation. *Psychological Reports*, 1975, *36*(1), 164.

Stang, D. J., McKenna, W., & Kessler, S. *Perceptions of academic psychology job applicants*. Washington, D.C.: American

Psychological Association, unpublished manuscript, 1978.

Stang, D. J., & Neer, K. *Sex differences in conformity?* Unpublished manuscript, Queens College, 1975.

Stang, D. J., & Neer, K. *An exploration of methodological factors affecting sex differences in conformity.* Unpublished manuscript, Queens College, 1976.

Stang, D. J., & O'Connell, E. J., Jr. The computer as experimenter in social psychological research. *Behavior Research Methods and Instrumentation,* 1974, *6*(2), 223–232.

Stang, D. J., & Russell, V. *The Talkative-quiet dimension: Some stereotypes and self-perceptions.* Unpublished manuscript, 1976.

Stang, D. J., & Seiler, L. H. No effect of absences on college course and instructor ratings. In *Improving College and University Teaching Yearbook,* 1977, 7–9.

Stang, D. J., & Solomon, R. Predicting student ratings of social psychology texts. *Teaching of Psychology,* 1976, *3*(3), 138–139.

Stang, D. J., & Wrightsman, L. S. *A dictionary of social behavior and social research methods.* Monterey, Calif.: Brooks/Cole, 1981.

Staples, F. R., & Walters, R. H. Anxiety, birth order and susceptibility to social influence. *Journal of Abnormal and Social Psychology,* 1961, *62*, 716–719.

Stark, R., & Glock, C. Y. *American piety: The nature of religious commitment.* Berkeley and Los Angeles: University of California Press, 1968.

Stark, R., & Glock, C. Y. *By their fruits: The consequences of religious commitment.* Berkeley and Los Angeles: University of California Press, 1969.

Staub, E. A child in distress: The influence of age and number of witnesses on children's attempts to help. *Journal of Personality and Social Psychology,* 1970, *14*, 130–140.

Staub, E. Helping a person in distress: The influence of implicit and explicit "rules" of conduct on children and adults. *Journal of Personality and Social Psychology,* 1971, *17*, 137–144. (a)

Staub, E. A child in distress: The influence of nurturance and modeling on children's attempts to help. *Developmental Psychology,* 1971, *5*, 124–132. (b)

Staub, E. Helping a distressed person: Social, personality, and stimulus determinants. In L. Berkowitz (Ed.), *Advances in experimental social psychology* (Vol. 7). New York: Academic Press, 1974.

Staub, E., & Sherk, L. Need for approval, children's sharing behavior, and reciprocity in sharing. *Child Development,* 1970, *41*, 243–252.

Steinzor, B. The spatial factor in face to face discussion groups. *Journal of Abnormal and Social Psychology,* 1950, *45*, 552–555.

Stern, W. *General psychology from the personal standpoint.* New York: Macmillan, 1938.

Sternbach, R. A., & Tursky, B. On the psychophysical power function in electric shock. *Psychonomic Science,* 1964, *1*(2) 217–218.

Stewart, A. J., & Winter, D. G. Self-definition and social definition in women. *Journal of Personality,* 1974, *42*, 238–259.

Stewart, J. C., & Scott, J. P. Lack of correlation between

leadership and dominance in a herd of goats. *Journal of Comparative and Physiological Psychology,* 1947, *40*, 255–264.

Stocker, T. L., Dutcher, L. W., Hargrove, S. M., & Cook, E. M. Social analysis of graffiti. *Journal of American Folklore,* 1972, *85*, 356–366.

Stogdill, R. M. Personal factors associated with leadership. *Journal of Psychology,* 1948, *25*, 35–71.

Stogdill, R. M. *Handbook of leadership.* New York: Free Press, 1974.

Stokols, D., Rall, M., Pinner, B., & Schopler, J. Physical, social, and personal determinants of the perception of crowding. *Environment and Behavior,* 1973, *5*(1), 87–117.

Stolz, H. R., & Stolz, L. M. *Somatic development of adolescent boys.* New York: Macmillan, 1951.

Storms, M. D., & Nisbett, R. E. Insomnia and the attribution process. *Journal of Personality and Social Psychology,* 1970, *2*, 319–328.

Stotland, E., & Blumenthal, A. The reduction of anxiety as a result of the expectation of making a choice. *Canadian Review of Psychology,* 1964, *18*, 139–145.

Stotland, E., & Canon, L. K. *Social psychology: A cognitive approach.* Philadelphia: Saunders, 1972.

Stotland, E., & Dunn, R. E. Identification, "oppositeness," authoritarianism, self-esteem, and birth order. *Psychological Monographs,* 1962, *76*, No. 528.

Stotland, E., & Hillmer, M. L., Jr. Identification, authoritarian defensiveness, and self-esteem. *Journal of Abnormal and Social Psychology,* 1962, *64*, 334–342.

Stouffer, S. A., Lumsdaine, A. A., Lumsdaine, M. H., Williams, R. M., Jr., Smith, M. B., Janis, I. L., Star, S. A., & Cottrell, L. S., Jr. *Studies in social psychology in World War II: The American soldier, combat and its aftermath.* Princeton, N.J.: Princeton University Press, 1949.

Strabilevitz, M., Strabilevitz, A., & Miller, J. E. Air pollutants and the admission rate of psychiatric patients. *American Journal of Psychiatry,* 1979, *136*, 205–207.

Strodtbeck, F. L. Husband-wife interaction over revealed differences. *American Sociological Review,* 1951, *18*, 141–145.

Strodtbeck, F. L. Family interaction, ethnicity, and achievement. In D. C. McClelland (Ed.), *Talent and society.* New York: Van Nostrand, 1958.

Strodtbeck, F. L., & Hook, L. N. The social dimension of a twelve-man jury table. *Sociometry,* 1961, *24*, 397–415.

Strodtbeck, F. L., James, R. M., & Hawkins, C. Social status in jury deliberations. *American Sociological Review,* 1957, *22*, 713–719.

Strodtbeck, F. L., & Mann, R. D. Sex role differentiation in jury deliberations. *Sociometry,* 1956, *19*, 3–11.

Stroebe, W., Insko, C. A., Thompson, V. D., & Layton, B. D. Effects of physical attractiveness, attitude similarity and sex on various aspects of interpersonal attraction. *Journal of Personality and Social Psychology,* 1971, *18*, 79–91.

Stroop, J. R. Is the judgment of the group better than that of the average member of the group? *Journal of Experimental Psychology,* 1932, *15*, 550–562.

Struening, E. Antidemocratic attitudes in a Midwestern

university. In H. Remmers (Ed.), *Antidemocratic attitudes in American schools.* Evanston, Ill.: Northwestern University Press, 1963.

Strümpfer, D. J. Fear and affiliation during a disaster. *Journal of Social Psychology,* 1970, *82,* 263–268.

Stukat, K. G. *Suggestibility: A factorial and experimental analysis.* Stockholm: Alqvist and Wiksell, 1958.

Suedfeld, P. Changes in intellectual performance and in susceptibility to influence. In J. P. Zubek (Ed.), *Sensory deprivation: Fifteen years of research.* New York: Appleton-Century-Crofts, 1969. (a)

Suedfeld, P. Introduction and historical background. In J. P. Zubek (Ed.), *Sensory deprivation: Fifteen years of research,* 1969. (b)

Suedfeld, P. Social isolation: A case for interdisciplinary research. *Canadian Psychologist,* 1974, *15,* 1–15.

Suedfeld, P., Bochner, S., & Matas, C. Petitioner's attire and petition signing by peace demonstrators: A field experiment. *Journal of Applied Social Psychology,* 1971, *1,* 278–283.

Sulman, F. G., Assael, M., Alpern, S., & Pfeifer, Y. Influence of artificial ionization of air on the electroencephalogram. *Israel Journal of Medical Sciences,* 1974, *16.* (Abstract)

Sulman, F. G., Pfeifer, Y., & Hirschman, M. [Effect of hot, dry, desert winds (Sharav, Hamsin) on the metabolism of hormones and minerals.] *Harokeach Haivri,* 1964, *10,* 401–404.

Sumner, W. G. *Folkways.* New York: Ginn, 1906.

Sundal, A. P., & McCormick, T. C. Age at marriage and mate selection, Madison, Wisconsin, 1937–1943. *American Sociological Review,* 1951, *16,* 37–48.

Sundstrom, E. *A study of crowding: Effects of intrusion, goal blocking and density on self-reported stress, self-disclosure and nonverbal behavior.* Unpublished doctoral dissertation, University of Utah, 1973.

Sung, Y. H. Effects of attitude similarity and favorableness of information on Bayesian decision making in a realistic task. *Journal of Applied Psychology,* 1975, *60,* 616–620.

Survey outlines employment patterns of women psychologists. *APA Monitor,* December 1971, p. 8.

Sutherland, E. *White collar crime.* New York: Dryden Press, 1949.

Szasz, T. *Law, liberty and psychiatry.* New York: Macmillan, 1963. (a)

Szasz, T. *The myth of mental illness: Foundations of a theory of mental illness.* New York: Hoeber-Harper, 1963. (b)

Taeuber, R., & Taeuber, A. *Negroes in cities.* Chicago: Aldine, 1965.

Taft, R. Coping with unfamiliar cultures. In N. Warren (Ed.), *Studies in cross-cultural psychology* (Vol. 1). London: Academic Press, 1976.

Tannenbaum, A. S. Reactions of members of voluntary groups: A logarithmic function of size of group. *Psychological Reports,* 1962, *10,* 113–114.

Tannenbaum, P. Mediated generalization of attitude change via the principle of congruity. *Journal of Personality and Social Psychology,* 1966, *3,* 493–500.

Tannenbaum, P., & Gengel, R. Generalization of attitude change through congruity principle relationships. *Journal of Personality and Social Psychology,* 1966, *3,* 299–304.

Tarter, D. E. Attitude: The mental myth. *American Sociologist,* 1970, *5,* 276–278.

Taylor, D. A. Some aspects of the development of interpersonal relationships. Social penetration processes. *Journal of Social Psychology,* 1968, *75,* 79–90.

Taylor, D. A., Altman, I., & Sorrentino, R. Interpersonal exchange as a function of rewards and costs and situational factors: Expectancy confirmation-disconfirmation. *Journal of Experimental Social Psychology,* 1969, *5,* 324–339.

Taylor, D. W., Berry, P. C., & Block, C. H. Does group participation when using brainstorming facilitate or inhibit creative thinking? *Administrative Science Quarterly,* 1958, *3,* 23–47.

Taylor, D. W., & Faust, W. L. Twenty questions: Efficiency in problem solving as a function of size of group. *Journal of Experimental Psychology,* 1952, *44,* 360–368.

Taylor, J. B. What do attitude scales measure: The problem of social desirability. *Journal of Abnormal and Social Psychology,* 1961, *62,* 386–390.

Taylor, S. E. On inferring one's attitudes from one's behavior: Some delimiting conditions. *Journal of Personality and Social Psychology,* 1975, *31,* 126–131.

Tedeschi, J. T. Attributions, liking and power. In T. L. Huston (Ed.), *Foundations of interpersonal attraction.* New York: Academic Press, 1974.

Tedeschi, J. T., & Lindskold, S. *Social psychology, interdependence, interaction, and influence.* New York: Wiley, 1976.

Teghtsoonian, M. Distribution by sex of authors and editors of psychological journals, 1970–1972: Are there enough women editors? *American Psychologist,* April 1974, 262–269.

Teichman, Y. Emotional arousal and affiliation. *Journal of Experimental Social Psychology,* 1973, *9,* 591–605.

Tennis, G. H., & Dabbs, J. M. Sex, setting and personal space: First grade through college. *Sociometry,* 1975, *38,* 385–394.

Terborg, J. R., & Ilgen, D. R. A theoretical approach to sex discrimination in traditionally masculine occupations. *Organizational Behavior and Human Performance,* 1975, *13,* 352–376.

Terman, L. M. A preliminary study of the psychology and pedagogy of leadership. *Pedagogical Seminary,* 1904, *11,* 413–451.

Tesser, A. *Toward a theory of self-generated attitude change.* Unpublished manuscript, University of Georgia, Athens, Institute for Behavioral Research and Department of Psychology, 1975.

Tesser, A. Attitude polarization as a function of thought and reality constraints. *Journal of Research in Personality,* in press.

Tesser, A., & Conlee, M. C. Some effects of time and thought on attitude polarization. *Journal of Personality and Social Psychology,* 1975, *31*(2), 262–270.

Tesser, A., & Cowan, C. L. *Some attitudinal and cognitive con-*

sequences of thought. Unpublished manuscript, University of Georgia, Athens, Institute for Behavioral Research and Department of Psychology, 1975.

Tesser, A., & Cowan, C. L. Some effects of thought and number of cognitions on attitude change. *Social Behavior and Personality,* in press.

Tesser, A., Gatewood, R., & Driver, M. Some determinants of gratitude. *Journal of Personality and Social Psychology,* 1968, *9,* 233–236.

Tesser, A., & Johnson, R. Dependence and thought as determinants of interpersonal hostility. *Bulletin of the Psychonomic Society,* 1974, *2,* 428–430.

Tesser, A., Rosen, S., & Conlee, M. C. News valence and available recipients as determinants of news transmissions. *Sociometry,* 1972, *35,* 619–628.

Test, M. A., & Bryan, J. H. The effects of dependency, models and reciprocity upon subsequent helping behavior. *Journal of Social Psychology,* 1969, *78,* 205–212.

Thayer, S. Lend me your ears: Racial and sexual factors in helping the deaf. *Journal of Personality and Social Psychology,* 1973, *28*(1), 8–11.

Theodore, A. *Professional women: The unchanging scene.* Paper presented at the annual meeting of the American Sociological Association, 1971.

Thibaut, J. W. An experimental study of the cohesiveness of underprivileged groups. *Human Relations,* 1950, *3,* 251–278.

Thibaut, J. W., & Kelley, H. H. *The social psychology of groups.* New York: Wiley, 1959.

Thibaut, J. W., & Riecken, H. W. Authoritarianism, status, and the communication of aggression. *Human Relations,* 1955, *8,* 95–120.

Thibaut, J. W., & Strickland, L. H. Psychological set and social conformity. *Journal of Personality,* 1956, *25,* 115–129.

Thiessen, D. D. Population density, mouse genotype, and endocrine function in behavior. *Journal of Comparative and Physiological Psychology,* 1964, *57,* 412–416.

Thiessen, D. D., Zolman, J. F., & Rodgers, D. A. Relation between adrenal weight, brain cholinesterase activity, and hole-in-wall behavior of mice under different living conditions. *Journal of Comparative and Physiological Psychology,* 1962, *55,*186–190.

Thistlewaite, D. L., & Kamenetsky, J. Attitude change through refutation and elaboration of audience counter-arguments. *Journal of Abnormal and Social Psychology,* 1955, *51,* 3–12.

Thomas, E. J., & Fink, C. F. Effects of group size. *Psychological Bulletin,* 1963, *60*(4), 371–384.

Thomas, E. J., Webb, S., & Tweedie, J. Effects of familiarity with a controversial issue on acceptance of successive persuasive communications. *Journal of Abnormal and Social Psychology,* 1961, *63,* 656–659.

Thomas, W. I. *Primitive behavior: An introduction to the social sciences.* New York: McGraw-Hill, 1937.

Thorndike, R. L. Factor analysis of social and abstract intelligence. *Journal of Educational Psychology,* 1936, *27,* 231–233.

Thorngate, W., & Love, D. *Historical trends in altruism* (Report No. 74-8). Edmonton, Alta.: University of Alberta, Social Psychology Laboratories, 1974.

Thornhill, M. A., Thornhill, G. J., & Youngman, M. B. A computerized and categorized bibliography on locus of control. *Psychological Reports,* 1975, *36,* 505–506.

Thrasher, F. M. *The gang.* Chicago: University of Chicago Press, 1927.

Thurber, J. The day the dam broke. In J. Thurber, *From my life and hard times.* New York: Harper & Row, 1961. (Originally published, 1933.)

Thurstone, L. L. Attitudes can be measured. *American Journal of Sociology,* 1928, *33,* 529–554.

Thurstone, L. L. Comment. *American Journal of Sociology,* 1946, *52,* 39–40.

Tidd, K. L., & Lockard, J. S. Monetary significance of the affiliative smile: A case for reciprocal altruism. *Bulletin of the Psychonomic Society,* 1978, *11*(6), 344–346.

Tinbergen, N. *The study of instinct.* Oxford: Clarendon Press, 1951.

Tinbergen, N. The curious behavior of the stickleback. *Scientific American,* 1952, *187*(6), 22–26.

Tippett, J., & Silber, E. Autonomy of self-esteem: An experimental approach. *Archives of General Psychiatry,* 1966, *14,* 372–385.

Tittle, C. R., & Hill, R. J. Attitude measurement and prediction of behavior: An evaluation of conditions and measurement techniques. *Sociometry,* 1967, *30,* 199–213.

Torrance, E. P. Some consequences of power differences on decision making in permanent and temporary three-man groups. *Research Studies* (State College of Washington), 1954, *22,* 130–140.

Tresemer, D. Fear of success: Popular but unproven. *Psychology Today,* 1974, *7*(10), 82–85.

Tresemer, D., & Pleck, J. Sex-role boundaries and resistance to social change. *Women's Studies,* 1974, *2,* 61–78.

Triandis, H. C. *Attitude and attitude change.* New York: Wiley, 1971.

Triandis, H. C., & Davis, E. Race and belief as determinants of behavioral intentions. *Journal of Personality and Social Psychology,* 1965, *2,* 715–726.

Triandis, H. C., & Fishbein, M. Cognitive interaction in person perception. *Journal of Abnormal and Social Psychology,* 1963, *67,* 446–453.

Triandis, H. C., & Osgood, C. E. A comparative factorial analysis of semantic structures of mono-lingual Greek and American college students. *Journal of Abnormal and Social Psychology,* 1958, *57,* 187–196.

Triandis, H. C., & Vassiliou, V. Frequency of contact and stereotyping. *Journal of Personality and Social Psychology,* 1967, *7,* 316–328.

Triplett, N. The dynamogenic factors in pacemaking and competition. *American Journal of Psychology,* 1897, *9,* 507–533.

Trope, Y., & Burnstein, E. Processing the information contained in another's behavior. *Journal of Experimental Social Psychology,* 1975, *11,* 439–458.

Trow, D. B. Autonomy and job satisfaction in task-oriented groups. *Journal of Abnormal and Social Psychology,* 1957, *54,* 204–209.

Tryon, R. C. Identification of social areas by cluster analysis: A general method with an application to the San Francisco Bay Area. *University of California Publications in Psychology,* 1955, *8*(1). (a)

Tryon, R. C. *Biosocial constancy of urban social areas.* Paper presented to the 63rd Annual Convention of the American Psychological Association, 1955. (b)

Tryon, R. C. *The social dimensions of metropolitan man* (Rev. title). Paper presented to the 67th Annual Convention of the American Psychological Association, 1959.

Tuddenham, R. D. Correlates of yielding to a distorted group norm. *Journal of Personality,* 1959, *27,* 272–284.

Tuddenham, R. D., MacBride, P., & Zahn, V. The influence of the sex composition of the group upon yielding to a distorted group norm. *Journal of Psychology,* 1958, *46,* 243–251.

Tumin, M. M. Some principles of stratification: A critical analysis. *American Sociological Review,* 1953, *18,* 387–394.

Turner, J. *Party and constituency: Pressures on Congress.* Baltimore: Johns Hopkins University Press, 1970.

Turner, J. L., Foa, E. B., & Foa, U. G. Interpersonal reinforcers: Classification, interrelationship, and some differential properties. *Journal of Personality and Social Psychology,* 1971, *19,* 168–180.

Tyler, L. E. *The psychology of human differences* (3rd ed.). New York: Appleton-Century-Crofts, 1965.

Tyler, T. R., & Sears, D. O. Coming to like obnoxious people when we must live with them. *Journal of Personality and Social Psychology,* 1977, *35,* 200–211.

Tylor, E. B. *Primitive culture. Researches in the development of mythology, philosophy, religion, language, art, and custom* (Vol. 1). New York: Holt, 1877.

Ulrich, R. E., & Azrin, N. H. Reflexive fighting in response to aversive stimulation. *Journal of the Experimental Analysis of Behavior,* 1962, *5,* 511–520.

Ulrich, R. E., Johnston, M., Richardson, J., & Wolff, P. The operant conditioning of fighting behavior in rats. *Psychological Record,* 1963, *13,* 465–470.

U.N. Department of Economic and Social Affairs. *Capital punishment.* New York: U.N. Educational, Scientific & Cultural Organization, 1962.

U.S. Department of Labor. *Americans volunteer* (Manpower Administration Research Monograph No. 10). Washington, D.C.: U.S. Government Printing Office, 1969.

U.S. Department of Labor. *Manpower report of the President: 1974.* Washington, D.C.: U.S. Government Printing Office, 1974.

U.S. Department of Labor. *Occupational projections and training data* (Bureau of Labor Statistics Bulletin No. 1918, GPO Stock No. 129-001-01949-1). Washington, D.C.: U.S. Government Printing Office, 1976.

Valenstein, E. S., Cox, V. C., & Kakolewski, J. W. Further studies of sex differences in taste preferences with sweet solutions. *Psychological Reports,* 1967, *20,* 1231–1234.

Valenstein, E. S., Kakolewski, J. W., & Cox, V. C. Sex differences in taste preference for glucose and saccharin solutions. *Science,* 1967, *156,* 942–943.

Valins, S. Cognitive effects of false heart-rate feedback. *Journal of Personality and Social Psychology,* 1966, *4,* 400–408.

Valins, S., & Baum, A. Residential group size, social interaction and crowding. *Environment and Behavior,* 1973, *5,* 421–440.

Valins, S., & Ray, A. A. Effects of cognitive desensitization on avoidance behavior. *Journal of Personality and Social Psychology,* 1967, *7,* 345–350.

Van Hooff, J. A. R. A. M. The facial displays of the Catarrhine monkey and apes. In D. Morris (Ed.), *Primate ethology.* Chicago: Aldine, 1967.

van Praag, H. M., & Korf, J. Monamine metabolism in depression: Clinical application of the probenecid test. In J. Barchas & E. Usdin (Eds.), *Serotonin and behavior.* New York: Academic Press, 1973.

Van Zelst, R. H. Sociometrically selected work teams increase production. *Personnel Psychology,* 1952, *5,* 175–185.

Vaughan, E. D. Misconceptions about psychology among introductory psychology students. *Teaching of Psychology,* 1977, *4*(3), 138–141.

Vaughan, G. M. The trans-situational aspect of conformity behavior. *Journal of Personality,* 1964, *32,* 335–354.

Veitch, R., & Griffitt, W. Good news, bad news: Affective and interpersonal effects. *Journal of Applied Social Psychology,* 1976, *6,* 69–75.

Verba, S., & Nie, N. H. *Participation in America.* New York: Harper & Row, 1972.

Vetter, B. M. More women for higher education. *Science,* 1972, *178.*

Vidulich, R. N., & Kaiman, I. P. The effects of information source status and dogmatism upon conformity behavior. *Journal of Abnormal and Social Psychology,* 1961, *63,* 639–642.

Von Vexkull, J. A stroll through the worlds of animals and men. In C. Schiller (Ed.), *Instinctive behavior.* New York: International University Press, 1957.

Vroom, V. H. *Work and motivation.* New York: Wiley, 1964.

Wagner, C., & Wheeler, L. Model need and cost effects in helping behavior. *Journal of Personality and Social Psychology,* 1969, *12,* 111–116.

Walker, E. L., & Heyns, R. W. *An anatomy for conformity.* Englewood Cliffs, N.J.: Prentice-Hall, 1962.

Walker, N. *Crime and punishment in Britain.* Edinburgh: Edinburgh University Press, 1965.

Walker, T. G. Behavior of temporary members in small groups. *Journal of Applied Psychology,* 1973, *58,* 144–146.

Wall, P. M. *Eye-witness identification in criminal cases.* Springfield, Ill.: Charles C Thomas, 1971.

Wallen, R. Sex differences in food aversions. *Journal of Applied Psychology,* 1943, *27,* 288–298.

Walster, E. *Did you ever see a beautiful conservative? A note.* Mimeographed report available from the author, 1971. (a)

Walster, E. Passionate love. In B. Murstein (Ed.), *Theories of attraction and love.* New York: Springer, 1971. (b)

Walster, E., Aronson, V., Abrahams, D., & Rottmann, L. Importance of physical attractiveness in dating behavior. *Journal of Personality and Social Psychology,* 1966, *4,* 508–516.

Walster, E., & Berscheid, E. Adrenaline makes the heart grow fonder. *Psychology Today,* 1971, *5*(1), 46–50.

Walster, E., & Prestholdt, P. The effect of misjudging another: Over-compensation or dissonance reduction? *Journal of Experimental Social Psychology,* 1966, *2,* 85–97.

Walster, E., & Walster, G. Effect of expecting to be liked on choice of associates. *Journal of Abnormal and Social Psychology,* 1963, *67,* 402–404.

Walters, R. H., & Karol, P. Social deprivation and verbal behavior. *Journal of Personality,* 1960, *28,* 89–107.

Walters, R. H., Marshall, W. S., & Shooter, J. R. Anxiety, isolation, and susceptibility to social influence. *Journal of Personality,* 1960, *28,* 518–529.

Walters, R. H., & Willows, D. Imitation behavior of disturbed children following exposure to aggressive and nonaggressive models. *Child Development,* 1968, *39,* 79–91.

Wanat, J. Political broadcast advertising and primary election voting. *Journal of Broadcasting,* 1974, *18,* 413–422.

Ward, C. Own height, sex, and liking in the judgment of the heights of others. *Journal of Personality,* 1967, *35,* 381–401.

Ward, C. D. Seating arrangement and leadership emergence in small discussion groups. *Journal of Social Psychology,* 1968, *74,* 83–90.

Warren, J. R. Birth order and social behavior. *Psychological Bulletin,* 1966, *65,* 38–49.

Washburn, M. F., Harding, L., Simmons, H., & Tomlinson, D. Further experiments on directed recall as a test of cheerful and depressed temperaments. *American Journal of Psychology,* 1925, *36,* 454–456.

Washburn, R. W. A scheme for grading the reactions of children in a new social situation. *Journal of Genetic Psychology,* 1932, *40,* 84–99.

Waters, H. F., & Malamud, P. Drop that gun, Captain Video. *Newsweek,* March 10, 1975, 81–82.

Watson, O. M., & Graves, T. D. Quantitative research in proxemic behavior. *American Anthropologist,* 1966, *68,* 971–985.

Watts, R. E. Influence of population density on crime. *Journal of the American Statistical Association,* 1931, *26,* 11–21.

Watts, W., & McGuire, W. Persistence of induced opinion change and retention of the inducing message contents. *Journal of Abnormal and Social Psychology,* 1964, *68,* 233–241.

Wegner, D. M., & Vallacher, R. R. *Implicit psychology: An introduction to social cognition.* New York: Oxford University Press, 1977.

Weiner, B. On being sane in insane places: A process (attributional) analysis and critique. *Journal of Abnormal Psychology,* 1975, *84,* 433–441.

Weiss, B., & Latres, V. *Behavioral toxicology.* New York: Plenum, 1972.

Weiss, J. M. Effects of coping behavior in different warning signal conditions on stress pathology in rats. *Journal of Comparative and Physiological Psychology,* 1971, *77,* 1–14.

Weiss, R. F., Buchanan, W., Alstatt, L., & Lombardo, J. P. Altruism is rewarding. *Science,* 1971, *171,* 1262–1263.

Weiss, W. Effects of the mass media of communications. In G. Lindzey & E. Aronson (Eds.), *Handbook of social psychology* (Vol. 5, 2nd ed.). Reading, Mass.: Addison-Wesley, 1969.

Weitz, S. Attitude, voice, and behavior: A repressed affect model of interracial interaction. *Journal of Personality and Social Psychology,* 1972, *24,* 14–21.

Weitzman, L. J., Eifler, D., Hokada, E., & Ross, C. Sex-role socialization in picture books for preschool children. *American Journal of Sociology,* 1972, *77,* 1125–1149.

Wells, W., & Siegel, B. Stereotyped somatypes. *Psychological Reports,* 1961, *8,* 77–78.

Wells, W. D. *Television and aggression: Replication of an experimental field study.* Unpublished manuscript, University of Chicago, 1973.

West, S. G., & Brown, T. J. Physical attractiveness, the severity of the emergency and helping: A field experiment and interpersonal simulation. *Journal of Experimental Social Psychology,* 1975, *11,* 531–538.

West, S. G., Whitney, G., & Schnedler, R. Helping a motorist in distress: The effects of sex, race, and neighborhood. *Journal of Personality and Social Psychology,* 1975, *31,* 691–698.

Westoff, C., & Rindfuss, R. R. Sex preselection in the United States: Some implications. *Science,* 1974, *184,* 633–636.

Wexler, D., Mendelsohn, J., Leiderman, P. H., & Soloman, P. Sensory deprivation: A technique for studying psychiatric aspects of stress. *Archives of Neurology and Psychiatry,* 1958, *79,* 225–233.

Weybrew, B. B. Human factors and the work environment. II. The impact of isolation upon personnel. *Journal of Occupational Medicine,* 1961, *3,* 290–294.

Wheeler, L. Toward a theory of behavioral contagion. *Psychological Review,* 1966, *73,* 179–192.

Wheeler, L. Social comparison and selective affiliation. In T. L. Huston (Ed.), *Foundations of interpersonal attraction.* New York: Academic Press, 1974.

White, R. C. The relation of felonies to environmental factors in Indianapolis. *Social Forces,* 1931, *10*(4), 498–509.

Whitehead, A. N. *The aims of education and other essays.* New York: The New American Library, 1949. (Originally published 1929.)

Whiting, B., & Edwards, C. P. A cross-cultural analysis of sex differences in the behavior of children aged three through 11. *Journal of Social Psychology,* 1973, *91,* 171–188.

Whiting, J. W. M. Effects of climate on certain cultural practices. In W. H. Goodenough (Ed.), *Explorations in cultural anthropology.* New York: McGraw-Hill, 1964.

Whittaker, J. O. Sex differences and susceptibility to interpersonal persuasion. *Journal of Social Psychology,* 1965, *66,* 91–92.

Whorf, B. L. In J. B. Carroll (Ed.), *Language, thought and reality.* New York: Wiley, 1956.

Whyte, W. F. *Street corner society*. Chicago: University of Chicago Press, 1943.

Whyte, W. F. *Street corner society* (2nd ed.). Chicago: University of Chicago Press, 1955.

Whyte, W. H., Jr. *The organization man*. New York: Simon & Schuster, 1956.

Wicker, A. W. Attitudes versus actions: The relationship of verbal and overt behavioural responses to attitude objects. *Journal of Social Issues*, 1969, *25*(4), 41–78.

Wicker, A. W. An examination of the "other variables" explanation of attitude-behavior inconsistency. *Journal of Personality and Social Psychology*, 1971, *19*, 18–30.

Wicklund, R. A. *Freedom and reactance*. Potomac, Md.: Erlbaum, 1974.

Wicklund, R. A., & Brehm, J. W. *Perspectives on cognitive dissonance*. Potomac, Md.: Erlbaum, 1976.

Wiener, M. Certainty of judgment as a variable in conformity behavior. *Journal of Social Psychology*, 1958, *48*, 257–263.

Wiggins, J. A., Dill, F., & Schwartz, R. D. On "status-liability." *Sociometry*, 1965, *28*, 197–209.

Wiggins, J. W. *Personality and prediction: Principles of personality assessment*. Reading, Mass.: Addison-Wesley, 1973.

Williams, J. *Personal space and its relation to extroversion-introversion*. Unpublished master's thesis, University of Alberta, 1963. (Cited in H. Patterson, 1968.)

Willis, F. N. Initial speaking distance as a function of the speakers' relationship. *Psychonomic Science*, 1966, *5*, 221–222.

Willis, R., & Bulatao, R. *Belief and ethnicity as determinants of friendship and marriage acceptance in the Philippines*. Paper presented at the 75th Annual Convention of the American Psychological Association, Washington, D.C., September 1967.

Willis, R. H. [Social influence and conformity—Some research perspectives.] *Acta Sociologica*, 1961, *5*, 100–114.

Wilner, D., Walkley, R. P., & Cook, S. W. Residential proximity and intergroup relations in public housing projects. *Journal of Social Issues*, 1952, *8*(1), 45–69.

Wilson, D. W., & Kahn, A. Rewards, costs, and sex differences in helping behavior. *Psychological Reports*, 1975, *36*, 31–34.

Wilson, E. O. Human decency is animal. *New York Times Magazine*, October 12, 1975. (a)

Wilson, E. O. *Sociobiology: The new synthesis*. Cambridge, Mass.: Belnap Press of Harvard University Press, 1975. (b)

Wilson, P. R. The perceptual distortion of height as a function of ascribed academic status. *Journal of Social Psychology*, 1968, *74*, 97–102.

Wilson, R. S. Personality patterns, source attractiveness, and conformity. *Journal of Personality*, 1960, *28*, 186–199.

Wilson, S. R. Leadership, participation, and self-orientation in observed and non-observed groups. *Journal of Applied Psychology*, 1971, *55*(5), 433–438.

Wilson, W., & Miller, H. Repetition, order of presentation, timing of arguments and measures as determinants of opinion change. *Journal of Personality and Social Psychol-*

ogy, 1968, *9*, 184–188.

Wilson, W., & Nakajo, H. Preference for photographs as a function of frequency of presentation. *Psychonomic Science*, 1965, *3*, 577–578.

Winch, R. F. *The modern family*. New York: Holt, 1952.

Winch, R. F. *Mate-selection: A study of complementary needs*. New York: Harper, 1958.

Winch, R. F., Ktsanes, T., & Ktsanes, V. The theory of complementary needs in mate selection: An analytic and descriptive study. *American Sociological Review*, 1954, *19*, 241–249.

Winterbottom, M. The relation of need for achievement in learning experiences to independence and mastery. In J. W. Atkinson (Ed.), *Motives in fantasy, action and society*. Princeton, N.J.: Van Nostrand, 1958.

Wishner, J. Reanalysis of "impressions of personality." *Psychological Review*, 1960, *67*, 96–112.

Witkin, H. A., Dyk, R. B., Faterson, H. F., Goodenough, D. R., & Karp, S. A. *Psychological differentiation*. Potomac, Md.: Erlbaum, 1974. (Originally published by Wiley, 1962.)

Witkin, H. A., & Goodenough, D. R. *Field dependence revisited* (ETS RB 77-16). Princeton, N.J.: Educational Testing Service, 1977.

Witkin, H. A., Goodenough, D. R., & Karp, S. A. Stability of cognitive style from childhood to young adulthood. *Journal of Personality and Social Psychology*, 1967, *7*, 291–300.

Witkin, H. A., Lewis, H. B., Hertzman, M., Machover, K., Meissner, P. B., & Wapner, S. *Personality through perception*. Westport, Conn.: Greenwood Press, 1972. (Originally published by Harper, 1954.)

Wohlwill, J. M. The physical environment: A problem for a psychology of stimulation. *Journal of Social Issues*, 1966, *22*, 29–38.

Wolf, A., & Weiss, J. H. Birth order, recruitment conditions, and volunteering preference. *Journal of Personality and Social Psychology*, 1965, *2*, 269–273.

Wolfenstein, M. *Disaster*. Glencoe, Ill.: Free Press, 1957.

Wolff, K. H. *The sociology of Georg Simmel*. Glencoe, Ill.: Free Press, 1950. (Reprinted by permission of the translator and publisher.)

Wolfgang, M. Crime: Homicide. In D. L. Sells (Ed.), *International encyclopedia of the social sciences* (Vol. 3). New York: Macmillan, 1968.

Wolfgang, M., & Ferracuti, F. *The subculture of violence: Towards an integrated theory in criminology*. London: Social Science Paperbacks, in association with Tavistock Publications, 1967.

Wong, K. L. Psychological differentiation as a determinant of friendship choice (Doctoral dissertation, City University of New York, 1976). *Dissertation Abstracts International*, 1977, *37*, 3638B. (University Microfilms No. 76-30,278)

Woodmansee, J. J., & Cook, S. W. Dimensions of verbal racial attitude: Their identification and measurement. *Journal of Personality and Social Psychology*, 1967, *7*, 240–250.

Worchel, P., & McCormick, B. Self-concept and dissonance reduction. *Journal of Personality*, 1963, *31*, 588–599.

Worchel, S. Cooperation and the reduction of intergroup conflict: Some determining factors. In W. G. Austin & S. Worchel (Eds.), *The social psychology of intergroup relations*. Monterey, Calif.: Brooks/Cole, 1979.

Worchel, S., & Brehm, J. W. Direct and implied social restoration of freedom. *Journal of Personality and Social Psychology*, 1971, *18*, 294–304.

Wright, B. A. Altruism in children and the perceived conduct of others. *Journal of Abnormal and Social Psychology*, 1942, *37*, 218–233.

Wrightsman, L. S. The effects of purported validity of a test on motivation and achievement. *Journal of Educational Research*, 1960, *54*, 153–156. (a)

Wrightsman, L. S. Effects of waiting with others on changes in level of felt anxiety. *Journal of Abnormal and Social Psychology*, 1960, *61*, 216–222. (b)

Wrightsman, L. S. Measurement of philosophies of human nature. *Psychological Reports*, 1964, *14*, 743–751.

Wrightsman, L. S. *Assumptions about human nature: A social-psychological approach*. Monterey, Calif.: Brooks/Cole, 1974.

Wrightsman, L. S. *Social psychology* (2nd ed.). Monterey, Calif.: Brooks/Cole, 1977.

Wrightsman, L. S., & Noble, F. C. Reactions to the President's assassination and changes in philosophies of human nature. *Psychological Reports*, 1965, *16*, 159–162.

Wyatt, R. J., Vaughan, T., Kaplan, J., Galanter, M., & Green, R. 5-hydroxytryptophan and chronic schizophrenia—A preliminary study. In J. Barchas & E. Usdin (Eds.), *Serotonin and behavior*. New York: Academic Press, 1973.

Wyer, R. S., & Goldberg, L. A probabilistic analysis of relationships among beliefs and attitudes. *Psychological Review*, 1970, *77*, 100–120.

Wylie, R. C. Children's estimates of their schoolwork ability, as a function of sex, race, and socioeconomic level. *Journal of Personality*, June 1963, *31*, 203–224.

Yarrow, M. R., Waxler, C. Z., & Scott, P. M. Child effects on adult behavior. *Developmental Psychology*, 1971, *5*, 300–311.

Yerkes, R. M., & Dodson, J. D. The relation of strength of stimulus to rapidity of habit-formation. *Journal of Comparative Neurological Psychology*, 1908, *18*, 459–482.

Younger, J. C., & Pliner, P. Obese-normal differences in the self-monitoring of expressive behavior. *Journal of Research in Personality*, 1976, *10*, 112–115.

Zacker, J. Authoritarian avoidance of ambiguity. *Psychological Reports*, 1973, *33*, 901–902.

Zajonc, R. B. A note on group judgments and group size. *Human Relations*, 1962, *15*, 177–180.

Zajonc, R. B. Social facilitation. *Science*, 1965, *149*, 269–274.

Zajonc, R. B. *Social psychology: An experimental approach*. Monterey, Calif.: Brooks/Cole, 1966.

Zajonc, R. B. Attitudinal effects of mere exposure. *Journal of Personality and Social Psychology Monograph*, 1968, *9*, 1–27.

Zajonc, R. B. Brainwash: Familiarity breeds comfort. *Psychology Today*, 1970, *3*(9), 33–35; 60–62.

Zajonc, R. B. Dumber by the dozen. *Psychology Today*, 1975, *40*(1), 37–43.

Zajonc, R. B., & Markus, G. B. Birth order and intellectual development. *Psychological Review*, 1975, *82*, 74–88.

Zajonc, R. B., & Rajecki, D. W. Exposure and affect: A field experiment. *Psychonomic Science*, 1969, *17*, 216–217.

Zander, A., Cohen, A. R., & Stotland, E. *Role relations in the mental health professions*. Ann Arbor: University of Michigan, Institute for Social Research, 1957.

Zander, A., & Van Egmond, E. Relationship of intelligence and social power to the interpersonal behavior of children. *Journal of Educational Psychology*, 1958, *49*, 257–268.

Zanna, M., Kiesler, C., & Pilkonis, P. Positive and negative attitudinal affect established by classical conditioning. *Journal of Personality and Social Psychology*, 1970, *14*, 321–328.

Zarcone, V. P., Hoddes, E., & Smythe, H. Oral 5-hydroxy-tryptophan effects on sleep. In J. Barchas & E. Usdin (Eds.), *Serotonin and behavior*. New York: Academic Press, 1973.

Zawadzki, B. Limitations of the scapegoat theory of prejudice. *Journal of Abnormal and Social Psychology*, 1948, *43*, 127–141.

Zax, M., & Takahashi, S. Cultural influences on response style: Comparisons of Japanese and American college students. *Journal of Social Psychology*, 1967, *71*, 3–10.

Zdep, S. M., & Oakes, W. F. Reinforcement of leadership behavior in group discussion. *Journal of Experimental Social Psychology*, 1967, *3*, 310–320.

Zelditch, M., Jr. Role differentiation in the nuclear family: A comparative study. In T. Parsons & R. Bales (Eds.), *Family, socialization and interaction process*. Glencoe, Ill.: Free Press, 1955.

Zibaida, G., Sieretzki, S., & Stang, D. J. *Physical attractiveness is not randomly distributed geographically*. Unpublished manuscript, Queens College, 1976.

Ziller, R. C. Group size: A determinant of the quality and stability of group decisions. *Sociometry*, 1957, *20*, 165–173.

Ziller, R. C., & Behringer, R. Group persuasion by the most knowledgeable member under conditions of incubation and varying group size. *Journal of Applied Psychology*, 1959, *43*(6), 402–406.

Ziller, R. C., & Behringer, R. D. A longitudinal study of the assimilation of the new child in the group. *Human Relations*, 1961, *14*, 121–133.

Zillman, D., Katcher, A., & Milavsky, B. Excitation transfer from physical exercise to subsequent aggressive behavior. *Journal of Experimental Social Psychology*, 1972, *8*, 247–259.

Zimbardo, P. G. The human choice: Individuation, reason and order, vs. deindividuation, impulse, and chaos. In the *Nebraska Symposium on Motivation* (Vol. 17). Lincoln: University of Nebraska Press, 1969.

Zimbardo, P. G., & Formica, R. Emotional comparison and self-esteem as determinants of affiliation. *Journal of Personality*, 1963, *31*, 141–162.

Zimbardo, P. G., Haney, C., Banks, W., & Jaffe, D. *The psychology of imprisonment: Privation, power, and pathology*.

Unpublished manuscript, Stanford University, 1972.

Zimbardo, P. G., Weisenberg, M., Firestone, I., & Levy, B. Communicator effectiveness in producing public conformity and private attitude change. *Journal of Personality*, 1965, *33*, 233–255.

Zimet, C. N., & Schneider, C. Effects of group size on interaction in small groups. *Journal of Social Psychology*, 1969, *77*, 177–187.

Zimmerman, E., & Parlee, M. B. Behavioral changes associated with the menstrual cycle: An experimental investigation. *Journal of Applied Social Psychology*, 1973, *3*, 335–344.

Zipf, S. G. Resistance and conformity under reward and punishment. *Journal of Abnormal and Social Psychology*, 1960, *61*, 102–109.

Ziv, A., Kruglanski, A. W., & Shulman, S. Children's psychological reactions to wartime stress. *Journal of Personality and Social Psychology*, 1974, *30*, 24–30.

Zlutnick, S., & Altman, I. Crowding and human behavior. In J. F. Wohwill & D. H. Carson (Eds.), *Environment and the social sciences: Perspectives and applications.* Washington, D.C.: American Psychological Association, 1972.

Znaniecki, F. Social groups as products of participating individuals. *American Journal of Sociology*, 1939, *44*, 799–811.

Zubek, J. P. (Ed.). *Sensory deprivation: Fifteen years of research.* New York: Appleton-Century-Crofts, 1969.

Zucker, I., & Wade, G. Sexual preferences of male rats. *Journal of Comparative and Physiological Psychology*, 1968, *66(3)*, 816–819.

Zucker, R. A., Manosevitz, J., & Lanyon, R. I. Birth order, anxiety, and affiliation during a crisis. *Journal of Personality and Social Psychology*, 1968, *8*, 354–359.

Zuckerman, M. Perceptual isolation as a stress situation. *Archives of General Psychiatry*, 1964, *11*, 255–276.

Zuckerman, M. Variables affecting deprivation results. In J. P. Zubek (Ed.), *Sensory deprivation: Fifteen years of research*, 1969.

Zuckerman, M., Albright, R. J., Marks, C. S., & Miller, G. L. Stress and hallucinatory effects of perceptual isolation and confinement. *Psychological Monographs*, 1962, *76*, No. 30.

Zuckerman, M., & Wheeler, L. To dispel fantasies about the fantasy-based measure of fear of success. *Psychological Bulletin*, 1975, *82*, 932–946.

Zung, W. W., & Green, R. L. Seasonal variation of suicide and depression. *Archives of General Psychiatry*, 1974, *30*, 89–91.

Name Index

Subject Index